PRENTICE HALL

MIDDLE GRADES MATH

TOOLS FOR SUCCESS

Course 1

*Prentice Hall dedicates
this mathematics program
to all mathematics educators
and their students.*

AUTHORS

Suzanne H. Chapin

Mark Illingworth

Marsha S. Landau

Joanna O. Masingila

Leah McCracken

CONSULTING AUTHORS

Sadie Chavis Bragg

Bridget A. Hadley

Vincent O'Connor

Anne C. Patterson

PRENTICE HALL

MIDDLE GRADES
MATH
TOOLS FOR SUCCESS

Course 1

Prentice
Hall

Glenview, Illinois
Needham, Massachusetts
Upper Saddle River, New Jersey

AUTHORS

Suzanne H. Chapin, Ed.D., Boston University, Boston, Massachusetts
Proportional Reasoning and Probability strands, and Tools for Problem Solving

Mark Illingworth, Hollis Public Schools, Hollis, New Hampshire
Graphing strand

Marsha S. Landau, Ph.D., Formerly, National Louis University, Evanston, Illinois
Algebra, Functions, and Computation strands

Joanna O. Masingila, Ph.D., Syracuse University, Syracuse, New York
Geometry strand

Leah McCracken, Lockwood School District, Billings, Montana
Data Analysis strand

CONSULTING AUTHORS

Sadie Chavis Bragg, Ed.D., Borough of Manhattan Community College, The City University of New York, New York, New York

Bridget A. Hadley, Mathematics Curriculum Specialist, Hopkinton, Massachusetts

Vincent O'Connor, Formerly, Milwaukee Public Schools, Milwaukee, Wisconsin

Anne C. Patterson, Volusia County Schools, Daytona Beach, Florida

Printed in the United States of America.

ISBN: 0-13-051960-X

5 6 7 8 9 10 04 03 02

Prentice
Hall

We are grateful to our reviewers, who advised us in the development stages and provided invaluable feedback, ideas, and constructive criticism to help make this program one that meets the needs of middle grades teachers and students.

REVIEWERS

All Levels
Ann Bouie, Ph.D., Multicultural Reviewer, Oakland, California

Dorothy S. Strong, Ph.D., Chicago Public Schools, Chicago, Illinois

Course 1
Darla Agajanian, Sierra Vista School, Canyon Country, California

Rhonda Bird, Grand Haven Area Schools, Grand Haven, Michigan

Gary Critselous, Whittle Springs Middle School, Knoxville, Tennessee

Rhonda W. Davis, Durant Road Middle School, Raleigh, North Carolina

Leroy Dupee, Bridgeport Public Schools, Bridgeport, Connecticut

Jose Lalas, Ph.D., California State University, Dominguez Hills, California

Richard Lavers, Fitchburg High School, Fitchburg, Massachusetts

Lavaille Metoyer, Houston Independent School District, Houston, Texas

Course 2
Raylene Bryson, Alexander Middle School, Huntersville, North Carolina

Susan R. Buckley, Dallas Public Schools, Dallas, Texas

Sheila Cunningham, Klein Independent School District, Klein, Texas

Natarsha Mathis, Hart Junior High School, Washington, D.C.

Jean Patton, Clements Middle School, Covington, Georgia

Judy Trowell, Arkansas Department of Higher Education, Little Rock, Arkansas

Course 3
Michaele F. Chappell, Ph.D., University of South Florida, Tampa, Florida

Bettye Hall, Math Consultant, Houston, Texas

Joaquin Hernandez, Barbara Goleman Senior High, Miami, Florida

Steven H. Lapinski, Henrico County Public Schools, Richmond, Virginia

Dana Luterman, Lincoln Middle School, Kansas City, Missouri

Loretta Rector, Leonardo da Vinci School, Sacramento, California

Elias P. Rodriguez, Leander Middle School, Leander, Texas

Anthony C. Terceira, Providence School Department, Providence, Rhode Island

STAFF CREDITS
The people who made up the *Middle Grades Math* team—representing editorial, design, marketing, page production, editorial services, production, manufacturing, technology, electronic publishing, and advertising and promotion—and their managers are listed below. Bold type denotes core team members. Barbara A. Bertell, Bruce Bond, Therese Bräuer, Christopher Brown, **Judith D. Buice**, Kathy Carter, Linda M. Coffey, Noralie V. Cox, Sheila DeFazio, Edward de Leon, Christine Deliee, Gabriella Della Corte, Jo DiGiustini, Robert G. Dunn, Barbara Flockhart, Audra Floyd, David B. Graham, Maria Green, Kristen Guevara, Jeff Ikler, Mimi Jigarjian, Elizabeth A. Jordan, Russell Lappa, Joan McCulley, Paul W. Murphy, Cindy A. Noftle, Caroline M. Power, Olena Serbyn, Dennis Slattery, Martha G. Smith, Kira Thaler Marbit, Robin Tiano, **Christina Trinchero**, **Stuart Wallace**, **Cynthia A. Weedel**, **Jeff Weidenaar**, **Mary Jane Wolfe**, Stewart Wood

We would like to give special thanks to National Math Consultants Ann F. Bell and Brenda Underwood for all their help in developing this program.

COURSE 1

Contents

CHAPTER 1 Using Statistics to Analyze Data

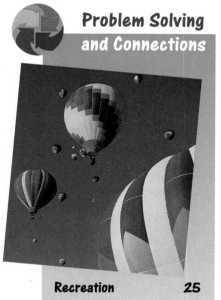

Problem Solving and Connections

Recreation	25
Art	4
Algebra	19
Music	23
Park Ranger	26
Animal Studies	27
Population	28

...and More!

CHAPTER PROJECT

Theme: Surveys
On Your Own Time

Conduct a Survey	*3*
Project Links	*7, 16, 36*
Finishing the Chapter Project	*37*
Web Extension	

ASSESSMENT

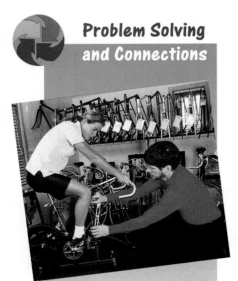

Problem Solving and Connections

Bicycle Designer 60
Fund-raising 62
Space 64
Health 66
Algebra 72
Hockey 73
Air Quality 76

...and More!

CHAPTER PROJECT

Theme: Patterns

Stepping Stones
Building a Fort 43
Project Links 47, 64, 76
Finishing the Chapter Project 77
Web Extension

CHAPTER 3 Adding and Subtracting Decimals

Problem Solving and Connections

Data Analysis 109
Accountant 87
Social Studies 88
Money 91
Nutrition 104
Sports 108
Amusement Parks 126

...and More!

ASSESSMENT

CHAPTER PROJECT

Theme: Consumer Issues
Name That Tune

Multiplying and Dividing Whole Numbers and Decimals

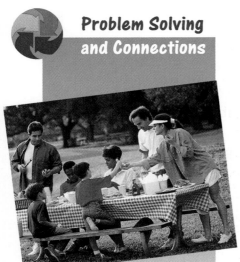

Problem Solving and Connections

...and More!

Picnics   144
Geometry   143
Coin Collecting 148
Veterinarian   159
Travel Time   160
Fuel Economy   164
Geography   171

ASSESSMENT

CHAPTER PROJECT

Theme: Planning Celebration!

Problem Solving and Connections

...and More!

CHAPTER PROJECT

Theme: Sports
Home Court Advantage

CHAPTER 6 Using Fractions

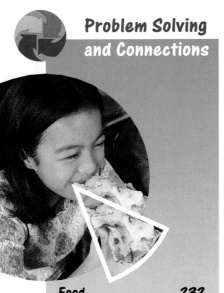

Problem Solving and Connections

...and More!

ASSESSMENT

CHAPTER PROJECT

Seeing Is Believing
Theme: Proofs

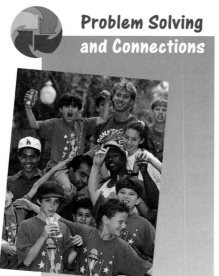

**Problem Solving
and Connections**

...and More!

CHAPTER
PROJECT

Theme: Astronomy
Planet of the Stars
Make a Scale Model   277
Project Links   284, 288, 295
Finishing the Chapter Project   319
  Web Extension

ASSESSMENT

Problem Solving and Connections

...and More!

Nature 360
Physical Education 332
Algebra 337
Art 339
Sailing 342
Optics 343
Cartoonist 348

CHAPTER PROJECT

Theme: Puzzles
Puzzling Pictures

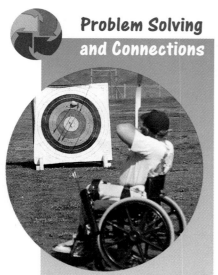

Problem Solving and Connections

Archery 400
Gardening 383
Conservation 393
Geometry 403
History 406
Carpenter 412
Package Design 414

...and More!

CHAPTER PROJECT

Theme: Technology
Home on the Web

Problem Solving and Connections

...and More!

CHAPTER PROJECT

Theme: History
The Time of Your Life

CHAPTER 11 Exploring Probability

Problem Solving and Connections

Board Game
Designer   506
Games   480
Consumer Issues   501
Data Analysis   502
Music   508
Track and Field   509
Tourism   512

...and More!

CHAPTER PROJECT

Theme: Statistics
Now Playing!
Design a Three-Choice System   *479*
Project Links   *491, 496, 506*
Finishing the Chapter Project   *517*
   Web Extension

ASSESSMENT

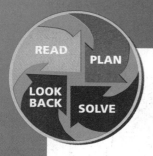

READ
PLAN
LOOK BACK
SOLVE

Tools for Problem Solving... An Overview

CONTENTS

To the Student:

The key to your success in math is your ability to use math in the real world—both now and in the future. To succeed you need math skill and some problem solving tools too. In this Problem Solving Overview, you'll learn how to use a four-step plan for problem solving, how to choose strategies for solving problems, how to best work in groups, and how to apply strategies to standardized tests.

As you work through the book, you'll find plenty of opportunities to improve your problem solving skills. The more you build on a skill, the better you'll get. And the better you get, the more confident you'll become. So keep at it!

Problem Solving Strategies

Draw a Diagram
Guess and Test
Look for a Pattern
Make a Model
Make a Table
Simulate a Problem
Solve a Simpler Problem
Too Much or Too Little Information
Use Logical Reasoning
Use Multiple Strategies
Work Backward

Tools for Problem Solving

The Four-Step Approach

You solve problems every day. Some problems are easy to solve. Others require good problem solving skills.

How you approach a problem can determine whether or not you solve it. Here is a four-step approach that many successful problem solvers use.

THE FOUR-STEP APPROACH

1. Read and understand the problem.
2. Plan how to solve the problem.
3. Solve the problem.
4. Look back.

As you follow each of the four steps, ask yourself questions about the problem.

SAMPLE PROBLEM...............

Sports A soccer field is 110 yards by 80 yards. A volleyball court is 20 yards by 10 yards. How many volleyball courts could you fit on a soccer field?

READ

Read for understanding. Summarize the problem.

Read the problem again. What information is given? What information is missing? Ask yourself: "What am I being asked to find or do?"

You can summarize the given information in the form of short notes like those below. You can also summarize what is being asked.

- soccer field — 110 yd × 80 yd
- volleyball court — 20 yd × 10 yd
- 1 soccer field = ? volleyball courts

PLAN

Decide a strategy.

Consider the strategies you know. Can you use one of them? Have you solved a similar problem before? If so, try the same approach.

This problem involves visualization. To see how many volleyball courts fit on a soccer field, you can draw a diagram.

SOLVE

Try the strategy.

Make a sketch and find how many volleyball courts fit.

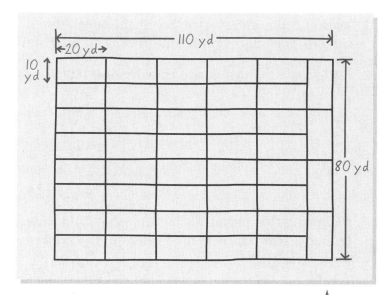

Eight volleyball courts fit down.

Five volleyball courts fit across.

Four more volleyball courts fit in the strip at the end of the soccer field.

$5 \times 8 + 4 = 44$

Therefore, 44 volleyball courts fit in the area of a soccer field.

LOOK BACK

Think about how you solved the problem.

This is an important step in solving a problem. Check that you answered the question. Does your answer make sense? Is there a different way to solve the problem?

Another way to solve the problem is to divide the area of a soccer field by the area of a volleyball court.

Area = length × width

Area of soccer field = 110 yd × 80 yd = 8,800 square yards

Area of volleyball court = 20 yd × 10 yd = 200 square yards

8,800 ÷ 200 = 44

This confirms that 44 volleyball courts can fit on a soccer field.

EXERCISES *On Your Own*

**Use the four-step approach to solve each problem.
Remember that there are many ways to solve problems.**

1. Juan, Lewin, and Ken arrive at the lunch line at the same time. In how many different orders can they stand in line?

2. *Patterns* Chandre made the arrangements below using pennies.

Following this pattern, Chandre used 55 pennies to make a triangle. How many pennies were in the bottom row of this large triangle?

3. *Home Improvement* Suppose you want new carpeting for a hallway 18 feet long and 1 yard wide. Each square yard of carpeting costs $25. Installation costs $55. Find the total cost of the new carpet.

4. *Jobs* Paulette and Camila rake leaves and mow lawns on Saturdays. Paulette charges $5 per hour and Camila charges $4 per hour. One day they worked for a combined total of 9 hours and together made $40. How much did each girl earn?

Using Strategies

A strategy can give you a head start in solving a problem. Some strategies you may have already learned include *Draw a Diagram, Make a Table, Look for a Pattern,* and *Guess and Test.*

There are many ways to solve problems. As you learn more about problem solving strategies, you can choose the ones that work best for you.

SAMPLE PROBLEM...

Design A landscape architect was asked to sketch some designs for a small rectangular pool with a fixed width of 1 foot to go in front of the new city courthouse. The pool requires 1-foot tiles around the sides. Here are his first three sketches.

A pool 1 foot long needs 4 square tiles. A pool 2 feet long needs 6 square tiles.

A pool 3 feet long needs 8 square tiles.

Suppose the pool is 6 feet long and follows the pattern in the drawings above. How many square tiles are needed?

•••

The solutions that follow use three different strategies. Ask yourself, "Which strategy would I use?"

Solution 1

STRATEGY: *Draw a Diagram*

The *Draw a Diagram* strategy helps you see the relationships in a problem. Sketch a simple picture that shows the information.

You may want to sketch several pictures. In this problem, for example, you could draw the next four pools in the pattern. Or just draw the pool that is 6 feet long.

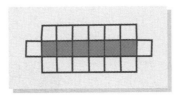

A 6-foot pool needs 14 square tiles.

Solution 2

STRATEGY: *Make a Table*

The *Make a Table* strategy is useful for organizing information so you can analyze it. Put the numbers in the problem into an ordered list like the one below.

Length of Pool	Number of Tiles
1	4
2	6
3	8
4	10
5	12
6	?

Solution 3

STRATEGY: *Look for a Pattern*

Patterns are all around us. They often occur in problems where there is a progression of data. You can find a rule that creates the pattern. Then use the rule to solve the problem.

The *Look for a Pattern* strategy often works well combined with the *Make a Table* strategy.

Length of Pool	Number of Tiles
1	4
2	4 + 2
3	4 + 2 + 2
4	4 + 2 + 2 + 2
5	4 + 2 + 2 + 2 + 2
6	4 + 2 + 2 + 2 + 2 + 2 = 14

The rule here is *add 2*.

The answer is the same. A 6-foot pool needs 14 square tiles.

EXERCISES *On Your Own*

1. *Zoology* The Stone Zoo has two cobras in its reptile collection. One is 8 inches longer than the other. The sum of their lengths is 152 inches. How long is each snake?

2. *Money* Suppose you have dimes, nickels, and pennies in your pocket. You reach in and pull out three coins. What different amounts of money could you could be holding?

3. *Sports* The officials of a soccer league make sure that all the players are called when games are canceled. They use a "telephone tree" to make the calls in rounds. The first person makes 2 phone calls. In the second round, 4 phone calls are made. In the third round, 8 phone calls are made. How many phone calls are made in the sixth round of calls?

4. *Design* If the pattern below continues, how many blocks are needed to make the tenth design in the sequence?

   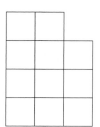

Working Together

Sometimes you may be asked to work in a cooperative group during math class. Sharing ideas and strategies with your classmates can help you become a better problem solver.

Solving problems in a group involves responsibility and cooperation. Usually classrooms have individual and group rules.

Here are some rules for individuals.

- You are responsible for your own work.
- You are responsible for your own behavior.

Here are some rules for groups.

- You must be willing to help other group members.
- All members should contribute to the solution.
- Group members should try to answer questions themselves before asking a teacher.

Part of working together is empowering one of your group members to speak for the entire group.

In a cooperative learning group, members work together to solve problems. Some members of the group may also have specific, individual responsibilities.

- The **recorder** takes notes and records information.

- The **researcher** finds necessary information that has not already been provided.

- Each member of the group should have general supplies such as paper and pencil, a calculator, and a ruler. The **organizer** makes sure that any unusual items, such as a stopwatch or masking tape, are also available.

- The **presenter** explains the group's strategies and solution to the rest of the class.

Though members of your group may have different roles, each must contribute if you are to come up with the best solution to the problem.

EXERCISES *On Your Own*

Solve each problem with your small group. Assign a role to each member of your group. Rotate the role assignments with each new exercise.

1. *Distance* What is the average number of paces taken by a member of your group when you walk a distance of 100 yards together?

2. *Geography* Suppose a planet has two hemispheres. In each hemisphere there are three continents. On each continent there are four countries. In each country there are five states. How many states are there on the planet?

3. *Time* In the morning, the school bell rings at 8:20, 9:05, 9:50, and 10:35. If this pattern continues, will the bell also ring at 11:20? At 12:35?

4. *Money* Eighty people went on the class trip to the local museum. Entrance fees were $2 for students and $3 for adults. The entrance fees totaled $168. How many people on the trip were students?

Preparing for Standardized Tests

Many standardized tests have multiple choice questions. You can use problem solving skills to answer multiple choice questions. Eliminating answers that don't make sense can help you choose the correct answer.

SAMPLE PROBLEM 1

Baking A recipe calls for $2\frac{2}{3}$ cups of sugar. To make half as much as the recipe calls for, how many cups of sugar should you use?

A. $5\frac{1}{3}$ **B.** $4\frac{2}{3}$ **C.** $1\frac{7}{8}$ **D.** $1\frac{1}{3}$ **E.** Not Here

Read and Understand If you make half the recipe, is the amount of sugar you need more than or less than $2\frac{2}{3}$ cups?

Why can you eliminate choices A and B?

Plan You can use the *Draw a Diagram* strategy to see relationships and find the answer.

Solve

Half of $2\frac{2}{3}$ is $1\frac{1}{3}$.

The correct answer is D.

Look Back Check your answer by adding $1\frac{1}{3} + 1\frac{1}{3} = 2\frac{2}{3}$.

Zack gets his household chores done by paying his little brother Mike to do them. Zack gives Mike 1¢ on Monday, 2¢ on Tuesday, 4¢ on Wednesday, and 8¢ on Thursday. According to this pattern, how much will Mike get on Sunday?

A. 64¢ **B.** 32¢ **C.** 10¢ **D.** 4¢ **E.** Not Here

Day	Pay
Mon	1¢
Tue	2¢
Wed	4¢
Thu	8¢
Fri	16¢
Sat	32¢
Sun	64¢

Make a table and look for a pattern.

Eliminate C and D because they don't follow the doubling pattern.

Find Mike's pay for Sunday.

The correct answer is A.

EXERCISES *On Your Own*

Use problem solving strategies and eliminate answers to find the correct answer.

1. Find the missing number in the sequence 1, 4, 9, 16, __, 36.
   A. 32 **B.** 25 **C.** 5 **D.** 3 **E.** Not Here

2. How many square brownies 2 inches on a side can be cut from a square pan 8 inches on a side?
   A. 64 **B.** 16 **C.** 4 **D.** 2 **E.** Not Here

3. Elizabeth bought milk for $1.10, carrots for $.69, cottage cheese for $1.29, and kidney beans for $.59. There was no tax. What was the bill for these items?
   A. $4.76 **B.** $3.76 **C.** $3.67 **D.** $2.48 **E.** Not Here

4. A rectangular garden is 30 feet by 25 feet. How many fence posts do you need to place one every 5 feet?
   A. 24 **B.** 22 **C.** 13 **D.** 6 **E.** Not Here

Using Statistics to Analyze Data

1

| WHAT YOU WILL LEARN IN THIS CHAPTER | • How to gather, display, and graph data | • How to find and use the range, mean, median, and mode | • How to use spreadsheets to analyze data |

ON YOUR OWN TIME

RING!!! The last bell of the day has rung. You and your classmates will soon head in different directions. Some of your classmates are on the same team or in the same club as you. Some of them are not. Do you know how much time your classmates spend on their favorite activities? You could guess the answers to the last question, but a more accurate method of finding the answers would be to collect real data.

Conduct a Survey For the chapter project you will survey 25 of your friends and classmates. You can choose the survey subject, such as how much time is spent on sports. You will organize and graph the data. Then you will make a presentation to your class to display your results.

Steps to help you complete the project:

• **How to solve problems by making tables**

PROBLEM SOLVING

3

Organizing and Displaying Data

What You'll Learn

▼ 1 To organize data into frequency tables

▼ 2 To make a line plot and find the range of data

...And Why

You can use frequency tables and line plots to collect and display data.

Here's How

Look for questions that
⣿ build understanding
✔ check understanding

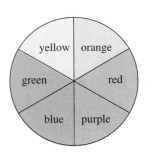

yellow | orange
green | red
blue | purple

 Blue is the favorite color of most Americans. In order, their next most favorite colors are red, green, purple, orange, and yellow.

Source: *3-2-1 Contact*

Work Together   *Organizing Data in a Table*

Art What's your favorite color? Suppose you want to find out the most popular color among students in your math class. Use the colors in the color wheel at the left below.

1. Record the favorite color of each student in a table.

2. Which color was the most popular? How many students picked each of the other colors?

3. ⣿*Draw a Conclusion* Describe how your table helps you organize the data.

THINK AND DISCUSS

▼ 1   *Making Frequency Tables*

A **frequency table** shows the number of times each type of answer occurs. Here's a sample of possible favorite color data.

■ EXAMPLE 1   *Real-World Problem Solving*

Organize responses to favorite color in a frequency table.

List the color choices.   Make a tally mark, |, to record the data.   Count the tally marks and record the frequency.

Favorite Color	Tally	Frequency
blue	⊞⊞⊞					9
purple	⊞⊞⊞			7
red					3
orange			1
yellow				2
green	⊞⊞⊞	5

4. ⣿*Reasoning* How many people responded in Example 1? Describe two ways you can find this number.

5. ✔ *Try It Out* The eye colors of ten students are brown, brown, blue, hazel, green, brown, green, hazel, hazel, and brown. Organize the eye color data in a frequency table.

▼2 *Using Line Plots and Finding the Range*

A **line plot** displays data using a number line.

■ **EXAMPLE 2** *Real-World Problem Solving*

Entertainment Suppose you work at Video Village. One night you kept track of the number of videos each customer rented. Make a line plot of the data given.

3, 5, 1, 2, 2, 1, 4, 1, 4, 2, 3, 3, 4, 1, 5, 2, 6, 2, 2, 4, 3, 1, 1, 2, 4, 2

①Write a title describing the data.

Number of Videos Rented at Video Village

③ Mark an x for each response.

②Draw a number line with the choices below it.

6. ▪**Look Back** How many customers rented videos at Video Village? How did you find this number?

7. ✔ *Try It Out* Make a line plot for the following set of data.
Ring sizes: 7, 5, 6, 6, $6\frac{1}{2}$, 8, 8, $5\frac{1}{2}$, $6\frac{1}{2}$, 9, 8, 5, $8\frac{1}{2}$, 7

The **range** is the difference between the greatest and the least values in a set of numerical data. In Example 2, the range of the number of videos each customer rents is $6 - 1$, or 5 videos.

8. *Geography* In 1852, surveyors made these six measurements of Mt. Everest to determine its height.

28,990 ft	28,992 ft	28,999 ft
29,002 ft	29,005 ft	29,026 ft

   a. What was the greatest height measured? The least height measured?
   b. ✔ *Try It Out* Find the range of the measurements.

1. *Social Studies* A town in Wales is named Llanfairpwllgwyngyllgogerychwyrndrobwllllantysiliogogogoch.
   a. Copy and complete the frequency table using the name of the Welsh town.
   b. *Writing* Describe the data recorded in your frequency table.

Letter	Tally	Frequency
a	|||	3
e	▣	▣
i	▣	▣
o	▣	▣
u	▣	▣

Wales

2. *Literature* The number of letters in each of the first 25 words of the book *The Story of Amelia Earhart* is shown below. Make a frequency table.

   6 3 4 2 3 5 3 7 3 4 3 3 4 3 3 3 6 6 3 5 3 2 3 7 5

Make a frequency table for each set of data.

3. cost of a CD player in several stores: $125, $122, $138, $135, $125, $122, $122, $125

4. lengths of words in a sentence: 5, 6, 3, 7, 4, 2, 3, 4, 6, 3, 4, 6, 2, 11, 5, 2, 5, 2, 4, 4, 3, 8

5. days in each month (nonleap year): 31, 28, 31, 30, 31, 30, 31, 31, 30, 31, 30, 31

6. results of tossing two coins: TT, TH, TT, HH, TH, TH, TH, HH, TT, TH, TH, TH, TT

7. students absent from class: 2, 0, 1, 1, 1, 0, 2, 3, 6, 2, 1, 0, 0, 0, 0, 6, 1, 1, 1, 1, 2, 0

8. goals in soccer games: 3, 2, 0, 0, 2, 2, 1, 3, 1, 1, 5, 1, 1, 0, 0, 1, 0, 1, 1, 3, 2, 0, 1, 4

Make a line plot for each set of data.

9. test scores: 85, 80, 85, 90, 90, 80, 75, 80, 75, 95, 85, 80, 75, 70, 80, 70, 90

10. heights of plants (in.): 10, 12, 15, 11, 12, 15, 13, 9, 14, 12, 11, 13, 10, 11, 11, 9, 12

11. speeds of runners (mi/h): 7, 7, 8, 8, 7, 9, 7, 7, 8, 9, 7, 7, 8, 8, 8, 9, 7, 8, 7, 9, 9, 8, 8, 7

12. shoe sizes: 6, 7, $4\frac{1}{2}$, $5\frac{1}{2}$, 5, 6, $8\frac{1}{2}$, 6, 4, $7\frac{1}{2}$, 8, $5\frac{1}{2}$, 9, 6, 4, 5, $6\frac{1}{2}$, 5, 6, 8, $5\frac{1}{2}$, 7

Find the range of each data set.

13. 4, 5, 3, 4, 5, 5, 5, 4, 5, 0

14. 80, 87, 85, 85, 82, 92, 80

15. $4\frac{1}{2}$, $5\frac{1}{2}$, 5, 6, 6, 4, $7\frac{1}{2}$, 8, $5\frac{1}{2}$, 7

16. a. *Research* Name the 8 states that begin with the letter *M*.
    b. *Data Collection* Ask 20 people to name as many states that begin with the letter *M* as they can. Record the states that each person correctly names in a frequency table.
    c. Display your results in a line plot.
    d. *Writing* Describe the results of your survey. What state was most often missed?

Use the line plot at the right for Exercises 17–19.

Science Test Grades

```
            ×
            ×
      ×     ×
      ×     ×     ×
      ×     ×     ×     ×
      ×     ×     ×     ×     ×
      ←─────────────────────────→
      A     B     C     D     F
```

17. What information is displayed in the line plot?

18. How many test grades are recorded in the line plot?

19. How many students received a grade of C or better?

20. *Sports* The prices of tickets available for a Texas Rangers' baseball game are $20, $18, $16, $12, $9, $10, $10, $9, $8, $6, and $4. Find the range.

21. *Social Studies* The birth states of the first 41 Presidents of the United States are shown at the right.
  a. Make a line plot of the data.
  b. In what four states were the most Presidents born?

22. a. *Reasoning* When would you use a frequency table?
  b. Why do you think it is called a *frequency table?*

23. *Writing* How are frequency tables and line plots alike? How are they different?

24. *Calculator* To the nearest inch, NASA requires that an astronaut be at least 59 in. and at most 76 in. tall. Find the height range.

Presidential Birth States

State	Tally	State	Tally
VA	ЖІІ ІІІ	NJ	І
MA	ІІІІ	IA	І
SC	І	MO	І
NY	ІІІІ	TX	ІІ
NC	ІІ	CA	І
NH	І	NE	І
PA	І	GA	І
KY	І	IL	І
OH	ЖІІ ІІ	AR	І
VT	ІІ		

Mixed Review

Find each answer. *(Previous Course)*

25. $243 + 43 + 817 + 36$

26. $592 - 418$

27. $23,427 - 4,798$

28. $1,585 - 371 + 19$

29. $15,904 - 6,086$

30. $18 + 39 + 22 + 7 + 11$

31. *Choose a Strategy* Jemika has six coins that total 52¢. What coins, and how many of each, does she have?

CHAPTER PROJECT

PROJECT LINK: COLLECTING DATA

Choose a survey topic. Identify seven or eight responses for students to choose. Decide how to organize the responses of your 25 friends or classmates. Collect and record the data in a table or chart.

1-2 Make a Table

READ PLAN LOOK BACK SOLVE

Problem Solving Strategies

Draw a Diagram
Guess and Test
Look for a Pattern
Make a Model
✔ Make a Table
Simulate a Problem
Solve a Simpler Problem
Too Much or Too Little
 Information
Use Logical Reasoning
Use Multiple Strategies
Work Backward

 READ

Read for understanding.
Summarize the problem.

 PLAN

Decide on a strategy.

 SOLVE

Try the strategy.

THINK AND DISCUSS

Sometimes you need to make a table to help you solve a problem. Use a table to list information in a logical way. Then you don't skip or leave out important parts of the answer.

SAMPLE PROBLEM..

Robert has a pocket full of coins. With just these coins, he can show you all possible ways to make 18¢. How many ways can Robert show you?

....

Think about the information you are given and what you are asked to find.

1. What does the problem ask you to find?

2. What types of coins must Robert have in his pocket? What is the value of each of these coins?

You can make a table to help you organize the possible ways to make 18¢.

3. Suppose Robert shows you only dimes and pennies. How many of each coin is needed to make 18¢?

4. Suppose Robert shows you one dime and one nickel. How many pennies are needed to make 18¢?

You can form an organized list of all possible ways to make 18¢.

Dimes	Nickels	Pennies
1	0	8
:	:	:
0	0	18

5. Copy and complete the table above.

6. Why does the number 2 not appear in the *Dimes* column?

7. How many ways can Robert make 18¢? Check your answer for reasonableness.

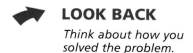 **LOOK BACK**

Think about how you solved the problem.

You can use the table you made to answer many other questions.

8. Find and describe any patterns in the numbers that appear in your table.

9. What is the minimum number of coins needed to make 18¢?

10. What is the maximum number of coins needed to make 18¢?

11. Ten coins total 18¢. Name the ten coins.

EXERCISES *On Your Own*

Make a table to solve each problem.

1. How many possible ways are there to make 28¢?

2. There is 16¢ in a bag. There are more nickels than pennies.
   a. What types of coins are in the bag?
   b. How many of each type of coin are in the bag?

3. *Rides* The carnival has two types of children's rides. Each race car seats 4 children and each tugboat seats 6 children. Altogether there are 28 race cars and tugboats that seat a total of 136 children. How many of each ride are there?

Use any strategy to solve each problem. Show all your work.

4. *Newspapers* Michael has a paper route. He earns 15¢ for each daily paper and 35¢ for each Sunday paper he delivers. Michael delivers twice as many daily papers each week as Sunday papers. How many of each type of paper does he deliver if he earns $13 each week?

5. *Games* Chris's favorite game uses three Velcro darts and a Velcro board like the one at the right. When a dart lands on a line, the higher value is counted. What possible scores can Chris get if all three darts hit the board?

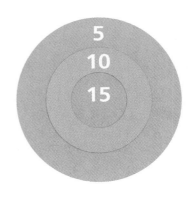

6. *Fruits* Six apples weigh the same as two grapefruits and two kiwis. A grapefruit weighs the same as eight kiwis. How many kiwis weigh as much as one apple?

7. *Transportation* Buses leave Boston for New York every 40 min. The first bus leaves at 5:10 A.M. What is the departure time closest to 12:55 P.M.?

8. *Supplies* Carlos spent $13 on pens, pencils, and notebooks. Pens cost $2. Pencils cost $1. Notebooks cost $4. How many combinations of school supplies could Carlos have bought?

9. *Jewelry* You want to make a single length of chain from the links shown below. Find the least number of links that must be opened and then closed to do this.

10. Sue, Kelly, and Carmen earned degrees in engineering, nursing, and law. Sue and the engineer plan to share an apartment. The nurse helps Carmen pack. Kelly's law firm specializes in corporate law. Who is the engineer?

11. *Clothes* Ken has a blue shirt, a yellow shirt, a white shirt, a pair of black pants, and a pair of jeans. How many different outfits does Ken have to choose from?

Mixed Review

Use the following data. *(Lesson 1-1)*
Student heights (inches): 53, 55, 60, 53, 57, 55, 52, 54, 53, 55

12. Make a frequency table.   13. Make a line plot.   14. Find the range.

15. *Book Club* Andrés is starting a book club. He is the only member now, but he plans to have each member find an additional 3 new members each month. How many members does Andrés expect to have after 6 months? *(Previous Course)*

SKILLS REVIEW

WHOLE NUMBER DIVISION

Before Lesson 1-3

Division is the opposite of multiplication. So you multiply the divisor by your estimate for each digit in the quotient. Then subtract. You repeat this step until you have a remainder that is less than the divisor.

■ EXAMPLE

Divide $23\overline{)1{,}158}$.

Step 1: Estimate the quotient.

$$1{,}158 \div 23$$ ← The dividend is 1,158. The divisor is 23.

$$1{,}200 \div 20 \approx 60$$ ← Mentally round 1,158 to the nearest hundred. Mentally round 23 to the nearest ten.

Step 2:

$$
\begin{array}{r}
6 \\
23\overline{)1158} \\
-138
\end{array}
$$

← Try 6 tens.

← 6 × 23 = 138 You cannot subtract so 6 tens is too much.

Step 3:

$$
\begin{array}{r}
5 \\
23\overline{)1158} \\
-115 \\
\hline
0
\end{array}
$$

← Try 5 tens.

← 5 × 23 = 115

← Subtract.

Step 4:

$$
\begin{array}{r}
50 \text{ R}8 \\
23\overline{)1158} \\
-115\downarrow \\
\hline
08 \\
-0 \\
\hline
8
\end{array}
$$

← Bring down 8.

← 0 × 23 = 0

← Subtract. The remainder is 8.

Step 5: Check your answer.

First compare your answer to your estimate.
Since 50 R8 is close to 60, the answer is reasonable.

Then find $50 \times 23 + 8$.

Divide. Check your answer.

1. $7\overline{)212}$
2. $9\overline{)376}$
3. $3\overline{)280}$
4. $8\overline{)541}$
5. $6\overline{)483}$

6. $1{,}058 \div 5$
7. $3{,}018 \div 6$
8. $5{,}072 \div 7$
9. $1{,}718 \div 4$
10. $3{,}767 \div 6$

11. $3{,}372 \div 67$
12. $19\overline{)1{,}373}$
13. $62\overline{)2{,}129}$
14. $4{,}165 \div 59$
15. $41\overline{)4{,}038}$

16. $2{,}612 \div 31$
17. $34\overline{)1{,}609}$
18. $1{,}937 \div 48$
19. $54\overline{)1{,}350}$
20. $1{,}850 \div 82$

21. *Writing* Describe how to estimate a quotient. Use the words *dividend* and *divisor* in your description.

1-3 Mean, Median, and Mode

What You'll Learn

▼ To find the mean

② To find the median or mode

...And Why

You can find the median length of comedy movies or discover which hobby is most popular.

Here's How

Look for questions that
- ▪ build understanding
- ✔ check understanding

Work Together

Finding Averages

Is your name longer than average? Let's find out!

1. Write the names of the students in your class on strips of graph paper as shown.

2. Find the average length of the names of the students in your group. Describe how your group found this number.

3. ▪ *Analyze* Compare your work with other groups. Did everyone find the average length of the names the same way? Explain.

uri

Gregory

Daria

Miki

Angela

THINK AND DISCUSS

1 *Finding the Mean*

You are probably familiar with the word *average*. In mathematics, an average is called a mean. The **mean** is the sum of the data divided by the number of data items.

■ EXAMPLE 1 *Real-World Problem Solving*

Airplanes Use the data table at the left. Find the mean wingspan of the jet airliners.

Step 1: Find the sum of the data.

Step 2: Divide the sum by the number of data items.

Method 1: Paper and Pencil

```
①  60        ②      50
   45            5)250
   44             − 25
   58              000
 + 43
  250
```

Method 2: Calculator

```
① 60 ⊞ 45 ⊞ 44 ⊞
   58 ⊞ 43 ▤ 250
② 250 ⊟ 5 ▤ 50
```

The mean wingspan of the jet airliners is 50 meters.

Wingspan of Jet Airliners

Type	Wingspan (meters)
Airbus A330	60
McDonnell Douglas DCB Super 63	45
Boeing 707	44
Ilyushin IL-96-300	58
Ilyushin IL-62	43

Source: *The Cambridge Factfinder*

4. The wingspan of the Concorde is 26 meters. Suppose you include this value with the set of data in Example 1.
 a. ⊞ *Estimation* Estimate the mean. Do you think the mean will be greater than or less than 50?
 b. ✔ *Try It Out* Find the mean.

5. ✔ *Try It Out* Find the mean of each data set.
 a. 23, 25, 19, 20, 21, 23, 23 **b.** 6, 3, 4, 6, 4, 5, 6, 4, 7

▼ *Finding the Median or Mode*

If the data set has an extreme high or low value, the median is a better measure to use. The **median** is the middle number in a set of ordered data.

Order the data.

18 3 20 17 22 20 19 ⟶ 3 17 18 19 20 20 22

↑
median

6. *Temperature* The daily temperatures (°F) at noon for one week are 86, 78, 92, 79, 87, 91, and 77.
 a. Order the data values.
 b. ✔ *Try It Out* Find the median.

When there is an even number of data items, you can find the median by adding the two middle numbers and dividing by 2.

■ **EXAMPLE 2** *Real-World Problem Solving*

Entertainment Find the median length of the comedy movies at the right.

Lengths of 10 Comedy Movies (min)				
111	105	100	101	101
92	87	96	92	95

111 105 100 101 101 92 87 96 92 95 ⟵ List the data.
87 92 92 95 96 100 101 101 105 111 ⟵ Order the data.

⟵ Identify the middle numbers.

$\frac{96 + 100}{2} = 98$ ⟵ Add and divide by 2.

The median is 98.

7. ✔ *Try It Out* Find the median of each data set.
 a. 78, 90, 88, 76, 102, 79, 80 **b.** 10, 5, 7, 13, 14, 12, 12, 10

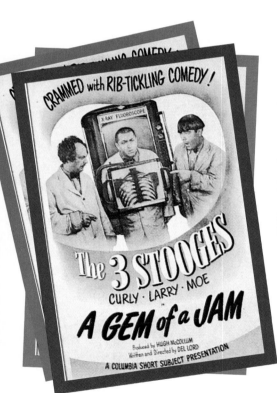

In the 1930s and early 1940s, the Three Stooges became popular in short films that played for 15–20 minutes before each feature film.

Data can also be described by the *mode*. The **mode** is the data value that appears most often. The mode is most helpful when the data are not numerical.

■ **EXAMPLE 3**   *Real-World Problem Solving*

The line plot shows the items collected by a group of students. Find the mode.

Collectibles

```
                    ×
      ×             ×
      ×             ×                       ×
      ×             ×             ×         ×
      ×             ×             ×         ×
      ×             ×             ×         ×          ×
   ───────────────────────────────────────────────────────
     Coins        Cards        Stamps  Comic Books    Other
```

The mode is cards because it appears most often.

A set of data can have more than one mode. There is no mode when all the data items occur the same number of times.

8. ⚓ *Look Back* Refer to Example 3. Suppose a student who collects stamps collects coins instead. Find the mode.

9. What would a line plot look like if the data set had no mode?

10. ✔ *Try It Out* Find the mean, median, and mode of each data set.
    a. 15 12 20 13 17 19   **b.** 95 80 92 91 98 94 94

EXERCISES *On Your Own*

Find the mean of each data set.

1. 12, 9, 11, 8, 9, 12, 9

2. 6, 5, 7, 5, 7, 6

3. 3, 2, 0, 2, 2, 3, 3, 1

4. 14, 18, 22, 19, 22, 9, 15

5. 18, 21, 19, 17, 19, 20

6. 125, 95, 115, 90, 100

7. 25, 13, 29, 26, 20, 19

8. 112, 112, 115, 109, 107

9. 0, 5, 25, 50, 75, 100, 25

Open-ended **Create a data set that is best described with the given measure. Then describe the data set.**

10. mode

11. mean

12. median

13. *Music* The line plot shows the number of songs on 30 recently released CDs.

Number of Songs on CDs

```
        x
        x
        x
        x       x
        x       x
    x   x   x   x
    x   x   x   x   x
x   x   x   x   x   x           x
x   x   x   x   x   x           x
──────────────────────────────────▶
10  11  12  13  14  15  16  17
```

a. Find the median and mode.
b. *Writing* Would it make sense to use the mean to describe these data? Why or why not?

Find the median of each data set.

14. 5, 7, 8, 7, 7, 5, 8

15. 14, 20, 24, 16, 20, 18

16. 88, 93, 87, 90, 88

17. 50, 52, 48, 52, 48, 52

18. 500, 450, 475, 450, 500

19. 820, 800, 775, 850

20. 350, 190, 40, 110, 230, 70

21. 17, 17, 17, 17, 17, 17

22. 5, 9, 5, 9, 5, 9

Find the mode of each data set.

23. 3, 2, 5, 2, 2, 5, 4, 3, 2

24. 100, 100, 100

25. 0, 1, 1, 1, 0, 1, 1, 0, 0, 0

26. 87, 92, 90, 89, 87, 91

27. 9, 10, 12, 9, 12, 11

28. 31, 28, 31, 30, 31, 30

29. 31, 31, 30, 31, 30, 31

30. T, H, T, T, H, H, H, T

31. 5, 6, 9, 8, 4, 7, 10, 3, 11

32. fish, beef, vegetarian, chicken, chicken, beef, chicken

33. Choose A, B, C, or D. Marc's teacher allows students to decide whether to record the mean, median, or mode of their test scores as their test score. Marc's score will be highest if he uses the mean. Which set of grades is Marc's?
  A. 74, 80, 92, 82, 92   **B.** 74, 80, 74, 82, 85   **C.** 74, 80, 92, 85, 74   **D.** 74, 80, 70, 71, 80

34. *Sports* In Major League baseball, a baseball is used for an average of five pitches before it is replaced. Find seven numbers that have a mean of 5.

Which measure—mean, median, or mode—best describes the data set? Explain your reasoning.

35. 54, 63, 47, 114, 51

36. 40, 50, 45, 30, 35

37. blue, red, blue, blue, white

38. 80, 80, 80, 55, 80

JOURNAL
Describe mean, median, and mode. Provide an example for each description.

Mixed Review

Find each answer. *(Previous Course)*

39. 2,057 − 569   **40.** 114 × 12   **41.** 248 ÷ 8   **42.** 37 × 27   **43.** 1,001 ÷ 13

44. *Patterns* At one point on a mountain road, the elevation is 4,000 ft. Two miles up the road, the elevation is 5,200 ft. Suppose this pattern continues. Predict the elevation six miles up the road from the starting point. *(Lesson 1-2)*

CHAPTER PROJECT

PROJECT LINK: ANALYZING DATA

Order the responses of your classmates by popularity. Find the mean, median, and mode of the data. Determine which measure is more typical of the responses. Explain why.

✓ CHECKPOINT 1

Lessons 1-1 through 1-3

Communications Use the table at the right.

1. Find the mean number of stations.

2. Find the median.   **3.** Find the mode.

Nutrition Use the data below for Exercises 4 and 5.
Grams of fat per serving for 25 popular breakfast cereals:
0, 1, 1, 3, 1, 1, 2, 2, 0, 3, 1, 3, 2, 0, 1, 0, 2, 1, 1, 0, 0, 0, 2, 1, 0

4. Make a frequency table.   **5.** Make a line plot.

6. How many possible ways are there to make $1 without using pennies?

States with the Most Public Radio Stations

State	Number of Stations
Alaska	15
California	23
Illinois	15
Michigan	20
Minnesota	17
New York	33
Ohio	20
Texas	15
Wisconsin	22

Source: *The Top 10 of Everything*

Choose the best answer.

1. Arturo played three games of miniature golf. His scores were 89, 84, and 94. What was his mean (average) score for the 3 games?

   A. 84   **B.** 89   **C.** 94   **D.** 287

2. Which measurement is most reasonable for the height of a refrigerator?

   F. 2 inches   **G.** 2 feet
   H. 2 yards   **J.** 2 miles

3. If Jeremy grows 3 more inches, he will be 6 feet tall. How tall is Jeremy now?

   A. 57 inches   **B.** 63 inches
   C. 69 inches   **D.** 75 inches

4. An ordinary shoe box has the top removed so that it is an open-topped box. How many sides does the box have after the top is removed?

   F. 3   **G.** 4   **H.** 5   **J.** 6

5. Forty-eight roses are to be split into 8 equal groups. Which of the following would you use to find the number of roses in each group?

   A. 48×8 **B.** $48 + 6$
   C. $48 - 8$ **D.** $48 \div 8$

Please note that items 6–9 have *five* answer choices.

6. A public library lent the following numbers of books each day for a week. Find the median.

        12 29 14 18 26 26 22

   F. 18   **G.** 21   **H.** 22   **J.** 26   **K.** Not Here

7. Melitha can make a silk bouquet in 15 to 20 minutes. What is a reasonable number of bouquets she can make in 240 minutes?

   A. less than 8
   B. between 8 and 11
   C. between 12 and 16
   D. between 17 and 20
   E. more than 20

8. The graph shows the number of laps Mackenzie swam each day.

   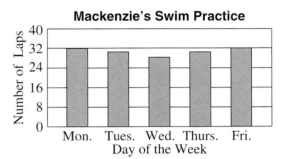

   How many total laps did Mackenzie swim?

   F. 32   **G.** 30
   H. 142   **J.** 152
   K. Not Here

9. Paul is taking a trip. His plane ticket will cost $198. His hotel will cost $65 per night. He budgets $35 per day for food and extras. He has saved $1,200. What else do you need to know to find if he has saved enough?

   A. the cost of luggage
   B. the number of rooms available
   C. the length of the vacation stay
   D. the number of flights per day
   E. the cost of plays he will attend

1-4 Using Spreadsheets to Organize Data

What You'll Learn

1. To organize data in a spreadsheet
2. To create formulas for spreadsheets

...And Why

Spreadsheets can help you organize data about CDs.

Here's How

Look for questions that
- build understanding
- ✔ check understanding

THINK AND DISCUSS

1 Using Spreadsheets

A compact disc can hold nearly 80 minutes of music. Do some types of CDs contain more music than other types?

You can use a **spreadsheet** to organize and analyze data. A **cell** is the spreadsheet box where a row and a column meet.

■ EXAMPLE 1 Real-World Problem Solving

Music The spreadsheet below shows the lengths of 15 CDs from five different categories. Identify the value of cell B5.

column B →

	A	B	C	D	E
1	Music Type	Disk 1 (min)	Disk 2 (min)	Disk 3 (min)	Mean Length (min)
2	Rock/Pop	40	44	45	
3	Rap	48	53	55	
4	Country	32	34	30	
5	Classical	45	54	51	
6	Jazz	41	53	44	

row 5 →

cell B5

The value in cell B5 is 45.

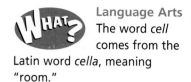
1. a. ✔ *Try It Out* What is the value of cell D4 in Example 1? What does this number mean?
   b. What cells are in row 2?

2. a. ⬛ *Look Back* Which cell in Example 1 contains the greatest value? The least value?
   b. What type of music is on the CD that contains the greatest amount of music? The least amount of music?

2 Creating Formulas

A computer automatically fills in the values for a cell of a spreadsheet if you tell it what calculations to do. A **formula** is a statement of a mathematical relationship. You can use a formula to tell the computer what to do.

■ EXAMPLE 2

Use the spreadsheet shown in Example 1.
a. Describe how to calculate the value of E2 without using a computer.

Without using a computer, find the mean of the values in row 2.

$$\frac{40 + 44 + 45}{3} = \frac{129}{3} = 43$$

The mean of the values in row 2 is 43.

b. *Algebra* Write the formula for cell E2.

To write the formula, use cell names instead of values.
Enter =(B2+C2+D2)/3 into cell E2.

3. ⬛ *Explain* Why are cell names used instead of numbers?

4. Use the spreadsheet in Example 1.
   a. ✔ *Try It Out* Write the formulas for cells E3 through E6.
   b. Find the mean lengths for each of the five types of music.

5. ⬛ *What If . . .* Explain what will happen to the value in E4 if each of the following occurs.
   a. the value in cell C4 increases
   b. the value in cell B4 decreases
   c. the value in cell B3 increases

Use the spreadsheet below for Exercises 1–14.

Each group of students created a video and received scores for originality, effort, and quality. Suppose their teacher entered all the data, but a "bug" in the program erased some of the data.

	A	B	C	D	E	F
1	Group	Originality	Effort	Quality	Total	Mean Score
2	Red	90	▦	80	▦	85
3	Orange	90	90	▦	▦	80
4	Yellow	95	100	75	▦	▦
5	Green	▦	80	80	▦	75
6	Blue	85	▦	85	▦	85

Identify the cell or cells that indicate each category.

1. Effort **2.** Mean Score **3.** Mean Score for Red **4.** Green

5. Total for Yellow **6.** Originality **7.** Quality for Blue **8.** Effort for Orange

9. Write the formulas that the teacher could have used to determine the values for cells E2 through E6.

10. Choose A, B, or C. Which formula could the teacher *not* have used to find the value for cell F2?
   A. =E2/3
   B. =(B2+B3+B4)/3
   C. =(B2+C2+D2)/3

11. *Writing* Explain how to find the value in cell D3.

 12. a. *Technology* Copy and complete the spreadsheet above.
   b. Which group created the most original video?
   c. Which group put the least effort into creating their video?
   d. Which group did the best job overall? Explain.

13. *Reasoning* Was it necessary to include column E in the spreadsheet to determine the mean score for each group? Explain.

14. *Number Sense* Why does the value in cell B5 have to be less than 80?

Use the spreadsheet below for Exercises 15–29.

Suppose a student works a part-time job and makes $6 per hour. The spreadsheet below shows a typical schedule for a week.

	A	B	C	D	E
1	Day	Time In (P.M.)	Time Out (P.M.)	Hours Worked	Amount Earned
2	9/15	3	5	▦	▦
3	9/17	4	6	▦	▦
4	9/19	3	6	▦	▦
5	9/20	1	6	▦	▦
6			Total:	▦	▦
7			Mean:	▦	▦

Write the value for the given cell.

15. C2   **16.** C5   **17.** B4   **18.** B2   **19.** C3   **20.** B5

Describe how to calculate the value of the given cell.

21. D2   **22.** E2   **23.** E6   **24.** D7   **25.** D5   **26.** E7

27. Write the formulas for the cells in columns D and E.

 28. a. *Computer* Make a spreadsheet like the one above. Enter formulas in columns D and E.
     b. Copy or print the completed spreadsheet.

29. a. How much does this student earn in a typical week?
     b. Which cell tells you this?

> **JOURNAL**
> Summarize what you know about spreadsheets. Include instructions for writing formulas using cells.

Mixed Review

Use the data 37, 11, 15, 16, 19, 11, 13, 20, and 11 to find the following. *(Lessons 1-1 and 1-3)*

30. range   **31.** mean   **32.** median   **33.** mode

34. *Temperature* At 9:00 P.M., the temperature was 42°F. By midnight, it had dropped 8 degrees. By 10:00 A.M., it had risen 15 degrees. Find the temperature at 10:00 A.M.
(Previous Course)

1-5 Reading and Understanding Graphs

What You'll Learn

▼ **1** To read and understand bar and line graphs

▼ **2** To read and understand circle graphs

...And Why

Reading graphs can help you discover information about recycling, in-line skating, and playing an instrument.

Here's How

Look for questions that
- ⁙ build understanding
- ✔ check understanding

THINK AND DISCUSS

1 ✔ *Reading Bar and Line Graphs*

You can display data using graphs. The type of graph you choose depends on the type of data you have collected and the idea you want to communicate. A **bar graph** is used to compare amounts.

■ **EXAMPLE 1**   *Real-World Problem Solving*

Recycling Use the bar graph below. How much money is earned by recycling newspapers?

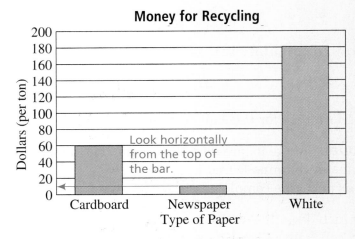

Money for Recycling

Look horizontally from the top of the bar.

Recycling newspapers earns $10 per ton.

1. **a.** ⁙*Look Back* Refer to Example 1. Order the types of paper from highest to lowest dollar amount per ton.
   b. How does the bar graph allow you to make these comparisons quickly?
   c. ⁙*Analyze* Describe the relationship between the heights of the bars and the dollars per ton of paper.

2. ✔ *Try It Out* How much is cardboard worth? How much is white paper worth?

3. ⁙ *What If . . .* Refer to Example 1. A neighborhood collected 15 tons of newspaper. How much money will they earn?

Paper has been made from recycled materials since early times. The Chinese invented paper in A.D. 105, using discarded rags and fishing nets. Trees were not cut down for paper-making until the 1850s.

Source: *Origins of Everything Under, and Including, the Sun*

A **line graph** shows how an amount changes over time.

■ **EXAMPLE 2**   *Real-World Problem Solving*

In-Line Skating Use the line graph below. How many in-line skaters were there in 1994?

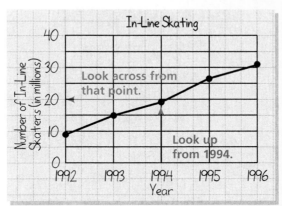

Source: IISA

There were about 20 million in-line skaters in 1994.

4. ⬣**Look Back** What trend does the line graph above show? Explain.

5. ✔ *Try It Out* Use the line graph in Example 2. Estimate how many in-line skaters there were in the year given.
   a. 1992   **b.** 1993   **c.** 1995   **d.** 1996

❷ *Reading Circle Graphs*

A **circle graph** compares parts to a whole. The entire circle represents the whole. Each wedge represents a part of the whole.

■ **EXAMPLE 3**   *Real-World Problem Solving*

Music Use the circle graph at the right. What instrument do more amateur musicians play than any other?

More amateur musicians play the piano than any other instrument.

Instruments Played by Amateurs

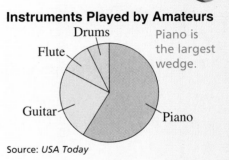

Source: *USA Today*

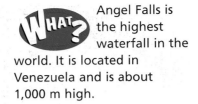

Angel Falls is the highest waterfall in the world. It is located in Venezuela and is about 1,000 m high.

Source: *The Information Please Almanac*

6. ✔ *Try It Out* Use the circle graph in Example 3. What instrument do the fewest amateur musicians play?

7. ⠿*Reasoning* Describe the relationship between the size of the circle wedges and the number of musicians in Example 3.

Work Together *Choosing the Most Appropriate Graph*

Work with a partner.

8. ⠿*Reasoning* Choose the most appropriate type of graph to display each set of data. Support your answer.
   a. students from each grade that are in the chorus
   b. school enrollment for each year from 1995 to the present
   c. heights of the ten highest waterfalls in the world

9. ⠿*Open-ended* Describe two situations that would best be displayed by each type of graph. Write each description on a separate index card. Then ask your partner to identify the most appropriate graph for each situation.

   a. bar graph   b. line graph   c. circle graph

EXERCISES *On Your Own*

Geography Use the bar graph at the right.

1. Which New England state has the greatest amount of land? The least amount of land?

2. Which New England states have about the same amount of land?

3. Compare the amount of land in Maine to the amount of land in Vermont.

Area of New England States

Food Use the circle graph at the right.

4. What is the least popular lunch choice for students? How do you know by looking at the circle graph?

5. Why is a circle graph a good graph to use to convince this school's cafeteria to improve their hot-lunch program?

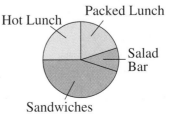

Lunch Choices

Hot Lunch · Packed Lunch · Salad Bar · Sandwiches

Recreation **For Exercises 6–9, use the line graph below.**

The Albuquerque International Balloon Fiesta

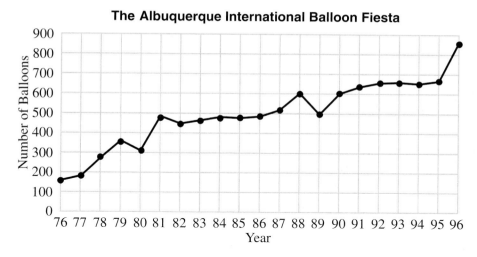

6. What overall trend does the line graph show?

7. During what periods did the number of balloons taking part in the Fiesta remain about the same?

8. During what years did the number of balloons taking part in the Fiesta increase the most?

9. How many balloons took part in the Fiesta in the year given?

    a. 1992   **b.** 1996   **c.** your birth year

Education **Use the circle graph at the right.**

Number of Teachers for the Typical Middle Grade Student

10. How many teachers do most middle grade students have?

11. Do about the same number of middle grade students have one teacher as have four teachers? Explain.

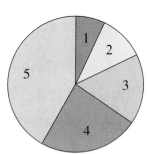

Choose the most appropriate type of graph to display each set of data. Explain your reasoning.

12. the number of left-handed students and the number of right-handed students in your math class

13. the number of cases of chicken pox in the United States for the years 1935, 1945, 1955, 1965, 1975, 1985, and 1995

14. the life spans of selected animals

15. the average annual temperature from 1990 to the present

Go for the Gold !

Olympic Awards

Beginning in 1994, Olympic winners received money as well as medals. The amount is based on the type of medal won.

The U.S. Olympic Committee says the awards provide "a way to pay for training, to stay in the sport longer."

Sports Use the article above for Exercises 16 and 17.

16. How much money does an Olympic gold medalist receive? A silver medalist? A bronze medalist?

17. *Writing* Describe the relationship between the length of the bar and the award amount for each type of Olympic medal.

18. *Data Analysis* What type of data is best displayed on a line graph?

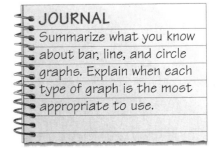

JOURNAL
Summarize what you know about bar, line, and circle graphs. Explain when each type of graph is the most appropriate to use.

Mixed Review

Find the mean, median, and mode. *(Lesson 1-3)*

19. 156, 159, 151, 155, 157, 155, 152

20. 10, 60, 18, 98, 54, 25, 67, 84

21. *Choose a Strategy* Find two consecutive positive numbers whose product is 462.

Math at Work

PARK RANGER

Do you enjoy working outdoors? Are you interested in history? If so, maybe a career as a park ranger is for you! Park rangers use mathematics to predict the number of visitors, measure rainfall and tree growth, plan trails, solve problems involving acid rain or deforestation, and construct time lines.

For more information about national parks, visit the Prentice Hall Web site: www.phschool.com

Making Bar and Line Graphs

What You'll Learn

▼ To make bar graphs
▼ To make line graphs

...And Why

You can make bar and line graphs to show trends in wildlife data.

Here's How

Look for questions that
▪ build understanding
✔ check understanding

U.S. Endangered Animals

Type of Animal	Number of Species
Mammals	55
Birds	74
Reptiles	14
Amphibians	7
Fish	65

Source: U.S. Fish and Wildlife Service

THINK AND DISCUSS

❶ *Making Bar Graphs*

Many animals face the danger of disappearing forever. The main causes are human activities like hunting and pollution and environmental changes.

■ **EXAMPLE 1** *Real-World Problem Solving*

Animal Studies Make a bar graph to display the data shown in the table at the left.

Draw and label the horizontal and vertical axes.

Choose an appropriate title.

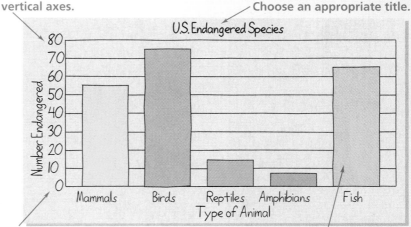

Choose a scale. The data goes from 7 to 74. Mark 0 to 80 in units of 10.

Draw bars of equal widths. The heights will vary.

1. ▪**Look Back** Refer to Example 1. How would you display this data in a bar graph where the bars are horizontal?

2. ▪**Reasoning** Suppose the vertical axis were marked in units of five. List an advantage and a disadvantage of using units of five instead of ten.

3. Choose a scale for the given data.
   a. 6, 3, 11, 14, 7   b. 125, 160, 52, 75, 180
   c. the average speeds of five animals ranging from 25 mi/h to 60 mi/h

2 Making Line Graphs

When you make a line graph, you use points instead of bars. These points are connected to show changes over time.

■ **EXAMPLE 2** *Real-World Problem Solving*

Population Make a line graph to display the changing population of Cleveland.

Population of Ohio Cities

Year	Cleveland	Columbus
1950	914,808	375,901
1960	876,050	471,316
1970	751,000	540,000
1980	574,000	565,000
1990	505,616	632,958

Source: Bureau of the Census

Draw and label the axes.

Choose an appropriate title

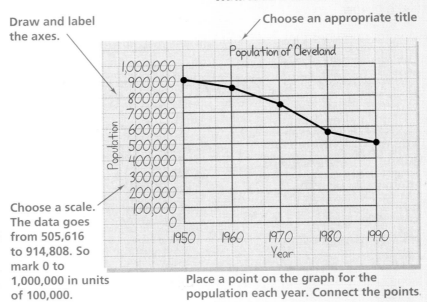

Choose a scale. The data goes from 505,616 to 914,808. So mark 0 to 1,000,000 in units of 100,000.

Place a point on the graph for the population each year. Connect the points.

4. a. **Look Back** What trend does the line graph in Example 2 show?

 b. Would changing the numbers marked on the vertical axis affect the trend? Explain.

5. a. ✔ *Try It Out* Make a line graph to display the population of Columbus. Use the data in Example 2. Describe the trend shown in the line graph.

 b. Make a bar graph to display the population of Columbus.

 c. **Analyze** Compare the graphs of parts (a) and (b).

Each graph below displays the same data. All three graphs are drawn incorrectly.

Weight of Your Backpack

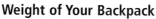
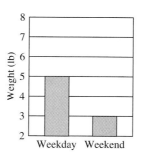 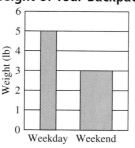 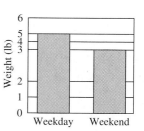

6. Analyze each graph and describe the error.

7. ✔ *Try It Out* Make a bar graph using the same data. Be sure your graph is drawn correctly.

EXERCISES *On Your Own*

Suppose you graphed the given data. Should you use units of 5, 10, 100, 1,000, or 5,000 for the scale? Explain.

1. 10,275 ft; 12,383 ft; 19,904 ft; 1,575 ft

2. $153, $215, $499, $385, $260, $428

3. 10,122 lb; 25,875 lb; 9,673 lb; 37,111 lb

4. 999, 56, 87, 156, 484, 525

5. 15 s, 27 s, 49 s, 8 s, 35 s, 59 s, 18 s, 33 s

6. $10,000; $17,000; $19,500; $15,900

Education **Use the table at the right.**

7. Choose A, B, or C. How would you best mark the scale used to graph the data?
A. units of 10 **B.** units of 100 **C.** units of 1,000

8. a. *Data Analysis* Make a line graph to display the number of schools with CD-ROMs.
   b. Make a line graph to display the number of schools with satellite dishes. Use the same scale you used in part (a).
   c. Describe the trend(s) shown in your line graphs.
   d. Which type of technology has increased at a higher rate? How is this shown on the graph?

Technology in Schools

Year	Number of CD-ROMs	Schools With Satellite Dishes
1992	5,706	1,129
1993	11,021	8,812
1994	24,526	12,580
1995	31,501	14,290

Source: Quality Education Data, Inc.

Architecture **Use the table at the right.**

9. *Writing* Would you use the same scale to graph the number of stories as the height? Why or why not?

10. Make a bar graph to display the number of stories in New York City's five tallest buildings.

11. Make a bar graph to display the height in feet of New York City's five tallest buildings.

Five Tallest Buildings in New York City

Building	Stories	Height
World Trade Center (North)	110	1,368 ft
World Trade Center (South)	110	1,362 ft
Empire State Building	102	1,250 ft
Chrysler Building	77	1,046 ft
American International Building	67	950 ft

Source: *World Almanac*

Choose a scale for the given data.

12. 8, 17, 12, 8, 7, 15, 13, 9   13. 8, 17, 25, 6, 49, 56, 64, 68   14. 121, 152, 123, 147, 164, 188

15. 68, 69, 70, 82, 99, 129, 56   16. 9, 11, 13, 10, 9, 9, 19, 12, 9   17. 12,235; 12,383; 18,911

18. 122, 199, 175, 196, 127   19. 15, 128, 75, 53, 90, 46, 2, 7   20. 36; 216; 1,296; 1,776; 842

Find the error in each graph.

21.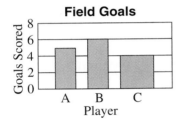

22.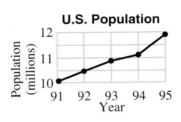

23.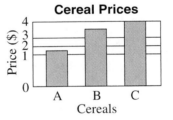

24. a. *Hobbies* Would you use a bar graph or a line graph to display the data in the table at the right? Explain your choice.
   b. Graph the data.

25. a. *Technology* Display the data in the spreadsheet below as a line graph.
   b. Display the data as a bar graph.
   c. Is the line graph or bar graph a better display of the data? Explain.

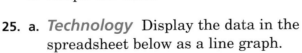

Top-Selling Stamp Sets

Stamp Set	Sales in Millions
The Civil War	46.6
Legends of The West	46.5
World War II	32.5
Jazz Musicians	26.5
Great Lakes Lighthouses	26.2

Source: The Associated Press

	A	B	C	D	E	F
1	Year	1950	1960	1970	1980	1990
2	U.S. Population (per square mile)	43	51	58	64	70

Mixed Review

Make a line plot of the data. *(Lesson 1-1)*

26. A, C, C, D, A, A, B, A, F   **27.** 16, 18, 18, 20, 18, 16, 17   **28.** 29, 36, 25, 29, 36, 29, 36, 26

29. S, L, XL, M, L, L, XL, L   **30.** 93, 87, 95, 87, 94, 95, 90   **31.** 1, 6, 6, 2, 5, 3, 1, 6, 4, 3, 6

**Name the type of graph that would be most appropriate.
Explain your choice.** *(Lesson 1-5)*

32. how the school's budget is spent

33. average monthly rainfall in Seattle, Washington

34. home prices from 1990 to the present

✓ CHECKPOINT 2 Lessons 1-4 through 1-6

Use the spreadsheet below for Exercises 1 and 2.

	A	B	C	D	E	F
1	Student	Test 1	Test 2	Test 3	Test 4	Mean Score
2	Justin	80	78	94	88	
3	Elizabeth	64	78	82	80	
4	Naomi	94	84	88	82	

1. Choose A, B, or C. What formula could you use to
determine the value in cell F4?
A. =(B2+B3+B4)/3   **B.** =(A4+B4+C4+D4+E4)/5   **C.** =(B4+C4+D4+E4)/4

2. Make a bar graph to display the mean scores for the students
listed in the spreadsheet.

Use the circle graph at the right.

3. Which branch of the U.S. armed forces received the most
Medals of Honor for service in the Vietnam War?

4. How many Medals of Honor were awarded for service in
the Vietnam War?

Vietnam Medals of Honor

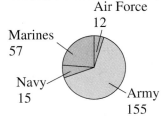

EXPLORATION

Other Methods of Displaying Data

After Lesson 1-6

You can use a *stem-and-leaf plot* or a *box-and-whisker plot* to display data. For example, the data shows the number of minutes it takes 27 students to get ready for school.

47 28 78 47 58 93 34 76 35 72 45 53 23
43 75 27 23 87 33 43 25 35 49 35 48 37 28

A **stem-and-leaf plot** orders the data and lets you see the values and frequencies.

stem ⟶ 5 8 ⟵ leaf

Time to Get Ready

```
2 | 3 3 5 7 8 8
3 | 3 4 5 5 5 7
4 | 3 3 5 7 7 8 9
5 | 3 8
6 |
7 | 2 5 6 8
8 | 7
9 | 3
```
Key: 2|3 means 23 min

A **box-and-whisker plot** shows you how the data are distributed and identifies only certain values.

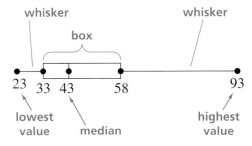

33 and 58 are the middle values of the bottom and top halves of the data, respectively.

Use the stem-and-leaf plot above for Exercises 1–3.

1. What does the stem 4 and leaf 7 represent?

2. How many students took more than 50 minutes?

3. a. *Reasoning* How would you use the stem-and-leaf plot to find the median and the mode of the data?
   b. What is the median? The mode?

Use the box-and-whisker plot at the right.

4. Find the median.

5. Find the highest and lowest values.

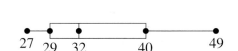

6. *Writing* What does 29 represent?

7. *Analyze* The right side of the box is wider. What does this tell you about the spread of the data?

Misleading Graphs

What You'll Learn

1 To recognize misleading line graphs

2 To recognize misleading bar graphs

...And Why

Misleading graphs are often used to persuade consumers.

Here's How

Look for questions that
- build understanding
- ✔ check understanding

THINK AND DISCUSS

1 *Misleading Line Graphs*

Sometimes people display data in a way that persuades you to see things their way for their own purposes. Even graphs that are correctly drawn can mislead the reader.

Both graphs below display recent basic monthly rates for Quality Cable Company.

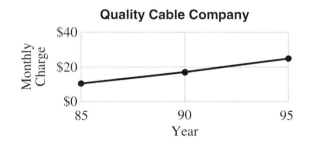

1. ▪*Reasoning* Which graph above is the cable company more likely to use to persuade you that an increase is justified? Explain.

2. a. What is the vertical scale of each graph above?
   b. ▪*Analyze* How does a change in the vertical scale affect the appearance of the data in the line graph? Explain.

3. ▪*Drawing Conclusions* In the first graph above, data items on the horizontal scale are spaced farther apart. How does this change the appearance of the data in the line graph?

▼2 *Misleading Bar Graphs*

Bar graphs can be misleading. Gaps in the scale make differences between the bar heights appear greater than they really are.

■ **EXAMPLE**   *Real-World Problem Solving*

Car Sales A company claims that it has dramatically increased its sales over the past three months. One of its advertisements shows the graph below. What is wrong with the company's claim? Explain.

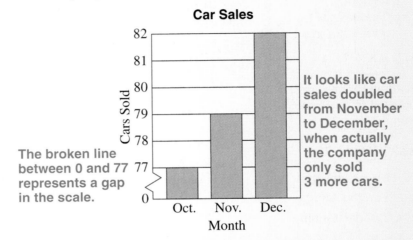

The broken line between 0 and 77 represents a gap in the scale.

It looks like car sales doubled from November to December, when actually the company only sold 3 more cars.

The graph is misleading because large portions of the bars are missing.

4. ✔ *Try It Out* Suppose the company wants to show that car sales have been constant over the past three months. Redraw the bar graph to support this claim.

EXERCISES *On Your Own*

Decide if each line graph appears misleading. Explain.

1.

2.
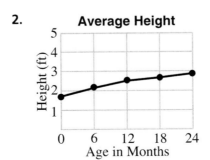

3.
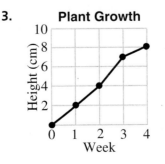

**Decide if each bar graph appears misleading. Explain.
Then redraw any misleading graph.**

4.
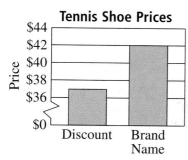
Tennis Shoe Prices

5.
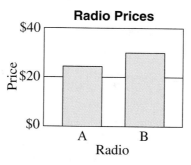
Radio Prices

6.
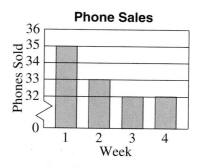
Phone Sales

Government **Each graph below came from one of the
sources given in Exercises 7–9. Match each graph with its
most likely source. Explain your choices.**

i.
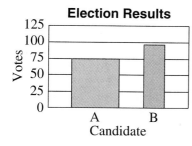
Election Results

ii.
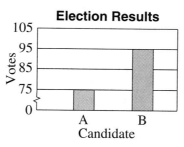
Election Results

iii.
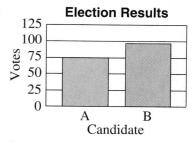
Election Results

7. Candidate B's ad

8. the school newspaper

9. Candidate A's ad

Data Analysis **Use the table at the right.**

10. Draw a line graph showing that the money pledged
increased greatly from 1988 to 1997.

11. Draw a line graph showing that the money pledged
increased slowly from 1988 to 1997.

12. *Writing* Explain how you drew the graphs in
Exercises 10 and 11 to get the desired results.

13. How is a gap in the scale of a graph represented?

14. How does a gap in the scale of a graph affect the
appearance of the data?

**Money Pledged
During a National Telethon**

Year	Dollars Pledged
1988	30,691,627
1989	32,074,566
1990	33,181,652
1991	34,096,773
1992	39,021,723
1993	41,132,113
1994	42,209,727
1995	44,172,186
1996	45,071,857
1997	45,759,368

15. *Open-ended* How might you redraw the graph below to show that recreation costs have increased dramatically?

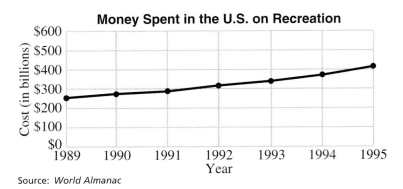

Money Spent in the U.S. on Recreation

Source: *World Almanac*

PORTFOLIO
For your portfolio, select one or two items from your work for this chapter. Consider the following:
• corrected work
• tables, data displays, graphs
Explain why you have included each selection.

Mixed Review

Mental Math **Add, subtract, multiply, or divide.** *(Previous Course)*

16. $300 + 700$ **17.** $10 + 110$ **18.** $100 - 10$ **19.** $1100 + 111$ **20.** $10 + 100 - 11$

21. $10,000 \div 10$ **22.** $100 \times 1,000$ **23.** $100 \div 10$ **24.** $10,000 \div 100$ **25.** $1,000 \times 1,000$

26. *Data Analysis* Draw a bar graph to display the data at the right. *(Lesson 1-6)*

27. *Data Analysis* Draw a pictograph to display the data at the right. (*Hint:* For help see "pictograph" in the Glossary/Study Guide.) *(Previous Course)*

28. *Choose a Strategy* Sumi earns $4.50 per hour baby-sitting. How many hours will she have to baby-sit to earn enough money to buy a portable CD player that costs $89.95?

Snowiest Cities

City	Average Snowfall
Albany, NY	about 65 in.
Boston, MA	about 40 in.
Juneau, AK	about 100 in.
Omaha, NE	about 30 in.

CHAPTER PROJECT

PROJECT LINK: DISPLAYING THE RESULTS

Display the data from your survey in three different ways.
• Consider different graphs as well as some type of table or chart.
• Which method do you think expresses the information the best? Why?

ON YOUR OWN TIME

Conduct a Survey The Project Link questions on pages 7, 16, and 36 should help you complete your project. Here is a checklist to help you gather the parts of your project together.

✓ your chosen topic, the choices, and the data you collected

✓ the mean, median, and mode of your data

✓ three different methods of displaying the data

Make a presentation to the class that displays the information neatly and accurately. Explain which display of information you feel is best and why you feel that way.

Reflect and Revise

Review your project with a friend or someone at home. Are your graphs complete and accurate? Would a different type of graph be more appropriate? Are any of your graphs misleading? How might the information you collected and graphed be used? If necessary, make changes to improve your project.

Web Extension
Prentice Hall's Internet site contains information you might find helpful as you complete your project. Visit www.phschool.com/mgm1/ch1 for some links and ideas related to surveys.

Organizing and Displaying Data

A **frequency table** lists data and shows the number of times each type of answer occurs. A **line plot** displays data on a horizontal line. The **range** is the difference between the greatest and the least values in a set of numerical data.

1. Make a frequency table showing the number of times each vowel appears in the paragraph above.

2. Make a line plot showing the number of times the words *the*, *and*, *a*, and *are* appear in the paragraph above.

Find the range of each data set.

3. 7, 8, 10, 6, 5, 7, 9, 4, 6

4. 90, 76, 88, 94, 81, 77, 80, 87

5. 4, 2, 12, 7, 3, 2, 10, 9, 6, 4

Problem Solving Strategies

You can make a table to organize possible solutions to a problem.

6. *Money* In how many ways can you make 21¢?

7. *Clothes* Kayla spent $48 on gym clothes. She bought at least one of each item. Shorts cost $16. T-shirts cost $8. Socks cost $2 a pair. How many ways could Kayla have bought gym clothes?

8. *Money* Suppose you have six coins that total $1. How many quarters do you have?

Mean, Median, and Mode

The **mean** is the sum of the data divided by the number of pieces of data. The **median** is the middle number in a set of ordered data. When there is an even number of data items, you can find the median by adding the two middle numbers and dividing by 2. The **mode** is the data value that appears most often.

Find the mean and median of each data set.

9. 34, 49, 63, 43, 50, 50, 26

10. 3, 7, 1, 9, 9, 5, 8

11. 14, 13, 16, 17, 24, 12, 13, 19

Find the mode of each data set.

12. M, S, XL, XL, M, L, M, L

13. 18, 18, 18, 18, 18, 18, 18

14. 8, 7, 10, 5, 6, 6, 8, 9, 5, 8

You use a **spreadsheet** to organize and analyze data. A **cell** is the spreadsheet box where a row and column meet. A **formula** is a set of instructions.

	A	B	C	D	E
1	Date	Kite Sales ($)	String Sales ($)	Book Sales ($)	Total Sales ($)
2	9/9/98	500	85	145	
3	9/10/98	750	65	125	

15. Which cells indicate kite sales?

16. What is the value of cell C3?

17. Write the formula for cell E2.

18. What is the value of cell E3?

A **bar graph** is used to compare amounts. A **line graph** shows how an amount changes over time. A **circle graph** compares parts to a whole.

19. Make a line graph to display the cost of tickets shown in the table at the right.

20. Make a bar graph to display the data you collected in the frequency table in Exercise 1.

Choose the most appropriate type of graph to display each set of data. Explain your reasoning.

21. your height on each birthday from birth to the present

22. the sales of different types of lunches in the cafeteria

Ticket Prices

Year	Ticket Cost
1970	$10.00
1975	$15.00
1980	$20.00
1985	$25.00
1990	$30.00

Decide if each graph appears misleading. Explain.

23.

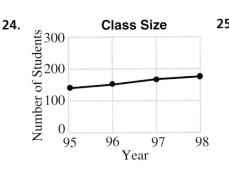

24.

25.

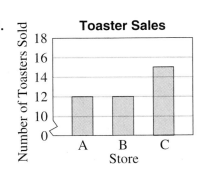

1. The numbers of children in 15 families are 1, 3, 2, 1, 3, 1, 2, 6, 2, 3, 3, 4, 3, 4, and 5.
   a. Make a frequency table.
   b. Make a line plot.

2. Find the mean, median, mode, and range of each set of data.
   a. 9, 8, 6, 6, 8, 1, 8, 2
   b. 31, 20, 31, 51, 27

3. How many ways can you have $1.05 with only dimes, nickels, and quarters?

4. **Choose A, B, or C.** If all the numbers in a set of data occur the same number of times, then the set has no ___?___.

   A. median   **B.** mean   **C.** mode

5. Use the circle graph at the right.
   a. What method do students use *most* to commute to school?
   b. What method do students use *least*?
   c. *Writing* Why is a circle graph better for displaying these data than a bar graph?

How Students Get to School

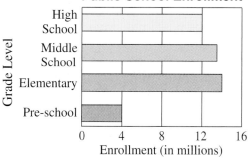

Use the spreadsheet below.

	A	B	C	D	E
1	Student	Quiz 1	Quiz 2	Quiz 3	Average
2	Yori	81	95	88	
3	Sarah	78	81	87	

6. What is the value of cell C3?

7. Write the formulas for cells E2 and E3.

8. *History*
   Use the data in the table at the right.
   a. Display the data in a line graph.
   b. Describe the trend.

Population of the American Colonies

Year	Population
1700	250,900
1710	331,700
1720	466,200
1730	629,400
1740	905,600

9. Create a data set with six numbers. The data set should have a mean of 40, a median of 41, and a range of 18.

10. Use the bar graph below.

Public School Enrollment

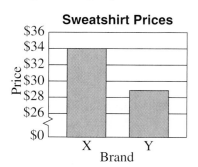

Source: U.S. Department of Education

   a. Which grade level has the *least* number of students enrolled?
   b. Which grade level has the *most*?
   c. Estimate the range.

11. Why is the graph below misleading?

Sweatshirt Prices

Choose the best answer.

1. Which measure is the greatest for these data? 81, 70, 95, 73, 74, 91, 86, 74

   A. mean
   B. median
   C. mode
   D. range

2. *Number Sense* When a number is divided by 13, the quotient is 15 and the remainder is less than 4. Which could be the number?

   A. 198   B. 200   C. 190   D. 206

3. *Data Analysis* What information does the bar graph shown *not* give you?

   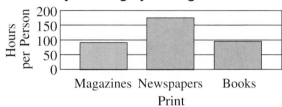

   Yearly Reading by Average Americans

   A. Americans spend more time reading newspapers than books.
   B. Americans spend about the same time reading magazines as books.
   C. Most Americans read the Sunday newspaper.
   D. Americans spend twice as much time reading newspapers as books.

4. *Estimation* Which product gives the best estimate of the product 519 × 36?

   A. 500 × 30
   C. 500 × 40
   B. 550 × 40
   D. 550 × 30

5. A business had weekly profits of $5,000, $3,000, $2,000, $2,500, and $5,000. Which measure might be misleading?

   A. mean
   C. mode
   B. median
   D. none of these

6. *Number Sense* The mean of three numbers is 19. The median is 22. What do you know about the other numbers?

   A. They are both between 19 and 22.
   B. The numbers must be 17 and 18.
   C. At least one of the numbers is between 19 and 22.
   D. If a number is 24, another must be 11.

7. Grapefruit juice is priced at three cans for $2.39. To the nearest cent, what is the cost of one can?

   A. $.08   B. $.79   C. $.80   D. $1.20

8. In one store portable radios sell for $90, $109, $79, and $60. Find the range.

   A. $60   B. $109   C. $49   D. $19

Use the line graph below for Exercises 9 and 10.

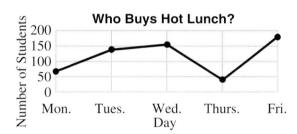

Who Buys Hot Lunch?

9. Estimate the median number of students buying hot lunch.

   A. 70   B. 140   C. 150   D. 120

10. How could you redraw the graph so it appears that about the same number of students buy lunch each day?

    A. Begin the vertical scale at 50.
    B. Use units of 10 instead of 50.
    C. Use units of 100 instead of 50.
    D. Display the data in a circle graph.

2

Patterns and Algebraic Thinking

STEPPING STONES

Do you see a pattern in the layers of this historic Mayan temple? How many pieces of material do you think were needed at the bottom of the structure compared to the top? Many buildings have mathematical patterns to their designs.

Building a Fort For this project you will build a model of a simple fort. You will record the changing value of the fort as you build up the walls layer by layer. You will look for patterns and write equations to describe the patterns.

Steps to help you complete the project:

• **How to solve problems by looking for a pattern**

2-1 Patterns and Number Sense

THINK AND DISCUSS

▼1 Extending Patterns

The first three designs in a pattern are shown at the right.

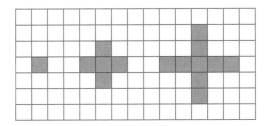

1. a. ▪ *Patterns* Sketch the fourth and fifth designs.
   b. How many shaded squares are in the fourth design? The fifth design?
   c. Imagine the sixth design. Describe the design in words.

You can form a number pattern from the design pattern above.

terms

1, 5, 9, . . .   ⟵ The three dots indicate that the pattern continues without end.

2. How are the first, second, and third terms in the number pattern related to the first, second, and third designs above?

3. What are the fourth and fifth terms in the number pattern?

To extend a number pattern, identify the number and operation used to get from one term to the next.

▪ EXAMPLE 1   Real-World Problem Solving

Patterns Use 50, 46, 42, 38, . . . to find the next three terms.

50, 46, 42, 38, . . .   ⟵ Subtract 4 from each term to get the next term.
  −4 −4 −4

50, 46, 42, 38, 34, 30, 26 ⟵ Continue the pattern to find the next three terms.
  −4 −4 −4 −4 −4 −4

The next three numbers in the pattern are 34, 30, 26.

② *Writing Rules for Number Patterns*

To describe the number pattern 1, 5, 9, 13, . . . use the following rule: *Start with the number 1, and add 4 repeatedly.*

Need Help? For practice with multiplying, see Skills Handbook page 540.

■ EXAMPLE 2

Patterns Find the next three terms in the number pattern 1, 3, 9, 27, ... Write a rule to describe the number pattern.

1, 3, 9, 27, . . .   ⟵ Multiply by 3 to get
 ×3 ×3 ×3   the next term.

1, 3, 9, 27, 81, 243, 729   ⟵ Continue the pattern to
 ×3 ×3 ×3 ×3 ×3 ×3   find the next three terms.

The next three terms are 81, 243, 729. The rule is *Start with the number 1, and multiply by 3 repeatedly.*

4. ✓*Try It Out* Find the next three terms in each number pattern. Write a rule to describe each number pattern.
   a. 4, 7, 10, 13, . . .   b. 5, 20, 80, 320, . . .

Work Together   *Graphing Number Patterns*

Kangaroo Hopping Speeds

Speed (km/h)	Length of Hop (m)
10	1.2
15	1.8
20	2.4
25	3.0
▪	▪

Biology At times you can predict the length of a kangaroo's hop.

5. a. Copy and complete the table at the left.
   b. Write two rules for the table: one to describe speed entries and one to describe length of hop entries.
   c. About how far does a kangaroo hop when it reaches a speed of 35 km/h?
   d. ▪*Estimation* Make a line graph to display the data. Estimate how far a kangaroo hops when it reaches the speed of 27 km/h.

1. a. Sketch the fifth and sixth designs in the pattern at the right.
   b. Use the designs to form a number pattern.
   c. Write a rule to describe the number pattern.
   d. How is this rule different from the one that describes the number pattern 1, 3, 5, 7, . . . ?

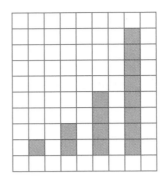

2. Write the first five terms in the following number pattern: *Start with the number 1, and multiply by 4 repeatedly.*

Sketch the next three designs in each pattern.

3.

4.

Find the next three terms in each number pattern.

5. 2, 4, 6, 8, 10, . . .

6. 1, 7, 49, 343, . . .

7. 2, 8, 14, 20, . . .

8. 8, 16, 24, 32, . . .

9. 13, 19, 25, 31, . . .

10. 24, 21, 18, 15, . . .

11. 64, 32, 16, 8, . . .

12. 1; 9; 81; 729; 6,561; . . .

13. 25, 50, 75, 100, . . .

14. *Astronomy* Edmund Halley (1656–1742) first saw the comet named for him in 1682. He correctly predicted that it would return about every 76 years.
   a. *Calculator* Based on Halley's calculations, when was the last time the comet appeared?
   b. When is the comet expected to return next? About how old will you be?
   c. *Writing* Did Edmund Halley see the comet a second time? Explain.

15. *Writing* Why is it important to tell what number to start with when describing the rule of a number pattern? Give an example.

16. *Reasoning* The Difference Engine is a computer designed by Charles Babbage (1791–1871). If you feed it a list of numbers, it will look for a pattern and continue the list. Why do you think the computer was given this name?

**Find the next three terms in each number pattern. Write
a rule to describe each number pattern.**

17. 6, 18, 54, 162, . . .

18. 1, 5, 25, 125, . . .

19. 2, 12, 22, 32, . . .

20. 7, 14, 21, 28, . . .

21. 120, 105, 90, 75, . . .

22. 78, 90, 102, 114, . . .

23. 127, 121, 115, 109, . . .

24. 2, 10, 50, 250, . . .

25. 1,458; 486; 162; 54; . . .

26. *Open-ended* Draw three figures in a design that follow a
pattern. State the rule of the pattern using numbers or words.

Mixed Review

Organize the data in a frequency table and in a line plot.
(Lessons 1-1 & 1-3)

27. ages: 14 15 9 10 9 18 9 14 15 11 8

28. points: 5 10 8 6 5 9 8 5 8 6

29. Find the mean, median, and mode of each set of data in
Exercises 27 and 28.

30. Forty-six members of the hiking club are going camping.
Each tent can hold four people. How many tents do they need
to take with them? *(Previous Course)*

CHAPTER PROJECT

PROJECT LINK: MODELING

Start by planning a foundation for a fort like the one shown
here. You can choose the shape and size of your foundation,
but use no more than 30 objects. Suppose each object
is worth 1 cent. Find the value
of your foundation layer. Now add
your first layer of the walls by
stacking an object on top of
each of the objects along the
outer edge. What is the value
of your fort with one
layer in the wall?

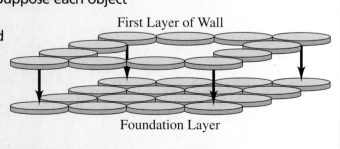

First Layer of Wall

Foundation Layer

2-2 Look for a Pattern

THINK AND DISCUSS

Patterns are everywhere! You use patterns every day to predict and plan.

Sample Problem

For practice, the speech coach asks each of the 15 members of the speech club to give a speech over the phone to every other member. What is the least number of phone calls needed?

READ

Read for understanding. Summarize the problem.

Think about the given information and what you are asked to find.

1. How many members belong to the speech club?

2. What does the problem ask you to find?

PLAN

Decide on a strategy.

You could draw diagrams and look for patterns in simpler cases. Record the minimum number of phone calls needed for each case.

3. How many calls are needed between 2 members?

4. How many calls are needed among 3 members?

5. How many calls are needed among 4 members?

6. How many calls are needed among 5 members?

 **SOLVE**

Try the strategy.

Record the information in a table like the one shown below. Look for a pattern.

Number of Members	Number of Calls	
2	1	+2
3	3	+3
4	6	+4
5	10	▨
6	▨	▨
7	▨	

7. a. How many calls are needed among 6 members? Among 7 members?

b. Describe the pattern.

8. Continue the pattern. Find the number of calls needed among all 15 members of the speech club.

 LOOK BACK

Think about how you solved the problem.

You could have used *Guess and Test* to find the number of calls needed.

9. Do you think *Guess and Test* would have been a good strategy to use to answer the problem? Why or why not?

EXERCISES *On Your Own*

Use *Look for a Pattern* to solve each problem.

1. Twelve people are at a party. Suppose each person shakes hands with each of the others exactly once. How many handshakes will there be altogether?

2. *Savings* Germaine plans to save $1 the first week, $2 the second week, $4 the third week, $8 the fourth week, and $16 the fifth week. If Germaine can continue this pattern, how much money will he save the twelfth week?

Choose any strategy to solve each problem. Show all your work.

3. *Jobs* Kieron wants to take his mother, father, and younger sister to the school play. Adults' tickets cost $6.00 and children's tickets cost $2.00. Kieron earns $3.50 per hour babysitting. How many hours will he have to work to buy two adults' and two children's tickets?

4. The student council is selling white, pink, and red carnations. The order slip at the right was accidentally torn. How many different combinations could have been ordered?

white
pink
red   1
TOTAL   6

5. *Cars* Suppose a car dealer sells at least 3 cars a day. On Monday morning, 50 cars are on the lot. By Friday evening of that week, what is the maximum number of cars the dealer can expect to have left?

6. There are 32 students in the chorus and 44 students in the band. There are 8 students who are in both the chorus and the band. How many students in all are enrolled in these two programs?

7. You open a book. The product of the page numbers you see is 600. What are the page numbers?

8. Hanukkah is a Jewish festival that lasts eight days. Two candles are lit on the first night of Hanukkah. Every night after that these candles are replaced and one more is added. How many candles have been used by the time Hanukkah ends?

Mixed Review

9. *Choose a Strategy* Don expects a grade above 80 in both English and math. How many possible ways are there for him to obtain an average grade of 93?

Find each answer. *(Previous Course)*

10. $918 + 79$ 11. $160 \div 8$ 12. $4,809 + 795$ 13. $1,287 \div 3$ 14. $695 \div 5$

15. Suppose you ask 100 people whether they prefer blueberry, raspberry, or vanilla yogurt. What type of graph would be appropriate to display your results? Explain. *(Lesson 1-5)*

What You'll Learn

▼ To find the value of expressions using the order of operations

▼ To compare values of expressions

...And Why

You can apply the order of operations to give you the mathematically correct answer for an expression.

Here's How

Look for questions that

⊞ build understanding

✔ check understanding

Even soccer equipment—shoes with cleats, socks, and shin guards—needs to be put on in a certain order.

Work Together   *Experimenting with Order of Operations*

Which operation does your calculator do first? Let's find out. An **expression** is a mathematical phrase.

1. ⊞ *Calculator* Compute the value of each expression below twice. First use paper and pencil. Then use a calculator.
   a. $18 + 12 \times 6$ **b.** $15 - 12 \div 3$ **c.** $(6 + 18) \div 3 \times 6$

2. **a.** ⊞ *Analyze* Compare your results in Question 1. Were the answers in each pair the same?
   b. Is it possible to get two different values? Explain.
   c. How might getting two values for one expression cause problems?

3. ⊞ *Summarize* Look at each calculator result. Decide which operation the calculator performed first for each expression.

THINK AND DISCUSS

▼ *Using the Order of Operations*

The order in which you calculate numbers matters. The **order of operations** gives you a set of rules to follow.

ORDER OF OPERATIONS

1. Do all operations within parentheses first.

2. Multiply and divide in order from left to right.

3. Add and subtract in order from left to right.

4. ✓ *Try It Out* Use the expression $3 + 2 \times 5 \times 4$.
   a. What would you do first? Why?
   b. Write the expression you have after the first step.
   c. What would you do next?
   d. What is the last step?
   e. Find the final value.

■ EXAMPLE 1

Find the value of the expression $30 - (6 + 2) \times 3$.

$30 - (6 + 2) \times 3$ ←Write the expression.

$30 - \quad 8 \times 3$ ←Add within the parentheses.

$30 - \quad 24$ ←Multiply 8 and 3.

$\quad 6$ ←Subtract 24 from 30.

5. ✓*Try It Out* Find the value of each expression.

a. $17 - 4 \times 2$ **b.** $3 + 5 \times 2 - 6$ **c.** $10 \div 2 + 3 \times 8$

CALCULATOR HINT

Some calculators perform operations strictly from left to right. If your calculator does not use the order of operations, you may need to insert parentheses. For example, enter 18 + 6 ÷ 3 as 18 ➕ 🄲 6 ➗ 3 🄳.

Most calculators use the order of operations. To find the value of $18 + 6 \div 3$ and $3 \times (5 + 2)$, use the keystrokes shown.

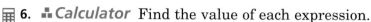

18 ➕ 6 ➗ 3 ▬ *20*

3 ✖ 🄲 5 ➕ 2 🄳 ▬ *21*

6. ⚏*Calculator* Find the value of each expression.

a. $24 - 10 \div 2$ **b.** $15 + 5 \times 2$ **c.** $18 \div (3 - 1)$

d. $16 \div 4 \times (13 - 9) \times 7$ **e.** $(69 - 13) + 60 \div 5$

▼2 *Comparing Values of Expressions*

Use the order of operations to compare values of expressions.

■ EXAMPLE 2

Replace ▦ with $<$, $>$, or $=$.

Use $(12 - 4) + 6 \div 2$ ▦ $12 - (4 + 6) \div 2$.

$(12 - 4) + 6 \div 2$ ▦ $12 - (4 + 6) \div 2$ ←Do operations within parentheses.

$8 \quad + 6 \div 2$ ▦ $12 - \quad 10 \div 2$ ←Divide on both sides.

$8 \quad + \quad 3$ ▦ $12 - \quad 5$ ←Add and subtract.

11 ▦ 7 ←Compare sides.

$11 > 7$

7. ✓*Try it Out* Replace ▦ with $<$, $>$, or $=$.

a. $(18 + 8) \div 2 + 4$ ▦ $18 + 8 \div 2 + 4$

b. $(24 + 11) \div (5 + 2)$ ▦ $(24 + 11) \div 5 + 2$

8. Replace ▦ with $<$, $>$, or $=$.

a. $5 + 0$ ▦ 5 (addition property of zero)

b. 5×0 ▦ 0 (multiplication property of zero)

Which operation would you perform first?

1. $8 - 2 \times 3$

2. $(40 - 16) \div 4$

3. $15 \times 8 \div 3$

4. $12 - 2 \times 3 \div 5$

5. $63 \div 7 \times (5 - 2)$

6. $12 - 9 \div 3 - 2$

Find the value of each expression.

7. $6 - 2 + 4 \times 2$

8. $3 + 3 \times 2$

9. $33 - (14 + 6)$

10. $4 \times 3 + 20 \div 5$

11. $6 \times (2 \times 5)$

12. $26 + 4 - 4 \times 2$

13. $400 \div (44 - 24)$

14. $12 + 8 \times 6$

15. $13 - (7 + 4)$

16. $45 \div 9 + 6 \times 3$

17. $7 \times (4 + 6) \times 3$

18. $13 + 5 \times 12 - 4$

19. *Reasoning* When would you add before multiplying?

20. *Writing* Explain the steps you would use to find the value of the expression $8 \div 4 \times 6 + (7 - 5)$.

21. a. Find the value of each expression.
  i. $(4 + 5) \times 5$ **ii.** $4 + (5 \times 5)$ **iii.** $4 + 5 \times 5$
  b. What do you notice about the values in part (a)?

22. The price of the apples at the right will be reduced by 20 cents. Next week the reduced price will double.
  a. To find next week's price, should you use $79 - 20 \times 2$ or $(79 - 20) \times 2$? Explain.
  b. Find the price of apples next week.

79¢ per lb

Replace ▧ with <, >, or =.

23. $(3 + 6) \times 4 \ \blacksquare\ 3 + 6 \times 4$

24. $(8 - 2) \times (6 + 1) \ \blacksquare\ (8 - 2) \times 6$

25. $2 + (12 \div 3) \ \blacksquare\ 2 + 12 \div 3$

26. $7 - 2 \times 0 \ \blacksquare\ (7 - 2) \times 0$

27. $2 \times (15 - 3) \ \blacksquare\ 2 \times 15 - 3$

28. $62 - 37 + 8 \ \blacksquare\ 62 - (37 + 8)$

▦ Place parentheses in each equation to make it true.

29. $12 + 6 \div 2 - 1 = 8$

30. $14 \div 2 + 5 - 1 = 1$

31. $1 + 2 \times 15 - 4 = 33$

32. $11 - 7 \div 2 = 2$

33. $14 - 3 - 2 \times 3 = 11$

34. $5 \times 6 \div 2 + 1 = 10$

Choose Use a calculator, paper and pencil, or mental math to find each answer.

35. $5 + 2 \times 0$

36. $(63 + 37) \div 5$

37. $160 \div (25 - 5)$

38. $4 \times (13 - 6)$

39. $(12 - 7) \times 5 + 1$

40. $13 \times (46 - 46)$

41. $(63 - 48) \times 1$

42. $(16 \times 4) \div (42 - 34)$

43. $18 \div 6 - (5 - 4)$

Insert operation symbols to make each equation true.

44. $(6 \blacksquare 9) \blacksquare 4 \blacksquare 6 = 10$

45. $(12 \blacksquare 8) \blacksquare (5 \blacksquare 1) = 20$

46. $14 \blacksquare 7 \blacksquare 2 \blacksquare 3 = 7$

47. *Open-ended* Write three expressions that equal 8, 9, and 10, respectively. Use the numbers 1, 2, 5, and 6, operation symbols, and the order of operations.

Mixed Review

48. Will has 2 copies of a *Batman* comic book valued at $35 each and an *Amazing Spiderman* comic valued at $170. Find the value of his comic collection. *(Previous Course)*

49. *Choose a Strategy* The lockers in the sixth-grade hallway are numbered 100 to 275. How many lockers are there?

✓ CHECKPOINT 1
Lessons 2-1 through 2-3

Find the value of each expression.

1. $8 + 13 \times 2$

2. $66 \div (2 + 4)$

3. $(1 + 12 - 7) \div 3$

Find the next three terms in each number pattern.

4. 9; 45; 225; 1,125; . . .

5. 54, 49, 44, 39, . . .

6. 0, 7, 14, 21, . . .

7. *Open-ended* Create a number pattern. List at least five terms. Then write a rule to describe the number pattern.

8. *Choose a Strategy* A bus can hold 44 passengers. It starts out empty and picks up 1 passenger at the first stop, 2 at the second stop, 3 at the third stop, and so on. If no one gets off of the bus, at which stop will the bus become full?

PROBLEM SOLVING PRACTICE

Choose the best answer.

1. Dennis works as a waiter. On five days he earned $25, $35, $45, $40, and $35 in tips. What was the mean (average) amount he earned each day?

   A. $34   B. $35
   C. $36   D. $180

2. For 4 days, Juanita kept a record of the number of laps she jogged around the school track. The numbers she recorded were 7, 11, 15, and 19. If she continues in the same pattern, how many laps will she jog on the fifth day?

   F. 20   G. 21
   H. 22   J. 23

3. Zachary is going to buy a new computer monitor that costs $392. He has already saved $295. How much more does he need to save?

   A. $687   B. $197
   C. $103   D. $97

4. Suki kept the following record of the number of sit-ups she did for 5 days in a row: 10, 18, 26, 34, 42. If she continues in the same pattern, how many sit-ups will she do on the sixth day?

   F. 44   G. 46
   H. 50   J. 52

5. Jill walks her dog three times every day. Each walk lasts from 10 to 20 minutes. How many times does she walk her dog in 1 year (365 days)?

   A. 375   B. 385
   C. 985   D. 1,095

Please note that items 6–9 have *five* answer choices.

6. Eric bought a stove costing $572 and a refrigerator costing $679. What was the total cost?

   F. $107
   G. $1,141
   H. $1,151
   J. $1,251
   K. Not Here

7. Marvella wants to save $1,000 to attend computer camp. So far she has saved $718. How much more does she need to save?

   A. $382
   B. $318
   C. $282
   D. $218
   E. Not Here

8. At an amusement park, each person pays $5 to enter plus $2 for each ride. Suppose each person pays for 9 rides. Which expression represents the total amount spent?

   F. $5 + 9 \times 2$
   G. $(5 + 9) \times 2$
   H. $(5 \times 9) + 2$
   J. $5 \times 9 \times 2$
   K. Not Here

9. A carton is packed with 24 cans that weigh 14 ounces each. What is the total weight of all the cans?

   A. 38 ounces
   B. 136 ounces
   C. 236 ounces
   D. 336 ounces
   E. Not Here

What You'll Learn

▼1 To model variable expressions

▼2 To evaluate variable expressions

...And Why

You can use models and algebra to evaluate expressions and solve an ancient puzzle.

Here's How

Look for questions that
- ▪ build understanding
- ✔ check understanding

THINK AND DISCUSS

▼1 *Modeling Variable Expressions*

A **magic square** is a special arrangement of numbers in a square. The rows, columns, and diagonals all have the same sum.

Magic Square

a	7	2
1	5	b
8	c	4

1. Find the magic square sum above. Explain how you found it.

A **variable** is a symbol, usually a letter, that stands for an unknown number.

2. ✓*Try It Out* Name the variables in the magic square above.

A **numerical expression** contains only numbers and operation symbols.

$$8 + 5 + 2$$

A **variable expression** contains at least one variable.

$$a + 7 + 2$$

3. a. What does the numerical expression $8 + 5 + 2$ represent?
    b. What does the variable expression $a + 7 + 2$ represent?
    c. ▪*Analyze* What is true about the values of both expressions?

Art In 1514, artist Albrecht Dürer included a 4-by-4 magic square in this mysterious and complex engraving.

Source: *Mathematical Puzzles & Diversions*

4. a. ⁛*Mental Math* What is the value of a in the magic square at the top of page 56?

b. Name another variable expression that you could use to find the value of a.

5. a. In the magic square at the top of page 56, what variable expressions could you use to determine the value of b? Of c?

b. ⁛*Mental Math* What is the value of b? Of c?

You can model numerical and variable expressions with tiles. Yellow tiles represent ones. Green tiles represent variables.

Expression	**Model**
$2 + 3$ ⟶	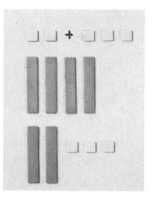
$4x$ (means $4 \times x$) ⟶	
$2x + 3$ ⟶	

■ **EXAMPLE 1**

Modeling Model the expression $3x + 1$ with algebra tiles.

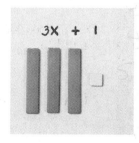

Model $3x$ with 3 green tiles and model 1 with 1 yellow tile.

6. ✓*Try It Out* Model each expression with algebra tiles.
a. $2x$ **b.** $4 + 1$ **c.** $x + 4$ **d.** $5x + 2$

▼ Evaluating Variable Expressions

You can evaluate a variable expression using algebra tiles.

■ EXAMPLE 2

Modeling Use algebra tiles to evaluate $2x + 1$ for $x = 3$.

Model the expression $2x + 1$.   Replace each green tile with 3 yellow tiles.

The value of $2x + 1$ for $x = 3$ is 7.

7. ✓*Try It Out* Use algebra tiles to evaluate $6 + 3t$ for $t = 2$.

You can evaluate a variable expression with numbers. Replace each variable with a number. Then follow the order of operations.

■ EXAMPLE 3

a. Evaluate $7b - 11$ for $b = 6$.
$$
\begin{aligned}
7b - 11 &= 7(6) - 11 &&\leftarrow\text{Replace } b \text{ with 6.}\\
&= 42 - 11 &&\leftarrow\text{Multiply 7 and 6.}\\
&= 31 &&\leftarrow\text{Subtract 11 from 42.}
\end{aligned}
$$

b. Evaluate $r(36 - s)$ for $r = 4$ and $s = 8$.
$$
\begin{aligned}
r(36 - s) &= 4(36 - 8) &&\leftarrow\text{Replace } r \text{ with 4 and } s \text{ with 8.}\\
&= 4(28) &&\leftarrow\text{Subtract 8 from 36.}\\
&= 112 &&\leftarrow\text{Multiply 4 and 28.}
\end{aligned}
$$

8. ✓*Try It Out* Evaluate each expression.
  a. $56 - 7x$ for $x = 5$ **b.** $a(1 + 2b)$ for $a = 5$ and $b = 3$

EXERCISES *On Your Own*

Modeling **Write a variable expression for each model.**

1.    **2.**    **3.**    **4.**

Modeling **Model each variable expression with tiles.**

5. $3x + 5$ **6.** $c + 3$ **7.** $5b + 2$ **8.** $x + 2$ **9.** $4 + 2x$ **10.** $7x$

Mental Math **Evaluate each expression for $x = 8$.**

11. $x + 12$ **12.** $80 \div x$ **13.** $7x$ **14.** $10 + 2x$ **15.** $x \div 2$ **16.** $2(x - 3)$

⊞ Choose **Use a calculator, mental math, or paper and pencil to evaluate each expression.**

17. $24 \div d$ for $d = 3$ **18.** $p + 8$ for $p = 6$ **19.** $3r - 2$ for $r = 65$

20. $8b - 12$ for $b = 6$ **21.** $n \div 10$ for $n = 30$ **22.** $75s$ for $s = 20$

23. $3(2c)$ for $c = 3$ **24.** $8 - 3y$ for $y = 2$ **25.** $6a + 8$ for $a = 7$

26. $6n - (m + 8)$ for $m = 20$ and $n = 15$ **27.** $5x - y$ for $x = 12$ and $y = 14$

28. $2r + st$ for $r = 7$, $s = 30$, and $t = 5$ **29.** $2abc$ for $a = 35$, $b = 3$, and $c = 10$

30. Copy and complete the magic square shown at the right. Find the values of r, s, and t.

4	9	r
s	7	3
6	5	t

Copy and complete each table by evaluating the expression for the given values of x.

31.

x	$x + 6$
1	7
4	10
7	▨
10	▨
▨	20

32.

x	$7x$
2	▨
4	▨
6	▨
8	▨
▨	70

33.

x	$100 - x$
20	▨
35	▨
50	▨
72	▨
▨	12

34.

x	$3x + 4$
0	▨
1	▨
▨	10
5	▨
10	▨

35. Choose A, B, C, D, or E. Use the expression $9x - 4$. Which value of x gives you a result of 50?

A. 10   **B.** 45   **C.** 5   **D.** 6   **E.** 7

36. *Writing* What is the difference between a numerical expression and a variable expression?

37. Reasoning Why is the symbol × used to show multiplication in numerical expressions but not in variable expressions?

38. Geometry The formula for the perimeter of a rectangular swimming pool is $2\ell + 2w$. The length ℓ of the pool is 24 ft and the width w is 12 ft. Find the perimeter.

JOURNAL
Describe a variable in your own words. Where have you seen variables used before? Give an example of a situation where a variable could be useful.

Mixed Review

Find the next three terms in each number pattern.
(Lesson 2-1)

39. 1, 4, 16, 64, . . .

40. 32, 35, 38, 41, . . .

41. 2,187; 729; 243; 81; . . .

42. Would you find the mean, median, or mode to discover the favorite pizza topping of the students in your class? Explain. *(Lesson 1-3)*

43. Margarite is standing in the middle of a line to buy concert tickets. There are 47 people in front of her. How many people are in the line? *(Previous Course)*

Math at Work

BICYCLE DESIGNER

What kind of bicycle would you like to own? With so many different types of bicycles to choose from, it could be a difficult decision. A bicycle designer combines mathematical, visual, and artistic skills to make special bicycle designs.

Bicycle designers use mathematical patterns to find the size and shape of the wheels, the number of gears, and how well these parts will work together for the cyclist. They also use math skills to find the size, shape, weight, and cost of materials.

For more information about designing bicycles, visit the Prentice Hall Web site: www.phschool.com

2-5 Writing Variable Expressions

What You'll Learn

▼ To describe variable expressions with word phrases

▼ To write variable expressions

...And Why

You can use variable expressions to describe fund-raising, food, and space flight situations.

Here's How

Look for questions that

▪ build understanding

✔ check understanding

Work Together
Exploring How to Write Expressions

1. ▪ **Think About It** Make a list of all the words or phrases you can think of that describe each operation: addition, subtraction, multiplication, and division.

2. ▪ **Analyze** Use your list to describe each numerical expression in as many different ways as you can.
   a. $5 + 8$ **b.** $10 - 4$ **c.** 10×3 **d.** $18 \div 6$

THINK AND DISCUSS

▼ Describing Variable Expressions

You can use a word phrase to describe a variable expression. Here are some examples.

Word Phrase	Variable Expression
the sum of m and 45	$m + 45$
22 more than a number	$n + 22$
w less than 55	$55 - w$
the product of w and 10	$10w$
the quotient of r and s	$r \div s$

3. ✓ **Try It Out** Write two word phrases for each variable expression.
   a. $b + 15$ **b.** $m - n$ **c.** $6x$ **d.** $18 \div p$

▼ Writing Variable Expressions

You can write a variable expression using a word phrase.

4. ✓ **Try It Out** Write a variable expression for each word phrase.
   a. five plus y **b.** 6 times q **c.** 2 less than x

5. Read the conversation below. Identify the word phrases in the conversation below that express mathematical ideas.

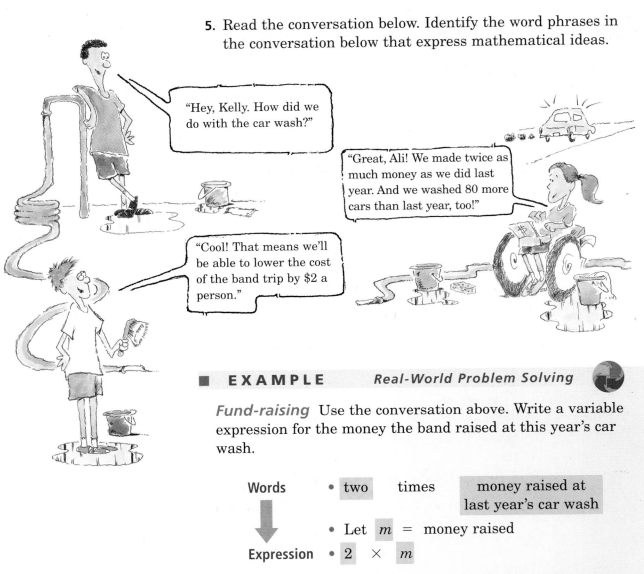

"Hey, Kelly. How did we do with the car wash?"

"Great, Ali! We made twice as much money as we did last year. And we washed 80 more cars than last year, too!"

"Cool! That means we'll be able to lower the cost of the band trip by $2 a person."

■ **EXAMPLE**   *Real-World Problem Solving*

Fund-raising Use the conversation above. Write a variable expression for the money the band raised at this year's car wash.

Words • two   times   money raised at last year's car wash

• Let m = money raised

Expression • 2   × m

A variable expression for the money raised this year is $2m$.

6. **What If . . .** Suppose the band raised $240 at last year's car wash. Evaluate the expression in the Example to find the money raised at this year's car wash.

7. a. ✓**Try It Out** Write a variable expression for the number of cars the band washed this year.

b. Suppose the band washed 50 cars last year. Find the number of cars washed at this year's car wash.

8. **Go a Step Further** Suppose t was the cost per person for the band trip before the car wash. Write a variable expression for the cost of the trip after the car wash.

Write two word phrases for each variable expression.

1. $z + 24$ **2.** $y - x$ **3.** $7s$ **4.** $g \div h$ **5.** $7 - x$

6. $t + 6$ **7.** $18 - h$ **8.** ab **9.** $21 \div m$ **10.** $4n$

What operation does the given word or phrase indicate?

11. more than   **12.** quotient   **13.** increased by   **14.** total   **15.** product

16. plus   **17.** less than   **18.** times   **19.** divided by   **20.** difference

21. Choose A, B, C, or D. Which word phrase does *not* describe the expression $36 - x$?

   A. 36 minus x **B.** 36 less than x **C.** 36 decreased by x **D.** a difference of 36 and x

22. *Food* The length of the largest lasagna in the United States was ten times its width.
   a. Write a variable expression for the length of the lasagna.
   b. Why is w a good variable to use to represent the width?
   c. The lasagna measured 7 ft wide. Evaluate the expression to find the length of the lasagna.

Write a variable expression for each word phrase.

23. 34 less than k **24.** 8 multiplied by x **25.** d more than 50   **26.** 23 times q

27. 7 increased by b **28.** r less than 13   **29.** h times 150   **30.** 4 added to e

31. eight less than s **32.** six more than a number   **33.** two inches taller than you

34. b divided by 3   **35.** the sum of r and s **36.** the product of three and m

37. *Amusement Rides* Suppose you ride one roller coaster all day. The ride lasts 45 seconds.
   a. Let t represent the number of times you go on the ride. Write a variable expression for the number of seconds you spend riding the roller coaster.
   b. *Reasoning* Write a variable expression for the number of minutes you spend riding the roller coaster.

38. *Writing* Do the phrases *twenty-two less than x* and *x less than twenty-two* result in the same variable expression? Explain.

39. *Space* At the end of a space flight, an astronaut's height can temporarily be 2 inches more than normal.
  a. Write a variable expression to describe an astronaut's height after flight.
  b. What variable did you use? What does it represent?

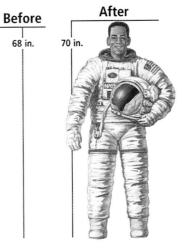

Before   After
68 in.   70 in.

In the absence of gravity, the cartilage disks in the spine expand. So an astronaut is temporarily 2 inches taller.

Write a variable expression for the rule in each table.

40.

x	
1	3
2	6
3	9
4	12

41.

a	
2	5
5	8
6	9
7	10

42.

m	
5	2
10	7
15	12
20	17

43.

p	
0	0
4	2
8	4
12	6

Mixed Review

44. President Eisenhower was born October 14, 1890, and died March 28, 1969. How old was he when he died? *(Previous Course)*

Use the spreadsheet below for Exercises 45 and 46. *(Lesson 1-4)*

	A	B	C
1	Title/Artist	Year	Weeks at No. 1
2	One Sweet Day/Mariah Carey and Boys II Men	1995	16
3	I Will Always Love You/Whitney Houston	1992	14
4	End of the Road/Boys II Men	1992	13
5	Hey Jude/Beatles	1968	9

Source: *The Top Ten of Everything*

45. What value is in cell B4?

46. What cells are in column C?

CHAPTER PROJECT

PROJECT LINK: RECORDING DATA

Continue adding layers to your fort. The final value must be within a budget of $2. Record the number of layers and the value of the fort. Describe the pattern. Write a numerical expression to relate layers to fort value.

Extra Practice, Lesson 2-5, page 523

Subtracting with Zeros

Before Lesson 2-6 →

When you subtract from a number with zeros, you may need to regroup more than once. Start by lining up the digits in the correct columns.

■ EXAMPLE 1

Subtract $3,020 - 86$.

Step 1

```
   110
3,020
-  86
    4
```

Step 2

```
 9 11
2 10 1 10
3,020
-  86
   34
```

Step 3

```
 9 11
2 10 110
3,020
-  86
2,934
```

■ EXAMPLE 2

Find each difference.

a. $908 - 273$

```
 8 10
 908
-273
 635
```

b. $602 - 174$

```
    9
 5 10 12
 602
-174
 428
```

c. $5,002 - 1,247$

```
     9 9
4 10 10 12
5,002
-1,247
3,755
```

Subtract.

1. 806 − 174	**2.** 240 − 63	**3.** 707 − 361	**4.** 5,060 − 3,221	**5.** 6,000 − 1,830	**6.** 8,000 − 5,274

7. $609 - 274$ **8.** $403 - 122$ **9.** $760 - 405$ **10.** $901 - 65$ **11.** $800 - 435$

12. $459 - 78$ **13.** $222 - 151$ **14.** $680 - 47$ **15.** $301 - 260$ **16.** $425 - 406$

17. $7,820 - 1,608$ **18.** $9,071 - 6,407$ **19.** $3,003 - 1,998$ **20.** $8,044 - 2,111$

21. $6,508 - 2,147$ **22.** $5,300 - 1,771$ **23.** $7,004 - 1,512$ **24.** $8,000 - 4,337$

25. a. Writing Explain what is meant by *regrouping*.
     b. When is regrouping necessary?

Modeling Equations That Use Addition or Subtraction

What You'll Learn

1 To define equations
2 To solve equations

...And Why

You can solve equations about anatomy.

Here's How

Look for questions that
🔳 build understanding
✔ check understanding

Work Together
Writing Numerical Expressions

Use the table at the right.

1. a. Write a numerical expression for the total number of bones in your arm and chest.
   b. Write a numerical expression for the total number of bones in your leg and spine.
   c. 🔳*Draw a Conclusion* What do you notice about the value of the expressions in parts (a) and (b)?

Bones in Your Body

Body Part	Number of Bones
Arm	32
Leg	31
Skull	29
Spine	26
Chest	25

THINK AND DISCUSS

1 Defining Equations

An **equation** is a mathematical sentence that contains an equal sign, =, read "is equal to." The equation acts like a balance scale.

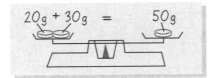
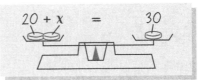

To **solve** an equation, replace the variable with a number that makes the equation true. This number is a **solution.**

■ EXAMPLE 1

State whether 29 is a solution to the equation $x - 15 = 12$.

$$x - 15 = 12$$
$$29 - 15 \stackrel{?}{=} 12 \quad \longleftarrow \text{Replace } x \text{ with 29.}$$
$$14 \neq 12 \quad \longleftarrow \text{Subtract. } (\neq \text{ means "is not equal to."})$$

The equation is false, so 29 is *not* a solution to $x - 15 = 12$.

2. ✓*Try It Out* State whether the given number is a solution to the equation.
   a. $y - 6 = 24$; 18
   b. $20 = p + 4$; 16
   c. $150 = k - 50$; 200
   d. $j + 30 = 70$; 100

▼ Solving Equations

You can use algebra tiles to find the solution to an equation. To *isolate the variable*, get the variable alone on one side of the equal sign.

■ EXAMPLE 2

Use algebra tiles to solve $x + 2 = 6$.

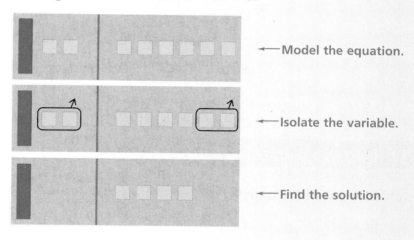

Model the equation.

Isolate the variable.

Find the solution.

The solution to $x + 2 = 6$ is 4.

3. **a.** What did you do to isolate the variable in Example 2?
   b. What operation does this action represent?

4. ✓*Try It Out* Use algebra tiles to solve each equation.
   a. $m + 4 = 7$
   b. $6 + k = 11$
   c. $9 = h + 3$

You can use mental math to solve equations involving addition or subtraction.

5. In the equation $r + 8 = 15$, what is the value of r?

6. In the equation $m - 4 = 10$, what is the value of m?

7. ⬛*Mental Math* Solve each equation.
   a. $8 = 3 + h$
   b. $a + 5 = 8$
   c. $m - 2 = 10$
   d. $15 = g - 5$
   e. $5 = n - 10$
   f. $8 = k + 7$

Sometimes it is not convenient to solve an equation using algebra tiles or mental math. Then you can use paper and pencil or a calculator.

■ **EXAMPLE 3**

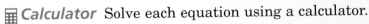 *Calculator* Solve each equation using a calculator.

a. $x + 3{,}687 = 5{,}543$

5543 ▭ 3687 ▭ *1856*

The solution is 1,856.

b. $x - 4{,}621 = 1{,}347$

1347 ▭ 4621 ▭ *5968*

The solution is 5,968.

8. **⸭ Look Back** Check the solution to Example 3a by replacing x with 1,856. Is the solution reasonable?

9. ✓ *Try It Out* When you solve the equation $x + 567 = 739$ using a calculator, what operation key do you use?

10. **⸭ Calculator** Solve each equation. Then check your solution.

a. $y - 432 = 127$

b. $12{,}597 = h + 6{,}954$

c. $183 = 119 + b$

d. $189 = p - 24$

EXERCISES *On Your Own*

Is each statement *true* or *false*?

1. $5 + 10 = 15$

2. $9 - 3 = 2$

3. $24 = 6 + 18$

4. $19 - 7 = 5 + 4$

5. **Choose A, B, C, or D.** Which value of x is a solution for the equation $x - 4 = 5$?

A. 6

B. 10

C. 9

D. 1

State whether the given number is a solution to the equation.

6. $h + 6 = 14$; 7

7. $k + 5 = 16$; 11

8. $p - 10 = 20$; 20

9. $18 = m - 4$; 22

10. $25 = 14 + y$; 11

11. $t - 5 = 25$; 15

12. $15 + x = 57$; 32

13. $c - 7 = 14$; 7

14. $r + 16 = 42$; 26

15. *Writing* Explain why the statement $4 + 6 = 10$ is true and the statement $3 + 7 = 12$ is false.

16. *Language* How is an equation like a sentence?

Modeling **Solve the equation shown in each model.**

17.

18.

19.

20.

21.

22.

Mental Math **Solve each equation mentally.**

23. $x + 2 = 7$

24. $c - 7 = 22$

25. $16 = k + 7$

26. $w - 7 = 10$

27. $6 + w = 9$

28. $20 = m - 66$

29. $x + 4 = 12$

30. $26 - p = 7$

Choose **Use algebra tiles, mental math, or a calculator to solve each equation. Check for reasonable solutions.**

31. $33 = k + 17$

32. $152 = p + 64$

33. $g + 8 = 84$

34. $437 + y = 512$

35. $62 + r = 83$

36. $y - 265 = 124$

37. $a - 64 = 65$

38. $6 + w = 9$

39. $x + 3 = 9$

40. $42 + h = 52$

41. $42 = 51 - m$

42. $45 = d + 28$

Use the article below for Exercises 43 and 44.

A DREAM COME TRUE

Dwight Collins was ten years old when he first thought about crossing the Atlantic Ocean. Twenty-six years later, he set a record by pedaling his boat, Tango, from Newfoundland to London in just 40 days—14 days faster than the previous record. Can you imagine pedaling 2,250 miles across the ocean? Not even a storm could stop Dwight Collins from making his dream come true!

43. Use the equation $r - 14 = 40$. Find the previous record r in days.

44. After the storm, Dwight still had 1,200 miles of pedaling to do. Use the equation $p + 1,200 = 2,250$. Find the number of miles Dwight had pedaled p before he sailed into the storm.

📱 Calculator **Solve and check each equation.**

45. $f + 1,478 = 3,652$

46. $10,006 = k - 67,948$

47. $z - 11,897 = 34,954$

48. $50,876 + s = 877,942$

49. $x - 6,781 = 10,384$

50. $18,943 = x - 11,256$

51. Open-ended Give an example of an equation that contains a variable. Then solve the equation.

52. Reasoning Explain what is meant by the statement "*addition and subtraction undo each other.*"

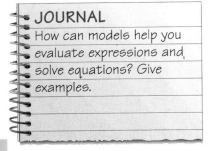
JOURNAL
How can models help you evaluate expressions and solve equations? Give examples.

Mixed Review

53. Data Analysis About how many more people own color sets than own black and white sets? *(Previous Course)*

54. Choose a Strategy A bookstore advertised the following sale: *Buy 3 books, get 1 book free!* How many books do you have to buy to get 4 free books?

Find the value of each expression. *(Lesson 2-3)*

55. $24 \div 3 - 2 \times 4$

56. $(63 + 87) - 6 \times 2$

How Many Own Televisions?

Type	Number of People
Color	90,258,000
Black and white	1,842,000
2 or more sets	59,865,000
1 set	32,235,000
Any type of set	92,100,000

Source: *Information Please Almanac*

✓ CHECKPOINT 2   Lessons 2-4 through 2-6

Evaluate each expression for $x = 7$.

1. $3x + 12$

2. $56 \div x$

3. $10 - x + 3$

4. $3(4 + x)$

5. $9x$

Write a variable expression for each word phrase.

6. 12 more than y

7. b increased by 5

8. 6 times w

9. r less than 20

Solve each equation.

10. $b + 25 = 75$

11. $256 = m - 129$

12. $6 = 4 + y$

13. $22 - p = 13$

14. Choose A, B, C, or D. Which expression has a value of 10 for $x = 8$?

A. $2x - 3$

B. $22 + x \div 3$

C. $3x - 22$

D. $3x - 14$

MATH TOOLBOX

Multiplying Whole Numbers

Before Lesson 2-7

When you multiply by a two-digit number, first multiply by the ones. Then multiply by the tens. Add the products. Remember zero times any number is zero.

■ EXAMPLE

Multiply 48×327.

Step 1: Multiply the ones.

$$\begin{array}{r} {}^{2\,5} \\ 327 \\ \times\ 48 \\ \hline 2,616 \end{array}$$

Step 2: Multiply the tens.

$$\begin{array}{r} {}^{1\,2} \\ 327 \\ \times\ 48 \\ \hline 2,616 \\ +\ 13,080 \end{array}$$

Step 3: Add the products.

$$\begin{array}{r} 327 \\ \times\ 48 \\ \hline 2,616 \\ +\ 13,080 \\ \hline 15,696 \end{array}$$

Multiply.

1. $\begin{array}{r} 312 \\ \times\ 53 \end{array}$
2. $\begin{array}{r} 456 \\ \times\ 71 \end{array}$
3. $\begin{array}{r} 906 \\ \times\ 20 \end{array}$
4. $\begin{array}{r} 915 \\ \times\ 27 \end{array}$
5. $\begin{array}{r} 808 \\ \times\ 60 \end{array}$
6. $\begin{array}{r} 409 \\ \times\ 70 \end{array}$

7. $\begin{array}{r} 25 \\ \times\ 46 \end{array}$
8. $\begin{array}{r} 601 \\ \times\ 63 \end{array}$
9. $\begin{array}{r} 62 \\ \times\ 88 \end{array}$
10. $\begin{array}{r} 430 \\ \times\ 80 \end{array}$
11. $\begin{array}{r} 87 \\ \times\ 31 \end{array}$
12. $\begin{array}{r} 970 \\ \times\ 40 \end{array}$

13. $\begin{array}{r} 54 \\ \times\ 26 \end{array}$
14. $\begin{array}{r} 780 \\ \times\ 62 \end{array}$
15. $\begin{array}{r} 881 \\ \times\ 77 \end{array}$
16. $\begin{array}{r} 440 \\ \times\ 67 \end{array}$
17. $\begin{array}{r} 68 \\ \times\ 46 \end{array}$
18. $\begin{array}{r} 82 \\ \times\ 17 \end{array}$

19. 415×76
20. 500×80
21. 320×47
22. 562×18
23. 946×37

24. 76×103
25. 32×558
26. 371×84
27. 505×40
28. 620×19

29. 607×50
30. 601×42
31. 400×26
32. 109×60
33. 298×70

34. 58×41
35. 30×600
36. 94×77
37. 163×47
38. 458×32

39. **a.** Multiply.
   i. 500×30 **ii.** 50×30 **iii.** 500×3 **iv.** 5×300 **v.** 50×300

   b. *Writing* How does the number of zeros in the numbers you multiply relate to the number of zeros in each product?

   c. *Reasoning* Does the product 500×40 fit the rule you found in part (b)? Why or why not?

Modeling Equations That Use Multiplication or Division

What You'll Learn

▼ To solve equations using models

▼ To solve equations using a calculator or mental math

...And Why

You can solve equations about sports teams.

Here's How

Look for questions that
- ⊞ build understanding
- ✔ check understanding

Work Together

Writing Equations from Data

Use the table shown at the right.

1. a. ⊞ *Mental Math* How many volleyball teams t can be formed with 30 students?
   b. ⊞ *Algebra* Does $6t = 30$ or $30t = 6$ describe this situation? Explain.
   c. Write equations for the number of basketball teams and the number of soccer teams.

Number of Players in Starting Lineup

Sport	Number of Players
Baseball	9
Basketball	5
Soccer	11
Volleyball	6

THINK AND DISCUSS

▼ Solving Equations Using Modeling

You can use algebra tiles to solve an equation with a whole number multiplied by a variable on one side.

■ EXAMPLE 1

Modeling Use algebra tiles to solve the equation $3x = 12$.

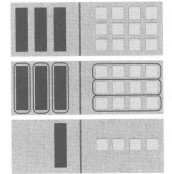

←— Model the equation.

←— Divide each side into 3 equal parts.

←— Keep one part on each side.

The solution is 4.

2. ✔*Try It Out* Use algebra tiles to solve each equation.
   a. $2x = 8$ b. $2x = 10$ c. $4x = 12$

▼2 Solving Using a Calculator or Mental Math

At times it is impractical to solve an equation using algebra tiles. You could use paper and pencil or a calculator instead.

■ EXAMPLE 2

🔢 **Calculator** Solve each equation using a calculator.

a. $125x = 1,875$

1875 ÷ 125 🟰 *15*

The solution is 15.

b. $x \div 21 = 85$

85 ✖ 21 🟰 *1785*

The solution is 1,785.

3. ⁂ **Look Back** Check the solution to Example (2a) by replacing x with 15. Is the solution reasonable?

4. ✓**Try It Out** When you solve the equation $x \div 429 = 6,864$, what operation key do you use?

🔢 **5.** ✓**Try It Out** Solve and check each equation.
a. $125v = 2,750$
b. $t \div 588 = 7,538$
c. $2,256 = g \div 1,111$
d. $3,456n = 41,472$

Sometimes you can solve equations mentally.

■ EXAMPLE 3   *Real-World Problem Solving*

Hockey A school spent $75 on chin straps for the hockey team. Each costs $3. How many straps did the school buy?

Words • total cost | equals | cost of one chin strap | times | number of straps

• Let c = number of chin straps bought

Equation • 75 = 3 × c

$75 = 3c$ ⟵ Ask yourself "What number times 3 equals 75?"

$75 = 3 \times 25$ ⟵ Use mental math.

The school bought 25 chin straps.

6. ⁂ **Mental Math** Solve each equation. Check your solution.
a. $5c = 35$
b. $n \div 2 = 30$
c. $100 = k \div 20$
d. $150 = 5h$
e. $11m = 121$
f. $b \div 10 = 1,000$

Certain algebraic properties can help you calculate mentally.

ALGEBRAIC PROPERTIES

Identity Properties

The sum of 0 and any number is that number.

Examples: $0 + 121 = 121; a + 0 = a$

The product of 1 and any number is that number.

Examples: $1 \times 75 = 75; x \times 1 = x$

Commutative Properties

Changing the order of addends or factors does not change the sum or product.

Examples: $7 + 8 = 8 + 7; 9 \times 5 = 5 \times 9$

Associative Properties

Changing the grouping of numbers does not change a sum or product.

Examples: $16 + (4 + 8) = (16 + 4) + 8$
$(7 \times 5) \times 2 = 7 \times (5 \times 2)$

7. ❖ *Reasoning* Why do you think it would be easier to find $(16 + 4) + 8$ mentally than $16 + (4 + 8)$?

8. ❖ *Mental Math* Use the commutative property to find $25 \times 42 \times 4$ mentally.

EXERCISES *On Your Own*

Modeling **Show the next step needed to solve the equation in each model.**

1.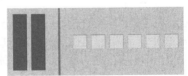

2.

3.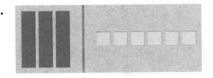

State whether the given number is a solution to the equation.

   4. $6h = 60$; 10   **5.** $g \div 8 = 7$; 64   **6.** $r \div 6 = 13$; 78

   7. $15 = 5p$; 3   **8.** $36 = m \div 3$; 12   **9.** $8c = 450$; 50

Modeling **Use algebra tiles to solve each equation.**

   10. $3x = 9$ **11.** $2m = 14$ **12.** $6x = 24$ **13.** $3x = 24$

   14. $4x = 12$ **15.** $7x = 14$ **16.** $20 = 4x$ **17.** $5x = 25$

18. *Modeling* **Use the model at the right.**
    a. Write an equation for the model.
    b. *Reasoning* Use algebra tiles to solve the equation.

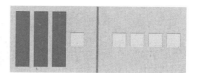

19. *Writing* Suppose you model and solve the equation $2x = 14$. Why do you divide each side of the equation into two equal parts?

Choose **Use algebra tiles, mental math, or a calculator to solve each equation.**

   20. $3m = 15$ **21.** $g \div 5 = 25$ **22.** $805 = 7b$ **23.** $6g = 24$

   24. $25h = 450$ **25.** $10 = k \div 20$ **26.** $y \div 43 = 1{,}204$ **27.** $n \div 3 = 14$

   28. $16 = 4h$ **29.** $525c = 86{,}625$ **30.** $h \div 20 = 9$ **31.** $90 = 6v$

   32. $e \div 2 = 88$ **33.** $75 = 15c$ **34.** $56d = 112$ **35.** $12 = r \div 9$

   36. $18{,}750 = 1{,}250k$ **37.** $d \div 1{,}000 = 100$ **38.** $400 = y \div 50$

39. **Choose A, B, C, or D.** Luchia participated in a swim-a-thon. Mr. Brown pledged $2.00 per lap. Luchia asked Mr. Brown for $44.00. Choose the equation that represents the number of laps Luchia swam.

    A. $2(44) = s$
    B. $2s = 44$
    C. $2 \div s = 44$
    D. $2 = 44s$

Calculator **Solve and check each equation.**

40. $x \div 23 = 56$

41. $4{,}731 = 57g$

42. $125p = 4{,}250$

43. $p \div 287 = 64{,}685$

44. $105{,}042 = 2{,}562s$

45. $s \div 62{,}409 = 289$

Match each equation below with the property it illustrates.

46. $47 \times 1 = 47$

47. $56 + 93 = 93 + 56$

48. $(9 \times 5) \times 2 = 9 \times (5 \times 2)$

A. Associative

B. Identity

C. Commutative

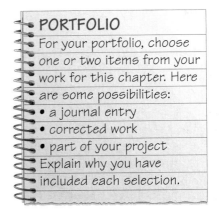

PORTFOLIO

For your portfolio, choose one or two items from your work for this chapter. Here are some possibilities:
• a journal entry
• corrected work
• part of your project
Explain why you have included each selection.

49. *Geometry* The area of a playground is given by the equation $A = w \times \ell$. The width w is 20 ft and the area A is 680 ft^2. Find the length of the playground.

50. *Pollution* A 9-gallon tank of gasoline produces about 180 pounds of carbon dioxide when it is burned.
  a. Write an equation to describe how much carbon dioxide one gallon of gasoline produces.
  b. Solve the equation.

Mixed Review

A record club sells CDs for $15.99 each plus a $2.38 shipping charge per order. *(Lesson 1-6)*

51. Make a table showing the cost of ordering 1, 2, 3, 4, or 5 CDs.

52. Graph the data in your table.

53. *Calendar* A year has two months in a row with a Friday the thirteenth. What months must they be? *(Previous Course)*

CHAPTER PROJECT

PROJECT LINK: CALCULATING

Write a sentence to describe how to calculate the value of the walls of your fort if you know the number of layers. Then write an equation to find the value of the fort.

CHAPTER PROJECT

STEPPING STONES

Building a Fort The Project Link questions on pages 47, 64, and 76 should help you to complete your project. Here is a checklist to help you gather the parts of your project together.

- ✔ determining the size of your foundation and the value of your fort with one layer in the wall
- ✔ a table, a description, and a numerical expression that fits your pattern
- ✔ a sentence describing how to calculate the value of your fort and an equation to find its value

Your final product will be a visual presentation of your fort, including a report with a diagram, a table, and calculations. You need to convince your teacher and the other members of the class that your fort is appropriate and within budget.

Be sure your work is neat and clear. Show your data and calculations. Write any explanations you think are necessary.

Reflect and Revise

Review your project with a friend or family member. Is your fort a reasonable size and shape? Is it within the $2 budget? Are your numerical expression and equation correct? If necessary, revise your project before presenting it to the class.

Web Extension

Prentice Hall's Internet site contains information you might find helpful as you complete your project. Visit www.phschool.com/mgm1/ch2 for some links and ideas related to patterns.

Patterns and Number Sense

Each number in a number pattern is called a term. You can describe a number pattern with a rule. A rule tells you the first term and what to do to get each of the following terms.

Find the next three terms in each number pattern.

1. 2, 6, 18, 54, . . .   **2.** 7, 19, 31, 43, . . .   **3.** 75, 65, 55, 45, . . .   **4.** 7, 14, 28, 56, . . .

5. Write the first five terms in the following number pattern:
Start with the number 5, and add 7 repeatedly.

Problem Solving Strategies

One strategy for solving a problem is to *Look for a Pattern.*

6. The cost of a 1-min call from Brookfield to the neighboring town Carnstown is 7 cents. The cost of a 2-min call is 15 cents, and a 3-min call is 23 cents. If this pattern continues, what would be the cost of a 5-min call?

The Order of Operations

The **order of operations** is a set of rules used in mathematics. You use these rules to find the value of numerical expressions.

- Do all operations within parentheses first.
- Multiply and divide in order from left to right.
- Add and subtract in order from left to right.

Find the value of each expression.

7. $2 \times 20 + 24 \div 4$ **8.** $5 + 4 \times 11$ **9.** $5 + 3 \times 12 - 4$ **10.** $(4 + 12) \div 4$

11. $21 \div 3 + 4 \times 2$ **12.** $8 \times (3 + 7) \times 3$ **13.** $45 \div 5 + 24 \div 6$ **14.** $16 \div (14 - 6)$

Replace each ▪ with <, >, or =.

15. $2 \times (12 - 3)$ ▪ $2 \times 12 - 3$ **16.** $(18 - 2) \times (6 - 2)$ ▪ $18 - 2 \times 6 - 2$

A **variable** is a symbol that stands for an unknown number. A **numerical expression** contains only numbers and operation symbols. A **variable expression** contains at least one variable. To evaluate a variable expression, replace each different variable with a number and then simplify.

Evaluate each expression.

17. $48 \div x$ for $x = 6$ **18.** $c - 7$ for $c = 56$ **19.** $14b$ for $b = 3$ **20.** $x \div 12$ for $x = 72$

21. $2ab + 3$ for $a = 4$ and $b = 3$ **22.** $h + 3k - 1$ for $h = 7$ and $k = 4$

Write a variable expression for each phrase.

23. 5 less than x **24.** y divided by p **25.** b more than 20   **26.** h times 4

27. The drama club sold twice as many tickets on Saturday as on Friday. Write a variable expression for the number of tickets sold on Saturday.

Modeling Equations   2-6, 2-7

An **equation** is a mathematical sentence that contains an equal sign. To **solve** an equation, replace the variable with a number that makes the equation true. The number that makes the equation true is a **solution**.

Solve each equation.

28. $x + 7 = 12$ **29.** $m + 348 = 781$ **30.** $r - 1{,}078 = 4{,}562$ **31.** $t \div 4 = 32$

32. $78x = 4{,}368$ **33.** $m - 8 = 15$ **34.** $4a = 32$ **35.** $x + 3 = 8$

36. **Choose A, B, C, or D.** Chandrelle bought a calculator for x dollars. She gave the clerk $40. She received $7 back. Which equation could you use to find the cost of the calculator?

   A. $7x = 40$ **B.** $x - 40 = 7$ **C.** $x \div 7 = 40$ **D.** $x + 7 = 40$

37. *Writing* Describe in your own words the difference between an expression and an equation.

1. a. Sketch the fourth and fifth designs in the pattern below.

  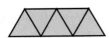

b. Use the designs to form a number pattern.
c. Write a rule to describe the number pattern.
d. Predict the number of triangles in the tenth design.

Find the next three terms in each number pattern. Write a rule to describe each number pattern.

2. 6, 10, 14, 18, . . .

3. 64, 32, 16, 8, . . .

4. 78, 69, 60, 51, . . .

5. 4, 12, 36, 108, . . .

6. Choose A, B, C, or D. Which number pattern can be described by this rule: *Start with the number 3, and add 7 repeatedly?*

A. 3, 21, 147, . . . **B.** 7, 10, 13, . . .
C. 1, 3, 7, . . . **D.** 3, 10, 17, . . .

7. Carol is training for a swim meet. She swims 4 laps per day the first week, 8 laps per day the second week, 12 laps per day the third week, and 16 laps per day the fourth week. She continues this pattern. How many laps per day will Carol swim in the eighth week?

8. Replace ■ with $<$, $>$, or $=$.
a. $3 + 2 \times 2$ ■ $3 + (2 \times 2)$
b. $6 + 14 \div 2$ ■ $(6 + 14) \div 2$

9. Evaluate $2a + b$ for $a = 5$ and $b = 18$.

10. *Mental Math* Solve each equation.
a. $14 = y - 8$ **b.** $2m = 26$

11. Write a variable expression for each model.

a.  **b.**

Find the value of each expression.

12. $500 + (12 - 8)$ **13.** $3 + 3 \times 4$

14. $8 \div 4 - 2$ **15.** $8 + 4 \div 2$

16. Write a variable expression for each word phrase.
a. 8 less than d **b.** twice q
c. c less than four **d.** six times x

17. Solve the equation shown in each model.

a.

b.

Solve each equation.

18. $25 + b = 138$ **19.** $n - 46 = 84$

20. $140 = 10y$ **21.** $k \div 12 = 3$

22. State whether the given number is a solution to the equation.
a. $x + 15 = 32$; 16
b. $21 - b = 13$; 8

23. *Writing* How would you use a calculator to solve $x - 562 = 1,455$?

Choose the best answer.

1. In a set of data, what name is given to the number found by subtracting the lowest number from the highest?

   A. mean   **B.** median
   C. mode   **D.** range

2. Which rule best describes the number pattern 4, 8, 12, 16, . . . ?

   A. Add 4 repeatedly.
   B. Start with 4, and add 4 repeatedly.
   C. Start with 4, and multiply by 2.
   D. Start with 4, and multiply by 2 repeatedly.

3. For a lake cruise, each of 127 people will pay $20 for a ticket. What is the total cost of all the tickets?

   A. $147   **B.** $154
   C. $2,440   **D.** $2,540

4. At a school play, adult tickets cost $7 and student tickets cost $4. The Baray family consists of 3 adults and 5 students. Which number sentence could be used to find T, the total cost in dollars for the family's tickets?

   A. $T = (4 \times 7) \times (5 \times 3)$
   B. $T = (4 \times 7) + (5 \times 3)$
   C. $T = (3 \times 7) + (5 \times 4)$
   D. $T = (3 + 7) \times (5 + 3)$

5. For a class project, 23 students have collected 925 golf balls that are being put into 23 wire baskets. Each basket will have the same number of balls. What is the greatest number of balls each basket can contain?

   A. 4   **B.** 39
   C. 40   **D.** 41

6. The circle graph below shows how Malinda budgets her income.

Malinda's Budget

Which statement is true?

   A. The biggest budget item is food.
   B. The amount for food and clothing is the same as for rent.
   C. She budgets more for insurance than for savings.
   D. The amount for savings is more than the amount for rent.

7. At a theme park each adult pays $20 and each student pays $12. Let R represent the total receipts for the day. Which sentence shows the total receipts for 320 adults and 578 students?

   A. $R = 20 + 12 + 320 + 578$
   B. $R = (20 \times 320) + (12 \times 578)$
   C. $R = 20 \times 320 \times 12 \times 578$
   D. $R = (20 + 350) \times (12 + 578)$

8. What is the value of $79 - 5 \times (3 + 10)$?

   A. 14   **B.** 70   **C.** 232   **D.** 962

9. Hank earns $25 each week on his paper route. So far he has earned $2,625. For how many weeks has he had the paper route?

   A. 105   **B.** 15
   C. 65,625   **D.** 2,600

Adding and Subtracting Decimals

3

| WHAT YOU WILL LEARN IN THIS CHAPTER | • How to read, write, and compare decimals | • How to add and subtract decimals | • How to use metric units of length, mass, and capacity |

Name that TUNE

Don't you just love to browse through a music store? But you love bargains, too! You have probably seen magazine ads that promise eight music CDs for only a penny. But is this really a bargain? Suppose that after you get your eight CDs, you must buy eight more CDs at regular club prices ($12.95–$17.95) over the next two years. Also, you must pay a shipping and handling charge per CD, including the eight CDs you got for a penny. Is the club still a good deal?

Compare Prices and Decide Your project will be to compare the costs of buying CDs through a CD club and at a store and to make a decision whether to join the club or not.

Steps to help you complete the project:

p. 95 Project Link: *Researching*
p. 102 Project Link: *Rounding and Estimating*
p. 121 Project Link: *Calculating*
p. 127 *Finishing the Chapter Project*

• How to solve problems using the guess and test method

3-1 Exploring Decimal Models

What You'll Learn

▼ 1 To model decimals

▼ 2 To explore equivalent decimals

...And Why

You can draw models to represent decimals and use your models to identify equivalent decimals.

Here's How

Look for questions that
- ⚬ build understanding
- ✔ check understanding

Tenths' Model

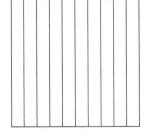

Hundredths' Model

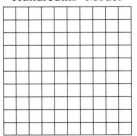

THINK AND DISCUSS

▼ 1 *Modeling Decimals*

Suppose you are in charge of cutting a huge, square birthday cake. One hundred people must be served. How would you cut the cake so that everyone receives an equal-sized piece?

To model the cake, draw a square with sides 10 centimeters long.

1. ⚬ **Modeling** Cut the "cake" vertically into ten equal strips. On your model, draw a line for each cut.

Since there are ten equal strips, one strip is *one tenth* of the cake. You can write one tenth as 0.1. Two strips are two tenths, or 0.2, of the cake.

2. **a.** How many strips are 0.3 of the cake?
   b. How many tenths are 0.8 of the cake?

3. ⚬ **Go a Step Further** Now cut the "cake" horizontally so that each strip is cut into 10 pieces. On your model, draw a line for each cut. How many pieces of cake do you have now?

One piece is *one hundredth* of the cake. You can write one hundredth as 0.01. Two pieces equal two hundredths, or 0.02.

4. **a.** How many pieces equal 0.07 of the cake?
   b. How many hundredths equal 0.43 of the cake?

■ EXAMPLE 1

Write a decimal for this model.

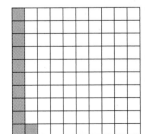

Eleven out of 100 pieces of the model are shaded.

The model represents eleven hundredths, or 0.11.

On October 18, 1989, a huge cake in the shape of the state of Alabama was made to celebrate the 100th birthday of the town of Fort Payne. The cake weighed 128,238.5 lb, including 16,209 lb of icing. A 100-year-old resident named Ed Henderson made the first cut.

Source: *Guinness Book of Records*

▼2 *Exploring Equivalent Decimals*

5. ⁂ *Modeling* Draw models to represent the decimals 0.7 and 0.70. What do you notice?

Decimals that represent the same amount are **equivalent.**

6. a. How many tenths describe the whole cake?
   b. How many hundredths describe the whole cake?
   c. ⁂ *Explain* Are the decimals 0.1 and 0.10 equivalent? Why or why not?

7. What whole number describes the whole cake?

■ EXAMPLE 2

How many hundredths are equivalent to five tenths?

Five tenths equals 0.5. Draw a model for 0.5. Five strips are shaded.

Then divide your model into hundredths. Fifty squares are shaded. This represents 0.50.

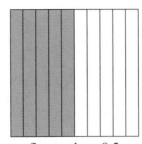

five tenths = 0.5

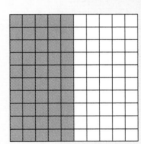

fifty hundredths = 0.50

0.50 = 0.5

---

8. ✔*Try It Out* How many hundredths are equivalent to nine tenths?

Work Together   *Applying Decimal Models to Money*

Suppose you have a dime and a penny.

9. ⁂*Modeling* Describe each coin as a decimal portion of a dollar. Draw models for one dollar, one dime, and one penny.

10. Draw models for one nickel and one quarter. Write the decimal representation for each coin.

Write a decimal for each model.

1.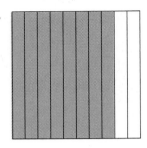

2.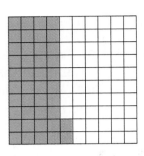

3.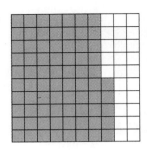

Draw a model for each decimal.

4. 0.6   5. 0.36   6. 0.3   7. 0.04   8. 0.2   9. 0.35

Write each decimal in words.

10. 0.08   11. 0.2   12. 0.56   13. 0.40   14. 0.65   15. 0.30

Write a decimal for the given words.

16. seven tenths   17. forty hundredths   18. five hundredths

19. five tenths   20. twenty-two hundredths   21. thirty-one hundredths

22. fifty-four hundredths   23. twelve hundredths   24. forty-seven hundredths

How many hundredths are equivalent to each amount?

25. two tenths   26. six tenths   27. eight tenths   28. ten tenths   29. four tenths

30. How many tenths are equivalent to sixty hundredths?

31. *Writing* Miki thinks this model shows 0.4. Paulo thinks it shows 0.40. Do you agree with Miki or with Paulo? Explain.

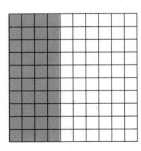

32. Suppose you want to cut a square birthday cake into 10 equal pieces. A vertical strip will not fit on a party plate, so you decide on a different shape.
   a. Draw a model that shows how you will cut the cake.
   b. Write a decimal number to represent one piece of cake.

33. *Open-ended* Imagine you are asked to invent a new coin. Describe your coin as a decimal portion of a dollar.

Estimation **Each square model represents 1. Write a decimal to estimate the amount shaded.**

34.

35.

36.

Mixed Review

37. An ant can lift 50 times its own body weight. Suppose a student weighing 85 lb could do the same. How much could the student lift? *(Previous Course)*

 Choose **Use tiles, mental math, or a calculator to solve each equation.** *(Lesson 2-7)*

38. $3x = 27$ **39.** $17 = y \div 9$ **40.** $a \div 10 = 210$ **41.** $950 = 5b$ **42.** $125 = y \div 5$

Compare using <, >, or =. *(Previous Course)*

43. $13 \times 7 \ \blacksquare \ 120 - 27$ **44.** $237 + 338 \ \blacksquare \ 25 \times 23$ **45.** $450 \div 90 \ \blacksquare \ 4500 \div 900$

Math at Work

ACCOUNTANT

Accountants usually work in some area of finance. They must enjoy working with numbers and know how to budget money well. Accountants use mathematics to prepare and analyze financial reports and tax returns, create budgets, and to manage company costs. Accountants' reports help people make good business decisions.

For more information about the field of accounting, visit the Prentice Hall Web site: www.phschool.com

Reading and Writing Whole Numbers and Decimals

What You'll Learn

1. To read and write whole numbers
2. To read and write decimals in expanded and standard forms

...And Why

You can write whole numbers and decimals to solve problems in social studies and sports.

Here's How

Look for questions that
- build understanding
- check understanding

THINK AND DISCUSS

1. Reading and Writing Whole Numbers

Social Studies The national debt is now over five trillion dollars. How large a number is this?

The position of a digit in a number determines the place value of that digit. The digits in a whole number are grouped into periods. A period has 3 digits, and each period has a name.

Trillions Period			Billions Period			Millions Period			Thousands Period			Ones Period		
Hundreds	Tens	Ones	Hundreds	Tens	Ones	Hundreds	Tens	Ones	Hundreds	Tens	Ones	Hundreds	Tens	Ones
	6	1	4	0	2	6	1	7	0	8	0	1	2	5

Read the number in each period followed by its period name.

61 trillion, 402 billion, 617 million, 80 thousand, 125

1. **Reasoning** As you move from left to right in the place value chart, how do the values increase or decrease?

2. Write each number in words.
   a. 56,789,445 b. 6,253,788,554 c. 45,568

To write a number in **standard form,** use commas to separate the periods. Add zeros if you need to so that each period has 3 digits.

Need Help? For more practice with whole numbers, see Skills Handbook pages 535 and 536.

■ EXAMPLE 1

Write 65 million, 3 thousand, 47 in standard form.

65 million + 3 thousand + 47 = 65,000,000 + 3,000 + 47

$$= 65,003,047$$

65 million, 3 thousand, 47 in standard form is 65,003,047.

3. ✔**Try It Out** Write each number in standard form.
   a. 232 billion, 753 thousand   **b.** 65 million, 2 thousand, 42

▼2 *Reading and Writing Decimals*

Two tenths and five hundredths is equivalent to twenty-five hundredths. One is expressed in expanded form, the other in standard form.

Expanded Form	=	**Standard Form**
0.2 + 0.05	=	0.25

two tenths and five hundredths = twenty-five hundredths

A number in **expanded form** shows the place and value of each digit. Look at 47.2586 in the place value chart below.

Hundreds	Tens	Ones		Tenths	Hundredths	Thousandths	Ten-Thousandths	Hundred-Thousandths
	4	7	.	2	5	8	6	

4. In the number 47.2586, the digit 2 is in the tenths place. What is the value of the 8?

When you read or write a decimal greater than 1, the word "and" tells you where to place the decimal point.

Gasoline prices are usually calculated to the *thousandths' place*. The number of gallons you buy is multiplied by the price. Then the total is rounded up to the nearest cent.

■ EXAMPLE 2   *Real-World Problem Solving*

Sports A marathon race is about twenty-six and twenty-one thousand, eight hundred seventy-five hundred-thousandths miles long. Write this number in standard form.

26   ⟵ Write the whole number part.
26.■ ■ ■ ■ ■   ⟵ Hundred-thousandths is 5 places to the right of the decimal point.
26.21875   ⟵ Place 21875 to the right.

Twenty-six and twenty-one thousand, eight hundred seventy-five hundred-thousandths in standard form is 26.21875.

5. ✔*Try It Out* Write each number in standard form.
  a. four and one hundred fifty-one thousandths
  b. two hundred forty-one and three ten-thousandths

EXERCISES *On Your Own*

Complete each statement.

1. 3,460,800 = ▨ million, ▨ thousand, ▨

2. 56,450,000,000 = ▨ billion, ▨ million

Write each number in words.

3. 205

4. 456,785

5. 6,745

6. 223,455,784

7. 45,654,332

Write each number in standard form.

8. eight hundred ninety

9. four thousand, six hundred

10. fourteen million

11. 478 thousand, 27

12. 240 million, 85 thousand, 11

13. 213 million, 125

14. 28 billion, 35 thousand, 40

15. 6 billion, 23 million, 158 thousand

16. 7 trillion, 2 million, 13 thousand

17. three hundred thousand, twenty

18. *Science* Scientists estimate the universe was formed about sixteen billion years ago. Write this number in standard form.

What is the value of the digit 4 in each number?

19. 0.4

20. 3.004

21. 1.28864

22. 42.3926

23. 4.0052

24. 530.34

25. 17.55643

26. 34,567.89

27. 433.0005

28. 3.40365

Write each number in words.

29. 352.3

30. 6.025

31. 11.2859

32. 70.009

33. 0.00657

34. *Open-ended* Write a decimal with 5 decimal places in standard form and in expanded form.

Write each number in standard form.

35. two and four hundred-thousandths

36. four hundred and seventy-five thousandths

37. 40 + 2 + 0.3 + 0.07 + 0.009 + 0.0004

38. 50 + 1 + 0.6 + 0.03

Money Write each amount as a decimal part of $1.00.

39. 8 dimes

40. 6 pennies

41. 49 pennies

42. 3 quarters

43. *Writing* Describe how the value of the digit 2 changes in each place in the number 22.222.

44. *Research* Earth revolves around the sun in 365.24 days. Find out how our calendar deals with the extra 0.24 day.

45. *Money* A mill is a very small unit of money that state governments sometimes use to calculate taxes. One mill is equivalent to one thousandth of a dollar ($.001).
  a. Write each amount as part of a dollar.
    i. 6 mills   **ii.** 207 mills   **iii.** 53 mills   **iv.** 328 mills
  b. About how many cents is each amount worth?

Biology Write each measurement in standard form.

46. Human fingernails grow about two thousandths of an inch a day.

47. A goat produces four and seven tenths pints of milk a day.

48. A flea can jump six hundred forty-six thousandths of a foot.

49. One beat of a housefly's wings takes about one thousandth of a second.

50. A bee's wing has a mass of five hundred-thousandths of a gram.

51. A tortoise moves seventeen hundredths of a mile per hour.

Mixed Review

52. Ten students took Mr. Yuji's science test. Their scores were 91, 84, 78, 84, 70, 93, 68, 89, 77, and 76. Find the mean, median, and mode of the scores. *(Lesson 1-3)*

53. Order the following numbers from greatest to least: 3,201,455; 2,684,387; 978,897; 2,852,238; 4,527,982; and 3,097,854. *(Previous Course)*

54. *Choose a Strategy* Evan saves two quarters and three nickels each day. At the end of 30 days, how much has he saved?

Comparing and Ordering Decimals

What You'll Learn

▼1 To compare decimals using models

▼2 To order decimals using place value

...And **Why**

You can order lists of data by comparing decimals.

Here's **How**

Look for questions that
- build understanding
- ✔ check understanding

QUICKreview

To compare numbers, use these symbols.
< is less than
= is equal to
> is greater than

Need Help? For practice with comparing and ordering whole numbers, see Skills Handbook p. 537.

THINK AND DISCUSS

▼1 *Comparing Decimals Using Models*

Social Studies Buenos Aires, Argentina, has an estimated population of 12.23 million people. About 12.79 million people live in Rio de Janeiro, Brazil. To compare the two populations, look at the whole number parts. They are the same. Now look at the decimal parts, 0.23 and 0.79.

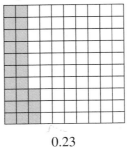
0.23

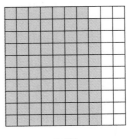
0.79

$0.23 < 0.79$, so $12.23 < 12.79$. Buenos Aires has an estimated population less than that of Rio de Janeiro.

1. Draw models for 0.7 and 0.72. Which number is greater?

You can also graph decimals on a number line to compare them. Numbers on a number line are greater as you move to the right.

2. Use <, =, or > to complete each statement.
 a. 0.7 ▇ 0.4 **b.** 0.4 ▇ 0.7 **c.** 0.7 ▇ 0.70

3. a. What decimals are at points *A* and *B?*
 b. Write two statements to compare the numbers.

4. ▪*Modeling* Use a number line to compare 0.13 and 0.08. How many hundredths are between the two decimals?

5. ▪*Analyze* How many numbers are between 0.8 and 0.9? Name three.

2 Ordering Decimals Using Place Value

You can compare decimals using place value. Start at the decimal point and move right, one place at a time.

Earth Science Which body of salt water is saltier, the Dead Sea or the Great Salt Lake?

Compare 0.28 and 0.205. Line up decimal points.

0.28	0.28	0.28
0.205	0.205	0.205
↑	↑	↑
same	same	8 > 0

The Dead Sea is saltier than the Great Salt Lake.

Salt per Liter in Major Bodies of Water

Water	Salt per Liter
Black Sea	0.018 kg
Caspian Sea	0.013 kg
Dead Sea	0.28 kg
Great Salt Lake	0.205 kg
Ocean (average)	0.035 kg

Source: *Natural Wonders of the World*

6. ✔*Try It Out* Which body of salt water is saltier, the Caspian Sea or the ocean? Refer to Example 1.

7. ⚬*Look Back* How could you use a model or number line to solve Example 1?

8. Use place value to compare each pair of decimals.
   a. 0.32 and 0.35   **b.** 0.14 and 0.041   **c.** 0.760 and 0.76

You can graph decimals on a number line to place them in order.

Order the bodies of water above from least to most salty.

Graph 0.018, 0.013, 0.28, 0.205, and 0.035 on a number line.

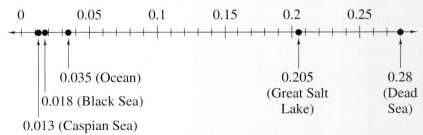

The bodies of water from least to most salty are Caspian Sea, Black Sea, the ocean, Great Salt Lake, and Dead Sea.

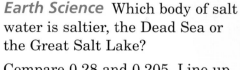

GEOGRAPHY People float easily in the salty water of the Dead Sea, between the countries of Israel and Jordan.

Israel and Jordan

Draw models for each pair of decimals. Explain how the models show which number is greater.

1. 0.4 and 0.5   **2.** 0.35 and 0.53   **3.** 1.42 and 1.44   **4.** 0.76 and 0.78   **5.** 0.2 and 0.02

6. *Writing* Explain how you can use place value to compare 1.679 and 1.697.

Use <, =, or > to complete each statement.

7. 0.58 ▓ 0.578   **8.** 5.7 ▓ 5.70   **9.** 0.37 ▓ 0.3651   **10.** 0.09 ▓ 0.002

11. 8.009 ▓ 8.079   **12.** 6.6 ▓ 6.2   **13.** 49.5 ▓ 49.05   **14.** 0.4389 ▓ 0.45

15. 0.06 ▓ 0.60   **16.** 3.968 ▓ 4.007   **17.** 0.05 ▓ 0.050   **18.** 0.2 ▓ 0.29

Graph each set of numbers on a number line.

19. 6.4, 6.04, 7.6, 6.59, and 7.2

20. 0.49, 0.34, 0.4, 0.3, and 0.38

21. **Choose A, B, C, or D.** Graph the decimals 0.2, 0.4, and 0.6 on a number line. Which statement is *not* true?

   A. 0.2 < 0.4 and 0.4 < 0.6   **B.** 0.2 < 0.4 and 0.2 < 0.6

   C. 0.2 < 0.6 and 0.6 < 0.4   **D.** 0.4 < 0.6 and 0.6 > 0.2

Astronomy **Read the article at the right. Use the information for Exercises 22–25.**

Light-Years Away

22. Which star is farthest from Earth? Which is closest to Earth?

23. Write the distances from Earth to each of the six stars in order from least to greatest.

24. Use <, =, and > to write three statements about the distances of any of these stars from Earth.

25. *Research* Look up the meaning of *light-year*. Why do you think astronomers use this measure?

26. What decimals are at points *A*, *B*, and *C*?

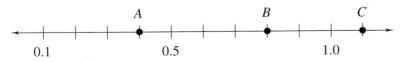

The brightest star in the sky is Sirius, which is about 8.7 light-years from Earth. The stars Alpha Centauri A and B are each about 4.37 light-years from Earth. Proxima Centauri is about 4.28 light-years away. Other stars are 6121 CygniB, about 11.09 light-years away, and Procyon B, about 11.4 light years away.

Find the value of each expression. *(Lesson 2-3)*

27. $4 - (24 \div 8) + 4$ **28.** $16 - 3 \times 2 + 5$ **29.** $55 \div (5 + 6) + 6$

Find each answer. *(Previous Course)*

30. $13,789 + 23,653$ **31.** $34,567 - 27,488$ **32.** 152×27 **33.** $585 \div 9$

34. *Choose a Strategy* A large stone weighs 5 times as much as a small brick. Together they weigh 30 lb. What is the weight of the stone?

CHAPTER PROJECT

PROJECT LINK: **RESEARCHING**

Research the prices of CDs at different stores in your area. Compare your prices with those of other students. Calculate the average price of a CD based on the prices you have found.

✓ CHECKPOINT 1

Lessons 3-1 through 3-3

Write each decimal in words.

1. 0.9   **2.** 0.01   **3.** 0.73   **4.** 0.60   **5.** 0.56   **6.** 0.99

Write each number as a decimal in standard form.

7. three tenths   **8.** two hundredths   **9.** $0.9 + 0.02$ **10.** $0.3 + 0.06$

Find the value of each underlined digit.

11. 5.$\underline{6}$8   **12.** 0.8$\underline{7}$0   **13.** $\underline{8}$.005   **14.** 4.20$\underline{3}$ **15.** 3.$\underline{6}$32   **16.** 1.1$\underline{11}$

Use <, =, or > to complete each statement.

17. 32.07 ▨ 32.070   **18.** 1.8 ▨ 1.08   **19.** 72.6 ▨ 7.62   **20.** 55.05 ▨ 55.50

21. 1.082 ▨ 1.28   **22.** 3.04 ▨ 3.040   **23.** 6.402 ▨ 6.042   **24.** 2.2 ▨ 2.22

25. *Open-ended* Make a list of five 6-digit whole numbers and decimals. Order the numbers from least to greatest.

Extra Practice, Lesson 3-3, page 524

3-4

Guess and Test

Problem Solving Strategies

- Draw a Diagram
- ✔ Guess and Test
- Look for a Pattern
- Make a Model
- Make a Table
- Simulate a Problem
- Solve a Simpler Problem
- Too Much or Too Little Information
- Use Logical Reasoning
- Use Multiple Strategies
- Work Backward

THINK AND DISCUSS

A good problem solving strategy is *Guess and Test*. First make a reasonable guess, and then test it against the given information. If your guess is incorrect, change it to make it more reasonable. Keep trying until you find the correct answer.

SAMPLE PROBLEM.................................

Handmade friendship bracelets use 20 cm of thread. Handmade rings use 8 cm of thread. Marny used a total of 184 cm of thread to make 14 items. How many friendship bracelets did she make?

 READ

Read for understanding. Summarize the problem.

Look at the given information. Decide what you are being asked to find.

1. **a.** How much thread is needed for a bracelet? A ring?
   b. How much thread did Marny use in all?
   c. How many items did Marny make?

2. What does the problem ask you to find?

 PLAN

Decide on a strategy.

Guess and Test is a good strategy to use.

3. Suppose you guess that Marny made 4 bracelets.
   a. ⬡*Reasoning* Why does this mean she made 10 rings?
   b. How many centimeters of thread are used to make 4 bracelets? 10 rings? Explain how you found each answer.
   c. Is a guess of 4 bracelets correct? Why or why not?
   d. ⬡*Writing* Should your next guess be higher or lower? Explain.

 **SOLVE**

Try the strategy.

You can organize your guesses in a table like the one below.

Bracelets	Rings	Thread	High/Low
5 × 20 cm = 100 cm	9 × 8 cm = 72 cm	172 cm	low
8 × 20 cm = 160 cm	6 × 8 cm = 48 cm	208 cm	high
▨	▨	▨	▨

4. In the table above you can see that 5 bracelets required too little thread and 8 bracelets required too much thread.
   a. What guess would be reasonable to make next?
   b. ▪ *Analyze* Is one of the guesses more reasonable to make than the other? Explain.
   c. Copy and complete the table above to test your next guess. Keep guessing until you find the correct answer.
   d. How many friendship bracelets did Marny make?

 **LOOK BACK**

Think about how you solved the problem.

Check your answer with the information given in the problem.

5. Is the total number of bracelets and rings 14? Is the total amount of thread used 184 cm?

EXERCISES *On Your Own*

Use *Guess and Test* to solve each problem.

1. *Fund-raising* Parents in Fullerton are raising money for the school by conducting a raffle. You can buy a ticket for a video game for $2 or a ticket for a remote-control car for $3. On Saturday, $203 was raised by selling 80 raffle tickets. How many remote-control car tickets were sold?

2. Place the digits 2, 3, 4, 6, and 8 in a copy of the figure at the right so the product in both directions is the same. Find the product.

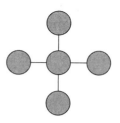

3. *Entertainment* Movie tickets cost $4.00 for children and $7.00 for adults. On Friday the theater collected $720 by selling 120 tickets. How many adult tickets were sold?

Use any strategy to solve. Show your work.

4. *Sports* In a race, Juan was behind Maria, but ahead of Noel. Noel was behind Juan, but ahead of Della. Order the students from fastest to slowest.

5. *School Outings* The 182 sixth-graders at the Fannie Lou Hamer Middle School are taking a trip to the museum. The entrance fee is $1.75 per pupil and $3.25 per adult. The bus fee is $189 per bus. Each bus holds 44 people. Find the total cost for the students and 14 adults to visit the museum.

6. *Literature* Millie, Bobbi, and Francesca are reading a mystery, a fantasy, and a biography. Each is reading a book type that does not begin with the same letter as her name. Francesca is reading *The Case of the Howling Wolves*. Who is reading a fantasy?

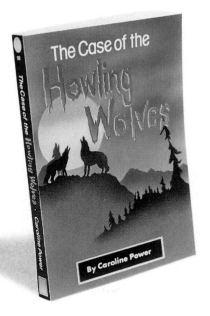

7. *Money* Suppose you save quarters and dimes in a jar. Last night you counted $6.75. The number of dimes is one more than the number of quarters. How many quarters are there?

8. *Consumer Issues* At the sub shop, you ate two slices of pizza and a small salad. You paid for your meal with a ten-dollar bill. Your change was $5.11. What was the price of your meal?

9. *Patterns* A train makes 5 stops. At the first three stops there are 3, 9, and 27 passengers. If the pattern continues, find the number of passengers at the fifth stop.

10. *Puzzles* The following is a *cryptarithm*, a puzzle in which each letter represents a different digit. Find a value for each letter. (*Hint:* What is the only possible value for M?)

$$\begin{array}{r} F\ U\ N \\ +\ \ I\ S \\ \hline M\ A\ T\ H \end{array}$$

Mixed Review

Write each number in words. *(Lesson 3-2)*

11. 973,430,624   12. 3,700,008   13. 16,765,803,578   14. 234,467,345,234,633

Find the value using the order of operations. *(Lesson 2-3)*

15. $5 + 2 \times 8 - 1$ 16. $16 \div 2 \times 3 - 20$ 17. $6 \times (2 + 9) \div 3$ 18. $26 + 2 \times (95 - 5)$

19. A mountain climber starts at an altitude of 2,830 ft above sea level and climbs 4,920 ft. The next day, she climbs another 3,130 ft. What is her final altitude? *(Previous Course)*

Modeling the Addition and Subtraction of Decimals

What You'll Learn

1 To model addition of decimals

2 To model subtraction of decimals

...And Why

You use decimals to add and subtract money.

Here's How

Look for questions that
- build understanding
- ✔ check understanding

QUICKreview

To find a sum, add. To find a difference, subtract.

Need Help? For practice adding and subtracting whole numbers, see Skills Handbook pages 538 and 539.

Work Together _____ *Investigating Decimal Addition*

1. **Modeling** Draw a model for 0.63.

2. Write 0.63 in expanded form.

3. Draw models for the sum 0.6 + 0.03.

4. Draw models for the sum 0.3 + 0.06.

THINK AND DISCUSS

1 *Modeling Addition of Decimals*

You can use models to find any sum.

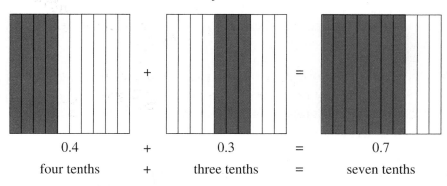

| 0.4 | + | 0.3 | = | 0.7 |
| four tenths | + | three tenths | = | seven tenths |

5. Use models to find each sum.
   a. 0.1 + 0.8　　b. 0.31 + 0.09　　c. 0.44 + 0.23

6. a. **Analyze** Use words to describe 0.8 + 0.5. What is the total number of tenths?
   b. Thirteen tenths is equivalent to one and ▓ tenths.
   c. You can write the sum as:
   $$\begin{array}{r} 0.8 \\ +\ 0.5 \\ \hline 1.3 \end{array}$$
   Draw a model showing that 0.8 + 0.5 = 1.3.

7. a. Three hundredths + nine hundredths = ▓ hundredths.
   b. Use decimals to write the sum described in part (a).
   c. **Modeling** Draw models to show this addition.

8. Add. Use models if they help you.

a. $\begin{array}{r} 0.31 \\ +\ 0.49 \end{array}$
b. $\begin{array}{r} 0.06 \\ +\ 0.55 \end{array}$
c. $\begin{array}{r} 1.50 \\ +\ 0.92 \end{array}$
d. $\begin{array}{r} 0.87 \\ +\ 0.56 \end{array}$

9. ▪ *Think About It* Why is it important to line up the decimal points?

 **Modeling Subtraction of Decimals**

You can also use models to subtract decimals.

■ **EXAMPLE**

Using models, find the difference 1.4 − 0.6.

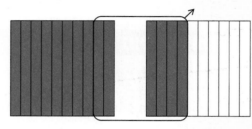

←Remove six tenths from fourteen tenths. Eight tenths remain.

1.4 − 0.6 = 0.8

10. ✔*Try It Out* Use models to find each difference.

a. 1.2 − 0.5   b. 0.92 − 0.75   c. 2.3 − 0.8

11. Think about the difference 0.52 − 0.07 in two ways.

a. ▪ *Modeling* Draw a model for 0.52. Remove 0.07. What is the answer?

b. Write the difference as:

$$\begin{array}{r} \overset{4\ 12}{0.\cancel{5}\cancel{2}} \\ -\ 0.07 \\ \hline 0.45 \end{array}$$

How could you check your answer?

c. ▪ *Analyze* The number 0.52 is equivalent to four tenths and twelve hundredths. How does the model show this?

12. Subtract. Use models if they help you.

a. $\begin{array}{r} 3.65 \\ -\ 0.57 \end{array}$
b. $\begin{array}{r} 5.8 \\ -\ 2.37 \end{array}$
c. $\begin{array}{r} 9.92 \\ -\ 4.74 \end{array}$

Use models to find each sum.

1. 0.9 + 0.4   **2.** 0.12 + 0.34   **3.** 0.67 + 0.33   **4.** 0.5 + 0.5

Use models to find each difference.

5. 1.2 − 0.5   **6.** 1.7 − 1.5   **7.** 0.88 − 0.57   **8.** 0.72 − 0.54

Use models to help you complete each statement.

9. 1.6 = one and ■ tenths = ■ tenths

10. 0.47 = ■ hundredths = ■ tenths and ■ hundredths

11. 2.5 = 2 ones and ■ tenths = 1 one and ■ tenths

12. 3 tenths and 1 hundredth = 2 tenths and ■ hundredths

Write the sum or difference statement shown by each model.

13.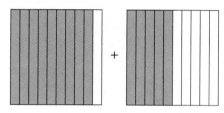

14.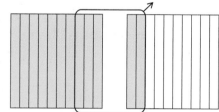

15.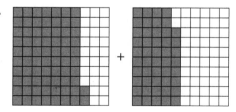

16.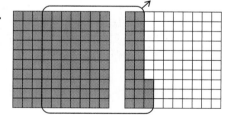

17. *Open-ended* Write a sum or a difference and find the answer in two different ways.

18. *Reasoning* Suppose you subtract hundredths from hundredths. Is an answer in terms of thousandths ever reasonable? Explain.

Add.

19. $0.65 + 4.23$ **20.** $0.83 + 0.67$ **21.** $3.93 + 7.14$ **22.** $0.85 + 6.09$

23. $0.32 + 0.12$ **24.** $3.46 + 9.17$ **25.** $5.52 + 0.99$ **26.** $7.11 + 5.93$

Subtract.

27. $8.63 - 4.39$ **28.** $2.34 - 0.73$ **29.** $8.2 - 1.93$

30. $8 - 3.62$ **31.** $6.04 - 2.49$ **32.** $3.74 - 2.81$

JOURNAL
Explain the different ways you can compare, order, add, and subtract decimals. List the advantages and disadvantages of each.

33. *Writing* Explain why five tenths and eleven hundredths is equivalent to six tenths and one hundredth. Model each sum to support your explanation.

Mixed Review

34. *Data Analysis* Refer to the graph at the right. The total amount of revenue was $1.61 billion. How much money came from merchandising? *(Lesson 1-5)*

Sources of Olympic Revenue
(Millions of dollars)

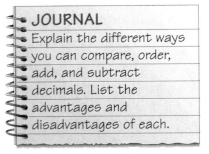

□ Broadcast rights   ▨ Merchandising
□ Corporate sponsors   □ Other
▨ Ticket sales

Source: Atlanta Committee for the Olympic Games

Write each number in standard form. *(Lesson 3-2)*

35. five and thirteen hundredths

36. nine hundred fifty thousandths

37. six hundred-thousandths

38. forty-three and fifteen ten-thousandths

Use mental math. *(Previous Course)*

39. $0 + 332$ **40.** $332 \div 1$ **41.** 30×20 **42.** $2{,}567 \times 1$ **43.** $40 \div 2$ **44.** 200×10

CHAPTER PROJECT

PROJECT LINK: ROUNDING AND ESTIMATING

You must buy eight CDs at regular club prices, which range from $12.95 to $17.95. Round these prices and estimate the total cost for the eight CDs. Will you use the higher price listed or the lower price? What number do you think best represents the price you'll usually have to pay? Explain.

SKILLS REVIEW

Rounding Whole Numbers

Before Lesson 3-6

Number lines can help you round numbers. On a number line, 5 is halfway between 0 and 10, 50 is halfway between 0 and 100, and 500 is halfway between 0 and 1,000. The acceptable method of rounding is to round 5 up to 10, 50 up to 100, and 500 up to 1,000.

■ EXAMPLE 1

Round 2,462 to the nearest ten.

2,462 is closer to 2,460 than to 2,470.

2,462 rounded to the nearest ten is 2,460.

■ EXAMPLE 2

Round 247,451 to the nearest hundred.

247,451 is closer to 247,500 than to 247,400.

247,451 rounded to the nearest hundred is 247,500.

Round each number to the nearest ten.

1. 65
2. 832
3. 4,437
4. 21,024
5. 3,545

Round each number to the nearest hundred.

6. 889
7. 344
8. 2,861
9. 1,138
10. 50,549

11. 6,411
12. 88,894
13. 13,735
14. 17,459
15. 6,059

Round each number to the nearest thousand.

16. 2,400
17. 16,218
18. 7,430
19. 89,375
20. 9,821

21. 15,631
22. 76,900
23. 163,875
24. 38,295
25. 102,359

26. *Writing* Describe a situation in which it is helpful to round data.

27. Explain how to round each of the numbers in Exercises 1–25 to the nearest ten thousand.

28. Suppose 31 is rounded to the nearest hundred. Is 0 a reasonable response? Why or why not?

3-6 Rounding and Estimating Data

THINK AND DISCUSS

1 Rounding Data

Do you ever wonder what is in the food you eat? For example, 0.138 of a kernel of corn is water.

To round 0.138 to the nearest hundredth, think about how you round whole numbers. The rules are similar.

Contents of Whole-Grain Field Corn

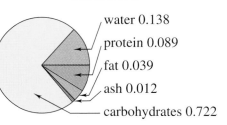

water 0.138
protein 0.089
fat 0.039
ash 0.012
carbohydrates 0.722

Locate the hundredths' place.

↓

0.1<u>3</u>8

Now look at the digit to the right.

0.13⑧

Is it ≥ 5?

You decide. Should you round 0.138 to 0.14 or to 0.13?

■ EXAMPLE 1

Round 0.138 to the nearest tenth.
You can use a number line or mental math.

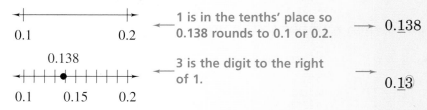

0.1   0.2

1 is in the tenths' place so 0.138 rounds to 0.1 or 0.2.

⟶ 0.<u>1</u>38

0.138

0.1   0.15   0.2

3 is the digit to the right of 1.

⟶ 0.1③

Since 3 < 5, 0.138 is closer to 0.1 than 0.2.
To the nearest tenth, 0.138 rounds to 0.1.

1. a. ✔**Try It Out** Round the other four decimals in the circle graph above to the nearest hundredth.
   b. Then round each decimal to the nearest tenth.

ROUNDING DECIMALS

Decide to which place you are rounding.

- **If the digit to the right of that place is greater than or equal to 5, round up.**

- **If the digit to the right of that place is less than 5, round down.**

2 Estimating Sums and Differences

You can use rounding to estimate a sum or a difference.

■ **EXAMPLE 2**   *Real-World Problem Solving*

To the nearest dollar, estimate the combined cost of the 1-gallon and 2-gallon tins of popcorn shown at the left.

$$
\begin{array}{ll}
\$\ 6.45 \ \longrightarrow & \$\ 6 \quad \longleftarrow \text{Round \$6.45 to the nearest dollar.} \\
\underline{+\ \$11.95} \ \longrightarrow & \underline{+\ \$12} \quad \longleftarrow \text{Round \$11.95 to the nearest dollar.} \\
& \$18
\end{array}
$$

The cost of the two tins is about $18.

2. ✔**Try It Out** Estimate the total cost of two 2-gallon tins.

3. ⬝**Estimation** About how much more does the largest tin of popcorn cost than the smallest tin? Use rounding to estimate.

To use **front-end estimation,** add the front-end digits, estimate the sum of the remaining digits, and add the results. The symbol ≈ means *is approximately equal to*.

■ **EXAMPLE 3**   *Real-World Problem Solving*

Use front-end estimation to estimate the total cost of three books marked $6.99, $7.25, and $15.80.

The books cost $6.99, $7.25, and $15.80.

Add the front-end digits, the dollars.	Estimate the cents.	Add.
$ 6.99	$ 6.99 ——$1	
$ 7.25	$ 7.25	$28
+ $15.80	+ $15.80 ——$1	$ 2
$28	$2	$30

The total cost of the three books is about $30.

Popcorn Prices

Size	Cost
1-gallon tin	$6.45
2-gallon tin	$11.95
3-gallon tin	$13.25
6-gallon tin	$19.95

4. a. ▦ *Calculator* Use a calculator to find the exact total cost of the three books in Example 3 on page 105.

  b. ⊹ *Look Back* How reasonable is the estimate?

5. a. ✔ *Try It Out* Use front-end estimation to estimate the total cost of the following items: jeans, $29.95; shirt, $12.50; shoes, $22.87; socks, $4.45.

  b. How reasonable is your estimate?

EXERCISES *On Your Own*

Round each decimal to the nearest hundredth. Then round each decimal to the nearest tenth.

1. 2.64372   **2.** 0.5817   **3.** 0.7352   **4.** 3.4746   **5.** 23.4546   **6.** 0.087

7. 0.6873   **8.** 2.7082   **9.** 4.0625   **10.** 2.0056   **11.** 491.2993   **12.** 1.001

13. *Open-ended* Write five different decimals that round to 6.7.

Round each number to the underlined place.

14. 1.3̲66   **15.** 0.401̲8   **16.** 5.12̲51   **17.** 0.006̲2   **18.** 2.319̲6   **19.** 0.6̲087

Use rounding or front-end estimation. Estimate each sum or difference to the nearest dollar.

20.	$4.89 + $3.97	21.	$8.97 − $2.15	22.	$5.19 − $2.79	23.	$6.15 + $8.86
24.	$14.65 + $ 3.85	25.	$9.93 − $3.26	26.	$16.81 + $11.49	27.	$12.44 − $ 8.25

28. *Consumer Issues* Regular unleaded gasoline costs $1.259/gal. You spend $5 on gasoline. About how many gallons did you buy?

29. *Reasoning* Is an estimate of 22 higher or lower than the sum of 6.83, 9.57, and 4.712? How can you tell? Is the estimate reasonable? Explain.

30. *Writing* Describe a situation in which you might want your estimate to be high. Then describe one in which you might want your estimate to be low.

31. *Research* Look through newspapers or magazines to find five decimals. Decide whether each decimal is an estimate. To which places were the decimals rounded?

32. Nutrition Use the chart at the right. Estimate and round to the nearest tenth.

Food	Sugar Content
Orange juice (4 oz)	0.417 oz
Plain granola bar	0.333 oz
Raisins (7 oz)	0.75 oz
Sherbet ($\frac{1}{2}$ cup)	1.166 oz
Soft drink (12 oz)	1.5 oz
Yogurt (8 oz)	1 oz

   a. About how much sugar is in a soft drink plus a granola bar? In one of everything?
   b. About how much more sugar is in $\frac{1}{2}$ cup of sherbet than in 8 oz of yogurt?
   c. About how much sugar is in the last three items combined?

33. Choose A, B, C, or D. Which sum might give you a low estimate of $19 and a high estimate of $22?
   A. $4.22 + $10.85 + $8.97
   B. $2.50 + $13.75 + $4.50
   C. $6.05 + $7.86 + $9.22
   D. $15.32 + $9.63 + $0.45

34. Is the last statement true or false? Explain your answer.

Tony has $10. He will have about $1 after buying pencils for $2.79, a notebook for $1.39, a ruler for $.85, and 3 pens for $1.69 each.

Use front-end estimation to estimate each total cost to the nearest dollar.

35. $1.29 + $3.52 + $8.89   **36.** $3.89 + $9.95 + $6.59   **37.** $23.56 + $33.33 + $1.50

38. $12.49 + $5.51 + $9.95   **39.** $1.29 + $3.52 + $8.89   **40.** $3.25 + $7.53 + $12.87

Mixed Review

Find the next three terms in each number pattern. Write a rule to describe each number pattern. *(Lesson 2-1)*

41. 2, 5, 10, 17, . . .   **42.** 5, 9, 13, 17, . . .   **43.** 1, 5, 25, 125, . . .   **44.** 1; 10; 100; 1,000; . . .

Solve each equation. *(Lessons 2-6 and 2-7)*

45. $a - 7 = 23$ **46.** $35 = 19 + c$ **47.** $54 = 3t$ **48.** $x \div 8 = 16$ **49.** $10y = 30$

50. A bookcase has three shelves. You place 20 books on each shelf. What is the total number of books in the bookcase? *(Previous Course)*

3-7 Adding and Subtracting Decimals

What You'll Learn

1 To add decimals

2 To subtract decimals

...And Why

You can do calculations with weights in decimal form.

Here's How

Look for questions that

 :: build understanding

 ✔ check understanding

THINK AND DISCUSS

1 *Adding Decimals*

If you estimate the answer before adding, you can tell if your answer is reasonable.

■ **EXAMPLE 1**

Find the sum 3.026 + 4.7 + 1.38.

Estimate: 3.026 + 4.7 + 1.38 ≈ 3 + 5 + 1 = 9

Add:
$$\begin{array}{r} 3.026 \\ 4.7 \\ + 1.38 \\ \hline \end{array}$$
$$\begin{array}{r} 3.026 \\ 4.700 \\ + 1.380 \\ \hline 9.106 \end{array}$$
← Line up decimal points and write zeros to make the columns even.

Check: 9.106 is reasonable since it is close to 9. ✓

1. :: **Writing** Explain why you can write 4.7 as 4.700.

2. ✔ **Try It Out** First estimate. Then find each sum.
   a. 6.5 + 0.6 + 3   **b.** 0.84 + 2 + 3.32   **c.** 9.008 + 2.115

2 *Subtracting Decimals*

You may need to regroup decimals when you subtract.

■ **EXAMPLE 2**   *Real-World Problem Solving*

Sports The official maximum weight of a basketball is 22.93 oz. The minimum weight is 21.16 oz. Find the range of weights. (Remember that range = maximum − minimum.)

Estimate: 22.93 − 21.16 ≈ 23 − 21 = 2

$$\begin{array}{r} \overset{8\ 13}{22.9\cancel{3}} \\ - 21.16 \\ \hline 1.77 \end{array}$$

← Regroup 9 tenths and 3 hundredths as 8 tenths and 13 hundredths.

← Subtract.

The range of standard weights for a basketball is 1.77 oz.

A properly inflated basketball should bounce between 1.2 m and 1.4 m if you drop it on a hard wooden floor from a height of about 1.8 m.

Source: *The Rules of the Game*

Need Help? For practice adding whole numbers, see Skills Handbook p. 538.

You can also use a calculator to add or subtract decimals.

■ **EXAMPLE 3**

Algebra Solve the equation $x + 5.22 = 20$.

$$x + 5.22 = 20$$
$$x + 5.22 - 5.22 = 20 - 5.22 \quad \longleftarrow \text{Subtract 5.22 from each side.}$$
$$20 \boxed{-} 5.22 \boxed{=} \mathit{14.78} \quad \longleftarrow \text{Use a calculator.}$$

Check: $14.78 + 5.22 = 20$ ✓

$x = 14.78$

3. Estimate the difference in Example 3. How reasonable is your estimate?

4. ✔*Try It Out* Solve each equation.
   a. $x + 2.25 = 5$ **b.** $x - 0.468 = 1.8$ **c.** $x - 37.63 = 50$

5. ⚏*Reasoning* Suppose you use a calculator to find $7.87 - 1.47$. Why will the display show 6.4 instead of 6.40?

Work Together
Subtracting Decimals Using Data

On September 7, 1997, Venus Williams became the first unseeded woman to play in the final of the U.S. Open Championship tennis tournament.

Data Analysis Most sports equipment has standard sizes.

Official Standard Weights

Type	Minimum Weight (oz)	Maximum Weight (oz)
Baseball	5	5.5
Football	14	15
Soccer ball	14	16
Softball	6.25	7
Tennis ball	2	2.06
Volleyball	9.17	9.88

6. List the types of sports balls from heaviest to lightest.

7. Find the range of standard weights for each sports ball.

8. ⚏*Analyze* Based on the given data, do you think the following statement is true or false: The heavier the ball, the smaller its range of standard weights is.

First estimate each sum. Then find the actual sum.

1. 0.6 + 3.4   **2.** 6.2 + 0.444   **3.** 8.001 + 0.77   **4.** 7 + 11.436 + 3.08

5. 4.035 + 8.99   **6.** 22.2 + 4.3   **7.** 9.76 + 3.45   **8.** 0.445 + 2.345 + 3

9. 0.5 + 4.6   **10.** 8.7 + 0.368   **11.** 9.011 + 0.45   **12.** 0.33 + 1.11 + 3.2

13. *Data Analysis* You have a $10 bill and a $5 bill. You wish to buy all the items on the list shown at the right. Can you afford to buy the 24-exposure film?

14. Jonah had $340.87 in his checking account. He withdrew $52 and wrote a check for $18.72. Find the new balance.

15. Choose A, B, C, or D. Suppose you place the digits 1–6 in the boxes ▪ ▪.▪ + ▪.▪ ▪ to give the greatest possible sum. What is the digit in the third box from the left?
    A. 2   **B.** 3   **C.** 2 or 3   **D.** 4

16. *Consumer Issues* At the movie theater, you order popcorn for $2.75 and two drinks for $1.50 each. You pay with a $10 bill. How much change will you get?

Things to Buy	
Poster	$4.99
Birthday Card	$1.25
Film (12 exposures)	$3.89
or	
(24 exposures)	$4.59
Wrapping paper	$2.49
Bow	$ .79

First estimate. Then find the difference.

17. 3.8 − 2.1   **18.** 9.1 − 6.05   **19.** 3.06 − 1.9

20. 4.068 − 1.29   **21.** 0.8 − 0.126   **22.** 8.91 − 6.08

23. 6.08 − 0.93   **24.** 18.2 − 9.26   **25.** 16.5 − 8.71

26. *Transportation* The length of the Eurotunnel between England and France is 49.94 km. The Seikan Tunnel in Japan is 53.9 km long. How much longer is the Seikan Tunnel?

27. *Data Analysis* Refer to the data at the right.
    a. Add the numbers in the chart. What does this sum mean?
    b. *Writing* What part of all the energy is produced from oil and coal? Is it more than half? Explain.
    c. *Estimation* Which two natural resources produce an amount of energy approximately equal to that of coal?
    d. Make a hundredths' model showing the part of all energy produced by each natural resource.

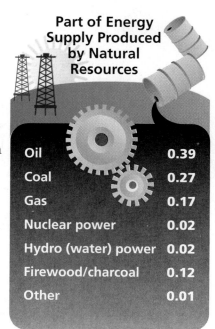

Part of Energy Supply Produced by Natural Resources

Oil	0.39
Coal	0.27
Gas	0.17
Nuclear power	0.02
Hydro (water) power	0.02
Firewood/charcoal	0.12
Other	0.01

Mental Math **Find each missing number.**

28. $6.4 + 3.1 = \blacksquare + 6.4$

29. $0.43 + \blacksquare = 0.43$

30. $(2.1 + 0.3) + 4 = 2.1 + (\blacksquare + 4)$

Algebra **Solve each equation.**

31. $12.45 = 3.44 + k$

32. $h - 0.455 = 3.44$

33. $x + 2.033 = 7.899$

34. $p - 45.678 = 65.887$

35. $34.768 = 12.356 + m$

36. $32.432 + c = 56.986$

37. *Data Analysis* When you order by mail, you usually pay for shipping and handling. Suppose the company bases the fee on the cost of the order. Use the information at the right and below.
   a. You order one adult sweatshirt, size XXL, and three children's T-shirts. How much do you pay without shipping and handling?
   b. Find the charge for shipping and handling your order.
   c. Suppose you order one of each item (size M for adult). Find the total cost, including shipping and handling.

Shipping and Handling Charges

Order Amount	Charge
Under $15.00	$2.95
$15.00–$24.99	$3.95
$25.00–$39.99	$4.95
$40.00–$49.99	$5.95
$50.00–$74.99	$6.95
$75.00–$99.99	$7.95
$100.00 and over	$8.95

HAPPY BIRTHDAY SHIRTS

#345 Adult Birthday Tee
(M – XL) $15.00
(XXL) $17.95

#355 Adult Birthday Sweatshirt
(M – XL) $29.50
(XXL) $29.95

#445 Child's Birthday Tee
$12.50

#455 Child's Birthday Sweatshirt
$16.95

Mixed Review

Evaluate each expression for $x = 10$. *(Lesson 2-4)*

38. $20 \div x$

39. $4x$

40. $4 + 2x$

41. $3x - 5$

Arrange the numbers in increasing order. *(Lesson 3-3)*

42. 0.05 5.55 0.505 0.55

43. 9.04 90.4 900.4 9.004

44. 60.92 603.8 68.3 62.9

45. Rod earns $10 for mowing one lawn. After mowing seven lawns, how much money has he earned? *(Previous Course)*

TECHNOLOGY

Spreadsheets and Bank Statements

After Lesson 3-7

Banks usually send you a monthly report, or a *statement*, for your account. The statement shows the money you put into the account (*deposits*), the money you take out of the account (*withdrawals*), and the *interest* you earned on the account. The balance is the amount of money in the account at a given time.

■ EXAMPLE

The spreadsheet below shows a portion of a bank statement.

	A	B	C	D	E	F
1	Date	Balance	Withdrawal	Deposit	Interest	End Balance
2	11/3	$73.47		$100.00		$173.47
3	11/14	$173.47	$98.00			$75.47
4	11/30	$75.47			$1.99	$77.46

a. What does the number in cell B2 represent?
   The number in cell B2, $73.47, shows the balance on 11/3.
b. How is the number in cell F2 calculated?
   The number in cell F2, $173.47, is the sum of the balance on 11/3 and the deposit on 11/3.

Refer to the spreadsheet above.

1. How was the amount in cell F3 calculated?

2. How was the amount in cell F4 calculated?

3. Which cells show the same amounts? Why?

4. Suppose you deposit $32.00 to the account in the Example on 12/2, withdraw $15.50 on 12/15, and receive interest of $1.25 on 12/30.
   a. Estimate your account balance on 12/31.
   b. Find the exact balance on 12/31.

3-8 Metric Units of Length

What You'll Learn

1 To use metric units of length

2 To choose appropriate units of measurement

...And Why

You can use metric units to measure common objects.

Here's How

Look for questions that
- ⚖ build understanding
- ✔ check understanding

Work Together — *Using Nonstandard Units of Length*

Suppose you invent a new unit of length. How about using the length of the cover of your favorite textbook?

1. Find the width of your desk in terms of your book's length. How many "books" wide is your desk?

2. ⚖ *Analyze* Compare your result with those of your classmates. Explain any differences you notice.

3. Is your book a good unit of measurement? Why or why not?

4. ⚖ *Reasoning* List some advantages and disadvantages of using your system of measurement.

5. Name two other objects you could use to measure the width of your desk.

THINK AND DISCUSS

1 *Using Metric Units of Length*

A **standard unit** of measurement is one on which everyone agrees. The **metric system** of measurement uses a decimal system. The standard unit of length is the **meter (m).**

Unit	Relationship to the Meter
kilometer (km)	1 km = 1000 m
meter (m)	*100cm = 1m*
centimeter (cm)	1 cm = 0.01 m
millimeter (mm)	1 mm = 0.001 m

1 cm

10 mm

6. ⚖ *Reasoning* How many centimeters are there in one meter?

7. ⚖ *What If . . .* Suppose you had a strip of paper 1 m long. How could you model centimeters on the paper?

8. a. **⁘Reasoning** One millimeter is one thousandth of a meter. To model millimeters, into how many equal parts would you divide a segment that represents 1 m?

   b. How many millimeters are there in one centimeter?

9. Complete the following. Use models if they help you.

   a. 100 cm = ▨ m
   b. ▨ m = 1 km
   c. ▨ mm = 1 m
   d. ▨ mm = 1 km
   e. ▨ mm = 1 cm
   f. 1 km = ▨ cm

When you need to measure short distances, you can use a centimeter ruler.

■ **EXAMPLE 1**

Find the length of the segment below. Use a metric ruler.

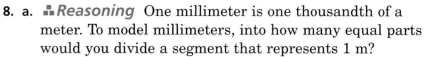

Align the zero mark on the ruler with one end of the segment.

Read the length at the other end of the segment.

The segment is 53 mm, or 5.3 cm, long.

10. a. **⁘Measurement** What do the smaller marks on the ruler represent?

    b. What do the numbers 0, 1, 2, 3, . . . represent?

11. ✔**Try It Out** Find each length in millimeters. Then find each length in centimeters.

    a. ▬▬▬▬
    b. ▬▬▬▬▬▬▬
    c. ▬▬▬▬▬▬▬▬▬

HISTORY
Ancient Egyptians based measures of length on the royal cubit, palm, and digit. The cubit (forearm) was the length from the elbow to the fingers. The palm was the width of the palm excluding the thumb. The digit was the width of the finger.

Source: *The Macmillan Dictionary of Measurement*

▼2 *Choosing Appropriate Units*

Before you measure an object you should first choose an appropriate unit of measure. Longer distances are measured in kilometers. Short distances are measured in millimeters.

■ EXAMPLE 2

Choose an appropriate metric unit of measure for each.

a. length of a pencil

A pencil is a lot shorter than a meter but a lot longer than a millimeter. The appropriate measure is centimeters.

b. height of your classroom

The height of the classroom is shorter than a kilometer but much longer than a centimeter. The appropriate measure is meters.

12. ✔*Try It Out* Choose an appropriate metric unit of measure for each.
   a. width of a playground
   b. length of a shirtsleeve
   c. width of a nailhead
   d. distance between towns

13. ▪*Writing* Explain why it is not convenient to measure long distances in small units or short distances in larger units.

14. ▪*Open-ended* Name two objects or distances you might measure using each unit.
   a. millimeter
   b. centimeter
   c. meter
   d. kilometer

EXERCISES *On Your Own*

Measurement **Find each length in millimeters. Then find each length in centimeters.**

1. ▬▬▬▬▬

2. ▬▬▬▬▬▬

3. ▬▬▬▬▬▬▬▬▬▬▬▬

4. ▬▬▬▬▬▬▬▬▬▬▬▬▬

5. **a.** Draw a segment that is 16 cm long.
   b. Draw a segment that is 128 mm long.
   c. Which segment is longer?

6. *Reasoning* The height of a table is about one meter. Explain how to estimate the height of your classroom from the floor to the ceiling using the height of that table. Is your estimate reasonable? Explain.

7. *Geometry* Find the perimeter of each figure. (*Hint*: The perimeter of a figure is the sum of the lengths of its sides.)

a.

b.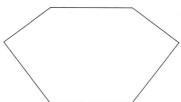

8. *Geometry* Draw a figure with a 20-cm perimeter.

9. *Geometry* A rectangular dog kennel measures 4 m by 5 m. What length of fence do you need to enclose the kennel? (*Hint*: A rectangle has two pairs of equal sides.)

10. *Open-ended* Describe some situations where you might need to know the distance around a figure.

11. a. *Geometry* Measure each side of the triangle at the right in centimeters.
   b. What is the distance around the triangle?

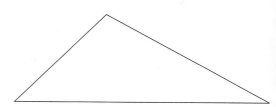

12. *Reasoning* The perimeter of a rectangular table is 8 m. The table is 1 m longer than it is wide. Find the length of each side. Explain how you got your answer.

Choose an appropriate metric unit of measure for each.

13. width of a highway   **14.** length of an eyelash   **15.** distance between cities

16. your height   **17.** width of your classroom door   **18.** width of your finger

19. length of your pen   **20.** length of your desk   **21.** width of your classroom

Is each measurement reasonable? If not, give a reasonable measurement.

22. The sidewalk is 30 km wide.   **23.** Your friend is about 160 cm tall.

24. Your pencil is 18 mm long.   **25.** A kitchen table is about 123 cm long.

26. a. *Reasoning* The width of a door is about 1 m. How can you estimate the length of a wall that contains the door?
   b. *Estimation* Estimate the length of your classroom wall using the method you just described.

27. *Writing* Read the article at the right. List some possible reasons why the metric system is not more widely used in this country. Do you think it should be more widely used? Why or why not?

U.S. Still Catching Up

THE UNITED STATES OFFICIALLY began to "go metric" in 1973. Since most of the rest of the world's countries were using the metric system, it seemed to be a good idea.

There has been little progress. Still, scientists use the metric system, and there are metric units on some highway signs and on some food and hardware items.

Mixed Review

Compare. Use >, <, or =. *(Lesson 3-3)*

28. 0.39 ▧ 0.399   **29.** 1.2 ▧ 1.02   **30.** 0.7 ▧ 0.0700   **31.** 4.6 ▧ 4.60   **32.** 5.5 ▧ 5.55

Write a variable expression. *(Lesson 2-5)*

33. 10 less than a number

34. the sum of a number and 5

35. Paper cups come in packages of 50. There are 576 students and teachers at Memorial Middle School. How many packages of paper cups should be purchased for the school picnic? *(Previous Course)*

✓ CHECKPOINT 2   *Lessons 3-4 through 3-8*

First estimate. Then find the sum or difference.

1. $\begin{array}{r} 1.25 \\ + 6.07 \\ \hline \end{array}$
2. $\begin{array}{r} 9.06 \\ - 0.8 \\ \hline \end{array}$
3. 5.59 + 12.6
4. 37 − 7.8
5. 789.456 + 564.9

Round each number to the underlined place value.

6. 12.0<u>4</u>1   **7.** <u>2</u>.40   **8.** 9.06<u>5</u>5   **9.** 53.8<u>5</u>   **10.** 0.4<u>4</u>32   **11.** 23.56<u>7</u>5

12. Choose A, B, or C. Suppose you wish to buy three items priced $2.09, $.59, and $1.46. Which is the best estimate of the total cost?
   A. $4.00   **B.** $3.50   **C.** $5.00

13. Find the length of the segment in millimeters and then in centimeters.

_____

3-9 Metric Units of Mass and Capacity

Work Together
Comparing Units of Measure

Look at a flyer or newspaper ad from a local grocery store.

1. Make a list of all the units of measurement shown in the ad.

2. Divide your list into categories according to the units used.

3. Compare two differently sized packages that are labeled with similar units of measurement.

4. ⁙ *Reasoning* Explain why differently sized packages may be labeled with the same measurements.

THINK AND DISCUSS

▼ Metric Units of Mass

Solids are sometimes measured in units of mass. **Mass** is a measure of the amount of matter in an object. The standard unit of mass is the **gram (g).** Another commonly used unit of mass is the kilogram (kg).

Unit	Relationship to the Gram
kilogram (kg)	1 kg = 1000 g
gram (g)	
milligram (mg)	1 mg = 0.001 g

5. Complete the following.

a. $1 \text{ g} = \blacksquare \text{ kg}$

b. $1 \text{ mg} = \blacksquare \text{ g}$

c. $1 \text{ mg} = \blacksquare \text{ kg}$

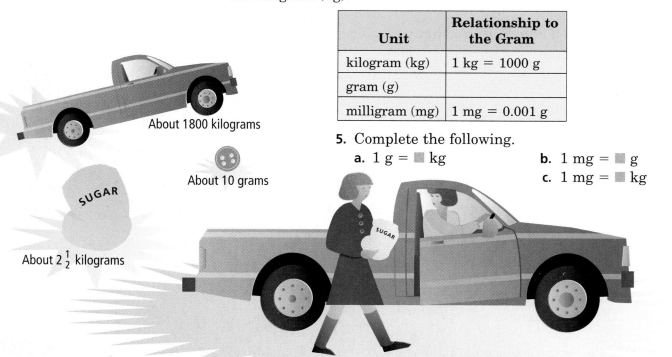

About 1800 kilograms

About 10 grams

SUGAR

About 2½ kilograms

SUGAR

■ EXAMPLE 1

Choose an appropriate metric unit of mass for each.

a. a pea   **b.** a baby   **c.** a car

a. A pea has about the same mass as a paper clip. An approximate unit of measure is the gram.
b. A baby has about the same mass as a few bags of sugar. The mass would be measured in kilograms.
c. A car's mass is a little less than that of a small truck. It is measured in kilograms.

6. ✔**Try It Out** Choose an appropriate metric unit of mass for each.

a. a notebook   **b.** a desk   **c.** a grain of sand

▼2 *Metric Units of Capacity*

Liquids are measured by units of capacity. **Capacity** is a measure of the amount of space an object occupies. The standard unit of capacity is the **liter (L).** Another commonly used unit of capacity is the milliliter (mL).

Unit	Relationship to the Liter
kiloliter (kL)	1 kL = 1000 L
liter (L)	
milliliter (mL)	1 mL = 0.001 L

A dewdrop is about 0.5 mL of water. A bottle of milk is about 1 L. A lake contains hundreds of thousands of kiloliters of water.

7. Complete the following.

a. 1 L = ▓ kL   **b.** 1 mL = ▓ L   **c.** 1 mL = ▓ kL

■ **EXAMPLE 2**

Choose an appropriate metric unit of capacity for each.

   a. a raindrop   **b.** carton of milk   **c.** swimming pool

  a. A raindrop has about the same capacity as a dewdrop. It is measured in milliliters.

  b. A carton of milk has about the same capacity as a soda bottle. It is measured in liters.

  c. The capacity of a swimming pool is a little less than that of a small pond. It is measured in kiloliters.

8. ✔*Try It Out* Choose an appropriate metric unit of capacity for each.

  a. a bottle of juice   **b.** a lake   **c.** a test tube

EXERCISES *On Your Own*

Choose an appropriate metric unit of mass for each.

1. a pen

2. a garbage can

3. a pin

4. a chair

5. a telephone

6. an eyelash

7. a potato

8. a shirt button

9. a mug

Choose an appropriate metric unit of capacity for each.

10. a flu shot

11. water used in a shower

12. Lake Michigan

13. tank of gasoline

14. bottle of sunscreen

15. a bucket of rainwater

16. cup of milk

17. a puddle

18. a drop of water

State whether each of the following is best measured in terms of mass or capacity.

19. a bottle of lamp oil

20. newspaper

21. bread

22. ears of corn

23. stick of butter

24. flour

25. box of rice

26. water in a fish tank

27. bricks

28. bag of oranges

29. orange juice

30. popcorn

Is each measurement reasonable? Explain.

31. A car has a mass of 1,200 kg.

32. You drink 2 L of water a day.

33. Your mass is 20 mg.

34. You use 4 mL of water to wash your hands.

35. A ladybug has a mass of 4 kg.

36. A cow produces 500 kL of milk a day.

***True* or *False*? If false, explain why.**

37. A tennis ball has a mass of about 58 mL.

38. A dime has a capacity of about 2.5 g.

39. 1,000 mg = 1 g   **40.** 10 L = 1,000 mL   **41.** 100 kg = 100,000 g

42. Your math book has a mass of 3 L.

43. *Open-ended* Name two things you might measure using each unit.
   a. milliliter   **b.** milligram   **c.** liter   **d.** kilogram

44. *Writing* Describe the advantages and disadvantages of using the metric system.

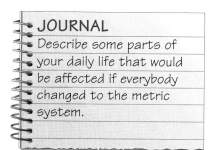

JOURNAL
Describe some parts of your daily life that would be affected if everybody changed to the metric system.

Mixed Review

Estimate using mental math. *(Lesson 3-6)*

45. $54.99 + $3.25   **46.** $5.49 − $2.99   **47.** $20.00 − $13.98   **48.** $23.89 + $3.78

Write in words. *(Lesson 3-2)*

49. 638,970   **50.** 0.35   **51.** 2.43   **52.** 67.08   **53.** 1,003.289   **54.** 0.0082

55. Randa received $25 for her birthday. Then she baby-sat and earned $13, $8.50, and $9.75. How much money does she have now? *(Lesson 3-7)*

CHAPTER PROJECT

PROJECT LINK: CALCULATING

The shipping and handling charge is $2.15 per CD. Calculate the shipping and handling costs for the total number of CDs you plan to buy. Calculate the average cost per CD. Don't forget to include the penny for the first eight CDs.

Choose the best answer.

1. At a concert, the attendance was 782 people. A reporter rounded the attendance to the nearest hundred. Which number is a reasonable estimate?

   A. 700   **B.** 780   **C.** 800   **D.** 1,000

2. Which metric length would be closest to the length of a baseball bat?

   F. 1 mm   **G.** 1 cm   **H.** 1 km   **J.** 1 m

3. Billie is stacking cubes. The first stack has 4 cubes, the second has 7 cubes, the third has 10 cubes, and the fourth has 13 cubes. If she continues the same pattern, how many more cubes will she need to complete two more stacks?

   A. 16 cubes   **B.** 19 cubes
   C. 35 cubes   **D.** 69 cubes

4. Five contestants received scores of 93.1, 90.9, 93.4, 98.4, and 90.7. Name the top three scores from greatest to least.

   F. 93.1, 90.9, 93.4   **G.** 90.7, 90.9, 93.1
   H. 98.4, 93.4, 93.1   **J.** 93.1, 93.4, 98.4

5. During which 10-year period was there a decrease in the population of Oak City?

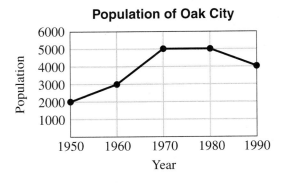

Population of Oak City

   A. 1950 to 1960   **B.** 1960 to 1970
   C. 1970 to 1980   **D.** 1980 to 1990

Please note that items 6 and 7 have *five* answer choices.

6. Mr Majko has only $20 to spend at the grocery store. He finds a steak costing $7.29, a roast costing $12.95, hamburger costing $3.95, and fish costing $6.25. Using estimation, he determines that he cannot buy all the items, but he can buy some of them and have less than $1 left in change. Which items could he buy?

   F. steak, hamburger, and fish
   G. roast and fish
   H. steak and roast
   J. roast and hamburger
   K. roast, hamburger, and fish

7. The number of people entering a garden show each day is shown by the graph. Each person pays $3 to enter, but the promoters have expenses of $580. How much profit will they make for the show?

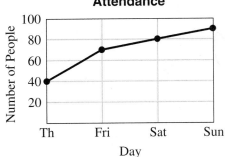

Garden Show Attendance

   F. $260   **G.** $360
   H. $840   **J.** $1,420
   K. Not Here

3-10 Measuring Elapsed Time

What You'll Learn

▼ To add and subtract measures of time

▼ To read, use, and make schedules

...And Why

You will use elapsed time to make and use schedules and to plan events.

Here's How

Look for questions that
▪ build understanding
✔ check understanding

Work Together

Investigating Elapsed Time

Look at the clocks at the right.

1. What time does Clock 1 show?

2. What time does Clock 2 show?

3. ▪ *Analyze* How much time has passed between the time on the first clock and the time on the second?

4. Copy and complete Clock 3 so that it shows fifteen minutes after four.

5. Draw a fourth clock showing the time 40 minutes after Clock 3.

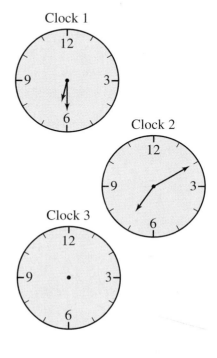

Clock 1

Clock 2

Clock 3

THINK AND DISCUSS

▼ Adding and Subtracting Measures of Time

The standard unit of time is the **second (s).**

Units of Time	
second (s)	
minute (min)	1 min = 60 s
hour (h)	1 h = 60 min = 3,600 s
day (d)	1 d = 24 h = 1,440 min
week (wk)	1 wk = 7 d = 168 h
year (yr)	1 yr ≈ 52 wk ≈ 365 d

6. ▪ *Reasoning* 1 h 20 min is equivalent to how many minutes? How many seconds? Explain how you got your answer.

The time between two events is called **elapsed time.** To calculate elapsed time, you can add or subtract hours and minutes. You may need to rewrite the hours and minutes.

■ **EXAMPLE 1**

Find the elapsed time between 1:45 P.M. and 3:27 P.M.
Subtract 1:45 from 3:27.

3:27 ⟶ 3 h 27 min ⟶ 2 h 87 min ⟵ Rewrite 3 h 27 min as 2 h 87 min.
1:45 ⟶ 1 h 45 min ⟶ − 1 h 45 min
1 h 42 min ⟵ Subtract.

The elapsed time is 1 h 42 min.

7. ✔*Try It Out* Find the elapsed time between 7:25 A.M. and 8:12 A.M. Then find the elapsed time between 8:45 P.M. and 10:25 P.M.

8. ⁂*Writing* Explain how you would find the elapsed time between 10:00 A.M. and 3:15 P.M. What extra step must you follow?

9. ⁂*Open-ended* What time do you get up in the morning on a school day? What time does school begin? Find the elapsed time.

2 *Reading, Using, and Making Schedules*

You use elapsed time when using schedules.

■ **EXAMPLE 2**   *Real-World Problem Solving*

Use the bus schedule at the left. Suppose you arrive at the Willson Street bus stop 5 minutes after the 11:50 A.M. bus has left.

a. How long do you have to wait for the next bus?

The buses run every 30 minutes. You will wait 25 minutes.

b. When do you arrive at Kagy Boulevard?

11:50 A.M. + 30 min = 11:80
= 11 h 80 min = 12 h 20 min

The next bus will arrive at 12:20 P.M. The trip takes 25 minutes. You will arrive at 12:45 P.M.

WK Bus Line

Buses Run Every 30 Minutes
Monday–Friday

Leave	Arrive
Willson St.	Kagy Blvd.
7:20 A.M.	7:45 A.M.
7:50 A.M.	8:15 A.M.
...	...
11:20 P.M.	11:45 P.M.
Kagy Blvd.	Willson St.
7:50 A.M.	8:15 A.M.
8:20 A.M.	8:45 A.M.
...	...
11:50 P.M.	12:15 A.M.

10. ✔Try It Out Lee is going to a party at 6:00 P.M. The party is a 5-minute walk from the bus stop on Kagy Boulevard. In order to be at the party on time, which bus should Lee take from Willson Street?

11. ⊞Reasoning By what time should Lee leave the party to catch a bus and be home by 9:00 P.M.?

EXERCISES *On Your Own*

Mental Math **How many minutes are in each amount of time?**

1. 1 h 30 min   2. 3 h 35 min   3. 2 h 59 min   4. 5 h 17 min

5. 10 h 15 min   6. 4 h 45 min   7. 6 h 12 min   8. 8 h 2 min

Find the elapsed time between each pair of times.

9. 8:25 A.M. and 10:52 A.M.   10. 8:35 P.M. and 9:18 P.M.   11. 5:25 P.M. and 11:11 P.M.

12. 6:45 A.M. and 9:02 A.M.   13. 4:25 A.M. and 7:24 A.M.   14. 3:25 A.M. and 4:37 P.M.

15. 3:27 P.M. and 7:32 P.M.   16. 9:25 A.M. and 11:12 P.M.   17. 2:25 P.M. and 2:59 A.M.

18. 1:09 P.M. and 8:12 A.M.   19. 10:25 A.M. and 11:58 P.M.   20. 3:59 P.M. and 5:01 P.M.

21. *Entertaining* Susan is having a party at 4:00 P.M. On the day of the party she needs to do the activities at the right.
   a. If Susan does the activities in the order given, at what time should she begin?
   b. Look more carefully at the activities. Which activities must be done in order? Could any be done at the same time? What is the latest time Susan could begin?
   c. Susan does not want to shower until she has frosted the cake. Does this change your answer?
   d. Susan decides she needs 25 minutes before the party to take care of last minute details. To allow for the extra 25 minutes, when should she begin her activities?

> decorate room (1 h)
> mix cake (40 min)
> bake cake (35 min)
> cool cake (45 min)
> frost cake (20 min)
> shower and dress (25 min)

22. Bonnie does the activities shown at the right after school but before her 6:00 P.M. dinner. School is out at 3:30 P.M.
   a. How much time does she have to visit neighbors?
   b. *Writing* Explain how you solved this problem.
   c. Make a schedule for Bonnie's afternoon.

Ride bike home	20 min
Feed the dog	10 min
Do homework	1 h
Visit neighbors	■
Help prepare dinner	35 min

23. **Party Planning** You plan a birthday party for your younger brother and make the schedule shown at the right.
    a. How long will the party last?
    b. How much time did you allow for the clown show? For lunch? For presents?
    c. The clown calls at 10:30 A.M. to say that he will not be at the party until noon. Make a new party schedule.

Party for Joey	
11:00 A.M.	Friends arrive, play outside.
11:30 A.M.	Clown show
12:15 P.M.	Lunch
1:00 P.M.	Open presents
2:00 P.M.	Friends leave

Amusement Parks Use the data at the right for Exercises 24–26.

24. Find the total time you would expect to spend for the Vortex ride at Kings Island.

25. Which ride has a wait time of 10 times the ride time?

26. Suppose you get to the park at 2:15 P.M. If you ride The Beast, Vortex, and The Racer, when will you be done?

Kings Island Amusement Park

Ride	Wait Time (min)	Ride Time (min:s)
The Beast	45	4:30
Vortex	30	2:30
The Racer	15	2:15
Beastie (for kids)	10	1:30

27. **Studying** Jackson has 3 h of homework tonight. He likes to take a $\frac{1}{2}$-h break. To finish by 9:30 P.M., what is the latest he can begin studying?

28. **Open-ended** Name at least five activities you do on Saturdays. Estimate the elapsed time for each activity.

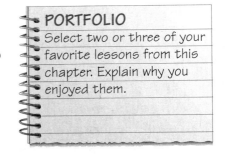

PORTFOLIO
Select two or three of your favorite lessons from this chapter. Explain why you enjoyed them.

Mixed Review

29. **Choose a Strategy** Mark does his laundry every six days beginning on the second day of the year. At the end of a year, how many times will he have done his laundry?

30. A teacher took a poll to see how many class members watched two or more hours of television each evening for a week. The data collected, beginning with Saturday, were 22, 13, 18, 11, 16, 2, 24. Draw an appropriate graph using the data. *(Lesson 1-6)*

What is the value of the digit 9 in each number? *(Lesson 3-2)*

31. 59,872   32. 0.94   33. 982,450   34. 12.0349   35. 6.0098   36. 9,007,321

CHAPTER PROJECT

Name that TUNE

Compare Prices and Decide The Project Link questions on pages 95, 102, and 121 will help you to complete your project. Here is a checklist to help you gather the parts of your project together.

✔ the average price of CDs in your area

✔ estimate of cost of eight CDs from the club

✔ cost of shipping and handling per CD

Write a report that summarizes whether you should join the CD club or not. Include any tables, lists, and calculations that helped you to make a decision. Show your work in organized steps. State other factors that helped you make your decision, such as the number of CDs you buy per year now and how much you spend on them. Include any advantages and disadvantages of joining the club.

Reflect and Revise

Share your report with a classmate or family friend. Is your report clear and logical? Are your calculations accurate? Have you included reasons for your decision? If necessary, revise your report.

Web Extension

Prentice Hall's Internet site contains information you might find helpful as you complete your project. Visit www.phschool.com/mgm1/ch3 for some links and ideas related to consumer issues.

Whole Numbers and Decimals
3-1, 3-2

Numbers that represent the same amount are **equivalent**. You can write decimals in **standard form**, **expanded form**, or in words.

How many hundredths are equivalent to each amount?

1. five tenths

2. two

3. 3.1

4. 0.9

5. $0.3 + 0.03$

6. **Choose A, B, C, or D.** Which of the following is five hundred twenty-five and five tenths in standard form?

A. 0.5255

B. 5255.5

C. 525.5

D. 500.255

Comparing and Ordering Decimals
3-3

You can compare and order decimals using place value or using a number line.

Use <, =, or > to complete each statement.

7. 1.839 ▧ 1.8380

8. 11.721 ▧ 6.731

9. 0.18 ▧ 0.081

10. 500.2 ▧ 50.02

11. Order 14.02, 14.2, 14.18, 14.1, and 14 from lowest to highest.

Problem Solving Strategies
3-4

A good problem solving strategy is *Guess and Test*.

12. Suppose your class is making plastic bird feeders in two sizes. Small bird feeders use 2 rods. Large bird feeders use 3 rods. The class used 103 rods to make 38 feeders. How many small bird feeders did the class make?

Addition and Subtraction of Decimals
3-5, 3-7

You can use models to find any sum or difference. You can also line up the decimal point and then add or subtract numbers in the same place value or you can use a calculator. Use estimation to check if answers are reasonable.

Add or subtract. Use models if they help you.

13. $0.5 + 0.2$ **14.** $0.99 - 0.76$ **15.** $1.741 - 0.81$ **16.** $62.24 - 8.598$ **17.** $337.4 + 20.08$

Rounding and Estimating Data   **3-6**

Rounding Decimals

Decide to which place you are rounding.

If the digit to the right of that place is greater than or equal to 5, round up.

If the digit to the right of that place is less than 5, round down.

To use **front-end estimation**, add the front-end digits, estimate the sum of the remaining digits, and then add the results.

Use rounding or front-end estimation. Estimate each sum or difference.

18. $\$5.82$
      $+ \$7.93$

19. 84.97
       $- 26.15$

20. 5.19
       $- 2.79$

21. 615.345
       $+ 8.86$

Metric Units of Length, Mass, and Capacity   **3-8, 3-9**

The **metric system** of measurement uses a decimal system. The **standard unit** of length is the **meter (m)**. The standard unit of **mass** is the **gram (g)**. The standard unit of **capacity** is the **liter (L)**.

Choose an appropriate unit of measure for each.

22. distance between planets   **23.** mass of a dog   **24.** capacity of a kitchen sink

25. *Writing* Explain how the metric units for length, mass, and capacity are similar. How are they different?

Measuring Elapsed Time   **3-10**

The time between two events is **elapsed time**. You use elapsed time when using schedules.

26. It's 6:00 P.M. Can Lori do everything on her list and still read for 25 minutes before her 9:30 P.M. bedtime? If she works continuously, at what time will she complete her to-do list?

Eat dinner	40 min
Homework	55 min
TV program	30 min
Feed dog	10 min

1. *Writing* Explain why thirteen hundredths are equivalent to one hundred thirty thousandths.

2. **Choose A, B, C, or D.** The value of the digit 3 in the number 24.1538 is ▦.

   A. three hundreds
   B. three tenths
   C. three hundredths
   D. three thousandths

3. **Choose A, B, C, or D.** Which of the following is *not* true for the number 5.836?

   A. 5.836 rounds to 5.84.
   B. 5.836 > 5.85
   C. The expanded form is
      5 + 0.8 + 0.03 + 0.006.
   D. It is read as "five and eight hundred thirty-six thousandths."

4. Compare. Use >, <, or =.
   a. 2.34 ▦ 2.4
   b. 8.97 ▦ 8.970
   c. 32.12 ▦ 32.42
   d. 12.82 ▦ 12.81

5. Place the digits 1 through 9 in the pattern below so that the sum is the same in both directions. What is the sum?

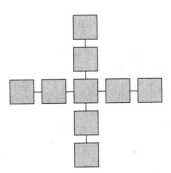

6. Graph 8.1, 8.2, 8.08, 8.15, and 8.03 on a number line.

7. Find each sum.
   a. 3.89 + 15.638
   b. 8.99 + 6.35
   c. 0.9356 + 0.208
   d. $4.38 + $2.74 + $1.17

8. *Estimation* Suppose your savings account has a balance of $129.55. You deposit $17.89 and withdraw $83.25. What is the approximate new balance?

9. Find each difference.
   a. $20 − $15.99
   b. 8.956 − 6.973
   c. 42.6 − 9.07
   d. 95.03 − 20.875

10. Find the perimeter by adding the lengths.

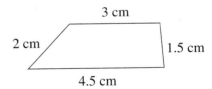

11. What unit of metric measure is appropriate for each item?
    a. length of a room
    b. length of a state border
    c. mass of a boat
    d. capacity of a cup

12. Jose plans to attend a beach party at 1:00 P.M. He needs to shower and dress (35 min), eat breakfast (25 min), do his chores (1 h 40 min), get his beach supplies (25 min), and bike to the party (20 min). Plan his schedule before he leaves for the beach party.

Choose the best answer.

1. Which is the decimal for thirty-four hundredths?

   A. 0.034
   B. 0.34
   C. 3.40
   D. 34.00

2. The winning speed of a car in an auto race was listed as 163.89 miles per hour. What is this speed rounded to the nearest mile per hour?

   A. 160 miles per hour
   B. 163 miles per hour
   C. 164 miles per hour
   D. 170 miles per hour

3. How would you find the range of five salaries?

   A. Add the salaries and divide by 5.
   B. Subtract the lowest salary from the highest.
   C. Arrange the salaries in order and choose the middle one.
   D. Choose the salary that occurs more than once.

4. Alfred bought a notebook costing $2.73 including tax. He gave the clerk $10. How much change should he have received?

   A. $7.27
   B. $7.73
   C. $8.73
   D. $12.73

5. All five items in a data set are multiplied by 10. How is the mode changed?

   A. It is multiplied by 10.
   B. It is multiplied by 50.
   C. It is multiplied by 2.
   D. The mode does not change.

6. What is a reasonable length for the length of the paper clip below?

   A. 5 mm
   B. 5 cm
   C. 5 m
   D. 5 km

7. Suppose you bought a shirt for x dollars with a twenty-dollar bill. The cashier gave you $5.35 back. Which equation could you use to find the cost of the shirt?

   A. $5.35x = 20$
   B. $x + 5.35 = 20$
   C. $20 \div x = 5.35$
   D. $5.35 - x = 20$

8. If 0.3 is represented by point B, what numbers could be represented by points A and C?

   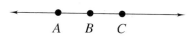

   A. A: 0.5, C: 0.7
   B. A: 0.03, C: 0.06
   C. A: 0.35, C: 0.4
   D. A: 0.2, C: 0.4

9. A hot-air balloon is 2,250 ft in the air. It is scheduled to land at 3:30 P.M. It descends 90 ft every minute. When should the balloonist start descending?

   A. 3:55 P.M.
   B. 3:05 P.M.
   C. 2:55 P.M.
   D. 2:45 P.M.

10. Without measuring, what is the best estimate for the total distance around the triangle below?

    A. 7 mm B. 7 cm C. 7 m D. 7 km

4

Multiplying and Dividing Whole Numbers and Decimals

WHAT YOU WILL LEARN IN THIS CHAPTER

- How to calculate products and quotients using decimals

- How to estimate decimal products and quotients

- How to explore databases

CELEBRATION

Suppose your class is planning to honor someone special in the community. Or you want to congratulate a winning team. You need to decide when and where the event will be, the types of decorations, the entertainment, and the refreshments. You may also need to decide how to raise funds for the celebration.

Plan a Celebration Your chapter project is to plan a celebration. You must decide how much it will cost and how much money each member of the class must raise. Your plan will include a list of supplies for the event and their costs.

Steps to help you complete the project:

p. 137   **Project Link:** *Researching*

p. 155   **Project Link:** *Calculating*

p. 162   **Project Link:** *Analyzing*

p. 175   *Finishing the Chapter Project*

• **How to recognize problems that have too much or too little information**

PROBLEM SOLVING

Estimating Products and Quotients

What You'll Learn

▼**1** To estimate products of numbers containing decimals

▼**2** To estimate quotients of numbers containing decimals

...And Why

Estimating makes it easier to solve problems that involve money.

Here's How

Look for questions that
- ▪ build understanding
- ✔ check understanding

Work Together _____ *Estimating with Decimals*

Wages Lisa's time card shows the hours she has worked this week. She gets paid $5.25/h. Let's estimate how much Lisa has earned this week.

1. What two numbers would you multiply to find how much Lisa has earned this week?

2. Estimate Lisa's earnings by rounding both numbers to the nearest whole number.

3. ▪*Reasoning* How does the estimated answer compare to the exact answer, $59.33? Is the estimate reasonable? Explain.

DH DH DH DH DH

Downtown Hardware

Employee

Lisa M. Smith

DAY	DATE	HOURS
MON	5/3	2.1
TUE		
WED	5/5	1.7
THU	5/6	3.5
FRI	5/7	4.0
SAT		
SUN		
TOTAL HOURS		11.3

DH DH DH DH DH

THINK AND DISCUSS

▼**1** Estimating Products

You can estimate a product by rounding each factor to the nearest whole number or by using **compatible numbers.** Compatible numbers are numbers that are easy to compute mentally.

▪ EXAMPLE 1

Estimate 26.03×3.31.

$$\begin{array}{rcr} 26.03 & \Rightarrow & 25 \\ \times\ 3.31 & \Rightarrow & \times\ 3 \\ \hline & & 75 \end{array}$$ ← Use compatible numbers such as 25 and 3.

The estimated product is 75.

4. ✔ ***Try It Out*** Estimate the product 3.89×16.03.

▼2 *Estimating Quotients*

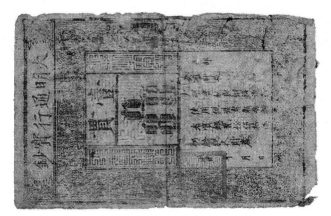

You can also use compatible numbers to estimate quotients.

The largest paper money ever created was the Chinese kwan note of the fourteenth century, shown at the right.

■ **EXAMPLE 2** *Real-World Problem Solving*

Money The Chinese kwan note was 92.8 cm long. The U.S. dollar bill is 15.6 cm long. About how many times as long as a dollar bill was the kwan note?

$92.8 \div 15.6$ ◄—— Write the numerical expression.
$90 \div 15 = 6$ ◄—— Use compatible numbers to divide.

The kwan note was about six times as long as a dollar bill.

5. ✔ *Try It Out* Use compatible numbers to estimate $37.1 \div 3.89$.

EXERCISES *On Your Own*

Estimation **Round each factor to the nearest whole number to estimate the product.**

1. 15.3×2.6 **2.** 2.25×16.91 **3.** 3.5×2.72 **4.** 0.95×22.8 **5.** 11.6×3.23

6. 15.25×3.9 **7.** 1.79×0.12 **8.** 4.01×0.62 **9.** 31.4×3.20 **10.** 37.1×3.89

Write a pair of compatible numbers. Then estimate.

11. 39.26×1.98 **12.** 18.8×4.3 **13.** 2.18×24.19 **14.** 41.5×18.75 **15.** 1.91×15.8

16. 3.5×8.9 **17.** 12.2×2.96 **18.** 5.3×7.49 **19.** 28.5×11.1 **20.** 14.8×10.658

21. *Mental Math* Suppose you earn $4.75/h mowing lawns. Estimate how much money you will earn in 3.5 h.

22. *Mental Math* Suppose you save $6.25 each week. Estimate how much you will save in one year.

23. Social Studies The Apennine Railroad Tunnel in Italy is 18.5 km long. The Seikan Tunnel in Japan is 2.9 times as long. Estimate the length of the Seikan Tunnel.

24. Packaging A volleyball weighs 283.5 g and a shipping crate weighs 595.34 g. Estimate the weight of a shipping crate containing 9 volleyballs.

Nutrition Use the chart below to answer Exercises 25–27.

Food	Serving Size	Protein (grams)
Canned Tuna	3 oz (drained)	24.4
Rye Bread	1 slice	2.3
Cheese Pizza	1 slice (14-in. pie)	7.8

25. About how many grams of protein are in 2 slices of cheese pizza?

26. About how many grams of protein are in 8 slices of cheese pizza?

27. Estimate how many grams of protein are in a sandwich consisting of 2 slices of rye bread and 2 oz of tuna.

Use compatible numbers to estimate each quotient.

28. $46.4 \div 4.75$ **29.** $39.3 \div 7.7$ **30.** $56.1 \div 6.9$ **31.** $17.33 \div 5.49$ **32.** $15.76 \div 2.51$

33. $65 \div 0.8$ **34.** $37.2 \div 6.12$ **35.** $79.8 \div 2.2$ **36.** $32.36 \div 1.87$ **37.** $149 \div 14.4$

38. $11.801 \div 2.9$ **39.** $101 \div 9.25$ **40.** $65.1 \div 2.89$ **41.** $73.09 \div 0.9$ **42.** $80.34 \div 7.82$

THE SOAP BOX DERBY

The Soap Box Derby held in Akron, Ohio, is a downhill race for cars without motors. The cars are built and driven by young people between the ages of 9 and 16. The cars race on a 953.75 ft downhill track.

One year more than 200 girls and boys from 35 states and 6 countries entered the race. Carolyn Fox, an 11-year-old from Salem, Oregon, was the winner of the Kit Car division. Her winning time was 28.27 seconds.

43. Estimation To find speed, divide the distance by the time. Estimate Carolyn Fox's average speed.

44. Suppose the track is 2.5 times its original length. A racer finishes the race in 52.56 s. Estimate the racer's average speed.

45. *Number Sense* Estimate 29.26×11.62.
   a. First use compatible numbers.
   b. Then estimate by rounding.
   c. Which method is closer to the exact answer? Why?

46. **Choose A, B, C, or D.** Between what two numbers is the quotient $18.7 \div 5$?

   A. 2 and 3   **B.** 3 and 4   **C.** 4 and 5   **D.** 5 and 6

47. *Jobs* Yvonne earned $33.25 in one week baby-sitting. She earns $3.50 per hour. Estimate the number of hours she worked.

48. *Savings* Suppose you saved $443.75 in one year. Estimate how much you saved each week.

49. *Library Science* The bill for 3 copies of a book is $38.85. Estimate the cost of 1 book. Is your estimate higher or lower than the book's actual cost?

50. *Writing* Suppose two different people estimate a product or quotient using compatible numbers. Will they always get the same result? Use examples to explain.

Mixed Review

Use the graph at the right for Exercises 51 and 52.
(Lesson 1-5)

51. If the braking distance is about 190 ft, how fast was the car traveling?

52. Find the braking distance for a car traveling 30 mi/h.

53. *Choose a Strategy* Name the ways you could make $.45 with no pennies.

54. A bus trip from Austin to San Antonio takes 2 h 57 min. What time will the bus arrive if it leaves Austin at 10:35 A.M.? *(Lesson 3-10)*

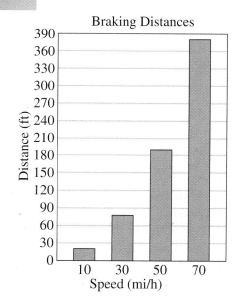

Braking Distances

CHAPTER PROJECT

PROJECT LINK: RESEARCHING

Brainstorm a list of all the celebration costs. Note the items you need to purchase and then research a reasonable price for each item. Decide the quantity you will need of each item. Be sure you have enough for every member of your class and the guest(s) of honor. Estimate the total cost of the event.

Decimals and Databases

After Lesson 4-1

You can use an electronic spreadsheet to create a *database*. An electronic database is powerful, because once you enter a set of data items, you can organize, reorganize, and recall that information for a variety of purposes.

For example, look at the comic book database screen shown below. You can organize this database to show all comics in the collection alphabetically or by their dollar value.

Here are some common database terms.
A *field* is a category within a database of information.
A *record* is a group of fields relating to one entry.
Sort is the computer command used to organize the fields.

	A	B	C	D
1	Issue Number	Title	Value	
2	270	Batman	8.00	
3	1	Indiana Jones	2.50	
4	99	Justice League	10.00	
5	28	Spiderman	335.00	
6	1	The Atom	750.00	

The **fields** are *Issue Number*, *Title*, and *Value*.

You could add a **field** to describe each comic's condition.

Each row is a **record**.

Source: *Overstreet Comic Book Price Guide*

Use the database screen above for Exercises 1–3.

1. How many records are shown in the database screen?

2. Suppose you sort the comics shown by value from greatest to least. Which comic would be listed first? Last?

3. Besides a field for each comic's condition, what other fields could you add?

4. *Writing* Think of a database you could create.
   a. Tell how the database would be useful to you.
   b. Show what fields would be contained in each record.
   c. Explain at least one way in which you might sort your database.

4-2 Exponents

What You'll Learn

1. To use exponents
2. To apply the order of operations to simplify powers and expressions

...And Why

Exponents make it easy to use multiple factors.

Here's How

Look for questions that
- build understanding
- ✔ check understanding

 Elis Stenman made the walls of his house by pasting and folding layers of newspaper. He used papers rolled into different sizes to make his furniture, which includes tables, chairs, lamps, and an upright piano.

Source: *The Kids' World Almanac of Records and Facts*

THINK AND DISCUSS

1 Using Exponents

Would you believe that Elis Stenman built a house and its furniture, including a piano, from about 100,000 newspapers? You can express 100,000 as $10 \times 10 \times 10 \times 10 \times 10$ or you can use an exponent.

$$10 \times 10 \times 10 \times 10 \times 10 = 10^5 \leftarrow \text{exponent}$$

5 factors   base

The **exponent** tells you how many times a number, or **base,** is used as a factor.

■ EXAMPLE 1

Write $5 \times 5 \times 5 \times 5$ using an exponent. Name the base and the exponent.

$5 \times 5 \times 5 \times 5 = 5^4$ ← The number 5 is used as a factor 4 times.

The base is 5 and the exponent is 4.

1. ✔ **Try It Out** Rewrite each expression using an exponent. Name the base and exponent.
   a. $7 \times 7 \times 7$ **b.** $2 \times 2 \times 2 \times 2 \times 2 \times 2$

You call a number that is expressed using an exponent a **power.** You read 10^5 as "ten to the fifth power."

In geometry, the exponents 2 and 3 have special names.

- The area of the square is 3×3, or 3^2. You read 3^2 as "three squared."

- The volume of the cube is $4 \times 4 \times 4$ or 4^3. You read 4^3 as "four cubed."

② Simplifying Powers

You can simplify a power by writing it as a product.

■ EXAMPLE 2

a. Simplify 4^3.

$$4^3 = 4 \times 4 \times 4 = 64$$

b. Simplify 1^2.

$$1^2 = 1 \times 1 = 1$$

2. ✔ Try It Out Simplify.

a. 3^4 b. 9^2 c. 5^3 d. 10^4

A calculator is helpful for exponents. You can use the $\boxed{x^2}$ key to square a number. Use the $\boxed{y^x}$ key to evaluate *any* power.

■ EXAMPLE 3

Use a calculator.

a. Simplify 26^2.

26 $\boxed{x^2}$ *676*

$$26^2 = 676$$

b. Simplify 6^8.

6 $\boxed{y^x}$ 8 $\boxed{=}$ *1679616*

$$6^8 = 1,679,616$$

3. ✔ Try It Out Use a calculator to simplify.

a. 31^2 b. 22^4 c. 15^5 d. 99^2

PROBLEM SOLVING HINT

The phrase *Please Excuse My Dear Aunt Sally* can help you to remember the order of operations. The first letter of each word in the phrase stands for an operation.

THE ORDER OF OPERATIONS

You can extend the order of operations to include powers.

1. Do all operations within parentheses first.
2. **Do all the work which has exponents.**
3. Multiply and divide in order from left to right.
4. Add and subtract in order from left to right.

EXAMPLE 4

a. Simplify $2 \times (4^2 - 5)$.

$$2 \times (4^2 - 5) = 2 \times (16 - 5) \qquad \longleftarrow 4^2 = 4 \times 4 = 16$$
$$= 2 \times 11 \qquad \longleftarrow \text{Subtract 5 from 16.}$$
$$= 22 \qquad \longleftarrow \text{Multiply 2 and 11.}$$

b. Simplify $2^3 - 9 \div 3$.

$$2^3 - 9 \div 3 = 8 - 9 \div 3 \qquad \longleftarrow 2^3 = 2 \times 2 \times 2 = 8$$
$$= 8 - 3 \qquad \longleftarrow \text{Divide 9 by 3.}$$
$$= 5 \qquad \longleftarrow \text{Subtract 3 from 8.}$$

4. ✔ *Try It Out* Simplify each expression.
a. $60 \div (6 + 3^2)$ **b.** $(3 + 7)^2 \div 5^2$

5. ▪*Reasoning* How can you use a calculator to simplify each expression in Example 4?

EXERCISES *On Your Own*

Name the base and the exponent.

1. 4^5 **2.** 3^2 **3.** 6^3 **4.** 7^9 **5.** 8^1 **6.** 10^3

Write using an exponent. Name the base and the exponent.

7. $6 \times 6 \times 6$ **8.** $3 \times 3 \times 3 \times 3 \times 3$ **9.** $8 \times 8 \times 8 \times 8$

10. $12{,}432 \times 12{,}432$ **11.** $1{,}500 \times 1{,}500 \times 1{,}500$ **12.** $4 \times 4 \times 4 \times 4 \times 4 \times 4$

Simplify each expression.

13. 5^4 **14.** 4^5 **15.** 7^3 **16.** 6^5 **17.** 8^4

18. $(10 - 8)^4 \times 3$ **19.** $5^3 \div 25$ **20.** $24^2 - 4^3$ **21.** $10^3 \div 1{,}000 + 10$

Geometry **Express each square's area (length × width) or cube's volume (length × width × height) using an exponent.**

22.   **23.**   **24.**

25. **a.** *Patterns* Copy and complete the table at the right.
   b. Look at the standard form numbers in the table. Explain how the number of zeros that follow the numeral 1 relate to the exponent.
   c. Extend and complete the table for 10^6, 10^7, 10^8.
   d. Add three rows to the top of the table. Look at the standard form column. Continue the pattern to write the three standard form numbers that precede 10.

Power	Standard Form
10^1	10
10^2	100
10^3	1,000
10^4	■
■	■

26. *Algebra* How would you write $n \times n \times n$ using exponents?

27. Look at the number pattern 1, 8, 27, 64, 125, 216, ... How does this number pattern relate to exponents?

28. *Entertainment* The size of the image of a motion picture is related to the distance of the projector from the screen. Use the table at the right.
   a. *Writing* Describe how the size of a motion picture is related to the distance from the projector to the screen.
   b. *Reasoning* A projector is 25 ft from the screen. How big will the image of the motion picture be?

Distance from Screen	Picture Size
1 unit	1 unit^2
2 units	4 units^2
3 units	9 units^2
4 units	16 units^2

Choose **Use a calculator, mental math, or paper and pencil to simplify each expression.**

29. 5^2 30. 2^3 31. 3^7 32. 22^3 33. 10^{10} 34. 11^7

35. $475 \div 5^2$ 36. $5 \times 3^2 - 10$ 37. 7×2^4 38. $2 \times 4^2 - 32$

39. $35 + 7 \times 2^4$ 40. $(56 - 4^2) \times 9$ 41. $3^3 - 2^4 + 30$ 42. $12 \times (60 - 2^5)$

43. $6^3 \div (2 \times 6) + 64$ 44. $498 + (2^{12} \div 2^4) \div (2^5 \times 2) - 2$

Mixed Review

Find each sum or difference. *(Lesson 3-7)*

45. $2.365 + 8.36$ 46. $10.25 - 7.86$ 47. $7.9 + 11.71$ 48. $20 - 13.07$ 49. $95.21 + 82.96$

Evaluate each expression for $x = 10$. *(Lesson 2-4)*

50. $4(x - 6)$ 51. $6x \div 3$ 52. $x + 27$ 53. $2(x + 10)$ 54. $(x \div 2) - 5$

55. *Grocery Shopping* Is $4.00 enough money to buy yogurt for $.79, blueberries for $1.59, and bread for $1.49? Explain. *(Lesson 3-6)*

4-3 The Distributive Property

What You'll Learn

▼ To find areas of rectangles

▼ To use the distributive property

...And Why

You'll use the distributive property to solve picnic planning problems and to do mental math.

Here's How

Look for questions that
- build understanding
- ✔ check understanding

Work Together ——————— Creating Area Models

Geometry On graph paper, draw rectangles with the dimensions shown below. Cut out the rectangles.

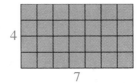

4   7

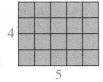

4   5

1. Find and record the number of squares in each rectangle.

2. Put the two rectangles end to end so the sides of equal length touch. What is the length and width of the new rectangle?

3. ▪*Reasoning* Find the number of squares in the new rectangle. How does this number relate to the numbers for the two smaller rectangles?

THINK AND DISCUSS

▼1 *Finding Areas of Rectangles*

Area is the number of square units in a figure. The area of a rectangle is equal to the product of its length and width. You write units of area in square units (units²).

w ℓ

Area = length × width
$A = \ell \times w$

4. ▪*Geometry* Use graph paper to draw a rectangle that is 5 units wide and 6 units long.
  a. Count the number of square units to find its area.
  b. Multiply the length times the width to find the area of the rectangle. Do you get the same result?
  c. Which method seems easier? Explain.

5. ✔*Try It Out* Find the area of a 3 ft-by-6 ft rectangle.

▼ Using the Distributive Property

Example 1 shows how you can use the **distributive property** to simplify an expression that has multiplication and addition.

■ **EXAMPLE 1**   *Real-World Problem Solving*

Picnics Suppose you want to cover the tops of two picnic tables. One table is 5 ft long and 3 ft wide. The other is 5 ft long and 4 ft wide. Find the minimum amount of paper you will need to cover the table tops.

Method 1
Find the area of each table top. Then add the areas.

Method 2
Place the tables side by side. Find the area of the combined table top.

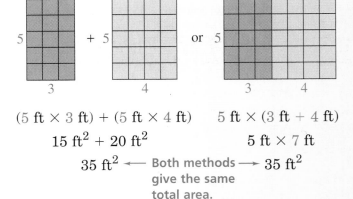

$$(5 \text{ ft} \times 3 \text{ ft}) + (5 \text{ ft} \times 4 \text{ ft}) \qquad 5 \text{ ft} \times (3 \text{ ft} + 4 \text{ ft})$$

$$15 \text{ ft}^2 + 20 \text{ ft}^2 \qquad\qquad 5 \text{ ft} \times 7 \text{ ft}$$

$$35 \text{ ft}^2 \longleftarrow \text{ Both methods } \longrightarrow 35 \text{ ft}^2$$
give the same
total area.

You will need at least 35 ft^2 of paper.

■ EXAMPLE 2

Use the distributive property to simplify the expression.
$$(3 \times 4) + (3 \times 7) = 3 \times (4 + 7)$$
$$= 3 \times 11$$
$$= 33$$

6. ✔*Try It Out* Use the distributive property to simplify.
a. $(13 \times 6) + (13 \times 4)$ **b.** $5 \times (9 + 20)$

You can use the distributive property to multiply mentally.

■ EXAMPLE 3

Mental Math Use the distributive property to find 8×59.
$$8 \times 59 = 8 \times (60 - 1) \quad \longleftarrow \text{Think of 59 as } 60 - 1.$$
$$= (8 \times 60) - (8 \times 1) \quad \longleftarrow \text{Multiply mentally.}$$
$$= 480 - 8 \quad \longleftarrow \text{Subtract mentally.}$$
$$= 472$$

7. ✔*Try It Out* Use the distributive property to multiply.
a. 4×59 **b.** 3×84 **c.** 6×49

THE DISTRIBUTIVE PROPERTY

Numbers added or subtracted within a set of parentheses can be multiplied by a number outside the parentheses.

Examples: $8 \times (5 + 3) = (8 \times 5) + (8 \times 3)$
$$8 \times (5 - 3) = (8 \times 5) - (8 \times 3)$$

EXERCISES *On Your Own*

1. *Index Cards* Standard index card sizes in the United States are 3 in. by 5 in., 4 in. by 6 in., and 5 in. by 8 in. Find the area of each card.

2. *Advertising* One side of a regular outdoor billboard is 14 ft by 48 ft. Find the maximum area covered by an advertisement on this billboard.

3. *Writing* Describe two ways to find the total area of the rectangle at the right.

Geometry Write an expression to represent the total area of each figure. Then, find the total area. Show all your work.

4.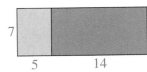

5.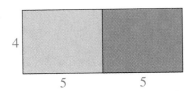

6.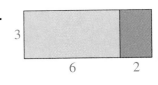

7. *Open-ended* Measure the length and the width of two different notebook covers. Find the area of each cover. Then find the combined area of both covers. Show two different ways to find the combined area.

8. *Reasoning* The formula for the area of a rectangle is *length × width*. What happens if you multiply *width × length* to find the area? Use an example to support your answer.

9. *Frames* The smallest ready-made picture frames measure 4 in. by 5 in. The largest frames measure 24 in. by 36 in.
   a. Find the area of each frame.
   b. How much greater area does the largest frame cover than the smallest?

10. *Washcloths* Typical washcloths range from 12 in. by 12 in. to 14 in. by 14 in.
   a. Find the minimum and maximum areas of washcloths.
   b. Find the range of the areas found in part (a).

Modeling Draw a rectangular model for each expression.

11. $8 \times (3 + 4)$
12. $(5 \times 8) + (5 \times 2)$
13. $6 \times (2 + 3)$
14. $(8 \times 8) + (8 \times 1)$

Find the missing numbers in each equation.

15. $6 \times (12 + 2) = (\blacksquare \times 12) + (6 \times \blacksquare)$

16. $(10 \times \blacksquare) - (\blacksquare \times \blacksquare) = 10 \times (6 - 3)$

17. $(8 \times 3) + (\blacksquare \times 4) = 8 \times (\blacksquare + 4)$

18. $3 \times (8 - 1) = (\blacksquare \times 8) - (3 \times \blacksquare)$

19. $8 \times (\blacksquare - 7) = (\blacksquare \times 13) - (8 \times \blacksquare)$

20. $\blacksquare \times (11 + 5) = (20 \times \blacksquare) + (\blacksquare \times 5)$

21. How can you use the distributive property to find 9×92?

22. *Sports* Look at the regulation-sized tennis court at the right.
   a. Find the rectangular area of the entire tennis court.
   b. Suppose you divided the entire court into four equal-sized sections. Estimate the area of each section.

36 ft

78 ft

Rewrite and simplify each expression.

23. $(4 \times 6) + (4 \times 3)$

24. $6 \times (20 - 4)$

25. $12 \times (4 + 10)$

26. $(5 \times 3) - (5 \times 2)$

27. $(13 \times 6) + (13 \times 4)$

28. $15 \times (3 + 20)$

29. $11 \times (50 - 4)$

30. $(25 + 12) \times 4$

31. $(6 \times 22) - (6 \times 18)$

Mental Math **Use the distributive property to simplify.**

32. 4×24

33. 2×66

34. 3×55

35. 6×210

36. 8×109

Mixed Review

Find the next three terms in each number pattern. *(Lesson 2-1)*

37. $5, 15, 45, 135, \ldots$ **38.** $3, 10, 17, 24, \ldots$ **39.** $25, 50, 100, 200, \ldots$ **40.** $91, 82, 73, 64, \ldots$

Draw a model for each decimal. *(Lesson 3-1)*

41. 0.75

42. 0.8

43. 0.06

44. 0.99

45. 0.1

46. 0.33

47. Mr. Garcia began work at 7:37 A.M. and finished at 4:19 P.M. He took a 45-minute lunch. How long did he work? *(Lesson 3-10)*

✓ CHECKPOINT 1

Lessons 4-1 through 4-3

Estimate using rounding.

1. 2.2×9.4

2. 26.28×1.71

3. 4.9×12.2

4. 99.6×9.8

Estimate using compatible numbers.

5. 39.4×2.34

6. 12.78×3.39

7. 28.75×51.23

8. 210×3.6

Simplify each expression.

9. 2^7

10. $7 \times 3^4 - 99$

11. $(2 \times 4^2) \div 8$

12. $50 \div (5^2 \div 5) + 4$

13. Choose A, B, C, or D. Find the total area of a rectangle that is 3 units long and 4 units wide plus a rectangle that is 3 units long and 6 units wide.

A. 25 square units **B.** 18 square units **C.** 30 square units **D.** 60 square units

Using Models to Multiply Decimals

What You'll Learn

▼ To model the multiplication of a decimal and a whole number

② To model the multiplication of two decimals

...And Why

You can use models to find the answers to problems involving hobbies.

Here's How

Look for questions that
- ⬛ build understanding
- ✔ check understanding

Work Together
Modeling Decimal Products

1. Model the sum $0.5 + 0.5 + 0.5 + 0.5$.
   a. How many squares do you need?
   b. How much of each square do you need to shade?
   c. How many tenths did you shade altogether?

2. a. How could you rewrite the addition expression as a multiplication expression?
   b. ⬛ *Think About It* Would the model for the multiplication expression look any different from the addition model?

THINK AND DISCUSS

▼ Multiplying Decimals and Whole Numbers

When you multiply a decimal and a whole number, you can use models to show multiplication as repeated addition.

⬛ **EXAMPLE 1** *Real-World Problem Solving*

Coin Collecting A collector buys two 1942 Mercury dimes. Each coin costs $.70. What is the total cost?

Write the cost of the coins as a sum and as a product. $0.7 + 0.7 = 2 \times 0.7$

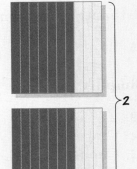

Shade 7 columns to represent $.70 or 0.7.

Shade two squares to model 2×0.7.

The shaded area is 14 tenths, or 1 whole and 4 tenths (1.4).
$2 \times 0.7 = 1.4$ or $2 \times \$.70 = \$1.40$

 The face on the Mercury dime is Miss Liberty. The wings on her cap represent freedom of thought. Many people mistook the cap and wings to represent the Greek god Mercury, so the coin became known as the "Mercury" dime.

▼2 *Modeling the Multiplication of Decimals*

You use just one square to model the multiplication of two decimals that are each less than 1.

3. a. ▪ *Modeling* Shade 3 rows blue. What number does this represent?

   b. Shade 8 columns red. What number does this represent?

   c. The purple (red and blue) area where the shading overlaps shows the product. How many squares are shaded purple?

   d. What decimal number does this represent?

   e. Write a multiplication sentence that describes the model.

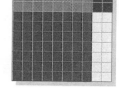

4. ▪ *Number Sense* When you multiply two decimals that are each less than 1, is your answer greater than or less than 1?

■ **EXAMPLE 2**

Model the product 1.5 × 0.5.

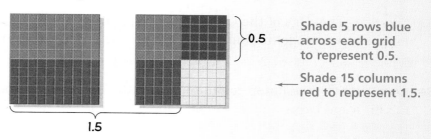

Shade 5 rows blue across each grid to represent 0.5.

Shade 15 columns red to represent 1.5.

1.5

The purple area represents 75 hundredths, or 0.75.

5. ✔ *Try It Out* Model the product 0.3 × 2.8.

EXERCISES *On Your Own*

Model each product.

1. 0.2 × 3

2. 6 × 0.5

3. 2 × 0.3

4. 3 × 0.6

5. 0.8 × 5

6. 4 × 0.4

7. 9 × 0.1

8. 0.3 × 7

9. 2 × 0.9

10. 4 × 0.8

11. 0.5 × 8

12. 7 × 0.5

13. 6 × 0.4

14. 0.7 × 6

15. 0.2 × 8

Write a multiplication sentence to describe each model.

16.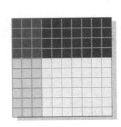

17.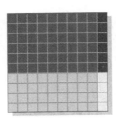

18.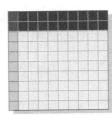

19.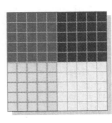

20.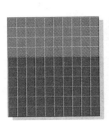

21.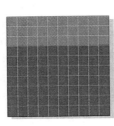

Model each product.

22. 2.2×0.4 23. 0.4×0.1 24. 0.7×0.2 25. 1.3×0.2 26. 1.7×0.5

27. 0.9×1.1 28. 0.4×0.6 29. 2.4×0.3 30. 0.1×0.1 31. 0.8×1.8

32. *Writing* Explain how to draw a model to find 1.2×0.4.

33. *Science* The eggs of the Cuban hummingbird are only 0.3 in. long. Draw a model to find the length of four eggs laid end to end.

34. *Computers* A palmtop computer is usually 3.4 in. deep and 6.3 in. wide. Draw a model to find the area of this computer.

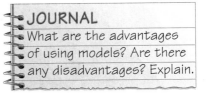

JOURNAL
What are the advantages of using models? Are there any disadvantages? Explain.

Mixed Review

Find the value of each expression. *(Lesson 2-3)*

35. $7 \times (2 + 4) - 4$ 36. $(3 + 7) \times 5 \div 5$ 37. $25 + 5 - 4 \times 7$ 38. $(2 \times 4) \times 3 - 1$

Find each sum or difference. *(Lesson 3-5)*

39. $0.2 + 0.18$ 40. $2.3 + 1.9$ 41. $3.15 + 0.8$ 42. $1.7 - 0.28$ 43. $0.98 - 0.8$

44. *Choose a Strategy* Suppose the distance to your aunt's apartment is 24 blocks. You walk 3 blocks, and then take the bus 16 blocks. How much farther is it to your aunt's?

4-5 Multiplying Decimals

What You'll Learn

▼ To multiply decimals and whole numbers

▼ To multiply two decimals

...And Why

You'll multiply decimals to solve problems in earth science and botany.

Here's How

Look for questions that
▪ build understanding
✔ check understanding

Need Help? For practice multiplying and dividing whole numbers, see the Skills Handbook pages 540–543.

Work Together Multiplying Decimals with a Calculator

Use a calculator to find each product. Then answer the questions.

31 ☒ 65   31 ☒ 6.5   3.1 ☒ 6.5   3.1 ☒ 0.65

1. Compare the numbers in each expression. How are they alike? How are they different?

2. Compare the products. How are they alike and different?

3. ▪ **Explain** For each expression, compare the number of decimal places in the original numbers and the number of decimal places in the product. What do you notice?

4. ▪ **Summarize** Write a rule for multiplying decimals. Use examples to test your rule.

THINK AND DISCUSS

1 *Multiplying Decimals and Whole Numbers*

To multiply a decimal and a whole number, first multiply as if both factors are whole numbers. Then place the decimal point so that there is the same number of decimal places in the product as in the decimal factor.

■ **EXAMPLE 1** *Real-World Problem Solving*

Earth Science North America is moving away from Europe at a rate of 0.8 inches per year. About how far will North America move in 5 years?

$$\begin{array}{r} 0.8 \quad \leftarrow\text{1 decimal place} \\ \times\ 5 \quad \leftarrow\text{no decimal places} \\ \hline 4.0 \quad \leftarrow\text{1 decimal place} \end{array}$$

In 5 years, North America will move about 4.0 inches farther away from Europe.

5. ✔ *Try It Out* About how far will North America move in 9 years?

② *Multiplying Two Decimals*

When both factors are decimals, you count the decimal places in both factors to find how many places are needed in the product.

■ **EXAMPLE 2** *Real-World Problem Solving*

Botany A eucalyptus tree in New Guinea grew 10.5 m in one year. How much will this tree grow in 2.5 years if it grows at the same rate?

Estimate: 10.5 × 2.5 ≈ 11 × 3 = 33

$$
\begin{array}{r}
10.5 \quad \longleftarrow \text{1 decimal place} \\
\times\ 2.5 \quad \longleftarrow \text{1 decimal place} \\
\hline
52\,5 \\
+\ 210 \\
\hline
26.25 \quad \longleftarrow \text{2 decimal places}
\end{array}
$$

The eucalyptus tree will grow about 26.25 m in 2.5 years. Since the estimate was 33 m, 26.25 m is a reasonable answer.

6. ❖*Number Sense* Explain how an estimated product can help you place the decimal point correctly in the exact product.

7. ✔*Try It Out* Find each product.
   a. 0.8 × 5.2   **b.** 1.3 × 13.8   **c.** 3.11 × 2.4   **d.** 0.9 × 2.26

■ **EXAMPLE 3**

Solve $n \div 0.13 = 0.02$. You can rewrite as $n = 0.02 \times 0.13$.

$$
\begin{array}{r}
0.13 \quad \longleftarrow \text{2 decimal places} \\
\times\ 0.02 \quad \longleftarrow \text{2 decimal places} \\
\hline
.0026 \quad \longleftarrow
\end{array}
$$
You need 4 decimal places. Insert two zeros and place the decimal point so that there are 4 decimal places in the product.

$n = 0.0026$

New Guinea

MULTIPLICATION OF DECIMALS

To multiply with decimals, first multiply as if you are multiplying whole numbers. Count the number of decimal places in the factors. Then place the decimal point in the product so that there is the same number of decimal places.

8. ✔ *Try It Out* Solve.
   a. $x \div 0.1 = 0.1$ b. $t \div 0.3 = 0.04$ c. $p \div 2.4 = 0.008$

9. a. ⋅⋅*Calculator* Find 2.5×10, 2.5×100, and $2.5 \times 1{,}000$.
   b. ⋅⋅*Reasoning* Compare the products. Write a rule for multiplying by 10, 100, or 1,000.

10. a. ⋅⋅*Calculator* Find 3×0.1, 3×0.01, and 3×0.001.
    b. Write a rule for multiplying by 0.1, 0.01, or 0.001.

The rules you wrote for multiplying by 10, 100, or 1,000 can help you multiply mentally.

■ EXAMPLE 4

Find $1{,}000 \times 0.26$ mentally.

$0.260 \Rightarrow 260$ ⟵ To multiply a decimal by 1,000, move the decimal point 3 places to the right.

$1{,}000 \times 0.26 = 260$

11. ✔ *Try It Out* Find 100×3.42 mentally.

EXERCISES *On Your Own*

Place the decimal point in each product.

1.	0.403	2.	2.33	3.	523	4.	22.76	5.	1842	6.	0.235
	× 5		× 8		× 0.5		× 3		× 0.22		× 55
	2015		1864		2615		6828		40524		12925

7.	3.14	8.	0.15	9.	37.3	10.	8.42	11.	93.3	12.	4.222
	× 10.1		× 0.31		× 0.5		× 6.7		× 1.6		× 0.3
	31714		00465		1865		56414		14928		12666

13. $3.2 \times 4.6 = 1472$ 14. $5.05 \times 3.14 = 158570$ 15. $4.50 \times 3.8 = 17100$

16. *Astronomy* The circumference of Earth is about 40,200 km at the equator. The circumference of Jupiter is 11.2 times as great. What is the circumference of Jupiter?

17. *Office Supplies* A ream consists of 500 sheets of paper. The thickness of one sheet of paper is 0.01 cm. Calculate the thickness of a ream of paper.

18. **Writing** In 1994, the average car traveled about 21.5 miles per gallon of gas. In 1974, the average was 13.4 miles per gallon. How much farther than the average 1974 car could the average 1994 car travel on 12 gallons of gas?

Find each product.

19. 1.9
× 9

20. 2.065
× 12

21. 35.15
× 25

22. 5.6
× 31

23. 6.108
× 35

24. 450
× 0.01

25. 2.065
× 1.2

26. 0.18
× 0.06

27. 3.1
× 0.04

28. 15.35
× 3.2

29. 0.96
× 0.12

30. 7.6
× 0.06

31. 0.7
× 1.5

32. 420
× 3.3

33. 0.56
× 1.1

34. 6.7
× 10.2

35. 0.33
× 0.45

36. 1.04
× 9.5

Calorie Counter

The energy in food and the energy you use are measured in calories. Not all foods have the same number of calories, and not all activities use the same number of calories. Your body weight is also a factor in the number of calories you use.

Exercise Read the article above. Use the expression and the chart for Exercises 37–39.

Weight × **Number of minutes of activity** **×** **Calories used per minute per pound**

37. Jim weighs 100 pounds. He jumps rope for 15 min. How many calories does he use?

38. Tara weighs 80 pounds and dances for 2 h. How many calories does she use?

39. How many calories will you use playing softball for 1 h 10 min? Would you use more calories playing soccer?

Activity	Calories/ min/lb
Dancing	0.05
Jumping rope	0.07
Roller skating	0.05
Running	0.10
Skateboarding	0.05
Playing soccer	0.05
Playing softball	0.04

Algebra Solve each equation.

40. $x \div 0.2 = 0.7$

41. $t \div 0.03 = 0.5$

42. $p \div 1.6 = 0.04$

43. $x \div 2.1 = 0.045$

44. $y \div 0.01 = 0.1$

45. $b \div 0.9 = 0.08$

46. $x \div 0.044 = 0.03$

47. $n \div 0.065 = 0.155$

Mental Math **Find each product.**

48. 6.2×10 **49.** 7.08×0.1 **50.** 3.5×10^3 **51.** 26×0.01 **52.** 3.25×100

53. 0.82×10^3 **54.** 10×25.7 **55.** 100×1.6 **56.** 0.47×10 **57.** 4.82×0.001

58. 57×0.1 **59.** $0.1 \times 1,000$ **60.** 10×9.25 **61.** $10^2 \times 0.008$ **62.** 3.2×0.01

63. Use a calculator to find 0.05×0.36. You will get 0.018 in the display. Why do you see 3 decimal places instead of 4 places?

64. *Marine Biology* Dolphins swim about 27.5 mi/h. A person can swim about 0.1 as fast. How fast can a person swim?

65. *Writing* Explain how multiplying 0.3×0.4 is like multiplying 3×4. How is it different?

***True* or *False?* Give an example to support each answer.**

66. The product of any decimal and zero is always zero.

67. If you change the order of two decimal factors, the product will change.

68. Any decimal multiplied by 1 is the original decimal.

Mixed Review

Solve each equation mentally. *(Lesson 2-6)*

69. $x - 5 = 3$ **70.** $y + 11 = 18$ **71.** $z - 8 = 7$ **72.** $2 + b = 21$ **73.** $a - 4 = 12$

Use <, =, or > to complete each statement. *(Lesson 3-3)*

74. $17.34 \ \blacksquare \ 17.051$ **75.** $0.1056 \ \blacksquare \ 0.15$ **76.** $6.225 \ \blacksquare \ 6.25$ **77.** $0.89 \ \blacksquare \ 0.888$

78. *Choose a Strategy* Karenna has a white blouse, a green blouse, a blue blouse, a plaid skirt, and a pair of striped pants. How many different outfits can she make?

CHAPTER PROJECT

PROJECT LINK: CALCULATING

Use the list of items and the prices you researched earlier to calculate the exact cost for the celebration event. How much will the event cost? How close to your estimated cost is your exact cost? Was your estimate reasonable? Explain.

EXPLORATION

Scientific Notation

After Lesson 4-5

The *Mars Pathfinder* went to Mars in 1997. The trip distance was more than 309 million miles. You can write this number in either standard form or *scientific notation*.

To write a number in scientific notation, you write the number as two factors. The first factor is any number between 1 and 10. The second factor is a number which is a power of 10, for example, numbers such as 10^2, 10^5, or 10^{11}.

Standard form:
309,000,000

Scientific notation:
3.09×10^8

■ EXAMPLE 1

Biology The average human body contains about 25,000,000,000 blood cells. Write the number in scientific notation.

$$25,000,000,000. = 2.5 \times 10^{10}$$

Move the decimal point to make a factor between 1 and 10. You use 2.5.

The exponent shows that in this example the decimal point moved **10** places to the left.

■ EXAMPLE 2

Write 4.99×10^6 in standard form.

$4.99 \times 10^6 = 4990000.$ ⟵ Move the decimal point **6** places to the right.

$= 4,990,000$

Write each number in scientific notation.

1. 34,000
2. 165,000,000,000
3. 654,321,987
4. 283,154.734

5. 800,000
6. 93,000,000,000,000
7. 9,415,027,392
8. 92.3421

Write each number in standard form.

9. 1.64×10^5
10. 9.0×10^6
11. 8.234×10^2
12. 9.2×10^{12}

13. *Open-ended* Use an almanac or the Internet to find data with large numbers. Write the data in scientific notation.

Using Models to Divide Decimals

What You'll Learn

▼1 To model dividing by tenths

▼2 To model dividing by hundredths

...And Why

You can divide decimals to solve problems when preparing food.

Here's How

Look for questions that
- build understanding
- ✔ check understanding

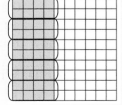

THINK AND DISCUSS

▼1 Modeling Dividing by Tenths

Measurement Alika is making fruit smoothies. She has 0.8 lb of strawberries. She uses 0.2 lb in each smoothie. The expression below represents the number of smoothies Alika can make.

$$0.8 \div 0.2$$

You can use a model to divide a decimal number by tenths.

1. Use the model at the right.
   a. How is 8 tenths, 0.8, shown?
   b. How is 2 tenths, 0.2, shown?
   c. How many groups of 0.2 are there in 0.8?
   d. **Calculator** Find the quotient 0.8 ÷ 0.2. How many smoothies can Alika make?

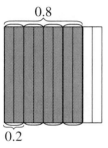

2. ✔**Try It Out** Draw a model to find each quotient.
   a. 0.8 ÷ 0.4   b. 0.9 ÷ 0.3   c. 1 ÷ 0.2

▼2 Modeling Dividing by Hundredths

You can also use a model to divide a decimal number by hundredths.

■ EXAMPLE

Find the quotient 0.4 ÷ 0.08.

Shade 4 columns to represent 0.4. →

Circle groups of 0.08. There are 5 groups. →

0.4 ÷ 0.08 = 5

3. ✔*Try It Out* Draw a model to find each quotient.
   a. $0.3 \div 0.06$ **b.** $0.9 \div 0.18$ **c.** $0.6 \div 0.12$

QUICKreview

Each number in a division
sentence has a special name.

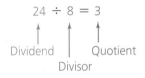

4. ⬛*Reasoning* In the sentence $0.8 \div 0.2 = 4$, the divisor, 0.2, represents the size of each group. What does the quotient, 4, represent?

Work Together   *Modeling Decimal Division*

Work with a partner. Draw a model to find each quotient. First decide how many decimal squares you need. Next shade your model to show the dividend. Then circle groups of equal size. In these problems the divisor tells you the size of each group.

     5. $1.8 \div 0.3$ **6.** $1.2 \div 0.2$ **7.** $2 \div 0.4$

EXERCISES *On Your Own*

Complete each sentence.

1.
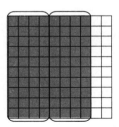
$\blacksquare \div 0.4 = 2$

2.
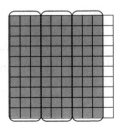
$0.9 \div 0.3 = \blacksquare$

3.
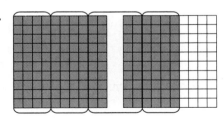
$\blacksquare \div 0.4 = 4$

4.
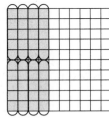
$0.3 \div 0.03 = \blacksquare$

5.
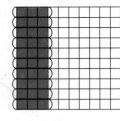
$0.4 \div \blacksquare = 8$

6.

$1 \div \blacksquare = 4$

7.
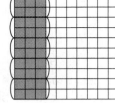
$0.3 \div \blacksquare = 5$

8. *Writing* Explain how to model $2.4 \div 0.6$.

9. **Choose A, B, C, or D.** What is the quotient $1 \div 0.25$?
      A. 4   **B.** 40   **C.** 0.4   **D.** 0.04

Draw a model to find each quotient.

10. $0.6 \div 0.2$ **11.** $1.6 \div 0.8$ **12.** $2 \div 0.5$ **13.** $1.2 \div 0.3$ **14.** $0.2 \div 0.2$

15. $1.5 \div 0.5$ **16.** $1.8 \div 0.3$ **17.** $2.4 \div 0.8$ **18.** $3 \div 0.6$ **19.** $2.8 \div 0.4$

20. $0.8 \div 0.16$ **21.** $1.35 \div 0.45$ **22.** $0.3 \div 0.15$ **23.** $0.9 \div 0.01$ **24.** $0.36 \div 0.18$

25. *Postage* Refer to the table at the right.
   a. Draw a model that shows how many times greater the postage for a 1-oz letter was in 1980 than in 1965.
   b. How many times greater was the postage in 1995 than in 1960?
   c. The table does not show the price of stamps for the years 1970, 1985, 1990, and 2000. What might be appropriate stamp prices for each of these years?

U.S. Postage for a 1-oz Letter

Year	Postage
1960	$.04
1965	$.05
1975	$.13
1980	$.15
1995	$.32

Mixed Review

Solve each equation. *(Lesson 2-7)*

26. $9a = 72$ **27.** $11x = 33$ **28.** $5y = 155$ **29.** $4b = 24$ **30.** $18c = 18$

31. *Choose a Strategy* Suppose you cut a piece of string in half and then cut those pieces in half. If you continue this process, how many pieces will you have after the fifth round of cuts?

Math at Work

VETERINARIAN

If you have a love for animals, then a career as a veterinarian might be right for you. These special doctors use their problem solving skills to diagnose medical problems, interpret laboratory data, perform surgery, and prescribe appropriate medicines for creatures that cannot describe their aches and pains.

For more information about being a veterinarian, visit the Prentice Hall Web site: www.phschool.com

4-7 Dividing Decimals by Whole Numbers

What You'll Learn

▼ To divide decimals by whole numbers

...And Why

You can divide decimals by whole numbers to find travel times.

Here's How

Look for questions that
- ⊞ build understanding
- ✔ check understanding

 The Great Seto Bridge crosses Japan's Inland Sea. It is the longest road and railway suspension bridge in the world.

Source: *Guinness Book of Records*

THINK AND DISCUSS

Dividing decimals is similar to dividing whole numbers. With decimals, you place a decimal point in the quotient.

■ **EXAMPLE**   *Real-World Problem Solving*

Travel Time The Great Seto Bridge is 7.64 mi long. How long would it take to cross the bridge if you were walking at 4 mi/h?

Estimate: 7.64 ÷ 4 ≈ 8 ÷ 4 = 2

$$
\begin{array}{r}
1.91 \\
4\overline{)7.64} \\
-4 \downarrow \\
\hline
36 \\
-36 \downarrow \\
\hline
04 \\
-4 \\
\hline
0
\end{array}
$$

◄— Divide as with whole numbers. Place the decimal point in the quotient above the decimal point in the dividend. Compare the answer and estimate to determine the reasonableness of the answer.

It would take 1.91 h, or almost 2 h, to walk across the bridge.

Japan

1. ✔*Try It Out* Find each quotient.
   a. $9.12 \div 6$ b. $385.6 \div 8$ c. $17.28 \div 12$ d. $77.35 \div 17$

2. ⚎*Go a Step Further* The answer to the Example is 1.91 hours or about 2 hours. Find how many minutes 1.91 hours is by multiplying 1.91×60 minutes.

You can use patterns to divide mentally.

3. a. ⚎*Patterns* Write the next three division equations for the pattern shown.

Dividend	Divisor		Quotient
2.9	÷ 10	=	0.29
2.9	÷ 100	=	0.029
2.9	÷ 1,000	=	0.0029

   b. What happens to the quotient as the divisor increases?
   c. How is the number of zeros in each divisor related to the number of places the decimal point "moves" left?
   d. ⚎*Writing* Find $0.8 \div 100$ mentally. Explain your method.

4. ⚎*Draw a Conclusion* Write a rule for dividing a decimal by 10, by 100, or by 1,000.

Need Help? For more practice dividing, see the Skills Handbook pages 542–543.

Work Together
Exploring Division Patterns

Work with a partner. Complete each statement.

5. $1.6 \div \blacksquare = 0.16$ 6. $1.6 \div \blacksquare = 0.016$
7. $1.6 \div 20 = \blacksquare$ 8. $1.6 \div 200 = \blacksquare$

EXERCISES *On Your Own*

Find each quotient.

1. $3\overline{)204}$ 2. $328.25 \div 13$ 3. $255.5 \div 7$ 4. $11\overline{)539}$

5. $7.5 \div 3$ 6. $15.40 \div 5$ 7. $3\overline{)\$19.80}$ 8. $30.15 \div 9$

9. $14\overline{)26.6}$ 10. $33\overline{)237.6}$ 11. $10.35 \div 3$ 12. $8\overline{)89.76}$

13. $569.36 \div 22$ 14. $22\overline{)\$1,057.10}$ 15. $4.08 \div 3$ 16. $114.24 \div 56$

17. **Choose A, B, C, or D.** Which quotient is greatest?

   A. $0.075 \div 5$ B. $0.75 \div 10$ C. $0.625 \div 25$ D. $7.5 \div 10$

18. Weather On Thursday, 1.4 in. of rain fell. On Friday, 2.2 in. of rain fell. What was the mean rainfall for the two days?

19. Hobbies A pack of 15 baseball cards costs $.75. How can you use the guess and test strategy to find the cost of one card?

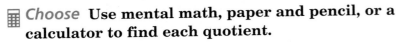

Choose Use mental math, paper and pencil, or a calculator to find each quotient.

20. $15\overline{)23.25}$

21. $\$20.70 \div 10$

22. $82\overline{)155.8}$

23. $1.5 \div 100$

24. $3 \div 100$

25. $12\overline{)\$96.36}$

26. $4.8 \div 100$

27. $3\overline{)7.32}$

28. $122.9 \div 10$

29. $8.17 \div 10$

30. $22\overline{)78.32}$

31. $15\overline{)664.5}$

32. Open-ended Describe a method for finding the thickness of a page in a book.

33. Writing How is dividing decimals different from dividing whole numbers?

34. Money A stack of 300 coins is 23.7 in. high. Find the thickness of one coin. Round to the nearest hundredth inch.

35. Research Find out the price of a jar of peanut butter at three stores in your town. Research just one size and brand. Find the mean price for that type of peanut butter.

Mixed Review

36. Choose a Strategy Solve if possible. If not, tell what additional information is needed.
  a. Twelve-year-old Jeron swam the 100-m freestyle in 29.56 s. His best time in 1993 was 29.6 s. What time does he need to swim in order to break the pool record?
  b. In how many ways can you have coins that total 15¢?

Compare. Write <, >, or = . *(Previous Course)*

37. 24×5 ▧ $600 \div 5$

38. $1,100 \div 100$ ▧ $110 \div 10$

39. 19×17 ▧ $176 + 83$

CHAPTER PROJECT

PROJECT LINK: ANALYZING

Suppose you decide to raise money for the celebration event by recycling cans. Using your calculated costs for the event, determine how much money each student in your class needs to raise.

4-8

Dividing Decimals by Decimals

What You'll Learn

▼ To divide decimals by decimals

...And Why

You can find gas mileage by dividing decimals by decimals.

Here's How

Look for questions that
∷ build understanding
✔ check understanding

THINK AND DISCUSS

To divide by a decimal, rewrite the divisor as a whole number.

■ EXAMPLE 1   Real-World Problem Solving

Pet Care Eric spent $3.12 on pet food. The food cost $0.06 per cup. How many cups of pet food did Eric purchase?

Find the quotient for $0.06\overline{)3.12}$

Multiply the divisor by a power of ten: $0.06 \times 100 = 6$
Multiply the dividend by the same number: $3.12 \times 100 = 312$

$$0.06\overline{)3.12} \quad \Rightarrow \quad \begin{array}{r} 52. \\ 6\overline{)312.} \\ -30 \\ \hline 12 \\ -12 \\ \hline 0 \end{array}$$

Estimate: Think $6 \times \blacksquare = 300$?
$6 \times 50 = 300$
Use the estimate to help place the first digit in the quotient.

Move both decimal points the same number of spaces to the right.

Check: $52 \times 0.06 = 03.12$ ✔

Compare the answer to the estimate. The quotient 52 is close to the estimate 50.

Eric purchased 52 cups of pet food.

1. ✔ **Try It Out** Find each quotient.
    a. $0.04\overline{)0.248}$ b. $38.125 \div 1.25$ c. $0.08\overline{)8.64}$

■ EXAMPLE 2

Find the quotient for $0.162 \div 0.54$.

$$0.54\overline{)0.162} \quad \Rightarrow \quad \begin{array}{r} 0.3 \\ 54.\overline{)16.2} \\ -16.2 \\ \hline 0 \end{array}$$

Estimate: Think $50 \times \blacksquare = 15.0$?
$54 > 16$ so write a zero in the ones place. $50 \times 0.3 = 15.0$
Place the first digit in the tenths place.

Move both decimal points.

Check: $0.3 \times 0.54 = 0.162$ ✔

$0.162 \div 0.54 = 0.3$

You can divide by decimals in many real-world situations.

■ **EXAMPLE 3** *Real-World Problem Solving*

Fuel Economy A family car travels 367.9 miles on 12.5 gallons of gas. To find the gas mileage to the nearest hundredth of a gallon, divide *miles driven* by *gallons of gas*.

Estimate: 367.9 ÷ 12.5 ≈ 360 ÷ 12 = 30

Use the estimate to place the first digit in the quotient.

$$
\begin{array}{r}
29.432 \\
125.\overline{)3679.000} \\
-250 \\
\hline
1179 \\
-1125 \\
\hline
540 \\
-500 \\
\hline
400 \\
-375 \\
\hline
250 \\
-250 \\
\hline
0
\end{array}
$$

12.5)367.9 ⟹

Move both decimal points the same number of spaces to the right.

← Add zeros when needed.

Divide to the thousandths place. Then round.

Round 29.432 to the hundredths place. Since the 2 in the thousandths place is less than 5, write 29.43. The gas mileage is about 29.43 mi/gal.

2. ✔ *Try It Out* Find the gas mileage to the nearest hundredth for a car that travels 335.6 miles on 15.6 gallons of gas.

3. *Reasoning* Suppose you are given a car's gas mileage to the nearest hundredth and the number of miles the car traveled. How would you find the amount of gas used?

You can use patterns to divide mentally.

Dividend	Divisor	Quotient
0.52 ÷	0.1	= ▪
0.52 ÷	0.01	= ▪
0.52 ÷	0.001	= ▪
0.52 ÷	0.0001	= ▪
0.52 ÷	0.00001	= ▪

4. **a.** ⬛*Patterns* Complete the equations at the right.

b. What happens to the quotient as the divisor decreases?

c. ⬛*Reasoning* How can you tell how many places to move the decimal point to the right?

d. Find $3.6 ÷ 0.01$ mentally. Explain what you did.

e. ⬛*Draw a Conclusion* Write a rule for dividing a decimal by 0.1, 0.01, or 0.001.

EXERCISES *On Your Own*

Find each quotient. Estimate first.

1. $29 ÷ 0.4$

2. $0.34\overline{)0.204}$

3. $51 ÷ 0.06$

4. $81 ÷ 5.4$

5. $0.5\overline{)66}$

6. $5.6\overline{)16.24}$

7. $0.04 ÷ 0.8$

8. $75.03 ÷ 6.1$

9. $6.497 ÷ 8.9$

10. $0.9\overline{)4.05}$

11. $0.1266 ÷ 0.6$

12. $7.1\overline{)39.05}$

13. $3.1\overline{)10.261}$

14. $91.8 ÷ 5.4$

15. $0.18\overline{)2.25}$

16. $1.048 ÷ 0.08$

Algebra **Solve each equation.**

17. $0.3x = 12.45$ **18.** $6.64y = 1.66$ **19.** $0.05r = 0.695$ **20.** $1.7g = 65.62$ **21.** $12.2x = 109.8$

22. **Choose A, B, or C.** Which expression is equivalent to three and eight-tenths divided by thirty-two thousandths?

A. $0.032 ÷ 3.8$ **B.** $3.8 ÷ 0.032$ **C.** $3.8 ÷ 0.32$

23. *Cost of Living* Use the chart at the right.
a. How many times greater was the price of milk in 1990 than in 1940?
b. How many times greater was the price of milk in 1980 than in 1950? Round to the nearest hundredth.

24. *School Supplies* A stack of paper measures 0.9 cm thick. Each piece of paper is 0.01 cm thick.
a. How many pieces of paper are in the stack?
b. Could each of 25 students get three pieces?

Average Milk Prices $\left(\frac{1}{2}\ \text{gal}\right)$

Year	Price
1940	$.25
1950	$.39
1960	$.49
1970	$.57
1980	$1.05
1990	$1.39

Choose Use mental math or paper and pencil to find each quotient. When necessary, round to the nearest hundredth.

25. $64.97 \div 3.2$

26. $0.09\overline{)4.05}$

27. $0.126 \div 0.6$

28. $26.03 \div 0.1$

29. $29.37 \div 4.45$

30. $5.04 \div 0.01$

31. $6.3\overline{)0.1386}$

32. $0.004 \div 0.01$

33. $6.4 \div 0.1$

34. $0.05\overline{)14.9}$

35. $0.99 \div 0.01$

36. $0.32 \div 0.002$

37. $3.25\overline{)26.8125}$

38. $3.8 \div 0.1$

39. $10.126 \div 2.3$

40. $0.85 \div 0.1$

41. *Fuel Economy* Find the gas mileage of a truck that travels 303.8 mi on 24.5 gal.

42. *Writing* Describe how to find the quotient $12.5 \div 0.04$.

Mixed Review

Write a variable expression for each word phrase. *(Lesson 2-5)*

43. x more than 14

44. 2 times v plus 2

45. p divided by q

46. 6 less than b

Write each number in words. *(Lesson 3-2)*

47. 45.927

48. 7,056

49. 457,258,654

50. 2.00008

51. 0.0054

52. *Choose a Strategy* Talisha got off the elevator at the 9th floor. She had already gone down 5, up 6, and down 3 floors. On what floor did she first enter the elevator?

✓ CHECKPOINT 2

Lessons 4-4 through 4-8

For each, find the product or quotient.

1. 5.2×6.3

2. 0.239×8.2

3. $0.13\overline{)2.132}$

4. $3.5154 \div 0.7$

5. Sam's shampoo costs $.12 per ounce. How many ounces are in a bottle that costs $2.88?

6. Cory has 0.275 L of pond water. If her test tubes are filled with 0.02 L each, how many test tubes can be completely filled?

7. *Jobs* Rosa earns $6.50 per hour as a cashier. For any time over 40 hours, she earns $9.75 per hour. Rosa worked 45 hours in a recent week. What were her wages that week?

Choose the best answer.

1. Which expression is equivalent to 100?

   A. $2^2 \times 5^2$
   B. 10^3
   C. $2^2 \times 2^5$
   D. $5^2 \times 2^3$

2. A group of 11 boys and 9 girls plans to go to a skating rink that charges $5 for each person. Which expression does *not* show the total amount the group will pay?

   F. $5 \times (11 + 9)$
   G. $(5 \times 11) + (5 \times 9)$
   H. $5 \times 11 \times 9$
   J. 5×20

3. Althea took a trip. On Monday she spent $12.53 for food, on Tuesday she spent $15.25 for food, and on Wednesday she spent $14.46 for food. What was the mean (average) amount Althea spent on food per day?

   A. $14.08
   B. $14.80
   C. $15.25
   D. $42.24

4. Which equation does *not* have 3 as its solution?

   F. $x + 2.3 = 5.3$
   G. $3.1x = 9.3$
   H. $x - 2 = 5.3$
   J. $x \div 3 = 1$

5. A ten-foot board is cut five times. Each cut is an equal distance from the previous cut. How many pieces of wood are there?

   A. 2 ft long   B. 5 pieces
   C. 6 pieces   D. 1 ft long

6. Which of the following is a solution to $x - 19 = 16 + 4 \times 2$?

   F. 5
   G. 24
   H. 40
   J. 43

Note that Exercises 7–10 have *five* answer choices.

7. A sheet of metal has a thickness of 0.006 in. What is the total thickness of a stack of 12 sheets?

   A. 72 in.   B. 7.2 in.
   C. 0.72 in.   D. 0.072 in.
   E. Not Here

8. A set of 5 videos costs $68.79. Estimate the cost of one video.

   F. less than $8
   G. less than $10
   H. between $10 and $11
   J. between $12 and $20
   K. more than $20

9. Pizza, salad, cake, and soft drinks are served at a party for 36 people. Each pizza serves 4 people. Each pound of salad and each cake serves 6 people. Each person drinks 2 soft drinks. Which cost is *not* needed to find the total cost of the food?

   A. cost of each pizza
   B. cost of each soft drink
   C. cost of renting the bowling alley
   D. cost of salad per pound
   E. cost of each cake

10. Cookies cost $.08 each. What is the greatest number you can buy with $2.00?

   F. 2   G. 16   H. 20
   J. 25   K. 160

4-9 Too Much or Too Little Information

Problem Solving Strategies

Draw a Diagram
Guess and Test
Look for a Pattern
Make a Model
Make a Table
Simulate a Problem
Solve a Simpler Problem
Use Logical Reasoning
Use Multiple Strategies
✔ Too Much or Too Little
   Information
Work Backward

THINK AND DISCUSS

Sometimes you do not have enough information to solve a problem. At other times, problems have more information than you need. You have to decide.

SAMPLE PROBLEM ....

Pablo is making a box kite out of wooden dowels and paper strips. The top and bottom of the kite are square. The sides of each square are 26.5 cm long. The dowels cost $2.20. Other supplies such as glue, string, and tape cost $4.27 altogether. The paper strips wrap around the kite. Paper strips are 13 cm wide and are sold by length in centimeters. Find the total length of the paper strips he will need. Pablo has $10.00 to spend on supplies and is wondering if he has enough money.

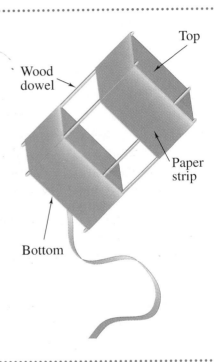

Top

Wood
dowel

Paper
strip

Bottom

READ

Read for understanding.
Summarize the problem.

PLAN

Decide on a strategy.

1. Think about the information that is given.
   a. What do you need to find out?
   b. What information do you need to solve the problem?

2. a. What is the shape of the top and bottom of the kite?
   b. What is the length of each side of the top and bottom squares?
   c. How can you use this information to solve the problem?
   d. Do you need to know the width of each paper?

3. You have decided what information you need. What unnecessary information is given?

SOLVE

Try the strategy.

4. One way to solve the problem is to find the perimeter of the square. Then double the perimeter to find the total length of paper needed for the two paper strips.
   a. What is the length of paper Pablo needs for the two strips?
   b. What is another way to solve the problem?

LOOK BACK

Think about how you solved the problem.

5. Let's find how much it will cost to make the kite.
   a. What information will help you find the total cost?
   b. What information is missing?

EXERCISES *On Your Own*

Solve if possible. If not, tell what additional information is needed.

1. *Transportation* Nathon bought two identical bicycle tires for a total of $21.90. The diameter of each tire is 20 in. The combined weight of the two tires is 2.9 lb.
   a. How much did each tire cost?
   b. What information did you use to solve part (a)?
   c. How much does one tire weigh?
   d. What information did you use to solve part (c)?

2. *Money* Matt buys some comic books. He hands the clerk $10.00 and receives $1.45 in change. Each comic book has the same price. How much does each comic book cost?

3. *Interior Decorating* A pair of curtains costs $69.99. Each curtain measures 45 in. by 98 in. The pair weighs 1.50 lb.
   a. How much does each curtain weigh?
   b. What unnecessary information is given?

4. *Savings* When Sasha was 7 years old, her mother started a college fund with $2,000. Every year she deposited the same amount into the account. Suppose she continues the pattern shown in the table. How much money will Sasha's mother have deposited when Sasha is 18 years old? (Note: Ignore interest earned.)

Sasha's College Fund

Sasha's Age	Total Amount Deposited
7 years old	$2,000
8 years old	$2,750
9 years old	$3,500
10 years old	$4,250

5. *Quilting* A quilt pattern has a 5-by-5 grid of squares. The design of the grid calls for alternating blue and red squares. How many squares of each color does the grid contain?

6. *Cost of Living* Use the chart at the right.
   a. How much more did bread cost in 1990 than in 1950?
   b. How many times greater was the price of a loaf of bread in 1970 than in 1940?

60 Years of Bread Prices (1-lb loaf)	
1930	$.04
1940	$.08
1950	$.14
1960	$.20
1970	$.24
1980	$.51
1990	$.69

Source: Bureau of Labor

7. *Horses* The record shoulder height for a horse is 78 in. A horse's height is measured in hands. One hand is about 4 in. What is the record shoulder height in hands?

8. *Jobs* Paul works for 2 hours each Monday, Wednesday, and Friday. He is saving to buy a bike that costs $245. He earns $6 per hour. How many weeks must he work to be sure he has enough money?

9. *Dressmaking* A dressmaker sent 250 dresses to several department stores. The dressmaker sent every store the same number of dresses. How many did each store receive?

10. *Telecommunications* The telephone company charged Ron for a phone call. The rates were $2.40 for the first minute and $.60 for each additional minute. For how many additional minutes was Ron charged?

11. *Hobbies* Mark collected 15 postcards. Some of the cards cost $.79 and some cost $1.19. He spent a total of $14.25. How many postcards of each price did he buy?

12. a. *Writing* Write a word problem with too much information.
    b. Write a word problem with too little information.

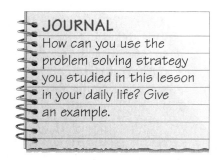

JOURNAL
How can you use the problem solving strategy you studied in this lesson in your daily life? Give an example.

Mixed Review

Use mental math to find each product or quotient.
(Lessons 4-5 and 4-7)

13. 2.3×10 14. $0.3 \div 10$ 15. 25.8×100 16. $28.7 \div 10$ 17. $579 \times 1,000$

Round each decimal to the nearest tenth. *(Lesson 3-6)*

18. 44.68 19. 8.146 20. 0.0519 21. 658.444 22. $8,291.09$

23. Marsha has 19 nickels. Jerry has 11 dimes. Who has more money? How much more? *(Previous Course)*

4-10 Patterns of Changing Metric Units

What You'll Learn

▼ To change metric units
② To use mental math to change units

...And Why

You often need to change metric units to solve problems in geography and nutrition.

Here's How

Look for questions that
▪ build understanding
✔ check understanding

THINK AND DISCUSS

① *Changing Metric Units*

Metric units are used in science and technology. They are universally recognized, and changes from one unit to another are easy to do.

You can rewrite one metric unit as another metric unit by multiplying or dividing by a power of 10.

Multiply to change from larger units to smaller units.

× 1,000   × 100   × 10

km   m   cm   mm

÷ 1,000   ÷ 100   ÷ 10

Divide to change from smaller units to larger units.

■ **EXAMPLE 1**   *Real-World Problem Solving*

Geography The distance from Earth's equator to the North Pole along the Earth's surface is 10,000,000 meters. What is the distance in kilometers?

$$\begin{array}{r} 10{,}000 \\ 1{,}000\overline{)10{,}000{,}000} \\ -\underline{1{,}000\phantom{{,}000}} \\ 0 \end{array}$$ ←—Divide by 1,000 to change m to km.

The equator is 10,000 km from the North Pole.

---

1. ▪**Look Back** In Example 1, you started with 10,000,000 meters.
   a. Is the meter a larger or smaller unit than the kilometer? smaller
   b. Is the answer greater than or less than 10,000,000? less than

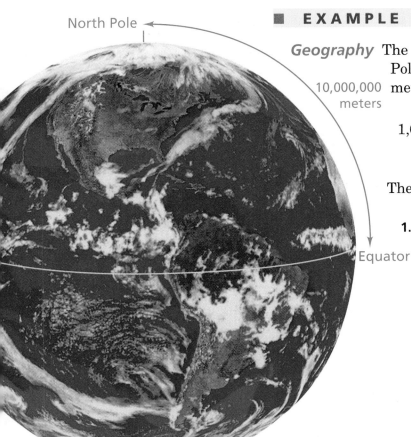

North Pole

10,000,000 meters

Equator

2. ✔**Try It Out** Complete each statement. Use the diagram on page 171 to help you decide whether to multiply or divide.
   a. One of the world's longest dogs measures 240 cm. How many meters long is this dog?

   240 cm = ▨ m

   b. A sprinter runs 60,000 m a week to train for the 400-m race event. How many kilometers is this?

   60,000 m = ▨ km

   c. The world's largest wave was about 3.36 kilometers tall. How many meters tall is this?

   3.36 km = ▨ m

QUICKreview

Common Metric Units

kL = kiloliter
L = **liter**
mL = milliliter

kg = kilogram
g = **gram**
mg = milligram

km = kilometer
m = **meter**
cm = centimeter
mm = millimeter

The most common metric units use the prefixes *kilo-*, *centi-*, and *milli-*.

Prefix	Meaning	Examples
kilo-	1,000	kilometer (1,000 m), kilogram (1,000 g)
centi-	$\frac{1}{100}$ or 0.01	centimeter (or 0.01 m), centigram (or 0.01 g)
milli-	$\frac{1}{1,000}$ or 0.001	milliliter (or 0.001 L), millimeter (or 0.001 m)

Knowing what the prefixes mean can help you more easily change units. For example, to write 2 kilometers as meters, you multiply 2 by 1,000 to get 2,000 meters.

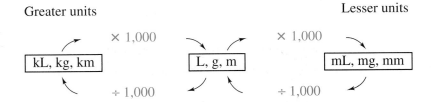

3. Change each measure to either liters, meters, or grams.
   a. 2,000 mL   b. 3.7 kL   c. 830 mL   d. 6,300 mg
   e. 0.5 km   f. 7,525 cm   g. 1.56 kg   h. 75 cm

4. ♣*Reasoning* When you are changing units, how do you decide whether you multiply or divide? Explain.

❷ Using Mental Math to Change Units

You can use mental math to multiply or divide by powers of 10. The important part of this process is deciding the direction and number of places to move the decimal point.

MULTIPLYING AND DIVIDING BY POWERS OF 10

To **multiply** by a power of 10, move the decimal point one place to the **right** for each zero in the power of 10.	To **divide** by a power of 10, move the decimal point one place to the **left** for each zero in the power of 10.

When you understand the pattern, you simply move the decimal point.

■ **EXAMPLE 2**   *Real-World Problem Solving*

Nutrition   A banana contains 950 mg of protein. How many grams of protein does a banana contain?

$$950 \text{ mg} \div 1{,}000 = \underline{\ \ ?\ \ } \text{ g} \quad \longleftarrow \begin{array}{l}\text{Divide by 1,000 to change}\\ \text{milligrams to grams.}\end{array}$$

$$950 \Rightarrow 0.950 \quad \longleftarrow \text{Move the decimal point 3 places to the left.}$$

A banana contains 0.95 g of protein.

5. ✔ *Try It Out* Complete each statement. Use the charts on pages 171 and 172 when needed.

    a. 102.4 mL = ▩ L   **b.** 745.3 cm = ▩ m

    c. 26.8 kg = ▩ g   **d.** 0.5L = ▩ mL

EXERCISES *On Your Own*

Change each measure to meters.

1. 1.3 km   **2.** 500 mm   **3.** 20 cm   **4.** 6 km   **5.** 3700 mm   **6.** 40 cm

Change each measure to liters.

7. 0.005 kL   **8.** 120 mL   **9.** 3070 mL   **10.** 0.61 kL   **11.** 503 mL   **12.** 6.4 kL

Change each measure to grams.

13. 8 kg   **14.** 7,000 mg   **15.** 0.24 kg   **16.** 34,000 mg   **17.** 500 mg   **18.** 0.07 kg

▦ **19. Choose A, B, C, or D.** Which is *not* equivalent to the others?
(*Hint:* Write each measure in meters.)

    A. 355.5 cm   **B.** 35.55 m   **C.** 0.03555 km **D.** 35,550 mm

20. *Quality Control* A bottle is supposed to contain 1 L of juice. The table shows several quality control test measurements.
a. Write each measurement in milliliters.
b. Which measurement is furthest away from 1 L? Explain.

Test #	Measurement
1	1,002.3 mL
2	1.001 L
3	999.7 mL
4	0.996 L

Complete each statement.

21. 8.6 mm = ■ cm

22. ■ m = 8,600 cm

23. 10,800 cm = ■ m

24. ■ km = 300,000 cm

25. 2.1 km = ■ m

26. 356 mm = ■ cm

27. 4,500 mL = ■ L

28. 35,000 mL = ■ L

29. ■ mL = 1.2 kL

30. 8.2 L = ■ mL

31. ■ mL = 0.5 kL

32. ■ L = 6,000 mL

33. *Writing* Suppose you want to make a bird feeder that holds about 500 mL of birdseed. Explain how you could make it out of an empty 2-L soft drink bottle.

34. *Nutrition* A cup of whole milk has 8.5 g of fat. A cup of skim milk has 400 mg of fat. Find the difference in fat content per cup.

35. *Physics* Light travels at 299,792,458 meters per second. How many kilometers does light travel in a second?

36. *Algebra* Write an expression for changing kilograms to grams.

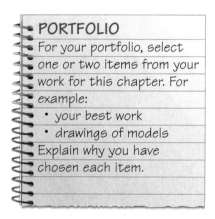

PORTFOLIO
For your portfolio, select one or two items from your work for this chapter. For example:
• your best work
• drawings of models
Explain why you have chosen each item.

Mixed Review

Choose an appropriate metric unit of measure for each.
(Lessons 3-8 and 3-9)

37. a tank of gas

38. a can of soda

39. a piano

40. a spoonful of honey

Write a word phrase for each variable expression.
(Lesson 2-5)

41. $x \div 5$

42. $s + 14$

43. $9a$

44. $42 - b$

45. $2c + 42$

46. *Choose a Strategy* Your town has 8 soccer teams. They are playing in a tournament. Each team will be out of the tournament after one loss. How many games will be played?

CHAPTER PROJECT

Plan a Celebration The Project Link questions on pages 137, 155, and 162 should help you to complete your project. Here is a checklist to help you gather the parts of your project together.

- ✔ the cost of individual items, the amount of each item needed, and the original estimate
- ✔ the actual cost of the event
- ✔ the amount each class member needs to raise

Now use what you have learned in the chapter to convince the class and your teacher that your plan should be adopted. Let them know that this celebration is well planned and affordable. Make a presentation including all your calculations in order to justify the expenses.

Reflect and Revise

Review your project with a friend or someone at home. Are your costs realistic? Are your calculations complete and accurate? Could items be cut to reduce the total amount that would need to be raised? Is the information presented in a clear and convincing manner? If necessary, make changes to improve your project.

Web Extension

Prentice Hall's Internet site contains information you might find helpful as you complete your project. Visit www.phschool.com/mgm1/ch4 for some links and ideas related to planning celebrations.

Estimating Products and Quotients 4-1

You can round to estimate decimal products and quotients. You can use compatible numbers to estimate products and quotients.

Estimate using rounding or compatible numbers.

1. 23.78×5.3 **2.** $34.1 \div 6.67$ **3.** 4.09×82.3 **4.** $84.6 \div 1.94$

Exponents 4-2

You can use an **exponent** to show how many times a number, or **base,** is used as a factor. A number expressed using an exponent is called a **power.** The order of operations includes powers.

Simplify each expression.

5. 4^7 **6.** $500 \div 5^2$ **7.** $100 - 2 \times 6^2$ **8.** $3^2 - 2^3 + 30$ **9.** $(4^2 - 1) \div 5^3$

10. *Writing* State the order of operations. Give an example.

The Distributive Property 4-3

You can use the **distributive property** to simplify expressions involving multiplication and addition or subtraction.

Complete each equation.

11. $5 \times 97 = (5 \times \blacksquare) + (5 \times 7)$ **12.** $8 \times 27 = 8 \times (\blacksquare - 3)$

Simplify using the distributive property.

13. $(11 \times 6) + (9 \times 6)$ **14.** $5 \times (4 + 12)$ **15.** $(8 \times 21) - (8 \times 9)$

16. 4×59 **17.** $9 \times (50 - 9) - 27$ **18.** $6 \times 3 + 6 \times 2 - 1$

Multiplying Decimals and Dividing Decimals 4-4, 4-5, 4-6, 4-7, 4-8

You can model multiplication and division of decimals.

19. Write a multiplication sentence to describe the model.

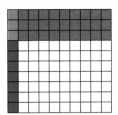

20. Write a division sentence to describe the model.

To multiply decimal numbers, count the number of decimal places in both factors to find how many places are needed in the product.

To divide by a decimal, "move" the decimal point in the divisor to make it a whole number. Then "move" the decimal point in the dividend the same number of places.

Find each product or quotient. Use models if they help you.

21. 3.215×0.04

22. 1.5×30.72

23. $4.5 \div 6$

24. $3.2\overline{)96}$

25. $1.25\overline{)8.3}$

26. $0.645 \times 1,000$

27. $7.2 \div 12$

28. 0.15×0.75

Problem Solving Strategies
4-9

Some problems have too much or too little information.

Solve if possible. If not possible, tell what additional information you need.

29. Mr. Chen's class wants to go to a game. Tickets cost $10. Food costs $7. Students will share evenly the $125 rental fee for a bus. How much will it cost each student?

30. Denika is 152.4 cm tall and weighs 44.5 kg. Her twin sister, Janika, is 1.1 cm taller and weighs 0.9 kg more. How tall is Janika?

Patterns of Changing Metric Units
4-10

You can change metric units by moving the decimal point.

Complete each statement.

31. ▓ m = 2.5 km

32. 57,000 mL = ▓ L

33. 1,257 mg = ▓ g

34. 8,090 L = ▓ kL

35. ▓ kg = 300,000 mg

36. 150 mm = ▓ cm

1. Estimate using rounding.
 a. 7.3×29.7
 b. 4.63×50.4
 c. 75.1×2.93
 d. 9.4×4.03

2. Estimate using compatible numbers.
 a. 21.14×4.89
 b. $17.9 \div 3.6$
 c. $98.13 \div 24.27$
 d. 38.95×2.78

3. Write a multiplication sentence for the model below.

4. Simplify each expression.
 a. 5^4
 b. $4^2 \times 2$
 c. $150 \div 5^2$
 d. $11 \times 21 - 4^2$

5. Choose A, B, C, or D. Which expression equals 108?
 A. $3^2 \times 2^2$
 B. $3^2 \times 2^3$
 C. $3^3 \times 2^2$
 D. $3^3 \times 2^3$

6. Complete.
 a. $8 \times 58 = (8 \times \blacksquare) + (8 \times 8)$
 b. $6 \times 73 = 6 \times (\blacksquare + 3)$

7. *Mental Math* Use mental math to simplify each expression.
 a. 5×102
 b. 4×58

8. Use the distributive property to simplify each expression.
 a. $5 \times (6 + 10)$
 b. $(7 \times 6) + (7 \times 5)$
 c. $9 \times (3 + 10)$
 d. $2 \times 19 + 2 \times 28$

9. *Writing* Explain how to model the quotient $0.6 \div 0.12$.

10. Find each product.
 a. $\begin{array}{r} 9.063 \\ \times\ 24 \\ \hline \end{array}$
 b. $\begin{array}{r} 0.85 \\ \times\ 0.06 \\ \hline \end{array}$
 c. $\begin{array}{r} 5.2 \\ \times\ 0.17 \\ \hline \end{array}$

11. *Entertainment* Jamal bought three tickets to a matinee movie. The matinee tickets cost $2.00 less than the evening movie tickets. Each matinee ticket cost $4.50. He paid with a $20-dollar bill and two quarters. How much change did Jamal receive?

12. Find each quotient.
 a. $3.2\overline{)8.832}$
 b. $45\overline{)\$32.85}$
 c. $0.4 \div 0.25$
 d. $63.72 \div 0.03$

13. *Shopping* Seedless grapes cost $1.79 per pound. Find the cost of a bunch of grapes that weighs 2.2 lb. Round your answer up to the next cent.

14. Complete each sentence.
 a. $672 \text{ mm} = \blacksquare \text{ cm}$
 b. $\blacksquare \text{ L} = 25{,}040 \text{ mL}$
 c. $35.1 \text{ kg} = \blacksquare \text{ g}$
 d. $\blacksquare \text{ L} = 0.125 \text{ kL}$
 e. $514 \text{ mg} = \blacksquare \text{ g}$
 f. $42.9 \text{ m} = \blacksquare \text{ cm}$

15. *Algebra* Write an expression for changing kilometers to centimeters.

16. Choose A or B. Which model represents 0.4×0.6?

A.   **B.**

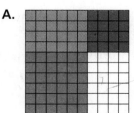
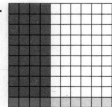

Choose the best answer.

1. Which rounded estimate represents the product 34.3 × 5.98?

   A. 34 × 6   **B.** 35 × 6
   C. 35 × 5   **D.** 34 × 5

2. What is the best unit of measurement to use to measure the length of a driveway?

   A. millimeters   **B.** centimeters
   C. meters   **D.** kilometers

3. Which number represents the median for this set of data? 50, 54, 62, 69, 70, 70, 81

   A. 70   **B.** 455
   C. 65   **D.** 69

4. Kevin bought six muffins for $2.39. He paid the cashier with three one-dollar bills and some pennies. He received no pennies in change. How many pennies must he have given the cashier?

   A. 1   **B.** 2   **C.** 3   **D.** 4

5. Where would you insert parentheses so that 6 − 2 × 9 ÷ 3 + 15 has the value 5?

   A. (6 − 2) × 9 ÷ 3 + 15
   B. 6 − (2 × 9) ÷ 3 + 15
   C. 6 − 2 × (9 ÷ 3) + 15
   D. 6 − 2 × 9 ÷ (3 + 15)

6. Which has a quotient equal to 0.317 ÷ 0.08?

   A. 317 ÷ 8   **B.** 31.7 ÷ 8
   C. 317 ÷ 0.8   **D.** 3.17 ÷ 8

7. Kiona has sixty-five cents in quarters, dimes, and nickels. (She has at least one of each of these coins.) What number of nickels can she *not* have?

   A. 1   **B.** 2   **C.** 3   **D.** 4

8. Which number is equal to 4.3?

   A. four and thirteen hundredths
   B. four hundred and three
   C. forty-three
   D. four and three tenths

9. In which set are the numbers all between 0.5 and 1.95?

   A. 0.504, 1.9, 1.951
   B. 0.194, 1, 1.94
   C. 0.618, 1, 1.009
   D. 0.6, 1.04, 2

10. Look at the table below. Which two students have the highest mean (average) scores?

Student	Test 1	Test 2	Mean
Keisha	100	88	▧
Justine	85	95	▧
Greg	77	83	▧
Pritpal	90	92	▧

   A. Pritpal and Justine
   B. Greg and Justine
   C. Justine and Keisha
   D. Keisha and Pritpal

11. Which equation is true given $y = 6$?

   A. $4y = 28$
   B. $88 + y = 92$
   C. $42 \div y = 6$
   D. $73 - y = 67$

12. Which rule best describes this number pattern? 1, 3, 5, 7, 9, 11, 13, . . .

   A. List only prime numbers.
   B. Add 2 repeatedly.
   C. Subtract 2 repeatedly.
   D. Multiply by 2 repeatedly.

Investigating Fractions

5

HOME COURT ADVANTAGE

In Malcolm's daydream, he is floating in the air on the way to a slam dunk. In reality, he is tossing pieces of paper into a wastebasket. He makes some shots, and he misses others.

Compare Basketball Statistics Your project will be to record and compare attempts and baskets made by the players on your own imaginary basketball team. You can shoot baskets with a real basketball on a real court, or you can toss pieces of paper into a wastebasket.

• How to solve problems by solving a simpler problem

PROBLEM SOLVING

Discovering Divisibility Rules

...gi... says our nation is "indivisible, with
...ce for all." The United States of America may not
...ut numbers are.

...c the numbers in the tables below.

Divisible by 2	Not Divisible by 2
0 14 202 5,756 798 80 120	9 13 467 4,005 99 42,975

a. ✎ **Writing** Write a definition of the word *divisible*.

b. Give two more numbers that are divisible by 2. Give two more that are not.

c. ✎ **Draw a Conclusion** Give a rule for numbers that are divisible by 2.

d. **Which** of the numbers in the table that are divisible by 2 are also divisible by 5? Divisible by 10?

e. Which of the numbers in the table that are not divisible by 2 are divisible by 5? Divisible by 10?

THINK AND DISCUSS

▼ Divisibility by 1, 2, 5, and 10

Divisibility is the ability of one whole number to divide into another with no remainder. The chart below gives divisibility rules for 1, 2, 5, and 10.

Divisible By	Rule
1	All numbers are divisible by 1.
2	All even numbers are divisible by 2.
5	Numbers ending in 5 or 0 are divisible by 5.
10	Numbers ending in 0 are divisible by 10.

An *even number* is a whole number that is exactly divisible by 2.
An *odd number* is a whole number that is *not* exactly divisible by 2.

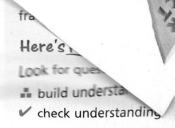

fra...

Here's...

Look for que...

⚏ build underst...

✔ check understanding

■ EXAMPLE 1

State whether the first number is divisible by the second.

a. 715; 5

Yes, 715 is divisible by 5, since it ends in 5.

b. 1,020; 10

Yes, 1,020 is divisible by 10, since it ends in 0.

2. ✔ Try It Out State whether 27,215 is divisible by 5 or 10.

▼2 Divisibility by 3 and 9

You can find whether a number is divisible by 3 by adding up the digits. If their sum is divisible by 3, then the number is, too.

■ EXAMPLE 2

Is 2,571 divisible by 3?

$2 + 5 + 7 + 1 = 15$ ◄— Find the sum of the digits.

$15 \div 3 = 5$ ◄— Find whether the sum is divisible by 3.

The sum of the digits is divisible by 3, so 2,571 is divisible by 3.

3. ✔ Try It Out Is 6,319 divisible by 3?

The divisibility rule for 9 is like the divisibility rule for 3.

4. a. ⁜ Mental Math Is 99 divisible by 9?
  b. What is the sum of the digits of the number 99? Is this sum divisible by 9?
  c. Is 66 divisible by 9?
  d. What is the sum of the digits of the number 66? Is this sum divisible by 9?
  e. ⁜ Reasoning Give a rule for divisibility by 9.

HISTORY
The Greek mathematician Plato (427?–348 B.C.) wrote about the number 5,040 in his work *The Laws*. He stated that 5,040 is divisible by 60 numbers, including 1 through 10.

Source: *Number Theory*

EXERCISES *On Your Own*

Find whether the first number is divisible by the second.

1. 525; 5   **2.** 848,960; 10   **3.** 2,385; 10   **4.** 36,928; 1   **5.** 4,673; 2   **6.** 53,559; 5

7. 99,718; 2   **8.** 202,470; 5   **9.** 60,714; 3   **10.** 22,996; 9   **11.** 757,503; 9   **12.** 333,335; 3

Mental Math **State whether each number is divisible by 1, 2, 3, 5, 9, or 10.**

13. 105 **14.** 15,345 **15.** 40,020 **16.** 70,641 **17.** 2,021,112 **18.** 8,516

Find the digit that makes each number divisible by 9.

19. 9,0▨5 **20.** 2,▨18 **21.** 34,76▨ **22.** ▨7,302 **23.** 2▨6,555 **24.** 19,76▨,228

25. *Open-ended* Find a four-digit number that is divisible by 1, 2, 3, 5, 9, and 10.

26. *Reasoning* If a number is divisible by 5, must it also be divisible by 10? Use an example to support your answer.

27. Choose A, B, C, or D. The five sides of the Pentagon in Washington, D.C., are equal in length. The perimeter of the building is divisible by 5 and 10. Which of the following could be the length of a side?

   A. 351 ft **B.** 352 ft **C.** 353 ft **D.** 357 ft

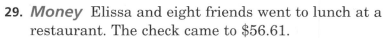

28. *Writing* Describe how you can use a calculator to tell if one number is divisible by another. Do you think it is easier to find divisibility using mental math or a calculator? Explain.

29. *Money* Elissa and eight friends went to lunch at a restaurant. The check came to $56.61.
   a. Can the group split the check into equal parts?
   b. Write a possible divisibility rule for dividing a decimal by 9. Use examples to support your answer.

30. Use the numbers at the right.
   a. Which numbers are divisible by both 2 and 3?
   b. *Calculator* Which numbers are divisible by 6?
   c. Use your results to write a divisibility rule for 6.

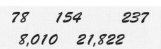

78   154   237
8,010   21,822

Mixed Review

Round to the place of the underlined digit. *(Lesson 3-6)*

31. 3.9<u>5</u>7 **32.** 34<u>5</u>.008 **33.** 32,<u>0</u>19.8 **34.** 16.9<u>3</u>07 **35.** 0.<u>5</u>2709 **36.** 42.0<u>6</u>52

37. Efra drinks two juice packs a day. Each pack contains 355 mL. How many liters of juice does she drink in one week? *(Lesson 4-10)*

5-2 Using Models and Factor Trees

A perfect number is a number that is the sum of all its factors except itself. The lowest perfect number is 6, since $6 = 1 + 2 + 3$. The next perfect number is 28.

Work Together *Experimenting with Composite Numbers*

1. Use graph paper. How many rectangles with different shapes can you form using exactly 12 squares?

2. What are the dimensions of each rectangle?

3. ▪ *Geometry* Does a 4-by-3 rectangle have the same shape as a 3-by-4 rectangle? Explain.

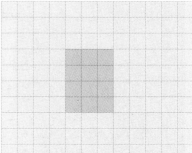

THINK AND DISCUSS

▼ *Prime and Composite Numbers*

The numbers 1, 2, 3, 4, 6, and 12 are factors of 12. One number is a **factor** of another if it divides into that number with no remainder.

4. ▪ *Reasoning* Compare the dimensions of the rectangles formed using exactly 12 squares to the factors of 12.

5. Draw rectangles to find all the factors of 17 and of 20.

You call a number that has exactly two factors, 1 and itself, a **prime number.** A number that has more than two factors is called a **composite number.**

6. ▪ *Modeling* Use a prime number of squares. How many rectangles with different shapes can you form?

7. Use a composite number of squares. Describe the number of rectangles with different shapes you can form.

8. ▪ *Explain* Why is the number 1 considered to be neither prime nor composite?

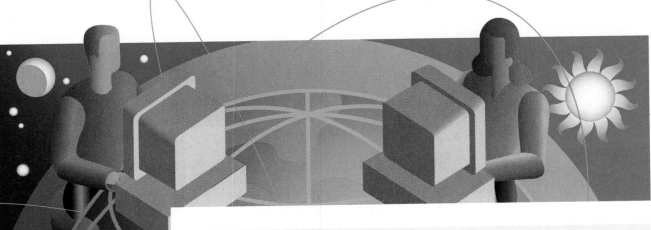

■ **EXAMPLE 1**

Tell whether 9 is prime or composite.

Draw the rectangles ← that can be made from exactly 9 squares.

The dimensions of the rectangles show that the factors of 9 are 1, 3, and 9. So, 9 is composite.

9. ✔ *Try It Out* Tell whether the number is prime or composite.
   a. 8   b. 23   c. 35   d. 46

▼2 *Prime Factorization*

A composite number is divisible by its prime factors. You can find these prime factors using a **factor tree.** Two factor trees for the number 36 are shown.

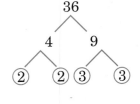

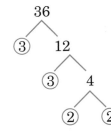

The greatest prime number found so far has 2,098,960 digits. It was found in 1999 over the Internet with a team of more than 2,000 partners.

10. a. ⁑*Reasoning* How are the two factor trees alike? How are they different?
    b. Name the prime factors of 36.

11. ⁑*Analyze* How can you use divisibility rules to begin a factor tree?

You can write a composite number as a product of its prime factors. This product is the **prime factorization** of the number. If you like, you can use exponents for factors that are repeated.

■ EXAMPLE 2

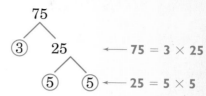

Find the prime factorization of 75 using a factor tree.

75 = 3 × 25

25 = 5 × 5

The prime factorization of 75 is $3 \times 5 \times 5$, or 3×5^2.

PROBLEM SOLVING HINT

Circle each prime factor as soon as it appears in your factor tree.

12. ✔*Try It Out* Find the prime factorization of 42.

EXERCISES *On Your Own*

1. The rectangles that can be formed using exactly 16 squares are shown below. List all the factors of 16.

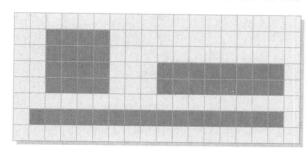

Sketch all the rectangles with different shapes that can be formed using exactly the given number of squares. List all the factors of each number. Tell whether each number is prime or composite.

2. 15	**3.** 3	**4.** 28	**5.** 21	**6.** 11	**7.** 18

Tell whether each number is prime or composite.

8. 55	**9.** 51	**10.** 103	**11.** 100	**12.** 59	**13.** 83
14. 43	**15.** 19	**16.** 72	**17.** 90	**18.** 44	**19.** 7
20. 80	**21.** 86	**22.** 93	**23.** 71	**24.** 150	**25.** 56

26. Writing Sketch all the rectangles with different shapes that can be formed using exactly 24 squares. Explain how to use your diagram to find the factors of 24 and to tell if 24 is a prime or composite number.

Copy and complete each factor tree.

27.

28.

29.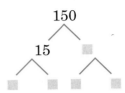

Find the prime factorization using a factor tree.

30. 30   **31.** 63   **32.** 120   **33.** 275   **34.** 50   **35.** 32

36. 45   **37.** 90   **38.** 143   **39.** 160   **40.** 108   **41.** 531

42. Use exponents to write the prime factorization $2 \times 2 \times 2 \times 3 \times 3 \times 5$.

43. Two prime numbers that differ by 2, such as 3 and 5, are called *twin primes*. Find all twin primes that are less than 100.

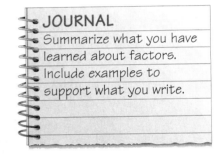

JOURNAL
Summarize what you have learned about factors. Include examples to support what you write.

Calculator Find the number with the given prime factorization.

44. $3 \times 17 \times 17 \times 17 \times 47$ **45.** $7 \times 7 \times 17 \times 23 \times 23$

Mixed Review

Write a decimal for the given words. *(Lesson 3-1)*

46. forty-five hundredths   **47.** nine tenths   **48.** six hundredths

Choose Use tiles, mental math, or a calculator to solve each equation. *(Lesson 2-6)*

49. $k + 8 = 14$ **50.** $m - 2 = 15$ **51.** $x + 96 = 117$ **52.** $58 = s - 19$ **53.** $456 - a = 20$

54. Choose a Strategy Guillermo has 20 dimes and nickels altogether. The total value of the coins is $1.35. How many dimes does Guillermo have?

Greatest Common Factor

What You'll Learn

▼ To find the greatest common factor by listing factors

▼ To find the greatest common factor using prime factorization

...And Why

You can use the greatest common factor to decide how to share items in a collection.

Here's How

Look for questions that
- ⊞ build understanding
- ✔ check understanding

Work Together
Investigating Common Factors

One set of classic comic books contains 18 books, and the other contains 24 books. Each set can be divided equally among the Collectors Club members present at the club meeting.

1. ⊞ **Number Sense** Is it possible only five members are present? Explain.

2. Is it possible only three members are present? Explain.

3. What must be true about the number of members present?

4. List all the possible numbers of members present. What is the greatest possible number?

THINK AND DISCUSS

▼ Finding the GCF By Listing Factors

Factors that are the same for two or more numbers are **common factors.** The **greatest common factor (GCF)** of two or more numbers is the greatest number that is a factor of every number.

■ EXAMPLE 1

Find the GCF of 18 and 30.

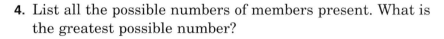

18: 1, 2, 3, 6, 9, 18
30: 1, 2, 3, 5, 6, 10, 15, 30   ⟵ List the factors for each number. Then circle the common factors.

The GCF is 6, the greatest of the common factors.

5. ✔ **Try It Out** Find the GCF of each set of numbers.
   a. 6, 21   b. 18, 45   c. 28, 42

6. ⊞ **Explain** How can you find the GCF of three numbers?

▼2 *Using Prime Factorizations to Find the GCF*

You can also use prime factorizations to find the GCF of a set of numbers.

■ **EXAMPLE 2**

Use prime factorizations to find the GCF of 27 and 36.

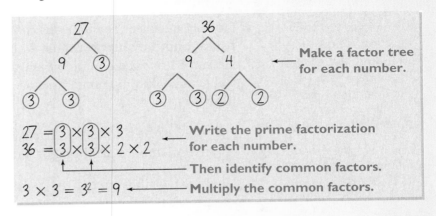

The GCF of 27 and 36 is 9.

7. ✔ *Try It Out* Use prime factorizations to find the GCF.
   a. 12, 32   **b.** 42, 90   **c.** 18, 48

8. a. Make a list to find the GCF of 28 and 33.
   b. Use prime factorizations to find the GCF of 28 and 33. Explain why the GCF is harder to find with this method.
   c. ♣ *Draw a Conclusion* When using prime factorizations, how do you know that the GCF of a set of numbers is 1?

EXERCISES *On Your Own*

Make a list to find the GCF of each set of numbers.

1. 14, 35   **2.** 24, 25   **3.** 10, 18   **4.** 15, 19   **5.** 24, 45   **6.** 11, 23

7. 9, 16   **8.** 25, 32   **9.** 30, 35   **10.** 26, 34   **11.** 12, 15, 21   **12.** 6, 8, 12

Use prime factorizations to find the GCF of each set of numbers.

13. 22, 104   **14.** 64, 125   **15.** 27, 30   **16.** 30, 49   **17.** 48, 54   **18.** 32, 40

19. 44, 52   **20.** 32, 56   **21.** 13, 120   **22.** 6, 57, 102   **23.** 17, 51, 85   **24.** 45, 90, 150

25. *Writing* What is the GCF of any two prime numbers? Explain.

26. *Open-ended* The GCF of 18 and some number is 6. What are three possible values for the number?

Mixed Review

Find each answer. *(Lessons 2-3 and 4-3)*

27. $8 - 2 \times 3 + 5$ **28.** $6 + 2 \times (12 \div 4)$ **29.** $(3 + 5) \times 10 - 4$ **30.** $7 - 5 \times (3 - 2)$

Add or subtract. Use models if they help you. *(Lesson 3-5)*

31. $0.8 + 0.5$ **32.** $1.2 - 0.7$ **33.** $0.56 + 0.9$ **34.** $2.59 - 0.83$ **35.** $1.8 - 0.09$

Find each product. *(Lesson 4-5)*

36. 0.24×7 **37.** 4.1×0.5 **38.** 6.2×1.1 **39.** 5.02×0.09 **40.** 6.35×2.6

41. *Choose a Strategy* The houses on Twelfth Avenue are numbered in order from 1 through 85. How many house numbers contain at least one digit 3?

Math at Work

PILOT

If you like to fly, then a career as a pilot may be right for you. Most pilots are involved in transporting people and cargo. Others have unusual tasks such as crop-dusting, testing aircraft, monitoring traffic, and rescuing injured persons. Pilots use their mathematical skills to choose a route, altitude, and speed that will provide the fastest, safest, and smoothest flight. Pilots must also calculate the speed they must reach in order to take off. To do this, they consider the height of the airport, the outside temperature, the weight of the aircraft, and the speed and direction of the wind.

For more information about being a pilot, visit the Prentice Hall Web site: www.phschool.com

PROBLEM SOLVING PRACTICE ★★★★★

Choose the best answer.

1. A quiz show contestant was asked to pick the equation having the solution $x = 20$. Which equation should she pick?

   A. $x - 20 = 40$
   B. $2x = 22$
   C. $x + 30 = 50$
   D. $x \div 2 = 40$

2. Boxes 12 inches tall are being stacked next to boxes 18 inches tall. What is the shortest height at which the stacks will be the same height?

   F. 216 inches
   G. 36 inches
   H. 32 inches
   J. 30 inches

3. Natraj has 36 students in his dance class. He plans to divide them into equal groups of 2 or more. What is the greatest number of students that a group can hold?

   A. 2
   B. 4
   C. 9
   D. 18

4. Tyrone has 30 oatmeal cookies and 48 chocolate chip cookies to package in plastic bags. Each bag must contain the same number of cookies. Tyrone wants one type of cookie in each bag. He also wants the greatest possible number in each bag. How many cookies can he put in each bag?

   F. 6
   G. 8
   H. 12
   J. 24

5. Mark subtracted 7.2 from 10. He got 2.8 for an answer. Which number sentence should he use to check his answer?

   A. $10 + 2.8 = 12.8$
   B. $10 \times 2.8 = 28$
   C. $2.8 + 7.2 = 10$
   D. $7.2 \times 10 = 72$

Please note that items 6–8 have *five* answer choices.

6. A family rented a car for 5 days. The cost was $9.95 per day plus $.18 per mile for each mile driven over 500 miles. The family drove 970 miles. Which number sentence could be used to find the total cost of renting the car?

   F. $T = (9.95 \times 5) + (970 - 500) \times 0.18$
   G. $T = (9.95 \times 5) + (970 \times 0.18)$
   H. $T = 9.95 \times 5 \times 970 \times 0.18$
   J. $T = 9.95 \times 5 + (970 + 500) \times 0.18$
   K. Not Here

7. Jolinda earns $5.75 per hour as a lifeguard. She works from 8 to 20 hours per week, depending on the weather. Which is a reasonable estimate of her weekly earnings?

   A. less than $20
   B. less than $40
   C. more than $40 but less than $120
   D. more than $120
   E. Not Here

8. A steak weighing 1.4 pounds cost $4.06. What was the cost per pound?

   F. $.29
   G. $.34
   H. $2.90
   J. $2.66
   K. $5.68

5-4 Using Fraction Models

What You'll Learn

▼ To model fractions
▼ To round fractions

...And Why

You'll use fractions for measurements in real-world situations, such as data collection.

Here's How

Look for questions that
⬛ build understanding
✔ check understanding

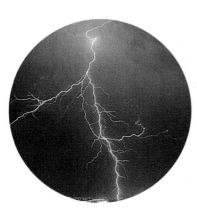

A flash of lightning lasts for about $\frac{1}{100}$ of a second. That's quicker than the blink of an eye!

THINK AND DISCUSS

▼ 1 Modeling Fractions

A **fraction model** shows a fraction's numerator and denominator as shaded parts and total parts.

numerator ⟶ $\frac{1}{6}$ ⟵ shaded part
denominator ⟶ ⟵ total parts

⬛ **EXAMPLE 1**

Name the fraction modeled.

a.

Four of six parts are shaded, so the fraction is $\frac{4}{6}$.

b.

Two of three parts are shaded, so the fraction is $\frac{2}{3}$.

1. ✔ **Try It Out** Name the fraction modeled.

a.    b.

2. Model the fractions $\frac{2}{6}$, $\frac{3}{4}$, $\frac{6}{10}$, and $\frac{4}{5}$.

3. ⬛ **Reasoning** What number is represented when *all* the parts in a fraction model are shaded? Explain.

▼ 2 Rounding Fractions

You can round fractions to the nearest half unit.

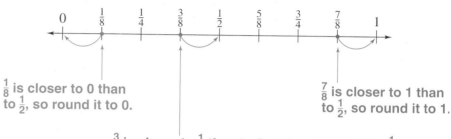

$\frac{1}{8}$ is closer to 0 than to $\frac{1}{2}$, so round it to 0.

$\frac{7}{8}$ is closer to 1 than to $\frac{1}{2}$, so round it to 1.

$\frac{3}{8}$ is closer to $\frac{1}{2}$ than to 0 or 1, so round it to $\frac{1}{2}$.

ROUNDING FRACTIONS

Round a fraction to 0 when the numerator is much less than the denominator. Examples: $\frac{1}{10}, \frac{2}{25}$

Round a fraction to $\frac{1}{2}$ when the numerator is about half the denominator. Examples: $\frac{3}{8}, \frac{23}{50}$

Round a fraction to 1 when the numerator is about equal to the denominator. Examples: $\frac{5}{6}, \frac{99}{100}$

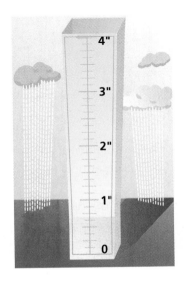

■ **EXAMPLE 2**   *Real-World Problem Solving*

⚘ *Weather* A science team uses a rain gauge to collect local rainfall data. It decides to round to the nearest half inch. How should the team round $\frac{11}{16}$ inch?

$\frac{11}{16}$ is closer to $\frac{1}{2}$ than to 0 or 1, so round to $\frac{1}{2}$ in.

The team should round $\frac{11}{16}$ inch to $\frac{1}{2}$ inch.

4. ✔ *Try It Out* Round each weight to the nearest half ounce.

   a. $\frac{9}{10}$ oz   **b.** $\frac{1}{64}$ oz   **c.** $\frac{5}{8}$ oz   **d.** $\frac{7}{16}$ oz   **e.** $\frac{30}{32}$ oz

EXERCISES *On Your Own*

Modeling **Name the fraction modeled.**

1.

2.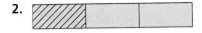

3.

4.

5.

6.

Modeling **Model each fraction.**

7. $\frac{1}{5}$ **8.** $\frac{9}{12}$ **9.** $\frac{3}{3}$ **10.** $\frac{3}{6}$ **11.** $\frac{7}{10}$ **12.** $\frac{8}{12}$

13. $\frac{5}{6}$ **14.** $\frac{4}{4}$ **15.** $\frac{4}{5}$ **16.** $\frac{1}{8}$ **17.** $\frac{4}{12}$ **18.** $\frac{2}{10}$

19. *Writing* How are the models at the right similar? How are they different?

20. Choose A, B, C, or D. Which figure models $\frac{3}{8}$?

A.   B.   C.   D.

Round each fraction to the nearest half unit.

21. [number line from 0 to 1 with $\frac{1}{2}$, $\frac{7}{8}$ marked, point near $\frac{7}{8}$]

22. [number line from 0 to 1 with $\frac{3}{16}$, $\frac{1}{2}$ marked, point near $\frac{3}{16}$]

23. [number line from 0 to 1 with $\frac{3}{10}$, $\frac{1}{2}$ marked, point near $\frac{3}{10}$]

24. Round each fraction at the right to the nearest half unit.

25. *Open-ended* Write three fractions that are close to 0, three that are close to $\frac{1}{2}$, and three that are close to 1.

26. *Time Management* Suppose you keep a record of how you spend your time, to the nearest half hour. How would you round 48 minutes? 20 minutes?

$$\frac{3}{30} \qquad \frac{7}{9} \qquad \frac{1}{10}$$

$$\frac{38}{45} \qquad \frac{17}{40} \qquad \frac{45}{100}$$

$$\frac{35}{80} \qquad \frac{5}{99} \qquad \frac{75}{80}$$

Mixed Review

First estimate. Then find the sum or difference. *(Lesson 3-7)*

27. $2.2 + 0.4$ **28.** $1.05 - 0.95$ **29.** $5.31 + 17.04$ **30.** $10.25 - 6.09$ **31.** $6.09 + 58.7$

32. *Choose a Strategy* Yuma drove 1,350 mi. His tank holds 15 gal. His car averaged 25 mi/gal. Gas costs $1.299 per gallon.
  a. How many tanks of gas did he use?   **b.** How much did the gas cost?

CHAPTER PROJECT

PROJECT LINK: RECORDING

You'll need five starters and two substitutes for your basketball team. Use the names of real players or make some up. If you use a ball of paper as a basketball, place your "foul line" about 10 ft from the trash can. Your first player should take 10 shots, your second player 9 shots, your third player 8 shots, and so on. Make a table to record the number of shots taken and the number of shots made by each player.

SKILLS REVIEW

Fractions and Rulers

After Lesson 5-4

A ruler helps you find the length of a segment.

The ruler below is marked in eighths of an inch.

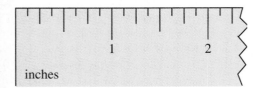

The ruler below is marked in sixteenths of an inch.

■ EXAMPLE

Find the length of each segment.

a.

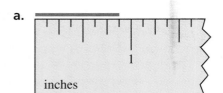

The ruler is marked in eighths of an inch. The segment is $\frac{7}{8}$ inch long.

b.

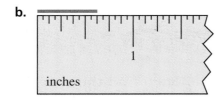

The ruler is marked in sixteenths of an inch. The segment is $\frac{10}{16}$ inch long. If you use a ruler that is marked in eighths, you find that the segment is $\frac{5}{8}$ inch long.

Find the length of each segment. Name each length in two ways.

1.

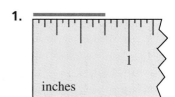

2.

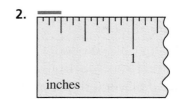

3.

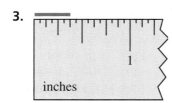

Use a ruler marked in sixteenths of an inch. Find the length of each segment. Name each length in two ways, if possible.

4. ▬▬▬▬▬▬

5. ▬▬▬▬▬

6. ▬▬▬

5-5 Equivalent Fractions

What You'll Learn

▼ To find equivalent fractions

▼ To write fractions in simplest form

...And Why

You can use equivalent fractions to make measurements and estimates.

Here's How

Look for questions that

▪ build understanding

✔ check understanding

Egypt

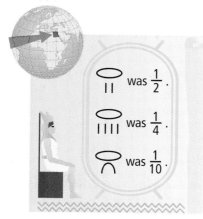

 HISTORY The ancient Egyptians wrote fractions by placing an oval above the symbols for their numbers.

Source: *The History of Mathematics*

THINK AND DISCUSS

▼ Finding Equivalent Fractions

The fraction models at the right show equivalent fractions.

Equivalent fractions are fractions that represent the same part of a whole.

1. a. ▪ **Modeling** What fraction is shown by the blue fraction model? The green fraction model?

   b. Model two other fractions with the same shaded area as the ones above.

   c. Name three fractions that are equivalent to $\frac{1}{2}$.

2. Model the fraction $\frac{4}{6}$. Model two other equivalent fractions.

You can form equivalent fractions by multiplying or dividing the numerator and denominator by the same nonzero number.

■ EXAMPLE 1

By what number can you multiply both the numerator and denominator of $\frac{3}{4}$ to get $\frac{9}{12}$?

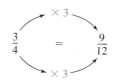 ◄——— Multiply the numerator and denominator by 3.

You can check the answer to Example 1 using fraction models.

The model for $\frac{9}{12}$ has 3 times as many shaded parts and 3 times as many total parts as the model for $\frac{3}{4}$.

3. ✔ **Try It Out** Write two fractions equivalent to each fraction.

   a. $\frac{1}{8}$ b. $\frac{2}{3}$ c. $\frac{4}{7}$ d. $\frac{5}{6}$ e. $\frac{10}{10}$

The fractions $\frac{6}{12}$ and $\frac{2}{4}$ are modeled below.

4. a. By what number can you divide both the numerator and denominator of $\frac{6}{12}$ to get $\frac{2}{4}$?

b. ⁂ *Explain* How is division by this number shown by the models?

c. Use division to find two other fractions equivalent to $\frac{6}{12}$.

❷ Writing Fractions in Simplest Form

You can write a fraction in **simplest form** by dividing both the numerator and denominator by their greatest common factor (GCF).

■ **EXAMPLE 2**

Write $\frac{20}{28}$ in simplest form.

20: ①, ②, ④, 5, 10, 20   List the factors for the numerator and
28: ①, ②, ④, 7, 14, 28   the denominator. Circle the common factors to find the GCF, 4.

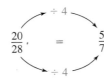

$\frac{20}{28}$, = $\frac{5}{7}$ Divide both the numerator and denominator by their GCF of 4.

The fraction $\frac{20}{28}$ written in simplest form is $\frac{5}{7}$.

5. ✔ *Try It Out* Write each fraction in simplest form.

a. $\frac{16}{18}$ **b.** $\frac{12}{16}$ **c.** $\frac{21}{24}$ **d.** $\frac{120}{150}$

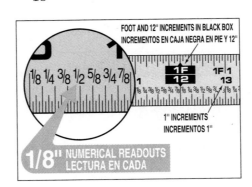

6. ⁂ *Measurement*
Refer to the tape rule at the left. Rewrite the labels for $\frac{1}{4}$ in., $\frac{1}{2}$ in., and $\frac{3}{4}$ in. as equivalent fractions in eighths of an inch.

EXERCISES On Your Own

1. **a.** *Modeling* Model the equivalent fractions $\frac{3}{5}$ and $\frac{6}{10}$.
   b. Model two other fractions equivalent to $\frac{3}{5}$ and $\frac{6}{10}$.

2. *Modeling* Model the fractions $\frac{9}{10}$ and $\frac{9}{12}$. Use the models to explain why the fractions are not equivalent.

Name the fractions modeled. Are they equivalent?

3.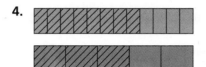

4.

5.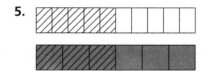

By what number can you multiply the numerator and denominator of the first fraction to get the second fraction?

6. $\frac{2}{5}, \frac{8}{20}$
7. $\frac{6}{7}, \frac{30}{35}$
8. $\frac{3}{4}, \frac{75}{100}$
9. $\frac{3}{8}, \frac{27}{72}$
10. $\frac{4}{9}, \frac{48}{108}$

By what number can you divide the numerator and denominator of the first fraction to get the second fraction?

11. $\frac{8}{48}, \frac{1}{6}$
12. $\frac{40}{50}, \frac{8}{10}$
13. $\frac{10}{32}, \frac{5}{16}$
14. $\frac{28}{49}, \frac{4}{7}$
15. $\frac{60}{150}, \frac{2}{5}$

Write two fractions equivalent to each fraction.

16. $\frac{1}{4}$
17. $\frac{10}{20}$
18. $\frac{4}{5}$
19. $\frac{15}{45}$
20. $\frac{6}{8}$
21. $\frac{1}{7}$

22. $\frac{12}{18}$
23. $\frac{9}{21}$
24. $\frac{7}{10}$
25. $\frac{3}{18}$
26. $\frac{6}{14}$
27. $\frac{6}{20}$

28. *Open-ended* Use some of the numbers 2, 3, 4, 6, 12, 18, and 24 to write three pairs of equivalent fractions.

29. *Traffic Planning* Two traffic engineers are writing about the average driving time between two towns. One engineer writes the time as 45, but the other writes it as $\frac{3}{4}$. What could explain the difference?

State whether each fraction is in simplest form. If not, write it in simplest form.

30. $\frac{5}{8}$
31. $\frac{4}{6}$
32. $\frac{10}{35}$
33. $\frac{4}{5}$
34. $\frac{24}{56}$
35. $\frac{21}{77}$

36. $\frac{25}{150}$
37. $\frac{3}{50}$
38. $\frac{15}{135}$
39. $\frac{17}{51}$
40. $\frac{10}{65}$
41. $\frac{120}{150}$

42. *Analyze* What is the only common factor of the numerator and denominator when a fraction is written in simplest form?

43. *Writing* Can you write a fraction in simplest form if you divide the numerator and denominator by a number other than the GCF? Explain.

44. *Reasoning* Can two different fractions that are written in simplest form also be equivalent to each other? Explain.

Mixed Review

Round each fraction to the nearest half. *(Lesson 5-4)*

45. $\frac{23}{25}$ **46.** $\frac{3}{40}$ **47.** $\frac{37}{80}$ **48.** $\frac{17}{100}$ **49.** $\frac{101}{196}$ **50.** $\frac{350}{400}$

Find each answer. *(Lesson 4-8)*

51. $19.2 \div 6$ **52.** $122 \div 6.25$ **53.** $0.3 \div 0.06$ **54.** $59.36 \div 7.42$

55. *Choose a Strategy* A flim is worth more than a flam. A flum is worth more than a flom. If a flam is worth less than a flom, which is greater, a flum or a flam?

✓ CHECKPOINT 1   *Lessons 5-1 through 5-5*

Mental Math **State whether each number is divisible by 1, 2, 3, 5, 9, or 10.**

1. 960   **2.** 243   **3.** 2,310   **4.** 5,070   **5.** 12,345

Find the prime factorization using a factor tree.

6. 40   **7.** 99   **8.** 960   **9.** 243   **10.** 2,310

Find the GCF of each set of numbers.

11. 48, 56   **12.** 7, 15   **13.** 15, 21   **14.** 24, 42, 72   **15.** 300, 450

Write each fraction in simplest form.

16. $\frac{12}{16}$ **17.** $\frac{64}{96}$ **18.** $\frac{21}{27}$ **19.** $\frac{9}{54}$ **20.** $\frac{18}{36}$

Simplifying Fractions

After Lesson 5-5

You can use a fraction calculator to simplify a fraction. The fraction calculator divides the numerator and denominator by a common factor and rewrites the fraction. Repeat the process until the fraction is in simplest form.

■ EXAMPLE

Use a fraction calculator to simplify $\frac{9}{27}$.

Press	Display	
9 **/** 27	**9/27**	←Enter the fraction.
Simp	SIMP N/D→n/d **9/27**	
=	N/D→n/d **3/9**	←The fraction is simplified once.
Simp	SIMP N/D→n/d **3/9**	
=	**1/3**	←The fraction is in simplest form.

In simplest form, $\frac{9}{27} = \frac{1}{3}$.

The display N/D ⟶ n/d can be written $\frac{N}{D} \longrightarrow \frac{n}{d}$. The symbols N and n represent the numerators. The symbols D and d represent the denominators.

Use a fraction calculator to simplify each fraction.

1. $\frac{18}{51}$ 2. $\frac{21}{49}$ 3. $\frac{102}{187}$ 4. $\frac{35}{56}$ 5. $\frac{20}{65}$

6. $\frac{17}{68}$ 7. $\frac{12}{15}$ 8. $\frac{28}{32}$ 9. $\frac{12}{30}$ 10. $\frac{45}{75}$

11. $\frac{24}{32}$ 12. $\frac{12}{96}$ 13. $\frac{35}{45}$ 14. $\frac{14}{63}$ 15. $\frac{40}{48}$

16. $\frac{105}{180}$ 17. $\frac{92}{132}$ 18. $\frac{39}{117}$ 19. $\frac{126}{324}$ 20. $\frac{200}{385}$

21. *Writing* Explain how you know whether the calculator uses the greatest common factor (GCF) when simplifying.

5-6 Mixed Numbers and Improper Fractions

What You'll Learn

▼ To write improper fractions

▼ To write mixed numbers

...And Why

You'll use mixed numbers and improper fractions for drawing and design.

Here's How

Look for questions that

⚫ build understanding

✔ check understanding

NEXT
2½ MI

The next time you're riding in a car, watch for mixed numbers. They are often on signs showing distances.

Work Together Comparing Numerators and Denominators

Investigate the fractions modeled below.

$\frac{4}{4}$ $\frac{5}{2}$ $\frac{1}{6}$

$\frac{1}{2}$ $\frac{11}{8}$ $\frac{3}{3}$

1. ⚫ **Number Sense** Which fractions equal 1? Compare their numerators to their denominators. (*Hint:* Use >, <, or =.)

2. Which fractions are less than 1? Compare their numerators to their denominators.

3. Which fractions are greater than 1? Compare their numerators to their denominators.

4. ⚫ **Draw a Conclusion** Write a general rule comparing the numerators and denominators of fractions.

THINK AND DISCUSS

▼ *Writing Improper Fractions*

An **improper fraction** has a numerator greater than or equal to its denominator. You can write an improper fraction greater than 1 as a **mixed number.** A mixed number shows the sum of a whole number and a fraction.

5. a. What improper fraction is modeled?
   b. How many whole cups are shaded?
   c. What additional fraction is shaded?

   d. ⚫ **Reasoning** The mixed number $1\frac{1}{4}$ describes the shaded portion. How does this number show the sum of a whole number and a fraction?

6. Describe the length shown at the right using both an improper fraction and a mixed number.

7. ⬛ *Reasoning* How would you write a whole number as an improper fraction?

You can use different methods to write a mixed number as an improper fraction.

■ EXAMPLE 1

Suppose you have $2\frac{1}{4}$ oranges. Write this quantity as an improper fraction.

Method 1 Use models.

$2\frac{1}{4}$ $\qquad\qquad\qquad$ $\frac{9}{4}$

$2\frac{1}{4}$ units $\qquad\qquad\qquad$ 9 fourths

Method 2 Use computation.

Multiply the denominator by the whole number.

Add the numerator.

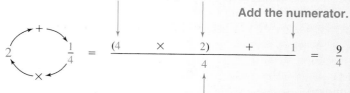

$$2 \,\frac{1}{4} = \frac{(4 \quad \times \quad 2) \quad + \quad 1}{4} = \frac{9}{4}$$

Write the result over the denominator, which stays the same.

The mixed number $2\frac{1}{4}$ can be written as $\frac{9}{4}$.

8. ⬛ *Choose* Use modeling or computation to write each mixed number as an improper fraction.

a. $1\frac{2}{3}$ $\qquad$ b. $5\frac{1}{5}$ $\qquad$ c. $4\frac{5}{6}$ $\qquad$ d. $3\frac{3}{10}$

9. ⬛ *Analyze* Which method do you prefer? Use examples to show what you mean.

2 *Writing Mixed Numbers*

Use division to write an improper fraction as a mixed number.

■ **EXAMPLE 2**   *Real-World Problem Solving*

Design   Suppose you are designing a chart for a school report. The chart has 28 rows of type. Each row is one eighth of an inch high. How much space do you need?

$\frac{28}{8}$ ←—Write an improper fraction.

$\begin{array}{r} 3R4 \\ 8\overline{)28} \\ \underline{24} \\ 4 \end{array}$ ←—Divide 28 by 8.

$3\frac{4}{8} = 3\frac{1}{2}$ ←—Express the remainder as a fraction and simplify.

You need $3\frac{1}{2}$ in.

10. ✔ *Try It Out* Write each improper fraction as a mixed number.

a. $\frac{15}{4}$ b. $\frac{49}{6}$ c. $\frac{40}{9}$ d. $\frac{27}{12}$

EXERCISES *On Your Own*

1. *Modeling* Are improper fractions greater than, less than, or equal to one? Use models to support your answer.

2. Choose A, B, C, or D. What mixed number represents the amount shaded?

A. $4\frac{3}{4}$ B. $3\frac{3}{4}$ C. $3\frac{15}{16}$ D. $3\frac{1}{4}$

Write each whole or mixed number as an improper fraction.

3. $1\frac{2}{5}$ **4.** $1\frac{5}{6}$ **5.** $2\frac{3}{4}$ **6.** $6\frac{3}{5}$ **7.** $2\frac{7}{8}$ **8.** $4\frac{1}{3}$

9. $\frac{4}{1}$ **10.** $3\frac{1}{4}$ **11.** $6\frac{7}{10}$ **12.** $2\frac{3}{16}$ **13.** $8\frac{4}{7}$ **14.** $10\frac{2}{5}$

Measurement **Describe each length using both an improper fraction and a mixed number.**

15.

16.

17. *Marine Biology* Find the mixed numbers in the article below. Write each mixed number as an improper fraction.

Philippines

Gifts from the Sea

Pearls are the only gems that come from the sea. They are also the only gems made by living things—mollusks.

The largest pearl was found in the Philippines in 1934. It was $9\frac{1}{2}$ in. long with a diameter of $5\frac{1}{2}$ in. The pearl weighed 14 lb 1 oz.

Write each improper fraction as a mixed number. Write each mixed number as an improper fraction.

18. $\frac{17}{5}$ **19.** $\frac{13}{7}$ **20.** $\frac{27}{5}$ **21.** $\frac{37}{12}$ **22.** $\frac{21}{4}$ **23.** $\frac{16}{5}$

24. $3\frac{5}{6}$ **25.** $\frac{9}{4}$ **26.** $\frac{17}{7}$ **27.** $1\frac{2}{9}$ **28.** $4\frac{3}{5}$ **29.** $\frac{19}{8}$

30. $\frac{23}{7}$ **31.** $\frac{13}{6}$ **32.** $1\frac{4}{5}$ **33.** $\frac{53}{23}$ **34.** $8\frac{2}{11}$ **35.** $\frac{37}{8}$

36. *Writing* Describe two situations in everyday life in which you have used mixed numbers.

37. *Physics* The formula to change temperature from degrees Celsius to degrees Fahrenheit is $\frac{9}{5}(°C) + 32 = °F$. Write the improper fraction in the formula as a mixed number.

38. *Research* Find out the heights, to the nearest inch, of several friends or family members. Record the heights in feet using mixed numbers.

Mixed Review

39. Alaina is at a football game. Her piano recital begins at 7:00 P.M. It takes her 15 min to get home, 20 min to eat supper, 25 min to change, and 10 min to get to the recital hall. What time should Alaina leave the game? *(Lesson 3-10)*

Simplify each answer. *(Lessons 4-2 and 4-3)*

40. $5^2 + 2 \times (6 + 4)$ **41.** $3^2 + 8^2$ **42.** $6^2 - 2 \times (8 + 1)$ **43.** $4 \times (9 - 2) \div 2^2$

44. An issue of *Teen Monthly* is $2.25. A yearly subscription costs $25.08. How much can you save by subscribing for a year? *(Lessons 3-7 and 4-5)*

Least Common Multiple

1 To find the least common multiple by listing multiples

2 To find the least common multiple using prime factorization

...And Why

You'll use the least common multiple to solve problems in astronomy.

Here's How

Look for questions that
- build understanding
- ✔ check understanding

Work Together _____ *Identifying Common Multiples*

Kristen and Dea get their hair cut at The Hair Fair. Kristen gets a haircut every sixth Saturday, and Dea gets one every fourth Saturday. Both look forward to the Saturdays they meet there.

1. Make a table that shows on which Saturdays Kristen and Dea each will be at The Hair Fair.

2. How often will they be there on the same day?

THINK AND DISCUSS

1 *LCM and Common Multiples*

A **multiple** of a number is the product of that number and a nonzero whole number. For example, 4, 8, and 12 are multiples of 4. Multiples shared by two or more numbers are **common multiples.** For example, 12 is a common multiple of 4 and 6.

3. ✔ *Try It Out* Name two more common multiples of 4 and 6.

The lowest common multiple of two or more numbers is their **least common multiple (LCM).**

■ EXAMPLE 1

Find the LCM of 6 and 8.

6: 6, 12, 18, 24, 30, . . . List the multiples of each number.
8: 8, 16, 24, 32, 40, . . . ← Then circle the lowest multiple the numbers have in common.

The LCM is 24, the lowest of the common multiples.

4. ✔ *Try It Out* Find the LCM of each set of numbers.
  a. 8, 10   **b.** 3, 9   **c.** 10, 15   **d.** 4, 5

5. ⊹ *Analyze* Explain how to find the LCM of three numbers.

■ **EXAMPLE 2**   *Real-World Problem Solving*

Astronomy In 1980, Jupiter and Saturn approached conjunction. That means they were aligned and appeared very close to each other in the night sky. Jupiter orbits the Sun about once every 12 years, and Saturn about once every 30 years. In what year will both planets return to these positions in their orbits simultaneously?

12: 12, 24, 36, 48, 60, 72, . . .
30: 30, 60, 90, 120, 150, . . . ←—Find the LCM of 12 and 30.
1980 + 60 = 2040 ←—Add the LCM to 1980.

Jupiter and Saturn will return to this position in 2040.

❷ *Finding the LCM Using Prime Factorizations*

You can also use prime factorizations to find the LCM.

■ **EXAMPLE 3**

Use prime factorizations to find the LCM of 15, 18, and 20.

$15 = 3 \times 5$
$18 = 2 \times 3 \times 3$ ←— Write the prime factorizations. Then circle all the different factors where they appear the greatest number of times.
$20 = 2 \times 2 \times 5$

$2 \times 2 \times 3 \times 3 \times 5 = 180$ ←—Multiply the circled factors.
The LCM is 180.

6. ✔ *Try It Out* Find the LCM of 5, 8, and 12.

EXERCISES *On Your Own*

Find the LCM of each set of numbers by making a list of their multiples.

1. 2, 12   **2.** 4, 9   **3.** 6, 10   **4.** 3, 5   **5.** 12, 15   **6.** 4, 12

7. 12, 20   **8.** 5, 6   **9.** 8, 12   **10.** 2, 3, 5   **11.** 3, 6, 8   **12.** 5, 6, 10

13. A number has both 8 and 10 as factors.
    a. *Reasoning* What is the lowest the number could be?
    b. Name four other factors of the number.

14. *Fitness* Suppose you jog every third day and swim every fourth day. You did both this morning. When will you next do both?

15. **Choose A, B, C, or D.** The LCM of a number and 15 is 120. What is the number?

    A. 20   **B.** 12   **C.** 6   **D.** 24

Use prime factorizations to find the LCM for each set of numbers.

16. 16, 24   17. 18, 24   18. 24, 32   19. 3, 4, 5   20. 14, 33   21. 75, 100

22. 4, 22   23. 20, 26   24. 3, 4, 9   25. 7, 8, 14   26. 22, 55, 60   27. 12, 18, 108

28. a. List the multiples of each number to find the LCM of 30, 40, and 50.
    b. Use prime factorizations to find the LCM of 30, 40, and 50.
    c. *Writing* Which method is more efficient? Explain.

29. a. For each pair, find the GCF, the LCM, the product of the two numbers, and the product of the GCF and LCM.
       i. 12 and 18   ii. 20 and 25   iii. 24 and 28
    b. *Writing* Look over your results. Describe the pattern.

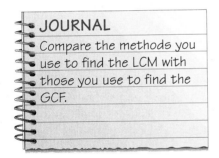

JOURNAL
Compare the methods you use to find the LCM with those you use to find the GCF.

Mixed Review

Find each product. (*Lesson 4-5*)

30. 1.9×0.8 31. 0.95×6 32. 36.18×4 33. 517.6×0.01 34. 4.25×0.32

Write a variable expression for each word phrase. (*Lesson 2-5*)

35. 28 less than k 36. 4 multiplied by h 37. y more than 12   38. 98 times a

39. *Choose a Strategy* A swim team can line up in 6 lanes with an equal number of swimmers in each lane. If only 5 lanes are used, two lanes each have an extra person. What is the least possible number of people on the swim team?

5-8 Comparing and Ordering Fractions

What You'll Learn

▼1 To compare fractions

▼2 To order fractions

...And Why

You'll compare and order fractions to make decisions in activities such as carpentry.

Here's How

Look for questions that
- ⚑ build understanding
- ✔ check understanding

Need Help? For practice in comparing and ordering whole numbers, see Skills Handbook p. 537.

THINK AND DISCUSS

▼1 Comparing Fractions

It is easy to compare fractions with the same denominator. The fraction with the larger numerator is greater. For example, as you can see from the model, $\frac{5}{6} > \frac{4}{6}$ because $5 > 4$.

1. ⚑ **Mental Math** Compare each pair using $<$, $>$, or $=$.

   a. $\frac{6}{8}, \frac{7}{8}$ b. $\frac{13}{15}, \frac{9}{15}$ c. $\frac{11}{12}, \frac{10}{12}$ d. $\frac{14}{24}, \frac{16}{24}$

You can compare fractions with unlike denominators by using equivalent fractions to find the least common denominator. The **least common denominator (LCD)** is the least common multiple (LCM) of the original denominators.

■ EXAMPLE 1

Compare $\frac{7}{24}$ and $\frac{5}{18}$. Use $<$, $>$, or $=$.

$24 = ② \times ② \times ② \times 3$ Find the LCD of the fractions by
$18 = 2 \times ③ \times ③$ finding the LCM of 24 and 18.
$2 \times 2 \times 2 \times 3 \times 3 = 72$ ◀—The LCD is 72.

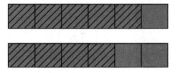

Write equivalent fractions using the LCD.

$21 > 20$ ◀—Compare the numerators.

Since $\frac{21}{72} > \frac{20}{72}$, then $\frac{7}{24} > \frac{5}{18}$.

2. ✔ **Try It Out** Compare each pair using $<$, $>$, or $=$.

   a. $\frac{4}{6} \blacksquare \frac{5}{8}$ b. $\frac{7}{12} \blacksquare \frac{9}{16}$ c. $\frac{4}{10} \blacksquare \frac{6}{15}$ d. $\frac{7}{8} \blacksquare \frac{9}{10}$

QUICKreview

To write equivalent fractions, multiply the numerator and the denominator by the same nonzero factor.

To compare mixed numbers, first compare the whole numbers. If the whole numbers are the same, compare the fraction parts.

■ **EXAMPLE 2**   *Real-World Problem Solving*

⚒ *Carpentry* "Measure twice, cut once" is the carpenter's motto. A carpenter needs a piece of lumber that is at least $6\frac{27}{32}$ inches wide. Is a $6\frac{3}{4}$-inch piece wide enough?

Since the whole numbers are the same, compare $\frac{27}{32}$ and $\frac{3}{4}$.

$$\frac{27}{32} = \frac{27}{32} \qquad \frac{3}{4} = \frac{24}{32} \quad \longleftarrow \text{ Write equivalent fractions.}$$

$$6\frac{27}{32} > 6\frac{24}{32} \quad \longleftarrow \text{ Compare.}$$

The $6\frac{3}{4}$-inch piece is not wide enough.

3. ✔ *Try It Out* Compare each pair using $<$, $>$, or $=$.
   a. $3\frac{2}{5} \blacksquare 2\frac{4}{5}$
   b. $1\frac{2}{3} \blacksquare 1\frac{5}{9}$
   c. $5\frac{7}{8} \blacksquare 6\frac{5}{6}$
   d. $2\frac{4}{7} \blacksquare 2\frac{12}{21}$
   e. $4\frac{2}{5} \blacksquare 4\frac{3}{7}$
   f. $3\frac{8}{12} \blacksquare 3\frac{3}{4}$

4. ⚒ *What If . . .* In Example 2, would a $6\frac{7}{8}$-inch piece of lumber be wide enough? Explain.

▼2 *Ordering Fractions*

You have used fraction models to *compare* fractions. You can also use models to *order* fractions.

5. ⚒ *Modeling* Use fraction models to order each set of fractions from least to greatest.
   a. $\frac{7}{10}, \frac{1}{10}, \frac{3}{10}$
   b. $\frac{3}{4}, \frac{3}{5}, \frac{3}{10}, \frac{3}{12}$

6. ⚒ *Mental Math* How are the fractions in Question 5(a) alike? Without using fraction models, how can you tell which fraction is the greatest?

7. ⚒ *Mental Math* How are the fractions in Question 5(b) alike? Without using fraction models, how can you tell which fraction is the greatest?

To order fractions with unlike numerators and denominators, use the LCD to write equivalent fractions. Then order the numerators.

■ **EXAMPLE 3**

Order from least to greatest: $\frac{3}{8}, \frac{2}{5}, \frac{7}{20}$.

$8 = ②\times②\times②$

$5 = 5$ ←——Find the LCM of 8, 5, and 20.

$20 = 2 \times 2 \times ⑤$

$2 \times 2 \times 2 \times 5 = 40$ ←——The LCD is 40.

$\frac{3}{8} = \frac{15}{40} \quad \frac{2}{5} = \frac{16}{40} \quad \frac{7}{20} = \frac{14}{40}$ ←——Write equivalent fractions.

$14 < 15 < 16$ ←——Arrange the numerators in order.

Since $\frac{14}{40} < \frac{15}{40} < \frac{16}{40}$, then $\frac{7}{20} < \frac{3}{8} < \frac{2}{5}$.

8. ✓Try It Out Order from least to greatest: $\frac{2}{6}, \frac{8}{21}, \frac{4}{14}$.

EXERCISES *On Your Own*

Compare using <, >, or =.

1. $2\frac{11}{16} \blacksquare 1\frac{13}{16}$

2. $\frac{13}{20} \blacksquare \frac{1}{4}$

3. $\frac{9}{24} \blacksquare \frac{3}{8}$

4. $\frac{15}{16} \blacksquare \frac{9}{10}$

5. $5\frac{4}{7} \blacksquare 5\frac{5}{7}$

6. $\frac{3}{11} \blacksquare \frac{1}{4}$

7. $3\frac{1}{4} \blacksquare 3\frac{1}{5}$

8. $\frac{2}{9} \blacksquare \frac{4}{15}$

9. Timothy ran $1\frac{3}{4}$ mi. Wenona ran $1\frac{7}{10}$ mi. Who ran farther?

10. *Shopping* Two bags of popcorn sell for the same price. One bag contains $1\frac{5}{8}$ oz. The other contains $1\frac{3}{4}$ oz. Which has more?

11. **Choose A, B, C, or D.** To compare $\frac{9}{24}$ and $\frac{5}{15}$, which would you do first? Explain.

  A. Find the LCM of 24 and 15.

  B. Simplify each fraction.

  C. Find the prime factorization of 24 and 15.

  D. Multiply 24×15 to find a common denominator.

12. **a.** Use models or equivalent fractions to tell whether each fraction is greater than, less than, or equal to $\frac{1}{2}$.

  i. $\frac{3}{5}$ **ii.** $\frac{5}{12}$ **iii.** $\frac{5}{8}$ **iv.** $\frac{2}{3}$

  b. *Writing* How can you use your results to compare $\frac{3}{5}$ and $\frac{5}{12}$? Can you use the results above to compare $\frac{3}{5}$ and $\frac{5}{8}$? Explain.

Order each set from least to greatest.

13. $\frac{2}{3}, \frac{2}{5}, \frac{2}{7}$

14. $\frac{4}{8}, \frac{5}{6}, \frac{7}{9}$

15. $1\frac{2}{3}, 1\frac{3}{4}, 1\frac{5}{6}$

16. $\frac{3}{5}, \frac{2}{7}, \frac{3}{8}$

17. $2\frac{8}{9}, 2\frac{17}{18}, 2\frac{5}{6}$

18. $\frac{11}{24}, \frac{5}{8}, \frac{5}{12}$

19. $\frac{7}{15}, \frac{1}{3}, \frac{7}{12}$

20. $1\frac{8}{11}, 2\frac{1}{4}, 1\frac{3}{4}$

21. $\frac{5}{7}, \frac{11}{14}, \frac{3}{4}$

22. $\frac{1}{5}, \frac{1}{8}, \frac{7}{40}, \frac{3}{10}$

23. $\frac{7}{12}, \frac{23}{40}, \frac{8}{15}, \frac{19}{30}$

24. $14\frac{7}{9}, 14\frac{3}{4}, 14\frac{13}{18}$

25. *Open-ended* Write three fractions and order them from least to greatest. State the method you used to order them.

26. *Music* Musical notes are based on fractions of a whole note.
   a. Order the fractions shown from greatest to least.
   b. Redraw the note symbols so they are in order.
   c. *Patterns* Is there a pattern to how the symbols change? Explain.

$\frac{1}{4}$ $\frac{1}{16}$ $\frac{1}{2}$ $\frac{1}{8}$

Fractions of a
Whole Note

Mixed Review

Mental Math **Change to minutes using mental math.** *(Lesson 3-10)*

27. 4 h 13 min

28. 2 h 27 min

29. 8 h 19 min

30. 10 h 16 min

31. 2 h 36 min

Find each product or quotient. *(Lessons 4-5 and 4-8)*

32. 3.7×83.5

33. 0.93×34.1

34. $401.5 \div 5$

35. $5.34 \div 0.6$

36. $3.705 \div 3.25$

37. *Choose a Strategy* A collector buys a stamp for $25, sells it for $30, buys it back for $33, and finally sells it for $35. How much did he make or lose in buying and selling the stamp?

CHAPTER PROJECT

PROJECT LINK: CALCULATING

Add a fourth column to your data table and write each player's shooting record as a fraction. Then compare and order the fractions. Rank your players from best to worst at foul shooting.

Fractions and Decimals

What You'll Learn

1 To write decimals as fractions

2 To write fractions as decimals

...And Why

You'll use fractions and decimals to solve construction problems.

Here's How

Look for questions that
- build understanding
- ✔ check understanding

QUICKreview

You read 0.225 as "two hundred twenty-five thousandths."

Work Together   *Using Decimal Models to Write Fractions*

1. **a.** What decimal does the model represent?
   b. Say the decimal in words.
   c. Write the decimal as a fraction.
   d. Complete this statement using the decimal and the fraction: ■ = ■.

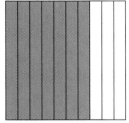

2. **a.** Find or draw a decimal square that models 0.05.
   b. Say the decimal in words.
   c. Write the decimal as a fraction.
   d. Simplify the fraction. Complete this statement using the fraction and the decimal: ■ = ■.

3. **Reasoning** How does writing the decimal in words help you to write the decimal as a fraction?

THINK AND DISCUSS

1 *Writing Fractions*

To write a decimal as a fraction, write the fraction as you would say the decimal. Then simplify it.

■ **EXAMPLE 1**

Write 0.225 as a fraction in simplest form.

$0.225 = \dfrac{225}{1,000}$ ◄——Write as a fraction.

$\dfrac{225}{1,000} \overset{\div 25}{\underset{\div 25}{=}} \dfrac{9}{40}$ ◄——Simplify. The GCF of 225 and 1,000 is 25.

$0.225 = \dfrac{9}{40}$

4. **✔ Try It Out** Write each decimal as a fraction in simplest form.
   a. 0.6   **b.** 0.35   **c.** 0.130   **d.** 0.85

If a decimal is greater than 1, it can be written as a mixed number.

■ **EXAMPLE 2**

Write 1.32 as a mixed number in simplest form.

$$1.32 = 1\frac{32}{100}$$ ←— Keep the whole number 1.

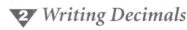

$\frac{32}{100} = \frac{8}{25}$ ←— Simplify the fraction. The GCF is 4.

$$1.32 = 1\frac{8}{25}$$

5. ✔ Try It Out Write each decimal as a mixed number in simplest form.

    a. 1.15   **b.** 3.14   **c.** 1.034   **d.** 2.155

▼2 *Writing Decimals*

You can write a fraction as a decimal by dividing the numerator by the denominator. The fraction symbol itself means division.

$$\frac{3}{4} \longrightarrow \begin{array}{r} 0.75 \\ 4\overline{)3.00} \\ -2\,8\downarrow \\ \hline 20 \\ -20 \\ \hline 0 \end{array}$$

You can also use a calculator.

■ **EXAMPLE 3**   *Real-World Problem Solving*

⊞ *Construction* A construction worker wants a drill with a diameter of no more than 0.6 inch. Can she use a $\frac{5}{8}$-inch drill?

Use a calculator to divide 5 by 8.

5 ⬛ 8 ⬛ *0.625*   ←— $\frac{5}{8} = 0.625$

Since 0.625 > 0.6, a $\frac{5}{8}$-inch drill is too big.

If its remainder is zero, the quotient is a **terminating decimal.** A quotient that repeats a digit or a group of digits without end is a **repeating decimal.**

$$0.4444 \ldots = 0.\overline{4} \quad \longleftarrow \quad \begin{array}{l} \text{The bar over the 4 means} \\ \text{that the digit 4 repeats.} \end{array}$$

■ **EXAMPLE 4**

Write each fraction as a decimal.

a. $\frac{4}{15}$

Use pencil and paper.

$$\begin{array}{r} 0.266 \\ 15\overline{)4.000} \\ -30 \\ \hline 100 \\ -90 \\ \hline 100 \\ -90 \\ \hline 10 \end{array}$$

$\longleftarrow$ The digit 6 repeats.

$$\frac{4}{15} = 0.2\overline{6}$$

b. $\frac{8}{11}$

Use a calculator.

8 ⊟ 11 ⊟ *0.72727272*

The digits 72 repeat.

$$\frac{8}{11} = 0.\overline{72}$$

6. ✔ *Try It Out* Write each fraction as a decimal. Use a bar to show repeating decimals.

a. $\frac{9}{20}$ **b.** $\frac{5}{9}$ **c.** $\frac{2}{3}$ **d.** $\frac{5}{11}$

7. a. How would you write $\frac{1}{3}$ as a decimal?
    b. How would you write 2 as a decimal?
    c. ■*Analyze* How can you use your results from parts (a) and (b) to write $2\frac{1}{3}$ as a decimal? Explain.

EXERCISES *On Your Own*

Write each decimal as a fraction or mixed number in simplest form.

1. 0.3	**2.** 0.004	**3.** 2.625	**4.** 1.35	**5.** 5.500
6. 0.075	**7.** 1.62	**8.** 0.15	**9.** 0.07	**10.** 10.02
11. 0.064	**12.** 4.44	**13.** 0.008	**14.** 3.12	**15.** 0.145
16. 5.875	**17.** 0.565	**18.** 66.6	**19.** 0.0015	**20.** 43.43

21. Money Pervis had $1 to spend. He bought a package of sunflower seeds for $.55. What fraction of his money did he spend?

22. Writing Explain the steps you would use to write 0.8 as a fraction in simplest form.

23. Open-ended Use decimal models and fraction models to show the decimal equivalents of two fractions.

Write each fraction or mixed number as a decimal.

24. $\frac{3}{20}$ **25.** $\frac{9}{50}$ **26.** $\frac{7}{32}$ **27.** $\frac{5}{6}$ **28.** $\frac{11}{16}$

29. $\frac{7}{8}$ **30.** $2\frac{4}{5}$ **31.** $10\frac{6}{8}$ **32.** $\frac{5}{12}$ **33.** $\frac{7}{20}$

34. $\frac{11}{8}$ **35.** $\frac{6}{11}$ **36.** $1\frac{1}{9}$ **37.** $\frac{14}{25}$ **38.** $\frac{7}{15}$

39. $4\frac{7}{10}$ **40.** $2\frac{7}{12}$ **41.** $\frac{5}{24}$ **42.** $\frac{7}{16}$ **43.** $3\frac{4}{11}$

44. Shopping Suppose you buy a quarter pound ($\frac{1}{4}$ lb) of roasted turkey at the delicatessen. What decimal should you see on the digital scale?

45. Finance Refer to the article below. A share of stock sold for $10\frac{5}{8}$. What is the equivalent decimal price?

| MCK | UPT | BIP | PRO |
| 8⅞ | 12½ | 25¾ | 14⅜ |

Stock Market Switches from $\frac{1}{8}$ to 0.125!

When it started in 1792, the stock market set the price of stocks in eighths of a dollar. | That's recently changed, and now stock prices are being quoted in decimals.

46. Number Sense Order each set of numbers from least to greatest.

a. $\frac{7}{8}$, 0.8, $\frac{9}{11}$, 0.87   **b.** 1.65, $1\frac{2}{3}$, $1\frac{3}{5}$, 1.7   **c.** $3\frac{1}{12}$, 3.1, $3\frac{1}{5}$, $3\frac{1}{20}$, 3.01

47. a. Calculator Write each fraction as a decimal: $\frac{17}{50}$, $\frac{1}{3}$, $\frac{8}{25}$, $\frac{26}{75}$.
b. Arrange the fractions in order from least to greatest.
c. Would you prefer to use equivalent fractions with a common denominator to order the numbers in part (a)? Explain.

Mixed Review

Find each product or quotient. *(Lessons 4-5 and 4-9)*

48. 0.07×4.8 **49.** $9.8 \div 2.8$ **50.** 5.03×2.4

51. $12.3 \div 1.5$ **52.** 0.58×0.6 **53.** $1.575 \div 0.25$

Data Analysis **Use the table at the right for Exercises 54 and 55.**

54. Copy and complete the chart. *(Lesson 3-7)*

55. *Patterns* Does the last column show a pattern? Why or why not? *(Lesson 2-1)*

Effect of Aging on Pupil Size

Age	Diameter of Pupils (mm)		
(yr)	daylight	night	difference
20	4.7	8.0	■
30	4.3	7.0	■
40	3.9	6.0	■
50	3.5	5.0	■
60	3.1	4.1	■
70	2.7	3.2	■
80	2.3	2.5	■

Source: *Sizes*

CHAPTER PROJECT

PROJECT LINK: COMPARING

You now have another way to compare the records of your players. Convert the fractions in your table to decimals. Use the decimals to rank your players. Does the order agree with the order you got when you compared fractions?

✓ CHECKPOINT 2

Lessons 5-6 through 5-9

Find the LCM of each set of numbers.

1. 16, 24, 32   **2.** 28, 56, 63   **3.** 40, 36, 18   **4.** 20, 10, 35

Write each fraction as a decimal.

5. $\frac{2}{5}$ **6.** $\frac{7}{100}$ **7.** $\frac{3}{8}$ **8.** $\frac{1}{6}$ **9.** $\frac{50}{9}$

Write each decimal as a fraction in simplest form.

10. 0.52   **11.** 0.04   **12.** 0.75   **13.** 15.025   **14.** 1.375

15. Choose A, B, C, or D. Which of the following is ordered from greatest to least?

A. 0.56, 0.055, 0.53, 0.52

B. 1.75, $\frac{3}{2}$, 1.25, 2.0

C. 3.47, $3\frac{1}{2}$, 3.6, $\frac{8}{3}$

D. $\frac{7}{8}$, 0.8, 0.75, $\frac{8}{11}$

5-10 Work Backward

THINK AND DISCUSS

Walking backward is dangerous, and talking backward will cause confusion. In math, however, *working backward* can be good for you. Sometimes you can work backward from a known result to find a fact at the beginning.

SAMPLE PROBLEM...

A teacher lends pencils to students. One day she gave out 7 pencils in the morning, collected 5 before lunch, and gave out 3 after lunch. At the end of the day she had 16 pencils. How many pencils did the teacher have at the start of the day?

....

READ

Read for understanding. Summarize the problem.

1. How many pencils did the teacher have at the end of the day?

2. How many times did the teacher give out pencils? Collect pencils?

3. Do you think she had *more than* or *fewer than* 16 pencils at the start of the day? Explain.

PLAN

Decide on a strategy.

You know that there were 16 pencils at the *end* of the day. Work backward to find out how many pencils the teacher had at the *start* of the day. Add each time she gave out pencils, and subtract each time she collected pencils.

SOLVE

Try the strategy.

4. What was the teacher's last action with pencils before the end of the day? How many pencils did she have just before that action?

5. Continue working backward to find the number of pencils the teacher had at the start of the day.

LOOK BACK

Think about how you solved the problem.

6. Check by starting with your answer and working *forward*. Do you have 16 pencils at the end of the day?

7. Some people may prefer to use *Guess and Test*. Solve the problem using 18 as your guess. Which strategy do you prefer? Explain.

EXERCISES *On Your Own*

Work backward to solve each problem.

1. If you multiply a number by 3, and then add 5, the result is 38. What is the number?

2. *Shopping* Bo spent half her money at a store in the mall. At another store, she spent half her remaining money and $6 more. She had $2 left. How much did Bo have when she arrived at the mall?

3. *Hobbies* Horace decided to sell all his baseball cards. He sold Juanita half his cards plus 1 card. Next he sold Ethan half the remaining cards. Then he sold Kyoko 13 cards. Finally, he sold the remaining 9 cards to Cleon. How many cards did Horace have at the start?

Use any strategy to solve each problem. Show your work.

4. *Games* A chess player won a chess tournament by winning three games. At each round, the loser was eliminated and the winner advanced to the next round. How many players were in the tournament?

5. *Calendar* Suppose March 27 is a Thursday. What day of the week is March 1?

6. *Cooking* Kathy and Bill baked some muffins. They put half away for the next day and divided the remaining muffins among their 3 sisters, each of whom received 3 muffins. How many muffins did Kathy and Bill bake?

7. *Biology* A bacterial population doubles in size every 6 minutes. Some bacteria are placed on a microscope slide, and in 2 hours the slide is covered. When was the slide half-covered?

8. *Writing* Why is it necessary to use opposite operations when working backward?

9. *Entertainment* At the grand opening of the Plex Cinema, every 15th customer got a free ticket. Every 10th customer got a free box of popcorn. Of the 418 ticket buyers, how many received both prizes?

10. *Scheduling* Aaron plans to study in the library after school. Then he has a track meet at 4:00 P.M. It takes him 5 min to change his clothes and 10 min to get to the track. Before the start of the race, Aaron needs to meet with his coach for 10 min and stretch for 15 min.
    a. When should Aaron leave the library?
    b. School lets out at 2:50 P.M. How much time can Aaron spend in the library?

11. *Savings* Each time Aretha's grandmother visits, she doubles the amount of money Aretha has saved and gives her $3 extra to spend. After her grandmother's most recent visit, Aretha had a total of $19. How much had Aretha saved?

12. *Health* Of 25 students, 11 need a dental check-up and 17 need an eye exam. Five students don't need either. How many need both?

13. *Money* Taesha has $1.35 in nickels and dimes. She has a total of 15 coins. How many of each coin does she have?

14. Box A has 9 green balls and 4 red balls. Box B has 12 green balls and 5 red balls. Suppose you want the fraction of green balls in Box A to equal the fraction of red balls in Box B. How many green balls must you move from Box A to Box B?

> PORTFOLIO
> For your portfolio, select one or two items from your work for this chapter. For example:
> • your best work
> • drawings of models
> • a journal entry
> Explain why you have chosen each item.

Mixed Review

Write a word phrase for each variable expression. *(Lesson 2-4)*

15. $a - 13$　　　16. $p \times 11$　　　17. $x \div 5$　　　18. $s + 14$　　　19. $(5 \times c) + 8$

Complete. *(Lesson 4-10)*

20. ▉ m = 54 cm　　　21. 18 km = ▉ m　　　22. 400 mm = ▉ cm　　　23. 850 mL = ▉ L

24. *Time Zones* The bus from Montreal to Chicago leaves at 5:43 A.M. and arrives at 4:54 P.M. The bus passes through one time zone, gaining an hour. How long is the trip? *(Lesson 3-10)*

CHAPTER PROJECT

HOME COURT ADVANTAGE

Compare Basketball Statistics Project Links on pages 195, 212, and 217 will help you complete your project. Here is a checklist to help you gather together the parts of your project.

✔ a table with the foul-shooting records of your basketball players

✔ shooting records ranked in order of fractions

✔ shooting records ranked in order of decimals

Make a poster to present your table and rankings to your class. You may wish to decorate the poster by adding a team name and logo, home made sports cards for some of your players, or a sketch of a team uniform. You could even make a tape-recorded interview with your top foul shooter!

Reflect and Revise

Review your poster with a classmate, a friend, or a family member. Are your calculations correct? Do your rankings correspond to your calculations? Is your table clearly presented? If necessary, make changes to improve your poster.

Web Extension

Prentice Hall's Internet site contains information you may find helpful as you complete your project. Visit www.phschool.com/mgm1/ch5 for some links and ideas related to sports.

Divisibility and Prime Factorization 　　　　　　　　5-1, 5-2

The rules for divisibility can help you find factors. A **prime number** has exactly two factors, 1 and itself. A **composite number** has more than two factors.

The **prime factorization** of a composite number is written as the product of the prime factors of the composite number.

State whether each number is divisible by 1, 2, 3, 5, 9, or 10.

1. 69 　　　　**2.** 146 　　　　**3.** 837 　　　　**4.** 405 　　　　**5.** 628 　　　　**6.** 32,870

7. Choose A, B, C, or D. Which number is a prime number?

　　A. 519 　　　**B.** 523 　　　**C.** 525 　　　**D.** 530

Find the prime factorization using a factor tree.

8. 72 　　　**9.** 120 　　　**10.** 33 　　　**11.** 80 　　　**12.** 234 　　　**13.** 345

GCF, LCM, and Rounding Fractions 　　　　　　　5-3, 5-4, 5-7

The **greatest common factor (GCF)** of two or more numbers is the greatest number that is a factor of every number.

The **least common multiple (LCM)** of two or more numbers is the lowest number that is a multiple of every number.

To round a fraction, compare the numerator to the denominator.

Find the GCF and the LCM of each set of numbers.

14. 40, 140 　　**15.** 28, 33 　　**16.** 24, 9 　　**17.** 15, 25 　　**18.** 18, 42, 60 　　**19.** 10, 12, 16

Round each fraction to the nearest half.

20. $\frac{54}{98}$ 　　**21.** $\frac{11}{12}$ 　　**22.** $\frac{1}{6}$ 　　**23.** $\frac{2}{9}$ 　　**24.** $\frac{19}{40}$ 　　**25.** $\frac{5}{11}$

26. *Writing* Explain the value of prime factorization in finding the GCF and the LCM. Include examples.

Equivalent Fractions and Simplest Form 5-5

You form **equivalent fractions** by multiplying or dividing the numerator and denominator by the same nonzero number.

To write a fraction in simplest form, divide both the numerator and the denominator by their GCF.

If the fraction is in simplest form, write two equivalent fractions. If not, write the fraction in simplest form.

27. $\frac{1}{8}$ **28.** $\frac{14}{28}$ **29.** $\frac{30}{50}$ **30.** $\frac{16}{18}$ **31.** $\frac{27}{72}$ **32.** $\frac{6}{21}$

Comparing and Ordering Fractions and Mixed Numbers 5-6, 5-8

An **improper fraction** has a numerator greater than or equal to its denominator. A **mixed number** shows the sum of a whole number and a fraction. Compare fractions by rewriting them using their **least common denominator (LCD)**.

Write each improper fraction as a mixed number. Write each mixed number as an improper fraction.

33. $4\frac{3}{4}$ **34.** $\frac{22}{5}$ **35.** $\frac{57}{7}$ **36.** $2\frac{3}{8}$ **37.** $\frac{30}{12}$ **38.** $5\frac{2}{11}$

39. Order from least to greatest: $1\frac{5}{6}, 1\frac{7}{9}, \frac{35}{36}, 1\frac{3}{4}$.

Fractions and Decimals; Problem Solving Strategies 5-9, 5-10

To express a decimal as a fraction, write the fraction as you would say the decimal. Then simplify the fraction. To write a fraction as a decimal, divide the numerator by the denominator. Write a bar over the digit or digits that repeat.

Write each decimal as a fraction in simplest form. Write each fraction as a decimal.

40. 0.04 **41.** 3.875 **42.** 2.14 **43.** $\frac{17}{40}$ **44.** $\frac{8}{9}$ **45.** $\frac{6}{11}$

46. At the first store, Tina spent $7. At the next store, she spent half of her remaining money. At the last store, she spent half of her remaining money and $3 more. Tina had $5 left. How much money did she have before shopping?

1. Writing
   a. Is 24,357 divisible by 5? Explain your answer.
   b. Is 24,357 divisible by 9? Explain your answer.

2. Choose A, B, C, or D. Which number is divisible by 2, 3, and 10?
   A. 375
   B. 430
   C. 2,328
   D. 5,430

3. List all the factors of each number. Tell whether each number is prime or composite.
   a. 33
   b. 54
   c. 19
   d. 102

4. Find the GCF of each set of numbers.
   a. 24, 36
   b. 20, 25, 30
   c. 45, 105
   d. 7, 19

5. Find the prime factorization of each number.
   a. 132
   b. 360

6. Name the fraction modeled.
   a.

   b.
   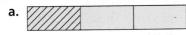

7. Estimation Round each fraction to the nearest half.
   a. $\frac{15}{16}$
   b. $\frac{2}{20}$
   c. $\frac{24}{50}$
   d. $\frac{40}{75}$

8. Name two fractions that are equivalent to each fraction.
   a. $\frac{6}{18}$
   b. $\frac{9}{24}$
   c. $\frac{18}{20}$
   d. $\frac{60}{100}$

9. Write each fraction in simplest form.
   a. $\frac{5}{45}$
   b. $\frac{34}{51}$
   c. $\frac{56}{128}$
   d. $\frac{120}{180}$

10. Find the LCM of each set of numbers.
   a. 4, 8
   b. 6, 11
   c. 18, 45
   d. 10, 12, 15

11. Write each improper fraction as a mixed number. Write each mixed number as an improper fraction.
   a. $3\frac{5}{6}$
   b. $\frac{43}{20}$
   c. $\frac{202}{50}$
   d. $5\frac{2}{3}$

12. Compare. Fill in the ■ with <, >, or =.
   a. $1\frac{2}{5}$ ■ $1\frac{1}{5}$
   b. $\frac{15}{4}$ ■ $\frac{17}{5}$
   c. $\frac{7}{14}$ ■ $\frac{1}{2}$
   d. $2\frac{3}{5}$ ■ $2\frac{7}{11}$

13. Choose A, B, or C. Lee jogged $\frac{1}{2}$ mi, Orlando jogged $\frac{2}{3}$ mi, and Holden jogged $\frac{3}{8}$ mi. Who jogged the longest distance?
   A. Lee
   B. Orlando
   C. Holden

14. Order the numbers in each set from least to greatest.
   a. $5\frac{3}{4}$, $5\frac{1}{8}$, $5\frac{2}{4}$
   b. $4\frac{4}{5}$, $3\frac{7}{10}$, $3\frac{3}{5}$
   c. $2\frac{1}{4}$, $1\frac{3}{4}$, $3\frac{2}{4}$
   d. $\frac{2}{9}$, $\frac{7}{36}$, $\frac{5}{18}$, $\frac{1}{2}$

15. Write each decimal as a fraction in simplest form.
   a. 0.4
   b. 0.82
   c. 0.025

16. Write each fraction as a decimal. Use a bar to show repeating decimals.
   a. $\frac{5}{8}$
   b. $\frac{7}{11}$
   c. $\frac{15}{45}$

17. Solve the following puzzle. When I add 2 to a number, subtract 5, and then multiply by 3, my result is 24. What is my number?

Choose the best answer.

1. Which number pattern can be described by the following rule? *Start with the number 12, and subtract 4 repeatedly.*

A. 12, 8, 4, . . .
B. 12, 8, 10, . . .
C. 12, 16, 24, . . .
D. 12, 24, 20, . . .

2. On Venus the length of a day is 243.01 Earth days. On Mercury the length of a day is 58.65 Earth days. How much longer than a Mercury day is a Venus day?

A. 301.66 Earth days
B. 215.64 Earth days
C. 195.46 Earth days
D. 184.36 Earth days

3. Which expression has a value of 13?

A. $3 + (2)^2$
B. $(3 + 2)^2$
C. $3^2 + 2^2$
D. $3^3 + 2^2$

4. A shirt costs $21.95 and a sweater costs $29.75. Which is the best estimate of the difference in costs?

A. $52   **B.** $9
C. $8   **D.** $7

5. Which decimal is equivalent to $\frac{3}{8}$?

A. 0.037   **B.** 0.38   **C.** 0.375   **D.** 3.75

6. Which word phrase describes the variable expression $2b - 8$?

A. eight minus two times b
B. two times b
C. two minus eight times b
D. two times b, minus eight

7. Which set of numbers has a GCF of 8?

A. 24, 36, 48
B. 56, 63, 42
C. 64, 24, 56
D. 56, 36, 28

8. Which fraction model does *not* equal $\frac{2}{3}$?

A.
B.
C.
D.

9. Which fraction is *not* equivalent to 0.125?

A. $\frac{5}{40}$ **B.** $\frac{125}{1000}$
C. $\frac{1}{8}$ **D.** $\frac{15}{200}$

10. The graph shows Erika's spelling scores for each week during the grading period. At the end of 6 weeks, her teacher drops the lowest score and finds the average of the remaining five scores to determine Erika's final score. What is the final score?

Erika's Spelling Scores

A. 7   **B.** 7.5
C. 8   **D.** 40

6

Using Fractions

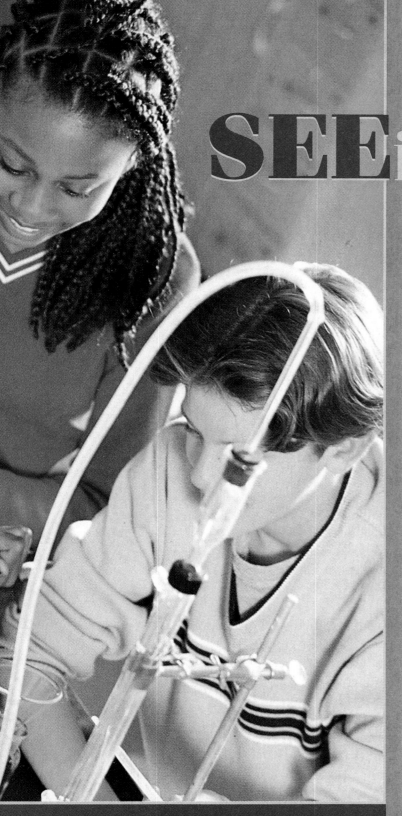

SEEing is Believing

Have you ever conducted a science experiment to prove that something is true? Scientists do not take someone else's word for something. Instead they plan to prove something is correct or incorrect. You can prove something in math class, too.

Design a Demonstration You will learn ways to add fractions and mixed numbers with unlike denominators, but can you prove these techniques *really* work? Your goal is to prove that they do by giving several demonstrations.

• How to solve problems by drawing a diagram

PROBLEM SOLVING

227

6-1 Estimating Sums and Differences

What You'll Learn

1 To estimate sums and differences by rounding fractions

2 To estimate sums and differences by rounding mixed numbers

...And Why

You can estimate measurements and rates of growth.

Here's How

Look for questions that
- build understanding
✔ check understanding

THINK AND DISCUSS

1 *Estimating with Fractions*

Look at the ruler at the right.

1. ▪ **Number Sense** Is each fraction closest to 0, $\frac{1}{2}$, or 1?

a. $\frac{1}{8}$　　　b. $\frac{7}{8}$　　　c. $\frac{3}{8}$　　　d. $\frac{15}{16}$

2. ▪ **Reasoning** Does $\frac{1}{4}$ round to 0 or to $\frac{1}{2}$? Explain.

You can estimate sums and differences of fractions by rounding to the nearest half.

■ EXAMPLE 1

Estimate.

a. $\frac{7}{12} + \frac{4}{5}$　　　　　　　　　　b. $\frac{9}{10} - \frac{1}{7}$

$\frac{7}{12} + \frac{4}{5}$　　　　　　　　　　　$\frac{9}{10} - \frac{1}{7}$

$\approx \frac{1}{2} + 1$ ← Round each fraction to the nearest $\frac{1}{2}$. → $\approx 1 - 0$

$\approx 1\frac{1}{2}$ ← Add or subtract the estimates. → ≈ 1

3. ✔ **Try It Out** Estimate each sum or difference.

a. $\frac{6}{7} + \frac{2}{9}$　　b. $\frac{7}{13} - \frac{3}{17}$　　c. $\frac{21}{44} + \frac{1}{99}$　　d. $\frac{12}{13} - \frac{1}{12}$

You can also use models to estimate sums.

4. ✔ **Try It Out** Write the fractions shown in the model. What does this model show you?

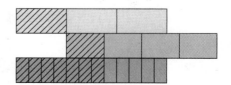

5. ▪ **Modeling** Represent $\frac{7}{8} + \frac{1}{2}$ with a model. Estimate the sum.

▼2 *Estimating with Mixed Numbers*

To estimate the sum or difference of mixed numbers, round each mixed number to the nearest whole number.

■ **EXAMPLE 2**   *Real-World Problem Solving*

Life Science The table at the right shows how one kudzu plant grew over five days.

Kudzu Plant Growth

Day	Height (ft)
1	$1\frac{1}{12}$
2	$1\frac{7}{8}$
3	$2\frac{3}{4}$
4	$3\frac{5}{8}$
5	$4\frac{7}{12}$

a. About how much did the kudzu plant grow from Day 1 to Day 2?

Subtract to find the growth in one day.

$$\begin{array}{cc} \text{Height} & - \quad \text{Height} \\ \text{on Day 2} & \quad \text{on Day 1} \end{array}$$

$$1\frac{7}{8} \quad - \quad 1\frac{1}{12}$$

$$\approx 2 - 1 \qquad \longleftarrow \text{Round each height to the nearest whole foot.}$$

$$\approx 1$$

The kudzu plant grew about 1 ft from Day 1 to Day 2.

b. Estimate the average growth per day for the kudzu plant.

$$\begin{array}{cl} \dfrac{\text{Average growth}}{\text{per day}} & = \dfrac{\text{Total growth}}{\text{Number of days}} \\[2mm] & = \dfrac{4\frac{7}{12} - 1\frac{1}{12}}{5} \quad \begin{array}{l} \longleftarrow \text{Subtract to find total growth.} \\ \longleftarrow \text{Divide by 5.} \end{array} \\[3mm] & \approx \dfrac{5 - 1}{5} \quad \begin{array}{l} \longleftarrow \text{Round each mixed number to the nearest whole number.} \end{array} \\[3mm] & \approx \dfrac{4}{5} \\[2mm] & \approx 1 \end{array}$$

The average growth is about 1 ft per day.

6. ✔*Try It Out* Estimate the height of the kudzu on Day 6 and Day 10.

7. Evaluate the reasonableness of your results in Question 6.

8. ⬝*Think About It* Why does it make sense to round a mixed number to the nearest *whole number* before adding or subtracting? Could you round to the nearest $\frac{1}{2}$ instead?

The kudzu plant, from Japan, was introduced to the United States in 1876. It grows fastest during the summer months. Under ideal conditions, a kudzu vine can grow 60 ft in a year.

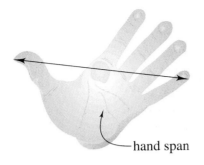

hand span

Work Together — *Measuring and Estimating*

9. ⛏*Measurement* Use an inch ruler to measure the hand span of each member of your group.

10. Record each measurement to the nearest half inch.

11. ⛏*Estimation* Estimate the difference between the greatest and least hand spans within your group.

EXERCISES *On Your Own*

Estimate each sum or difference to the nearest $\frac{1}{2}$.

1. $\frac{1}{4} + \frac{1}{8}$
2. $\frac{7}{8} - \frac{1}{4}$
3. $\frac{7}{8} + \frac{3}{5}$
4. $\frac{11}{20} - \frac{2}{15}$
5. $\frac{13}{30} + \frac{19}{20}$

6. $\frac{9}{16} - \frac{1}{4}$
7. $\frac{15}{16} + \frac{7}{15}$
8. $\frac{13}{16} - \frac{3}{8}$
9. $\frac{1}{10} + \frac{81}{100}$
10. $\frac{70}{80} - \frac{2}{5}$

11. $\frac{15}{28} + \frac{11}{12}$
12. $\frac{6}{7} - \frac{43}{80}$
13. $\frac{5}{6} + \frac{4}{9}$
14. $\frac{11}{12} - \frac{1}{15}$
15. $\frac{47}{50} + \frac{22}{25}$

16. *Number Sense* Will the sum of many different fractions less than $\frac{1}{4}$ ever be greater than 1? Support your answer.

17. *Estimation* Use the table at the right. Suppose you place a dime, a penny, a nickel, and a quarter side-by-side as shown below. Estimate the total length of the coins.

U.S. Coins

Coin	Diameter (in.)
Dime	$\frac{11}{16}$
Penny	$\frac{3}{4}$
Nickel	$\frac{13}{16}$
Quarter	$\frac{15}{16}$

Estimate each sum or difference.

18. $7\frac{7}{8} + 8\frac{5}{12}$
19. $12\frac{9}{10} - 4\frac{3}{8}$
20. $3\frac{3}{4} + 1\frac{2}{5}$
21. $25\frac{6}{7} - 13\frac{3}{4}$
22. $2\frac{9}{10} + 43\frac{13}{14}$

23. $11\frac{9}{16} - 10\frac{5}{8}$
24. $7\frac{8}{11} + 4\frac{10}{13}$
25. $4\frac{2}{3} - \frac{5}{6}$
26. $29\frac{1}{8} + 30\frac{8}{11}$
27. $76\frac{6}{23} - 45\frac{2}{5}$

28. $3\frac{9}{10} + 5\frac{3}{8}$
29. $78\frac{3}{4} - 57\frac{17}{23}$
30. $13\frac{7}{43} + 22\frac{1}{8}$
31. $2\frac{5}{7} - \frac{1}{2}$
32. $34\frac{3}{7} + 16\frac{9}{17}$

33. *Sewing* Fabric costs $4.96 per yard. Suppose you need $1\frac{5}{8}$ yd of a solid-color fabric and $\frac{3}{4}$ yd of a print fabric for a quilt. About how much will the fabric cost?

34. *Measurement* At the beginning of the summer, Jocelyn, Carlos, and Amanda measured their heights. At the end of the summer, Carlos, Jocelyn, and Amanda measured their heights again. Refer to the table at the right.

a. About how much did Amanda grow during the summer?

b. About how much did Carlos and Jocelyn grow during the summer? Which of the three grew the most?

Heights

Person	June	Sept.
Jocelyn	$61\frac{7}{8}$ in.	$62\frac{1}{4}$ in.
Carlos	$60\frac{3}{4}$ in.	$61\frac{5}{8}$ in.
Amanda	$59\frac{1}{8}$ in.	$60\frac{5}{8}$ in.

35. *Geometry* You plan to put a fence around your garden, shown at the right. About how much fencing will you need?

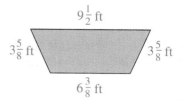

36. *Writing* Finalists in a contest to build the tallest tower of cans build towers $7\frac{7}{8}$ ft, $7\frac{3}{4}$ ft, and $7\frac{15}{16}$ ft high. If you round each height to the nearest foot, is an estimate of the difference in height reasonable? Explain.

Mixed Review

Write each fraction in simplest form. *(Lesson 5-5)*

37. $\frac{45}{60}$ **38.** $\frac{36}{64}$ **39.** $\frac{75}{350}$ **40.** $\frac{49}{63}$ **41.** $\frac{96}{100}$ **42.** $\frac{112}{400}$

Organize each set of data in a frequency table and in a line plot. *(Lesson 1-1)*

43. ages of first cousins at a family reunion: 16 15 9 10 9 13 9 12 15 11 8 20

44. points scored by gymnasts on the balance beam: 8.5 8.8 8.4 8.4 8.5 9 8.6 8.1 8.5 9

45. *Choose a Strategy* Akira spent one third of his money, then spent $6, and then spent half the money he had left, leaving him with exactly $4. How much money did he start with?

CHAPTER PROJECT

PROJECT LINK: RESEARCHING

Look around for items that are typically divided into equal parts, or fractions. Some suggestions are rulers, pizzas, and cakes. How are these items usually divided—into halves, thirds, eighths? Make a list of items you could use to demonstrate the proofs you develop. Gather as many of these items as you can.

6-2 Modeling Like Denominators

What You'll Learn

1 To add fractions with like denominators

2 To subtract fractions with like denominators

...And Why

You can solve problems involving portions of pizza and apple pie.

Here's How

Look for questions that
- ⊞ build understanding
- ✔ check understanding

THINK AND DISCUSS

1 *Adding Fractions with Like Denominators*

Food A pizza is cut into eight equal pieces. Suppose you eat two pieces and your friend eats three pieces. What portion of the pizza has been eaten? What portion of the pizza is left? You can model this problem with circles.

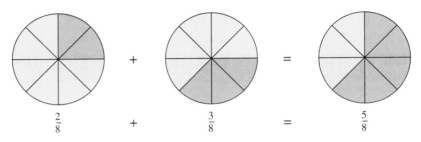

$$\frac{2}{8} \qquad + \qquad \frac{3}{8} \qquad = \qquad \frac{5}{8}$$

1. ✔**Try It Out** What fraction represents the amount of pizza you have eaten? What fraction represents the amount of pizza your friend has eaten? What portion of the pizza has been eaten?

You can use fraction models to show addition problems.

■ **EXAMPLE 1**

Find $\frac{1}{10} + \frac{5}{10}$. Write the answer in simplest form.

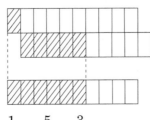

$$\begin{array}{r} \frac{1}{10} \\ + \frac{5}{10} \\ \hline \end{array}$$

Add the numerators. The denominators remain the same.

$$\frac{1}{10} + \frac{5}{10} = \frac{3}{5}$$

$$\frac{6}{10} = \frac{3}{5}$$

Simplify. Divide the numerator and denominator by the GCF of 2.

2. ✔**Try It Out** Add. Write each answer in simplest form.

a. $\frac{2}{5} + \frac{1}{5}$ b. $\frac{1}{6} + \frac{1}{6}$ c. $\frac{3}{10} + \frac{7}{10}$ d. $\frac{5}{8} + \frac{1}{8}$

QUICKreview

To write an improper fraction as a mixed number, divide the numerator by the denominator.

The sum of fractions is sometimes greater than 1.

3. **⁘Algebra** Write the addition sentence for the model shown below. Write the sum as a mixed number in lowest terms.

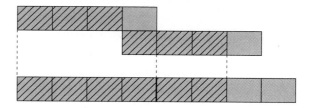

▼2 Subtracting Fractions with Like Denominators

Suppose an apple pie was cut into twelve equal pieces. There are three pieces left. You eat one piece. What portion of the pie is left?

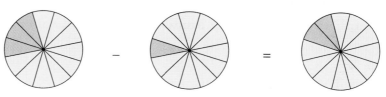

4. **⁘Algebra** Write a subtraction sentence for the problem above.

You can also use fraction models to subtract.

■ EXAMPLE 2

Find $\frac{3}{12} - \frac{1}{12}$. Write the answer in simplest form.

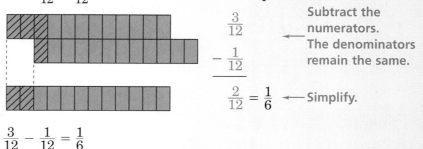

$$\frac{3}{12}$$

$$-\frac{1}{12}$$

Subtract the numerators. The denominators remain the same.

$$\frac{2}{12} = \frac{1}{6}$$ ← Simplify.

$$\frac{3}{12} - \frac{1}{12} = \frac{1}{6}$$

5. **✔Try It Out** Subtract. Write each answer in simplest form.

a. $\frac{3}{5} - \frac{2}{5}$ **b.** $\frac{3}{4} - \frac{1}{4}$ **c.** $\frac{7}{10} - \frac{3}{10}$ **d.** $\frac{5}{12} - \frac{1}{12}$

6. **⁘Algebra** Explain the steps you would follow to solve the equation $\frac{3}{8} + x = \frac{7}{8}$.

7. **⁂ Open-ended** Write a problem that could be solved using the equation in Question 6. Solve the problem. Justify your solution.

EXERCISES *On Your Own*

Algebra **Write an addition sentence for each model.**

1.

2.
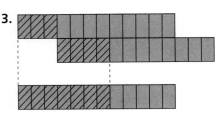

3.

Find each sum. Write each answer in simplest form.

4. $\frac{3}{5} + \frac{1}{5}$ 5. $\frac{7}{12} + \frac{5}{12}$ 6. $\frac{2}{6} + \frac{3}{6}$ 7. $\frac{3}{10} + \frac{2}{10}$ 8. $\frac{1}{3} + \frac{1}{3}$

9. $\frac{5}{12} + \frac{5}{12}$ 10. $\frac{3}{4} + \frac{1}{4}$ 11. $\frac{1}{2} + \frac{1}{2}$ 12. $\frac{1}{4} + \frac{2}{4}$ 13. $\frac{9}{16} + \frac{3}{16}$

14. $\frac{1}{20} + \frac{3}{20} + \frac{5}{20}$ 15. $\frac{27}{100} + \frac{41}{100} + \frac{3}{100}$ 16. $\frac{4}{15} + \frac{1}{15} + \frac{7}{15}$ 17. $\frac{19}{50} + \frac{9}{50} + \frac{7}{50}$

18. *Modeling* Draw a model to represent $\frac{4}{5} + \frac{3}{5} = \frac{7}{5}$. Write $\frac{7}{5}$ as a mixed number. Compare the result to your model.

Algebra **Write a subtraction sentence for each model.**

19.

20.

21.
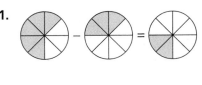

Is each answer correct? Write *yes* or *no*. If *no*, write the correct answer in simplest form.

22. $\frac{3}{10} + \frac{3}{10} = \frac{4}{5}$ 23. $\frac{7}{12} - \frac{3}{12} = \frac{5}{6}$ 24. $\frac{5}{6} + \frac{4}{6} = 1\frac{1}{2}$ 25. $\frac{3}{4} - \frac{1}{4} = \frac{1}{2}$ 26. $\frac{11}{12} - \frac{5}{12} = 2\frac{1}{12}$

27. *Measurement* A piece of thread is $\frac{9}{16}$ in. long. Another piece of thread is $\frac{7}{16}$ in. long.
   a. To compare their lengths, would you add or subtract?
   b. Compare their lengths. Justify your solution.

Find each difference. Write each answer in simplest form.

28. $\frac{7}{10} - \frac{4}{10}$ **29.** $\frac{4}{5} - \frac{2}{5}$ **30.** $\frac{5}{6} - \frac{1}{6}$ **31.** $\frac{3}{4} - \frac{2}{4}$ **32.** $\frac{10}{12} - \frac{5}{12}$

33. $\frac{2}{3} - \frac{1}{3}$ **34.** $\frac{9}{10} - \frac{3}{10}$ **35.** $\frac{2}{4} - \frac{1}{4}$ **36.** $\frac{8}{12} - \frac{5}{12}$ **37.** $\frac{9}{10} - \frac{7}{10}$

Algebra **Find x.**

38. $\frac{5}{6} - \frac{1}{6} = x$ **39.** $\frac{3}{10} + x = \frac{8}{10}$ **40.** $x + \frac{2}{5} = \frac{4}{5}$ **41.** $x = \frac{2}{8} + \frac{5}{8}$ **42.** $x - \frac{1}{3} = \frac{1}{3}$

43. *Cooking* Peanut sauce is commonly used as a base for stews and soups in Nigeria, Ghana, and Sierra Leone.
  a. To make the sauce spicier, you decide to double the amount of cayenne. How much cayenne will you use?
  b. You decide to use equal amounts of apple and apricot juices. How much of each type of juice will you use?

Peanut Sauce
2 cups chopped onion
1 tablespoon peanut oil
¼ tablespoon cayenne
¼ teaspoon ground ginger
1 ripe banana
1 cup tomato juice
½ cup apple or
  apricot juice
½ cup peanut butter
½ teaspoon salt

44. *Modeling* In an archery tournament, Zwena hit the target 9 times out of 12. What fraction of Zwena's arrows did not hit the target? Draw a model to show your solution.

45. *Open-ended* Write a problem that could be solved using one of the equations from Exercises 38–42.

46. *Writing* The flag of Thailand is at the right. Describe what each statement could represent on the flag.
  a. $\frac{1}{6} + \frac{1}{6} = \frac{1}{3}$ **b.** $\frac{6}{6} - \frac{4}{6} = \frac{1}{3}$

Mixed Review

Write using an exponent. *(Lesson 4-2)*

47. $6 \times 6 \times 6 \times 6$ **48.** $22 \times 22 \times 22$ **49.** $5.8 \times 5.8 \times 5.8 \times 5.8 \times 5.8$

Find the GCF of each set of numbers. *(Lesson 5-3)*

50. 14, 21   **51.** 10, 15, 20   **52.** 13, 17   **53.** 36, 27   **54.** 24, 60, 72

55. *Choose a Strategy* Jan and Leah earn money running errands for neighbors. Leah earns $1.25 more per hour than Jan. If together they earned $15.75 for 3 hours of work, how much did each earn per hour?

6-3 Unlike Denominators

What You'll Learn

▼1 To use fraction models to add and subtract fractions with unlike denominators

▼2 To use equivalent fractions to add and subtract fractions with unlike denominators

...And Why

You can add fractions of distances with different denominators.

Here's How

Look for questions that
- build understanding
- ✔ check understanding

THINK AND DISCUSS

1 Using Fraction Models

You can use fraction models when the denominators are different.

■ **EXAMPLE 1**

Model the sum $\frac{1}{4} + \frac{2}{3}$.

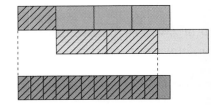

←— Use the fraction model for $\frac{1}{4}$.

←— Use the fraction model for $\frac{2}{3}$.

←— Find a fraction model to represent the sum.

$$\frac{1}{4} + \frac{2}{3} = \frac{11}{12}$$

Sometimes even when the fractions have different denominators, you can use other fraction models to add or subtract.

■ **EXAMPLE 2**

Model the difference $\frac{1}{2} - \frac{1}{3}$.

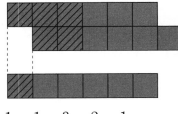

←— Use the $\frac{3}{6}$ fraction model for $\frac{1}{2}$.

←— Use the $\frac{2}{6}$ fraction model for $\frac{1}{3}$.

←— Subtract: $\frac{3}{6} - \frac{2}{6}$.

$$\frac{1}{2} - \frac{1}{3} = \frac{3}{6} - \frac{2}{6} = \frac{1}{6}$$

1. ✔**Try It Out** Model each sum or difference.

a. $\frac{3}{5} + \frac{1}{10}$ b. $\frac{5}{6} - \frac{2}{3}$ c. $\frac{1}{3} + \frac{1}{4}$ d. $\frac{5}{12} - \frac{1}{4}$

To write equivalent fractions, you must first find the least common denominator (LCD) of the fractions.

2. a. ✔Try It Out What is the LCD of $\frac{1}{2}$ and $\frac{1}{5}$?

 b. ▪Go a Step Further Write equivalent fractions for $\frac{1}{2}$ and $\frac{1}{5}$ using the LCD you found in part (a).

■ **EXAMPLE 3**

Find the sum $\frac{7}{8} + \frac{1}{6}$.

Estimate: $\frac{7}{8} + \frac{1}{6} \approx 1 + 0 = 1$

The LCD of $\frac{7}{8}$ and $\frac{1}{6}$ is 24. ←—Find the LCM of 8 and 6.

$$\begin{array}{l} \frac{7}{8} = \frac{7 \times 3}{8 \times 3} = \frac{21}{24} \\ + \frac{1}{6} = \frac{1 \times 4}{6 \times 4} = \frac{4}{24} \\ \hline \phantom{+ \frac{1}{6} = \frac{1 \times 4}{6 \times 4}} = \frac{25}{24} \\ \phantom{+ \frac{1}{6} = \frac{1 \times 4}{6 \times 4}} = 1\frac{1}{24} \end{array}$$

←——The LCD is 24. Write the fractions with the same denominators.

←——Add the numerators.

←——Write the answer as a mixed number. The answer is close to the estimate.

---

3. ✔Try It Out Find each sum or difference.

 a. $\frac{2}{9} + \frac{1}{6}$ **b.** $\frac{7}{8} - \frac{1}{2}$ **c.** $\frac{7}{8} + \frac{1}{10}$ **d.** $\frac{4}{5} - \frac{2}{3}$

Sometimes you must add or subtract fractions to solve equations.

■ **EXAMPLE 4**

Algebra Solve the equation $\frac{1}{2} + x = \frac{14}{15}$.

$$\frac{1}{2} + x = \frac{14}{15}$$ ←—Write the equation.

$$\frac{1}{2} + x - \frac{1}{2} = \frac{14}{15} - \frac{1}{2}$$ ←—Subtract $\frac{1}{2}$ from each side.

$$x = \frac{14}{15} - \frac{1}{2}$$

$$x = \frac{28}{30} - \frac{15}{30}$$ ←—Write equivalent fractions.

$$x = \frac{13}{30}$$ ←—Subtract.

4. ✔Try It Out Solve each equation.

 a. $\frac{3}{4} + x = \frac{11}{12}$ **b.** $x - \frac{1}{12} = \frac{5}{6}$ **c.** $\frac{5}{8} + x = \frac{11}{12}$

Algebra **Write a number sentence for each model shown.**

1.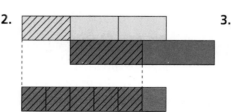

2.

3.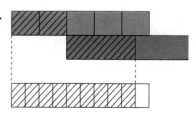

Model each statement.

4. $\frac{3}{4} - \frac{1}{2} = \frac{1}{4}$

5. $\frac{1}{5} + \frac{1}{2} = \frac{7}{10}$

6. $\frac{3}{4} - \frac{1}{3} = \frac{5}{12}$

7. $\frac{5}{6} - \frac{1}{3} = \frac{3}{6}$ or $\frac{1}{2}$

Model each sum or difference.

8. $\frac{1}{3} + \frac{1}{6}$

9. $\frac{9}{10} - \frac{3}{5}$

10. $\frac{1}{3} + \frac{1}{2}$

11. $\frac{4}{5} - \frac{1}{10}$

12. $\frac{2}{3} + \frac{1}{12}$

13. $\frac{1}{6} + \frac{1}{3}$

14. $\frac{11}{12} - \frac{3}{4}$

15. $\frac{2}{3} + \frac{1}{4}$

16. $\frac{7}{12} - \frac{1}{4}$

17. $\frac{1}{2} - \frac{3}{10}$

Estimation **Is each answer greater than or less than 1?**

18. $\frac{1}{8} + \frac{1}{4}$

19. $\frac{4}{5} - \frac{1}{2}$

20. $\frac{1}{2} + \frac{3}{4}$

21. $\frac{6}{7} - \frac{4}{5}$

22. $\frac{3}{4} + \frac{5}{12}$

23. *Art* Suppose you use $\frac{3}{4}$ yd of felt on the top of a bulletin board display. Then you use another $\frac{2}{3}$ yd on the bottom of the display. How much felt do you use altogether?

24. *Geology* Two students explore a cove along an old road. One student explores $\frac{1}{3}$ mi of the cove. The other explores $\frac{1}{4}$ mi of the cove at the opposite end. How much of the cove do they explore altogether?

Find each sum or difference. Use equivalent fractions.

25. $\frac{1}{3} + \frac{2}{5}$

26. $\frac{13}{16} - \frac{1}{4}$

27. $\frac{4}{5} - \frac{1}{2}$

28. $\frac{3}{4} + \frac{1}{3}$

29. $\frac{4}{5} + \frac{1}{6}$

30. $\frac{7}{10} - \frac{1}{4}$

31. $\frac{3}{8} + \frac{4}{5}$

32. $\frac{5}{6} + \frac{1}{4}$

33. $\frac{5}{6} - \frac{1}{2}$

34. $\frac{7}{8} - \frac{1}{3}$

35. $\frac{7}{12} + \frac{2}{3}$

36. $\frac{8}{9} + \frac{5}{6}$

37. $\frac{7}{12} - \frac{1}{3}$

38. $\frac{2}{3} - \frac{1}{5}$

39. $\frac{5}{12} + \frac{7}{9}$

40. $\frac{11}{20} + \frac{3}{4}$

41. $\frac{17}{20} - \frac{2}{5}$

42. $\frac{3}{4} - \frac{1}{5}$

43. $\frac{9}{10} - \frac{7}{8}$

44. $\frac{11}{12} + \frac{9}{10}$

Social Studies Use the data at the right for Exercises 45–47.

45. List the countries in order from least to greatest population.

46. Are the populations of Costa Rica and Nicaragua together greater than or less than the population of Honduras?

47. Which country has a population almost equal to the populations of Belize and Honduras combined?

Algebra Find x. Write the answer in simplest form.

48. $x - \frac{1}{2} = \frac{1}{6}$ 49. $\frac{2}{5} + x = \frac{7}{10}$ 50. $x + \frac{2}{5} = \frac{5}{12}$

51. $x - \frac{2}{3} = \frac{3}{4}$ 52. $\frac{1}{10} + x = \frac{7}{12}$ 53. $x - \frac{2}{3} = \frac{7}{12}$

54. **Writing** Describe two different ways to find the sum of $\frac{1}{6}$ and $\frac{3}{4}$.

Choose Use any method to add or subtract.

55. $\frac{5}{8} + \frac{9}{12}$ 56. $\frac{11}{30} - \frac{1}{5}$ 57. $\frac{2}{5} + \frac{1}{2}$ 58. $\frac{3}{4} - \frac{1}{3}$

59. **Number Sense** A package of sliced ham weighs $\frac{1}{2}$ lb. Another package of sliced ham weighs $\frac{3}{4}$ lb. You buy both packages. Do you have enough ham to serve $\frac{1}{3}$ lb to each of four persons?

Population of Central America	
Country	**Portion of Population**
Belize	$\frac{1}{125}$
Costa Rica	$\frac{11}{100}$
El Salvador	$\frac{9}{50}$
Guatemala	$\frac{8}{25}$
Honduras	$\frac{17}{100}$
Nicaragua	$\frac{3}{25}$
Panama	$\frac{2}{25}$

Mixed Review

Name the type of graph (bar, line, or circle graph) most appropriate for each situation below. Support your answer. *(Lesson 1-5)*

60. average cost of lunch at six restaurants

61. change in taxes paid from 1950 to 2000

62. number of senior citizens', adults', and children's tickets sold at an art museum in one day

63. *Choose a Strategy* The last Friday of a certain month is the 28th day of the month. On what day of the week is the first day of that month?

Estimate each sum or difference.

1. $\frac{1}{4} + \frac{5}{8}$ **2.** $\frac{46}{47} - \frac{19}{23}$ **3.** $5\frac{3}{4} + 3\frac{3}{5}$ **4.** $12\frac{67}{68} + 5\frac{1}{62}$ **5.** $2\frac{1}{2} - \frac{11}{12}$

Write an addition or subtraction sentence for each model.

6. 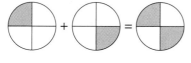   **7.** 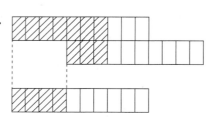   **8.**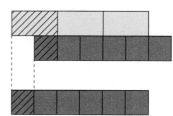

Find each sum or difference. Write the answer in simplest form.

9. $\frac{2}{5} + \frac{1}{5}$ **10.** $\frac{7}{9} - \frac{4}{9}$ **11.** $\frac{7}{8} - \frac{3}{8}$ **12.** $\frac{1}{8} + \frac{1}{4}$ **13.** $\frac{5}{6} - \frac{1}{3}$ **14.** $\frac{1}{5} - \frac{1}{10}$

15. *Open-ended* Write and solve an equation requiring the addition or subtraction of fractions.

Math at Work

CHEF

Generally, there are two types of chefs—institutional chefs and restaurant chefs. No matter where a chef works, he or she will measure, mix, and cook meals according to given recipes.

The art of cooking requires skill in many areas of mathematics. Knowing how to weigh and measure with both metric and customary measures is essential to following a recipe. A knowledge of estimation, ratio, and proportion will help a chef determine quantities and serving sizes.

 For more information about a career as a chef, visit the Prentice Hall Web site: www.phschool.com

6-4 Adding Mixed Numbers

What You'll Learn

▼ To add mixed numbers mentally

▼ To add mixed numbers by renaming

...And Why

Adding measurements sometimes involves adding mixed numbers.

Here's How

Look for questions that
- build understanding
- ✔ check understanding

 The giant tortoise is one of the slowest-moving animals. The slowest giant tortoise ever recorded crawled only 15 feet in 43.5 seconds.

Source: *Guinness Book of World Records*

Work Together

Using Mixed Numbers

Cut some string into each of the following lengths: $1\frac{3}{8}$ in., $2\frac{1}{4}$ in., $1\frac{7}{8}$ in., $3\frac{1}{8}$ in., and $5\frac{3}{4}$ in. Place two of the pieces end to end.

1. **▪Algebra** Estimate the sum of the length of the two pieces and then add. Write an addition sentence for the sum.

2. Repeat Question 1 for several different pairs of string pieces.

3. **▪Measurement** Check each addition sentence by measuring the total length of each pair of pieces.

THINK AND DISCUSS

▼ **Adding Mixed Numbers Mentally**

One way to add mixed numbers is to compute the whole number and fraction parts separately.

■ **EXAMPLE 1** **Real-World Problem Solving**

Zoology Suppose a giant tortoise traveled $8\frac{1}{4}$ yd in one minute and $7\frac{1}{2}$ yd in the next minute. What total distance did it travel during these two minutes?

Words	•	1st minute	+	2nd minute	=	Total distance traveled

Equation	•	$8\frac{1}{4}$	+	$7\frac{1}{2}$	=	d

$8 + 7 = 15$ ⟵ Add the whole numbers.

$\frac{1}{4} + \frac{1}{2} = \frac{1}{4} + \frac{2}{4} = \frac{3}{4}$ ⟵ Add the fractions.

$15 + \frac{3}{4} = 15\frac{3}{4}$ ⟵ Combine the two parts.

The giant tortoise traveled $15\frac{3}{4}$ yd.

4. ✔**Try It Out** Find the sum $10\frac{1}{8} + 6\frac{3}{16}$.

2 Adding Mixed Numbers by Renaming

Sometimes the sum of the fraction part is an improper fraction. If so, rename it as a mixed number.

■ EXAMPLE 2

Find the sum $15\frac{3}{4} + 3\frac{1}{2}$.

Estimate: $15\frac{3}{4} + 3\frac{1}{2} \approx 16 + 4 = 20$

$$15\frac{3}{4} \qquad = 15\frac{3}{4}$$

The LCD is 4. Write the fractions with the same denominators.

$$+ \ 3\frac{1}{2} = \ 3\frac{1 \times 2}{2 \times 2} = \ 3\frac{2}{4}$$

$$= 18\frac{5}{4}$$

Add whole numbers. Add fractions.

$$= 18 + 1\frac{1}{4}$$

Rename $\frac{5}{4}$: $\frac{5}{4} = \frac{4}{4} + \frac{1}{4} = 1\frac{1}{4}$

Add the whole numbers.

$$= 19\frac{1}{4}$$

The answer is close to the estimate.

5. ✔*Try It Out* Find each sum.

a. $3\frac{5}{6} + 5\frac{11}{12}$ b. $12\frac{3}{8} + 6\frac{3}{4}$ c. $7\frac{3}{5} + 13\frac{2}{3}$

6. ⚏*Open-ended* Write two mixed numbers whose sum is a whole number.

To solve some equations, you may need to add mixed numbers.

■ EXAMPLE 3

Algebra Solve the equation $x - 8\frac{11}{16} = 5\frac{3}{8}$.

$$x - 8\frac{11}{16} = 5\frac{3}{8}$$

$$x - 8\frac{11}{16} + 8\frac{11}{16} = 5\frac{3}{8} + 8\frac{11}{16}$$

Add $8\frac{11}{16}$ to each side.

$$x = (5 + 8) + (\frac{3}{8} + \frac{11}{16})$$

Separate whole numbers from fractions.

$$x = 13 + (\frac{6}{16} + \frac{11}{16})$$

Add the whole numbers. Then add the fractions.

$$x = 13 + \frac{17}{16}$$

$$x = 13 + 1\frac{1}{16}$$

Rename the improper fraction.

$$x = 14\frac{1}{16}$$

Add.

The solution is $14\frac{1}{16}$.

7. ✔*Try It Out* Solve each equation.

a. $x - 3\frac{5}{8} = 12\frac{3}{4}$ b. $4\frac{1}{12} = x - 11\frac{2}{3}$ c. $x - 7\frac{1}{5} = 2\frac{3}{10}$

EXERCISES *On Your Own*

Mental Math **Add.**

1. $1 + \frac{1}{6}$ 2. $3 + 1\frac{2}{3}$ 3. $9\frac{2}{3} + 5\frac{2}{3}$ 4. $4\frac{1}{2} + 4\frac{1}{2}$ 5. $5\frac{3}{5} + 3\frac{2}{5}$

Find each sum.

6. $8 + 1\frac{2}{3}$ 7. $3\frac{1}{6} + 2$ 8. $8\frac{1}{5} + 3\frac{3}{4}$ 9. $11\frac{3}{8} + 2\frac{1}{16}$ 10. $9\frac{1}{12} + 8\frac{3}{4}$

11. $1\frac{1}{4} + 6\frac{1}{2}$ 12. $3\frac{1}{3} + 1\frac{1}{6}$ 13. $9\frac{1}{16} + 4\frac{7}{8}$ 14. $7\frac{3}{5} + 21\frac{1}{10}$ 15. $33\frac{1}{3} + 23\frac{2}{5}$

16. $7\frac{1}{10} + 3\frac{2}{5}$ 17. $6\frac{1}{4} + 2\frac{3}{5}$ 18. $2\frac{5}{16} + 1\frac{1}{4}$ 19. $10\frac{1}{4} + 3\frac{1}{3}$ 20. $27\frac{5}{8} + 23\frac{1}{4}$

21. *Writing* Explain how you can mentally find the sum below.
$5\frac{1}{3} + 3\frac{4}{5} + 2\frac{2}{3} + 6\frac{1}{5}$

Complete to rename each mixed number.

22. $2\frac{11}{10} = 3\frac{\blacksquare}{10}$ 23. $4\frac{11}{6} = 5\frac{\blacksquare}{6}$ 24. $\frac{9}{4} = 2\frac{\blacksquare}{4}$ 25. $5\frac{\blacksquare}{12} = 6\frac{1}{12}$ 26. $7\frac{4}{7} = 6\frac{\blacksquare}{7}$

27. *Open-ended* Write a mixed number containing an improper fraction. Rename your mixed number.

Find each sum.

28. $2\frac{3}{4} + 1\frac{5}{8}$ 29. $4\frac{5}{8} + 1\frac{1}{4}$ 30. $3\frac{1}{3} + 2\frac{5}{6}$ 31. $1\frac{2}{3} + 3\frac{5}{6}$ 32. $4\frac{3}{5} + 1\frac{2}{3}$

33. $1\frac{7}{8} + 1\frac{1}{4}$ 34. $4\frac{5}{12} + 1\frac{1}{2}$ 35. $6\frac{4}{5} + 2\frac{1}{3}$ 36. $5\frac{8}{9} + 7\frac{1}{6}$ 37. $17\frac{3}{5} + 12\frac{7}{10}$

38. $33\frac{3}{4} + 33\frac{5}{6}$ 39. $41\frac{9}{10} + 2\frac{3}{4}$ 40. $13\frac{2}{3} + 2\frac{1}{24}$ 41. $10\frac{3}{5} + 1\frac{7}{10}$ 42. $4 + 13\frac{5}{6}$

43. *Tides* A mark on the side of a pier shows that the water is
$4\frac{7}{8}$ ft deep. When the tide is high, the depth increases by $2\frac{3}{4}$ ft.
a. What is the depth of the water when the tide is high?
b. Did you add or subtract to find the answer to part (a)?
Justify your solution.

44. *Number Sense* Explain why the sum of two mixed numbers is not always a mixed number.

Algebra **Solve each equation for x.**

45. $x - \frac{9}{10} = 23\frac{3}{10}$ **46.** $32\frac{4}{5} = x - 1\frac{3}{5}$ **47.** $12\frac{1}{2} = x - 15\frac{1}{6}$ **48.** $17\frac{11}{12} = x - 6\frac{5}{6}$

49. $x - \frac{5}{6} = 3\frac{1}{2}$ **50.** $x - 11\frac{1}{12} = 11\frac{1}{12}$ **51.** $x - 17\frac{2}{3} = 14\frac{1}{4}$ **52.** $x - 10\frac{1}{6} = \frac{5}{12}$

53. $x - 23\frac{1}{2} = \frac{5}{6}$ **54.** $12\frac{7}{12} = x - \frac{3}{4}$ **55.** $x - 3\frac{1}{2} = 6\frac{3}{4}$ **56.** $34\frac{3}{8} = x - \frac{5}{8}$

57. $x - 70\frac{5}{6} = 100\frac{1}{2}$ **58.** $x - \frac{4}{5} = 3\frac{1}{2}$ **59.** $23\frac{5}{6} = x - 12\frac{7}{8}$ **60.** $x - 40\frac{1}{6} = 3\frac{9}{10}$

61. *Carpentry* A nail is driven through a $3\frac{1}{2}$-in. wooden board. The nail extends beyond the board by $1\frac{5}{8}$ in. How long is the nail?

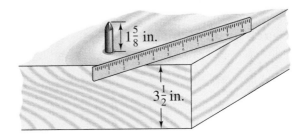

62. *Cooking* One recipe uses $1\frac{3}{4}$ c milk, and another uses $1\frac{1}{2}$ c milk. You have about 3 c milk at home. Do you have enough milk for both recipes? Explain.

63. **Choose A, B, C, or D.** Which two mixed numbers have a sum of $6\frac{3}{5}$?

   A. $3\frac{1}{10}$ and $2\frac{6}{5}$ **B.** $3\frac{2}{10}$ and $2\frac{6}{5}$ **C.** $3\frac{2}{10}$ and $3\frac{6}{5}$ **D.** $3\frac{3}{5}$ and $2\frac{5}{5}$

64. *Number Sense* The sides of a triangle have lengths $5\frac{1}{2}$ in., $3\frac{7}{8}$ in., and $2\frac{1}{4}$ in. Is a 12-in. piece of string long enough to fit around the triangle? Explain.

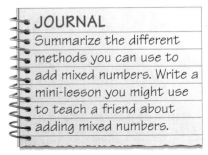

65. *Geometry* Fencing costs $5 per foot. How much will the fence cost for a $4\frac{1}{2}$ ft-by-$3\frac{1}{4}$ ft rectangular flower garden?

Mixed Review

Use the distributive property to find each product. *(Lesson 4-3)*

66. 24×5 **67.** 99×26 **68.** 68×8 **69.** 95×4 **70.** 53×7 **71.** 41×9

Find the next three terms in each number pattern. *(Lesson 2-1)*

72. 2, 4, 6, 8, ▇, ▇, ▇   **73.** 12, 36, 108, 324, ▇, ▇, ▇   **74.** 6, 12, 18, 24, ▇, ▇, ▇

75. *Choose a Strategy* Kyle counted 12 wheels on the cycles in the Homecoming Parade. His friend Leilani counted 7 cycles in all. The only cycles allowed were unicycles, bicycles, and tricycles. How many cycles of each type were in the parade?

TECHNOLOGY

Using a Fraction Calculator to Compute

After Lesson 6-4

You can use a fraction calculator to add and subtract fractions.

■ EXAMPLE 1

Find the difference: $\frac{5}{6} - \frac{3}{8}$

Estimate: $\frac{5}{6} - \frac{3}{8} \approx 1 - \frac{1}{2} \approx \frac{1}{2}$

Enter 5 $\boxed{/}$ 6 $\boxed{-}$ 3 $\boxed{/}$ 8 $\boxed{=}$ *11/24*

$\frac{5}{6} - \frac{3}{8} = \frac{11}{24}$

You can also use a fraction calculator to add mixed numbers and to simplify the answer when necessary.

■ EXAMPLE 2

Find the sum: $1\frac{3}{4} + 3\frac{1}{2}$

Estimate: $1\frac{3}{4} + 3\frac{1}{2} \approx 2 + 3\frac{1}{2} \approx 5\frac{1}{2}$

Enter 1 $\boxed{\text{UNIT}}$ 3 $\boxed{/}$ 4 $\boxed{+}$ 3 $\boxed{\text{UNIT}}$ 1 $\boxed{/}$ 2 $\boxed{=}$ *4 u 5/4*

To rename this number, press $\boxed{\text{Ab/c}}$ $\boxed{=}$ *5 u 1/4*

$1\frac{3}{4} + 3\frac{1}{2} = 5\frac{1}{4}$

Find each sum or difference.

1. $\frac{3}{4} - \frac{2}{5}$

2. $\frac{5}{8} + \frac{1}{4}$

3. $\frac{9}{10} - \frac{1}{5}$

4. $\frac{8}{9} + \frac{1}{12}$

5. $\frac{11}{12} - \frac{3}{8}$

6. $\frac{4}{5} + \frac{1}{20}$

7. $\frac{3}{10} - \frac{2}{9}$

8. $\frac{22}{25} + \frac{9}{100}$

9. $\frac{5}{9} - \frac{2}{5}$

10. $\frac{2}{3} + \frac{4}{5}$

11. $9\frac{3}{4} + 3\frac{3}{4}$

12. $5\frac{3}{8} + 8\frac{1}{8}$

13. $11\frac{8}{9} - 7\frac{1}{2}$

14. $6\frac{9}{10} + 2\frac{1}{12}$

15. $18\frac{5}{12} - 9\frac{1}{2}$

16. $1\frac{1}{10} + 8\frac{1}{12}$

17. $13\frac{5}{12} - 5\frac{1}{3}$

18. $4\frac{1}{4} + 2\frac{1}{3}$

19. $14\frac{3}{10} - 3\frac{1}{2}$

20. $7\frac{8}{9} - 3\frac{1}{6}$

21. *Writing* How can you use a fraction calculator to simplify an improper fraction?

6-5 Subtracting Mixed Numbers

What You'll Learn

1 To subtract mixed numbers mentally

2 To subtract mixed numbers by renaming

...And Why

To find differences in length and width, you often must subtract mixed numbers.

Here's How

Look for questions that
- build understanding
- ✔ check understanding

THINK AND DISCUSS

1 *Subtracting Mixed Numbers Mentally*

Use the scale drawings of animal tracks below.

1. Which is wider, the coyote's track or the red fox's track?

2. Which is longer, the coyote's track or the gray wolf's track?

3. Is the length or the width of the gray wolf's track greater?

Coyote
$2\frac{1}{2}$ in. Length
2 in. Width

Red Fox
$2\frac{1}{4}$ in. Length
$2\frac{1}{8}$ in. Width

Gray Wolf
$4\frac{1}{8}$ in. Length
$3\frac{3}{4}$ in. Width

To find the difference between two measurements, you subtract.

■ **EXAMPLE 1** *Real-World Problem Solving*

Biology How much wider is the gray wolf's track than the red fox's?

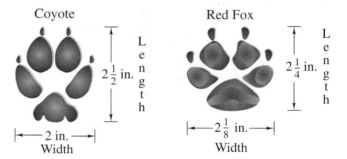

| Words | Width of gray wolf's paw track | − | Width of red fox's paw track | = | Difference in width |

| Equation | $3\frac{3}{4}$ in. | − | $2\frac{1}{8}$ in. | = | w |

$3 - 2 = 1$ ←── Subtract the whole numbers.

$\frac{3}{4} - \frac{1}{8} = \frac{6}{8} - \frac{1}{8} = \frac{5}{8}$ ←── Subtract the fractions.

$1 + \frac{5}{8} = 1\frac{5}{8}$ ←── Combine the two parts.

The gray wolf's track is $1\frac{5}{8}$ in. wider than the red fox's track.

4. ✔Try It Out How much longer is the coyote's track than the red fox's track?

▼2 Subtracting Mixed Numbers by Renaming

Sometimes you need to rename before you can subtract.

The cheetah is the fastest animal on land for distances up to 350 yd. The pronghorn antelope is faster than the cheetah after 350 yd.

■ **EXAMPLE 2**   *Real-World Problem Solving*

Suppose an antelope ran $43\frac{1}{2}$ yd while a cheetah ran $63\frac{1}{4}$ yd. How much farther did the cheetah run than the antelope?

Words	•	Distance run by cheetah	−	Distance run by antelope	=	Difference in distance

Equation	•	$63\frac{1}{4}$ yd	−	$43\frac{1}{2}$ yd	=	d

Estimate: $63\frac{1}{4} - 43\frac{1}{2} \approx 63 - 44 = 19$

Since $\frac{1}{4}$ is less than $\frac{1}{2}$, you must rename $63\frac{1}{4}$ before you can subtract.

$$63\frac{1}{4} = 62 + 1\frac{1}{4} = 62\frac{5}{4}$$ ←— Rename $63\frac{1}{4}$ as $62\frac{5}{4}$.
$$-\ 43\frac{1}{2} = 43\frac{1 \times 2}{2 \times 2} = 43\frac{2}{4}$$ ←— Write an equivalent fraction for $\frac{1}{2}$.
$$= 19\frac{3}{4}$$ ←— Subtract the whole numbers and fractions. The answer is close to the estimate.

The cheetah ran $19\frac{3}{4}$ yd farther than the antelope.

5. ⬛Look Back Check your answer to Example 2 by adding.

You can also use equations to solve problems.

■ **EXAMPLE 3**

Algebra Solve the equation $4\frac{1}{2} + x = 6\frac{1}{3}$

$$4\frac{1}{2} + x = 6\frac{1}{3}$$
$$4\frac{1}{2} + x - 4\frac{1}{2} = 6\frac{1}{3} - 4\frac{1}{2}$$ ←— Subtract $4\frac{1}{2}$ from both sides.
$$x = 6\frac{2}{6} - 4\frac{3}{6}$$ ←— Write equivalent fractions.
$$= 5\frac{8}{6} - 4\frac{3}{6}$$ ←— Rename. $6\frac{2}{6} = 5 + 1\frac{2}{6} = 5\frac{8}{6}$.
$$= 1\frac{5}{6}$$ ←— Subtract whole numbers and then fractions.

6. ✓*Try It Out* Solve each equation.

a. $x + 1\frac{3}{4} = 3\frac{1}{4}$

b. $5\frac{1}{2} + x = 7\frac{5}{8}$

EXERCISES *On Your Own*

Mental Math **Subtract.**

1. $9\frac{2}{3} - 5\frac{2}{3}$

2. $1 - \frac{1}{6}$

3. $3 - 1\frac{2}{3}$

4. $4\frac{1}{2} - 4\frac{1}{2}$

5. $12\frac{3}{4} - 10\frac{1}{4}$

Find each difference.

6. $7\frac{3}{4} - 3\frac{3}{8}$

7. $2\frac{5}{16} - 1\frac{1}{4}$

8. $9\frac{4}{5} - 4\frac{3}{5}$

9. $21\frac{1}{8} - 11\frac{1}{16}$

10. $15\frac{11}{12} - 11\frac{1}{2}$

11. $12\frac{1}{4} - 4\frac{1}{8}$

12. $3\frac{2}{3} - 1\frac{1}{6}$

13. $6\frac{4}{5} - 2\frac{1}{4}$

14. $41\frac{11}{12} - 27\frac{5}{6}$

15. $70\frac{9}{10} - 45\frac{4}{5}$

16. $10\frac{1}{10} - 3\frac{2}{5}$

17. $3\frac{3}{8} - 1\frac{3}{4}$

18. $4\frac{5}{12} - 1\frac{1}{2}$

19. $6\frac{1}{5} - 2\frac{2}{3}$

20. $3\frac{2}{3} - 1\frac{3}{4}$

21. $18\frac{1}{2} - 1\frac{2}{3}$

22. $4\frac{3}{8} - 1\frac{7}{16}$

23. $3\frac{1}{16} - 2\frac{1}{2}$

24. $4\frac{1}{4} - 1\frac{2}{3}$

25. $25\frac{5}{8} - 17\frac{15}{16}$

26. $2\frac{1}{4} - 1\frac{7}{8}$

27. $4\frac{1}{12} - 1\frac{11}{12}$

28. $5\frac{5}{8} - 2\frac{7}{16}$

29. $11\frac{2}{3} - 3\frac{5}{6}$

30. $10\frac{9}{10} - 3\frac{11}{12}$

31. *Writing* Explain how you can mentally find the difference $12\frac{1}{4} - 10\frac{3}{4}$.

32. **Choose A, B, C, or D.** Which two mixed numbers have a difference of $4\frac{2}{5}$?

A. $12\frac{7}{10}$ and $8\frac{4}{5}$

B. $16\frac{3}{10}$ and $12\frac{1}{2}$

C. $7\frac{1}{10}$ and $2\frac{7}{10}$

D. $13\frac{1}{5}$ and $9\frac{2}{5}$

33. *Patterns* Write the next two numbers in the pattern below.

$9\frac{1}{3}, 8\frac{1}{6}, 7, 5\frac{5}{6}, 4\frac{2}{3}, \blacksquare, \blacksquare.$

34. Explain how you could have used subtraction to answer Exercise 33.

Biology **Use the data at the right for Exercises 35–37.**

35. Rewrite the table showing the lengths of the cones from shortest to longest.

36. Find the difference in length between the shortest cone and the longest cone.

37. *Estimation* Which two cones differ in length by about $\frac{1}{2}$ in.?

Spruce Tree	Length of Cone (in.)
White	$1\frac{5}{8}$
Norway	$5\frac{1}{2}$
Black	$\frac{7}{8}$
Red	$1\frac{1}{4}$

Data Analysis Use the table at the right for Exercises 38–40.

38. How much farther did Heike Drechsler jump than Chioma Ajunwa?

39. What is the difference in length between the 1960 and 1996 winning long jumps?

40. Find the difference between the longest winning jump and the shortest winning jump shown.

Women's Olympic Long Jump Winners

Year	Winner	Distance
1960	Vera Krepkina, U.S.S.R.	20 ft $10\frac{3}{4}$ in.
1964	Mary Rand, Great Britain	22 ft 2 in.
1968	Viorica Viscopoleanu, Romania	22 ft $4\frac{1}{2}$ in.
1972	Heidemarie Rosendahl, West Germany	22 ft 3 in.
1976	Angela Volgt, East Germany	22 ft $\frac{1}{2}$ in.
1980	Tatiana Kolpakova, U.S.S.R.	23 ft 2 in.
1984	Anisoara Scanclu, Romania	22 ft 10 in.
1988	Jackie Joyner-Kersee, U.S.	24 ft $3\frac{1}{2}$ in.
1992	Heike Drechsler, Germany	23 ft $5\frac{1}{4}$ in.
1996	Chioma Ajunwa, Nigeria	23 ft $4\frac{1}{2}$ in.

Algebra Solve each equation for x.

41. $x + 7\frac{1}{2} = 16\frac{3}{4}$ **42.** $18\frac{5}{6} = x + 12\frac{7}{8}$ **43.** $20\frac{15}{16} = x + 10\frac{1}{4}$ **44.** $x + 24\frac{3}{4} = 56\frac{1}{8}$

45. $31\frac{1}{5} + x = 40\frac{1}{2}$ **46.** $34\frac{1}{3} = x + 11\frac{7}{12}$ **47.** $x + 8\frac{1}{2} = 12\frac{3}{4}$ **48.** $5\frac{7}{8} + x = 10\frac{5}{16}$

49. $56\frac{1}{8} = x + 41\frac{1}{4}$ **50.** $x + 9\frac{1}{3} = 16\frac{3}{4}$ **51.** $33\frac{1}{4} + x = 45\frac{1}{2}$ **52.** $18\frac{1}{9} = x + 13\frac{7}{18}$

53. *Carpentry* A $3\frac{5}{8}$-in. nail is driven through a wooden door. The nail extends beyond the door by $\frac{7}{8}$ in.
  a. How thick is the door?
  b. What operation did you use in part (a)? Why?

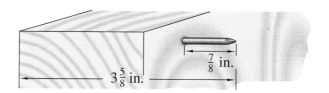

Mixed Review

Write each fraction as a decimal. Write each decimal as a fraction in simplest form. *(Lesson 5-9)*

54. $\frac{17}{20}$ **55.** 0.48   **56.** 0.06   **57.** $\frac{3}{25}$ **58.** 0.152   **59.** $\frac{21}{25}$

Round to the place of the underlined digit. *(Lesson 3-6)*

60. 2<u>0</u>,567   **61.** 9,<u>3</u>48,120   **62.** 0.0<u>9</u>3   **63.** 5.6<u>1</u>84   **64.** 6,4<u>5</u>6   **65.** 0.13<u>2</u>9

66. *Choose a Strategy* The Rotary Club has $140 in savings. The dues from 8 new members raised the amount to $198. Find the dues collected from each new member.

Draw a Diagram

Problem Solving Strategies

✔ Draw a Diagram
  Guess and Test
  Look for a Pattern
  Make a Model
  Make a Table
  Simulate a Problem
  Solve a Simpler Problem
  Too Much or Too Little
   Information
  Use Logical Reasoning
  Use Multiple Strategies
  Work Backward

THINK AND DISCUSS

Drawing a diagram is a strategy you can use to solve many problems. A diagram helps you to see a problem and its solution more clearly.

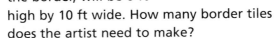

An artist is creating a tiled wall for the Native American wing of a museum. The border will be made of tiles containing Native American designs. Each tile is a square that measures $\frac{1}{2}$ ft on a side. The tiled wall, including the border, will be 6 ft high by 10 ft wide. How many border tiles does the artist need to make?

READ

Read for understanding. Summarize the problem.

Identify the information you need to use to solve the problem.

1. What size and shape are the border tiles?

2. What size and shape is the tiled wall? Do the dimensions include the border?

3. Is the problem asking you to find the total number of tiles the artist needs to make for the tiled wall? Explain.

PLAN

Decide on a strategy.

If you draw a diagram of the tiled wall, you can then draw in the border. If you use graph paper, you can count the number of border tiles needed.

4. What measurement will each unit on the graph paper represent?

5. How many units high and wide will your diagram be?

SOLVE

Try the strategy.

Draw a diagram to "see" the problem and its solution.

6. If one unit on the graph paper represents $\frac{1}{2}$ ft, how many feet in height will your diagram represent? How many feet in width?

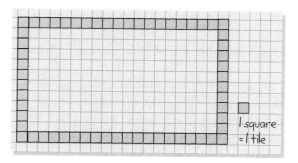

7. Use the diagram to find the number of border tiles the artist needs to make.

LOOK BACK

Think about how you solved the problem.

8. How did the diagram help you solve this problem? Evaluate your solution for reasonableness.

9. Do you think this problem would be difficult to solve without drawing a diagram? Explain.

10. Instead of drawing a diagram, one student followed the steps below. Find the number of border tiles needed for each side of the wall: top, 20; bottom, 20; left side, 12; right side, 12. Then add: 20 + 20 + 12 + 12 = 64 border tiles. What is wrong with this solution?

EXERCISES *On Your Own*

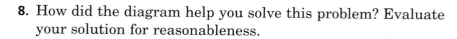

Draw a diagram to solve each problem.

1. *Pets* Suppose you have 24 ft of fence for a rectangular dog kennel. Each side will be a whole number of feet (no fractions). List all possible dimensions for the kennel. Which will give your dog the greatest area?

2. *Gardening* Your brother is planting flowers along the edge of a rectangular flower bed. He will place the plants 6 inches apart. The perimeter of the garden measures 7 feet. How many plants will your brother need?

3. **Carpentry** Jo is making a bookcase with wood that is $\frac{3}{4}$ in. thick. The bookcase has four shelves. One shelf is used for the top of the bookcase, and one is used for the bottom. The space between shelves is 12 in. Find the total height of the bookcase.

4. **Rugs** Elisha has a rug in her living room that is 12 ft by 18 ft. She wants to cut it into two smaller rectangular rugs that can be placed in other rooms. Show how she can make one cut and end up with two rugs the same size and shape.

Use any strategy to solve each problem. Show your work.

5. **Patterns** A store owner is stacking boxes for a window display. The top row will have one box. The second row will have three boxes. The third row will have five boxes. If this pattern continues, how many boxes will the tenth row have?

6. **Commuting** William drives about 24 mi total to and from work each day. He works five days each week and takes two weeks of vacation each year. About how many miles does William drive to and from work in one year?

7. **Food** Juan is making sandwiches for a party. Each sandwich has one type of bread, one type of cheese, and one type of meat. There are two choices each for bread, cheese, and meat. How many different sandwiches can Juan make?

8. **Marketing** To celebrate its opening day, a store is offering a free gift to every 15th customer. The store manager expects about 100 customers each hour. About how many gifts will the store offer by the end of its 12-h opening day?

9. **Scheduling** Britta needs to get to work by 9:30 A.M. She must drive her son to school, which takes 12 min. She will also drop off some dry cleaning. From school to the dry cleaners takes about 15 min. From the dry cleaners to work takes about 18 min. When should Britta leave home?

10. **Sports** A basketball team sold 496 raffle tickets and collected $396.80. Expenses totaled $75.98. How much did each ticket sell for?

Mixed Review

11. **Data Analysis** Draw a bar graph of the information found in the table at the right. *(Lesson 1-6)*

12. What metric unit would you use to measure the height of your school? The amount of juice in a glass? *(Lessons 3-8 and 3-9)*

13. Give the information needed to solve the following problem. Suppose you bought 3 boxes of juice. How much did you pay for them? *(Lesson 4-9)*

Number of Known Species	
Beetles	290,000
Bees/wasps	103,000
Butterflies/moths	112,000
Seed plants	248,400

Source: *The Diversity of Life*

6-7 Modeling the Multiplication of Fractions

What You'll Learn

▼1 To multiply fractions by fractions

▼2 To multiply whole numbers by fractions

...And Why

Sometimes you will need to find a fraction of a fraction.

Here's How

Look for questions that
- ⸬ build understanding
- ✔ check understanding

Work Together — *Finding a Fraction of a Fraction*

Let's pretend you are sharing an apple with a friend.

1. Use a circular piece of paper to represent the apple. Cut the "apple" into two equal pieces. What portion of the apple does each piece of paper represent? Take one piece.

2. Now cut your piece of "apple" into two equal pieces. Give one piece to your friend. What portion of your piece of "apple" does your friend have?

3. ⸬*Number Sense* What portion of the whole "apple" does each of you have?

THINK AND DISCUSS

▼1 *Multiplying Fractions by Fractions*

You can use area models to multiply fractions by fractions. The word "of" means multiplication when used mathematically.

■ **EXAMPLE 1**   *Real-World Problem Solving*

Community Planning A town plans to use one half of a square park for a picnic area. One third of the picnic area will be a playground. What portion of the park will be a playground?

 ← Picnic area = $\frac{1}{2}$ of the park; shade half of a rectangle.

 ← Divide the park area horizontally into thirds. Draw diagonal lines for $\frac{1}{3}$ of the shaded area.

One sixth of the park will be a playground.

4. ✔ **Try It Out** Suppose one fourth of the playground is for baseball. What portion of the park is for baseball?

5. ⠿ **Modeling** Draw an area model to show $\frac{2}{3}$ of $\frac{3}{4}$.

You can also multiply to find a fraction of a fraction.

■ **EXAMPLE 2**

Find $\frac{2}{3}$ of $\frac{1}{2}$.

$$\frac{2}{3} \text{ of } \frac{1}{2} \longrightarrow \quad \frac{2}{3} \times \frac{1}{2} \qquad \longleftarrow \text{Multiply the fractions.}$$

$$= \frac{2 \times 1}{3 \times 2} \qquad \longleftarrow \begin{array}{l}\text{Multiply the numerators.}\\ \text{Multiply the denominators.}\end{array}$$

$$= \frac{2}{6} = \frac{1}{3} \qquad \longleftarrow \text{Simplify.}$$

So, $\frac{2}{3}$ of $\frac{1}{2} = \frac{1}{3}$.

6. ✔ **Try It Out** Find each product.

   a. $\frac{2}{3}$ of $\frac{3}{4}$ **b.** $\frac{1}{4}$ of $\frac{2}{5}$ **c.** $\frac{3}{4}$ of $\frac{1}{8}$ **d.** $\frac{1}{2}$ of $\frac{2}{3}$

▼2 *Multiplying Whole Numbers by Fractions*

To solve some problems, you will need to multiply a fraction and a whole number. The model below shows how you can do this.

1	1	1	1
$1 \times \frac{2}{3}$	$1 \times \frac{2}{3}$	$1 \times \frac{2}{3}$	$1 \times \frac{2}{3}$

$$4 \times \frac{2}{3} = \frac{2}{3} + \frac{2}{3} + \frac{2}{3} + \frac{2}{3}$$
$$= \frac{8}{3}$$
$$= 2\frac{2}{3}$$

You can change a whole number to an improper fraction with a denominator of 1 and then multiply two fractions.

■ **EXAMPLE 3**

Find the product $\frac{3}{4} \times 5$.

$$\frac{3}{4} \times 5 = \frac{3}{4} \times \frac{5}{1} \qquad \longleftarrow \text{Write 5 as } \frac{5}{1}.$$

$$= \frac{3 \times 5}{4 \times 1} \qquad \longleftarrow \text{Multiply the numerators and denominators.}$$

$$= \frac{15}{4} = 3\frac{3}{4} \qquad \longleftarrow \text{Rewrite as a mixed number.}$$

7. ✔ *Try It Out* Find each product.

    a. $\frac{1}{9} \times 10$ **b.** $\frac{4}{5} \times 12$ **c.** $\frac{2}{3} \times 11$ **d.** $\frac{3}{8} \times 7$

If the denominator of one fraction and the numerator of the other have a common factor, you can simplify before multiplying.

■ **EXAMPLE 4**   *Real-World Problem Solving*

School Play Suppose 12 students tried out for speaking parts in the school play. Two thirds of the students will get speaking parts. How many students will speak in the play?

$$\frac{2}{3} \text{ of } 12 = \frac{2}{3} \times \frac{12}{1}_{\,4} \qquad \longleftarrow \text{Write 12 as } \frac{12}{1}.$$

$$= \frac{2}{_1 3} \times \frac{\cancel{12}}{1} \qquad \longleftarrow \begin{array}{l}\text{Divide both 12 and 3 by}\\ \text{their GCF of 3.}\end{array}$$

$$= \frac{2 \times 4}{1 \times 1} = \frac{8}{1} = 8 \qquad \longleftarrow \text{Multiply and simplify.}$$

8. ✔ *Try It Out* Find each product.

    a. $\frac{1}{2}$ of 16   **b.** $\frac{2}{5}$ of 25   **c.** $\frac{3}{8}$ of 24   **d.** $\frac{5}{6}$ of 30

EXERCISES *On Your Own*

Modeling **What number sentence is represented by each model?**

1.   **2.**   **3.**

Modeling **Draw a model to represent each product.**

4. $\frac{1}{4}$ of $\frac{1}{3}$ **5.** $\frac{1}{2}$ of $\frac{3}{4}$ **6.** $\frac{3}{4}$ of $\frac{1}{4}$ **7.** $\frac{1}{5}$ of $\frac{5}{8}$ **8.** $\frac{4}{5}$ of $\frac{5}{16}$

9. Choose A, B, C, or D. Which product does the model at the right represent?

    A. $\frac{3}{4} \times \frac{2}{3}$ **B.** $\frac{1}{3} \times \frac{1}{3}$ **C.** $\frac{3}{4} \times \frac{1}{3}$ **D.** $\frac{1}{3} \times \frac{2}{3}$

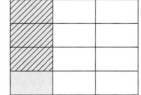

10. *Open-ended* Choose two fractions. Model their product.

11. *Research* Find out what fraction of your town's population is of school age. What portion of those are in first grade?

Find each product.

12. $\frac{1}{2}$ of $\frac{1}{4}$

13. $\frac{3}{5} \times \frac{2}{3}$

14. $\frac{5}{8} \times \frac{2}{7}$

15. $\frac{5}{6}$ of $\frac{3}{10}$

16. $\frac{2}{5} \times \frac{7}{8}$

17. $\frac{1}{5}$ of $\frac{1}{2}$

18. $\frac{1}{2}$ of $\frac{1}{5}$

19. $\frac{2}{5} \times \frac{1}{8}$

20. $\frac{1}{2}$ of $\frac{1}{3}$

21. $\frac{3}{5} \times \frac{3}{4}$

22. $\frac{2}{5}$ of 7

23. $\frac{5}{6} \times 13$

24. $\frac{3}{8} \times 11$

25. $\frac{9}{10}$ of 31

26. $\frac{5}{8} \times 3$

27. $\frac{2}{3}$ of 16

28. $\frac{7}{10} \times 80$

29. $\frac{3}{4}$ of 23

30. $\frac{6}{11} \times 77$

31. $\frac{1}{2}$ of 55

32. *Landscaping* Suppose two thirds of your yard will be grass. The rest will be plants. Three fourths of the plant area will have flowers. What portion of the yard will have flowers?

33. *Population* The U.S. population is about 265 million. About one fourth of the population is 17 years of age or under. About half of this group is female. About how many people in the United States are females 17 years of age or younger?

34. *Writing* Explain how multiplying $\frac{3}{10}$ and $\frac{2}{10}$ is similar to multiplying 0.3 and 0.2.

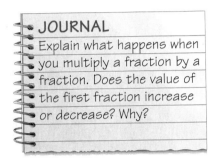
JOURNAL
Explain what happens when you multiply a fraction by a fraction. Does the value of the first fraction increase or decrease? Why?

Mixed Review

Is each number prime or composite? *(Lesson 5-2)*

35. 61

36. 51

37. 78

38. 79

39. 113

40. 129

Find the value of the digit 3 in each number. *(Lesson 3-2)*

41. 108.39

42. 38.22

43. 0.523

44. 345,650

45. 0.0293

46. 3,589,192

47. *Choose a Strategy* The lengths of three rods are 4 cm, 6 cm, and 9 cm. Arrange these rods to measure 11 cm.

CHAPTER PROJECT

PROJECT LINK: DEMONSTRATING

Using some of the items you have gathered, create a demonstration showing the addition of fractions that have the same denominator. You could use a ruler to add eighths of an inch, a measuring cup to add thirds of a cup of water, or a clock to add sixths of an hour. Make sure you prove that the two fractions add up to the expected sum.

PROBLEM SOLVING PRACTICE

Choose the best answer.

1. Bryan walked $1\frac{3}{4}$ mi, $2\frac{3}{4}$ mi, 3 mi, and $3\frac{1}{2}$ mi on consecutive days. Find the mean number of miles he walked for the four days.

   A. $1\frac{3}{4}$ mi   B. $2\frac{3}{4}$ mi

   C. $2\frac{7}{8}$ mi   D. 11 mi

2. What is the length of the nail below in inches?

   F. $1\frac{1}{4}$ G. $1\frac{3}{8}$

   H. $1\frac{1}{2}$ J. $1\frac{3}{4}$

3. Three paint brushes have widths of $\frac{1}{2}$ in., $\frac{3}{8}$ in., and $\frac{3}{4}$ in. Order the widths from least to greatest.

   A. $\frac{1}{2}$ in., $\frac{3}{4}$ in., $\frac{3}{8}$ in.

   B. $\frac{3}{8}$ in., $\frac{1}{2}$ in., $\frac{3}{4}$ in.

   C. $\frac{3}{4}$ in., $\frac{1}{2}$ in., $\frac{3}{8}$ in.

   D. $\frac{1}{2}$ in., $\frac{3}{8}$ in., $\frac{3}{4}$ in.

4. Today two neighbors water their lawns. After today the first will water her lawn every 4 days. The other will water hers every 5 days. How many days will pass before they water their lawns on the same day again?

   F. 8 days   G. 9 days

   H. 10 days   K. 19 days

5. Alice needed $4\frac{5}{6}$ yd of ribbon for a project. She bought 5 yd of ribbon. How many extra inches of ribbon did Alice buy?

   A. 3   B. 6   C. 9   D. 12

Please note that items 6–9 each have *five* answer choices.

6. A cookie recipe calls for $1\frac{1}{2}$ cups of molasses, $\frac{3}{4}$ cup of water, and $\frac{1}{2}$ cup of milk. How many cups of liquid does the recipe call for in all?

   F. $1\frac{5}{8}$ cups   G. $1\frac{3}{4}$ cups

   H. 2 cups   J. $2\frac{3}{4}$ cups

   K. Not Here

7. A picket fence is made of pickets that are $4\frac{1}{2}$ ft long. Pierre is using boards for each picket that are $5\frac{1}{4}$ ft long. How much must he trim from each board to make a picket?

   A. $\frac{1}{4}$ ft   B. $\frac{3}{4}$ ft

   C. $1\frac{1}{4}$ ft   D. $9\frac{3}{4}$ ft

   E. Not Here

8. At a book fair, paperbacks sell at 3 for $2 and hardbacks sell at 3 for $5. Sheila has $10 to spend on books. If she spends all of her money, which of the following could she buy?

   F. 3 paperbacks and 6 hardbacks
   G. 12 hardbacks
   H. 15 paperbacks
   J. 6 paperbacks and 6 hardbacks
   K. 20 paperbacks

9. Suppose you earn $4.75 per hour and work $3\frac{1}{2}$ hours, 4 days per week. What is your weekly salary?

   A. $8.25   B. $12.25   C. $16.63

   D. $66.50   E. Not Here

6-8 Multiplying Mixed Numbers

What You'll Learn

▼ To estimate products of mixed numbers

② To multiply mixed numbers

...And Why

You can find the areas of rectangular shapes.

Here's How

Look for questions that
- build understanding
- ✔ check understanding

The smallest newspaper was dated September 5, 1885. It was called "Tid Bits from all the Most Interesting Books, Periodicals and Newspapers in the World." The newspaper was owned by Mark Sundquist of Shoreline, Washington.

Source: *Guinness Book of Records*

THINK AND DISCUSS

① Estimating Products of Mixed Numbers

You can estimate area by estimating the length and width and multiplying. Often you must estimate products of mixed numbers.

■ **EXAMPLE 1**   *Real-World Problem Solving*

Newspapers The smallest newspaper ever printed had a page size of $2\frac{1}{8}$ in. wide by $2\frac{3}{4}$ in. long. Estimate the area of the page.

$$\textbf{area} = \textbf{width} \times \textbf{length}$$
$$= \quad 2\frac{1}{8} \quad \times \quad 2\frac{3}{4}$$
$$\approx 2 \times 3 \qquad \leftarrow \text{Round each mixed number to the nearest whole number.}$$
$$\approx 6 \qquad \leftarrow \text{Multiply.}$$

The area of the page is about 6 square inches (in.²).

1. ✔*Try It Out* The largest page size ever used for a newspaper measured $55\frac{3}{4}$ in. long by $39\frac{1}{6}$ in. wide. Estimate the area of the page.

2. **Estimation** Estimate each product.
   a. $12\frac{1}{2} \times 10\frac{2}{3}$ b. $2\frac{5}{6} \times 4\frac{1}{7}$ c. $7\frac{7}{12} \times 2\frac{1}{5}$

② Multiplying Mixed Numbers

You can use area models to multiply mixed numbers.

The area of a rectangle $1\frac{1}{2}$ in. wide by $2\frac{1}{4}$ in. long is shown below.

$$1\frac{1}{2} \times 2\frac{1}{4} = 1 + 1 + \frac{1}{4} + \frac{1}{2} + \frac{1}{2} + \frac{1}{8} = 3\frac{3}{8} \text{ in.}^2$$

To multiply mixed numbers, write each mixed number as an improper fraction.

■ EXAMPLE 2

CALCULATOR HINT

You can use a fraction calculator to find products of mixed numbers.

Find the product $2\frac{2}{3} \times 3\frac{1}{4}$.

Estimate: $2\frac{2}{3} \times 3\frac{1}{4} \approx 3 \times 3 \approx 9$

$$2\frac{2}{3} \times 3\frac{1}{4} = \frac{8}{3} \times \frac{13}{4} \quad \longleftarrow \text{Write each mixed number as an improper fraction.}$$

$$= \frac{\overset{2}{8}}{3} \times \frac{13}{\underset{1}{4}} \quad \longleftarrow \text{Simplify by dividing both 8 and 4 by the GCF, 4.}$$

$$= \frac{2 \times 13}{3 \times 1} \quad \longleftarrow \text{Multiply.}$$

$$= \frac{26}{3} = 8\frac{2}{3} \quad \longleftarrow \text{Simplify.}$$

Check: $8\frac{2}{3} \approx 9$ ✔

$$2\frac{2}{3} \times 3\frac{1}{4} = 8\frac{2}{3}$$

3. ✔**Try It Out** Find each product.

   a. $3\frac{1}{8} \times 3\frac{1}{5}$ **b.** $7\frac{1}{3} \times 3\frac{3}{4}$ **c.** $10\frac{4}{5} \times 1\frac{2}{3}$

4. ■**Explain** List the steps for finding $6\frac{2}{3} \times 1\frac{1}{5}$. Then multiply. Evaluate the reasonableness of the result.

Sometimes you need to know how much work you can do in a given amount of time.

■ EXAMPLE 3   *Real-World Problem Solving*

Typing Suppose you can type one page in $\frac{1}{3}$ h. How long will it take you to type a $2\frac{1}{2}$-page research paper?

Total time	=	time per page	×	number of pages
	=	$\frac{1}{3}$	×	$2\frac{1}{2}$

$$= \frac{1}{3} \times \frac{5}{2} \quad \longleftarrow \text{Write } 2\frac{1}{2} \text{ as } \frac{5}{2}.$$

$$= \frac{1 \times 5}{3 \times 2} = \frac{5}{6} \quad \longleftarrow \text{Multiply.}$$

It will take $\frac{5}{6}$ h, or 50 min, to type a $2\frac{1}{2}$-page paper.

5. ■**Look Back** Evaluate the reasonableness of your answer to Example 3.

6. ✔**Try It Out** If your friend can type one page in $\frac{1}{4}$ h, how long will it take him to type a $3\frac{1}{2}$-page paper?

Estimate each product.

1. $3\frac{1}{2} \times 1\frac{1}{4}$ 2. $14\frac{2}{3} \times 5\frac{1}{3}$ 3. $7\frac{3}{4} \times 9\frac{1}{2}$ 4. $15\frac{9}{10} \times 3\frac{1}{5}$

5. $2\frac{3}{4} \times 6\frac{1}{8}$ 6. $5\frac{1}{2} \times 10\frac{3}{10}$ 7. $9\frac{1}{5} \times 5\frac{7}{12}$ 8. $9\frac{5}{7} \times 10\frac{1}{3}$

9. *Baking* Estimate the area of the cookie sheet shown at the right.

10. *Writing* Describe some items that have an area you can find by multiplying mixed numbers.

Find each product.

11. $4\frac{1}{2} \times 7\frac{1}{2}$ 12. $3\frac{2}{3} \times 6\frac{9}{10}$ 13. $6\frac{1}{2} \times 7\frac{2}{3}$ 14. $8\frac{1}{2} \times 8\frac{1}{2}$

15. $4\frac{1}{9} \times 3\frac{3}{8}$ 16. $2\frac{1}{5} \times 10\frac{1}{2}$ 17. $2\frac{2}{5} \times 1\frac{1}{6}$ 18. $2\frac{1}{2} \times 10\frac{1}{2}$

19. $3\frac{1}{5} \times 1\frac{7}{8}$ 20. $7\frac{5}{6} \times 4\frac{1}{2}$ 21. $1\frac{2}{3} \times 5\frac{9}{10}$ 22. $1\frac{5}{8} \times 2\frac{2}{3}$

23. $3\frac{3}{4} \times 5\frac{1}{3}$ 24. $1\frac{1}{12} \times 6\frac{1}{2}$ 25. $4\frac{1}{2} \times 3\frac{5}{6}$ 26. $1\frac{2}{3} \times 3\frac{9}{16}$

27. *Geometry* Find the area of the rectangle at the right.

28. *Business* Letter-size hanging folders measure $9\frac{3}{8}$ in. $\times$ $11\frac{3}{4}$ in. Find the area of one side of a hanging folder.

$3\frac{1}{2}$ in.

$1\frac{1}{4}$ in.

29. *Sewing* A quilt pattern shows a square with $4\frac{1}{2}$-in. sides. Patty wants to reduce each side to $\frac{2}{3}$ the length shown on the pattern. Find the dimensions of the reduced square. Solve the problem two different ways.

Data Analysis **Use the information at the right for Exercises 30 and 31.**

30. *Carpentry* Davar is building the floor of a deck. He will place 32 "2-by-4" boards side by side with $\frac{1}{4}$ in. space between each pair of boards. How wide will the floor of the deck be?

31. *Construction* Simon loaded his truck with a single stack of boards. The stack had three "2-by-6" boards and six "2-by-2" boards. How high is the stack?

Standard Lumber Sizes

Lumber Name	Thickness (in.)	Width (in.)
"1-by-4"	$\frac{3}{4}$	$3\frac{1}{2}$
"2-by-2"	$1\frac{1}{2}$	$1\frac{1}{2}$
"2-by-4"	$1\frac{1}{2}$	$3\frac{1}{2}$
"2-by-6"	$1\frac{1}{2}$	$5\frac{1}{2}$

Find the LCM of each set of numbers. *(Lesson 5-7)*

32. 8, 12, 6   **33.** 5, 6, 15   **34.** 9, 15, 18   **35.** 36, 40   **36.** 10, 20, 50   **37.** 35, 36, 180

Mental Math **Find each answer.** *(Lesson 4-7)*

38. $3.9 \div 10$ **39.** $19.1 \div 100$ **40.** $0.82 \div 1{,}000$ **41.** $0.367 \div 10$ **42.** $307.9 \div 1{,}000$

43. *Choose a Strategy* Linda bought 4 movie tickets with a $20 bill. Each ticket cost $4.25. How much change did she get?

CHAPTER PROJECT

PROJECT LINK: MODELING

Now create a demonstration to calculate the sum of fractions with unlike denominators. See whether or not the sum agrees with the measured results. Again, use items you have gathered, visual models, or other methods. Expand your demonstration to illustrate the addition of mixed numbers.

✓ CHECKPOINT 2   Lessons 6-4 through 6-8

Find each sum or difference.

1. $6\frac{3}{4} + 4\frac{1}{8}$ **2.** $8\frac{7}{16} - 3\frac{1}{4}$ **3.** $13\frac{1}{3} + 15\frac{1}{6}$ **4.** $8\frac{3}{10} - 3\frac{2}{5}$ **5.** $5\frac{3}{5} + 2\frac{2}{3}$

Solve each equation.

6. $x - 3\frac{1}{2} = 6\frac{3}{4}$ **7.** $x + 14\frac{3}{4} = 38\frac{3}{8}$ **8.** $3\frac{7}{16} = x + 2\frac{7}{8}$ **9.** $8\frac{5}{6} = x - 4\frac{7}{8}$

10. Choose A, B, C, or D. Suppose $\frac{7}{8}$ of the area of a geometric drawing is red. A circle makes up $\frac{3}{10}$ of the red part. What portion of the geometric drawing is a red circle?

   A. $\frac{20}{21}$ **B.** $\frac{10}{18}$ **C.** $\frac{21}{80}$ **D.** $\frac{24}{70}$

Find each product.

11. $\frac{4}{5} \times \frac{1}{8}$ **12.** $\frac{5}{12}$ of 36   **13.** $3 \times \frac{3}{4}$ **14.** $\frac{3}{8}$ of 27   **15.** $3\frac{2}{3} \times 3\frac{1}{11}$

Dividing Fractions and Mixed Numbers

What You'll Learn

▼ To divide fractions

❷ To divide mixed numbers

...And Why

You can calculate how many items you can make from a given amount of material.

Here's How

Look for questions that

🔡 build understanding

✔ check understanding

Work Together
Investigating Fraction Division

What happens when you divide a number by $\frac{1}{2}$? Use a fraction calculator or a ruler model.

1. Divide several different numbers by $\frac{1}{2}$. Copy and complete the table at the right.

Number	Fraction	Quotient
10	$\frac{1}{2}$	■
5	$\frac{1}{2}$	■
3.8	$\frac{1}{2}$	■
$9\frac{1}{4}$	$\frac{1}{2}$	■
■	$\frac{1}{2}$	■

2. 🔡 **Number Sense** When you divide a number by $\frac{1}{2}$, is the quotient greater than or less than the number? Explain.

THINK AND DISCUSS

❶ *Exploring Division of Fractions*

You and three friends equally share $\frac{1}{2}$ of a cantaloupe. What portion of the whole cantaloupe does each friend eat?

3. 🔡 *Modeling* Use the circle at the right to represent the cantaloupe. Four of you will share $\frac{1}{2}$ of the cantaloupe. So divide $\frac{1}{2}$ of the circle into four equal pieces. What portion of the cantaloupe does each of you eat?

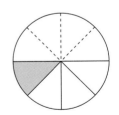

4. 🔡 *Algebra* Write a division sentence to describe the situation in Question 3. Explain its meaning.

5. You can also think of this as a multiplication problem. Each friend gets $\frac{1}{4}$ of $\frac{1}{2}$ of the cantaloupe. Find the product $\frac{1}{4} \times \frac{1}{2}$.

6. 🔡 *Reasoning* You used both multiplication and division to solve the cantaloupe problem. What did you notice about the two expressions $\frac{1}{2} \times \frac{1}{4}$ and $\frac{1}{2} \div 4$?

The numbers 4 and $\frac{1}{4}$ are **reciprocals.** The numerators and denominators have been switched.

7. **Reasoning** Find each product. What do you notice?

   a. $4 \times \frac{1}{4}$ b. $\frac{2}{3} \times \frac{3}{2}$ c. $\frac{1}{2} \times \frac{2}{1}$ d. $8 \times \frac{1}{8}$ e. $\frac{9}{2} \times \frac{2}{9}$

8. ✔**Try It Out** Write the reciprocal of each number.

   a. $\frac{2}{3}$ b. $\frac{1}{9}$ c. 5   d. 1   e. $\frac{7}{4}$

9. **Draw a Conclusion** What do you know about a number and its reciprocal?

You will use reciprocals to divide with fractions.

■ **EXAMPLE 1**   *Real-World Problem Solving*

Nancy has 3 yd of ribbon. It takes $\frac{3}{8}$ yd to make one bow. How many bows can Nancy make if she uses all the ribbon?

Words	•	Yards of ribbon	÷	Amount needed for each bow	=	Number of bows
Equation	•	3	÷	$\frac{3}{8}$	=	b

$3 \div \frac{3}{8} = \frac{3}{1} \times \frac{8}{3}$ ⟵ Rewrite 3 as $\frac{3}{1}$. Multiply 3 by the reciprocal of $\frac{3}{8}$.

$= \frac{{}^1 3 \times 8}{1 \times 3_1}$ ⟵ Simplify. Then multiply.

$= 8$

Nancy can make 8 bows with 3 yd of ribbon.

10. ✔**Try It Out** Find each quotient.

   a. $4 \div \frac{1}{3}$ b. $\frac{6}{7} \div \frac{3}{4}$ c. $5 \div \frac{5}{7}$ d. $\frac{4}{5} \div \frac{3}{8}$

You can also use a model to solve Example 1.

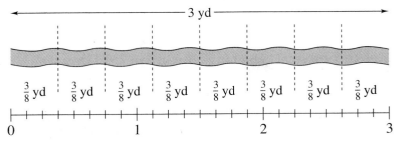

▼2 Division of Mixed Numbers

To divide mixed numbers, first write each mixed number as an improper fraction.

■ **EXAMPLE 2** **Real-World Problem Solving**

Food Leroy made 30 c of soup. How many $1\frac{1}{4}$-c servings of soup does he have?

Divide: $30 \div 1\frac{1}{4}$

$$30 \div 1\frac{1}{4} = 30 \div \frac{5}{4} \quad \longleftarrow \text{Write } 1\frac{1}{4} \text{ as } \frac{5}{4}.$$

$$= \frac{30}{1} \times \frac{4}{5} \quad \longleftarrow \text{Multiply by the reciprocal of } \frac{5}{4}.$$

$$= \frac{\overset{6}{\cancel{30}} \times 4}{1 \times \underset{1}{\cancel{5}}} \quad \longleftarrow \text{Simplify. Then multiply.}$$

$$= 24$$

Leroy has 24 $1\frac{1}{4}$-c servings of soup.

11. ✔*Try It Out* Find the quotient $25 \div 3\frac{3}{4}$.

EXERCISES *On Your Own*

Use a circle to model the situations of Exercises 1 and 2.

1. Two people equally share $\frac{2}{3}$ of a pizza.   **2.** Three people equally share $\frac{3}{4}$ of a cheese wheel.

3. *Modeling* Draw a diagram. Show how many pieces of string $\frac{1}{3}$ ft long you can cut from a $3\frac{1}{3}$-ft piece.

Write the reciprocal of each number.

4. $\frac{4}{5}$ **5.** 3   **6.** $\frac{2}{10}$ **7.** $\frac{1}{5}$ **8.** $3\frac{1}{2}$ **9.** $2\frac{5}{6}$

Mental Math **Find each quotient mentally.**

10. $6 \div \frac{1}{2}$ **11.** $5 \div \frac{1}{3}$ **12.** $3 \div \frac{1}{8}$ **13.** $7 \div \frac{1}{5}$ **14.** $8 \div \frac{1}{4}$ **15.** $12 \div \frac{1}{3}$

16. *Measurement* How many $\frac{1}{4}$ in. are in $\frac{1}{2}$ ft? Draw a diagram that shows the problem and your solution.

17. Suppose you cut canvas into pieces. The canvas is $\frac{3}{4}$ yd long. How many pieces $\frac{1}{8}$ yd long can you cut?

Find each quotient.

18. $5 \div \frac{3}{8}$ **19.** $15 \div \frac{3}{4}$ **20.** $\frac{4}{9} \div \frac{3}{5}$ **21.** $12 \div \frac{1}{3}$ **22.** $15 \div \frac{5}{8}$

23. $42 \div \frac{6}{7}$ **24.** $75 \div \frac{1}{2}$ **25.** $\frac{5}{8} \div \frac{3}{4}$ **26.** $\frac{1}{5} \div \frac{1}{3}$ **27.** $\frac{8}{9} \div \frac{2}{3}$

28. $45 \div 2\frac{1}{2}$ **29.** $15\frac{1}{2} \div 2$ **30.** $52 \div 3\frac{1}{4}$ **31.** $12 \div 3\frac{1}{3}$ **32.** $32 \div 5\frac{1}{3}$

33. $2\frac{1}{5} \div 2\frac{1}{2}$ **34.** $6\frac{1}{2} \div \frac{1}{4}$ **35.** $1\frac{3}{4} \div 4\frac{3}{8}$ **36.** $2\frac{2}{5} \div 7\frac{1}{5}$ **37.** $7\frac{2}{3} \div \frac{2}{9}$

38. *Writing* Write a problem that can be solved by dividing 10 by $\frac{1}{3}$. Solve your problem at least two different ways.

39. *Measurement* How many $\frac{1}{2}$-c servings are in an 8-c pitcher of juice? Evaluate the reasonableness of your solution.

40. **Choose A, B, C, or D.** Which quotient is greater than 1?

   A. $\frac{3}{5} \div \frac{3}{5}$ **B.** $\frac{1}{4} \div \frac{3}{4}$ **C.** $\frac{1}{3} \div 4$ **D.** $2 \div \frac{1}{4}$

41. *Apples* Suppose you cut 3 apples into eighths. How many pieces of apple would you have?

42. *Baking* How many $\frac{1}{2}$-in. thick cookies can you slice from a roll of cookie dough 1 ft long?

43. *Bird Seed* You have a 15-lb bag of bird seed.
  a. If the birds you feed eat $1\frac{1}{2}$ lb of seed each day, how many days will your seed last?
  b. Did you multiply or divide to find your answer to part (a)? Why?

44. *Measurement* Alex decides to use a $\frac{1}{4}$-gal jug to fill a 5-gal jar. How many times must Alex pour liquid from the jug into the jar to fill it?

Mixed Review

Find each quotient. *(Lesson 4-8)*

45. $25 \div 0.5$ **46.** $3.2 \div 0.8$ **47.** $0.75 \div 0.25$ **48.** $0.144 \div 1.2$ **49.** $14.4 \div 0.006$

50. Find a three-digit number divisible by 1, 2, 3, and 5. *(Lesson 5-1)*

51. *Choose a Strategy* Taro, Alma, and Wanell are a pharmacist, a teacher, and a stockbroker. Taro first met the teacher and the stockbroker, who were already acquainted, at a fund-raiser. The teacher knows Alma. Match each person with the correct occupation.

MATH TOOLBOX

SKILLS REVIEW

The Customary System

Before Lesson 6-10

The customary system of measurement was established for the British Empire in 1824. The most commonly used units for length, weight, and capacity are shown below.

Length

12 inches (in.) = 1 foot (ft)

3 feet = 1 yard (yd)

5,280 feet = 1 mile (mi)

Weight

16 ounces (oz) = 1 pound (lb)

2,000 pounds = 1 ton (T)

Capacity

8 fluid ounces (fl oz) = 1 cup

2 cups (c) = 1 pint (pt)

2 pints = 1 quart (qt)

4 quarts = 1 gallon (gal)

EXAMPLE

Choose an appropriate unit of measure for each.

a. the height of a tall building

You usually measure the height of a building in feet.

b. weight of a pencil

The weight of a pencil is measured in ounces.

c. amount of lemonade in a glass

The amount of lemonade in a glass is usually measured in fluid ounces.

Choose an appropriate unit of measure for each.

1. weight of a car

2. length of a backyard

3. amount of water in a tub

4. height of a tall tree

5. amount of water in a mug

6. weight of a bag of sugar

Open-ended **For each unit, think of something you would measure with that unit. Give examples from your daily life.**

7. mile **8.** yard **9.** ton **10.** pound **11.** cup **12.** quart

13. *Writing* Why is it important to choose appropriate units of measure?

6-10

Changing Units in the Customary System

What You'll Learn

▼ To change units of length, weight, and capacity

▼ To compare amounts by expressing them in the same units

...And Why

You can compare lengths, weights, and capacity.

Here's How

Look for questions that
- ▪ build understanding
- ✔ check understanding

THINK AND DISCUSS

▼ Changing Units

Fractions and mixed numbers are commonly used with the customary system of measurement. For example, you may buy $1\frac{1}{2}$ gal of milk for your family. Or you may need $1\frac{1}{4}$ c of flour for a recipe.

You can multiply or divide to change units of measurement.

1. a. ✓ *Try It Out* How many inches are in 2 ft?
   b. How many tons are in 10,000 lb?

2. ▪ *Number Sense* How do you know when to multiply and when to divide?

To solve many problems, you change units of measurement. To do this, you need to know how the units are related.

■ **EXAMPLE 1** *Real-World Problem Solving*

Sewing Suppose you need $8\frac{1}{2}$ ft of fabric for a sewing project. Fabric is sold in yards. About how many yards of fabric should you buy?

Ask yourself how many yards equal $8\frac{1}{2}$ ft.

$$3 \text{ ft} = 1 \text{ yd} \quad \longleftarrow \text{Write the relationship between feet and yards.}$$

$$8\frac{1}{2} \text{ ft} \div 3 = \blacksquare \quad \longleftarrow \text{Divide } 8\frac{1}{2} \text{ by 3.}$$

$$= 8\frac{1}{2} \times \frac{1}{3}$$

$$= \frac{17}{2} \times \frac{1}{3}$$

$$= \frac{17}{6} = 2\frac{5}{6}$$

You need $2\frac{5}{6}$ yd of fabric, or about 3 yd.

3. *Try It Out* How many yards are equivalent to $14\frac{3}{4}$ ft?

You may need to change units when you add or subtract measurements in the customary system.

■ **EXAMPLE 2**

Find 8 lb 3 oz − 4 lb 7 oz.

		You cannot subtract 7 from 3.
8 lb 3 oz →	7 lb 19 oz	← Since 1 lb = 16 oz,
− 4 lb 7 oz	− 4 lb 7 oz	rename 8 lb 3 oz as 7 lb 19 oz.
	3 lb 12 oz	← Subtract.

8 lb 3 oz − 4 lb 7 oz = 3 lb 12 oz

4. ✓*Try It Out* Add or subtract.

a.　　7 ft 10 in.
　　− 4 ft 11 in.

b.　　5 lb 4 oz
　　+ 3 lb 14 oz

c.　　6 gal 2 qt
　　− 2 gal 3 qt

▼2 Comparing Amounts

It is easy to compare amounts when they are expressed in the same units.

■ **EXAMPLE 3**　　*Real-World Problem Solving*

Entertaining Suppose you are planning a party. You invite 24 guests. You want to serve at least 2 c of fruit punch to each guest. You plan to fill a $3\frac{1}{2}$-gal punchbowl. Will you have enough punch?

$$\frac{24}{\text{guests}} \times \frac{2\text{ c}}{\text{per guest}} = 24 \times 2 = 48\text{ c} \quad \leftarrow \begin{array}{l}\text{Calculate the amount}\\\text{of punch you need.}\end{array}$$

You will need 48 c of punch.

$3\frac{1}{2}$ gal = $(3\frac{1}{2} \times 4)$ qt = $\frac{7}{2} \times 4$ = 14 qt　　← Change gallons to quarts.

14 qt = (14 × 2) pt = 28 pt　　← Change quarts to pints.

28 pt = (28 × 2) c = 56 c　　← Change pints to cups.

There are 56 c in $3\frac{1}{2}$ gal. You need only 48 c, so you have enough punch.

5. ▪*Look Back* Solve the problem in Example 3 by asking yourself "How many gallons are equivalent to 48 c?"

Complete each statement.

1. 9 ft = ▓ yd
2. 32 oz = ▓ lb
3. 16 qt = ▓ gal
4. 6,000 lb = ▓ T

5. 6 lb = ▓ oz
6. ▓ ft = 48 in.
7. 32 c = ▓ pt
8. 3 mi = ▓ ft

9. $6\frac{1}{4}$ ft = ▓ yd
10. $1\frac{3}{4}$ mi = ▓ ft
11. $2\frac{1}{2}$ qt = ▓ pt
12. $1\frac{1}{2}$ gal = ▓ qt

13. 24 oz = ▓ lb
14. $4\frac{1}{2}$ T = ▓ lb
15. $4\frac{1}{4}$ c = ▓ fl oz
16. $\frac{1}{2}$ lb = ▓ oz

17. $3\frac{1}{2}$ yd = ▓ ft
18. 880 yd = ▓ mi
19. $5\frac{1}{2}$ ft = ▓ in.
20. 7,000 lb = ▓ T

21. *Reasoning* What operation do you use to change–
   a. inches to feet?
   b. yards to feet?
   c. gallons to cups?

22. *Wildlife* In some parts of Alaska, moose actually cause traffic jams. An adult moose weighs about 1,000 lb. How many tons does an adult moose weigh?

23. *Architecture* The Washington Monument in Washington, D.C., is 555 ft $5\frac{1}{8}$ in. tall. How many inches tall is it?

24. *Writing* Describe a situation from daily life in which you need to change from one unit of measure to another.

25. *Cooking* Cranberry mousse requires 32 fl oz nonfat plain yogurt. How many cups is this?

Add or subtract. Rename when necessary.

26.
```
  4 ft 10 in.
+ 1 ft  9 in.
```

27.
```
  5 yd 1 ft
- 1 yd 2 ft
```

28.
```
  3 gal 3 qt
+ 3 gal 1 qt
```

29.
```
  17 lb 12 oz
-  9 lb 13 oz
```

30. *Geometry* Find the distance in feet around the square at the right.

6 in.

6 in.

31. *Nutrition* Read the article below. Suppose six adults are served a $2\frac{1}{2}$-lb roast beef for dinner. Each adult will eat about the same amount. Should they eat the whole roast? Explain.

LATEST NEWS *from the* AMERICAN HEART ASSOCIATION

THE American Heart Association recommends that an adult eat no more than 6 oz (2–3 servings) of cooked poultry, fish, or lean red meat each day. Meat, fish, and poultry are the major contributors of iron, zinc, and B vitamins in most American diets.

32. *Data Analysis* Use the recipe at the right. Odetta bought a 6-fl oz container of nonfat plain yogurt. Did Odetta buy enough yogurt to make Avocado Cream? Explain.

33. *Number Sense* You have a set of 20 encyclopedias. Each book is $1\frac{7}{8}$ in. thick. Your shelf is 3 ft wide. Will the set of books fit on one shelf? Explain.

34. *Geography* The Mont Blanc Tunnel goes through a mountain and connects Italy and France. Its length is 7.2 mi.
a. What is the length of the tunnel in feet?
b. Did you multiply or divide to find the answer to part (a)? Why?

35. *Energy* La Grande Complexe is a hydroelectric power facility in Canada. One of its dams, LG2, has a channel that allows 750,000 gal of water to pass through per second.
a. How many gallons pass through LG2 in 1 min?
b. A gallon of water weighs about 8 lb. About how many tons of water pass through the dam's channel in 1 s?

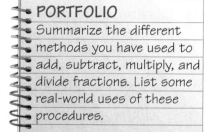

Avocado Cream
a sauce for quesadillas, salads, and tortilla chips

1 ripe avocado

juice of 1 lime

$\frac{1}{2}$ cup nonfat plain yogurt

Compare using <, >, or =.

36. 85 in. ■ 8 ft

37. $3\frac{1}{2}$ lb ■ 56 oz

38. $2\frac{1}{2}$ gal ■ 25 pt

39. $1\frac{1}{2}$ T ■ 4,000 lb

40. $6\frac{1}{2}$ pt ■ 2 qt

41. 24 fl oz ■ 3 c

42. 6,750 lb ■ $3\frac{3}{4}$ T

43. $1\frac{1}{2}$ lb ■ 10 oz

44. $5\frac{1}{2}$ yd ■ 180 in.

45. 252 in. ■ 25 ft

46. 16 yd ■ 50 ft

47. 3 qt ■ 96 oz

PORTFOLIO
Summarize the different methods you have used to add, subtract, multiply, and divide fractions. List some real-world uses of these procedures.

Mixed Review

Place a decimal point in each product. *(Lesson 4-5)*

48. $5.9 \times 0.46 = 2714$

49. $0.08 \times 0.09 = 00072$

50. $0.3 \times 0.2 = 0006$

Write each improper fraction as a mixed number. Write each mixed number as an improper fraction. *(Lesson 5-6)*

51. $\frac{49}{5}$

52. $5\frac{2}{3}$

53. $\frac{49}{6}$

54. $12\frac{3}{4}$

55. $8\frac{5}{6}$

56. $\frac{21}{8}$

57. *Choose a Strategy* You have five coins with a total value $.75. Two of the coins are quarters. What are the other coins?

CHAPTER PROJECT

SEEing is Believing

Design a Demonstration The Project Link questions on pages 231, 256, and 261 should help you complete your project. Here is a checklist to help you gather the parts of your project together.

- ✔ list of materials used for your experiment
- ✔ step-by-step descriptions of the procedures you followed
- ✔ calculations of the sums
- ✔ a summary table comparing your calculated and measured sums

Present your demonstration of fractions to your class. Your proofs should convince any nonbelievers.

Reflect and Revise

Show your proofs to some of your classmates. Discuss whether or not these same techniques would work to show subtraction of fractions and mixed numbers. Work together to devise a method for proving that fraction multiplication techniques work. Are your proofs logical and correct? Are your calculations accurate? Revise your demonstration or proofs as necessary.

Web Extension
Prentice Hall's Internet site contains information you might find helpful as you complete your project. Visit www.phschool.com/mgm1/ch6 for some links and ideas related to proofs.

Chapter 6 Finishing the Chapter Project

6 WRAP UP

Estimating Sums and Differences 6-1

You can estimate the sum or difference of fractions by rounding each fraction to the nearest half. To estimate the sum or difference of mixed numbers, round each mixed number to the nearest whole number.

Estimate each sum or difference.

1. $\frac{15}{16} - \frac{7}{12}$ 2. $\frac{6}{11} + \frac{7}{8}$ 3. $7\frac{3}{5} - 3\frac{1}{6}$ 4. $4\frac{4}{9} + 1\frac{8}{15}$

Adding and Subtracting Fractions 6-2, 6-3

You can use models to add or subtract fractions.

To add or subtract fractions with unlike denominators, first find a common denominator. Use equivalent fractions.

Write an addition or subtraction sentence to describe each model.

5.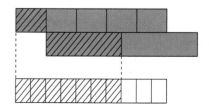

6.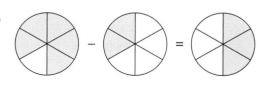

Find each sum or difference.

7. $\frac{2}{9} + \frac{5}{9}$ 8. $\frac{5}{6} - \frac{2}{6}$ 9. $\frac{1}{3} + \frac{3}{4}$ 10. $\frac{5}{6} - \frac{4}{5}$ 11. $\frac{5}{8} - \frac{3}{10}$

Adding and Subtracting Mixed Numbers 6-4, 6-5

To add or subtract mixed numbers, compute the whole number and fraction parts separately. When subtracting, start with the fractions first.

Find each sum or difference.

12. $2\frac{3}{5} + 3\frac{2}{5}$ 13. $6\frac{2}{5} - 2\frac{3}{4}$ 14. $3\frac{7}{8} + 1\frac{2}{12}$ 15. $4\frac{9}{10} - \frac{5}{6}$ 16. $15\frac{5}{12} - 10\frac{7}{9}$

Sometimes it's helpful to draw a diagram when solving a problem.

17. Mrs. Cruz bought a rectangular piece of carpet that is 12 ft wide and 18 ft long. She will carpet her rectangular bathroom, square office, and a hallway measuring 4 ft wide and 18 ft long.
    a. Draw a diagram to show how she can make the three carpets with two cuts.
    b. Find the dimensions of the bathroom and office.
    c. Find the area of each room and the combined area of all three rooms.

To multiply fractions, multiply the numerators and then multiply the denominators. To divide fractions, multiply by the reciprocal of the divisor. To find $\frac{2}{3} \div \frac{5}{6}$, multiply $\frac{2}{3} \times \frac{6}{5}$.

Simplify before multiplying when possible. Divide numerators and denominators by any common factors.

Write mixed numbers as improper fractions.

Find each product or quotient.

18. $\frac{3}{5} \times \frac{5}{6}$ 19. $\frac{2}{3} \div 8$ 20. $2\frac{1}{6} \times 3\frac{3}{4}$ 21. $2\frac{3}{8} \div 2\frac{1}{2}$

You can multiply or divide to change units of measurement.
To compare amounts, express them in the same units.

Complete each statement.

22. $5\frac{1}{2}$ pt = ▓ c   23. 880 in. = ▓ ft   24. $2\frac{1}{2}$ gal = ▓ c   25. 12,000 lb = ▓ T

26. In baseball, the distance from the pitcher to the batter is 60 ft 6 in. How far is this in yards?

27. *Writing* Explain why it is useful to be able to change units of measurement.

1. Estimate each sum or difference.

   a. $\frac{3}{4} + \frac{1}{9}$
   b. $\frac{11}{12} - \frac{1}{10}$
   c. $14\frac{7}{8} + 10\frac{3}{8}$
   d. $34\frac{65}{66} - 12\frac{1}{16}$

2. *Modeling* Draw a model to find each sum or difference.

   a. $\frac{1}{4} + \frac{1}{4}$
   b. $\frac{11}{12} - \frac{5}{12}$

3. Find each sum. Write the answer in simplest form.

   a. $\frac{1}{5} + \frac{11}{15}$
   b. $\frac{7}{12} + \frac{3}{8}$
   c. $4\frac{1}{2} + 6\frac{2}{15}$
   d. $5\frac{4}{5} + 3\frac{1}{2}$

4. Find each difference. Write the answer in simplest form.

   a. $\frac{3}{4} - \frac{2}{5}$
   b. $\frac{5}{6} - \frac{4}{15}$
   c. $7\frac{7}{8} - 5\frac{17}{32}$
   d. $12\frac{9}{10} - 4\frac{3}{5}$

5. Kelsey tutored for $3\frac{3}{4}$ h on Tuesday and $7\frac{1}{3}$ h on Saturday.

   a. About how many more hours did Kelsey tutor on Saturday than on Tuesday?
   b. About how much time did Kelsey tutor altogether?

6. *Writing* Explain how you can mentally find the sum $3\frac{1}{4} + 2\frac{2}{3} + 5\frac{3}{4} + 1\frac{1}{3}$.

7. Roscoe grew $4\frac{1}{4}$ in. over a two-year period. If he grew $2\frac{1}{2}$ in. the first year, how many inches did Roscoe grow during the second year?

8. Four students are waiting in line. Joe is behind Sarah, Noton is in front of Max, and Sarah is behind Max. In which order are the students standing?

9. *Mental Math* Solve for x.

   a. $\frac{3}{10} + x = \frac{8}{10}$
   b. $x + \frac{2}{5} = \frac{4}{5}$

10. *Algebra* Solve for x.

    $3\frac{5}{8} + x = 7\frac{1}{8}$

11. Find each product.

    a. $\frac{3}{8}$ of 64
    b. $\frac{2}{5} \times 45$
    c. $3\frac{1}{3} \times 2\frac{3}{4}$
    d. $4\frac{3}{10} \times 2\frac{1}{2}$

12. Estimate each product.

    a. $10\frac{9}{10} \times 5\frac{1}{5}$
    b. $9\frac{5}{12} \times 6\frac{11}{12}$

13. Find each product or quotient.

    a. $2\frac{1}{5} \times 2\frac{3}{4}$
    b. $3\frac{3}{8} \times 4\frac{4}{5}$
    c. $10\frac{1}{2} \div \frac{1}{2}$
    d. $6\frac{3}{4} \div 4\frac{1}{2}$

14. **Choose A, B, C, or D.** A sales representative completed $\frac{4}{7}$ of a 1,394-mi business trip. About how many miles of the trip remain?

    A. about 400
    B. about 600
    C. about 800
    D. about 1,000

15. A doll maker uses $1\frac{7}{8}$ yd of material to make one doll. How many dolls can be made from a piece of material that is 45 yd long?

16. Tung has an income of \$2,640 each month. He spends $\frac{1}{5}$ of his income on rent. How much does Tung spend on rent?

Complete each statement.

17. 30 yd = ▧ ft
18. $14\frac{1}{2}$ gal = ▧ c
19. 108 fl oz = ▧ pt
20. $5\frac{3}{4}$ ft = ▧ yd
21. ▧ ft = 86 in.
22. 150 lb = ▧ oz

Choose the best answer.

1. Which is *not* equivalent to five tenths?
   A. 0.05
   B. $\frac{5}{10}$
   C. 0.5
   D. fifty hundredths

2. Summer vacation is 68 days long. If $\frac{3}{4}$ of vacation has gone by, how many days are left?
   A. 12 days
   B. 51 days
   C. 23 days
   D. 17 days

3. Which set of numbers is ordered from least to greatest?
   A. $0.67, \frac{2}{3}, \frac{7}{10}, \frac{3}{4}$
   B. $\frac{1}{4}, \frac{6}{25}, 0.23, \frac{2}{9}$
   C. $1\frac{1}{4}, 1\frac{2}{7}, 1.3, 1\frac{1}{3}$
   D. $0.37, \frac{3}{8}, \frac{1}{3}, 0.4$

4. Which is *not* a true statement?
   A. $0.04 > 0.01$
   B. $0.48 < 0.4798$
   C. $0.014 < 0.02$
   D. $29.6 > 29.06$

5. A calculator sells for $18.64. Sales tax is $1.49. How much money do you need to buy the calculator?
   A. $19.03
   B. $17.15
   C. $33.54
   D. $20.13

6. Which set of numbers has a GCF of 3?
   A. 15, 30, 45
   B. 6, 30, 24
   C. 24, 36, 9
   D. 36, 27, 18

7. Describe how to find $1\frac{3}{4}$ divided by $\frac{1}{2}$.
   A. Multiply $1\frac{3}{4}$ and $\frac{1}{2}$.
   B. Find $\frac{7}{4} \div 2$.
   C. Multiply $\frac{1}{2}$ and $\frac{4}{7}$.
   D. Multiply $\frac{7}{4}$ and 2.

8. Which of the following is *not* a solution to the given equation?
   A. $4a = 20; 5$
   B. $x + 9.5 = 10; 0.5$
   C. $y \div 5 = 35; 7$
   D. $b + 53.7 = 100; 46.3$

9. Your bowling scores one day were 125, 137, and 92. How would you find the mean score?
   A. Subtract 92 from 137.
   B. Choose the middle score.
   C. Find the total and divide by 3.
   D. Add all three scores.

10. A table is shown below. What type of graph should be made from the information?

Sizes of Eggs

Size	Ounces per Dozen
Jumbo	30
Extra large	27
Large	24
Medium	21
Small	18
Peewee	15

   A. a line plot
   B. a bar graph
   C. a line graph
   D. a circle graph

11. What is the value of the expression $5 + 7(6 - 1) \div 2$?
   A. 18
   B. 20
   C. 22.5
   D. 30

12. Estimate the solution to the equation $x - 17.16 = 33.4$.
   A. about 16
   B. about 50
   C. about 2
   D. about 0.5

7

Ratios, Proportions, and Percents

Planet
of the Stars

When you look up at the stars in the sky, you don't think about how far away they are. Stars appear a lot closer than they really are, and the same is true of planets. The huge distances between planets make it impossible for books to show how vast our solar system really is.

Make a Scale Model In this chapter, you will make scale models of two planets. You will compare sizes and distances for each planet and calculate the ratios involved in your scale model.

- **How to solve problems by solving a simpler problem**

PROBLEM SOLVING

7-1 Exploring Ratios

What You'll Learn

▼ To explore the
    meaning of ratio

...And Why

Ratios help you relate
numbers to other
numbers.

Here's How

Look for questions that
- build understanding
✔ check understanding

THINK AND DISCUSS

Can you sit boy, girl, boy, girl, . . . in your class?

1. **Data Collection**
   Collect data from your
   class to complete the table
   at the right.

Students in Your Class

Total Number of Students	▪
Number of Girls	▪
Number of Boys	▪

2. Use the data in the table to write each fraction.
   a. $\dfrac{\text{number of boys}}{\text{total number of students}}$
   b. $\dfrac{\text{number of girls}}{\text{total number of students}}$

The fractions you wrote in Question 2 are called *ratios*. A **ratio**
compares two numbers by division. You can compare a part to its
whole, a part to another part, or the whole to one of its parts. For
example, suppose you made 3 cups of party mix (whole) using
2 cups of cereal (part A) and 1 cup of pretzels (part B).

Type of Ratio	Statement	Ways to Write Ratio
part A to whole	2 c cereal to 3 c mix	2 to 3, 2 : 3, or $\frac{2}{3}$
whole to part B	3 c mix to 1 c pretzels	3 to 1, 3 : 1, or $\frac{3}{1}$
part A to part B	2 c cereal to 1 c pretzels	2 to 1, 2 : 1, or $\frac{2}{1}$

■ **EXAMPLE**   *Real-World Problem Solving*

Camp Suppose you are at camp. There are 3 counselors
and 7 campers in every cabin. Write each ratio below in
three ways.

  a. counselors to people in the cabin

    $\dfrac{3}{10}$ ⟵ $\dfrac{\text{counselors}}{\text{people in the cabin}}$ 3 to 10   3 : 10

  b. campers to counselors

    $\dfrac{7}{3}$ ⟵ $\dfrac{\text{campers}}{\text{counselors}}$ 7 to 3   7 : 3

3. ✓*Try It Out* There are 3 times as many peanuts as almonds in a mixture of nuts. Write each ratio in three ways.
   a. peanuts to almonds   **b.** almonds to peanuts

4. ⁂*Open-ended* Name two situations where you might use ratios.

EXERCISES *On Your Own*

Write a ratio in three ways for each comparison.

1. plates to bowls

2. cups to bowls

3. bowls to cups

4. plates to cups

Draw a picture to represent each ratio.

5. 4 stars to 8 moons

6. $\dfrac{2 \text{ apples}}{6 \text{ bananas}}$

7. $\dfrac{1 \text{ c rhubarb}}{2 \text{ c strawberries}}$

8. 3 big tiles : 7 small tiles

9. 3 shirts to 5 shorts

10. 1 red tile : 3 white tiles

Write a ratio in three ways for each statement.

11. Combine 1 part ginger ale to 2 parts fruit juice.

12. There are 120 students for every 5 teachers.

13. There are 14 girls to 12 boys in your class.

14. Add 2 parts cream for every 1 part powder.

A drama club sold 35 student tickets, 24 adult tickets, and 11 discount tickets. Write each ratio in three ways.

15. student tickets to adult tickets

16. adult tickets to student tickets

17. adult tickets to discount tickets

18. student tickets to total tickets

19. adult tickets to total tickets

20. discount tickets to total tickets

21. *Research* Find two examples of ratios in a newspaper. You might try the sports pages or look in a supermarket ad.

Open-ended **Describe a situation with the following ratio.**

22. 1 : 2   **23.** $\frac{6}{1}$ **24.** 2 to 3   **25.** $\frac{3}{1}$ **26.** 10 to 1   **27.** 3 : 5

Write a ratio to represent each comparison.

28. sunglasses to caps

29. bats to balls

30. the number of vowels (not counting y) to consonants in the alphabet

31. the number of vowels (not counting y) to consonants in your first name

32. *Writing* Is 2 : 1 the same ratio as 1: 2? Explain your reasoning.

Mixed Review

Find each sum or difference. Use models if they help you.
(Lesson 3-5)

33. $37.5 + 68.7$ **34.** $13.3 - 5.68$ **35.** $18.62 - 0.84$ **36.** $9.99 + 3.7$

Write two fractions equivalent to each fraction. *(Lesson 5-5)*

37. $\frac{21}{30}$ **38.** $\frac{7}{8}$ **39.** $\frac{25}{525}$ **40.** $\frac{6}{15}$ **41.** $\frac{16}{24}$ **42.** $\frac{5}{8}$

43. *Choose a Strategy* The number of homes rented by a real estate agent for each of the first five months of the year has been 11, 9, 13, 8, and 20. Find the monthly average. Use it to estimate the number of rentals for the entire year.

7-2 Equal Ratios and Unit Rates

What You'll Learn

▼ 1 To write equal ratios
▼ 2 To find unit rates

...And Why

You use equal ratios and unit rates to compare quantities and prices.

Here's How

Look for questions that
▪ build understanding
✔ check understanding

THINK AND DISCUSS

1 Writing Equal Ratios

You can write a ratio in simplest form the same way you write a fraction in simplest form.

1. Write each ratio in simplest form.
   a. $25 : 75$ **b.** $50 : 150$ **c.** $4 : 12$ **d.** $13 : 39$

2. What do you notice about the answers to Question 1?

Like equivalent fractions, **equal ratios** are names for the same number. You can find equal ratios by multiplying or dividing each term in a ratio by the same nonzero number.

▪ **EXAMPLE 1**   *Real-World Problem Solving*

Food Write three ratios equal to the ratio $\dfrac{3 \text{ c of unpopped corn}}{24 \text{ qt of popcorn}}$.

$$\overset{\times 2}{\underset{\times 2}{\frac{3}{24} = \frac{6}{48}}} \quad \overset{\div 3}{\underset{\div 3}{\frac{3}{24} = \frac{1}{8}}} \quad \overset{\times 4}{\underset{\times 4}{\frac{3}{24} = \frac{12}{96}}}$$

Cups of unpopped corn ⟶
Quarts of popcorn ⟶

Three ratios equal to $\frac{3}{24}$ are $\frac{6}{48}$, $\frac{1}{8}$, and $\frac{12}{96}$.

3. ▪ *Look Back* Refer to Example 1. How much popcorn can you expect from 9 c of unpopped corn?

4. ▪ *Reasoning* When you multiply or divide the numerator and the denominator by the same number, you get an equal ratio. Justify this statement. Give an example.

5. ✔ *Try It Out* Write three ratios equal to the ratio given.
   a. $6 : 8$ **b.** 10 to 35 **c.** $\dfrac{21}{42}$ **d.** $12 : 18$

The ratios in Question 1 are equal because the simplest form of each ratio is the same. Equal ratios have the same simplest form.

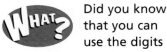
■ **EXAMPLE 2**

Are the given ratios equal?

a. 8 c sugar : 12 c flour and 10 c sugar : 15 c flour

$$\overset{\div 4}{\frac{8}{12}} = \frac{2}{3} \qquad \overset{\div 5}{\frac{10}{15}} = \frac{2}{3}$$ ← Write each ratio in simplest form.
$$\underset{\div 4}{} \qquad \underset{\div 5}{}$$

$2 : 3 = 2 : 3$ ← Compare ratios.

The ratios 8 : 12 and 10 : 15 are equal.

b. $\dfrac{25 \text{ A's and B's}}{75 \text{ grades}}$ and $\dfrac{50 \text{ A's and B's}}{125 \text{ grades}}$

$$\overset{\div 25}{\frac{25}{75}} = \frac{1}{3} \qquad \overset{\div 25}{\frac{50}{125}} = \frac{2}{5}$$ ← Write each ratio in simplest form.
$$\underset{\div 25}{} \qquad \underset{\div 25}{}$$

$\dfrac{1}{3} \neq \dfrac{2}{5}$ ← Compare ratios.

The ratios $\dfrac{25}{75}$ and $\dfrac{50}{125}$ are *not* equal.

6. ✓**Try It Out** Are the given ratios equal?
   a. 9 : 45 and 6 : 30   b. 15 to 12 and 5 to 4   c. $\dfrac{20}{4}$ and $\dfrac{1}{5}$

▼② *Finding Unit Rates*

A **rate** is a ratio that compares two quantities measured in different units. The rate $\dfrac{46 \text{ mi}}{2 \text{ h}}$ compares miles traveled to hours of travel. A **unit rate** compares a quantity to a unit of one.

■ **EXAMPLE 3**   *Real-World Problem Solving*

A car traveled 300 miles on 12 gallons of gas. Find the unit rate in miles per gallon (mi/gal).

miles ⟶ $\dfrac{300}{12}$ ← Write the comparison as a ratio.
gallons ⟶

$$\overset{\div 12}{\frac{300}{12}} = \frac{25}{1}$$ ← Divide the numerator and the denominator by the denominator.
$$\underset{\div 12}{}$$

The unit rate is $\dfrac{25 \text{ mi}}{1 \text{ gal}}$, or 25 mi/gal.

7. ✓**Try It Out** Find the unit rate for each situation.
   a. 144 players on 12 teams   b. $19.50 for 3 shirts

Write three ratios equal to the given ratio.

1. 6 : 18   2. $\frac{4}{24}$ 3. 8 to 10   4. 30 : 40   5. 3 : 8   6. $\frac{32}{36}$

7. $\frac{50}{100}$ 8. 9 to 81   9. 8 : 14   10. $\frac{14}{42}$ 11. 20 to 25   12. $\frac{1}{10}$

Write each ratio in simplest form.

13. $\frac{6}{15}$ 14. 75 : 15   15. $\frac{42}{50}$ 16. 8 : 36   17. $\frac{18}{12}$ 18. 32 : 90

19. $\frac{18}{3}$ 20. 50 : 150   21. $\frac{24}{30}$ 22. 64 : 96   23. $\frac{45}{25}$ 24. 72 : 24

25. *Earth Science* Earth's ratio of water to land is 7 : 3. Write three ratios equal to this ratio.

26. *Reasoning* Carlos tells you he ate $\frac{1}{3}$ of a pizza. Raylene says she ate $\frac{9}{27}$, and Maggie says she ate $\frac{2}{6}$. You want to know who ate the most pizza. Which of these ratios do you find easier to use? Why?

27. *Sports* A team won 8 of the 12 games it played. Write the ratio of games won to games played in simplest form.

28. *Jobs* You earn $135 for working 20 hours. Find your unit rate in dollars per hour.

Use the article below for Exercises 29–31.

Sign on the Dotted Line

Autographs from famous people are sometimes worth big money.

Clark Gable's autograph is worth $100. Lucille Ball's autograph is worth $75. President Harry Truman's autograph is worth $40 and Hillary Clinton's autograph is worth $100.

Button Gwinnett signed the Declaration of Independence, and his autograph recently sold for $100,000.

Write each ratio in simplest form.

29. the price of President Truman's autograph to Clark Gable's

30. the price of Lucille Ball's autograph to Button Gwinnett's

31. the price of Lucille Ball's autograph to Hillary Clinton's

Find the value that makes the ratios equal.

32. $\dfrac{5}{10}, \dfrac{\blacksquare}{20}$ **33.** $25 : 75$, $1 : \blacksquare$ **34.** 6 to 9, $\blacksquare$ to 3   **35.** $\dfrac{\blacksquare}{15}, \dfrac{25}{75}$

Find the unit rate for each situation.

36. 336 mi in 12 h   **37.** read 66 pages in 2 h   **38.** type 110 words in 5 min

39. 16 mi in 4 h   **40.** 30 min for 5 customers   **41.** $24 for 8 toys

42. *Swimming* Crystal will pay $126 for 28 swimming lessons. Bill will pay $30 for 6 lessons. Who is paying more per lesson? How much more is the person paying?

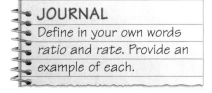

JOURNAL
Define in your own words ratio and rate. Provide an example of each.

43. *Sports* In the last three softball practices, Julie ran a total of 7.5 miles. Find her unit rate for miles run per practice.

44. *Writing* How does a unit rate help you compare prices in a grocery store? Give an example.

Mixed Review

Solve each equation. *(Lesson 2-6 and 2-7)*

45. $x - 58 = 107$ **46.** $3y = 51$ **47.** $a + 39 = 87$ **48.** $b \div 6 = 36$ **49.** $15c = 105$

50. At the copy center it costs $33.75 to print every 1,000 copies. What is the cost of printing 5,000 copies? *(Lesson 4-5)*

CHAPTER PROJECT

PROJECT LINK: WRITING RATIOS

Your class's solar system model will be based on a 2-mm diameter for Pluto. For each of your two assigned planets, write the ratio of the planet's real diameter to the real diameter of Pluto. (Use the data at the right.) How many times bigger than Pluto is each of your assigned planets?

Body	Diameter (mi)	Mean Distance from Sun (millions of miles)
Sun	865,120	0
Mercury	3,030	36.0
Venus	7,520	67.2
Earth	7,926	93.0
Mars	4,216	141.7
Jupiter	88,724	483.9
Saturn	74,560	885.0
Uranus	31,600	1,781.6
Neptune	30,600	2,790.2
Pluto	1,860	3,670.7

7-3 Solving Proportions

What You'll Learn

▼ To recognize proportions
▼ To solve proportions

...And Why

You can solve proportions related to crafts, school supplies, science, and music.

Here's How

Look for questions that
▪ build understanding
✔ check understanding

THINK AND DISCUSS

▼ Recognizing Proportions

A **proportion** is an equation that states two ratios are equal.

$$\frac{1}{2} = \frac{4}{8}$$

A proportion is true only if the ratios are equal.

1. Use the statements below for parts (a), (b), (c), and (d).

   I. $\frac{180}{42} \overset{?}{=} \frac{30}{7}$ **II.** $\frac{7}{8} \overset{?}{=} \frac{21}{24}$ **III.** $\frac{3}{15} \overset{?}{=} \frac{8}{20}$ **IV.** $\frac{16}{30} \overset{?}{=} \frac{8}{15}$

   a. Rewrite each statement so the ratios are in simplest form.
   b. Is each statement a proportion? How do you know?
   c. Multiply the blue numbers for each statement. Then multiply the red numbers.
   d. ▪ *Draw a Conclusion* What do you notice about the products?

You can use **cross products** to tell if two ratios form a proportion. The cross products of a proportion are *always* equal. In the equation $\frac{1}{2} = \frac{4}{8}$, 1×8 and 2×4 are the cross products.

■ EXAMPLE 1   Real-World Problem Solving

Crafts In 4 hours, one weaver made 10 baskets. In 20 hours, another weaver made 50 baskets. Are the two weavers working at the same pace?

$\frac{\text{hours}}{\text{baskets}} \longrightarrow$ $\frac{4}{10} \overset{?}{=} \frac{20}{50}$ ◄—Write a possible proportion.

$4 \times 50 \overset{?}{=} 10 \times 20$ ◄—Write the cross products.

$200 = 200$ ◄—Multiply.

The ratios are proportional. So both weavers are working at the same pace.

2. ✓*Try It Out* Does each pair of ratios form a proportion?

   a. $\frac{3}{9}, \frac{6}{18}$ b. $\frac{9}{10}, \frac{18}{30}$ c. $\frac{33}{39}, \frac{55}{65}$ d. $\frac{9}{27}, \frac{7}{21}$

▼2 Solving Proportions

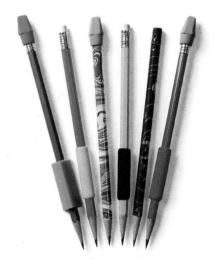

QUICK review

Multiplying or dividing the numerator and the denominator by the same number is the same as multiplying or dividing by 1.

$\frac{1}{3} \times \frac{6}{6} = \frac{1}{3} \times 1$

$\frac{12}{32} \div \frac{4}{4} = \frac{12}{32} \div 1$

Sometimes you can use mental math to find the missing term in a proportion.

$$\overset{\times 6}{\underset{\times 6}{\frac{1}{3}}} = \frac{6}{\blacksquare}$$

Use the same operation on the numerator and the denominator.

$$\overset{\div 4}{\underset{\div 4}{\frac{12}{32}}} = \frac{\blacksquare}{8}$$

3. ⬛**Mental Math** Find the missing term in each proportion above.

You can also use cross products to solve proportions.

■ EXAMPLE 2

Find the value of n in $\frac{n}{312} = \frac{5}{24}$.

$\frac{n}{312} = \frac{5}{24}$

$n \times 24 = 312 \times 5$ ←— Write the cross products.

$24n = 1{,}560$ ←— Multiply.

$\frac{24n}{24} = \frac{1{,}560}{24}$ ←— Divide both sides by 24.

$n = 65$

Proportions can help you solve problems involving rates.

■ EXAMPLE 3 *Real-World Problem Solving*

▦ **School Supplies** Pencils at the school store are 2 for $.15. Find the cost of 21 pencils.

$\dfrac{\text{pencils}}{\text{cost (\$)}} \longrightarrow \dfrac{2}{0.15} = \dfrac{21}{c}$ ←— Let c represent the cost.

$2 \times c = 0.15 \times 21$ ←— Write the cross products.

$.15 \boxed{\times} 21 \boxed{\div} 2 \boxed{=} 1.575$ ←— Use a calculator to solve.

$c = 1.575$

Round to the next cent. So 21 pencils cost $1.58.

▦ **4.** ✓**Try It Out** Use a calculator, paper and pencil, or mental math. Find the value of each variable.

  a. $\frac{9}{39} = \frac{3}{y}$ **b.** $\frac{k}{17} = \frac{20}{34}$ **c.** $\frac{2}{9} = \frac{25}{x}$ **d.** $\frac{96}{144} = \frac{n}{12}$

5. ⬛**Reasoning** How could you use a pattern to find the cost of the pencils in Example 3?

WHAT? The familiar eraser on the end of a pencil wasn't introduced until about 1860. Some teachers objected because they felt that students would make more errors if they could correct them easily.

Does each pair of ratios form a proportion?

1. $\frac{1}{2}, \frac{50}{100}$

2. $\frac{10}{20}, \frac{30}{40}$

3. $\frac{4}{12}, \frac{6}{8}$

4. $\frac{42}{6}, \frac{504}{72}$

5. $\frac{9}{11}, \frac{63}{77}$

6. $\frac{93}{60}, \frac{62}{40}$

7. $\frac{18}{9}, \frac{6}{3}$

8. $\frac{4}{9}, \frac{3}{5}$

9. $\frac{10}{16}, \frac{6}{14}$

10. $\frac{24}{54}, \frac{8}{18}$

11. Write the cross products of the proportion $\frac{3}{4} = \frac{9}{12}$.

12. **a.** Do the ratios $\frac{45}{50}$ and $\frac{18}{20}$ form a proportion? How do you know?

   b. *Reasoning* How else could you decide whether the ratios in part (a) form a proportion?

13. Use the numbers 2, 5, 6, and 15. Write as many proportions as possible.

14. *Open-ended* Describe a situation requiring a proportion.

Mental Math **Find the missing term in each proportion.**

15. $\frac{48}{\blacksquare} = \frac{4}{7}$

16. $\frac{9}{12} = \frac{\blacksquare}{48}$

17. $\frac{4}{18} = \frac{6}{\blacksquare}$

18. $\frac{\blacksquare}{55} = \frac{18}{22}$

19. $\frac{\blacksquare}{42} = \frac{5}{6}$

▦ *Choose* **Use a calculator, paper and pencil, or mental math. Find the value of each variable.**

20. $\frac{10}{3} = \frac{c}{12}$

21. $\frac{12}{n} = \frac{4}{21}$

22. $\frac{3}{11} = \frac{15}{a}$

23. $\frac{42}{g} = \frac{7}{10}$

24. $\frac{25}{6} = \frac{d}{30}$

25. $\frac{b}{9} = \frac{3}{27}$

26. $\frac{7}{2} = \frac{77}{w}$

27. $\frac{72}{c} = \frac{8}{3}$

28. $\frac{16}{27} = \frac{4}{m}$

29. $\frac{h}{2} = \frac{3}{16}$

30. *Food* A flavor of frozen yogurt has 65 calories in 2 oz. How many calories are in 10 oz of that frozen yogurt?

31. *Science* A glacier moves about 12 in. every 8 h. About how far does the glacier move in 72 h?

32. *Sports* Youth soccer teams in Hopkinton have 22 players and 3 coaches. How many coaches are needed for 196 players?

33. Suppose you get paid $7 for 2 h of baby-sitting, and you were paid $17.50 last night. How long did you baby-sit?

34. *Music* A piano has 88 keys. The ratio of white keys to black keys is 52 to 36. A piano maker has 676 white keys.
   a. How many black keys does the piano maker need to have the correct ratio of white keys to black keys?
   b. How many pianos can be built? Explain.

35. *Writing* Describe two different ways to solve a proportion.

Find each difference. *(Lesson 6-3)*

36. $\frac{8}{9} - \frac{2}{3}$ **37.** $\frac{7}{8} - \frac{3}{4}$ **38.** $\frac{1}{2} - \frac{3}{16}$ **39.** $\frac{27}{32} - \frac{1}{2}$ **40.** $\frac{13}{15} - \frac{2}{3}$ **41.** $\frac{9}{10} - \frac{3}{4}$

Use compatible numbers to estimate. *(Lesson 4-1)*

42. $9.36 \div 5.1$ **43.** 17.56×9.31 **44.** 24.83×3.07 **45.** $16.31 \div 4.07$ **46.** 39.2×3.201

47. Abraham Lincoln, who was 1.93 m tall, was the tallest U.S. president. Would he have fit through an 80 cm-by-200 cm doorway? By how many centimeters would the doorway have been taller or shorter than Lincoln? *(Lesson 4-10)*

CHAPTER PROJECT

PROJECT LINK: CALCULATING

You know three pieces of data: the diameter of Pluto, the diameters of your assigned planets, and the scale diameter of Pluto. Use proportions to find the scale-model diameters of your planets. Then make two-dimensional drawings of the planets.

✓ CHECKPOINT 1   Lessons 7-1 through 7-3

Write two ratios equal to the given ratio.

1. $\frac{10}{15}$ **2.** 20 to 34   **3.** 18 : 40   **4.** $\frac{23}{44}$ **5.** 4 to 7   **6.** $\frac{10}{30}$

Find the unit rate for each situation.

7. You can buy 3 tacos for $2.67.   **8.** A package of 6 batteries costs $2.10.

Find the value of each variable.

9. $\frac{21}{36} = \frac{7}{n}$ **10.** $\frac{x}{42} = \frac{3}{7}$ **11.** $\frac{m}{12} = \frac{6}{9}$ **12.** $\frac{6}{45} = \frac{2}{n}$ **13.** $\frac{54}{c} = \frac{9}{13}$

14. Choose A, B, C, or D. A bookstore sold 24 paperbacks, 6 hardcovers, 38 magazines, and 5 calendars. What was the ratio of magazines sold to paperbacks sold?

   A. 24 : 38   **B.** 19 to 31   **C.** $\frac{19}{12}$ **D.** 12 : 24

7-4 Solve a Simpler Problem

READ PLAN LOOK BACK SOLVE

THINK AND DISCUSS

When solving a problem, you may find it helpful to solve a similar, simpler problem first.

SAMPLE PROBLEM..

Imagine you are playing the video game Treacherous Tunnel. You have two choices for entering the next level of the game. You don't want to use Choice 1 because it takes too long. Your goal is to use Choice 2 and follow the correct path within the time limit.

Treacherous Tunnel

Choose a path. Travel Time: 1 min

Choice 1 This path has diamonds in bunches of 2, 3, 4, and so on, to 100. You must collect all the even-numbered bunches. If you miss any, or if you collect odd-numbered bunches, the game ends.

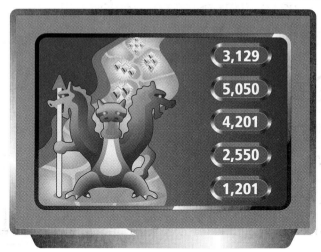

3,129
5,050
4,201
2,550
1,201

Choice 2 A three-headed creature guards the path. One of the numbers at the left is the total number of diamonds you could collect in Choice 1. If you select the wrong number, the creature will not let you pass, and the game ends.

Think about the information you have and what you need to find.

READ

Read for understanding. Summarize the problem.

1. Read Choices 1 and 2 carefully. What is your goal?

2. What numbers will you add to find the number you should select in Choice 2?

3. What numbers in Choice 2 can you eliminate? Why?

PLAN

Decide on a strategy.

One strategy for finding the sum of all even numbers from 2 through 100 is to solve a simpler problem first. Start with all even numbers from 2 through 20: 2, 4, 6, 8, 10, 12, 14, 16, 18, 20. Look for shortcuts to find this sum.

SOLVE

Try the strategy.

4.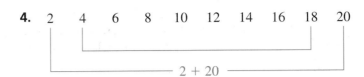

2   4   6   8   10   12   14   16   18   20

2 + 20

a. Continue to add pairs. What sum do you get each time?
b. How many even numbers did you start with?
c. How many pairs do you have?
d. How can you use the number of pairs to find the sum?

5. Look at the original problem and use the same method.
   a. What are the first and last numbers you will add? What is the sum of these two numbers?
   b. There are 50 even numbers from 2 to 100. How many pairs can you make?
   c. Show with examples that each pair has the same sum.
   d. What is the sum of all the even numbers from 2 to 100? This is the number you will select in the video game.

LOOK BACK

Think about how you solved the problem.

6. a. Explain how solving a simpler problem helped you find the answer to the original problem.
   b. Why is this strategy better than finding the sum by hand or with a calculator?

EXERCISES *On Your Own*

Solve by using a simpler problem.

1. *Traffic* A traffic light was installed exactly 1 year ago. The traffic light changes every 30 seconds. How many times has the traffic light changed since it was installed?
   a. Break the problem into simpler problems. How many times does the light change in 1 minute? In 1 hour?
   b. Solve the problem. Explain your solution.

2. Find the sum of all whole numbers from 1 to 100.
   a. What smaller set of numbers could you start with?
   b. How will you make pairs?
   c. Solve the problem and explain your solution.

Use any strategy to solve each problem. Show your work.

3. *Biology* A baby's heart beats about 120 times per minute. How many times does a baby's heart beat in a year?

4. *Consumer Issues* A 3-pack of flowering plants costs $1.59. A flat of these plants costs $11.59. There are 24 plants in a flat. Suppose you want to buy 30 plants. What is the least amount of money you could spend?

5. *Savings* Suppose you save a quarter every day. How much will you have saved in 1 year? In 10 years?

6. *Biology* In every quart of blood in your body, you have about 19 fluid ounces of plasma. An average adult has about 5 quarts of blood. About how many quarts are plasma?

7. A line of 1,500 people is waiting to see a museum exhibit. Every 20 min, a guard allows 55 people to enter. The exhibit is open for 8 h. Will all 1,500 people get in?

8. *Consumer Issues* Tickets to the circus are $6.50 per person. The cost of a ticket decreases to $5.00 per person for groups of ten or more people.
   a. How much do you save over the regular ticket price if you buy 18 tickets?
   b. How much would your class save on a trip to the circus?

Mixed Review

Simplify each expression. *(Lessons 2-3, 3-7, 4-5, and 4-7)*

9. $7 \times 8 + 4$

10. $2.2 + 3.1 \times 7$

11. $9.8 \div 2 \times 4.2$

12. $7.7 - 2.3 \div 4$

Complete. *(Lesson 6-10)*

13. $17 \text{ qt} = \blacksquare \text{ pt}$

14. $7\frac{1}{2} \text{ yd} = \blacksquare \text{ ft}$

15. $8,000 \text{ lb} = \blacksquare \text{ T}$

16. $3.75 \text{ gal} = \blacksquare \text{ pt}$

Draw a model to find each product. *(Lesson 4-4)*

17. 0.9×0.2
18. 1.6×0.7
19. 1.2×0.4
20. 2.1×0.6
21. 1.5×1.1
22. 0.3×1.9

23. *Choose a Strategy* Eight birds and some squirrels are at the backyard feeder. You count 24 legs. How many squirrels are there?

7-5 Scale Drawings

What You'll Learn

1 To enlarge or reduce designs by making a scale drawing

2 To find the actual size of an object

...And Why

Architects use proportions to make scale drawings called blueprints.

Here's How

Look for questions that

▪ build understanding

✔ check understanding

THINK AND DISCUSS

▼**1** *Enlarging or Reducing Designs*

Architects, advertisers, and fashion designers all make drawings *to scale*. You can use graph paper to reduce or enlarge designs. The designs below were created on centimeter graph paper.

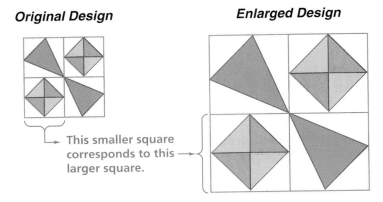

Original Design **Enlarged Design**

This smaller square corresponds to this → larger square.

1. a. ▪*Measurement* Find the length of the squares in each design.
   b. What is the ratio of the enlarged design to the original design?

2. a. Make a drawing of the original design using a ratio of 3 cm to 1 cm (original design).
   b. Explain the steps you used to make your drawing.
   c. ▪*Reasoning* Suppose your ratio is 0.5 cm to 1 cm (original design). How would your method be different?

A **scale** is a ratio that compares a length on a model (usually listed first) to the actual length of the real object (second).

3. Use the drawing at the left. Write the scale as a ratio in fraction form.

4. ▪*Explain* Why should a scale drawing show the scale?

1 cm : 30 cm

▼2 Finding the Actual Size of an Object

A scale drawing should be proportional to the actual size of the object so the scale can be used to calculate its actual size.

■ **EXAMPLE**

1 mm : 10 m

Architecture Use the scale drawing at the left to find the actual height of the skyscraper.

$\frac{\text{drawing (mm)}}{\text{actual (m)}}$ ⟶ $\frac{1}{10}$ ◄—Write the scale as a ratio.

The building is 34 mm high. ◄—Measure the height of the model.

$\frac{\text{drawing (mm)}}{\text{actual (m)}}$ ⟶ $\frac{1}{10} = \frac{34}{h}$ —Write a proportion. Let h represent the actual height.

$1 \times h = 10 \times 34$ ◄—Write the cross products.

$h = 340$

The actual height of the skyscraper is about 340 m.

5. **✓ Try It Out** Use each scale drawing to find the actual size.

a.

speedboat
1 cm : 3 m

b.

lizard
1 cm : 9 cm

EXERCISES *On Your Own*

Write the scale used for each scale drawing.

1. a 10-in. drawing of a 40-ft boat

2. a 2-in. model of a 8-ft car

3. a 4-ft model of a 100-ft building

4. a 15-in. drawing of a 300-ft fence

Make a scale drawing of each design. Use a scale of 3 cm to 1 cm (original design).

5.

6.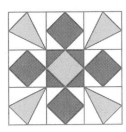

7.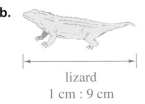

8.

9. Geography Shrink the map at the right. Use a scale of 0.5 cm to 1 cm (actual length).

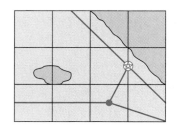

10. Architecture The height of a wall in a blueprint is 3 in. The actual wall is 96 in. high. Find the scale of the blueprint.

Use a map scale of 1 cm : 100 km. How many kilometers equal each of these lengths on the map?

11. 4 cm   **12.** 2.5 cm   **13.** 0.7 cm   **14.** 12 cm

Use a map scale of 1 cm : 100 km. How many centimeters equal each distance?

15. 125 km   **16.** 80 km   **17.** 4,000 km   **18.** 450 km

A scale model measures 2 cm × 7 cm. Find the dimensions of the actual object with the given scale.

19. 1 cm : 5 m   **20.** 1 cm : 2 km   **21.** 1 cm : 1 m   **22.** 1 cm : 80 m

23. 2 cm : 6 m   **24.** 1 cm : 0.5 m   **25.** 1 mm : 1 km   **26.** 1 cm : 2.5 m

27. Open-ended Create a scale drawing of an object.

Use the article below for Exercises 28–31. Copy and complete the table.

SCALING
DOWN

Have you ever noticed the detail in a toy car? Designers try to make toy cars look real. A designer chooses a car to model and then selects a size for the toy. Next each piece on the real car is scaled down. To determine the scale, the designer uses the ratio $\frac{\text{size of toy car}}{\text{size of real car}}$.

	Part	Toy Size	Actual Size
	Car	3 in.	100 in.
28.	Door handle	▓	5 in.
29.	Headlight	▓	8 in.
30.	Front bumper	▓	6 ft
31.	Rear window	▓	4.5 ft

Use each scale drawing to find the actual size.

32.

whale
1 cm to 3 m

33.

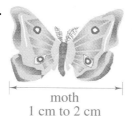

moth
1 cm to 2 cm

34.

goat
1 mm to 6 cm

35.

0.25 in. : 9 in.

chair

36. *Writing* Why would you want to see the blueprint of a house before construction starts?

37. Use the designs at the right.
  a. The original design is on a 4 × 6 grid. What are the dimensions of the new *distorted* design?
  b. *Reasoning* Why is it not in scale with the original?

Original Design   *Distorted Design*

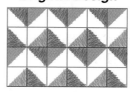
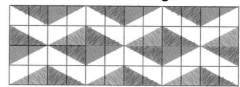

Mixed Review

Find each quotient. Round to the nearest hundredth, if necessary.
(Lesson 4-8)

38. $36.45 \div 2.1$ **39.** $6.4 \div 0.56$ **40.** $7.12 \div 4.4$ **41.** $4.8 \div 3.2$ **42.** $11.22 \div 1.1$

Find a number that satisfies the given conditions.
(Lesson 5-1)

43. a four-digit number divisible by 2, 3, 5, and 10

44. a four-digit number divisible by 2, 3, 5, and 9

45. Hank gets ready for school in 45 min. He can walk to school in 22 min. What time should he get up if school starts at 8:05 A.M.? *(Lesson 3-10)*

CHAPTER PROJECT

PROJECT LINK: ANALYZING DATA

Use ratios, proportions, and the data on page 284 to find the scale distances from the sun to your two assigned planets.

EXPLORATION

Indirect Measurement

After Lesson 7-5

You can use *similar figures* to find measurements that cannot be found directly, like the height of a tree on a sunny day.

■ EXAMPLE

Look at the triangles formed by the person and her shadow and then those formed by the tree and its shadow. The triangles are similar. Write and solve a proportion to find the height of the tree.

$$\frac{\text{person's height}}{\text{length of her shadow}} \longrightarrow \frac{5 \text{ ft}}{3 \text{ ft}} = \frac{x \text{ ft}}{15 \text{ ft}} \longleftarrow \frac{\text{tree's height}}{\text{length of tree's shadow}}$$

$$5 \times 15 = 3x \quad \longleftarrow \text{Solve the proportion.}$$

$$\frac{75}{3} = x$$

$$25 = x$$

The tree is 25 feet tall.

Find the missing length in each drawing.

1.

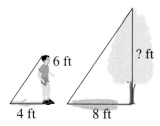

2.

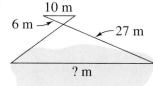

3.

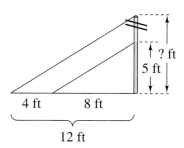

4.

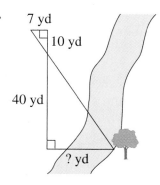

5. *Writing* Think of a situation when you have had to use indirect measurements to estimate the size or height of something. How did you make your estimate?

Percent Sense Using Models

What You'll Learn

▼ To model percents

...And Why

You can use models to help you understand the meaning of percents.

Here's How

Look for questions that
- build understanding
✔ check understanding

THINK AND DISCUSS

When you compare a number to 100 you are finding a **percent.**
You can write the ratio $\frac{75}{100}$ as 75%.

Words	Ratio	Percent
75 out of 100	$\frac{75}{100}$	75%

1. ᚚ*Open-ended* Where have you seen percents used?

2. Write each statement as a percent.
   a. 9 flashlights out of every 100 flashlights are defective.
   b. 45 cables of the 100 cables are not working.

You can model percents with 10 × 10 square grids.

■ EXAMPLE

Modeling What percent of the grid is shaded?

$$\frac{\text{amount shaded}}{\text{the whole}} = \frac{15 \text{ squares}}{100 \text{ squares}}$$

Write the ratio as a percent.

$$\frac{15}{100} \longrightarrow 15\%$$

So 15% of the grid is shaded.

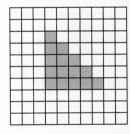

3. a. What percent of the grid in the Example is *not* shaded?
   b. ᚚ*Reasoning* How could you find the answer to part (a) without counting squares?

4. ✓*Try It Out* What percent of each grid is shaded?

a.
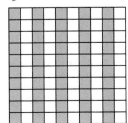

b.
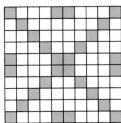

5. ⊹*Estimation* Estimate each percent. Choose 25%, 50%, or 75%.

  a. About what percent of the fish tank is full?

  b. About what percent of the pizza is eaten?

Work Together
Writing Percents Using Data

6. ⊹*Measurement* Use a centimeter tape measure to find each measure.

  a. length of your arm

  b. circumference of your head

  c. width of your smile

  d. length of your thumb

QUICKreview

100 cm = 1 m

7. What percent of a meter is each measurement in Question 6?

8. ⊹*Analyze* Why is it easier to use metric units than it is to use customary units in this activity?

EXERCISES *On Your Own*

Modeling **Model each percent using a 10 × 10 square grid.**

1. 5%   **2.** 100%   **3.** 75%   **4.** 37%   **5.** 90%   **6.** 18%

7. *Entertainment* Use the table at the right.

  a. What percent of those surveyed watch more than 21 hours of TV per week? What percent watched less than 15 hours?

  b. *Writing* How can you use your results from part (a) to find the missing percent in the table?

  c. Find the missing percent.

Write each statement as a percent.

8. 11 students out of 100 students are left handed.

9. 97 days out of 100 days last summer were sunny.

10. 4 radios out of every 100 radios arrive damaged.

11. 85 answers out of 100 answers are correct.

How Much TV Do We Watch?

Hours Per Week	Percent
Less than 7	17
7 to 14	29
15 to 21	▪
22 to 28	12
29 to 35	9
36 to 42	4
43 to 49	2
50 to 70	3
71 or more	1
No response	1
	100

Source: *TV Guide*

Use the design at the right for Exercises 12 and 13.

12. **a.** What percent of the design is made up of each pattern?

   i. 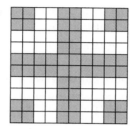 **ii.** ☐ **iii.** ☐ **iv.** ☐ **v.** ☐

   b. Find the sum of the percents in part (a).

13. *Open-ended* Draw your own design. Use at least three patterns. How many squares should you start with?

Modeling **What percent of each grid is shaded? What percent is *not* shaded?**

14. 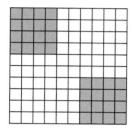   15.

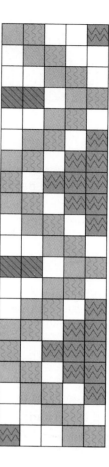

16. *Sports* Thirty-five percent of a group said football is their favorite sport. What percent did *not* choose football?

Number Sense **Use the numbers 1 through 100.**

17. What percent are multiples of 3? 18. What percent are odd? 19. What percent are prime? 20. What percent have at least one 7?

Mixed Review

Find each sum or difference. (*Lessons 6-4 and 6-5*)

21. $3\frac{2}{5} - 2\frac{1}{6}$ 22. $7\frac{9}{10} + 7\frac{5}{6}$ 23. $4\frac{1}{3} - 2\frac{5}{6}$ 24. $3\frac{1}{3} + \frac{3}{4}$ 25. $1\frac{4}{5} + 4\frac{3}{4}$

Write each decimal as a fraction or mixed number in simplest form. (*Lesson 5-9*)

26. 0.84   27. 5.25   28. 5.6   29. 28.825   30. 6.1   31. 7.9

32. *Choose a Strategy* There are 30 students in a math class. Twelve belong to the computer club, 8 to the hiking club, and 3 to both. How many belong to neither?

Percents, Fractions, and Decimals

What You'll Learn

▼1 To write percents as fractions and decimals

▼2 To write decimals and fractions as percents

...And Why

You will better understand numbers in real-world situations, such as those related to animals or earth science.

Here's How

Look for questions that
▪ build understanding
✔ check understanding

Work Together
Modeling Percents

Work in groups. Use a 10×10 grid for each model.

1. **a.** Model the percents 30%, 75%, 20%, and 50%.
   b. Model the fractions $\frac{3}{4}$, $\frac{1}{2}$, $\frac{3}{10}$, and $\frac{1}{5}$.
   c. Model the decimals 0.2, 0.5, 0.75, and 0.3.
   d. ▪*Reasoning* Match each percent model with an equivalent fraction model and an equivalent decimal model.

2. Express each shaded area as a percent, as a fraction in simplest form, and as a decimal.

   a.

   b.

THINK AND DISCUSS

▼1 *Writing Percents as Fractions and Decimals*

You can use what you know about percents to write a percent as a fraction and then as a decimal.

■ EXAMPLE 1

Write 36% as a fraction in simplest form and as a decimal.

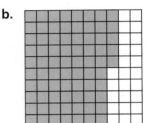

$36\% = \frac{36}{100}$ ← Write the percent as a fraction with a denominator of 100.

$\frac{36}{100} = \frac{9}{25}$ ← Write the fraction in simplest form.

$\frac{36}{100} = 0.36$ ← Write the fraction as a decimal, or move the decimal point 2 places to the right.

$36\% = 0.36$ ←

3. ✓*Try It Out* Write each percent as a fraction in simplest form and as a decimal.
   a. 25% **b.** 66% **c.** 4%

4. ✓*Try It Out* Ninety-nine percent of all kinds of plants and animals that have ever lived are now extinct. Write 99% as a fraction and then as a decimal.

▼2 *Writing Decimals and Fractions as Percents*

Sometimes you need to write a fraction as a decimal first, before writing the equivalent percent.

■ EXAMPLE 2

Earth Science About $\frac{7}{10}$ of Earth's surface is covered by water. Write $\frac{7}{10}$ as a decimal and as a percent.

$$7 \div 10 = 0.7 \quad \longleftarrow \text{Divide or simply write as a decimal.}$$

$$\frac{7}{10} = \frac{70}{100} = 70\% \quad \longleftarrow \begin{array}{l}\text{Write as a fraction with a denominator} \\ \text{of 100 or move the decimal point} \\ \text{2 places to the right.}\end{array}$$

$$0.7 = 70\% \quad \longleftarrow$$

5. ✓*Try It Out* Write each fraction as a decimal and then as a percent.
   a. $\frac{4}{5}$ **b.** $\frac{14}{25}$ **c.** $\frac{5}{8}$ **d.** $\frac{7}{20}$

6. How would you write 0.285 as a percent?

You can use a calculator to write a fraction as a percent.

■ EXAMPLE 3

▦ *Calculator* Use a calculator to write the fraction $\frac{2}{3}$ as a percent.

2 ⃞ 3 ⃟ *0.6666666* ✕ 100 ⃟ *66.666666* ≈ 66.7%

The fraction $\frac{2}{3}$ is about 66.7%.

▦ **7.** ⸭*Calculator* Write each fraction as a percent. Then round the percents to the nearest tenth.
   a. $\frac{1}{3}$ **b.** $\frac{7}{8}$ **c.** $\frac{8}{11}$ **d.** $\frac{2}{9}$

Modeling **Model each number on a 10 × 10 grid.**

1. 0.8   **2.** 91%   **3.** 0.72   **4.** $\frac{2}{5}$ **5.** 6%   **6.** $\frac{11}{20}$

Write each percent as a decimal and then as a fraction in simplest form.

7. 15%   **8.** 75%   **9.** 88%   **10.** 18%   **11.** 50%   **12.** 14%

13. 7%   **14.** 70%   **15.** 62.5%   **16.** 33%   **17.** 27.4%   **18.** 2%

19. 42%   **20.** 22%   **21.** 17%   **22.** 0.5%   **23.** 44%   **24.** 5%

25. *Physical Science* The air we breathe is about 80% nitrogen and 20% oxygen. Write each percent as a fraction in simplest form and as a decimal.

26. Write 58% as a decimal and as a fraction in simplest form.

Use the graph at the right for Exercises 27–29.

27. In what percent of lunch bags are you likely to find fruit?

28. **Choose A, B, C, or D.** Which of the following can you *not* conclude from the graph?
   A. About one fourth of the lunch bags contained fruit.
   B. Almost 10% of the lunch bags contained a sandwich.
   C. Fruit was in almost twice as many lunch bags as cookies.
   D. Students don't take drinks in their lunch bags.

29. *Research* Take a lunch bag survey in your class. Make a graph to show your results.

30. Copy and complete the table below. Write each fraction in simplest form.

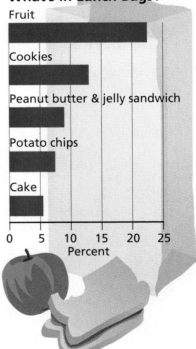

What's in Lunch Bags?

Fraction	Decimal	Percent
▨	▨	22%
▨	0.78	▨
$\frac{22}{25}$	▨	▨
▨	0.55	▨
$\frac{4}{5}$	▨	▨

Write each fraction or decimal as a percent.

31. $\frac{19}{20}$ 32. 0.65 33. $\frac{7}{50}$ 34. $\frac{1}{4}$ 35. 0.7 36. 0.34

37. 0.03 38. $\frac{1}{8}$ 39. 0.11 40. $\frac{3}{200}$ 41. 1.00 42. $\frac{8}{20}$

43. 0.99 44. $\frac{3}{10}$ 45. 0.01 46. 0.005 47. $\frac{12}{30}$ 48. $\frac{2}{25}$

49. *Writing* Describe how to write a decimal as a percent.

50. *Reasoning* How are fractions, decimals, and percents alike? How are they different?

51. a. The table shows the fraction of high school students who graduated from 1940 to 1990. Write each fraction as a percent.

Year	1940	1950	1960	1970	1980	1990
Graduates	$\frac{1}{4}$	$\frac{17}{50}$	$\frac{11}{25}$	$\frac{11}{20}$	$\frac{69}{100}$	$\frac{77}{100}$

Source: *Universal Almanac*

b. Graph the data in the table. Make a line graph.
c. *Data Analysis* Use your graph to predict the percent of high school graduates in the year 2000.

Calculator **Write each fraction as a percent. Round percents to the nearest tenth.**

52. $\frac{1}{6}$ 53. $\frac{4}{15}$ 54. $\frac{7}{11}$ 55. $\frac{12}{45}$ 56. $\frac{78}{98}$ 57. $\frac{1}{7}$

58. $\frac{6}{13}$ 59. $\frac{17}{30}$ 60. $\frac{4}{9}$ 61. $\frac{2}{15}$ 62. $\frac{7}{18}$ 63. $\frac{18}{21}$

Mixed Review

Use <, =, or > to complete each statement. *(Lesson 3-3)*

64. 0.112 ■ 0.121 65. 0.9985 ■ 0.998 66. 0.0009 ■ 0.001 67. 1.9 ■ 11.9

Simplify using the distributive property. *(Lesson 4-3)*

68. $(2.5 \times 16) + (2.5 \times 14)$ 69. $4 \times (6 - 2) - 2$ 70. $(2.08 \times 20) + (8.9 \times 20)$

71. *Choose a Strategy* A hotel has 28 rooms at $74 per day, 152 rooms at $93 per day, 317 rooms at $112 per day, and 18 rooms at $136 per day. To the nearest dollar, what is the average cost of a room?

Extra Practice, Lesson 7-7, page 528

Choose the best answer.

1. The ratio of a team's wins to losses is exactly 4 to 3. The team could have—

   A. 12 wins and 10 losses
   B. 16 wins and 9 losses
   C. 16 wins and 12 losses
   D. 30 wins and 40 losses

2. The distance between school and the library is 0.8 kilometers. How many meters is 0.8 kilometers?

   F. 0.0008 meters   **G.** 8 meters
   H. 80 meters   **J.** 800 meters

3. Matthew wrote 24 letters in 15 seconds. Lydia wrote 18 letters in 10 seconds. Which statement is true?

   A. Matthew writes faster than Lydia.
   B. Lydia writes faster than Matthew.
   C. Matthew wrote 6 more letters than Lydia during the same time period.
   D. Matthew and Lydia together wrote at a rate of 42 letters in 25 seconds.

4. Janelle is practicing for a shot put competition. Each day she plots on a number line the longest distance she threw for on that day. Which point best represents a distance of 9.05 meters?

   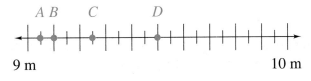

   F. *A*   **G.** *B*   **H.** *C*   **J.** *D*

5. Which pair is equivalent to $\frac{2}{5}$?

   A. 4% and 0.04   **B.** 25% and 0.025
   C. 25% and 0.25   **D.** 40% and 0.4

6. At one car dealer, $\frac{2}{5}$ of the vehicles sold during the year were sport utility vehicles. What percent of the vehicles sold were sport utility vehicles?

   F. 2.5%   **G.** 20%   **H.** 25%   **J.** 40%

7. For the proportion $\frac{9}{20} = \frac{n}{100}$, which statement is *not* true?

   A. $900 = 20n$ **B.** $\frac{900}{20} = n$
   C. $\frac{9}{100} = \frac{n}{20}$ **D.** $\frac{100}{n} = \frac{20}{9}$

Please note that items 8–10 each have *five* answer choices.

8. A car traveled 279.9 miles on 9.8 gallons of gasoline. A good estimate for the miles per gallon that the car traveled is—

   F. less than 20 miles per gallon
   G. 20 miles per gallon
   H. 25 miles per gallon
   J. 30 miles per gallon
   K. 40 miles per gallon

9. A scale model of an airplane is 7.5 inches long. The scale used to make the model was 1 inch : 5 feet. What is the length of the original airplane?

   A. 1.5 inches   **B.** 1.5 feet
   C. 37.5 inches   **D.** 37.5 feet
   E. Not Here

10. A garage charges $2.00 for the first 90 minutes and $1.00 for each additional half-hour. Which equation can you use to find the cost of parking for 4 hours?

    F. $C = 2.00 + 4(1.00)$
    G. $C = 2.00 + 2.5(1.00)$
    H. $C = 2.00 + 5(1.00)$
    J. $C = 4(2.00 + 1.00)$
    K. Not Here

Estimating with Percents

What You'll Learn

▼ To estimate percents using models

▼ To estimate a percent using mental math

...And Why

You often estimate percents when you shop or leave a tip in a restaurant.

Here's How

Look for questions that

▪ build understanding

✔ check understanding

THINK AND DISCUSS

▼ Estimating Percents Using Models

Estimating percents when you shop helps you make smart consumer decisions. You can use models to estimate percents.

■ **EXAMPLE 1**   *Real-World Problem Solving*

Sales A jacket is on sale for 60% of the regular price of $49.95 (or 40% off). Is $25 enough to buy the jacket?

Step 1 Make a model with ten equal sections.

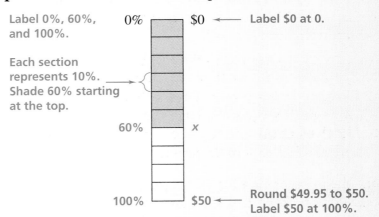

Label 0%, 60%, and 100%.

Each section represents 10%. Shade 60% starting at the top.

Label $0 at 0.

Round $49.95 to $50. Label $50 at 100%.

Step 2 Find the dollar value of each section.

$$100\% \text{ dollar value} \div \frac{\text{total number}}{\text{of sections}} = \frac{\text{dollar value of}}{\text{each section}}$$

$$\$50 \quad \div \quad 10 \quad = \quad \$5$$

Each section represents $5. Six sections represent 6 × 5, or $30. So $25 is not enough to buy the jacket.

1. What does the shading in the model in Example 1 represent?

2. Copy the model in Example 1 on graph paper. Write dollar amounts for 20%, 40%, 60% and 80%.

3. ✔*Try It Out* What dollar amount does the shaded part of the model at the left represent?

▼2 *Estimating Percents Using Mental Math*

You can use mental math to estimate the added cost of sales tax.

■ **EXAMPLE 2**   *Real-World Problem Solving*

Music You buy a CD for $14.99. The sales tax is 6%.
Estimate the sales tax and the final cost.

$14.99 ≈ $15.00	◀— Round to a convenient place.
6% ⟶ 6¢ per dollar	◀— Think of the percent as cents per dollar.
15 × 6 = 90	◀— Multiply mentally.
15 + 0.90 = 15.90	◀— Add the estimates.

The sales tax is about $.90. The final cost is about $15.90.

4. ✓*Try It Out* Estimate the sales tax and final cost for a hat that costs $18.59 with a sales tax of 5%.

5. ⊞*Think About It* Why wouldn't you want to round the price of an item down before estimating the sales tax?

You can use mental math to determine the amount of a tip.

■ **EXAMPLE 3**   *Real-World Problem Solving*

Dining Out You and two friends eat at a local restaurant. Estimate a 15% tip for a bill of $16.22.

$16.22 ≈ $16.00 ◀— Round to a convenient place.

First estimate 10% of the bill.

10% = 0.10	◀— Think of the percent as a decimal.
0.10 × 16 = 1.60	◀— Multiply mentally.

Half of $1.60 is $.80. So $.80 is about 5%.

$$10\% + 5\% = 15\%$$
$$\downarrow \quad\quad \downarrow \quad\quad \downarrow$$
$$1.60 + 0.80 = 2.40$$

So a 15% tip is about $2.40.

6. ✓*Try It Out* Estimate a 15% tip for each bill amount given.
  a. $18.29   **b.** $23.40   **c.** $41.63

7. ⊞*Look Back* Estimate a 20% tip for the bill in Example 3.

What dollar amount does each shaded part represent?

1. 0% — $0
    80% — x
    100% — $80

2. 0% — $0
    20% — x
    100% — $110

3. 0% — $0
    60% — x
    100% — $45

4. 0% — $0
    90% — x
    100% — $33

Draw a model to help you estimate each amount.

5. 90% of 41   **6.** 20% of 486   **7.** 10% of 129   **8.** 60% of 40

9. 25% of 53   **10.** 75% of 98   **11.** 15% of 21   **12.** 80% of 160

13. *Shopping* All items in a store are marked at 70% of the
    original price. Estimate the sale price of each item.
    a. a T-shirt regularly priced at $16.99   **b.** a jacket regularly priced at $129

14. *Sports* A baseball mitt is on sale for 75% of the original
    price of $39.99. Estimate the sale price of the mitt.

15. The regular price for a pair of boots is $23.99. They are on
    sale for 80% of the regular price. Estimate the sale price.

16. *Reasoning* The regular price of a chair is $349. Estimate
    the amount saved at each sale below.
    a. 20% off   **b.** 30% off   **c.** 75% off

17. *Recreation* Use the skateboard ad at the right.
    a. *Reasoning* What percent of the regular price of the
    skateboard is the sale price?
    b. *Estimation* Estimate the cost of the skateboard.
    c. Is $22 enough to buy the skateboard on sale?

18. *Pediatrics* By the age of two, a child's height is
    usually about 50% of its full adult height. Estimate
    the adult height of a 2-year-old whose height is 2 ft 9 in.

20% OFF $32

Estimate each amount.

19. 50% of 89   **20.** 10% of 302   **21.** 25% of 43   **22.** 30% of 295   **23.** 1% of 512

24. 25% of 59   **25.** 60% of 789   **26.** 90% of 49   **27.** 10% of 872   **28.** 75% of 23

29. 15% of 201   **30.** 50% of 37   **31.** 5% of 411   **32.** 40% of 81   **33.** 25% of 78

Use the sales tax chart at the right. Estimate the sales tax and final cost of each item below in each state.

State Sales Tax

State	Tax
Colorado	3%
Florida	6%
Georgia	4%
Massachusetts	5%
New Jersey	7%

Source: *The World Almanac and Book of Facts*

34. in-line skates: $75   **35.** dictionary: $14.59

36. poster: $9.99   **37.** calculator: $18.50

38. game: $21.03   **39.** erasers: $.79

40. *Eating Out* A meal costs $5.83. Estimate each tip.
  a. 10% tip   **b.** 15% tip   **c.** 20% tip

41. *Writing* Suppose 10% of a bill is $4.36. How can you use this to find a 20% tip? A 15% tip?

42. a. *Jobs* Miguel received the following tips. Estimate the value of each.
   i. 15% of $4.20   **ii.** 10% of $4.75   **iii.** 12% of $6.00
  b. Which tip was for the greatest amount?

Mixed Review

Find each product or quotient. *(Lessons 6-8 and 6-9)*

43. $3\frac{1}{3} \div 1\frac{1}{2}$ **44.** $1\frac{1}{5} \times 4\frac{1}{3}$ **45.** $7\frac{2}{3} \div 8\frac{7}{10}$ **46.** $12 \times 4\frac{8}{9}$ **47.** $3\frac{5}{6} \div 3\frac{3}{10}$

Find the GCF of each set of numbers. *(Lesson 5-3)*

48. 54, 72   **49.** 85, 95   **50.** 16, 20, 36   **51.** 30, 15, 60   **52.** 9, 27, 54   **53.** 14, 21, 84

54. What metric unit would you use to measure each item?
   (Lessons 3-8 and 3-9)
  a. length of a bridge   **b.** weight of a cat   **c.** amount of juice

55. *Choose a Strategy* Suppose a team is out of a soccer tournament if it loses a game. If 63 games must be played to determine the champion, how many teams were entered?

7-9 Finding a Percent of a Number

What You'll Learn

1 To find a percent of a number using a model or a calculator

2 To find a percent of a number using proportions

...And Why

Your safe exercise range can be found by calculating the percent of a number.

Here's How

Look for questions that
- **⊞** build understanding
- **✔** check understanding

THINK AND DISCUSS

▼ Using Modeling or a Calculator

Your heart rate increases when you exercise. A safe exercise range is between 60% and 80% of your maximum *safe heart rate*. Your maximum safe heart rate is 220 minus your age.

■ **E X A M P L E 1**   *Real-World Problem Solving*

Fitness Find the safe exercise range for a 12-year-old.
    220 − 12 = 208   ←— Find the maximum safe heart rate.

Method 1 Use a model.

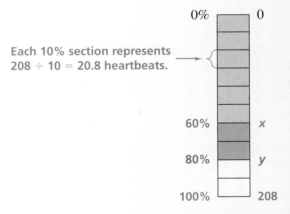

Each 10% section represents
208 ÷ 10 = 20.8 heartbeats.

60% of 208 is 6 sections × 20.8 = 124.8 ≈ 125 heartbeats
80% of 208 is 8 sections × 20.8 = 166.4 ≈ 166 heartbeats

Method 2 Use a calculator and the percent key to multiply.

    208 ✕ 60 % ▤ *124.8* ≈ 125
    208 ✕ 80 % ▤ *166.4* ≈ 166

Both methods give the same result. The safe exercise range for a 12-year-old is about 125 to 166 heartbeats per minute.

1. a. **✓Try It Out** Find the safe exercise ranges for a 20-year-old and for a 50-year-old.
  b. How does the safe exercise range change as a person grows older?

▼2 *Using Proportions*

You can also write a proportion to find the percent of a number.

■ EXAMPLE 2

Find 30% of 80.

$$30\% = \frac{30}{100}$$

Use a model to write a proportion.

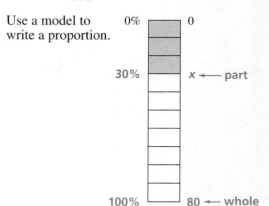

$$\frac{30}{100} = \frac{x}{80}$$ ⟵ Write a proportion.

$$30 \times 80 = 100 \times x$$ ⟵ Write the cross products.

$$2{,}400 = 100x$$ ⟵ Multiply.

$$\frac{2{,}400}{100} = x$$

$$24 = x$$ ⟵ Divide.

30% of 80 is 24.

2. ✓*Try It Out* Find each percent. Use any method.
   - a. 75% of 84
   - b. 37% of 140
   - c. 80% of 255
   - d. 10% of 56
   - e. 50% of 786
   - f. 43% of 61

For some problems, one method may be more appropriate or convenient than another.

3. a. ⁂*Choose* Which method would you use to answer each question? Explain your reasoning. Use a 24-hour day.
   - i. Catherine spends 25% of her day in school. How many hours does Catherine spend in school each day?
   - ii. Ian practices the piano for 5% of the day. For how many hours does Ian practice the piano each day?
   b. ⁂*Reasoning* Describe how to calculate the percents in part (a) using mental math.

Modeling **Use a model to find each percent.**

1. 20% of 48　　**2.** 50% of 288　　**3.** 90% of 72　　**4.** 30% of 305　　**5.** 25% of 112

Find each percent. Use a model or a calculator.

6. 12% of 90　　**7.** 5% of 86　　**8.** 35% of 120　　**9.** 15% of 60　　**10.** 70% of 240

11. 66% of 99　　**12.** 7% of 50　　**13.** 18% of 170　　**14.** 63% of 450　　**15.** 44% of 165

16. 8% of 235　　**17.** 55% of 91　　**18.** 75% of 32　　**19.** 12% of 72　　**20.** 22% of 288

Sports **Use the table at the right for Exercises 21–23. There were 250 boys and 250 girls surveyed. Use any method.**

21. How many girls swam?

22. How many boys swam?

23. How many girls sailboarded?

24. *Savings* During the summer Rosa earned $950. She saved 40%. How much money did she save?

25. Nail biting is a hard habit to kick. About 40% of children and teenagers bite their nails. A town has 1,618 children and teenagers. How many would you expect to be nail biters?

Teens Who Participated in Water Sports During One Year

Water Sport	Boys	Girls
Swimming	62%	76%
Waterskiing	13%	13%
Boating	15%	15%
Scuba Diving	9%	4%
Surfing	7%	3%
Sailboarding	4%	2%

Source: Teenage Research Unlimited

Language **Estimate the number of letters you expect in each passage given below. Use the table below.**

Frequency of Vowels in Written Passages

Letter	A	E	I	O	U	Y
Frequency	8%	13%	6%	8%	3%	2%

26. number of E's in a passage of 300 letters

27. number of A's in a passage of 1,400 letters

28. number of U's in a passage of 235 letters

29. number of I's in a passage of 695 letters

30. *Reasoning* Why don't the percents in the table above add up to 100%?

Use a proportion to find each percent.

31. 20% of 180   **32.** 55% of 160   **33.** 15% of 320   **34.** 5% of 230   **35.** 75% of 680

36. 15% of 90   **37.** 65% of 80   **38.** 11% of 600   **39.** 40% of 40   **40.** 72% of 325

41. In the United States, about 46% of the population wears glasses or contact lenses.
  a. In a group of 85 people, how many people would you expect to wear glasses or contact lenses?
  b. *Writing* Explain how you found your answer to part (a) and why you chose that method.
  c. How many people in your classroom would you expect to wear glasses or contact lenses?

42. *Entertainment* A dance club printed 400 tickets for its annual show and sold 85% of them. How many tickets did it sell?

43. *Sports* The Lions won 75% of their 28 games this year. How many games did they win?

44. About 67% of a person's body weight is water. Suppose a person weighs 114 lb. About how many pounds are water?

45. *Simple interest* earned on a savings account is found by multiplying the amount deposited, the interest rate, and the number of years. Suppose you deposited $1,000 at an interest rate of 4% for 5 years. Find the simple interest earned.

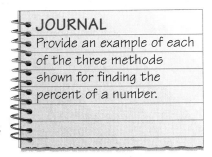

JOURNAL
Provide an example of each of the three methods shown for finding the percent of a number.

Mixed Review

Complete each statement. *(Lesson 4-10)*

46. 10.3 m = ▒ km   **47.** 56,930 mg = ▒ kg   **48.** 253 L = ▒ kL   **49.** 36 mm = ▒ cm

Estimate each sum or difference. *(Lesson 6-1)*

50. $2\frac{2}{5} + 2\frac{1}{4}$ **51.** $18\frac{1}{4} - 12\frac{3}{5}$ **52.** $2\frac{1}{20} + 1\frac{1}{3}$ **53.** $11\frac{7}{8} - \frac{5}{6}$ **54.** $8\frac{3}{4} + 4\frac{2}{3}$

55. *Choose a Strategy* Suppose one day you save 1 dime and the second day you save 2 dimes. Each day you save 1 more dime than the day before. How much money will you have after 2 weeks?

Modeling **Use a 10 × 10 grid to model each percent.**

1. 17%   **2.** 46%   **3.** 89%   **4.** 71%   **5.** 2%   **6.** 110%

Write each fraction or decimal as a percent.

7. $\frac{6}{8}$ **8.** 0.45   **9.** 0.67   **10.** $\frac{15}{25}$ **11.** $\frac{19}{20}$ **12.** 0.07

Estimation **Estimate each percent.**

13. 10% of 72   **14.** 80% of 41   **15.** 40% of 59   **16.** 25% of 191   **17.** 60% of 54

18. *Travel* A map has a scale of 1 cm : 75 km. The distance on the map from Hondo to Cheyenne is 3.5 cm. What is the actual distance?

19. **Choose A, B, C, or D.** Which method should *not* be used to find 88% of 40?

   A. 0.88 × 40   **B.** $\frac{88}{100} \times 40$ **C.** 88 [%] [×] 40 [=]   **D.** $\frac{40}{n} = \frac{88}{100}$

Math at Work

INTERNET HELP PROVIDER

If you enjoy surfing the Internet, making computer art, or exploring Web life, then a career as an Internet help provider might be for you. Help providers educate people about technical writing and are involved in Web page design. Consulting and technical drawing are also responsibilities of an Internet help provider.

Technical drawing and design require a knowledge of geometry and proportion. Technical writing requires good problem solving and logical reasoning skills.

For more information about Internet help providers, visit the Prentice Hall Web site: www.phschool.com

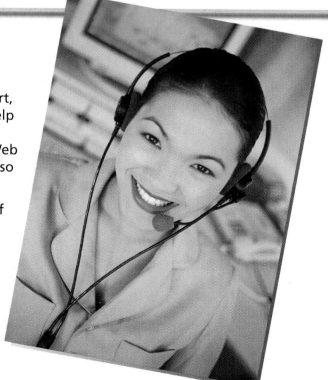

7-10 Data and Circle Graphs

What You'll Learn

▼ To sketch circle graphs

...And Why

You can use circle graphs to display data about television, reading, and the environment.

Here's How

Look for questions that
- ⁘ build understanding
- ✔ check understanding

Work Together

Applying Data to Circle Graphs

Texas A&M University asked children between 4 years old and 12 years old how they received money. Here are the results.

Allowance	Doing Chores	Earned Outside the Home	Gifts
54%	20%	10%	16%

Source: *The Book of Lists for Kids*

Circle graphs provide a good visual display of percent data. Work with a partner to make a circle graph for the data above.

1. Make a strip 10 cm long. Leave a tab at the end as shown.

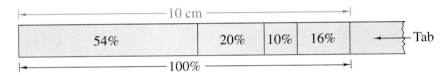

2. Since 10 cm = 100 mm, each millimeter represents 1% of the strip. Mark the strip with the percentages given in the table.

3. Shape the strip into a percent ring and tape the ends. Be sure to align the beginning and end of the strip.

4. ⁘*Modeling* Use a compass. Draw a circle slightly larger than your percent ring. Place a dot at the center of the circle.

5. Use your percent ring to mark the percentages around the circumference of the circle. Use a ruler to connect the marks to the center of the circle.

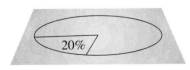

6. ⁘*Estimation* Label your graph and give it a title. Does each section appear to equal the percents in the table above?

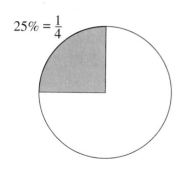

$25\% = \frac{1}{4}$

THINK AND DISCUSS

Most of the time a sketch of a circle graph gives you adequate information. You can sketch a circle graph by estimating a percent and using its fraction equivalent. For example, $24\% \approx 25\%$, which equals $\frac{1}{4}$. So shade a section that is about $\frac{1}{4}$ of the whole.

7. Each percent is approximately what fraction of the whole?
    a. 52%   **b.** 26%   **c.** 32%   **d.** 74%

You can use math skills you already know to sketch a circle graph.

■ **EXAMPLE**   *Real-World Problem Solving*

Environment Sketch a circle graph showing the willingness of teen drivers to use the bus more often.

What Teen Drivers Will Do for Air Quality

Option	Very Willing	Somewhat Willing	Not Very Willing	Don't Know
Use Bus More Often	22%	25%	50%	3%
Car Pool More Often	49%	26%	23%	2%

Source: Gallup Organization

Estimate the size of each section using the table above.

Very Willing ⟶ 22% is a little less than $\frac{1}{4}$ of the whole circle.

Somewhat Willing ⟶ 25% is $\frac{1}{4}$ of the whole circle.

Not Very Willing ⟶ 50% is $\frac{1}{2}$ of the whole circle.

Don't Know ⟶ 3% is the part of the circle left.

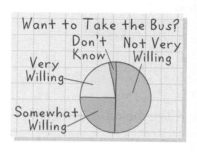

⟵ Draw a circle.

Divide the circle into two parts for the 50% section. The 25% section is half of the remaining section. Then estimate the 22% and 3% sections.

Label each section and give your graph a title.

8. ⬧ *Estimation* Sketch a circle graph for the percentages given.
    a. 23%, 51%, 26%   **b.** 33%, 32%, 35%   **c.** 74%, 13%, 13%

9. ✔**Try It Out** Refer to the Example. Sketch a circle graph showing the willingness of teens to car pool more often.

10. **⸬Analyze** Look at the Example and Question 9. Which option for preserving air quality seems more likely to succeed? Why?

11. **a.** A section that is $\frac{1}{8}$ of a circle graph would be what percent of the whole?
    b. Explain how you would sketch a circle graph with a shaded section equal to $\frac{1}{8}$ of the whole.

EXERCISES *On Your Own*

Sketch a circle graph with a shaded section equal to the fraction given.

1. $\frac{1}{2}$ 2. $\frac{3}{4}$ 3. $\frac{1}{6}$ 4. $\frac{1}{3}$ 5. $\frac{4}{10}$ 6. $\frac{7}{8}$

Estimation **Sketch a circle graph for the percentages given.**

7. 25%, 75%   8. 36%, 64%   9. 42%, 58%   10. 10%, 40%, 50%

11. 60%, 30%, 10%   12. 12%, 26%, 62%   13. 45%, 45%, 8%, 2%   14. 5%, 14%, 33%, 48%

15. 24%, 76%   16. 34%, 32%, 34%   17. 48%, 25%, 27%   18. 59%, 41%

19. 42%, 19%, 39%   20. 55%, 45%   21. 20%, 75%, 5%   22. 8%, 92%

Data Analysis **The table below shows the results of 1,000 adults surveyed. Use the table for Exercises 23 and 24.**

Amount of Time Adults Think They Spend Reading for Pleasure

Too much	Too little	About right	Don't know
7%	73%	16%	4%

Source: Gallup Organization

23. *Estimation* Sketch a circle graph for the data.

24. How many adults responded "Don't know"? "Too little"? "About right"?

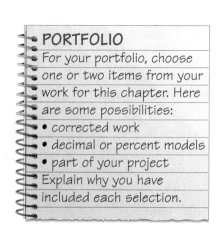

PORTFOLIO
For your portfolio, choose one or two items from your work for this chapter. Here are some possibilities:
• corrected work
• decimal or percent models
• part of your project
Explain why you have included each selection.

25. The graph at the right is labeled incorrectly. Trace the circle graph and move each percent label to the correct section.

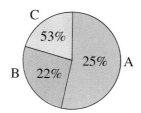

26. *Open-ended* List the things you do on a Saturday. Estimate the hours you spend on each activity. Write each time as a percent of a 24-hour day. Make a circle graph using your data.

27. *Fund-raising* Display the data below in a circle graph.

**Percent of Money Raised from
La Monte Middle School Fund-raisers**

Car Wash	Paper Drive	Book Sale	Food Stand
42%	28%	18%	12%

28. *Data Analysis* Use the graph at the right.
   a. *Estimation* Estimate the percent of total ad hours spent on each type of product.
   b. *Calculator* Find the percent of total ad hours spent on each type of product.
   c. Compare your estimates in part (a) to the actual percents you found in part (b). How close were your estimates?

29. *Writing* Why should the percents that make up a circle graph always total 100%?

30. *Sports* Out of 160 students, 22 play lacrosse, 41 play soccer, 19 play field hockey, and 78 don't play. Sketch a circle graph of the data.

**Kinds of Ads During
604 Hours of Kid's TV**

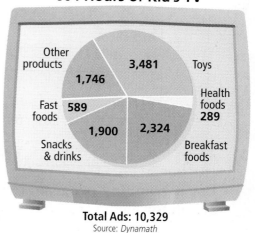

Total Ads: 10,329
Source: *Dynamath*

Mixed Review

Find the LCM of each set of numbers. *(Lesson 5-7)*

31. 15, 25, 75   **32.** 6, 10, 15   **33.** 3, 12, 19   **34.** 9, 12, 81   **35.** 24, 40, 60

Find the value of each expression. *(Lesson 4-2)*

36. $6^2 + 7^3$ **37.** $4^3 + 3^2 \times 8$ **38.** $10^3 - 5^2 + 2^3$ **39.** $3^3 + 5^2 \times 1^{10}$

40. *Choose a Strategy* Suppose you can arrange the chorus singers in rows of 10, 12, or 15 with no one left over. What is the least possible number of singers?

Constructing Circle Graphs

After Lesson 7-10

Many spreadsheet applications have graphing capabilities. To make a circle graph on a computer, enter the data in a spreadsheet. Highlight the data you wish to graph. Then choose "circle graph" from the menu.

■ EXAMPLE

The data in the table below were entered in a spreadsheet program. Use a computer to graph the data.

How Sierra Spends Her Time on Weekdays

Activity	Amount of Time
At School	6 hours
Chores	1 hour
Homework	2 hours
Play/Recreation	4 hours
Eating	3 hours
Sleeping	8 hours

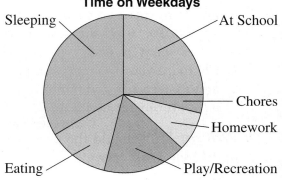

How Sierra Spends Her Time on Weekdays

Use a graphing program to make a circle graph for each set of data.

1. Ages of People Eating at Freddy's Fast Food

Age	Under 12	12–18	19–30	31–50	Over 50
Number of People	80	120	60	30	70

2. How Theo Spends His Weekly Allowance

Categories	Food	School	Fun	Savings	Other
Amount Spent	$4	$5	$6	$2	$1

3. How Often Adults Need to Search for Keys

Categories	Never	Once a Year	Once a Month	Once a Week	Once a Day
Number of Responses	31	15	23	9	2

Planet of the Stars

Make a Scale Model The Project Link questions on pages 284, 288, and 295 will help you complete your project. Here is a checklist to help you gather the parts of your project together.

✔ ratios of the diameter of each of your two planets to the real diameter of Pluto

✔ two-dimensional drawings of your two planets

✔ scaled distances from the sun to your two planets

Present your scale model of your two planets and all your calculations to the class. Include all necessary dimensions. You may want to describe the distance each of your planets is from the sun in terms of distances your classmates would understand.

Reflect and Revise

Meet with other students who also chose one of your planets to compare data. Compare any differences that you find and revise your calculations if necessary. Is your model neat and legible? Is it attractive but informative? Could your scale model be improved? If necessary, revise parts of your project.

Web Extension

Prentice Hall's Internet site contains information you might find helpful as you complete your project. Visit www.phschool.com/mgm1/ch7 for some links and ideas related to astronomy.

Ratios and Rates
7-1, 7-2

A **ratio** is a comparison of two numbers.

A **rate** is a ratio that compares two measures with different units.

Write each ratio as a fraction in simplest form.

1. 20 to 80
2. 15 : 35
3. 33 : 77
4. 14 to 56
5. 17 : 51

6. A moonrat is a member of the hedgehog family. An adult male's body is about 45 cm long. In three different ways, write the ratio to compare a moonrat's body length to 1 m. (1 m = 100 cm)

7. A package of three videotapes is on sale for $5.97. A package of two videotapes is on sale for $3.76. Find the unit rate for each. Which package has the higher unit cost?

Proportions and Scale Drawings
7-3, 7-5

A **proportion** is an equation stating that two ratios are equal. You can use cross products to find the missing term in a proportion.

A **scale** is a ratio that compares length on a drawing or model to the actual length of an object.

Find the value of n.

8. $\frac{3}{5} = \frac{n}{35}$
9. $\frac{6}{9} = \frac{18}{n}$
10. $\frac{n}{6} = \frac{12}{24}$
11. $\frac{32}{n} = \frac{8}{4}$
12. $\frac{n}{15} = \frac{5}{25}$

13. $\frac{17}{51} = \frac{3}{n}$
14. $\frac{n}{28} = \frac{9}{12}$
15. $\frac{45}{n} = \frac{30}{48}$
16. $\frac{0}{108} = \frac{n}{9}$
17. $\frac{96}{144} = \frac{4}{n}$

Use a centimeter ruler and the scale drawing at the right.

18. Find the actual length of the bicycle.

19. Find the actual diameter of the front wheel.

1 cm : 1 m

20. The scale on a landscape blueprint is 1 in. : 6 ft. A stone wall is 4 in. long on the blueprint. How long is the wall?

21. A drawing of a leatherback turtle has a scale of 2 cm : 1 m. The drawing of the turtle is 3 cm long. How long is the turtle?

Solving a similar, simpler problem can help you see new ways to solve a given problem.

22. A clock chimes once every 30 min. How many times will it chime in the month of June?

23. How many days have passed since you were born?

A **percent** is a ratio that compares a number to 100. You can write a percent as a decimal or as a fraction.

Write each as a percent, as a fraction in simplest form, and as a decimal.

24. 24 cm out of 100 cm

25. 55 students out of 100 students

26. 3 hats out of 25 hats

27. 5 pens out of 20 pens

28. 40 heads out of 100 coin tosses

29. 2 days out of 10 days

30. Write 65% as a decimal and as a fraction in simplest form.

31. An office chair is on sale for 80% of the regular price of $87.95. Estimate the sale price.

32. Choose A, B, C, or D. Find the best estimate for 72% of 90.

A. 72 B. 45 C. 63 D. 90

You can use a model, a calculator, or a proportion to find a percent of a number.

You can make a circle graph to show percent data.

Find each percent.

33. 75% of 40 **34.** 23% of 19 **35.** 60% of 80 **36.** 10% of 235 **37.** 5% of $15.98

38. Use the data at the right to sketch a circle graph.

Ways We Get to School

Car	Bus	Bike	Walk
24%	57%	4%	15%

1. **Choose A, B, C, or D.** Which is another way to write the ratio 6 : 3?

   A. 3 : 6   **B.** 6, 3

   C. $\frac{3}{6}$ **D.** 6 to 3

2. *Writing* Are the ratios 9 apples to 12 apples and 6 apples to 10 apples equal? Explain your answer.

3. Use the figure below. Write a ratio comparing the shaded regions to the unshaded regions as a fraction in lowest terms.

   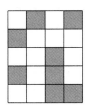

4. **Choose A, B, C, or D.** Find a ratio equal to $\frac{3}{12}$.

   A. $\frac{9}{24}$ **B.** $\frac{4}{1}$

   C. $\frac{8}{32}$ **D.** $\frac{5}{15}$

5. Solve for n.

   a. $\frac{21}{35} = \frac{9}{n}$ **b.** $\frac{n}{63} = \frac{4}{14}$

6. *Geometry* A scale drawing has a scale of 1 cm to 1.5 m. A tree in the drawing measures 4.5 cm. Find the height of the tree.

7. Write each as a percent.

   a. $\frac{11}{20}$ **b.** 0.7

8. Write each as a fraction in lowest terms.

   a. 38%   **b.** 0.62

9. Express each as a decimal.

   a. $\frac{6}{20}$ **b.** 55%

   c. 6%   **d.** $\frac{78}{100}$

10. *Estimation* Choose the best estimate for $\frac{5}{12}$. Explain how you arrived at your estimate.

    A. 50%   **B.** 40%   **C.** 30%

11. Draw a model to show each percent.

    a. 75% of 200

    b. 30% of 210

12. Find each percent.

    a. 52% of 96

    b. 20% of 400

    c. 38% of 150

13. Use the data in the table below to make a circle graph.

    Favorite Types of Books

Mysteries	Biographies	Fiction	Humor
22%	13%	55%	10%

14. The class treasury totals $210. Forty percent of this was earned from the art show. How much money was earned from the art show?

15. Gerald bought art supplies that totaled $15.78. The sales tax is 3%. Estimate the amount of the tax and the total cost of the art supplies.

16. Estimate a 15% tip on each bill.

    a. $25.35

    b. $9.35

Choose the best answer.

1. Which number is *not* a prime factor of 2,420?

   A. 2

   B. 3

   C. 5

   D. 11

2. Find the value of the expression $3 + b^2$ when $b = 5$.

   A. 64

   B. 28

   C. 16

   D. 13

3. What is a step to find the difference $5\frac{1}{4} - 3\frac{2}{3}$?

   A. Subtract $\frac{1}{4}$ from $\frac{2}{3}$.

   B. Write $5\frac{1}{4}$ as $5\frac{3}{12}$.

   C. Find the difference $5 - 3\frac{2}{3}$.

   D. Write $3\frac{2}{3}$ as $2\frac{5}{3}$.

4. Sukie boarded the school bus at 7:48 A.M. and arrived at school at 8:13 A.M. How many minutes did she spend on the bus?

   A. 13 min

   B. 15 min

   C. 25 min

   D. 65 min

5. Which expression is equivalent to 35×10?

   A. $35 \times (100 \div 10)$

   B. $35 \times (100 \times 10)$

   C. $35 + (100 \times 10)$

   D. $35 + (100 + 10)$

6. Find the mean of the following allowances: $4, $2, $2.50, $4, $3.

   A. $4.00

   B. $2.50

   C. $2.75

   D. $3.10

7. Which number is the *best estimate* for 21.7×0.03?

   A. 66

   B. 6.6

   C. 0.66

   D. 0.066

8. The mass of a package is 1.1 kilograms. How many grams are equivalent to 1.1 kilograms?

   A. 0.11 g

   B. 11 g

   C. 110 g

   D. 1,100 g

9. The regular price of a jacket is $46.95. However, during a sale there is a 20% discount off the regular price. It is reasonable to assume that the sale price will be —

   A. more than $10 but less than $20

   B. more than $20 but less than $30

   C. more than $30 but less than $40

   D. more than $40 but less than $50

10. If you continue the pattern below, which figure will have 11 blocks?

    A. the 5th

    B. the 6th

    C. the 10th

    D. the 11th

11. Which is the best buy?

    A. a half-dozen muffins, if a dozen cost $6.59

    B. a half-dozen muffins for $3.19

    C. a half-dozen muffins if each costs $.59

    D. a half-dozen muffins if muffins cost $1.19 for 2

12. What is the reciprocal of $4\frac{2}{5}$?

    A. $2\frac{4}{5}$

    B. $\frac{5}{2}$

    C. $\frac{1}{4}$

    D. $\frac{5}{22}$

8 Tools of Geometry

Puzzling Pictures

Do you remember putting together simple puzzles when you were younger? Those designed for little children are often made of wood and are made of large pieces. The pieces have straight sides so that the child can put the puzzle together easily.

Create a Puzzle Imagine that the photograph of the San Antonio, Texas, Riverwalk at the left was a puzzle. Your project is to make an attractive but challenging puzzle for your classmates to solve. Include as many geometric shapes as you can.

- How to solve problems using logical reasoning

Steps to help you complete the project:

Points, Lines, and Planes

What You'll Learn

▼ To identify and work with points, lines, segments, and rays

② To investigate relationships between special pairs of lines

...And Why

You can accurately describe and identify geometric figures.

Here's How

Look for questions that
■ build understanding
✔ check understanding

THINK AND DISCUSS

▼ Exploring Points, Lines, Segments, and Rays

You can easily find a particular star in the sky if you can see the group, or constellation, to which it belongs. The stars are points on an imaginary geometric figure.

A **point** has no size, only location. A small dot made by a pencil tip can represent a point. Points A, B, and C are shown.

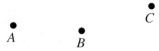

1. ✓*Try It Out* Give an example of a physical model of a point.

A **line** continues without end in opposite directions. It has no thickness. You can name a line by using two points on the line. For example, one name for this line is $\overleftrightarrow{DE}$ (read as "line DE").

2. ✓*Try It Out* What are some other names for the line above?

3. Name something that could be a physical model of a line.

A **plane** is a flat surface that extends indefinitely in four directions. It has no thickness.

4. Name something that could be a physical model of a plane.

A **segment** is part of a line. It is made up of two points and all the points of the line that joins the two points. You name a segment by the two *endpoints*. This is $\overline{RS}$ (read as "segment RS").

5. ✓*Try It Out* Give another name for $\overline{RS}$.

6. ✓**Try It Out** Draw $\overleftrightarrow{JK}$ and $\overline{JK}$. Explain the difference.

7. ⚓**Open-ended** Draw a line and label several points on it. Name your line. Name four different segments.

A **ray** is part of a line. It consists of one endpoint and all the points of the line on one side of the endpoint. To name a ray, you name the endpoint first and then any other point on the ray. This is $\overrightarrow{GH}$ (read as "ray GH").

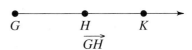

8. ✓**Try It Out** Give another name for $\overrightarrow{GH}$.

9. ⚓**Think About It** Describe $\overrightarrow{YX}$. How is $\overrightarrow{YX}$ different from $\overrightarrow{XY}$? What part of $\overleftrightarrow{XY}$ do $\overrightarrow{YX}$ and $\overrightarrow{XY}$ have in common?

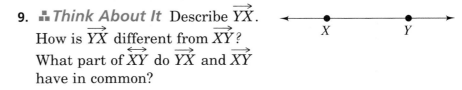

If a line can be drawn through a set of points, the points are **collinear.** If no one line can be drawn through all the points, the points are **noncollinear.**

collinear points **noncollinear points**

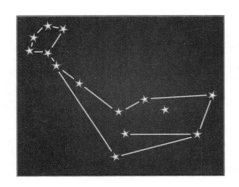

The stars that form the constellation Cetus can be represented by points. These points are connected here with segments to help you see the shape of Cetus.

Source: *Encyclopedia Americana*

▼2 *Special Pairs of Lines*

There are two possible relationships between two lines that lie in a plane: either they intersect or they are parallel. **Parallel lines** are lines in the same plane that do not intersect. **Parallel segments** lie in parallel lines.

Some lines are horizontal or vertical.

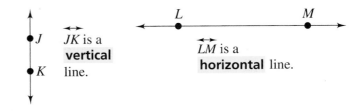

$\overleftrightarrow{JK}$ is a **vertical** line.

$\overleftrightarrow{LM}$ is a **horizontal** line.

This game involves sticks that can be parallel or intersecting. The sticks are removed one by one. The object of the game is to not let the marbles fall between the sticks.

Skew lines are lines that lie in different planes. They are neither parallel nor intersecting.

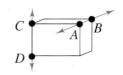

$\overleftrightarrow{AB}$ and $\overleftrightarrow{CD}$ are skew.

■ **EXAMPLE**

Does each pair of lines appear to be parallel or intersecting?

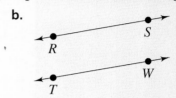

a. $\overleftrightarrow{AB}$ and $\overleftrightarrow{CD}$ are intersecting lines, even though the point of intersection is not shown.

b. $\overleftrightarrow{RS}$ and $\overleftrightarrow{TW}$ are parallel. No matter how far you extend them, they will not intersect.

Work Together   *Drawing Points and Lines*

10. Draw a point. How many lines can you draw through a point? How many vertical lines can you draw through a point?

11. ⁝ *What If . . .* Draw two points. How many lines can you draw through two points? Can you draw a horizontal line through your two points? Explain.

12. ⁝ *Go a Step Further* Draw three points. Then draw all the lines that go through any two points. Arrange the three points so that you get a different number of lines.

EXERCISES *On Your Own*

Match each figure with its name.

1.

2.

3.

4. E ●————————● F →

a. $\overleftrightarrow{EF}$ b. $\overrightarrow{EF}$ c. $\overrightarrow{FE}$ d. $\overline{EF}$

Use the diagram at the right for Exercises 5 and 6.

5. Name the line in several different ways.

6. Name four different rays.

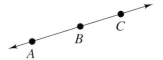

Refer to the diagram below for Exercises 7–12. Name each of the following.

7. three collinear points

8. three noncollinear points

9. three segments

10. three rays

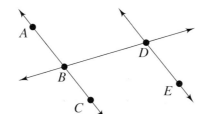

11. two lines that appear to be parallel

12. two pairs of intersecting lines

Draw each of the following.

13. five collinear points

14. three noncollinear points

15. two noncollinear points

16. a. *Open-ended* Arrange four points in as many different positions as you can. For each arrangement, draw all lines that go through at least two of the points.

b. *Reasoning* If you have four points on a plane, how many lines go through at least two of the points?

Name each pair of segments in each figure that appear to be parallel.

17.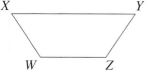

18.

19.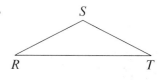

Complete each sentence with *sometimes*, *always*, or *never*.

20. Two points are ▦ collinear.

21. Two parallel lines are ▦ intersecting.

22. Four points are ▦ collinear.

23. A segment ▦ has two endpoints.

24. A ray ▦ has two endpoints.

25. A line ▦ has two endpoints.

26. Horizontal lines are ▦ parallel.

27. Skew lines ▦ intersect.

Use the article below to answer Exercise 28.

28. **a.** *Astronomy* How could you describe geometrically the position of the moon, Earth, and sun during a solar eclipse?
   b. *Reasoning* These planets are very large. Why can we think of them as points?

(((**Eclipses**)))

EARTH IS ABOUT 248,550 mi from the moon and 93,000,000 mi from the sun. The diameters of Earth and the moon are about 7,910 mi and 2,200 mi, respectively. The diameter of the sun is about 865,400 mi. A solar eclipse occurs when the moon comes between the sun and Earth.

29. *Writing* Write a description of the figure at the right that would help someone to draw a copy of the figure.

30. *Reasoning* In how many ways can three lines that lie on one plane be related? Draw sketches to show some ways.

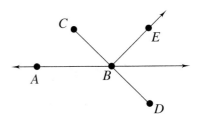

Look at the diagram at the right for Exercises 31–36. Name each of the following.

31. a pair of parallel lines   32. a pair of intersecting lines

33. a pair of skew lines   34. a vertical line

35. a horizontal line   36. a pair of vertical lines

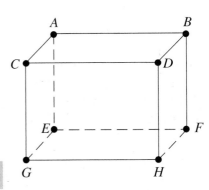

Mixed Review

Simplify each expression. *(Lesson 4-2)*

37. 17^2 38. 4.2^2 39. $3 \times (2 + 6)^2$ 40. $359 - 6^3$ 41. $(52 \div 2) - 2^4$

Estimate each sum or difference. *(Lesson 6-1)*

42. $6\frac{1}{5} - 2\frac{7}{8}$ 43. $4\frac{1}{2} + 5\frac{7}{10}$ 44. $3\frac{5}{16} + \frac{7}{8}$ 45. $2\frac{7}{12} - 1\frac{2}{3}$ 46. $9\frac{5}{8} - 4\frac{1}{5}$

47. You work in groups in math class. Each group must have the same number of students. If 36 students are in your class, what size groups are possible? *(Lesson 5-2)*

8-2 Exploring Angles

What You'll Learn

1 To estimate and measure angles

2 To classify angles as acute, right, obtuse, or straight

...And Why

You can understand exercise directions involving angle measures.

Here's How

Look for questions that
- build understanding
- ✔ check understanding

THINK AND DISCUSS

1 *Estimating and Measuring Angles*

More than 3,000 years ago, the Babylonians discovered that it takes about 360 days for the sun to travel in a circular path. They divided the path into 360 equal parts. We now call each of these parts a **degree.**

An **angle** is made up of two rays with a common endpoint.

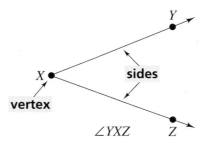

∠YXZ

1. a. ✓*Try It Out* Name the vertex and sides of the angle.
   b. Describe what the three letters represent in ∠YXZ.
   c. Use three letters to give the angle another name.

2. **Look Back** Sometimes you can name an angle with a number, like ∠1, or by the name of the vertex. What one-letter name would you use for ∠YXZ? Explain.

3. a. ✓*Try It Out* How many angles are shown at the right? Name them.
   b. **Reasoning** Why can't you use a single letter to name any of the angles?

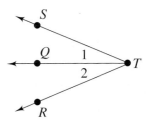

The legs of this camera tripod form angles with each other and meet at the vertex. The legs are sides of the angles.

You can use a *protractor* to measure the size of an angle. The units of measurement are degrees. Use the symbol ° for degrees.

■ **EXAMPLE 1**   *Real-World Problem Solving*

Physical Education Measure the angle formed by the football player's leg and the ground.

First, extend the sides of the angle so that they will intersect the scale on the protractor.

③ Read the scale where it intersects the second side of the angle.

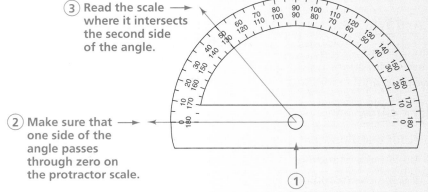

② Make sure that one side of the angle passes through zero on the protractor scale.

① Place the center point of the protractor on the vertex of the angle.

The angle measures 50°.

4. ⁂**Reasoning** Most protractors have two scales. How do you decide which number to read?

5. ⁂**Reasoning** Does changing the lengths of the sides of the angle change the measurement of the angle? Explain.

6. ✔*Try It Out* Use a protractor to measure each angle.

a.    b.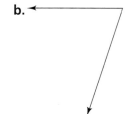

2 Classifying Angles

You can use measures to classify angles.

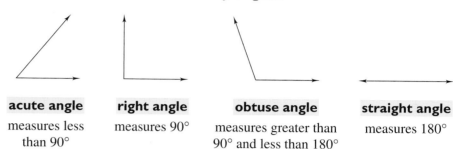

acute angle
measures less than 90°

right angle
measures 90°

obtuse angle
measures greater than 90° and less than 180°

straight angle
measures 180°

■ EXAMPLE 2   Real-World Problem Solving

Art In this drawing, what type of angle does the dinosaur make with the ground?

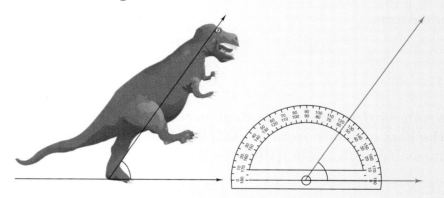

The angle measures 55°. Since 55° < 90°, the dinosaur makes an acute angle with the ground.

Many museum models of *Tyrannosaurus rex* show the dinosaur in an upright, tail-dragging position. Scientists now believe that *Tyrannosaurus rex* actually walked at an angle, using its tail for balance.

7. ✓*Try It Out* Classify the angles in Question 6 on page 332 as acute, right, obtuse, or straight.

8. How would you use your protractor to draw a 110° angle?

Lines that intersect to form right angles are **perpendicular.** The symbol ⌐ on a diagram indicates that lines are perpendicular and that an angle is a right angle.

9. Name all the right angles formed by the perpendicular lines, $\overleftrightarrow{AB}$ and $\overleftrightarrow{CD}$, shown.

10. ♣*Open-ended* Find examples of perpendicular lines in your classroom.

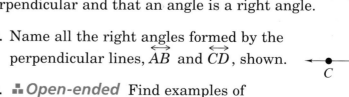

Name the vertex and sides of each angle.

1.

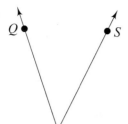

2.

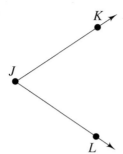

3.

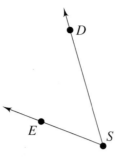

4.

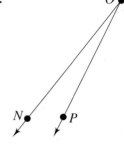

5. Name three angles in the diagram at the right. Then name each angle in a different way.

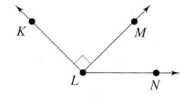

Use a protractor to draw angles with the following measures.

6. 30°	**7.** 135°	**8.** 90°	**9.** 45°	**10.** 120°	**11.** 60°
12. 125°	**13.** 75°	**14.** 82°	**15.** 154°	**16.** 52°	**17.** 165°

Estimation **Estimate the measure of each angle. Choose the best estimate from 30°, 60°, 90°, 120°, 150°. Then measure each angle with a protractor.**

18.

19.

20.

21.

22.

23.

Classify each angle as *acute, right, obtuse,* or *straight.*

24.

25.

26.

27.

28.

29. *Photography* A 50-mm camera lens has a 45° viewing angle. What kind of angle is this?

30. *Writing* Must two acute angles have the same measure? Must two right angles? Two obtuse angles? Two straight angles? Explain.

31. **a.** Draw two perpendicular lines, $\overleftrightarrow{RS}$ and $\overleftrightarrow{TW}$.
    b. How many right angles are formed?

32. Name all the right angles formed by the perpendicular lines $\overleftrightarrow{ST}$ and $\overleftrightarrow{WX}$ at the right.

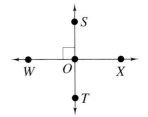

33. *Reasoning* What angles can you draw accurately without using a protractor? Explain.

34. *Open-ended* Draw an obtuse $\angle DEF$, an acute $\angle NOP$, and a straight $\angle KJQ$.

35. **Choose A, B, C, or D.** Which measure is *not* a measure of one of the angles shown at the right?

   A. 60°   **B.** 90°   **C.** 120°   **D.** 150°

36. **a.** *Measurement* Find the measure of each angle in the figure at the right.

   i. $\angle AGF$ **ii.** $\angle DGB$ **iii.** $\angle BGE$ **iv.** $\angle EGC$
   b. List all the obtuse angles shown.
   c. List all the right angles shown.
   d. List all the straight angles shown.

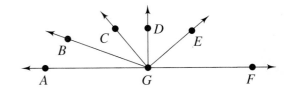

Mixed Review

Write three equal ratios for each given ratio. (*Lesson 7-2*)

37. 3 : 5   **38.** 5 to 9   **39.** $\frac{1}{6}$ **40.** 14 : 32   **41.** 16 to 20   **42.** $\frac{48}{80}$

Find the GCF. (*Lesson 5-3*)

43. 18, 27   **44.** 52, 78   **45.** 84, 28   **46.** 10, 15, 25   **47.** 4, 18, 144   **48.** 9, 36, 56

49. *Choose a Strategy* Suppose you have a 3-qt container and a 5-qt container. Without marking the containers, how could you measure exactly 1 qt of water?

Basic Constructions

After Lesson 8-2

A *bisector* is a line perpendicular to a segment and passing through the midpoint of the segment.

An *angle bisector* is a ray that divides the angle into two congruent angles.

■ EXAMPLE 1

Use a compass and straightedge to construct the perpendicular bisector of $\overline{AB}$.

A   B

Open the compass to more than half the length of $\overline{AB}$. Put the tip of the compass at A. Draw a part of a circle that intersects $\overline{AB}$.

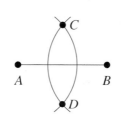

Put the tip of the compass at B, keeping the compass open to the same width. Then draw a part of a circle that intersects $\overline{AB}$. The curves intersect at two points. Label these points C and D. $\overleftrightarrow{CD}$ intersects $\overline{AB}$ at its midpoint M.

Point M is the midpoint of $\overline{AB}$.

■ EXAMPLE 2

Use a compass and straightedge to construct the angle bisector of $\angle E$.

Put the tip of the compass at E. Draw a part of a circle that intersects the sides of $\angle E$. Label the points of intersection F and G.

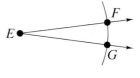

Put the compass tip at F and then at G. With the same compass opening, draw intersecting parts of circles. Label the point of intersection H. Draw $\overleftrightarrow{EH}$. $\overleftrightarrow{EH}$ is the bisector of $\angle FEG$.

1. Copy $\overline{JK}$ at the right. Then construct the perpendicular bisector of $\overline{JK}$.

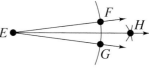

2. Copy $\angle L$ at the right. Then construct the angle bisector of $\angle L$.

3. **Writing** Explain how you can use what you know about perpendicular bisectors and angle bisectors to construct angles of 90° and 45°.

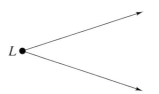

8-3 Special Pairs of Angles

What You'll Learn

▼ To identify congruent, complementary, supplementary, interior, and exterior angles

...And Why

You can find the measure of unknown angles based on the measures of other angles.

Here's How

Look for questions that
- ⣿ build understanding
- ✔ check understanding

Work Together
Investigating Angles

1. Use a ruler to draw a straight line on your paper. Then draw a second line parallel to the first.

2. Now draw a line that intersects the pair of parallel lines.

3. ⣿ *Analyze* Measure the four angles formed at each intersection. What do you notice?

THINK AND DISCUSS

Sometimes, two angles have a special relationship.

Complementary angles

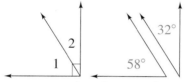

two angles, the sum of whose measures is 90°

Supplementary angles

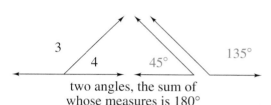

two angles, the sum of whose measures is 180°

■ EXAMPLE

Algebra Find the measure of ∠AEB .

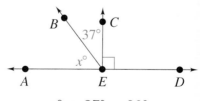

∠AEB and ∠BEC are complementary. The sum of their measures is 90°.

$$x° + 37° = 90°$$ ⟵ Write an equation.

$$x° + 37° - 37° = 90° - 37°$$ ⟵ Subtract 37° from each side.

$$x° = 53°$$

The measure of ∠AEB is 53°.

4. ✓*Try It Out* Refer to the Example. Find the measure of the angle that is supplementary to ∠AEB.

In the Work Together, you drew a line intersecting a pair of parallel lines. This line is a **transversal.** The transversal forms eight angles with the pair of parallel lines.

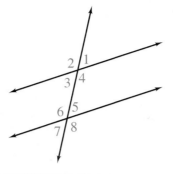

∠s 1, 2, 7, and 8 are outside the parallel lines. They are **exterior angles.**

∠s 3, 4, 5, and 6 are between the parallel lines. They are **interior angles.**

Congruent angles are angles that have the same measure.

5. ✓*Try It Out* Use the diagram above to name each of the following.
   a. a pair of congruent angles
   b. two pairs of supplementary angles
   c. two supplementary angles that are both exterior
   d. two supplementary angles, one of which is interior and one of which is exterior

EXERCISES *On Your Own*

Complete each sentence with *sometimes, always,* or *never*.

1. Two acute angles are ▦ complementary.
2. Two obtuse angles are ▦ complementary.
3. Two obtuse angles are ▦ supplementary.
4. Two right angles are ▦ supplementary.

Algebra **Find the measure of each angle marked $x°$.**

5.
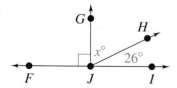

6.
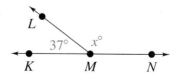

7.
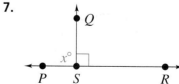

8. *Cheese* One half of a cheese wheel is cut into two unequal wedges. One wedge forms an angle whose measure is 65°. Find the angle formed by the other wedge. (*Hint:* The sum of the angles formed by all three wedges is 360°.)

9. **Architecture** The Leaning Tower of Pisa makes an angle of about 5° with a vertical line. What is the measure of the acute angle that the tower makes with the ground? What is the measure of the obtuse angle?

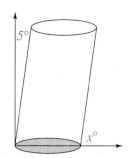

10. **Writing** Explain how to draw a pair of supplementary angles without using a protractor.

11. **Art** The photograph at the right shows *Oblique House* by American artist Mary Lucier. Which angles are congruent? Complementary? Supplementary?

12. **Open-ended** Draw a pair of complementary angles. What is the measure of each angle?

13. **Research** Find out how complementary and supplementary angles are used in carpentry.

Use the diagram at the right to name each of the following.

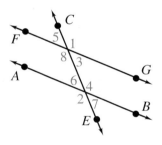

14. the transversal

15. two interior angles

16. two exterior angles

17. two pairs of supplementary angles

Mixed Review

Draw a model to find each quotient. *(Lesson 4-6)*

18. $0.2 \div 0.04$ 19. $0.9 \div 0.03$ 20. $1.5 \div 0.1$ 21. $0.8 \div 2$ 22. $0.24 \div 0.04$

23. **Choose a Strategy** To purchase a car that cost $12,800, Ms. Jackson paid $2,400 in cash and agreed to pay $535 each month for 24 months. How much interest did she pay by purchasing the car this way?

CHAPTER PROJECT

PROJECT LINK: IDENTIFYING

The diagram shows a puzzle known as a tangram. Identify the geometric shapes used to form the large square.

What You'll Learn

▼ To identify triangles by their angles or by their sides

...And Why

Different types of triangles are used in games, drafting, and optics.

Here's How

Look for questions that
▪ build understanding
✔ check understanding

Work Together
_____ *Forming Different Triangles*

On geoboards, form as many of the triangles described below as you can. Try to form two triangles with different shapes that fit each description.

1. Draw each triangle on dot paper.
   a. a triangle with three acute angles
   b. a triangle with one right angle
   c. a triangle with one obtuse angle
   d. a triangle with one right angle and one obtuse angle
   e. a triangle with no sides that have the same length
   f. a triangle with two sides that have the same length

2. ▪ **Look Back** Which of the above triangle(s) could you *not* form on your geoboard? Explain.

THINK AND DISCUSS

Segments that have the same length are called **congruent segments.**

You can classify triangles by angle measures or by the number of congruent sides.

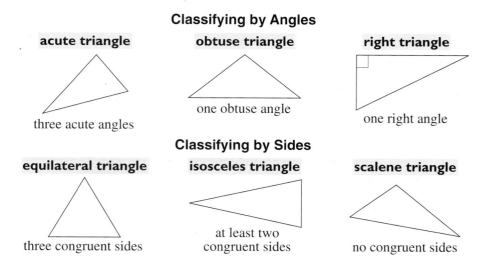

Classifying by Angles

acute triangle

three acute angles

obtuse triangle

one obtuse angle

right triangle

one right angle

Classifying by Sides

equilateral triangle

three congruent sides

isosceles triangle

at least two congruent sides

scalene triangle

no congruent sides

3. ⚎ *Think About It* Can an isosceles triangle be an acute triangle? Can a right triangle be an acute triangle? Explain.

4. Can a scalene triangle be an acute triangle? Can it be an obtuse triangle?

5. Can an equilateral triangle be an acute triangle? Can it be a right triangle? Explain.

6. ⚎ *Reasoning* Suppose a triangle is both isosceles and obtuse. What is the best name for such a triangle?

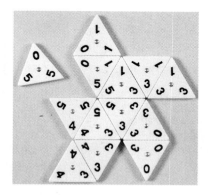

 Triominoes is a game similar to dominoes. It is played with triangular pieces instead of the rectangles used in dominoes.

■ **EXAMPLE**   *Real-World Problem Solving*

Games Judging by appearance, give all the names you can for the triangle formed by each triomino. What is the best name?

The triangle has three acute angles. It is acute.

The triangle has at least two congruent sides. It is isosceles.

The triangle has three congruent sides. It is equilateral.

The best name is equilateral because every equilateral triangle is both acute and isosceles.

7. ⚎ *Visual Thinking* Why do you think triominoes are equilateral triangles?

EXERCISES *On Your Own*

Classify each triangle with given side lengths as *scalene*, *isosceles*, or *equilateral*.

1. 3, 3, 5   2. 8, 8, 8   3. 6, 9, 4   4. 7, 9, 14   5. 5, 8, 5   6. 6, 8, 6

7. 12, 7, 9   8. 3, 4, 5   9. 6, 8, 10   10. 11, 11, 11   11. 4, 4, 9   12. 3, 6, 7

Classify each triangle with given angle measures as *acute*, *right*, or *obtuse*.

13. 90°, 35°, 55°   14. 15°, 60°, 105°   15. 30°, 90°, 60°   16. 120°, 35°, 25°

17. 85°, 70°, 25°   18. 45°, 45°, 90°   19. 100°, 30°, 50°   20. 60°, 60°, 60°

Judging by appearance, name all the triangles shown below that fit each description.

21. equilateral triangle

22. isosceles triangle

23. scalene triangle

24. acute triangle

25. right triangle

26. obtuse triangle

a.

b.

c.

d.

e.

f.

27. *Sailing* A triangular sail allows a boat to sail in any direction—even into the wind. Judging by appearance, give all the names you can for the triangle in the photo at the right. What is the best name for it?

28. *Writing* Must an equilateral triangle be an isosceles triangle? Why or why not? Must an isosceles triangle be an equilateral triangle? Why or why not?

29. *Reasoning* Use a metric ruler and protractor to measure the sides and angles of each triangle below. Classify each of the triangles by side lengths. What do you notice?

 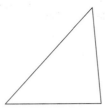 

30. a. *Drafting* Measure the sides and angles of each drafting triangle at the right.

  b. Classify each triangle according to its angle measures and side lengths. Then choose the best name for each triangle.

  c. How are the triangles alike? How are they different?

31. *Optics* A triangular prism can be used to bend rays of light. Give all the names you can to this triangle. What is the best name?

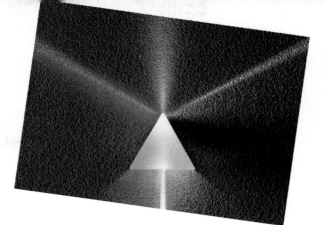

Sketch each triangle. If you can't sketch a triangle, explain why.

32. an acute isosceles triangle

33. an obtuse scalene triangle

34. a right isosceles triangle

35. an acute equilateral triangle

36. an acute scalene triangle

37. an obtuse right triangle

38. a right scalene triangle

39. an obtuse isosceles triangle

40. a right equilateral triangle

41. an obtuse equilateral triangle

> **JOURNAL**
> Make a list of the places in which you might see triangles in everyday life. Classify the triangles used in each situation. Are some types more common than others?

Mixed Review

Find each percent. *(Lesson 7-9)*

42. 80% of 20

43. 96% of 32

44. 30% of 192

45. 68% of 90

46. 17% of 500

Compare. Use >, <, or =. *(Lesson 5-8)*

47. $\frac{3}{8} \blacksquare \frac{2}{4}$

48. $\frac{2}{3} \blacksquare \frac{6}{15}$

49. $\frac{7}{10} \blacksquare \frac{84}{120}$

50. $\frac{19}{25} \blacksquare \frac{9}{15}$

51. $\frac{99}{100} \blacksquare \frac{199}{200}$

52. Brett had $80. He spent $5 on cement, 4 times as much as that on bricks, and bought 3 gallons of paint for $11 each. How much change did he receive?

CHAPTER PROJECT

PROJECT LINK: DRAWING

Your puzzle must include at least one of each of the following triangles: right, equilateral, isosceles, and scalene. Try drawing a rectangular puzzle on a piece of paper.

Work Together
Investigating Polygons

Some of the figures shown are polygons.

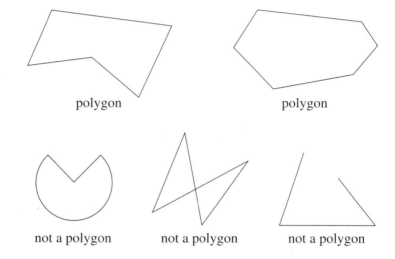

polygon   polygon

not a polygon   not a polygon   not a polygon

1. a. **Analyze** How are the polygons alike?
   b. How do the polygons differ from the figures that are not polygons?
   c. **Writing** Write a definition for a polygon. Share your definition with the class.

2. Use your definition to tell which of these figures are polygons. Does your definition work? If not, how would you change it?

   a.    b.    c.

   d.   e.    f.

A **polygon** is a closed shape formed by line segments that do not cross.

A **convex** polygon is one that a rubber band could fit around snugly, without any gaps and without crossing itself.

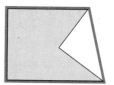

The red band does not fit snugly. This polygon is not convex.

3. Which of the following polygons are convex? Explain.

a.  b. 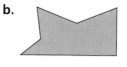 c.   d.

From now on, unless stated otherwise, assume that the polygons discussed are convex.

You can name a polygon according to the number of sides.

Polygon	Number of Sides
Triangle	3
Quadrilateral	4
Pentagon	5
Hexagon	6
Octagon	8
Decagon	10

The surface of this soccer ball is made up of hexagons and pentagons.

■ EXAMPLE

Name each polygon.

a.

b.

c.

This polygon has five sides. It is a pentagon.

This polygon has eight sides. It is an octagon.

This polygon has four sides. It is a quadrilateral.

4. ✔*Try It Out* Name each polygon.

a.    b.    c.

EXERCISES *On Your Own*

State whether each polygon is convex.

1. 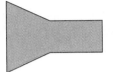   **2.**    **3.**    **4.**   **5.**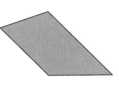

6. Is a circle a polygon? Explain.   **7.** *Open-ended* Draw two nonconvex polygons.

Name each polygon.

8.   **9.**   **10.**   **11.**

12.   **13.**    **14.**   **15.**

16. a. An *interior* angle is formed by two sides of a polygon that share a common vertex. How many interior angles does each polygon have?
    i. triangle   **ii.** quadrilateral   **iii.** pentagon
    iv. hexagon   **v.** octagon   **vi.** decagon

b. *Writing* What is the relationship between the number of sides and the number of interior angles in a polygon? Why does this relationship exist?

17. *Reasoning* What characteristics do triangles, quadrilaterals, and pentagons have in common?

18. **Botany** The Raft of the
Treetops allows botanist
Francis Hallé and his team to
investigate the top of the rain
forest without having to climb
the trees.

   a. What shape is the platform?

   b. Draw a polygon shaped like
the platform. Instead of
dividing it into six triangles,
divide it into four triangles.

   c. Draw a polygon shaped like the
platform. Divide it into a
quadrilateral and two triangles.

19. The *diagonal* of a polygon is a segment that connects
two vertices that are not next to each other. The
quadrilateral at the right has two diagonals.

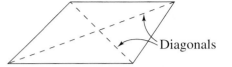

Diagonals

   a. Draw a hexagon. How many diagonals does it have?

   b. How many diagonals does a triangle have? Explain.

20. **Language** A prefix is a syllable at the beginning of a word
that helps describe the object.

   a. List three words, besides *triangle*, that have the prefix *tri-*.

   b. List three words, besides *quadrilateral*, that have the
prefix *quad-*.

   c. For each of your words, state what the prefix tells you
about it.

Mixed Review

**Find each product or quotient. Write each answer in
simplest form.** *(Lessons 6-8 and 6-9)*

21. $6\frac{1}{2} \times \frac{1}{10}$ **22.** $1\frac{5}{6} \div 3\frac{2}{3}$ **23.** $7\frac{1}{5} \times 7\frac{1}{5}$ **24.** $3\frac{3}{4} \div 6\frac{3}{10}$ **25.** $6\frac{2}{3} \times 2\frac{7}{10}$

Use mental math to complete each statement. *(Lesson 4-10)*

26. $2.07 \text{ g} = \blacksquare \text{ mg}$ **27.** $0.6 \text{ L} = \blacksquare \text{ kL}$ **28.** $89 \text{ m} = \blacksquare \text{ mm}$ **29.** $440 \text{ cm} = \blacksquare \text{ km}$

30. **Choose a Strategy** Suppose you have 20 dimes and nickels
altogether. The total value of the coins is $1.35. How many
dimes do you have?

Use the figure at the right for Exercises 1–10. Name each of the following.

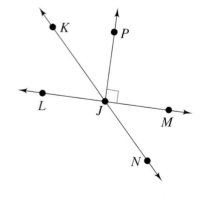

1. two lines

2. a right angle

3. three collinear points

4. an acute angle

5. an obtuse angle

6. a straight angle

7. three noncollinear points

8. an angle that measures 133°

9. a pair of parallel lines

10. a pair of perpendicular lines

11. Choose A, B, C, or D. Judging by appearance, classify the triangle at the right.

    A. right scalene **B.** acute isosceles

    C. equilateral **D.** obtuse isosceles

How many sides does each of the following polygons have?

12. a decagon

13. an octagon

14. a quadrilateral

15. a hexagon

Math at Work

CARTOONIST

If you enjoy reading comics and draw well, a career as a cartoonist may be right for you. Some cartoonists produce comic strips meant for amusement. Others create illustrations for stories, articles, books, or advertisements. Editorial cartoons can dramatize the news. Cartoonists can work for newspapers, advertising agencies, or other commercial firms. They use their mathematics skills to create cartoons using lines, angles, measures, and perspective.

For more information about cartoonists, visit the Prentice Hall Web site: www.phschool.com

Classifying Quadrilaterals

What You'll Learn

▼ To identify quadrilaterals

▼ To classify quadrilaterals

...And Why

There are many different types of four-sided figures, some of which have special names.

Here's How

Look for questions that

⚓ build understanding

✔ check understanding

Work Together
Drawing Quadrilaterals

1. Using a geoboard or dot paper, show each of the following.
   a. a quadrilateral with two pairs of parallel sides and no right angles
   b. a quadrilateral with four right angles and two pairs of congruent sides
   c. a quadrilateral with four congruent sides and no right angles
   d. a quadrilateral with four congruent sides and four right angles
   e. a quadrilateral with one pair of parallel sides

2. Name 3 characteristics your quadrilaterals have in common.

THINK AND DISCUSS

▼ *Identifying Quadrilaterals*

Certain quadrilaterals have special names because they have characteristics that differ from those of other quadrilaterals.

Parallelogram	**Rectangle**	**Rhombus**

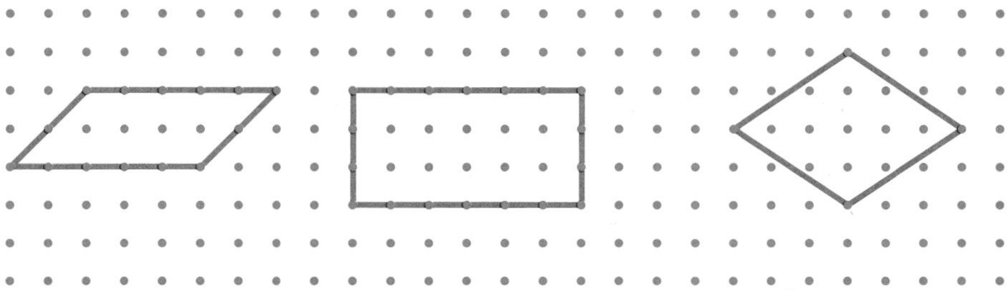

a quadrilateral with both pairs of opposite sides parallel

a parallelogram with four right angles

a parallelogram with four congruent sides

3. ⚓*Open-ended* Find several examples of rectangles in your classroom.

4. ⚓*Reasoning* Can a rhombus be a rectangle? Explain.

Square

Trapezoid

a rectangle with
four congruent sides

a quadrilateral
with exactly one
pair of parallel sides

5. a. ⚒ *Think About It* Is every square a rectangle? Is every
rectangle a square? Explain.

b. Is every square a rhombus? Is every rhombus a square?
Explain.

c. ⚒ *Reasoning* What is the best name for a rhombus that
is also a rectangle?

6. ⚒ *Reasoning* Can a trapezoid be a parallelogram? Explain.

▼2 *Classifying Quadrilaterals*

You can classify quadrilaterals as you classified triangles in
Lesson 8-4. First look at all the characteristics. Then decide on
the best name.

■ **EXAMPLE**   *Real-World Problem Solving*

Judging by appearance,
give all the names you can
for the quadrilateral in
the picture at the right.
What is the best name?

Both pairs of opposite sides
are parallel. It is a parallelogram.

The four sides are congruent. It is a rhombus.

The best name is rhombus, because every rhombus is a
quadrilateral and a parallelogram.

7. ✓*Try It Out* Give all the names you can for
the polygon at the right. What is the best name?

Use the shapes at the right for Exercises 1 and 2.

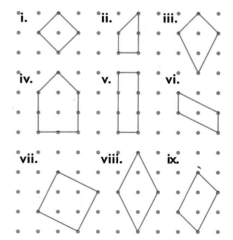

1. Identify the polygons that have each name.
   a. quadrilateral **b.** parallelogram **c.** rhombus
   d. rectangle **e.** square **f.** trapezoid

2. Which shape is not used? Why?

Sketch an example of each quadrilateral.

3. a parallelogram **4.** a square **5.** a trapezoid

6. a rectangle **7.** a rectangle that is not a square

8. a rhombus that is not a square

9. a quadrilateral that is not a trapezoid or a parallelogram

Complete each sentence with *All*, *Some*, or *No*.

10. ▨ quadrilaterals are parallelograms.

11. ▨ trapezoids are parallelograms.

12. ▨ parallelograms are quadrilaterals.

13. ▨ squares are rectangles.

14. ▨ rhombuses are rectangles.

15. ▨ rectangles are trapezoids.

16. ▨ quadrilaterals are trapezoids.

17. ▨ rectangles are parallelograms.

18. ▨ parallelograms are trapezoids.

19. ▨ rectangles are rhombuses.

List all the names that apply to each quadrilateral.
Choose from *parallelogram*, *rectangle*, *rhombus*, *square*,
and *trapezoid*. Then circle the best name.

20.

21.

22.

23.

24. *Writing* Describe the relationships among the following
    figures: rectangle, rhombus, square.

25. a. Four trapezoids are shown at the right. What do you notice about each pair of nonparallel sides?

   b. When sides of a triangle have this same characteristic, what special name do you give the triangle?

   c. *Reasoning* What special name could you use for trapezoids like this? Why does this name fit?

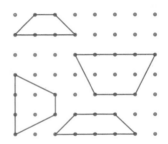

Name all the types of quadrilaterals that fit each description.

26. four congruent sides   **27.** four right angles   **28.** parallelogram

29. Draw three copies of the trapezoid at the right.

   a. Draw a line on one trapezoid that divides it into two trapezoids.

   b. Draw a line on the second trapezoid that divides it into a parallelogram and a triangle.

   c. Draw a line on the third trapezoid that divides it into a rhombus and a trapezoid.

30. Choose A, B, C, or D. Which name does *not* appear to describe quadrilateral *RSTU*?

   A. square   **B.** rhombus   **C.** trapezoid   **D.** parallelogram

Mixed Review

Find the value of *n*. *(Lesson 7-3)*

31. $\frac{1}{2} = \frac{n}{10}$ **32.** $\frac{15}{25} = \frac{3}{n}$ **33.** $\frac{7}{9} = \frac{21}{n}$ **34.** $\frac{n}{5} = \frac{20}{60}$ **35.** $\frac{n}{3} = \frac{9}{18}$

36. *Choose a Strategy* Payat bought 3 shirts for $14 each and a pair of pants for $23. How much of his clothing budget does Payat have left?

CHAPTER PROJECT

PROJECT LINK: PLANNING

Your puzzle must also include at least one of each of the following polygons: quadrilateral, pentagon, hexagon, rhombus, trapezoid, and parallelogram. Draw a new puzzle that includes these shapes as well as the four triangle types.

8-7

Use Logical Reasoning

THINK AND DISCUSS

You often can use logical reasoning to solve problems involving relationships among groups of objects or people.

SAMPLE PROBLEM..

The 6th-grade class at Fairfield Middle School surveyed 130 7th- and 8th-grade students to find out how they earn money. The survey showed that 45 students baby-sit, 32 have paper routes, 28 do yard work, and 12 have after-school office jobs. Each student who works does only one kind of work, except for 15 who baby-sit *and* do yard work. How many students earn money by either baby-sitting or doing yard work (or both)? How many students do not earn money?

 READ

Read for understanding. Summarize the problem.

1. Think about the information you are given and what you are asked to find.
   a. How many students were surveyed? How did they earn money?
   b. How many students did two different kinds of work?
   c. What does the problem ask you to find?

 PLAN

Decide on a strategy.

Logical Reasoning is a good strategy to use here. You can draw a diagram to show the different ways students earn money. Draw a rectangle to represent all the 7th- and 8th-grade students.

In the rectangle, draw a circle to represent each type of work. Label your circles *B* (for baby-sitting), *P* (for paper routes), *Y* (for yard work), and *O* (for office jobs).

2. Which circles should overlap? Why?

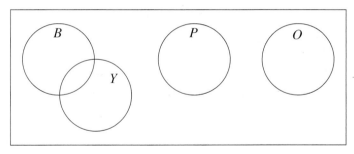

Write 15 where *B* and *Y* overlap. Write 32 in *P* and 12 in *O*.

SOLVE

Try the strategy.

3. What number should be in *B*? How many students have you included already? What number should be in the part of *B* that does not overlap *Y*? Write it in.

4. How many students earn money only by doing yard work? What number should be in the part of *Y* not overlapping *B*? Place all known data in the diagram.

Use the information above to answer the questions in the problem.

5. Find the total number of students who earn money by either baby-sitting or doing yard work (or both).

6. **a.** Add the numbers on your diagram. How does this number compare to the number of students surveyed? Explain.
   b. If you subtract the sum from 130, what does the result represent? Where would you write that number? Why?

LOOK BACK

Think about how you solved the problem.

Make sure that you have clearly stated your answers to the questions in the problem.

7. Draw a diagram like the one shown at the right. Label it to show the relationships among quadrilaterals.

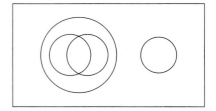

EXERCISES *On Your Own*

Use *Logical Reasoning* to solve each problem.

1. *Sports* There are 20 students on the intramural tennis team. Eight students play only singles and eight students play both singles and doubles. How many students play only doubles?

2. *Buttons* In a box of 39 buttons, 25 buttons have four holes, 18 are red, and 13 have four holes and are also red. The rest of the buttons have two holes or are colors other than red.
   a. How many buttons have four holes but are not red?
   b. How many red buttons have two holes?
   c. How many buttons do not have four holes and are not red?

Use any strategy to solve each problem. Show your work.

3. *Weather* Did you know that $\frac{1}{2}$ in. of rain is equal to about 4 in. of snow? In April 1921, 6 ft 4 in. of snow fell during a 24-h period in Silver Lake, Colorado. How much rain would have fallen if it had not been cold enough to snow?

4. *Clothes* Suppose you have three pairs of pants, four sweaters, and five shirts. How many days can you wear an outfit consisting of a pair of pants, a sweater, and a shirt before you wear the same outfit again?

5. *Food* In a restaurant, 37 customers ordered lunch between 11:30 A.M. and 12:30 P.M. Of those customers, 25 ordered soup with their lunch, 16 ordered salad with their lunch, and 8 ordered both soup and salad.
   a. How many customers ordered soup but no salad?
   b. How many customers did not order soup or salad?

6. *Baseball Cards* Suppose you have a baseball card collection and you decide to sort your cards. When you put your cards in piles of two, you have one card left over. You also have one left over when you put the cards in piles of three or piles of four. But when you put them in piles of seven, you have none left over. What is the least possible number of cards in your collection?

7. *Money* How many coin combinations total exactly 17¢?

8. *Lemonade* To make lemonade, you need 3 c water for every 2 c lemon juice. Suppose you want to make 10 gal of lemonade. How many cups of lemon juice do you need?

Mixed Review

Complete each statement. *(Lesson 6-10)*

9. 8,800 lb = ▒ T ▒ lb   10. 18 qt = ▒ gal ▒ qt   11. 60 fl oz = ▒ c ▒ fl oz

Find each quotient. *(Lesson 4-8)*

12. $53.7 \div 1.2$ 13. $46.2 \div 2.4$ 14. $101.536 \div 3.8$ 15. $38.13 \div 8.2$ 16. $250.56 \div 11.6$

17. The temperature is 70°F at 10:00 A.M. It increases 2 degrees every hour. What is the temperature at 4:00 P.M.? *(Lesson 3-10)*

8-8 Congruent and Similar Figures

What You'll Learn

▼ To determine if figures are congruent

▼ To determine if figures are similar

...And Why

You can use congruent and similar figures in architecture and construction.

Here's How

Look for questions that

⚓ build understanding

✔ check understanding

Work Together
Investigating Similarity

1. ⚓*Modeling* Draw four identical triangles on dot paper. Cut out the four triangles. Put the triangles on top of each other. Check that they have the same size and shape.

2. a. Arrange the four triangles so that they form a larger triangle that has the same shape as the original triangle. None of the triangles should overlap.

   b. Draw your arrangement on dot paper. How do the lengths of the sides of the original triangle and the lengths of the sides of the larger triangle compare?

3. ⚓*Analyze* Show how to arrange nine identical triangles to form a larger triangle with the same shape. How do the lengths of the sides of the larger triangle compare to the lengths of the sides of the original triangle?

THINK AND DISCUSS

▼ Identifying Congruent Figures

Figures that have the same size and shape are **congruent.** Congruent figures have congruent *corresponding* sides and angles.

Two figures can be congruent even if one of the figures is turned.

Two figures can also be congruent even if one appears to be flipped over.

4. ⚓*Reasoning* How could you check that the trapezoids shown are congruent?

You can see congruent and similar triangles in Arizona's Navajo Bridge. The bridge crosses the Colorado River.

5. ✓*Try It Out* Which of the triangles below are congruent to the triangle at the right?

A.   B.    C.

2 *Identifying Similar Figures*

Similar figures have the same shape, but are not necessarily the same size. Similar figures have congruent angles.

The matching parts of similar figures are called **corresponding parts.** Corresponding parts of similar figures are proportional.

6. ■*Reasoning* Must two congruent figures be similar? Why or why not?

■ EXAMPLE

Which triangles below are similar to the triangle at the right?

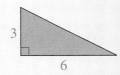

a.

$$\frac{2}{1} \stackrel{?}{=} \frac{4}{2}$$
$$2 = 2 \checkmark$$
similar

b.

$$\frac{2}{3} \stackrel{?}{=} \frac{4}{4}$$
$$\frac{2}{3} \neq 1$$
not similar

c.

$$\frac{2}{3} \stackrel{?}{=} \frac{4}{6}$$
$$\frac{2}{3} = \frac{2}{3} \checkmark$$
similar

7. ✓*Try It Out* Which of the following triangles are also similar to the one in the Example above?

a. 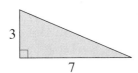   b.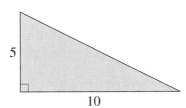

1. Which of the figures below appear to be congruent to the trapezoid at the right?

A.   B.   C.   D.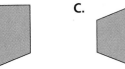

2. *Open-ended* Use dot paper to draw four congruent triangles in different positions.

3. *Writing* Explain how you decide if two figures are congruent.

4. List the pairs of triangles below that appear to be congruent.

A.  B.   C.   D.  E.   F.

5. **Choose A, B, C, or D.** Which figure below is not congruent to the figure at the right?

A.   B.   C.   D. 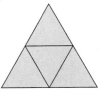...

A.   B.   C.   D.

6. Which rectangles are similar to the rectangle at the right?

A.   B.   C. D.

Tell whether the triangles appear to be *congruent*, *similar*, or *neither*.

7. 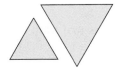 8.  9. 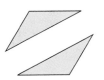 10.

11. *Patterns* How many congruent triangles are in the diagram at the right? How many similar triangles are there?

12. *Home Improvement* Suppose you are replacing a window. Should the replacement be congruent to or similar to the original? Explain your reasoning.

13. *Measurement* List the pairs of figures below that are similar.

       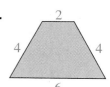

A. B. C. D. E. F.

G. H. I. J. K. L.

14. *Reasoning* Are congruent figures similar? Are similar figures congruent? Explain.

15. a. Use dot paper to draw several rhombuses, none of which are congruent. Include squares and nonsquares. If possible, make each one a different shape.
   b. Are all rhombuses similar? Explain.
   c. Are all squares similar? Explain.

16. Use a protractor to draw a triangle with two angles measuring 45° and 60°. Then draw a second triangle that is not congruent to the first triangle, but that has angles measuring 45° and 60°. What appears to be true of the two triangles?

Mixed Review

Write each improper fraction as a mixed number.

(Lesson 5-6)

17. $\frac{38}{6}$ **18.** $\frac{49}{8}$ **19.** $\frac{47}{3}$ **20.** $\frac{63}{4}$ **21.** $\frac{18}{5}$ **22.** $\frac{29}{12}$

Write each as a percent. *(Lesson 7-7)*

23. 18 boards out of 100 boards are warped.   **24.** 86 seats out of 100 seats are occupied.

25. *Choose a Strategy* In a class of 40 students, 29 wore jeans, 18 wore sneakers, and 10 wore both jeans and sneakers. How many wore neither jeans nor sneakers?

CHAPTER PROJECT

PROJECT LINK: DESIGNING

Prepare the plan for your puzzle. Make sure it includes two triangles that are congruent and two triangles that are similar but not congruent.

Line Symmetry

What You'll Learn

▼ To determine whether a figure has line symmetry

...And Why

Symmetry is very important in art, design, and photography.

Here's How

Look for questions that
⊞ build understanding
✔ check understanding

THINK AND DISCUSS

You often see symmetry in nature—in the human body, in flowers, insects, birds, and in many other living things. Symmetrical designs are appealing to the eye. They often are used in fabrics, flags, architecture, masks, art, and pottery.

A figure has **line symmetry** if a line could be drawn to divide the figure into two congruent halves that are mirror images of each other. The line is called a **line of symmetry.**

1. Does the butterfly at the left below have any lines of symmetry? How many?

2. ⊞*Modeling* Draw an equilateral triangle. Sketch all the lines of symmetry. How many lines of symmetry does an equilateral triangle have?

3. How many lines of symmetry does a square have?

■ **E X A M P L E**   *Real-World Problem Solving*

Nature How many lines of symmetry does each figure have? Describe each line of symmetry as horizontal, vertical, or neither.

a.

The leaf has one vertical line of symmetry.

b.

The snowflake has one horizontal line of symmetry, one vertical, and four that are neither horizontal nor vertical.

4. ♣ *Reasoning* How could you check whether a figure has line symmetry?

5. ✓*Try It Out* How many lines of symmetry does each figure have? Describe each line of symmetry as horizontal, vertical, or neither.

a.

b.

Work Together

Looking at Symmetry

6. Fold a sheet of paper. Cut out a shape that will have the fold line as a line of symmetry.

7. Fold a sheet of paper into quarters. Cut out a shape that will have two perpendicular lines of symmetry.

EXERCISES *On Your Own*

Does each figure have line symmetry? If it does, trace the figure and draw all the lines of symmetry.

1.

2.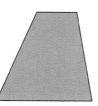

3.

4.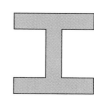

5.

6.

7.

8.

How many lines of symmetry does each figure have? Describe each line of symmetry.

9.

10.

11.

Copy each figure on dot paper. Complete the figure so that the line is a line of symmetry.

12.

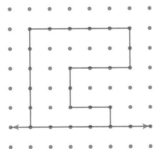

13.

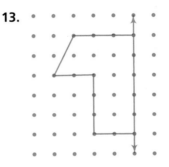

14.

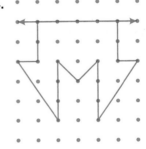

15. Trace the hexagon at the right. Draw each line of symmetry.

16. **a.** Draw three isosceles triangles like those shown below. Draw all the lines of symmetry for each triangle.

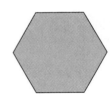

   b. *Open-ended* Draw three scalene triangles. Draw all the lines of symmetry for each triangle.
   c. *Writing* Describe the lines of symmetry of scalene, equilateral, and isosceles triangles.

17. Which capital letters have line symmetry?
   A B C D E F G H I J K L M
   N O P Q R S T U V W X Y Z

18. The word **CODE** has a horizontal line of symmetry. Find another word that has a horizontal line of symmetry.

19. The word **MOW**, written vertically, has a vertical line of symmetry. Find another word like that.

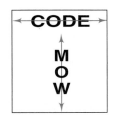

20. a. *World Flags* Find all the lines of symmetry of each flag.

    b. Design a flag that has at least one line of symmetry.
    c. Design a flag that has no line of symmetry.

Tell whether each dashed line is a line of symmetry.

21.
    22.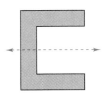

23.
    24.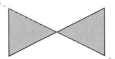

> JOURNAL
> Look through nature books and magazines. List as many occurrences of symmetry in natural objects as you can find.

Mixed Review

Find each product. *(Lesson 4-5)*

25. 70.3×70.55 **26.** 9.07×0.025 **27.** 21.51×21.49 **28.** 1.7×1.78 **29.** 0.0145×0.12

Estimate each sum or difference. *(Lesson 6-1)*

30. $\frac{1}{10} + \frac{1}{3}$ **31.** $\frac{1}{2} - \frac{1}{6}$ **32.** $\frac{4}{9} + \frac{1}{6}$ **33.** $\frac{5}{8} - \frac{1}{6}$ **34.** $\frac{3}{4} - \frac{9}{16} + \frac{1}{2}$

35. *Choose a Strategy* Thirty-two teams are competing in a single-elimination tournament. How many games will the winning team have to play?

8-10 Investigating Circles

THINK AND DISCUSS

Designers and engineers use geometric figures to model real objects.

A **circle** is the set of points in a plane that are the same distance from a given point, the *center*. You name a circle by its center.

Circle O

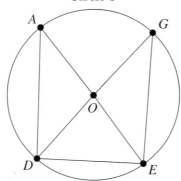

$\overline{OG}$, $\overline{OA}$, $\overline{OD}$ and $\overline{OE}$ are radii (plural of **radius**) of circle O.

$\overline{AE}$ and $\overline{DG}$ are **diameters** of circle O.

$\overline{AD}$, $\overline{DE}$, and $\overline{GE}$ are **chords** of circle O.

You can model a Ferris wheel with a circle and segments inside the circle.

1. ✔ *Try It Out* Name a radius of the model of the Ferris wheel at the right.

2. ✔ *Try It Out* Name a diameter of the model.

3. ✔ *Try It Out* Name a chord of the model.

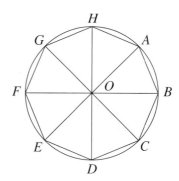

4. a. Use a compass to draw a circle. Label the center S.
   b. Draw a radius of your circle. Label it $\overline{ST}$.
   c. Did you and your classmates draw $\overline{ST}$ the same way?
   d. ⊞ Reasoning How many different radii can a circle have? How many diameters can a circle have?

The length of a radius r is the distance from the center to any point on the circle. The length of a diameter d is the distance from a point on the circle, through the center, to another point on the circle.

5. **a.** Choose a point on your circle other than T. Label it U. Draw diameter $\overline{UV}$. Compare the lengths of $\overline{UV}$ and $\overline{ST}$.
   b. ⚬Reasoning What is the relationship between the length of a radius and the length of a diameter for any given circle? Explain.

CIRCLES

The length of the diameter of a circle is equal to twice the length of the radius. ($d = 2r$ or $r = \frac{d}{2}$)

■ **EXAMPLE**   *Real-World Problem Solving*

Amusement Parks The first Ferris wheel had a diameter of 250 ft. What was its radius?

$$d = 250 \quad \longleftarrow \text{Write an equation.}$$
$$2r = 250 \quad \longleftarrow \text{Substitute } 2r \text{ for } d.$$
$$\frac{2r}{2} = \frac{250}{2} \quad \longleftarrow \text{Divide each side by 2.}$$
$$r = 125 \quad \longleftarrow \text{Simplify.}$$

The length of the radius was 125 ft.

6. ✓*Try It Out* Find the length of the radius of a circle whose diameter is 8 cm.

7. ⚬*Measurement* Draw and measure several chords of circle S above. What is the longest chord of a circle called?

8. ⚬*Explain* A model of a Ferris wheel, like the one at the right, contains many angles. Some of the angles, like $\angle APB$, are **central angles.** Why do you think they have this name?

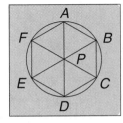

9. **a.** Name the 6 acute central angles shown in circle P above.
   b. ⚬*Measurement* Measure one acute central angle.
   c. ⚬*Reasoning* The 6 central angles are congruent. What is the sum of their measures?

EXERCISES On Your Own

Name each of the following for circle O.

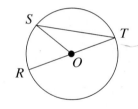

1. three radii   2. a diameter   3. two chords   4. two central angles

5. Draw a circle that has radius $\overline{RT}$, diameter $\overline{WX}$, and chords $\overline{WT}$ and $\overline{TX}$.

Find the unknown length for each circle.

6. $r = 10$ in.; $d = $ ▨   7. $d = 140$ ft; $r = $ ▨   8. $d = 5$ m; $r = $ ▨   9. $r = 46$ cm; $d = $ ▨

10. $d = 22$ cm; $r = $ ▨   11. $r = 12$ m; $d = $ ▨   12. $r = 35$ mi; $d = $ ▨   13. $d = 4$ mm; $r = $ ▨

14. $r = 7$ km; $d = $ ▨   15. $d = 0.25$ ft; $r = $ ▨   16. $r = 0.6$ mi; $d = $ ▨   17. $d = 12.4$ m; $r = $ ▨

18. *Writing* A graphic designer wants to describe the drawing at the right in words. Write a description for him. Remember to use geometric terms such as *radius*, *diameter*, and *chord*.

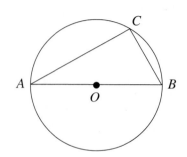

19. *Leisure* The diameter of a circular swimming pool is 20 ft. What is the radius?

20. *Open-ended* Draw a circle and several chords with different lengths. Measure the distance from the center of the circle to each chord. Describe the relationship between the lengths of the chords and the distances from the center of the circle.

21. a. *Measurement* Find the measure of $\angle AXB$.
    b. Judging by appearance, classify the triangles shown for circle X.

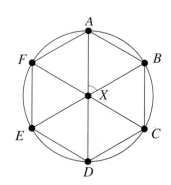

22. *Reasoning* Draw and label a circle. Then draw a central angle of your circle. If you increase or decrease the size of your circle, what happens to the measure of the central angle?

23. **Choose A, B, C, or D.** Circle P has 8 congruent central angles. What is the measure of $\angle APC$?

   A. 45°   **B.** 60°

   C. 90°   **D.** 120°

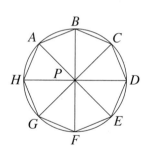

24. *Data Analysis* Make a circle graph that shows the information at the right. *(Lesson 7-10)*

Favorite Fruit	
Apples	50%
Oranges	25%
Other	25%

Find the prime factorizations using a factor tree.
(Lesson 5-2)

25. 60   **26.** 144   **27.** 500   **28.** 496   **29.** 1,240   **30.** 5,070

31. *Choose a Strategy* There are 30 students in a math class. Of these students, 12 belong to the computer club, 8 to the hiking club, and 3 to both. How many belong to neither?

✓ CHECKPOINT 2   *Lessons 8-6 through 8-10*

1. *Writing* In your own words, describe a square.

2. The Cool Café had 63 customers. All of them had dinner. Twenty of the customers ordered an appetizer, and 36 had dessert. Complete the diagram at the right.
   a. How many customers ordered an appetizer but no dessert with their dinner?
   b. How many customers had dinner only?

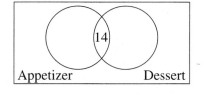

3. a. Which of the figures shown below appear to be congruent?
   b. Which figures appear to be similar?

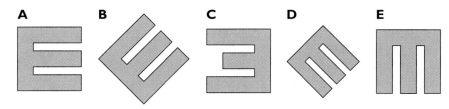

4. Choose A, B, C, or D. Which figure has the most lines of symmetry?

   A. a square   **B.** a right isosceles triangle
   C. a scalene triangle   **D.** an equilateral triangle

Find the unknown length for each circle.

5. $r = 10$ in.; $d = $ ▓   **6.** $d = 180$ ft; $r = $ ▓   **7.** $d = 5$ m; $r = $ ▓   **8.** $r = 46$ cm; $d = $ ▓

Investigating Angles of a Triangle

After Lesson 8-10

You can use geometry software to investigate relationships among angles of a triangle.

Open a new geometry window. Use the polygon feature to draw a triangle. Label the vertices A, B, and C. Use the angle-marking feature to mark the three interior angles.

 polygon feature

 angle-marking feature

color-linking feature

Open a new spreadsheet window. Use the color-linking feature to link each interior angle to a cell in the spreadsheet.

Drag the vertex of one angle so that the angle measure changes.

	A	B	
1	Angle A	54	
2	Angle B	66	
3	Angle C	60	
4	Sum	=B1+B2+B3	

Enter the formula to find the sum of the three angles.

1. How does this affect the other angle measures?

2. How does it affect the sum of the angle measures?

3. Drag the vertex of another angle. What do you notice?

4. What can you conclude about the sum of the measures of the interior angles of a triangle?

Use the segment tool to extend one of the sides of the triangle. Mark the exterior angle ($\angle ACF$) it forms with the other side. Open a new spreadsheet window. Link this angle to a cell in the spreadsheet.

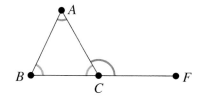

Study the relationship between the measure of the exterior angle and the sum of the measures of the two opposing interior angles.

5. What do you notice?

6. What can you conclude about the exterior angle and the two opposing interior angles?

	A	B	
1	Angle A	55	
2	Angle B	65	
3	Sum Angles A and B	=B1+B2	
4	Angle ACF	120	

Choose the best answer.

1. How many lines of symmetry does a nonsquare rectangle have?

   A. 0   **B.** 1   **C.** 2   **D.** 4

2. A nickel is approximately 21 mm across. What is this distance expressed in centimeters?

   F. 21,000 cm   **G.** 2,100 cm
   H. 210 cm   **J.** 2.1 cm

3. Which of the following polygons is *not* a quadrilateral?

   A. trapezoid   **B.** parallelogram
   C. rhombus   **D.** pentagon

4. What is the area of a rectangle 9 m wide and 70 cm high?

   F. 6,300 cm^2 **G.** 630 cm^2
   H. 63 m^2 **J.** 6.3 m^2

5. Name two triangles in the diagram that are *not* congruent.

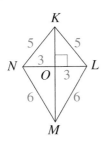

   A. triangles *KNO* and *KLO*
   B. triangles *MON* and *MOL*
   C. triangles *NKL* and *NML*
   D. triangles *KMN* and *KML*

6. What are all the factors of 100?

   F. 2 and 5   **G.** $2^2 \times 5^2$
   H. 2, 4, 5, 10, 20, 25, and 50
   J. 1, 2, 4, 5, 10, 20, 25, 50, and 100

7. If a quadrilateral has at least two lines of symmetry, then it *cannot* be which of the following?

   A. rhombus   **B.** square
   C. rectangle   **D.** trapezoid

8. In a fishing contest, the weights of the four heaviest fish are plotted on a number line. Which point shows the weight for a fish weighing $4\frac{3}{8}$ pounds?

   F. point *M*   **G.** point *N*
   H. point *P*   **J.** point *Q*

Please note that items 9 and 10 each have *five* answer choices.

9. On a scale drawing, the scale shown is 1 in. : 10 ft. The length of a room is 2.5 in. on the drawing. How long is the actual room?

   A. 4 in.   **B.** 25 in.   **C.** 4 ft
   D. 25 ft   **E.** Not Here

10. A triangular table top has the dimensions shown below.

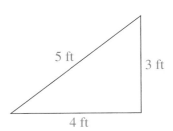

   A smaller table is similar in shape, but the longest side is 2.5 feet long. How long is the shortest side of the smaller table?

   F. 1.5 ft   **G.** 2 ft
   H. 6 ft   **J.** 8 ft
   K. Not Here

What You'll Learn

▼ 1 To explore translations and reflections

▼ 2 To explore rotations

...And Why

Translations, reflections, and rotations are widely used in interior design.

Here's How

Look for questions that

⬦ build understanding

✔ check understanding

Work Together
Investigating Slides, Flips, and Turns

1. Fold an index card in half. Cut out a geometric shape along the fold line. Cut an extra piece from one side of the fold.

2. Unfold the index card.
   a. Use the card as a stencil. Draw the shape on a sheet of paper.
   b. Without turning or lifting the stencil, slide it to the right. Draw the shape again.

3. Flip the stencil over, so that the front is face down. Draw the shape again.

4. Turn your stencil so the top is now at the bottom. Draw the shape.

5. Flip the shape again so the front is face up again. Draw the shape.

6. ⬦*Analyze* How are the shapes alike? How are they different? Are all of your drawings congruent? Explain.

 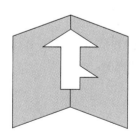  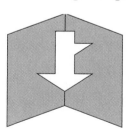 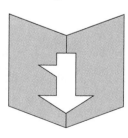

THINK AND DISCUSS

▼ 1 Exploring Translations and Reflections

You can say that the first shape was moved to the right to become the second shape. A **translation** moves a figure so that every point moves the same distance in the same direction. The new shape is called the **image** of the original shape.

7. ⁂*Reasoning* Why is a translation also called a *slide?*

■ **EXAMPLE 1**

Draw two translations of the shape at the right.

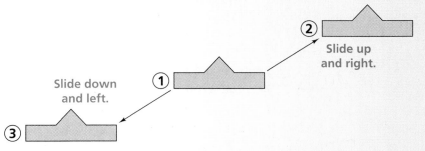

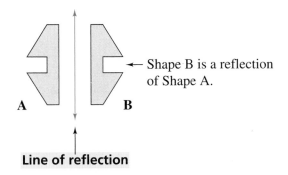

Shapes ② and ③ are translations of shape ①.

8. ✓*Try It Out* Draw two translations of the shape at the right.

Another way of moving a figure is to reflect it. A **reflection** is a figure flipped across a line. The new figure is a mirror image of the original figure.

Shape B is a reflection of Shape A.

A   B

Line of reflection

9. ✓*Try It Out* Place a mirror on the line of reflection above, perpendicular to the page. What do you notice?

10. ✓*Try It Out* Draw the reflection of each shape over the line of reflection.

a.

b.

c.

▼ *Exploring Rotations*

A rotation turns, or rotates, a shape. Imagine you have a cutout of the letter E, which you place on a piece of cardboard. Suppose you insert a pin through the corner, as shown by the black dot at the right.

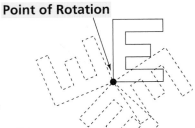

Point of Rotation

11. ▪ *Writing* Describe each image of the letter E as you rotate the cutout once around the point of rotation.

A rotation can be described in terms of the number of degrees by which the original figure has been rotated.

12. ▪ *Reasoning* Suppose you rotate the letter E so it is back where it started. How many degrees have you turned it?

■ **EXAMPLE 2**

Which of the following is a rotation of the shape at the right?

A.   B.   C.

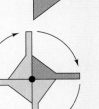

Imagine you place a pin at any point on the shape. Picture some stages of the rotation.

Shape B is the only one that you will see. Shape A is a reflection over a vertical line. Shape C is a reflection over a horizontal line.

   is a rotation of   .

13. ✓*Try It Out* Which of the following is a rotation of the figure at the right?

A.   B.   C.

Draw two translations of each shape.

1.
2.
3.
4.

5. *Interior Design* Describe all the translations of the figure in the fabric shown below.

Draw a reflection of each shape. Use the dashed line as the line of reflection.

6.
7.
8.
9.

10. The art at the right shows part of a figure and part of its reflection. Copy the diagram. Complete the figure. Then complete the image.

11. *Writing* Describe how translations and reflections are alike and how they are different. Include examples.

Tell whether each shows a translation or a reflection.

12.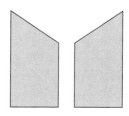
13.
14.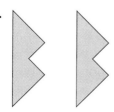

Decide if each figure is a rotation of the shape at the right.

15.

16.

17.

18.

19.

20.

21. Identify all rotations of the shape at the right.

A. 　　B. 　　C. 　　D.

E.　　F.　　G.　　H.

22. *Open-ended* Design a wallpaper pattern that consists of translations, reflections, and rotations of one basic figure.

23. *Reasoning* Why are rotations also called *turns*?

Mixed Review

Find each difference. Write the answer in simplest form.
(Lesson 6-5)

24. $14\frac{1}{3} - 5\frac{2}{9}$　　25. $25 - 17\frac{2}{3}$　　26. $27\frac{1}{2} - 5\frac{3}{4}$　　27. $9\frac{3}{5} - 4\frac{1}{5}$　　28. $19\frac{3}{5} - 6\frac{7}{10}$

Write each number in words. *(Lesson 3-2)*

29. 0.73　　30. 0.009　　31. 386.908　　32. 4,273.15　　33. 407,683.07　　34. 0.03902

35. *Choose a Strategy* Eight people shake hands with each of the others exactly once. What is the total number of handshakes exchanged?

CHAPTER PROJECT

Puzzling Pictures

Create a Puzzle The Project Link questions on pages 339, 343, 352, and 359 will help you to complete your project. Here is a checklist to help you gather the parts of your project together.

- ✔ list of geometric shapes
- ✔ different types of triangles
- ✔ list of polygons
- ✔ congruent and similar triangles

Your finished tangram should have 8–12 polygonal pieces. Your practice puzzles were drawn on paper. Redraw your final design on a rectangular piece of thin cardboard. Paste a piece of wall paper, a magazine picture, a photograph, or a drawing on the other side of the cardboard. Cut out the pieces of your puzzle.

Reflect and Revise

Make a checklist of the requirements for your puzzle. Use the checklist to see if your tangram satisfies all the requirements. How few pieces can you have and still satisfy all the requirements?

Exchange puzzles with a classmate and put them together as quickly as possible.

Web Extension
Prentice Hall's Internet site contains information you might find helpful as you complete your project. Visit www.phschool.com/mgm1/ch8 for some links and ideas related to puzzles.

Points, Lines, Planes, and Angles   8-1, 8-2, 8-3

A **point** has no size, only location. A **line** continues without end in opposite directions. A **plane** is a flat surface that extends indefinitely in four directions. A **segment** has two endpoints. A **ray** is a part of a line with one endpoint.

If a line can be drawn through a set of points, the points are **collinear**. **Parallel lines** are lines in the same plane that do not intersect. **Skew lines** are lines that lie in different planes.

An **angle** is made up of two rays with a common endpoint. **Complementary angles** have measures whose sum is 90°. **Supplementary angles** have measures whose sum is 180°. **Congruent angles** are angles that have the same measure.

You can classify angles as **acute**, **right**, **obtuse**, or **straight**.

1. Draw three noncollinear points A, B, and C.   2. Draw parallel lines $\overleftrightarrow{JK}$ and $\overleftrightarrow{MN}$.

3. How many segments are in the figure at the right? How many rays are in the figure? How many lines are in the figure?

Classify each angle as *acute*, *right*, *obtuse*, or *straight*.

4.   5.   6.

Triangles, Polygons, and Quadrilaterals   8-4, 8-5, 8-6

You can classify triangles by their angles as **acute**, **obtuse**, or **right**, and by their sides as **equilateral**, **isosceles**, or **scalene**.

A **polygon** is a closed shape formed by line segments that do not cross.

7. **Choose A, B, C, or D.** When $\overline{XZ}$ is drawn in parallelogram $WXYZ$, two congruent equilateral triangles are formed. What kind of figure is $WXYZ$?

   A. rectangle   **B.** rhombus   **C.** trapezoid   **D.** square

You can often use *Logical Reasoning* to solve problems.

8. Of 26 students, 3 read *The Yearling* and *Where the Red Fern Grows*, 11 read only the first book, and 7 students read neither book. How many read only the second book?

Figures that have the same size and shape are **congruent**. **Similar** figures have the same shape, but not necessarily the same size. A **line of symmetry** divides a figure into two congruent parts.

Do the triangles appear to be congruent, similar, or neither?

9.   10.

11. *Writing* Describe the lines of symmetry of a rhombus and a square.

A **circle** is the set of points in a plane that are the same distance from a given point. A **radius** has one endpoint at the center and one endpoint on the circle. A **diameter** has two endpoints on the circle and passes through the center. A **chord** has two endpoints on the circle.

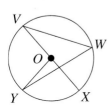

Name the following for circle O.

12. three radii

13. a diameter

14. three chords

A figure can be moved to make a **translation** (slide), a **reflection** (flip), or a **rotation** (turn).

15. *Open-ended* Draw a translation, a reflection, and a rotation of the shape at the right.

1. Draw three noncollinear points and label them X, Y, and Z. Draw $\overleftrightarrow{XY}$. Then draw a line through Z that appears to be parallel to $\overleftrightarrow{XY}$.

2. What is the best estimate for the measure of $\angle PQR$?

   A. 80°
   B. 100°
   C. 135°
   D. 150°

3. Measure each angle. Classify each as *acute*, *obtuse*, or *right*.

   a.
   b.

   c.
   d.

4. What is the best classification for triangle ABC?

   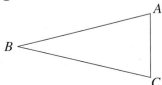

5. **Writing** In the polygons below, *diagonals* are drawn from one vertex. How many diagonals can you draw from one vertex of a hexagon? From one vertex of a 7-sided polygon? From one vertex of a 100-sided polygon? Explain your reasoning.

6. Draw a circle O and any chord $\overline{AB}$ that is not a diameter. Draw $\overline{OA}$, $\overline{OB}$, and the radius that is perpendicular to $\overline{AB}$. Make as many statements as you can about the angles, segments, and triangles in your diagram.

7. In order to conclude that $MNOP$ is a rhombus, what do you have to know?

   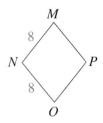

   A. $\overline{MO}$ is perpendicular to $\overline{NP}$.
   B. $\overline{MO}$ has length 8.
   C. $\overline{MP}$ and $\overline{PO}$ have length 8.
   D. $\overline{NP}$ and $\overline{MO}$ are congruent.

8. Of the 16 boys in Mrs. Stern's math class, seven play soccer and five are in the band. Four play football, but they do not participate in any other activity. Two students play soccer *and* play in the band. How many students participate in none of the three activities?

9. a. Draw two triangles that appear to be congruent.
   b. Draw two triangles that appear to be similar but not congruent.

10. Draw a quadrilateral with the given number of lines of symmetery.
    a. 0   b. 1   c. 2   d. 4

11. Draw a translation, a reflection, and a rotation of the shape at the right.

Choose the best answer.

1. What information does the circle graph below *not* tell you?

   A. Jen purchased lunch more often than she brought it from home.
   B. Jen purchased hot and cold lunches about as often.
   C. Jen brought lunch from home more often than she purchased cold lunch.
   D. Jen purchased hot lunch more often than she brought lunch from home.

   Jen's School Lunches

   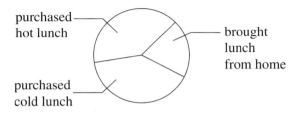

   purchased hot lunch — brought lunch from home — purchased cold lunch

2. If bagels cost $2 per dozen, how would you find the cost of 5 bagels?

   A. $2 × 5 × 12   B. $2 ÷ 12 × 5
   C. $2 × 12 ÷ 5   D. $2 ÷ 5 × 12

3. Which set of decimals below is ordered from least to greatest?

   A. 0.2, 0.02, 0.22   B. 0.15, 0.51, 1.05
   C. 0.24, 0.3, 0.05   D. 0.49, 0.4, 0.05

4. The Amazon River in South America carries one sixth of Earth's water that flows into oceans. About what percent of the water that flows into oceans is this?

   A. 17%   B. 12.5%   C. 10%   D. 6%

5. If 31.2 × ■ = 0.00312, ■ must be—

   A. 10,000 B. 1,000   C. 0.001   D. 0.0001

6. What is the value of $3 + 4 \times 2^3$?

   A. 515   B. 56   C. 35   D. 27

7. What information do you *not* need to know in order to solve the problem?

   At Ma's Restaurant, a cheese sandwich costs 99¢, a salad costs 20¢ less than a cheese sandwich, and milk costs 75¢. If you have $3.00, can you buy two cheese sandwiches and milk for lunch?

   A. the cost of a cheese sandwich
   B. the cost of a salad
   C. the cost of milk
   D. You have $3.00.

8. To solve a puzzle, you must solve the equation $4x = 8.8$. The solution is—

   A. 2.2   B. 4.8   C. 22   D. 35.2

9. Which of the following is *not* equivalent to a rate of 60 miles per hour?

   A. 180 miles in 3 hours
   B. 90 miles in 1.5 hours
   C. 240 miles in 3 hours
   D. 30 miles in 30 minutes

10. What can you conclude from the line plot below?

    A. Most absences occurred on Monday and Friday.
    B. The mean number of absences per day was 2.5.
    C. Only one person was absent on Wednesday because of a field trip.
    D. At least one person was absent twice that week.

    Number of Students Absent

    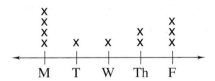

Geometry and Measurement

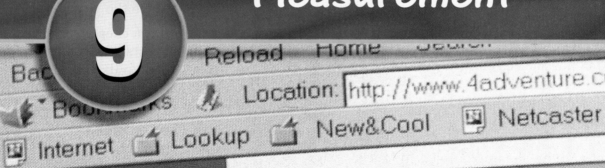

9

Attractions

What's New?

Press Room

Conservation Update

Vacation Packages

Ticket Prices

Park Hours

Directions

Just For Fun

WHAT YOU WILL LEARN IN THIS CHAPTER

- How to estimate and find areas of geometric figures

- How to find and use pi

- How to find surface area and volume of rectangular prisms

orida/trame.html

Sea World
of Florida

TURED ATTRACTION

West at Sea World" celebrates

best of the Florida Keys—

right here—in Orlando.

Feed dolphins, touch

g rays, experience endangered sea

les—all while basking in the famous

rida Keys spirit!

• How to solve a
problem by making
a model

THEME:
TECHNOLOGY

Home *on the* Web

Have you ever "surfed" the
Internet? If so, you may see a
dolphin like the one at the left. Such
pictures are so attractive that they
almost beg you to read the page.
Other pages do not look as exciting.
The World Wide Web can provide
quick access to useful information.
Unfortunately, many Web pages use
lots of space to say very little.

Design a Home Page For this
project you will research Web home
pages. You will then create your own
home page.

Estimating Area

What You'll Learn

▼ To estimate area

...And Why

You can solve problems involving gardening and geography by estimating area.

Here's How

Look for questions that
- build understanding
- ✔ check understanding

THINK AND DISCUSS

You can find the area of any figure by finding the number of *square units* that cover it.

1. ✔**Try It Out** How many square units are in each figure? Describe your method for finding each area.

a.
b.
c.

Some of the standard units of area are square centimeters (cm^2), square meters (m^2), square inches (in.^{2}), square feet (ft^2), square yards (yd^2), and square miles (mi^2).

2. ■**Open-ended** Name some other units of area.

The figure below is on centimeter graph paper.

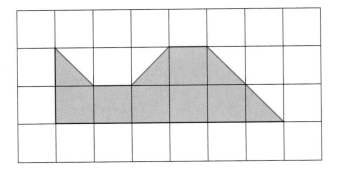

3. a. What is the area of each square of the graph paper?
   b. ✔**Try It Out** What is the area of the shaded figure?
   c. ■**Explain** How did you find the area?
   d. ■**Go a Step Further** Suppose each square represents 9 m^2. What is the area of the figure?

You can estimate area by using a grid. Decide whether each square is full, almost full, about half full, or almost empty.

■ **EXAMPLE**   *Real-World Problem Solving*

Gardening Estimate the area of the flower bed in the drawing below. Each square represents 1 m².

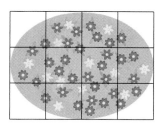

The 2 center squares are full. The 6 squares in the middle of the sides are almost full. The 4 corner squares are about half full.

$$2 + 6 + (4 \times \frac{1}{2}) = 2 + 6 + 2$$
$$= 10$$

The area is about 10 m².

4. ✔*Try It Out* Below is a drawing of a lake. Each square represents 4 mi². Estimate the area of the lake.

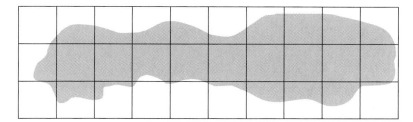

Sydney, Australia

Work Together
Estimating Area from Maps

5. *Geography* Work with a partner. Each square represents an area 240 mi by 240 mi. Estimate the area of Australia.

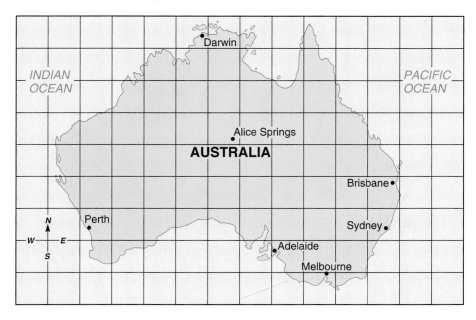

The area of each square is 1 cm². Find the area of each
figure.

1.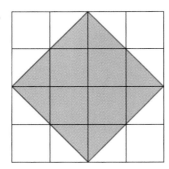

2.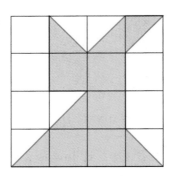

3.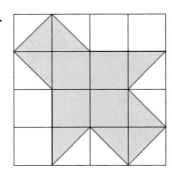

Each square represents 1 in.² Estimate the area of each
figure.

4.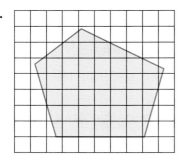

5.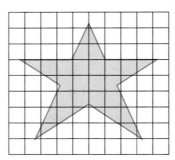

6.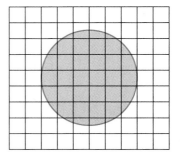

Each square represents 4 cm². Estimate the area of each
figure.

7.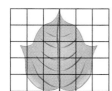

8.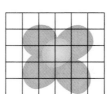

9.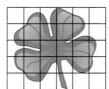

10. Choose A, B, C, or D. Each square represents 100 m².
Which is the best estimate for the area of the figure at
the right?

    A. 3,000 m²   **B.** 1,550 m²   **C.** 15.5 m²   **D.** 15.5 cm²

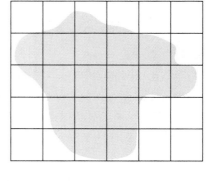

11. *Writing* Explain why estimating area is sometimes more
useful than actually measuring area. Give an example to
support your answer.

12. Which region has the greatest area? The least area? Explain.

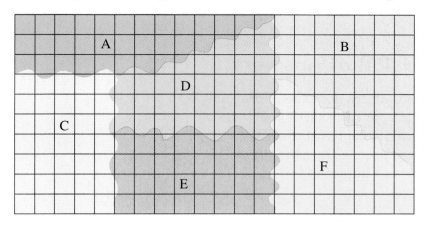

13. *Open-ended* Place your hand, with your fingers touching, on centimeter graph paper. Trace around your hand. On a second sheet of centimeter graph paper, trace around your hand with your fingers spread apart.
   a. Estimate the area of each hand.
   b. *Reasoning* Why might there be differences in your two estimates for part (a)?

14. *Reasoning* How many square feet are in a square yard? How many square inches are in a square yard? Use drawings to illustrate your answer.

Mixed Review

Find each sum or difference. Use equivalent fractions.
(Lessons 6-2 and 6-3)

15. $\frac{1}{5} + \frac{3}{5}$ **16.** $\frac{4}{9} - \frac{3}{9}$ **17.** $\frac{7}{8} + \frac{1}{4}$ **18.** $\frac{14}{21} - \frac{3}{7}$ **19.** $\frac{5}{12} + \frac{4}{6}$ **20.** $\frac{23}{25} - \frac{1}{5}$

Write a ratio in three ways for each statement. *(Lesson 7-1)*

21. two black kittens in a litter of 6

22. eight A-students in a class of 24

23. 1 cup butter for every 2 cups sugar

24. 4 cartons for 24 bottles

25. *Choose a Strategy* Mr. Delgado is growing sunflowers to sell at the school plant sale. He plants $2\frac{1}{2}$ dozen seeds each day, but $\frac{3}{4}$ dozen seeds of each $2\frac{1}{2}$ dozen seeds planted do not grow. On how many days must Mr. Delgado plant to have a total of at least 8 dozen sunflower plants?

Extra Practice, Lesson 9-1, page 530

EXPLORATION

Precision of Answers

Before Lesson 9-2

Sometimes you use numbers that are not exact. For example, measurements are *approximate*, or not exactly *precise*. The *precision* of a number refers to its degree of exactness. Measurements cannot be more precise than the measuring tool used. In science, precision is very important.

■ EXAMPLE 1

To what degree of precision can you measure a length using the ruler at the right?

The ruler is divided into sixteenths of an inch, so you can measure a length to the nearest sixteenth of an inch.

■ EXAMPLE 2

Find the length of the line segment at the right using the given measuring tool.

The centimeter ruler is divided into tenths of a centimeter, or millimeters. Since the line segment is closer to 7.6 cm or 76 mm than it is to 7.7 cm or 77 mm, its length is 7.6 cm or 76 mm.

To what degree of precision can you measure a given length using each measuring tool?

1.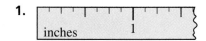

2.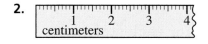

3.

Find the length of each line segment using the measuring tool directly below it.

4.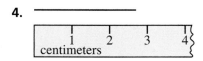

5.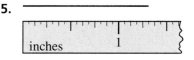

6.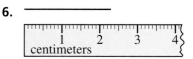

7. *Writing* Describe five items for which a centimeter measure would be reasonable. For example, a pencil could reasonably be described as 7.5 cm long.

9-2 Perimeters and Areas of Rectangles

What You'll Learn

▼ To find perimeters and areas of rectangles

▼ To find perimeters and areas of squares

...And Why

Finding the area of a figure helps you solve problems involving landscaping.

Here's How

Look for questions that

▪ build understanding

✔ check understanding

THINK AND DISCUSS

▼ 1 Measuring Rectangles

Suppose you are planning a vegetable garden. You plan to have 12 square garden plots arranged into a rectangle. Each plot measures 1 meter along each side.

1. a. ▪ *Reasoning* How can you arrange the 12 plots to have the least perimeter?

   b. How can you arrange the plots to have the greatest perimeter?

2. a. What is the area of the arrangement with the least perimeter?

   b. What is the area of the arrangement with the greatest perimeter?

   c. ▪ *Explain* Will the area change if you arrange the plots in a nonrectangular shape? Why or why not?

Perimeter measures the distance around a figure. When you do not have sides or squares to count, you can find the perimeter P of a rectangle by adding each length ℓ and width w: $\ell + w + \ell + w$, which is $2\ell + 2w$, or $2(\ell + w)$.

The area of a figure is the amount of surface it covers. It is measured in square units. You can find the area A of a rectangle by multiplying the length ℓ and the width w.

PERIMETER AND AREA OF A RECTANGLE

$P = 2(\ell + w)$

$A = \ell \times w$

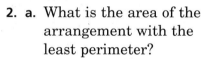

■ **EXAMPLE 1**   *Real-World Problem Solving*

Landscaping Find the perimeter and area of the backyard.

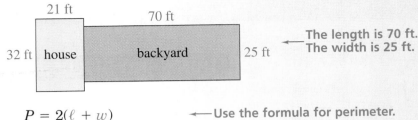

The length is 70 ft.
The width is 25 ft.

$P = 2(\ell + w)$ ◄——Use the formula for perimeter.
$\quad = 2(70 + 25)$
$\quad = 2 \times 95 = 190$ ft

$A = \ell \times w$ ◄——Use the formula for area.
$\quad = 70 \times 25 = 1{,}750$ ft^2

The perimeter is 190 ft. The area of the backyard is 1,750 ft^2.

3. ▪ *Number Sense* In Example 1, why was the area given in square feet and the perimeter in feet?

4. ✔ *Try It Out* Find the perimeter and area of each rectangle.
   a. $\ell = 8$ ft, $w = 5$ ft   **b.** $\ell = 12$ in., $w = 7$ in.

5. ▪ *What If . . .* Suppose the length of the backyard in Example 1 were cut by one half.
   a. How would the area of the backyard change?
   b. How would the backyard's perimeter change?

▼**2** *Measuring Squares*

A square is a rectangle with 4 sides of equal measure. The perimeter P is 4 times the length of each side s, or $4s$. You can find the area A by squaring the length of a side, or s^2.

PERIMETER AND AREA OF A SQUARE

$P = 4s$
(Perimeter = 4 × side)

s

s

$A = s \times s = s^2$
(Area = side × side)

■ EXAMPLE 2

A square's perimeter is 32 cm. Find its area.

$$P = 4s$$ ← Use the formula for perimeter to find the measure of a side.
$$32 = 4s$$
$$\frac{32}{4} = \frac{4s}{4}$$ ← Solve for s.
$$8 = s$$

$$A = s^2$$ ← Use the formula for area.
$$A = 8^2 = 64$$

The area of the square is 64 cm^2.

6. ✔**Try It Out** Find the area of a square with perimeter 8 ft.

Work Together   *Relating Perimeter and Area*

Use square tiles to form the following rectangles. Record the results on graph paper.

7. ▪**Modeling** Form at least two rectangles whose areas (in square units) are less than their perimeters (in units).

8. Form at least one rectangle whose area is equal to its perimeter.

9. Form at least two rectangles whose areas are greater than their perimeters.

EXERCISES *On Your Own*

Find the perimeter and area of each rectangle.

1.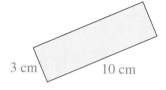
3 cm   10 cm

2.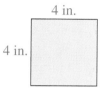
4 in.
4 in.

3.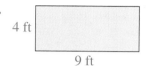
4 ft
9 ft

4.
16 m
8 m

5. a. **Landscaping** How much fencing do you need to enclose a rectangular pool area that is 24 ft by 66 ft?
   b. Suppose you use fence sections 3 ft wide. How many sections will you need?

Find the perimeter and area of each rectangle.

6. $\ell = 6$ cm, $w = 3$ cm

7. $\ell = 15$ yd, $w = 10$ yd

8. $\ell = 5$ mm, $w = 20$ mm

9. $\ell = 7$ yd, $w = 12$ yd

10. $\ell = 1.5$ m, $w = 0.25$ m

11. $\ell = 7.2$ cm, $w = 3.7$ cm

Use a centimeter ruler to measure the length and width of each rectangle. Then find the perimeter and area.

12.

13.

14.

15.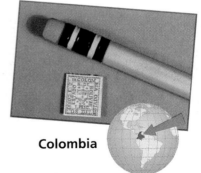

Choose **Use a calculator, paper and pencil, or mental math to solve.**

16. The area of a rectangle is 24 in.^{2}. One side is 6 in. What is the perimeter?

17. The perimeter of a rectangle is 22 ft. The width is 4 ft. What is the length? The area?

18. *Stamp Collecting* The world's smallest stamp, shown at right, was issued in Colombia from 1863 to 1866. It measured 0.31 in. by 0.37 in. Find the stamp's area.

19. *Gardening* Suppose you would like a garden with an area of 18 ft^2. You have a garden space 6 ft long. How wide should it be?

20. **Choose A, B, C, or D.** A rectangle is 15.95 m by 8.25 m. Which of the following is the best estimate for the area?

A. about 48 m   **B.** about 48 m^2 **C.** about 128 m   **D.** about 128 m^2

Colombia

Find the perimeter and area of each square.

21. $s = 4.5$ in.

22. $s = 13$ m

23. $s = 21$ mm

24. $s = 50$ mi

25. $s = 1.5$ cm

26. $s = 4.1$ km

27. $s = 100$ ft

28. $s = 12.5$ in.

29. The area of a rectangular parking lot is 24 yd^2. Find all the possible whole-number dimensions in yards.

30. The perimeter of a rectangle is 10 m. Find all the possible whole-number dimensions in meters.

31. *Writing* Suppose you know the area of a rectangle. Can you then find its perimeter? Why or why not? Use examples to illustrate your answer.

32. *Mental Math* Estimate the area of the rectangle at the right.

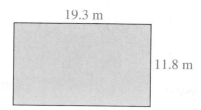

19.3 m

11.8 m

Find the area of each square with the given perimeter.

33. 8 cm **34.** 20 m **35.** 48 in. **36.** 10 mi

37. The perimeter of a square is 16 in.
 a. What is its area?
 b. Suppose the length of the square's sides is cut in half. How would the perimeter and area change?

38. *Home Improvement* A homeowner is buying square tiles for her dining room floor. The room is 10 ft by 15 ft. She can choose tiles that are 1 ft on a side or 2 ft on a side.
 a. How many tiles does she need if she chooses 1-ft^2 tiles?
 b. How many 1-ft^2 tiles does it take to cover the same area as one 4-ft^2 tile?

Mixed Review

Find each quotient. *(Lessons 4-7 and 4-8)*

39. $90\overline{)360}$ **40.** $11.85 \div 7.9$ **41.** $45\overline{)58.5}$ **42.** $2.262 \div 8.7$ **43.** $7\overline{)0.161}$

44. *Baby-sitting* Sheila baby-sits for $4\frac{3}{4}$ hour each Saturday and each Sunday. She plans to baby-sit for $3\frac{1}{2}$ weekends next month. Find the total number of hours she will work next month. *(Lesson 6-8)*

CHAPTER PROJECT

PROJECT LINK: RESEARCHING

Visit the home pages of several Web sites. Find an example of a home page that has a lot of words and pictures. Also find a home page that *does not* have a lot of words or pictures. Create a bookmark or record the addresses of the sites so you can return to them later.

What You'll Learn

▼ To find the areas of parallelograms and triangles

▼ To find the areas of complex figures

...And Why

You can use the areas of parallelograms and triangles to solve conservation problems.

Here's How

Look for questions that

⚫ build understanding

✔ check understanding

Work Together

Comparing Areas

1. a. Draw a nonrectangular parallelogram on graph paper. Draw a perpendicular segment from one vertex to the base.

   b. Cut the parallelogram out. Cut along the perpendicular segment.

   c. ⚫*Patterns* Rearrange the two figures to form a rectangle.

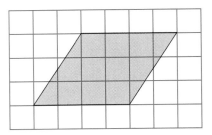

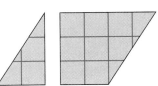

2. a. What is the area of the rectangle?

   b. ⚫*Explain* What do you think was the area of the original parallelogram? Why?

   c. ⚫*Analyze* Repeat this activity. Make three different-sized parallelograms. Are the results similar?

3. ⚫*Patterns* Draw two congruent triangles on centimeter graph paper. Cut out and arrange the triangles to form a parallelogram. How does the area of each triangle compare to the area of the parallelogram?

THINK AND DISCUSS

▼ Areas of Parallelograms and Triangles

Any side of a parallelogram or triangle can be considered the base, with length b. The height h of the parallelogram or triangle is the length of a perpendicular segment, or *altitude,* from a vertex to the line containing the base.

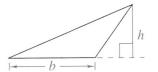

The area of a parallelogram is *the same as* the area of a rectangle with the same dimensions. The area of a triangle is *half* the area of a parallelogram with the same base length and height.

> **AREAS OF PARALLELOGRAMS AND TRIANGLES**
>
> Area of a parallelogram = base length × height = bh
>
> Area of a triangle = $\frac{1}{2}$ × base length × height = $\frac{1}{2}bh$

■ **EXAMPLE 1** *Real-World Problem Solving*

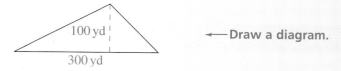

A nature conservancy is a group that buys land in order to preserve it in its natural state.

Conservation A nature conservancy plans to buy a triangular plot of land. The plot has a base length of 300 yards and a height of 100 yards. What is the plot area?

←— Draw a diagram.

100 yd
300 yd

$A = \frac{1}{2}bh = \frac{1}{2} \times 300 \times 100$ ←— Use the formula for the area of a triangle.
$ = 15{,}000$

The area is 15,000 yd^2.

4. ⁘ ***What If . . .*** Suppose the base length of the triangular plot of land in Example 1 were doubled. Find the new area.

5. ✔ ***Try It Out*** Find the area of a triangle with base 30 m and height 17.3 m.

▼2 *Areas of Complex Figures*

Sometimes it helps to split a figure into smaller polygons. Then you can find the area of each polygon and add.

■ **EXAMPLE 2**

Find the area of the figure below.

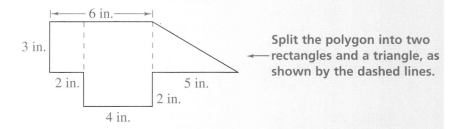

Split the polygon into two rectangles and a triangle, as shown by the dashed lines.

Area of smaller rectangle = $3 \times 2 = 6$ in.^{2}
Area of larger rectangle = $5 \times 4 = 20$ in.^{2}
Area of triangle = $\frac{1}{2}(5 \times 3) = \frac{1}{2} \times 15 = 7.5$ in.^{2}

Find the area of each of the polygons.

6 in.^{2} + 20 in.^{2} + 7.5 in.^{2} = 33.5 in.^{2} ◄—— Add the three areas.

6. ✔*Try It Out* Find the area of the figure at the right.

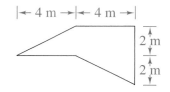

7. ▪*Look Back* Show another way that you can split the figure in Example 2 to find the area.

EXERCISES *On Your Own*

Find the area of each parallelogram.

1. $b = 4$ ft, $h = 9$ ft

2. $b = 10$ in., $h = 7$ in.

3. $b = 6$ km, $h = 8$ km

4. $b = 20$ yd, $h = 34$ yd

5. $b = 2.4$ cm, $h = 4$ cm

6. $b = 3.7$ m, $h = 6.3$ m

Find the area of each triangle.

7. $b = 12$ in., $h = 9$ in.

8. $b = 5$ cm, $h = 10$ cm

9. $b = 4$ yd, $h = 8$ yd

10. $b = 14$ km, $h = 14$ km

11. $b = 3.5$ m, $h = 7$ m

12. $b = 5.3$ cm, $h = 6.5$ cm

Find each area. Use units².

13.

14.

15.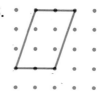

16.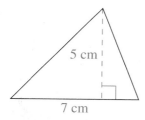

5 cm

7 cm

17.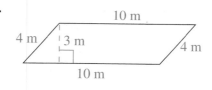

10 m

4 m   3 m   4 m

10 m

18.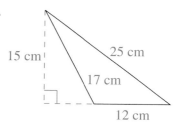

15 cm   25 cm

17 cm

12 cm

19. Measurement Use a centimeter ruler to measure the sides of the triangle at the right. Measure to the nearest millimeter. Then find its perimeter and its area.

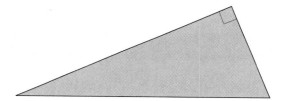

20. Choose A, B, C, or D. A right triangle and a rectangle have equal bases and equal heights. How do their perimeters compare? (*Hint:* Use *Guess and Test.*)

  A. The perimeter of the triangle is greater.
  B. The perimeter of the rectangle is greater.
  C. The perimeters are equal.
  D. It is impossible to tell.

Find the area of each parallelogram. Use units².

21.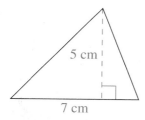

D   6   C

5

A   B

22.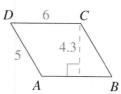

D   6   C

5   4.3

A   B

23.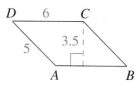

D   6   C

5   3.5

A   B

24. a. Copy the trapezoid onto paper. Split it into two triangles with 3 cm heights. Then find the area.
  b. Writing Explain how you can find the area of this trapezoid by splitting it into two triangles.

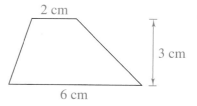

2 cm

3 cm

6 cm

Copy each figure on dot paper. Then find each area. Use units².

25.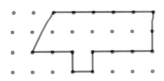

26.

27.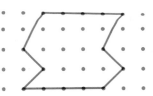

28. Find the area of the figure at the right.

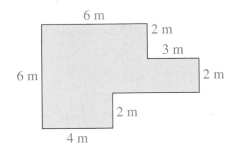

6 m

2 m

3 m

6 m

2 m

2 m

4 m

JOURNAL

Describe the relationship between the areas of parallelograms and triangles. Draw diagrams as part of your explanation.

Mixed Review

Find each product. *(Lesson 6-8)*

29. $3\frac{5}{8} \times \frac{1}{2}$

30. $5\frac{3}{5} \times 3\frac{3}{4}$

31. $2\frac{2}{3} \times 8\frac{3}{4}$

32. $4\frac{1}{6} \times 1\frac{7}{8}$

33. $12\frac{3}{5} \times 2\frac{1}{2}$

Use a protractor to draw angles with the following measures. *(Lesson 8-2)*

34. $32°$

35. $173°$

36. $92°$

37. $104°$

38. $12°$

39. $45°$

40. The club wants to buy 8 pizzas at $6.99 each and some juice. Kevin thinks that each of the 32 club members should pay $1.75. Barbara thinks they need to pay $2.00 each. Who do you think made a better estimate? Explain. *(Lesson 4-1)*

✓ CHECKPOINT 1
Lessons 9-1 through 9-3

1. How much lace do you need to trim a 72 in. × 48 in. rectangular tablecloth?

2. A rectangle is 35 in. long. Its width is 5 in. What are its perimeter and area?

Find the area of each figure.

3. rectangle: $\ell = 7$ in., $w = 12$ in.

4. square: $s = 8.5$ cm

5. parallelogram: $b = 13$ m, $h = 6$ m

6. triangle: $b = 50$ ft, $h = 40$ ft

Extra Practice, Lesson 9-3, page 530

EXPLORATION

Tessellations

After Lesson 9-3

A *tessellation* is a repeated geometric design. It covers a plane with no gaps or overlaps. Brick walls and tiled floors are examples of tessellations.

■ EXAMPLE 1

Name the polygon used to form the tessellation below.

←—Find the figure that repeats. It is a triangle.

The tessellation above is formed by a triangle.

You can use more than one type of polygon to form a tessellation.

■ EXAMPLE 2

Form a tessellation using the polygons at the right.

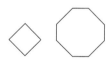

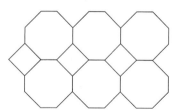

←—Arrange the polygons with no gaps or overlaps.

Trace each figure. Can you use it to form a tessellation? If so, sketch the tessellation.

1.

2.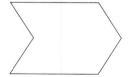

3.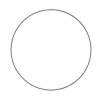

4.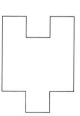

5. *Open-ended* Use tiles, dot paper, or cutouts to create a tessellation from squares and equilateral triangles.

9-4 Gathering Data to Explore π

What You'll Learn

▼ To estimate π and the circumference of a circle

▼ To use π to find the circumference of a circle

...And Why

You can use the circumference of a circle to solve entertainment and sports problems.

Here's How

Look for questions that
■ build understanding
✔ check understanding

THINK AND DISCUSS

▼ *Estimating π and Circumference*

Suppose you design the circular stage shown below. How will the size of the stage affect the number of red and blue lights you need?

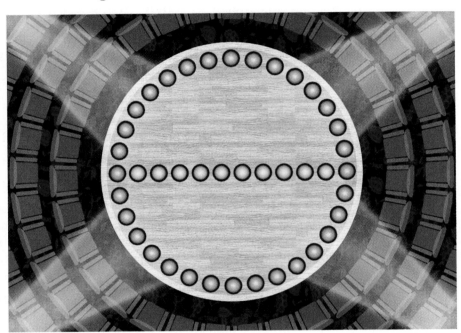

QUICK review

The distance across a circle (through its center) is the *diameter*. The *radius* is half the length of the diameter. For example, if the diameter is 10 in., the radius is 5 in.

The distance around a circle is its **circumference.** You can use the relationship between the circumference and diameter of a circle to solve the stage problem.

1. **a.** First explore the ratio of the circumference of a circle to its diameter $\left(\frac{C}{d} = \blacksquare\right)$. Use a string and a centimeter ruler to measure the circumference and diameter of at least three different circles. Measure to the nearest tenth of a centimeter. Make a table with columns C, d, and $\frac{C}{d}$. Record your results.

   b. ■*Writing* What pattern do you see in the ratio $\frac{C}{d}$?

   c. ■*Analyze* How does the number of red lights you need compare to the number of blue lights? Does that change if the circle changes?

2. a. ✔*Try It Out* Use your results from Question 1 to help estimate the circumference of the circle at the right.

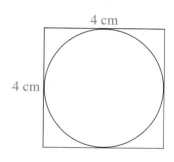

4 cm

4 cm

b. Find the square's perimeter.

c. ⠿*Think About It* Is the circumference of the circle less than or greater than the perimeter of the square? Does this make sense? Explain.

You can use the relationship between the circumference and diameter of a circle to solve problems.

3. Suppose you design the circular stage to have an 83-ft diameter. The light bulbs are 1 ft apart.

a. ✔*Try It Out* Estimate the circumference of the stage.

b. ⠿*Explain* How did you find your estimate?

c. ⠿*Draw a Conclusion* Will 200 red light bulbs be enough to go completely around the stage? Explain.

4. Suppose the drummer sits 25 ft from the center of the stage.

a. ⠿*Spatial Reasoning* Draw a diagram that shows the drummer's path as the stage goes around once in one minute.

b. What is the diameter of the circle made by the drummer's path?

c. ⠿*Analyze* Estimate the circumference of the circle made by the drummer's path in 1 minute.

d. About how far does the drummer travel in 1 second?

e. ⠿*Draw a Conclusion* Write the speed at which the drummer travels on the stage as feet per second (ft/s). Will the drummer travel faster than 10 mi/h?

QUICKreview

5,280 ft = 1 mi

The ratio $\frac{C}{d}$ equals a number close to 3 that is called pi. The rounded value 3.14 is often used to represent the value of pi. We use the symbol π (read as "pi") to stand for this value.

5. ⠿*Number Sense* Which point on the number line represents π? Explain.

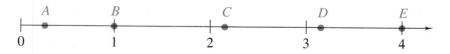

2 *Using π to Find Circumference*

You can use $\frac{C}{d} = \pi$ to find a circle's circumference C if you know its diameter d. Since $\frac{C}{d} = \pi$, $C = \pi d$.

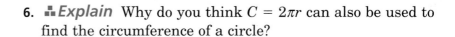

CIRCUMFERENCE OF A CIRCLE

$C = \pi d$ (Circumference = pi × diameter)

$C = 2\pi r$ (Circumference = 2 × pi × radius)

6. ⁝ *Explain* Why do you think $C = 2\pi r$ can also be used to find the circumference of a circle?

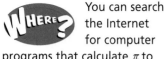 You can search the Internet for computer programs that calculate π to many decimal places. There are many Web sites devoted to π.

Computers can approximate the value of π to thousands of decimal places. You can use the value 3.14 to solve most problems. Also, many calculators have a π key.

7. ⁝ *Calculator* Press the π key on your calculator. What is the result?

■ EXAMPLE   *Real-World Problem Solving*

Archery A regulation archery target has a circle with a 48-in. diameter. Find the circumference of a regulation target.

Estimate: $C = \pi d = \pi \times 48 \approx 3 \times 50 = 150$

Calculate: π × 48 ▣ *150.7964474* ← Use a calculator. When necessary, round the answer to the nearest unit.

The circumference is about 151 in.

8. ✔*Try It Out* Find the circumference for each circle with the given radius or diameter. Round the answer to the nearest unit.
   a. $d = 1$ ft
   b. $r = 13.5$ cm
   c. $r = 22$ in.
   d. $d = 30$ m

9. ⁝ *Think About It* The archery target at the left is a regulation one. Use the information in the Example. Estimate the length of the sides of the square around the target.

You can use the circumference formula to find a circle's diameter if you know its circumference.

PROBLEM SOLVING HINT
Draw a diagram. Show the tire track and the point where the pebble makes a mark.

10. How good a detective are you? A pebble stuck in a bicycle's tire left a mark in the tire track every 69 in.
    a. *Reasoning* What is the circumference of the tire? How do you know?
    b. Estimate the diameter of the tire.
    c. *Calculator* Use the π key. Find the diameter of the tire. Round the answer to the nearest half inch.

EXERCISES *On Your Own*

Estimate the circumference of a circle with the given radius or diameter. (*Hint:* To estimate, use 3 for π.)

1. $d = 5$ cm
2. $d = 11$ m
3. $r = 1$ in.
4. $r = 3$ m
5. $d = 40$ mi

Calculator **Find the circumference of a circle with the given radius or diameter. Round the answer to the nearest unit.**

6. $d = 15$ ft
7. $d = 50$ m
8. $r = 17$ in.
9. $r = 64$ m
10. $d = 200$ ft

11. $d = 3.9$ m
12. $r = 9.5$ in
13. $d = 17.5$ ft
14. $r = 0.39$ km
15. $d = 3,183$ m

16. **Choose A, B, C, or D.** If you double the radius of a circle, what happens to the circumference?

    A. The circumference remains the same.
    B. The circumference is doubled.
    C. The circumference is tripled.
    D. The circumference is quadrupled.

17. Find the diameter and radius of a circle with a circumference of 62.8 mm.

18. *Pets* A dog tied to a post gets exercise by running in a circle. One day the dog ran around the post 100 times with the 10-ft rope stretched tightly. (Assume that the rope did not wrap around the post.) Did the dog run at least 1 mi?

19. *Bicycles* A bicycle popular in the late 1800s had a large wheel in the front and a smaller wheel in the back. If the diameter of the large wheel was 3 ft, about how far would the bicycle travel as that wheel made one full turn?

🖩 Calculator Find the diameter of a circle with the given circumference. Round the answer to the nearest tenth of a unit.

20. 192 ft   **21.** 85 cm   **22.** 22.5 in.   **23.** 56 m   **24.** 1,273 mm

25. 2 yd   **26.** 27.5 ft   **27.** 68.7 cm   **28.** 3.75 in.   **29.** 19.67 m

🖩 Choose For Exercises 30 and 31, use 3.14 for π or use the **π** key on a calculator.

30. *Drafting* Suppose you want to draw a circle with a circumference of 10 cm. How wide should you set your compass (to the nearest 0.1 cm)?

31. *Cycling* The diameter of a bicycle's wheel is 28 in. About how many times does each wheel make a complete circle when the bicycle travels 1,000 ft?

Mixed Review

Name each polygon. *(Lesson 8-5)*

32.   **33.**   **34.**   **35.**

Compare using <, >, =. *(Lesson 5-8)*

36. $\frac{5}{8} \blacksquare \frac{11}{16}$ **37.** $\frac{7}{10} \blacksquare \frac{7}{8}$ **38.** $\frac{121}{500} \blacksquare \frac{1}{2}$ **39.** $\frac{9}{36} \blacksquare \frac{7}{28}$ **40.** $\frac{5}{8} \blacksquare \frac{11}{12}$ **41.** $\frac{2}{5} \blacksquare \frac{1}{4}$

42. *Choose a Strategy* At a gift shop, Nara bought twice as many cards as Ann. Ann bought 3 fewer cards than Jamil but three more than Kamala. Ann bought 8 cards. How many cards did each of the others buy?

CHAPTER PROJECT

PROJECT LINK: DIAGRAMING

Draw a diagram of the two Web home pages you have chosen. Draw a rectangle, triangle, or circle around each block of text or graphic (photograph or artwork) on the page. Label each area as text, graphic, or white space. Save these diagrams for use later.

Area of a Circle

What You'll Learn

▼1 To find the area of a circle

▼2 To find combined areas of circles and polygons

...And Why

You can use the area of a circle to find areas on a basketball court.

Here's How

Look for questions that
▪ build understanding
✔ check understanding

Work Together   *Exploring the Area of a Circle*

Use a compass to draw a circle with radius 7 cm on centimeter graph paper. With a ruler, divide the circle into eight congruent wedges as shown.

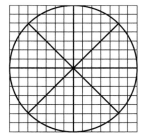

1. ▪ *Geometry* About how many square centimeters are in the circle? What is the circumference of the circle?

Cut out the circle and the eight wedges you drew. Rearrange the wedges into the figure shown below.

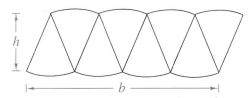

2. a. What quadrilateral is the new figure similar to?
   b. ▪ *Estimation* Estimate the base length b and height h.
   c. Use your answers to parts (a) and (b) to estimate the area of the new figure. (*Hint:* Use the formula $A = b \times h$.)
   d. How does the number of square centimeters in the uncut circle compare to the number of square centimeters in the new figure?

THINK AND DISCUSS

▼1 *Finding Area of a Circle*

You can use this formula to find the area A of a circle.

Area of a Circle

$$A = \pi \times r \times r = \pi r^2$$

■ **EXAMPLE 1**

▦ *Calculator* Find the area of a circle with radius 5 cm. Round your answer to the nearest tenth of a unit.

Estimate: $A = \pi r^2 \longrightarrow A \approx 3 \times 5^2 = 3 \times 25 = 75$

Use a calculator.

[π] [×] 5 [x^2] [=] **78.539816** ←— $A = \pi r^2$

The area is about 78.5 cm^2.

3. ✓ *Try It Out* Find the area of a circle with the given radius or diameter. Round each answer to the nearest tenth of a unit.
   a. $r = 11$ mi **b.** $d = 16$ in. **c.** $d = 10.5$ m **d.** $r = 5.5$ cm

▦ 4. **a.** ⠿*Calculator* Find the area of a circle with radius 7 cm.
   b. How does this area compare to the number of square centimeters you counted for the circle in Question 1?

▼2 *Finding Areas of Circles and Polygons*

You can find the area of a figure that contains polygons and circles.

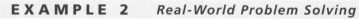

■ **EXAMPLE 2**   *Real-World Problem Solving*

Basketball The shaded foul shot area at the right contains half a circle and a rectangle. Find the area of the shaded region.

Area of rectangle:

$\ell \times w = 19 \times 12 = 228$

Area of circle:

The radius is $\frac{1}{2}d$ or 6 ft.

$A = \pi r^2$

$A \approx 3.14 \times 6^2 = 3.14 \times 36 = 113.04$

$\genfrac{}{}{0pt}{}{\text{area of}}{\text{rectangle}} + \frac{1}{2}\genfrac{}{}{0pt}{}{\text{area of}}{\text{circle}} = 228 + \frac{1}{2}(113.04) = 284.52$

The area of the shaded region is about 284.52 ft^2, or $284\frac{1}{2}$ ft^2.

5. In the diagram at the right, the 3-point area of a basketball court is shaded.

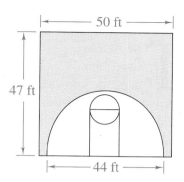

a. ▪Explain Describe how to find the area of the shaded region.

b. ✓Try It Out Find the area. Use 3.14 for π.

EXERCISES On Your Own

▦ Calculator **Find the area of each circle. Round each answer to the nearest tenth of a unit.**

1.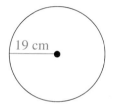
19 cm

2.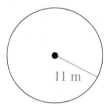
11 m

3.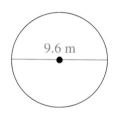
9.6 m

4.
87 yd

Mental Math **Estimate the area of each circle with the given radius or diameter.** (*Hint:* To estimate, use 3 for π.)

5. $r = 2$ in.   6. $d = 2$ m   7. $r = 10$ cm   8. $r = 5$ in.   9. $d = 6$ mm   10. $r = 20$ cm

Find the area of each circle with the given radius or diameter. Round each answer to the nearest tenth of a unit.

11. $d = 20$ m   12. $d = 9$ ft   13. $d = 4$ yd   14. $r = 6$ cm   15. $r = 15$ in.   16. $r = 1.3$ m

17. $r = 3$ mm   18. $r = 10$ ft   19. $r = 4$ in.   20. $d = 13$ m   21. $d = 11$ ft   22. $d = 2.4$ m

23. $r = 4.4$ m   24. $d = 2$ ft   25. $r = 12$ ft   26. $d = 10$ ft   27. $r = 2.5$ m   28. $d = 0.5$ m

29. **Communications** You can pick up the radio signal for station WAER FM 88 in Syracuse, New York, within a 45-mi radius of the station. What is the approximate area of the broadcast region? Use 3.14 for π.

30. *Writing* Which is larger: a pan with a radius of 10 in. or a pan with a diameter of 18 in.? Explain.

FOLLOW THE SUN

The Aztecs used their accurate knowledge of astronomy and mathematics to make a calendar called The Sun Stone. They carved the calendar on a circular stone 3.6 meters in diameter. The Aztecs began working on the calendar in 1427 and completed the work in 1479. The center circle of the stone shows the face of Tontiuh, the Aztec sun god. The 20 squares in the second ring name the 20 days of each Aztec month. There were 18 Aztec months.

31. Find the area of the Sun Stone. Use 3.14 for π.

32. How long did it take the Aztecs to complete the calendar?

33. How many days were in the Aztec calendar?

Calculator Find the area of each circle with the given radius or diameter. Round each answer to the nearest tenth of a unit.

34. $r = 9$ cm   **35.** $d = 7$ cm   **36.** $r = 3.2$ m   **37.** $d = 8$ ft   **38.** $d = 14$ in.   **39.** $r = 1$ mm

40. $r = 7.5$ in.   **41.** $r = 18$ m   **42.** $d = 20$ ft   **43.** $d = 11$ in.   **44.** $r = 44$ cm   **45.** $d = 15$ ft

46. $d = 4.5$ m   **47.** $d = 17$ in.   **48.** $r = 12$ in.   **49.** $r = 25$ in.   **50.** $d = 1.5$ m   **51.** $r = 0.5$ cm

Calculator Find the area of each shaded region. Round to the nearest unit.

52.

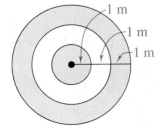

3 m

10 m

53.

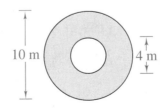

10 m

4 m

54.

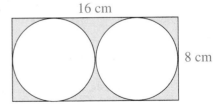

16 cm

8 cm

55.

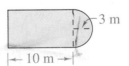

1 m

1 m

1 m

56.

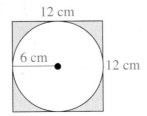

12 cm

6 cm

12 cm

⊞ *Calculator* Find the area of each figure. Use units². Round each answer to the nearest tenth.

57.

58.

59.

60. *Games* Use the hopscotch drawing at the right.
   a. Suppose the sides of each square equal 2 ft. Find the area of the hopscotch drawing.
   b. Suppose the sides of each square equal 1.5 ft. Find the area of the hopscotch drawing.
   c. Compare the areas in parts (a) and (b). Which do you think would be easier to hop on without going outside the lines? Explain your reasoning.

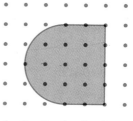

Mixed Review

Classify each triangle with the given angle measures as *acute*, *right*, or *obtuse*. *(Lesson 8-4)*

61. 25°, 45°, 110°   **62.** 90°, 30°, 60°   **63.** 80°, 50°, 50°   **64.** 60°, 70°, 50°

Estimate each amount. *(Lesson 7-8)*

65. 39% of 50   **66.** 98% of 725   **67.** 9% of 25   **68.** 60% of 31   **69.** 41% of 200

70. *Choose a Strategy* Karim owns an office supply store. He sells a lap desk for two times his cost plus $4.25. The lap desk sells for $17.75. What is Karim's cost?

CHAPTER PROJECT

PROJECT LINK: CALCULATING

For each home page you diagramed, calculate the total text or graphic area and the area of the home page screen. Write these areas as the ratio $\frac{\text{area with text or graphic}}{\text{area of home page screen}}$. Next, write this ratio as a percent.

Three-Dimensional Figures

What You'll Learn

▼ To identify three-dimensional figures

...And Why

You can recognize three-dimensional figures in architecture.

Here's How

Look for questions that
- 🔡 build understanding
- ✔ check understanding

THINK AND DISCUSS

Figures, such as those modeled by the Houston skyline buildings below, do not lie in a plane. These figures are called **three-dimensional figures.** The flat surfaces are called **faces.**

A **prism** is a three-dimensional figure with two parallel and congruent polygonal faces. In a prism, these faces are called **bases.** You name a prism by the shape of its bases. When you draw a prism, use dashed lines to show segments you cannot see.

■ EXAMPLE

Name the prism shown.

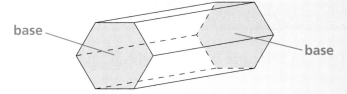

base — base

Each base is a hexagon. So the figure is a hexagonal prism.

1. ✓*Try It Out*
   Name each prism.

   a.

   b.

   c.

   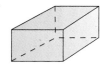

An **edge** is a segment where two faces meet. A **vertex** is a point where edges meet. A **cube** is a prism with six congruent faces.

2. How many faces, edges, and vertices are in the figure?

3. How many faces are "hidden from view" in this drawing?

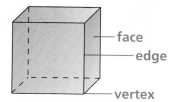

A **pyramid** has one polygonal base. You name a pyramid by the shape of its base.

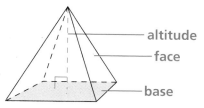

4. ✓*Try It Out* What name would you give each pyramid?

a. b. c.

5. ⬛*Draw a Conclusion* What shape is any face of a pyramid that is not the base?

Some three-dimensional figures do not have polygonal faces. A cylinder has two circular, parallel, and congruent bases. A cone has one circular base and one vertex. A sphere has no base.

cylinder   cone   sphere

6. ⬛*Analyze* How are a cylinder and a cone alike? How are they different?

Work Together

Work with a partner. A **net** is a pattern that you cut out and fold to form a three-dimensional figure.

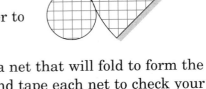

7. **a.** ▪*Predict* Name the three-dimensional figure you can form from the net shown.

b. Copy the net onto centimeter graph paper. Cut, fold, and tape it to check your answer to part (a).

8. ▪*Spatial Reasoning* Draw a net that will fold to form the figure given. Then cut, fold, and tape each net to check your answer.

a. rectangular prism **b.** triangular pyramid **c.** cylinder

---

EXERCISES *On Your Own*

Name each prism.

1. 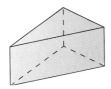 **2.** **3.** **4.**

Sketch each three-dimensional figure.

5. cylinder   **6.** rectangular prism   **7.** triangular pyramid   **8.** cone

9. square pyramid   **10.** cube   **11.** hexagonal prism   **12.** sphere

13. *Spatial Reasoning* How many of the following nets could you fold to form a box without a top? Which nets are these?

A.   **B.**   **C.**   **D.**

E.   **F.**   **G.**   **H.**

For each photo, identify the largest three-dimensional figure.

14.

15.

16.

17.

Spatial Reasoning **Name the figure you can form from each net.**

18.

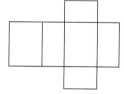

19.

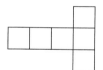

20.

21.

22. **a.** Identify the figure at the right.
    b. How many faces, edges, and vertices are in the figure?

23. *Writing* Describe, in your own words, a square pyramid.

24. **a.** What shape is each face of a cube?
    b. How do the lengths of the edges of a cube compare?

25. **Choose A, B, C, or D.** Which of the following is *not* a possible view of a cylinder?

A.

B.

C.

D.

Complete each sentence with *All*, *Some*, or *No*. *(Lesson 8-6)*

26. ▦ trapezoids are parallelograms.

27. ▦ rhombuses are rectangles.

28. ▦ rectangles are squares.

29. ▦ parallelograms are quadrilaterals.

30. Make a cutout of the letter K. Trace around the letter K. Draw a black dot on the letter K. Then show two rotated images of the letter K. *(Lesson 8-11)*

31. Mr. Dawson, the gardener, increased his sale of rose bushes this year by 20%. By what fraction did he increase his sales? *(Lesson 7-7)*

CHAPTER PROJECT

PROJECT LINK: DESIGNING

Design your own Web home page about yourself, your family, or your class. Neatly sketch the page. On a separate sheet, describe other Web pages to which your home page would be linked.

Math at Work

CARPENTER

If you like to work with your hands, you might find carpentry an interesting career. Carpenters use a wide array of tools such as power saws, planers, sanders, and lathes to shape raw wood into finished pieces. A good understanding of measurement and the ability to visualize in three dimensions are essential skills for a successful carpenter.

For more information about carpentry, visit the Prentice Hall Web site: www.phschool.com

Spatial Reasoning

After Lesson 9-6

Stack 6 cubes as shown at the right. The number of cubes you can "see" depends on how you look at the stacks.

From the front, you see

From the right side, you see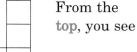

From the top, you see

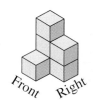

Front   Right

■ EXAMPLE

Use the drawings below. How many cubes are in a possible model?

Front View

Right Side View

Top View

Use blocks to make a model that matches each view. Count the blocks.

There are 11 blocks in this model although other models are possible.

Use blocks to create each group of blocks. Draw the front view, right side view, and top view of each group.

1.

2.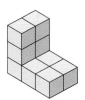

3.

Use the drawings below. How many cubes may be in each group?

4.

Front View   Right Side View   Top View

5.

Front View   Right Side View   Top View

Exploring Surface Area

THINK AND DISCUSS

The **surface area** (SA) of a rectangular prism is the sum of the areas of all the faces. A rectangular prism has three pairs of congruent sides or faces.

$$\text{Area of top} = \text{Area of bottom}$$
$$\text{Area of front} = \text{Area of back}$$
$$\text{Area of left side} = \text{Area of right side}$$

SURFACE AREA OF A RECTANGULAR PRISM

SA of a rectangular prism $= 2(\ell \times w) + 2(\ell \times h) + 2(w \times h)$

■ **EXAMPLE**   *Real-World Problem Solving*

Package Design Package designers want to find the surface area of the juice box below. Multiply each area by 2 and find the sum.

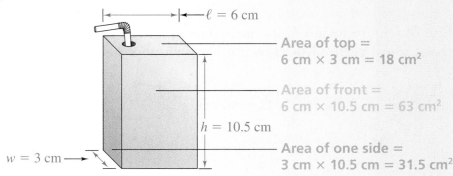

$\ell = 6$ cm

Area of top = 6 cm × 3 cm = 18 cm²

Area of front = 6 cm × 10.5 cm = 63 cm²

$h = 10.5$ cm

Area of one side = 3 cm × 10.5 cm = 31.5 cm²

$w = 3$ cm

Areas of top and bottom	+	Areas of front and back	+	Areas of other sides	=	Surface Area
$2(\ell \times w)$	+	$2(\ell \times h)$	+	$2(w \times h)$	=	▨
2(18)	+	2(63)	+	2(31.5)	=	▨
36	+	126	+	63	=	225

The surface area of the juice box is 225 cm².

1. ✓ *Try It Out* Find the surface area of each prism.

a.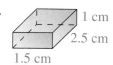
1 cm
2.5 cm
1.5 cm

b.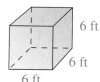
6 ft
6 ft
6 ft

c.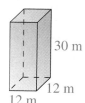
30 m
12 m
12 m

2. ⁙ *Think About It* How can you use a net to find the surface area of a rectangular prism? Explain.

3. a. What shape are the faces of the cube at right?

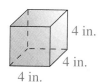
4 in.
4 in.
4 in.

   b. ⁙ *Reasoning* What shortcuts can you use to find the surface area of the prism shown?

   c. How would the surface area of the cube change if the length of the sides were doubled?

Work Together

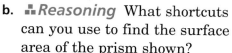

Finding Surface Area

Work with a partner to find the surface area of an object.

4. a. ⁙ *Open-ended* Select an object in your class that is a rectangular prism.

   b. ⁙ *Measurement* Measure the length, width, and height of the object.

   c. Make a three-dimensional sketch of the object. Label the length, width, and height.

   d. Find the surface area of the object.

EXERCISES *On Your Own*

Spatial Reasoning **Find the surface area of each figure. Each small cube measures 1 cm on a side.**

1.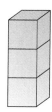

2.

3.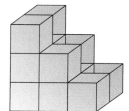

4.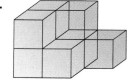

Name the prism you can build from each net. Find the surface area of each prism.

5.
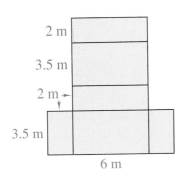
2 m
3.5 m
2 m
3.5 m
6 m

6.
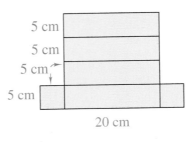
5 cm
5 cm
5 cm
5 cm
20 cm

7.
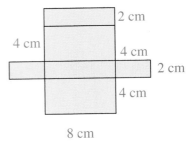
2 cm
4 cm
4 cm
2 cm
4 cm
8 cm

8. a. Draw a net that you could fold to form the rectangular prism at the right

b Find the surface area of the prism.

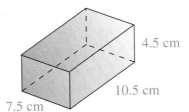
4.5 cm
10.5 cm
7.5 cm

▦ *Choose* **Use a calculator, paper and pencil, or mental math to find the surface area of each rectangular prism.**

9.
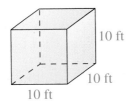
10 ft
10 ft
10 ft

10.
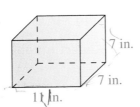
7 in.
7 in.
1 ḭ in.

11.
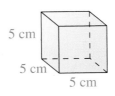
5 cm
5 cm
5 cm

12.
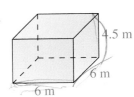
4.5 m
6 m
6 m

13.
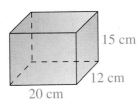
15 cm
12 cm
20 cm

14.
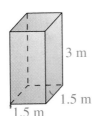
3 m
1.5 m
1.5 m

15.
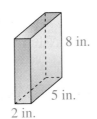
8 in.
5 in.
2 in.

16.
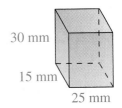
30 mm
15 mm
25 mm

17. Choose A, B, or C. Which whole piece of wrapping paper below can *not* be used to wrap the box at the right?

4 in.
9 in.
15 in.

A.
20 in.

28 in.

B.
36 in.

18 in.

C.
40 in.
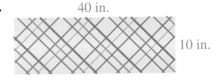
10 in.

18. Construction You have been hired to paint the walls in the room shown below.

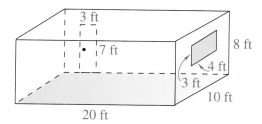

   a. Find the area of the two walls that do not have doors or windows.

   b. Find the total area of the surface you will paint on the other two walls. (Assume that you will not paint the door or the window.)

   c. What is the surface area of the region you will paint?

   d. A gallon of paint covers about 400 ft^2. How many gallons do you need?

19. Writing Suppose you know the area of the top, front, and one side of a rectangular prism. How can you find its surface area?

20. Reasoning The surface area of the cube shown at the right is 24 cm^2. What is the length of each edge?

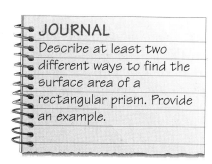

JOURNAL

Describe at least two different ways to find the surface area of a rectangular prism. Provide an example.

Mixed Review

21. Use the parallelogram at the right. Show four different ways in which the figure can be cut into congruent parts. *(Lesson 8-8)*

A scale model measures 3 cm × 5 cm. Find the dimensions of the actual object with the given scale. *(Lesson 7-5)*

22. 1 cm : 3 cm   **23.** 4 cm : 6 m   **24.** 1 cm : 0.5 m   **25.** 1 mm : 1 km

26. Choose a Strategy Ms. Spencer bought a rake for $9.00, a lawn mower for $250.00, and three garden hoses. She spent a total of $284.50. How much did she pay for each garden hose?

9-8 Volume of a Rectangular Prism

What You'll Learn

▼ To find the volume of a rectangular prism

▼ To find a missing dimension of a rectangular prism

...And Why

You can find the volume of everyday objects such as cereal boxes.

Here's How

Look for questions that
- build understanding
- ✔ check understanding

Work Together

Discovering Volume

Spatial Reasoning Work with a partner.

1. a. **Open-ended** Find the number of centimeter cubes that would fit inside a small box.

   b. **Summarize** Describe the method you used.

2. Next use the centimeter cubes to build rectangular prisms. Use the dimensions in the table. After you have built each prism, count how many cubes the prism contains. Copy and complete the table.

3. a. *Patterns* Look at your completed table. How do the length, width, and height of a prism relate to the total number of cubes?

   b. Write a formula for finding the number of cubes within a rectangular prism.

Length ℓ	Width w	Height h	Number of Cubes
3	4	2	24
5	6	4	
8	1	3	
4	4	4	
6	3	6	

THINK AND DISCUSS

▼ *Finding Volume*

The **volume** of a three-dimensional figure is the number of cubic units needed to fill the space inside the figure.

Volume = length × width × height

$$V = \ell w h$$

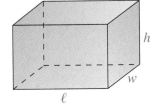

Area measures two dimensions, *length* and *width*, in square units. Volume measures three dimensions, *length*, *width*, and *height*, in cubic units, such as cubic centimeters (cm^3), cubic meters (m^3), or cubic inches ($in.^3$).

■ EXAMPLE 1   *Real-World Problem Solving*

Food Find the volume of the cereal box shown. Use the formula $V = \ell w h$.

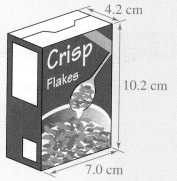

$$V = \ell \times w \times h$$

$$V = 7.0 \times 4.2 \times 10.2 = 299.88$$

The volume is 299.88 cm^3, or about 300 cm^3.

4. ✓**Try It Out** Find the volume of each rectangular prism with the given dimensions.
   a. $\ell = 8$ ft, $w = 7$ ft, $h = 10$ ft
   b. $\ell = 4$ cm, $w = 2.5$ cm, $h = 7$ cm

▼2 *Finding a Dimension*

If you know the volume and two dimensions of a prism, you can find the third dimension.

■ EXAMPLE 2

The volume of a rectangular prism is 105 $in.^3$ The height of the prism is 5 in. The length is 7 in. Find the missing dimension.

$$V = \ell \times w \times h \qquad \longleftarrow \text{Use the volume formula.}$$
$$105 = 7 \times w \times 5 \qquad \longleftarrow \text{Substitute.}$$
$$105 = 35w$$
$$\frac{105}{35} = \frac{35w}{35} \qquad \longleftarrow \text{Divide each side by 35.}$$
$$w = 3$$

Check: $105 = 7 \times 3 \times 5$ ✓

The missing dimension is the width. The width is 3 in.

5. ✓*Try It Out* Find the missing dimension for each prism.
 a. $V = 180$ cm^3, $w = 4$ cm, $h = 9$ cm
 b. $V = 168$ m^3, $w = 2$ m, $\ell = 7$ m
 c. $V = 336$ ft^3, $\ell = 8$ ft, $h = 6$ ft

6. ▪*Reasoning* The volume of a rectangular prism is 36 m^3.
 The area of the base is 9 m^2. What is the height of the prism?

EXERCISES *On Your Own*

1. Choose A, B, C, or D. Each cube of the rectangular prism at
 the right measures 1 cm on each side. If the top level of cubes
 is removed, what is the volume of the remaining prism?

 A. 45 cm^3 **B.** 60 cm^3 **C.** 48 cm^3 **D.** 40 cm^3

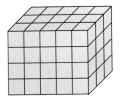

Find the volume of each rectangular prism.

2.
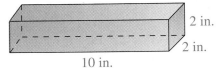
2 in.
2 in.
10 in.

3.
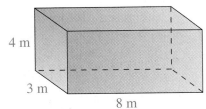
4 m
3 m
8 m

4.
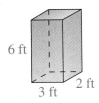
6 ft
3 ft
2 ft

5.
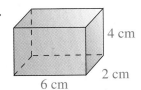
4 cm
2 cm
6 cm

6.
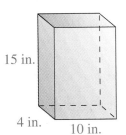
15 in.
4 in.
10 in.

7.
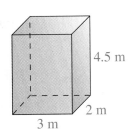
4.5 m
2 m
3 m

8.
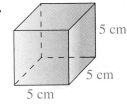
5 cm
5 cm
5 cm

Mental Math **Find the volume of the rectangular prism
with the given dimensions.**

9. $\ell = 6$ ft, $w = 1$ ft, $h = 7$ ft

10. $\ell = 2$ in., $w = 6$ in., $h = 5$ in.

11. $\ell = 10$ ft, $w = 4$ ft, $h = 8$ ft

12. $\ell = 6$ yd, $w = 9$ yd, $h = 10$ yd

13. *Writing* How could you write the formula for the volume of
 a cube in a different way than $V = \ell wh$? Explain.

Find the volume of each rectangular prism with the given dimensions.

14. $\ell = 5$ mm, $w = 4$ mm, $h = 9$ mm

15. $\ell = 14$ cm, $w = 7$ cm, $h = 2.5$ cm

16. $\ell = 2.4$ m, $w = 3.1$ m, $h = 5.4$ m

17. $\ell = 4$ mm, $w = 4$ mm, $h = 7$ mm

18. $\ell = 1.5$ mm, $w = 1.5$ mm, $h = 4$ mm

19. $\ell = 5$ cm, $w = 8$ cm, $h = 11$ cm

20. *Swimming Pools* A swimming pool is 24 m long and 16 m wide. The average depth of the water is 2.5 m.
   a. What is the volume of the water?
   b. *Measurement* Units of capacity such as liters (L) are used to measure the volume of liquids. A volume of 1 m^3 is equivalent to 1,000 L. What is the capacity, in liters, of the swimming pool?

21. Choose A, B, C, or D. A rectangular prism is 2 m long, 50 cm wide, and 1 m high. What is its volume?
   A. 100 m^3
   B. 100 cm^3
   C. 1 m^3
   D. $10,000$ cm^3

22. *Draw a Conclusion* How do the volumes of these prisms compare? How do the surface areas compare?

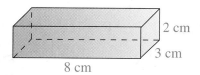
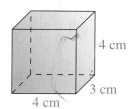

The volume and two dimensions of a rectangular prism are given. Find the third dimension.

23. $V = 154$ yd^3, $h = 11$ yd, $w = 2$ yd

24. $V = 120$ cm^3, $w = 4$ cm, $h = 6$ cm

25. $V = 108$ ft^3, $\ell = 6$ ft, $w = 2$ ft

26. $V = 140$ ft^3, $w = 4$ ft, $h = 7$ ft

27. $V = 180$ in.^{3}, $w = 3$ in., $h = 12$ in.

28. $V = 256$ cm^3, $\ell = 8$ cm, $w = 4$ cm

Number Sense **Find the whole-number dimensions of all possible prisms that have the given volume.**

29. $V = 32$ cm^3

30. $V = 48$ cm^3

31. $V = 54$ m^3

32. $V = 24$ in.^{3}

33. *Reasoning* A ton of coal fills a bin that is 3 ft by 4 ft by 4 ft. Find the dimensions of a bin that would hold 2 tons.

Mixed Review

Find the missing length in each circle. *(Lesson 8-10)*

34. $d = \blacksquare$ cm, $r = 13$ cm   **35.** $d = 142$ ft, $r = \blacksquare$ ft   **36.** $d = \blacksquare$ m, $r = 37$ m

Find each quotient. *(Lesson 6-9)*

37. $3\frac{5}{8} \div \frac{1}{2}$ **38.** $12 \div 3\frac{3}{4}$ **39.** $16\frac{4}{5} \div \frac{3}{5}$ **40.** $4\frac{1}{6} \div \frac{1}{3}$ **41.** $2\frac{1}{4} \div \frac{1}{8}$

42. *Gardening* Lahela has a rectangular vegetable garden with an area of 15 ft². If the width of the garden is $2\frac{1}{2}$ ft, what is the length of the garden? *(Lesson 9-2)*

✓ CHECKPOINT 2 *Lessons 9-4 through 9-8*

Find the circumference of each circle. Round each answer to the nearest unit. Find the area of each circle. Round each answer to the nearest tenth of a unit.

1.
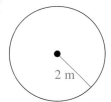
2 m

2.

13 in.

3.
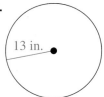
6 km

Identify each three-dimensional figure.

4.

5.

6.

7.

Find the surface area and volume of each figure.

8.
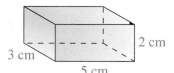
3 cm   2 cm   5 cm

9.
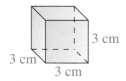
3 cm   3 cm   3 cm

10.
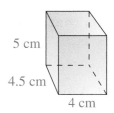
5 cm   4.5 cm   4 cm

PROBLEM SOLVING PRACTICE

Choose the best answer.

1. An odometer on a car measured the distance between two cities as 163.9 miles. What is this distance rounded to the nearest ten?

   A. 160 miles   **B.** 163 miles
   C. 164 miles   **D.** 170 miles

2. A circular mirror has a diameter of 12 inches. What is the circumference of the mirror rounded to the nearest inch? Use 3.14 for π.

   F. 24 in.   **G.** 38 in.
   H. 113 in.   **J.** 452 in.

3. If the ratio of dogs to cats in a kennel is exactly 3 to 2, then the kennel could have —

   A. 9 dogs and 4 cats
   B. 4 dogs and 6 cats
   C. 12 dogs and 8 cats
   D. 15 dogs and 8 cats

4. What is the perimeter of a rectangular pen that is 10 feet wide by 20 feet long?

   F. 30 ft   **G.** 60 ft
   H. 200 ft   **J.** 400 ft

5. Look at the drawing of a fish below. Which drawing shows a reflection of the fish?

   A.   **B.**

   C.   **D.**

6. Suppose you are cutting out geometric shapes to make a collage. Which of the following figures are *always* similar?

   F. two triangles
   G. two rectangles
   H. two squares
   J. two parallelograms

Please note that items 7 and 8 each have *five* answer choices.

7. Aldo made a scale drawing of his room. The room is 12 feet long by 9 feet wide. He used the scale 1 inch : 6 feet. Find the dimensions of the scale drawing.

   A. 72 feet by 63 feet
   B. 72 inches by 63 inches
   C. 2 feet by $1\frac{1}{2}$ feet
   D. 2 inches by $1\frac{1}{2}$ inches
   E. Not Here

8. Sampson plans to carpet the patio around the pool. Which procedure should he use to find the shaded area?

   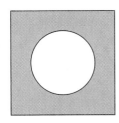

   F. Find the area of the square and add the area of the circle.
   G. Find the area of the square and subtract the area of the circle.
   H. Find the area of the square and subtract the circumference of the circle.
   J. Find the perimeter of the square and add the area of the circle.
   K. Find the perimeter of both figures.

9-9

Make a Model

Problem Solving Strategies

Draw a Diagram
Guess and Test
Look for a Pattern
✔ Make a Model
Make a Table
Simulate a Problem
Solve a Simpler Problem
Too Much or Too Little
 Information
Use Logical Reasoning
Use Multiple Strategies
Work Backward

THINK AND DISCUSS

Sometimes words are not enough to help you visualize a problem. A physical model can help you solve problems. Architects and engineers make models to help solve problems.

SAMPLE PROBLEM..

Danica collects pennies. She keeps her pennies in a box. The dimensions of the inside of the box are 21 cm wide by 30 cm long by 21 cm high. About how many pennies will the box hold?

READ

Read for understanding. Summarize the problem.

1. Think about the information you are given and what you are asked to find.
   a. What does the problem ask you to find?
   b. Are you given all the information you need? What else do you need to know?

PLAN

Decide on a strategy.

Making a model will help you solve the problem. If you have some pennies, you can model how many pennies are needed to form one layer that fits inside the bottom of the box. Make a model of the box by drawing a rectangle 21 cm wide and 30 cm long.

2. You can stack pennies to find how many layers might fit in the box. Do you need to have a stack of pennies 21 cm high in order to find out how many layers will fit in the box? Why or why not?

SOLVE

Try the strategy.

3. Work with your group to make models you can measure.
   a. How many pennies can you fit in a row 21 cm long?
   b. How many pennies will fit in a stack of pennies 21 cm high?

4. a. How many pennies will fit in one layer?
   b. About how many pennies will fit in the box?

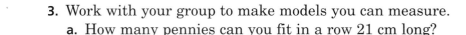

5. How reasonable is your final estimate for the number of pennies that will fit in the box? Explain.

EXERCISES *On Your Own*

Make a model to solve each problem.

1. *Coins* Lincoln's head is right-side-up on the penny on the left. If you roll the penny halfway around the other penny, will Lincoln's head be right-side-up, upside-down, or neither?

2. *Woodworking* It takes Clara 12 min to cut a log into 4 pieces. How long will it take her to cut a log that is the same size into 5 pieces?

3. *Jobs* Chris works in a grocery store after school. He stacked grapefruit in the shape of a square pyramid. There was one grapefruit on the top level, four on the next level, and nine on the next level. If there were eight levels in all, how many grapefruit did Chris stack?

Use any strategy to solve each problem. Show all your work.

4. *Gardening* Todd planted 60 seeds in his garden. Not all of the seeds grew into plants. Thirty more seeds grew into plants than did not grow at all. How many of the 60 seeds grew into plants?

5. *Geometry* A square game board is 16 in. long and 16 in. wide. A square that measures 2 in. × 2 in. is cut from each corner of the board. What is the perimeter of the original game board? Of the new game board?

6. *Savings* Maria is saving her money to buy some basketball shoes that cost $72. She has $17 right now. Each week Maria earns $12 by mowing her neighbor's lawn. In how many weeks will she be able to buy the shoes?

7. Jafar's birthday cake is cube shaped, with icing on the top and four sides. He cut it as shown at the right.

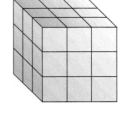

   a. How many cuts did Jafar make?

   b. Into how many pieces did he cut the cake?

   c. *Spatial Reasoning* How many of the pieces did not have any icing?

8. a. *Patterns* Find three numbers that continue the pattern.

           1, 2, 4, ▨, ▨, ▨

   b. Find another three numbers that continue the pattern in a different way.

9. *Geometry* What are the whole-number dimensions of the rectangular prism with a volume of 12 cubic units and the greatest possible surface area?

10. *Literature* The numbered pages in the book *Why Do Clocks Run Clockwise?* run from 1 to 251. How many of these page numbers contain at least one number 2?

11. Rachel wants to make a fenced rectangular area in her backyard for her dog Jesse. She has 36 m of fencing. What are the whole-number dimensions (in meters) of the different rectangular regions she can fence?

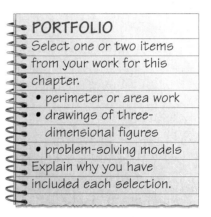

PORTFOLIO

Select one or two items from your work for this chapter.
 • perimeter or area work
 • drawings of three-dimensional figures
 • problem-solving models
Explain why you have included each selection.

Mixed Review

How many lines of symmetry does each figure have?
(Lesson 8-9)

12.   **13.**   **14.**   **15.** ⬭

Write each statement as a percent. *(Lesson 7-6)*

16. 10 boys in a class of 25   **17.** 7 silk scarves out of 21   **18.** 15 tables out of 50

19. Draw three collinear points and four noncollinear points.
(Lesson 8-1)

20. *Choose a Strategy* A local bus picked up 3 passengers at its first stop. At every stop thereafter, it picked up 2 more passengers than at the previous stop. How many passengers got on at the fifth stop?

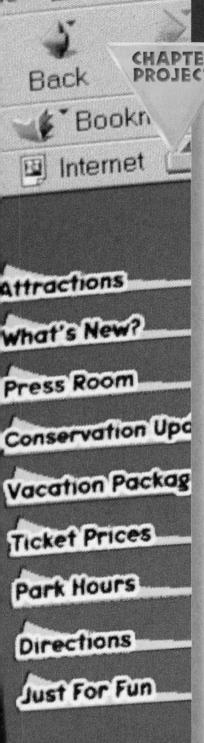

Home on the Web

Design a Home Page Project Links on pages 391, 402, 407, and 412 can help you work on the different parts of your project. Here is a checklist to help you gather together those parts.

- ✔ diagrams of two Web pages you evaluated
- ✔ calculations that show the measurement of areas on the home page
- ✔ calculations that show the percent of text and graphics on each page
- ✔ a sketch of the Web page you designed, with descriptions of its links to other Web pages

Prepare a presentation that explains what you learned from analyzing Web pages. Describe how you used what you learned to design your own home page. What factors other than space use affect the quality of a Web page?

Reflect and Revise

Exchange home pages with other students. Did the pages you and your classmates created use space better than the Web pages you studied? Make changes to improve your home page.

Web Extension

Prentice Hall's Internet site contains information you might find helpful as you complete your project. Visit www.phschool.com/mgm1/ch9 for some links and ideas related to the World Wide Web.

Perimeter and Area of Polygons
9-1, 9-2, 9-3

Perimeter is the distance around a figure.

Area is the number of square units inside a figure. The formula for area of a parallelogram is $A = bh$. The formula for area of a triangle is $A = \frac{1}{2}bh$.

1. Estimate the area of the figure. Assume each square represents 1 m^2.

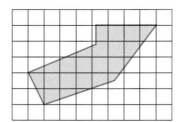

2. Find the area and perimeter of the parallelogram.

1.5 cm   2 cm   9 cm

3. A rectangular yard has an area of 72 m^2. One side is 8 m long. How much fence do you need to enclose the entire yard?

4. Find the area of a triangle with a base 12 cm and height 7.6 cm.

Circumference and Area of Circles
9-4, 9-5

Use the symbol π to stand for the ratio $\frac{\text{circumference}}{\text{diameter}}$. The formula for the area of a circle is $A = \pi r^2$.

Find the circumference of each circle with the given radius or diameter. Round each answer to the nearest unit.

5. $r = 6$ in.   6. $r = 3.8$ m   7. $d = 24.5$ cm   8. $d = 37.6$ ft

Calculator **Find the area of each circle. Round each answer to the nearest tenth of a unit.**

9.

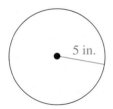

5 in.

10.

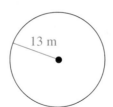

13 m

11.

4.7 m

Three-Dimensional Figures

Three-dimensional figures are figures such as boxes, cans, and buildings that do not lie in a plane. Most three-dimensional figures have flat, polygonal surfaces called **faces**. Where two faces meet, the resulting segment is called an **edge**. Each point where edges meet is a **vertex**.

A **prism** is a three-dimensional figure with two parallel and congruent polygonal faces, called **bases**. A prism is named for the shape of its base.

12. a. Identify the figure at the right.

    b. Find the number of faces, edges, and vertices.

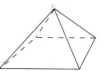

13. *Writing* Give a description of a rectangular prism.

Surface Area and Volume

The **surface area** of a rectangular prism is the sum of the areas of all its faces.

The **volume** of a three-dimensional figure is the number of cubic units needed to fill the space inside the figure. The formula for the volume of a rectangular prism is $V = \ell wh$.

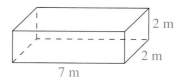

14. Find the surface area and the volume of the rectangular prism at the right.

15. Choose A, B, C, or D. Which could not be the dimensions of a rectangular prism with a volume of 60 m^3?

    A. 1 m by 1 m by 60 m   **B.** 4 m by 15 m by 2 m

    C. 3 m by 4 m by 5 m   **D.** 1 m by 6 m by 10 m

Problem Solving Strategies

Sometimes making a model can help you solve a problem.

16. You have 12 square tables. One person can sit on each side. You need to arrange the tables so that at least one side of each table is touching another table. How many people can you seat?

17. Suppose you have a heavy 3-ft wide cube with the letter K on top. If you flip the cube end over end in one straight line over a distance of 18 feet, where will the letter K end up? Draw a picture to show the path and final position of the letter K.

1. Find the area of the figure below. Assume that each square represents 1 cm^2.

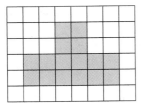

2. Find the area and perimeter of a square with sides 6 m.

3. The perimeter of a rectangle is 32 ft. One dimension is 9 ft. Find the area.

4. Find the area of the figure below.

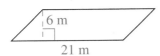

6 m
21 m

5. Find the area of a parallelogram with base 12 cm and height 7 cm.

6. Find the area of a triangle with base 9.2 m and height 19.3 m.

7. Find the area of the triangle below.

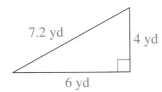

7.2 yd
4 yd
6 yd

8. *Writing* Which is larger: a pie plate with a radius of 5 in., or a pie plate with a diameter of 9 in.? Explain.

9. What is the surface area of a box with length 8 ft, width 5 ft, and height 4 ft?

10. Find the circumference of a circle with the given radius or diameter. Round to the nearest unit.
    a. r = 10 km
    b. d = 12 cm
    c. d = 7.4 yd
    d. r = 27 m

11. a. Identify the figure at the right.
    b. Find the number of faces, edges, and vertices.

12. A rectangular prism is 17 m long, 3 m wide, and 5 m high. Find its volume.

13. The volume of a rectangular prism is 504 cm^3. The area of the base is 72 cm^2. Find the height of the prism.

14. The volume and two dimensions of a rectangular prism are given. Find the third dimension.
    a. V = 189 cm^3, h = 7 cm, w = 3 cm
    b. V = 1,080 in.^{3}, h = 15 in., w = 6 in.
    c. V = 360 ft^3, h = 9 ft, w = 4 ft

15. **Choose A, B, C, or D.** Which could be a net for a cube with an open top?

    A.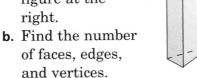
    B.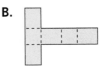

    C.
    D.

Choose the best answer.

1. To the nearest tenth of a unit, what is the area of a circle with a 6-cm diameter?

   A. 12.0 cm^2 B. 28.3 cm^2

   C. 36.0 cm^2 D. 113.4 cm^2

2. What is the median cost of peanut butter per serving? Use the table below.

Peanut Butter Prices (3 tbsp serving)	
Sticky Stuff	22¢
Grandma's Choice	20¢
Shop Along	19¢
All Natural	22¢
Cityside	14¢
Nutty Taste	22¢

   A. 20¢   B. 20.5¢

   C. 21¢   D. 22¢

3. What do you do first to evaluate the expression $3.9 + 4.1 \times 16 - 6 \div 4.8$?

   A. Add 3.9 and 4.1.

   B. Multiply 4.1 by 16.

   C. Subtract 6 from 16.

   D. Divide 6 by 4.8.

4. Find the volume of the open box made by folding the sides of the net below.

   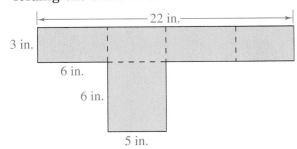

   A. 14 in.^{3} B. 66 in.^{3}

   C. 90 in.^{3} D. 165 in.^{3}

5. Which is a good estimate of the quotient $358.2 \div 0.67$?

   A. 50   B. 60

   C. 500   D. 6,000

6. Which is the GCF of 20, 35, and 100?

   A. 5   B. 10   C. 100   D. 700

7. Which equation is *not* an example of the distributive property?

   A. $12(6.2) + 12(3.8) = 12(6.2 + 3.8)$

   B. $0.75(8.869) + 0.25(8.869) = 1(8.869)$

   C. $19.1(80) = 19.1(100) - 19.1(20)$

   D. $8.1(1.9 + 3.5) = (8.1 + 1.9)(3.5)$

8. Which display would you use to show your height for each year since birth?

   A. line plot   B. line graph

   C. pictograph   D. circle graph

9. Which statement is false?

   A. A nonrectangular parallelogram and a rectangle can have the same area.

   B. A square is always a parallelogram.

   C. You can divide a parallelogram into two congruent triangles.

   D. Two rectangles with the same area always have the same perimeter.

10. The difference between two fractions is $2\frac{7}{12}$. Which fractions might have been used?

    A. $4\frac{1}{3}$ and $2\frac{11}{12}$

    B. $4\frac{1}{4}$ and $1\frac{2}{3}$

    C. $4\frac{2}{3}$ and $2\frac{11}{12}$

    D. $4\frac{1}{2}$ and $1\frac{3}{4}$

10

Algebra: Integers and Graphing

WHAT YOU WILL LEARN IN THIS CHAPTER

- How to model addition and subtraction of integers

- How to graph functions

- How to create and use a coordinate system

The TIME of your life

Do you know an older person who has lived an interesting life? That person could probably tell you a lot of stories about his or her life, but you could tell stories about your life, too. You may not have lived as long, but there have been important times in your life, and there will be other important times in your future.

Draw a Time Line Your project will be to build a time line of your life—past and future. Think about time lines you have seen in your social studies classes. You will get a chance to apply math skills such as ratios, measurements, scale drawings, and integers.

Steps to help you complete the project:

- **How to use multiple strategies to solve problems**

PROBLEM SOLVING

What You'll Learn

▼ To graph integers on a number line

▼ To compare and order integers

...And Why

You can use integers in sports such as football and golf.

Here's How

Look for questions that

• build understanding

✔ check understanding

QUICKreview

To graph a number on a number line, draw a point at that number.

THINK AND DISCUSS

▼ Positive and Negative Numbers

Suppose you are playing football and your team moves 4 yd forward. You can say your new position is *positive* 4 yd, or +4 yd. If your team gets pushed back 3 yd, your new position is *negative* 3 yd, or −3 yd.

You can graph these numbers on a number line.

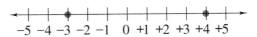

1. ✔*Try It Out* Write negative 5 as a number. Then draw a number line and graph negative 5.

2. On the same number line, graph the numbers −1, 3, and 0.

The numbers . . . −3, −2, −1, 0, +1, +2, +3, . . . are **integers.**

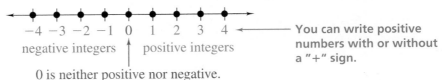

negative integers   positive integers

You can write positive numbers with or without a "+" sign.

0 is neither positive nor negative.

Two numbers that are the same distance from 0 on a number line, but in different directions, are **opposites.**

■ EXAMPLE 1

Name the opposite of 3.

3 and −3 are both 3 units from zero.

The opposite of 3 is −3.

3. ✔*Try It Out* Name the opposite of each integer.

    a. 4   **b.** −6   **c.** 15   **d.** 8   **e.** −120   **f.** 32

4. 🔸*Open-ended* Name two integers that are opposites. How far from 0 is each integer?

5. a. What is the opposite of positive nine yards in football?
   b. Write the numbers from part (a) as integers.

 You can use the ⊞ key to write the opposite of a number.

$$5 \;\boxed{+/-} \rightarrow -5 \qquad\qquad 5 \;\boxed{+/-}\;\boxed{+/-} \rightarrow 5$$

6. ✔*Try It Out* A calculator displays -12. Suppose you press the ⊞ key. What will the calculator display?

7. 🔸*Explain* Why do you think the ⊞ key is called the "change-sign" key?

QUICKreview

The values of numbers on a number line increase as you move from left to right.

▼ *Comparing and Ordering Integers*

In golf, scores are related to an established number of strokes called *par*. A score of 1 *under* par can be represented as -1. A score of 3 *over* par can be represented as 3.

■ **EXAMPLE 2**   *Real-World Problem Solving*

Golf Suppose your golf score is 1 under par (-1). Your friend's score is 5 under par (-5). Who has the lower score?

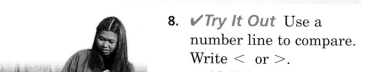

-5 is to the left of -1.
Therefore, $-5 < -1$ or $-1 > -5$.

Your friend's score of -5 is the lower score.

8. ✔*Try It Out* Use a number line to compare. Write $<$ or $>$.
   a. 10 ▦ 6
   b. -7 ▦ 0
   c. 3 ▦ -4
   d. -13 ▦ -11

9. ⚕*Reasoning* Complete with *always*, *sometimes*, or *never*.

   a. 0 is ▓ greater than a negative integer.

   b. 0 is ▓ greater than a positive integer.

   c. A negative integer is ▓ less than another negative integer.

■ **EXAMPLE 3**   *Real-World Problem Solving*

Golf The table shows the scores of five golfers in a professional tournament. Order the scores from least to greatest.

Golfer	Score
Jonathan Lomas	2
Tiger Woods	0
Padraig Harrington	−4
Greg Norman	3
Shigeki Maruyama	−2

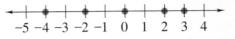

← Graph each score on a number line.

−4, −2, 0, 2, 3 ← Write the scores from left to right.

In order from least to greatest, the scores are −4, −2, 0, 2, and 3.

10. ✔*Try It Out* Order from least to greatest: 7, −4, 11, 0, −8.

EXERCISES *On Your Own*

Name the integer that is represented by each point.

1. *M*   **2.** *N*

3. *P*   **4.** *Q*

5. Graph these integers on a number line: 6, −9, 7, −1, 0, 3.

Write an integer to represent each situation.

6. earnings of $25   **7.** 14 degrees below zero   **8.** a debt of $100

9. At 1,565 ft deep, the Carlsbad Caverns are the United States' deepest caves.

10. *Geography* Mt. Whitney in California has an elevation of 4,418 m.

Name the opposite of each integer.

11. 13   **12.** −8   **13.** 150   **14.** −212   **15.** −1   **16.** 3,999

17. Name three pairs of situations that are opposites. For example, walk up two stairs and walk down two stairs.

18. *Writing* Describe what integers and opposites are. Include number lines in your descriptions.

▦ *Calculator* **Name the integer that results from each key sequence.**

19. 8 ⊡

20. 9 ⊡ ⊡

21. 6 ⊡ ⊡ ⊡

22. *Weather* List the temperatures from least to greatest.

- Normal body temperature is about 37°C.

- An average winter day on the polar icecap is −25°C.

- The warmest day ever in Canada was 45°C.

- Water freezes at 0°C. Ski resorts can make artificial snow at this temperature.

- The coldest day ever in Alaska was −62°C.

Compare. Write <, >, or =.

23. −7 ▦ 2

24. −12 ▦ −9

25. −17 ▦ −23

26. −4 ▦ 2

27. 0 ▦ −8

28. 1 ▦ −7

29. −12 ▦ −5

30. −3 ▦ −7

Order from least to greatest.

31. −2, 3, 4, −1

32. 3, −2, 0, −7

33. 4, −5, −2, 3, −1

34. −10, 8, 0, −6, 5

Open-ended **Name an integer between the given integers.**

35. −7, 3

36. 0, −6

37. −5, −13

38. −1, 2

39. −9, 0

Mixed Review

Find the area of each circle. *(Lesson 9-5)*

40. $r = 6$ in.

41. $d = 24$ mm

42. $r = 7$ m

43. $d = 11$ in.

44. $r = 8.5$ mm

45. *Choose a Strategy* Tina has an appointment at 8:15 A.M. tomorrow. She wants to arrive at least 10 minutes early. It takes her one hour to get ready and 35 minutes to drive there. What time should Tina plan to get up?

Inequalities and Absolute Values

You can use a number line to show *inequalities* and *absolute values*.

Karen bikes more than 2 mi but less than 3 mi. Frank bikes 3 mi or more. These distances can be described as *inequalities*.

You can write an inequality as a statement that compares two expressions.

Symbols

$<$ means *is less than*.
$\leq$ means *is less than or is equal to*.
$>$ means *is greater than*.
$\geq$ means *is greater than or is equal to*.

■ EXAMPLE 1

Write and graph the distances biked by Karen and Frank.

$$2 < d < 3 \qquad\qquad d \geq 3 \qquad \longleftarrow \text{Let } d = \text{distance.}$$

 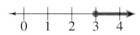

An *open* dot means the number *is not* included.

A *closed* dot means the number *is* included.

The *absolute value* of a number is its distance, in either direction, from zero on a number line. Since direction does not matter, there are no negative absolute values.

The symbol for absolute value is a vertical rule before and after a number. For example: $|-10|$

■ EXAMPLE 2

Find $|-2|$.

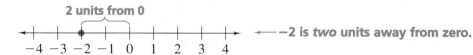

2 units from 0

$\longleftarrow$ –2 is *two* units away from zero.

Therefore, $|-2| = 2$.

Graph each inequality.

1. $x > 3$ **2.** $x \leq 3$ **3.** $x < 0$ **4.** $x \geq -1$ **5.** $x < -2$

Find each value.

6. $|-4|$ **7.** $|17|$ **8.** $|-65|$ **9.** $|0|$ **10.** $|-2|$ **11.** $|180|$

10-2

Modeling Integers

What You'll Learn

▼ To use models to represent positive integers, negative integers, and zero

...And Why

Modeling will help you add and subtract integers.

Here's How

Look for questions that
∴ build understanding
✔ check understanding

THINK AND DISCUSS

You can use colored tiles to model integers. Yellow tiles represent positive integers. Red tiles represent negative integers.

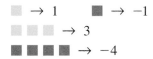

1. ∴*Modeling* What integer is represented by each set of tiles?
   a. ■■
   b. ▨▨▨▨▨▨▨
   c. ▨▨▨▨▨▨
   d. ■■■■■

2. Which integers in Question 1 are opposites?

3. ∴*Draw a Conclusion* What do you notice about the sets of tiles that represent a number and its opposite?

4. ✔*Try It Out* Use tiles to model each integer and its opposite.
   a. 4   b. −3   c. 2   d. −8

Suppose you earned $1 and then spent $1. Then ▨ represents the $1 that you earned, and ■ represents the $1 that you spent. You have *no more or less* money than before.

These tiles are a *zero pair*. ⟶

5. ∴*What If . . .* Suppose you have seven positive tiles. How many negative tiles do you need to represent zero?

6. Suppose you have ten negative tiles. How many positive tiles do you need to represent zero?

7. Suppose you have four positive tiles and two negative tiles. How many tiles of each color do you need to represent zero?

You can use pairs of tiles that represent zero to write integers when you have tiles of both colors together.

■ **EXAMPLE**

Write the integer that is represented by ■ ■ ■ ■ ■ ▫ ▫ .

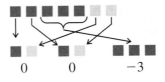

Group the pairs of tiles ← that represent zero.
Then remove them.

0   0   −3

■ ■ ■ ■ ■ ▫ ▫ = −3 ← Write the integer that the remaining tiles represent.

8. ✔*Try It Out* Write the integer that is represented by the tiles.

a. ■ ■ ■ ▫ ▫

b. ■ ■ ■
   ■ ■ ▫

c. ■ ■ ■ ▫
   ▫ ▫ ▫ ▫
   ▫ ▫ ▫ ▫

9. a. What integer is represented by ■ ■ ▫ ▫ ▫ ▫ ?
   b. What integer is represented by ▫ ▫ ▫ ▫ ▫ ■ ■ ■ ?
   c. How do the answers to parts (a) and (b) compare?
   d. ⁂*Writing* How many ways are there to represent an integer with tiles? Explain.

EXERCISES *On Your Own*

Modeling **Model each integer and its opposite.**

1. −2   2. 6   3. −4   4. 1   5. −5   6. 9

Write the integer that is represented by each set of tiles.

7. ▫ ▫ ▫
   ■ ■
   ■

8. ■ ■ ▫ ▫
   ▫ ▫ ▫ ▫
   ■ ▫ ▫

9. ■ ■ ■ ▫
   ■ ■ ▫
   ■ ▫ ▫

10. ■ ■ ▫
    ▫ ▫ ▫
    ■

11. ▫ ▫ ▫ ▫
    ▫ ■ ■ ▫

12. ■ ■ ■
    ▫ ■ ▫
    ■ ▫

13. ■
    ■ ■ ■ ▫
    ■

14. ■ ■ ■ ▫
    ■ ▫ ▫
    ■ ■

15. *Writing* Explain how you can use tiles to represent integers. Include examples and diagrams.

Modeling **Model each integer in two ways.**

16. 1   **17.** −7   **18.** 0   **19.** −1   **20.** 5   **21.** −3

22. Choose A, B, C, or D. Which of the integers modeled is *not* equal to the others?

    A. ■ ■   **B.** ▨   **C.** ▨ ■ ▨   **D.** ■ ■ ▨ ▨ ▨

23. *Modeling* Write the integer that is represented by each combination.
    a. 3 negative tiles and 7 positive tiles
    b. 12 negative tiles and 8 positive tiles
    c. 15 negative tiles and 9 positive tiles

24. *Reasoning* Suppose you have 6 uncolored tiles, a yellow crayon, and a red crayon.
    a. Show all the different ways you can color the tiles so that when placed together they represent various integers.
    b. List all the integers that the tiles could represent.

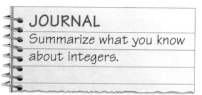

JOURNAL
Summarize what you know about integers.

Mixed Review

Find each sum or difference. *(Lessons 6-4 and 6-5)*

25. $8\frac{1}{3} + 2\frac{1}{6}$ **26.** $15\frac{6}{9} - 13\frac{5}{12}$ **27.** $6\frac{5}{12} + 12\frac{5}{8}$ **28.** $23\frac{2}{3} - 4\frac{1}{2}$ **29.** $26 - 4\frac{1}{9}$

Evaluate each expression for $a = 2$ and $b = 4$. *(Lesson 2-4)*

30. $a + a$ **31.** $72 \div b$ **32.** $2ab$ **33.** $a \times 0$ **34.** $2a - b$ **35.** $a + b \div 6$

36. *Estimation* Suppose you want to buy 2 sets of pencils that cost $3.75 each and some markers that cost $2.31. The total sales tax is $.30. You have a ten-dollar bill. Do you have enough money? Explain. *(Lesson 3-7)*

CHAPTER PROJECT

PROJECT LINK: CALCULATING

Plan a time line about 3 ft long. It should show a lifetime of about 80 yr. Use what you learned about ratios and scale drawings in Chapter 7 to choose a scale for your time line. What distance will you use between the one-year marks?

What You'll Learn

▼ **1** To use models to add integers with like signs

▼ **2** To use models to add integers with unlike signs

...And Why

You can add integers to keep score in contests.

Here's How

Look for questions that
- ⁂ build understanding
- ✔ check understanding

THINK AND DISCUSS

▼ **1** *Adding Integers with Like Signs*

Toadstool the Frog is a contestant in the Frogville Double Jump. Each frog gets two jumps. A frog's total score is the sum of the distances of the two jumps. When a frog jumps in the wrong direction, the distance is recorded as a negative number. The chart shows Toadstool's practice jumps.

Toadstool's Practice Jumps

Round	1st Jump	2nd Jump	Total
1	3 ft	7 ft	■
2	−5 ft	−2 ft	■
3	6 ft	−4 ft	■
4	−7 ft	3 ft	■
5	4 ft	−4 ft	■

You can use tiles to model Toadstool's jumps. To find the sum for his first round, write this number sentence.

$$3 \quad + \quad 7 \quad = \quad ■$$

1. Complete the number sentence above. How many total feet did Toadstool jump in his first round?

2. Show how tiles can be used to find the sum 5 + 4.

3. ⁂*Reasoning* Complete the sentence: Adding two positive integers always results in a ■ integer.

■ **EXAMPLE 1**

Find the sum of Toadstool's jumps in his second round.

$$-5 \quad + \quad -2 \quad = \quad -7$$

←—Use tiles to model each integer.

←—Then count the tiles.

Toadstool jumped a total of −7 ft.

The largest frog in the world was found in Cameroon in Africa. It was 14.5 in. long and weighed 8 lb 1 oz. The world's smallest frog species lives in Cuba. An adult of this species is less than $\frac{1}{2}$ in. long.

Source: *The Guinness Book of Records*

4. ✔*Try It Out* Use tiles to find each sum.
  a. $-8 + (-1)$ **b.** $-3 + (-6)$ **c.** $-12 + (-9)$

5. a. What do you notice about the sign of the sum of two negative integers?
  b. ♣*Reasoning* Complete: Adding two negative integers always results in a ▇ integer.

▼ Adding Integers with Unlike Signs

You can also use models to add integers that have unlike signs.

■ **EXAMPLE 2**

Use the table on page 442. What is the sum of Toadstool's two jumps in his third round?

Model with tiles.
←Combine tiles to make zero pairs.
Write the integer
$6 \quad + \quad -4 = \qquad\qquad 2$ ←that the remaining tiles represent.

The sum is 2 ft.

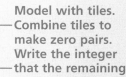

6. ✔*Try It Out* Use tiles to find each sum.
  a. $-5 + 9$ **b.** $-8 + 3$ **c.** $7 + (-7)$

7. ♣*Draw a Conclusion* What do you notice about the sign of the sum of a positive integer and a negative integer?

ADDING INTEGERS

The sum of two positive numbers is positive. The sum of two negative numbers is negative.

Examples: $3 + 5 = 8$ $-3 + (-5) = -8$

To add two numbers with different signs, find the difference between the two numbers without considering their signs. The sum has the same sign as the number that is farthest from 0 on a number line.

Examples: $-3 + 5 = 2$ $3 + (-5) = -2$

8. ▪ *Explain* What is the sum of a number and its opposite? Give examples to justify your answer.

Work Together

Adding Integers

Work with a partner. Place 10 red and 10 yellow algebra tiles in a paper bag. Make a score card like the sample at the right.

Tiles	Player A	Player B
1	1	−1
2	2	−2
3	−1	3
4	4	2
5	■	■
6	■	■
7	■	■
8	■	■
Total	■	■

9. Remove 1 tile from the bag. Write the integer that the tile represents. Replace the tile.

10. Now your partner removes 1 tile, writes the integer, and replaces the tile.

11. Continue removing tiles and writing integers. During each round, increase the number of tiles you remove by 1. For example, remove two tiles in the second round, three tiles in the third round, and so on.

12. At the end of 8 rounds, find your score. Cross out any zeros. Model the remaining integers with tiles. Your score is the sum of these integers.

13. ▪ *Analyze* Compare your scores. Who had the greater score?

EXERCISES *On Your Own*

Use tiles to find each sum.

1. $1 + 5$
2. $-2 + (-6)$
3. $0 + (-9)$
4. $4 + 3$
5. $-9 + (-5)$
6. $-11 + 4$
7. $10 + (-10)$
8. $-1 + 4$
9. $3 + (-8)$
10. $-6 + 2$

Write a numerical expression for each model. Find the sum.

11. ■■ + ■
    ■■   ■

12. ▫▫▫ + ▫▫
    ▫▫   ▫

13. ■■ + ▫▫▫▫
         ▫▫▫▫

14. ▫▫ + ■■
    ▫   ■■

15. ■ + ▫▫▫
    ■   ▫▫▫

16. ■■■ + ▫▫▫
    ■■■   ▫▫

Mental Math **State whether the sum is positive or negative.**

17. $16 + 14$ **18.** $-16 + (-14)$ **19.** $-16 + 18$ **20.** $16 + -15$ **21.** $16 + -18$

Choose **Use tiles, paper and pencil, or mental math to find each sum.**

22. $9 + (-4)$ **23.** $-8 + (-7)$ **24.** $-15 + 6$ **25.** $-11 + 11$ **26.** $0 + (-8)$

27. $-6 + 11$ **28.** $7 + (-11)$ **29.** $12 + (-5)$ **30.** $8 + (-4)$ **31.** $5 + (-5)$

Open-ended **Write an addition exercise involving a positive integer and a negative integer with each of the following types of sums.**

32. negative   **33.** zero   **34.** positive

Compare. Write <, >, or =.

35. $-7 + (-3)$ ▩ $7 + 3$ **36.** $5 + (-5)$ ▩ $-1 + 1$ **37.** $-2 + 8$ ▩ $-8 + 2$

38. *Writing* Explain how you could use tiles to model the score of a golfer as she plays 18 holes.

39. *Office Mail* The mailroom of a large company is on the 15th floor. A mail clerk delivers mail by first going up 5 floors in the elevator. Next he goes down 3 floors. Then he goes down 4 floors. Where is he in relation to the mailroom?

40. *Money* Suppose you earned $12 on Saturday running errands. On Monday, you spent $8. On Friday, you earned $7 baby-sitting. How much money did you have then?

41. *Sports* A football team gained 6 yd on one play. On the next play, the team lost 11 yd. Write the total gain or loss of yards as an integer.

42. *Weather* At 7:30 A.M. on January 22, 1943, the temperature was $-4°F$ in Spearfish, South Dakota. At 7:32 A.M., the temperature had risen an amazing 49 degrees! What was the temperature then?

43. Use the table on page 444. After 4 rounds, did Player A or Player B have the greater score? Explain.

44. Copy the Magic Integer Square. Arrange the integers −4, −3, −2, −1, 0, 1, 2, 3, 4 so they add up to zero in all eight directions (vertically, horizontally, and diagonally).

Magic Integer Square

?	?	?
?	?	?
?	?	?

Mental Math **Group opposites to get a sum of 0. Add the remaining integers.**

45. −4 + 7 + 4 + (−2)

46. 6 + (−3) + (−8) + 3

47. 8 + (−9) + (−8) + 9

48. −7 + 5 + (−1) + 7 + (−7)

Mixed Review

Find the value of *n*. *(Lesson 7-3)*

49. $\frac{4}{6} = \frac{n}{9}$

50. $\frac{22}{25} = \frac{n}{200}$

51. $\frac{3}{7} = \frac{21}{n}$

52. $\frac{9}{27} = \frac{n}{42}$

53. $\frac{9}{10} = \frac{27}{n}$

Find each quotient. *(Lessons 4-7 and 4-8)*

54. 10.2 ÷ 3

55. 8.45 ÷ 0.25

56. 37.1 ÷ 14

57. 128.31 ÷ 1.3

58. 0.125 ÷ 0.025

59. Kay bought a case of shampoo. She sold 11 bottles to Sabrina and still had 25 bottles left. How many bottles were in the case? *(Lesson 2-6)*

✓ CHECKPOINT 1
Lessons 10-1 through 10-3

Compare. Write <, >, or =.

1. 2 ▨ 5

2. −4 ▨ −8

3. −3 ▨ 0

4. 6 ▨ −6

5. −11 ▨ −10

6. Graph on a number line: 2, −5, 3, 1, −7, −2.

7. What integer is represented by ■ ■ ■ ▨ ▨ ▨ ▨ ?

Use tiles to represent each integer and its opposite.

8. 6

9. −5

10. −2

11. 8

12. −3

13. 4

Find each sum.

14. −2 + (−3)

15. 7 + (−5)

16. −9 + 9

17. −1 + (−11)

18. −3 + 6

Extra Practice, Lesson 10-3, page 531

Choose the best answer.

1. A digital scale measured the weight of a baby as 7.819 pounds. What is the weight rounded to the nearest tenth of a pound?

   A. 7 pounds
   B. 7.8 pounds
   C. 7.9 pounds
   D. 8 pounds

2. On a test, Alexis was asked to write $2 \times 2 \times 2 \times 5 \times 5$ in exponential notation. Which should she have written?

   F. $8^3 \times 25^2$
   G. $3 \times 2 \times 5 \times 2$
   H. $2^3 \times 5^2$
   J. $3^2 \times 2^5$

3. The width of a doorway is 95 cm. What is the width in meters?

   A. 0.95 m
   B. 9.5 m
   C. 950 m
   D. 9,500 m

4. Billy buys 80 ounces of fudge. How many pounds of fudge is this?

   F. 5 lb
   G. $6\frac{2}{3}$ lb
   H. 8 lb
   J. 10 lb

5. Look at the drawing of a sailboat.

   Which drawing shows a translation of the sailboat?

   A.
   B.
   C.
   D.

6. Which point is located at (4, 2)?

   F. point M
   G. point N
   H. point P
   J. point Q

   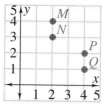

Please note that Exercises 7 and 8 each have *five* answer choices.

7. Four flag styles are available. Each flag is made up of 8 triangles. The cost of the flag depends on the types of triangles used. Red silk triangles cost $9.50 each. White cotton triangles cost $4.50 each.

   Suppose you pick a flag that has both horizontal line symmetry and vertical line symmetry. How much would the flag cost?

   A. $41
   B. $46
   C. $51
   D. $56
   E. Not Here

8. The graph shows the results of a survey in which 200 people named their favorite dessert. How many people preferred ice cream?

   Favorite Dessert

   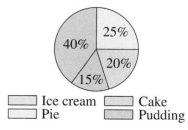

   F. 8
   G. 40
   H. 50
   J. 80
   K. Not Here

10-4 Modeling Subtraction of Integers

What You'll Learn

1 To model the subtraction of integers

2 To use models to solve equations with integers

...And Why

You can subtract integers to solve problems involving weather.

Here's How

Look for questions that
- build understanding
- ✓ check understanding

THINK AND DISCUSS

▼ Modeling Subtraction of Integers

You can use tiles to subtract integers.

■ EXAMPLE 1

Use tiles to find $-8 - (-6)$.

 ←— Start with 8 negative tiles.

 ←— Take away 6 negative tiles.

 ←— Two negative tiles remain.

$-8 - (-6) = -2$

1. ✓Try It Out Use tiles to find each difference.
  a. $12 - 4$ **b.** $-10 - (-3)$ **c.** $-15 - (-9)$

You may need to add zero pairs to subtract.

■ EXAMPLE 2

Use tiles to subtract $4 - (-3)$.

Start with 4 positive tiles.
←—There are not enough negative tiles to take 3 negative tiles away.

 ←—Add 3 zero pairs.

Take away 3 negative tiles.
There are 7 positive tiles left.

$4 - (-3) = 7$

2. a. What is the total value of the 3 zero pairs? Explain.
  b. Did adding 3 zero pairs affect the value of 4? Explain.

❷ Using Models to Solve Equations

You can use tiles to solve equations with integers.

■ EXAMPLE 3   *Real-World Problem Solving*

Weather Between dawn and noon, the temperature rose 9 degrees Celsius. At noon it was 5°C. What was the temperature at dawn? Let t = temperature at dawn.

Words • Temperature at dawn plus Rise in temperature equals Temperature at noon

Equation • $\quad t \quad + \quad 9 \quad = \quad 5$

$t + 9 = 5$ ⟵ Solve for t.

$t = 5 - 9$ ⟵ Subtract 9 from each side.

⟵ Use tiles to subtract 5 − 9.
Start with 5 positive tiles.

⟵ There are not enough positive tiles to take 9 away. Add 4 zero pairs.

⟵ Take away 9 positive tiles. There are 4 negative tiles left.

$5 - 9 = -4$

So $t = -4$. The temperature at dawn was $-4°C$.

3. ✔*Try It Out* Solve each equation.
  a. $x + 4 = 2$ **b.** $p + 8 = 3$ **c.** $y + 7 = 1$

4. a. Find $5 + (-9)$. Compare your answer to Example 3.
  b. ⬥*Draw a Conclusion* Does your comparison suggest a rule for subtracting integers? Explain.

SUBTRACTING INTEGERS

You can subtract an integer by *adding its opposite*.
Examples:

$10 - 6 = 10 + (-6) = 4$ $6 - 10 = 6 + (-10) = -4$

$10 - (-6) = 10 + 6 = 16$ $6 - (-10) = 6 + 10 = 16$

The Mount Washington Observatory in New Hampshire records weather conditions at the top of the highest peak in the northeastern United States. The temperature on the peak ranges from –47°F to 72°F (–44°C to 22°C).

Need Help? For practice in subtracting whole numbers, see Skills Handbook page 539.

5. ✔ **Try It Out** Find each difference.
   a. $12 - 19$ b. $-10 - 5$ c. $-5 - (-11)$

Work Together _____ *Subtracting Integers*

Play the Great Integer Game! You will need yellow and red tiles, a green number cube, and a red number cube.

- Work in groups. Each player starts with 3 positive and 3 negative tiles. Put the remaining tiles in the game pile.

- Roll the cubes. Subtract the number on the red cube from the number on the green cube. Take the resulting number of tiles away from your tiles and place them in the game pile.

- If you don't have enough tiles to put in the game pile, take zero pairs from the game pile in order to make your number.

- The winner is the first person to run out of tiles.

6. As you play, each person should complete a recording sheet.

Tiles at start of turn	Your Roll Green − Red	Taking away tiles	Tiles at end of turn

EXERCISES *On Your Own*

Write a numerical expression for each model. Find the difference.

1.

2.

3.

Modeling **Use tiles to find each difference.**

4. $14 - 8$ 5. $7 - 12$ 6. $-8 - 4$ 7. $-1 - (-5)$ 8. $4 - (-6)$

9. $9 - 5$ 10. $-2 - 7$ 11. $6 - 9$ 12. $-3 - 3$ 13. $5 - (-1)$

14. *Writing* Describe how to use tiles to subtract integers. Include examples with both positive and negative integers.

Algebra **Solve each equation.**

15. $b + 11 = -2$ **16.** $7 + a = 4$ **17.** $t - 20 = -5$ **18.** $12 + b = -1$ **19.** $x + 8 = 0$

Choose **Use tiles, pencil and paper, or mental math to find each difference.**

20. $1 - 6$ **21.** $-13 - 8$ **22.** $-4 - (-15)$ **23.** $-5 - 3$ **24.** $-12 - 17$

25. $-3 - (-7)$ **26.** $-1 - 6$ **27.** $-6 - (-6)$ **28.** $11 - 15$ **29.** $0 - 10$

Compare. Write <, >, or =.

30. $12 + (-3) \blacksquare 12 - 3$ **31.** $-1 - 5 \blacksquare -5 - 1$ **32.** $6 - 11 \blacksquare 11 - 6$

33. $-9 + 7 \blacksquare 7 - 9$ **34.** $-4 - (-9) \blacksquare -4 + 9$ **35.** $8 - (-8) \blacksquare -8 + 8$

Geography **The map shows the time zones for North America. The numbers indicate the time (in hours) compared to the time at the starting zone.**

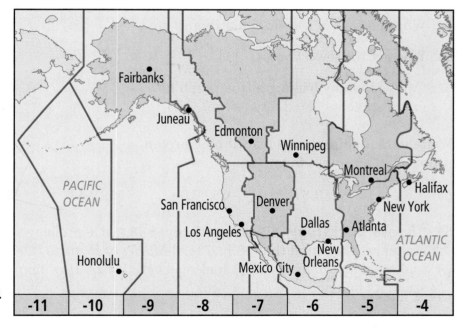

36. Complete with *add* or *subtract*: For each zone you travel west, you $\blacksquare$ 1 h. For each zone you travel east, you $\blacksquare$ 1 h.

37. It is midnight on New Year's Eve at Times Square in New York City. What time is it in Los Angeles?

38. It is 2:30 P.M. in the starting zone. What is the time in Denver?

39. It is 8:15 A.M. in San Francisco. What time is it in Dallas?

40. *Research* Find the names of the various time zones on the map above.

Patterns **Find the next three integers in each pattern.**

41. 12, 7, 2, −3, ■, ■, ■

42. 19, 13, 7, 1, ■, ■, ■

43. −12, −9, −6, −3, ■, ■, ■

Open-ended **Use positive and negative integers to write two different subtraction sentences for each exercise.**

44. ■ − ■ = 0

45. ■ − ■ = 8

46. ■ − ■ = −5

47. ■ − 3 = ■

48. a. Find −3 + (−3) + (−3) + (−3).
   b. Write part (a) as a multiplication sentence.
   c. How could you write your answer to part (b) as a division sentence?

Mixed Review

Use the graph for Exercises 49–52. *(Lesson 1-5)*

49. How many candidates were there?

50. What percent of the votes did Bianca get?

51. Who got the fewest votes?

52. Can you tell by looking at the graph how many students voted for George?

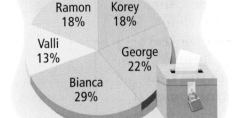

Student Council Election Results

Ramon 18% Korey 18% Valli 13% George 22% Bianca 29%

Write each decimal as a fraction or mixed number in simplest form. *(Lesson 5-9)*

53. 1.6

54. 0.375

55. 0.09

56. 0.57

57. 2.125

58. 0.72

59. *Choose a Strategy* A teacher surveyed 48 sixth-grade students. She found that 18 had read *Mariel of Redwall*, 20 had read *Mossflower*, and 11 had read both books. How many students had not read either book?

CHAPTER PROJECT

PROJECT LINK: DRAWING

Draw your time line on a sheet of paper about 3 ft long. Use marks of different lengths to show the one-year, five-year, and ten-year divisions. Label the current year "0" so that your past lies on the negative side of the time line and your future lies on the positive side.

Solving Two-Step Equations

After Lesson 10-4

A *two-step equation* is an equation with two operations. You can use algebra tiles to solve two-step equations. Use the same methods you used to solve one-step equations.

■ EXAMPLE

Solve $2x - 1 = -7$.

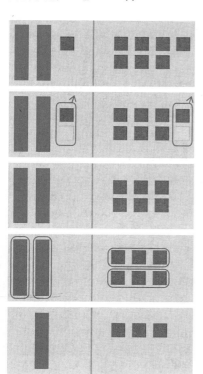

Model the equation. Notice that $2x - 1$ is shown as $2x + (-1)$.

Make zero pairs to get the x-tiles alone on one side of the equation.

Simplify each side. You now have a one-step equation, $2x = -6$.

Divide each side of the equation into 2 equal parts.

Find the solution.

The solution to $2x - 1 = -7$ is -3.

Use algebra tiles to solve each equation.

1. $2x + 3 = 5$ **2.** $3x - 4 = 2$ **3.** $2x - 4 = 4$ **4.** $4x + 3 = -5$ **5.** $5x - 6 = 4$

6. $4x - 1 = 3$ **7.** $3x + 5 = -1$ **8.** $2x + 7 = -1$ **9.** $2x - 1 = -7$ **10.** $3x - 6 = 3$

11. $5x - 2 = -7$ **12.** $2x - 1 = 5$ **13.** $4x - 9 = -1$ **14.** $6x + 3 = -3$ **15.** $2x + 4 = 4$

16. *Writing* Explain why $2x - 1$ can be written as $2x + (-1)$.

10-5 Use Multiple Strategies

Problem Solving Strategies

Draw a Diagram
Guess and Test
Look for a Pattern
Make a Model
Make a Table
Simulate a Problem
Solve a Simpler Problem
Too Much or Too Little
  Information
Use Logical Reasoning
✓ Use Multiple Strategies
Work Backward

THINK AND DISCUSS

Sometimes you need to use more than one strategy to solve a problem.

SAMPLE PROBLEM..

Malcolm finished first in the flying ring contest held at his school's playing field. The field had scoring zones worth 1, 3, 5, 7, and 9 points. All five of Malcolm's throws landed in a scoring zone. Which of these total scores could be Malcolm's total score? **4 24 37 47**

Throwing • Spot

 READ

*Read for understanding.
Summarize the problem.*

1. How many times did Malcolm throw the ring?

2. What scores were possible on each throw?

3. Was 0 a possible score for one of Malcolm's throws?

 PLAN

Decide on a strategy.

Use Logical Reasoning and *Look for a Pattern* to eliminate some of the scores in the list above. Then *Guess and Test* possible throw combinations.

SOLVE

Try the strategy.

The only possible scores for a throw were 1, 3, 5, 7, or 9 points. Think logically about the possible total scores for 5 throws.

4. What was the highest total score Malcolm could get?

5. What was the lowest total score he could get?

6. Which two scores in the list can you now eliminate?

Now you can *Look for a Pattern* to find if Malcolm could get the remaining scores of 24 or 37. Notice that all the possible scores for a single throw are *odd* numbers. Look for a pattern in the sums of odd numbers.

7. Is the sum of two odd numbers odd or even?

8. Is the sum of three odd numbers odd or even?

9. Is the sum of four odd numbers odd or even?

10. Is the sum of five odd numbers odd or even?

Now that you know what kind of number results from adding five odd numbers, can you eliminate one of the two remaining totals?

11. Which score was not possible? Why?

LOOK BACK

Think about how you solved the problem.

12. Which was the only possible total score? *Guess and Test* to confirm your answer.

13. What are two other possible total scores that Malcolm could have thrown? Explain.

EXERCISES *On Your Own*

Use one or more strategies to solve each problem. Show all your work.

1. *Time* The old town clock loses 10 minutes every 2 days. On May 1 the clock showed the correct time. If the clock continues to lose time at the rate noted, on what date will the clock again show the correct time?

2. *Gardening* A gardener wants to fence in the greatest possible area using 200 ft of fencing. Find the best length and width for the garden.

3. *Navigation* Suppose you launched a raft on the Ohio River at Pittsburgh, Pennsylvania. Your raft drifted at a steady 3 miles per hour for 9 hours less than exactly 2 weeks. When your raft landed at Cairo, Illinois, you had traveled the entire length of the Ohio River. How long is the river?

4. *Statistics* There are 48 members of the band. Of these, 10 are left-handed and 19 wear eyeglasses. There are 27 members who are *not* left-handed and who do *not* wear eyeglasses. How many left-handed members wear eyeglasses?

5. *Weather* A pilot left Helena, Montana. The thermometer outside her plane showed a temperature rise of 100 degrees on her way to Houston, Texas. She then went on to Marshall, Minnesota, where she saw a 71-degree drop. When she reached Portland, Maine, the temperature was 12 degrees, a full 14 degrees warmer than Marshall. What was the temperature in Helena that morning?

6. *Customer Service* Suppose a customer would like no more than 6 one-dollar bills in change. In how many different ways can you give change from a $100 bill for a $79 purchase?

7. *Biology* Suppose the average blink of an eye takes $\frac{1}{5}$ of a second, and you blink 25 times per minute. You traveled at an average speed of 50 miles per hour for 12 hours. How many miles would you have traveled with your eyes closed?

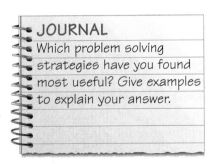

JOURNAL
Which problem solving strategies have you found most useful? Give examples to explain your answer.

8. *Geometry* Suppose you have a 4-cm stick and an 8-cm stick. You want to use a third stick to form a triangle. What whole-number lengths (in centimeters) can you use?

Mixed Review

Estimate using rounding or compatible numbers. *(Lesson 4-1)*

9. $90.88 \div 14.2$ 10. 6.7×4.1 11. 26.50×4 12. $1.03 \div 0.3$ 13. 7.6×5.1

Complete. *(Lesson 6-10)*

14. 3 gal = ■ pt   15. 6 lb = ■ oz   16. 11 ft = ■ in.   17. 12 yd = ■ ft   18. 3 T = ■ lb

19. *Choose a Strategy* Two numbers have a sum of 34 and a product of 273. What are the two numbers?

10-6 Graphing Functions

...And Why

▼ To make a function table

▼ To graph functions

...And Why

You can use functions to solve problems involving sports, time, and wages.

Here's How

Look for questions that
■ build understanding
✔ check understanding

THINK AND DISCUSS

① *Making Function Tables*

Sometimes one set of data depends on another. This kind of relationship is called a **function.**

In football, for example, the number of points scored by field goals is a function of the number of field goals kicked. The table shows the points scored for different numbers of field goals.

Input (Field Goals)	Output (Points)
1	3
2	6
3	9
4	12
5	■

A table like the one above is called a **function table.** It shows the *input* and the *output* of the function. The input is the number of field goals and the output is the number of points.

1. **a.** You can describe the relationship between field goals and points as *number of field goals* × 3 = *number of points.* What is the output for an input of 5 field goals?
   b. How many field goals would be needed to score 21 points?

■ **EXAMPLE 1** *Real-World Problem Solving*

Time You can describe the relationship between hours and minutes as *number of hours* × 60 = *number of minutes.* Each hour equals 60 minutes. Make a function table for minutes as a function of hours.

Multiply each input by 60 to get each output.

Input (hours)	Output (minutes)
1	60
2	120
3	180
4	240
5	300

2. ✔ Try It Out Each day equals 24 hours. Make a function table for hours as a function of days.

▼ Graphing Functions

You can graph the input and output of a function. You can extend the graph to find other values of the function.

■ **EXAMPLE 2**   *Real-World Problem Solving*

Jobs Wages are a function of the number of hours you work. Suppose you earn $5 per hour. Graph the function. Then use the graph to find the wages you would earn for 6 hours.

Input (hours)	1	2	3	4
Output (dollars)	5	10	15	20

←—Make a table.

Draw the points and a line.

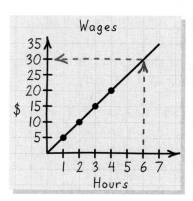

Mark the point on the line that represents 6 hours.

Through this point, draw a horizontal line that intersects the vertical axis.

You would earn $30 for 6 hours.

3. a. ⁙*Patterns* Does the result $30 for 6 hours of work fit the pattern in the table? Explain.

   b. ⁙*Open-ended* Use the graph above. Estimate how many hours you would need to work to purchase a CD player and 3 CDs. Explain your estimation.

4. ⁙*Algebra* Let *h* stand for the number of hours worked. Write a variable expression that represents your wages in Example 2.

5. ✔ Try It Out Each touchdown in football scores 6 points. Make a function table and a graph to show points as a function of touchdowns.

Work Together

Work with a partner to copy and complete the table below.

6. Sporty Goods sells T-shirts for $9 each. There is no shipping charge. Better still, you have a coupon that gives you $2 off the total.

   a. ⠿*Algebra* Let n stand for the number of T-shirts you order. Write an expression to represent the final price for T-shirts purchased at Sporty Goods.

   b. Make a prediction for the final price of 7 T-shirts.

   c. Graph the data in the table to check your predictions.

Sporty Goods

Number of T-shirts	Final Price ($)
1	7
2	▦
3	▦
4	▦

EXERCISES *On Your Own*

Complete each function table.

1.

Input	Output
1	4
2	8
3	12
4	▦
5	▦

2.

Input	Output
3	5
4	6
5	7
6	▦
7	▦

3.

Input	Output
10	30
15	45
20	60
25	▦
30	▦

Measurement **Make a function table for each function.**

4. feet as a function of yards

5. inches as a function of feet

6. months as a function of years

7. centimeters as a function of meters

Graph each function.

8.

Hours	Wages
1 h	$7
2 h	$14
3 h	$21
4 h	$28

9.

Time	Distance
5 min	15 mi
6 min	18 mi
7 min	21 mi
8 min	24 mi

10.

Correct Answers	Score
12 answers	60 points
13 answers	65 points
14 answers	70 points
15 answers	75 points

11. *Writing* Are all tables of data function tables? Explain using examples.

12. Use your graphs from Exercises 8–10.
  a. Find the wages for 6 hours.
  b. Find the distance for 11 minutes.
  c. Find the score for 18 correct answers.

13. Choose A, B, or C. Three companies offer to sew your team name RANGERS on your uniforms. Pro Lettering charges $2 per letter. Uniforms-R-Us charges $1 per letter plus a fee of $5. Speedy Lettering charges a flat fee of $15. Which graph shows the fees of the company that would charge you least? (*Hint:* Each graph shows only the cost for 1 to 6 letters.)

A.

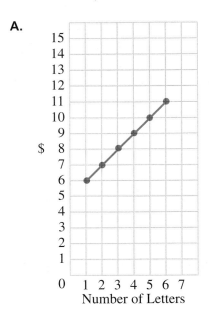

Number of Letters

B.

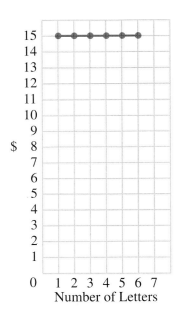

Number of Letters

C.

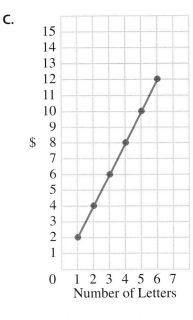

Number of Letters

14. *Patterns* You can draw diagonals from one vertex inside a polygon to create triangles. As the number of sides of a polygon increases, the number of triangles you can make also increases. Complete the function table. Then graph the number of triangles within a polygon as a function of the number of sides.

Number of Sides	Number of Triangles
3 sides	1
4 sides	2
5 sides	3
6 sides	■
7 sides	■

 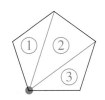 

15. Mail Order Goalposters sells football kicking tees by mail for $3 each. There is a shipping charge of $5 no matter how many kicking tees you order.

  a. Complete the function table to show the final price for the purchase of two, three, and four tees.

  b. *Writing* Write a word equation that explains the cost of buying any number of football kicking tees by mail.

Goalposters

Number of Tees	Final Price ($)
1	8
2	■
3	■
4	■

16. Geometry The sum of the measures of the angles of a regular polygon is a function of the number of sides. Complete the function table. Then graph the function.

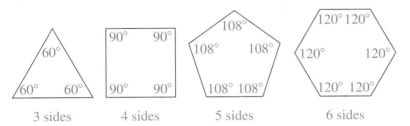

3 sides   4 sides   5 sides   6 sides

Regular Polygons

Number of Sides	Sum of Measures of Angles
3	180°
4	360°
5	540°
6	■

Mixed Review

Find the area of each square given its perimeter. *(Lesson 9-2)*

17. 60 cm   **18.** 19.2 m   **19.** 6.8 ft   **20.** 12 m   **21.** $\frac{1}{2}$ ft   **22.** 36.4 cm

Find each percent. *(Lesson 7-9)*

23. 75% of 36   **24.** 200% of 14   **25.** 25% of 115   **26.** 33% of 21   **27.** 6% of 75

28. Choose a Strategy Two student tickets and one adult ticket to a concert cost $19. One student ticket and three adult tickets cost $29.50. Find the cost of each kind of ticket.

CHAPTER PROJECT

PROJECT LINK: GRAPHING

Make a list of entries for your time line. Include milestones such as learning to walk or crawl. Add events that have shaped who you are, such as making new friends, learning valuable lessons, or gaining new skills or confidence. Place these events on the negative side of your time line.

TECHNOLOGY

Using a Graphing Calculator

After Lesson 10-6

A graphing calculator makes it easy to graph equations.

Start by finding the **ON** key. Then find CLEAR . This key clears, or erases, the numbers on the calculator screen. ENTER is used to enter data and commands.

■ EXAMPLE

Use a graphing calculator to graph $y = x + 2$.

Press Y= . Your screen should look like the one at the right.

Press X,T,θ ➕ 2 ENTER to enter the equation.

Press ZOOM and select **ZStandard** to view the graph in the standard viewing window. You can select other commands from the **ZOOM** menu to zoom in and out.

Press GRAPH to display the graph. If your graph does not look like the one at the right, ask for help.

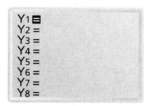

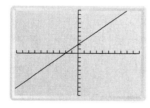

Use a graphing calculator to graph each equation. Sketch each graph on graph paper.

1. $y = x$

2. $y = x + 1$

3. $y = x + 2$

4. $y = x + 3$

5. $y = x - 1$

6. $y = x - 2$

7. $y = x - 3$

8. $y = x - 4$

9. $y = 2x$

10. $y = 4x$

11. $y = 6x$

12. $y = 8x$

13. $y = 3x + 1$

14. $y = 5x - 2$

15. $y = 4x + 2$

16. $y = 2x - 4$

17. a. Look at your graphs for Exercises 1−4. What happens to the graph as the number that is added increases?
   b. Look at your graphs for Exercises 5−8. What happens when the number that is subtracted increases?

18. *Reasoning* Look at your graphs for Exercises 9−12. The number multiplied by x is called its *coefficient*. What happens to the graph as the coefficient changes?

10-7

Graphing on the Coordinate Plane

...And Why

1. To use a coordinate plane to graph points
2. To name the coordinates of points and the quadrants of the coordinate plane

...And Why

The coordinate plane allows you to graph data so you can see trends and tendencies.

Here's How

Look for questions that
- build understanding
- ✔ check understanding

Work Together

Exploring Coordinates

Work with a partner. You need rubber bands and two geoboards. Agree on a system for locating points on the geoboard.

1. **Geometry** Create a figure on a geoboard with a rubber band. Don't let your partner see the figure you have created!

2. Your partner should ask questions about each line segment of your figure. Answer each question using your location system.

3. Your partner tries to guess the shape and to duplicate it on a geoboard. Compare your partner's version to your own.

4. **Analyze** Switch roles and repeat the activity. Were the guesses accurate? Why or why not?

THINK AND DISCUSS

1 Graphing Points

You can identify points by using a coordinate plane. The **coordinate plane** is formed by the intersection of two number lines.

origin, the point where axes intersect	**y-axis,** or vertical number line
	x-axis, or horizontal number line

You can graph points on a coordinate plane. Each point has 2 *coordinates*, which form an **ordered pair.**

The *x-coordinate* tells how far to move left or right along the *x*-axis. $(-2, 4)$ The *y-coordinate* tells how far to move up or down along the *y*-axis.

The coordinates $(0, 0)$ describe the origin. You move *left* from the origin to graph a negative *x*-coordinate. You move *down* from the origin to graph a negative *y*-coordinate.

■ EXAMPLE 1

Graph point *A* with coordinates $(3, -2)$.

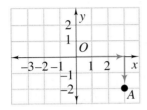

Move 3 units to the right from the origin.

Move 2 units down from the *x*-axis.

Draw a point and label it *A*.

5. ✔*Try It Out* Graph each point on a coordinate plane.
  a. $(-4, -4)$ b. $(-3, 1)$ c. $(1, -2)$ d. $(0, 5)$

▼2 *Naming Coordinates and Quadrants*

You can name the coordinates of points that are already graphed.

A *scatter plot* is a graph of data from two different sets. The two sets of data are plotted as ordered pairs.

■ EXAMPLE 2   *Real-World Problem Solving*

Dogs Find the coordinates of point *B* on the scatter plot.

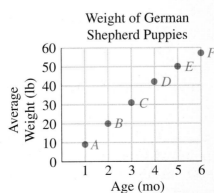

Weight of German Shepherd Puppies

Source: The German Shepherd Dog Web Site

Start at the origin.

Move 2 units to the right. The first coordinate is 2.

Then move up from the *x*-axis. The second coordinate is 20.

The coordinates of point *B* are $(2, 20)$.

6. ✔Try It Out Find the coordinates of points C, D, and E on the scatter plot.

The coordinate plane has four *quadrants*.

7. In which quadrant is the point $M(-2, 5)$ located?

8. ⬛ Reasoning In which quadrants are the x-coordinates of the points positive numbers?

9. ⬛ Reasoning In which quadrants are the y-coordinates of the points negative numbers?

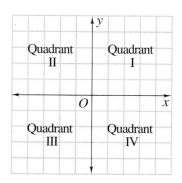

EXERCISES *On Your Own*

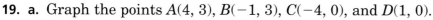

Graph each labeled point on a coordinate plane.

1. $G(-4, 1)$ **2.** $R(1, -4)$ **3.** $L(0, 8)$ **4.** $F(-5, -2)$ **5.** $S(2, 2)$ **6.** $H(-1, 0)$

Name the point with the given coordinates.

7. $(1, 2)$ **8.** $(-2, -6)$ **9.** $(3, -3)$ **10.** $(0, -5)$ **11.** $(3, 0)$

Write the coordinates of each point.

12. C **13.** D **14.** K **15.** Q **16.** N

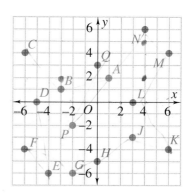

17. Point M is at $(6, 4)$. Which point has opposite coordinates?

18. a. Graph the points $M(-5, -3)$, $N(2, -4)$, and $P(0, 1)$ on a coordinate plane.
   b. *Geometry* Connect the points in order. What shape do you see?

19. a. Graph the points $A(4, 3)$, $B(-1, 3)$, $C(-4, 0)$, and $D(1, 0)$.
   b. Connect the points in order. What shape do you see?
   c. *Geometry* What is the most specific name you can use to describe figure $ABCD$? Explain.

20. *Language* Why do you think the point where the x-axis and y-axis intersect is called the *origin*?

Identify the quadrant in which each point lies.

21. $(3, 2)$ **22.** $(-17, 2)$ **23.** $(-6, -40)$ **24.** $(9, -11)$ **25.** $(-1, 100)$ **26.** $(38, 38)$

27. Choose A, B, C, or D. Which point is in Quadrant IV?

  A. $(-2, 2)$ **B.** $(2, -2)$ **C.** $(-2, -2)$ **D.** $(2, 2)$

28. In which quadrant are all coordinates positive?

29. What are the signs for the x-coordinates and the y-coordinates for all the points in the second quadrant?

30. Three corners of a rectangle have coordinates $(4, 2)$, $(4, 7)$, and $(-3, 2)$. Find the coordinates of the fourth corner.

Where on Earth Are You?

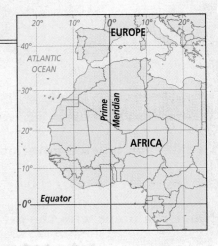

How CAN YOU TELL SOMEONE ELSE WHERE YOU ARE ON EARTH? Geographers have given Earth a coordinate system so that locations can be described easily. Imagine a coordinate plane wrapped around the planet. The equator is the "horizontal axis" and the prime meridian is the "vertical axis."

Distances on Earth's coordinate system are measured in *degrees*. Degrees north or south of the equator are called *degrees of latitude*. Degrees east or west of the prime meridian are called *degrees of longitude*.

31. Refer to the article above. On what continent is the location 30° N latitude, 20° E longitude? On what continent is 40° N latitude, 20° E longitude?

32. *Research* Use a map to locate your town to the nearest degree of latitude and nearest degree of longitude.

33. *Writing* How are a map and the coordinate plane alike? How are they different?

Crafts **Some quilt makers use coordinate grids to plan their patterns before they stitch their quilts.**

34. The Monkey Wrench pattern shown at right is from an African American story quilt. Find the coordinates of the pattern points.

35. *Open-ended* Create your own quilt pattern. Draw the pattern on a grid and name the coordinates of the points.

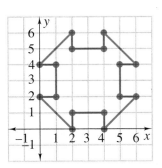

Geography Map makers use a coordinate system. On many maps, coordinates refer to a rectangular area of the map, instead of a specific point.

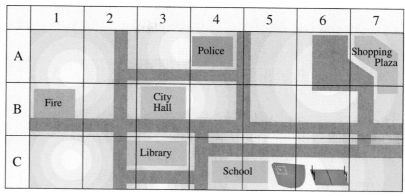

36. What do the letters A−C identify? What do the numbers 1−7 identify?

37. What is located in section B3?

38. What are the coordinates of the school and its nearby playing fields?

Mixed Review

Classify the triangle with the given side lengths as scalene, isosceles, or equilateral. *(Lesson 8-4)*

39. 4 m, 4 m, 4m   **40.** 2 ft, 8 ft, $8\frac{1}{2}$ ft   **41.** 7 m, 24m, 25m   **42.** 4 in., 3 in., 4 in.

Evaluate each expression for $x = 8$. *(Lesson 2-4)*

43. $3x - 2$ **44.** x^2 **45.** $2x + 10$ **46.** $0.5x$ **47.** $12 \div x$ **48.** $4x$

49. Norma bought a bicycle for \$126.90 at a store having a $\frac{1}{3}$-off sale. What was the bike's original price? *(Lessons 7-4 and 7-9)*

✓ CHECKPOINT 2
Lessons 10-4 through 10-7

Name the point with the given coordinates.

1. $(-1, -3)$ **2.** $(0, 2)$ **3.** $(2, -2)$ **4.** $(-4, 1)$

Write the coordinates of each point.

5. J **6.** M **7.** B **8.** F

9. D **10.** H **11.** C **12.** K

Find each sum or difference.

13. $-10 - 10$ **14.** $-215 + 343$ **15.** $451 - (-134)$ **16.** $-1,035 - 961$

10-8 Applying Integers and Graphs

What You'll Learn

❶ To find profit and loss

❷ To draw and interpret graphs involving integers

...And Why

You can use profit and loss and graphs to solve business problems.

Here's How

Look for questions that

⠿ build understanding

✔ check understanding

THINK AND DISCUSS

❶ Finding Profit and Loss

Businesses keep track of the money they receive (income) and the money they spend (expenses). The *balance* is the company's profit or loss.

Expenses

Income

To find the balance, add the income (positive numbers) and the expenses (negative numbers) together.

positive balance = *profit*   negative balance = *loss*

You can use a calculator and the key to find balances.

■ EXAMPLE 1   *Real-World Problem Solving*

▦ *Accounting* Find Video Mania's profit or loss for February.

Add income to expenses.

12739 ⊞ 9482 ± ▤ *3257*

The balance is positive. So, there is a profit.

Income and Expenses for Video Mania		
Month	Income	Expenses
Jan.	$11,917	–$14,803
Feb.	$12,739	–$9,482
March	$11,775	–$10,954
April	$13,620	–$15,149

Video Mania had a profit of $3,257.

1. ✔*Try It Out* Find the profit or loss for each month.
   a. January   b. March   c. April

2 Making a Graph

Businesses use line graphs to look at the trends of their monthly balances.

■ **EXAMPLE 2**   *Real-World Problem Solving*

Business Draw a line graph of the monthly profits and losses for Hobby & Toy Town.

Income and Expenses for Hobby & Toy Town			
Month	Profit/Loss	Month	Profit/Loss
January	−$1,917	July	$933
February	−$682	August	$1,110
March	$303	September	−$417
April	$781	October	−$824
May	−$150	November	$1,566
June	$250	December	$1,945

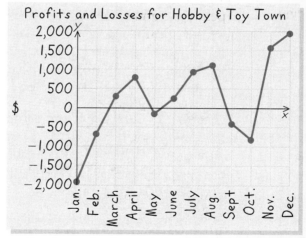

Put the dollar amounts on the vertical axis.

Balances vary from −$1,917 to $1,945. Make a scale from −$2,000 to $2,000. Use intervals of 500.

Put the months on the horizontal axis.

Graph a point for each monthly balance. Connect the points.

2. ⬚*Analyze* In which months was there a profit?

3. In which month did the greatest loss occur?

4. In which month did Hobby & Toy Town come closest to breaking even?

5. Which month's balance showed the greatest change from the previous month?

You can use a spreadsheet program to find profit and loss.

■ **EXAMPLE 3**   *Real-World Problem Solving*

 *Technology* Use a spreadsheet and the data from Example 1 on page 468 to find Video Mania's year-to-date profit or loss for February.

The spreadsheet below calculates the year-to-date balances. Cell E3 shows the combined balances for the first two months, January and February.

	A	B	C	D	E
1	Month	Income	Expenses	Profit/Loss	Year-to-date Profit/Loss
2	January	$11,917	−$14,803	−$2,886	−$2,886
3	February	$12,739	−$9,482	$3,257	$371
4	March				
5	April				

Video Mania had a year-to-date profit of $371 for February.

6. ⁘*Think About It* To write the formula for cell E3, enter =E2+D3 into cell E3. How would you write the formula for cell E4? For E5?

7. ✔*Try It Out* Copy and complete the spreadsheet above.

8. ⁘*Data Analysis* Draw a line graph that shows the year-to-date balances for Video Mania for January, February, March, and April.

9. ⁘*Summarize* Describe the status of Video Mania, based on its balance for the first four months of the year.

EXERCISES *On Your Own*

▦ *Calculator* **Use a calculator to find each sum or difference.**

1. $-435 + 628$

2. $581 - (-57)$

3. $-321 - 789$

4. $-2,044 - (-1,806)$

5. $-212 + 234$

6. $246 - (-38)$

7. $-459 - 659$

8. $-3,265 - (-1,958)$

Choose Use a calculator, mental math, or paper and pencil.

9. $-12 + 5$

10. $38 - 64$

11. $29 - (-18)$

12. $-100 + 800$

13. $-245 + 245$

14. $1,434 + (-672)$

15. $850 - 1,050$

16. $-8,126 - (-134)$

What scale and intervals would you use to graph each data set?

17. $-2, 3, 2, 4, -4, 1, -1, 3$

18. $-34, 98, 12, -71, 53, -95$

19. $4, 68, 50, 41, -13, -18, 27$

20. $-20, 7, -9, 4, 18, 5, -1, 9$

21. $-89, 89, 74, -22, 14, -45$

22. $-32, -24, -14, -23, 0, 4, 16$

23. a. Use the data at the right. Find the balance for each day.

  b. Draw a line graph to display the balances.

24. Choose A, B, C, or D. Which day should have the highest point on the graph for Exercise 23?

  A. Tuesday **B.** Thursday
  C. Saturday **D.** Sunday

Day	Expenses	Income
Mon.	-$85	$94
Tues.	-$60	$78
Wed.	-$22	$13
Thurs.	-$73	$90
Fri.	-$49	$37
Sat.	-$16	$15
Sun.	-$36	$19

Computer Copy or use a spreadsheet like the one below.

	A	B	C	D
1	Week	Income	Expenses	Profit/Loss
2	2/1–2/7	$4,257	-$6,513	▦
3	2/8–2/14	$3,840	-$2,856	▦
4	2/15–2/21	$4,109	-$3,915	▦
5	2/22–2/28	$3,725	-$4,921	▦
6	Totals	▦	▦	▦

25. What formulas would you enter in cells D2 through D5?

26. What formula should be entered in cell B6? Explain.

27. Enter the formulas to find the unknown values.

28. What was the balance for the month? Was it a loss or profit?

29. *Writing* Describe two types of graphs you could use to show the data. Explain the advantages and disadvantages of each.

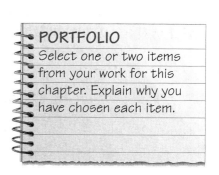

PORTFOLIO
Select one or two items from your work for this chapter. Explain why you have chosen each item.

Use prime factorization to find the GCF of each set of numbers. *(Lesson 5-3)*

30. 8, 12, 14   **31.** 2, 5, 10   **32.** 15, 25, 45   **33.** 9, 12, 18   **34.** 36, 45, 945

The volume and two dimensions of a rectangular prism are given. Find the third dimension. *(Lesson 9-8)*

35. $V = 48 \text{ m}^3, h = 3 \text{ m}, \ell = 2 \text{ m}$ **36.** $V = 3,240 \text{ m}^3, h = 15 \text{ m}, w = 8 \text{ m}$

37. *Choose a Strategy* Mercedes is a computer salesperson at RayState Computers. Her salary is $1,150 per month. In addition, she earns 12% of her monthly sales over $5,000.
   a. What did Mercedes earn in October if her computer sales totaled $11,640?
   b. The following amounts were subtracted from Mercedes's October earnings: 6.2% for Social Security, 18% for federal income tax, 4% for state income tax, and $40.35 for health insurance. What was the amount of Mercedes's paycheck?

Math at Work

METEOROLOGIST

If you enjoy studying earth science and working with computer models, consider a career as a meteorologist. Meteorologists apply mathematical relationships to create short- and long-range weather forecasts. They study air pressure, temperature, humidity, and wind velocity. In addition, meteorologists apply their knowledge of Earth's atmosphere to air pollution control, the study of global warming, and research about the ozone layer.

For more information about meteorology, visit the Prentice Hall Web Site: www.phschool.com

The TIME of your life

Draw a Timeline Project Links on pages 441, 452, and 461 helped you complete the side of your time line that represents the past. Here is a checklist to help you gather together the parts of your project.

- ✔ an appropriate scale for a 3-ft time line
- ✔ a 3-ft time line labeled with appropriate divisions and 0
- ✔ past major events identified on your time line

Complete the time line for your future. List events or changes that you think will be important. What do you think will happen? What do you want to happen? Consider life changes such as getting married and having children. Consider education and career goals. Show your time line to your class. Explain why you chose the events you did. Add details to your time line to make it more attractive. Make the print bold enough to be readable. Add colors, and attach photographs, magazine pictures, or artwork.

Reflect and Revise

Review your time line with a classmate, friend, or family member. Did you choose an appropriate scale? Does your time line have enough details? Is it attractive? If necessary, make changes to improve your time line.

Web Extension

Prentice Hall's Internet site contains information you might find helpful as you complete your project. Visit www.phschool.com/mgm1/ch10 for some links and ideas related to history.

Integers and Opposites

Opposites are two numbers that are the same distance from 0 on the number line, but in opposite directions. The set of **integers** is the set of whole numbers and their opposites.

To compare integers, think of the number line. The integer farther to the right is the greater integer.

1. What integer represents 7 degrees below zero?

2. Name the opposite of each integer.
   a. -7 **b.** 1 **c.** -8 **d.** -14 **e.** 89 **f.** -100

3. Write three numbers that are between -4 and -5. Are these numbers integers? Explain.

4. *Writing* Explain how to order the following integers from least to greatest: $3, -1, -13, 5, 0$.

Compare using <, >, or =.

5. $-9 \ \blacksquare \ -11$ **6.** $4 \ \blacksquare \ -13$ **7.** $-21 \ \blacksquare \ 16$ **8.** $0 \ \blacksquare \ 9$ **9.** $6 \ \blacksquare \ 11$

Write the integer represented by each set of tiles.

10.   **11.**   **12.**   **13.**

Modeling Addition and Subtraction of Integers

To add integers, model each integer with tiles. If possible, combine tiles to make zero pairs and remove as many zero pairs as possible. Write the integer that the remaining tiles represent.

To subtract integers, model the first integer with tiles. Take away the second number of tiles. (You may need to add zero pairs.) Write the integer that the remaining tiles represent.

Find the sum or difference.

14. $9 + (-4)$ **15.** $-13 + 6$ **16.** $1 - (-7)$ **17.** $-2 - 8$ **18.** $-3 - (-3)$

19. $7 + (-5)$ **20.** $-18 + 4$ **21.** $3 - (-9)$ **22.** $-5 - 5$ **23.** $-4 - (-8)$

Making Function Tables and Graphing Functions 10-6

You can represent functions using a **function table** or a graph.
Both methods show the function's *input* and *output*.

24. The cost of a 1-min telephone call is $.10. The cost of a 2-min
call to the same place is $.20. A 3-min call is $.30.
  a. Make a function table and a graph for the data.
  b. *Writing* Explain how you could use the graph to find the
    cost of an 8-min call.

Graphing on the Coordinate Plane 10-7

The **coordinate plane** is formed by the intersection of the *x-axis*
and the *y-axis*. Every point on the plane can be described by an
ordered pair of numbers (*x, y*). These *coordinates* tell how far a
point is from the **origin**, (0, 0).

Name the point with the given coordinates.

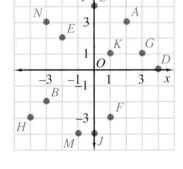

25. (0, 4)   **26.** (3, 1)   **27.** (−3, 3)

28. (2, 3)   **29.** (−4, −3)   **30.** (1, 1)

Write the coordinates of each point.

31. *B*   **32.** *F*   **33.** *J*

34. *E*   **35.** *D*   **36.** *M*

Problem Solving Strategies and Graphing Applications 10-5, 10-8

You can use multiple strategies to solve problems.

A *profit and loss* statement is a table of *income* and *expenses*.
Income is listed as a positive number. Expenses are listed as
negative numbers.

37. Find Royale Bakery's balance for each month. Graph the
  balances. Over four months, was there a profit or a loss?

38. Two people live 36 mi apart. They leave their homes at
  10:00 A.M., riding bicycles toward each other. The first
  person averages 8 mi/h, and the second person averages
  10 mi/h. At what time will they meet?

Income and Expenses for Royale Bakery		
Month	Income	Expenses
Jan.	$1,314	−$828
Feb.	$2,120	−$120
March	$1,019	−$1,285
April	$1,438	−$765

1. Compare. Write $<$, $>$, or $=$.
   a. $18 \blacksquare -24$ b. $-15 \blacksquare -9$
   c. $27 \blacksquare -27$ d. $-3 \blacksquare -4$

2. Write the integer that is represented by the tiles.
   a. ▨▨▨■   b. ■■■■▨

3. Use tiles to model each integer and its opposite.
   a. -1 b. 6 c. -2 d. -9

4. Compare using $<$, $>$, or $=$.
   a. $-13 + 4 \blacksquare 13 + (-4)$
   b. $7 + (-8) + (-1) \blacksquare 7 + (-9)$

5. The temperature was 4°F at midnight. By 6:00 A.M. the temperature had risen 22 degrees. What was the temperature at 6:00 A.M.?

6. Use tiles to find each sum or difference.
   a. $-11 + (-4)$ b. $-12 - 4$
   c. $6 - (-3)$ d. $-5 + 5$

7. Solve $d + 6 = -3$.

8. a. Complete the function table below.

Input	Output
5	40
6	48
7	56
8	▨
9	▨

   b. Graph the function.

9. Graph each point on a coordinate plane.
   a. $A (1, 1)$ b. $B (2, 0)$
   c. $C (-3, -2)$ d. $D (4, -1)$

10. **Choose A, B, C, or D.** On a corrected math quiz, a student got –2 points on the first question, –1 on the second, –3 on the third, –2 on the fourth, and –1 on the fifth. A perfect score was 50 points. What was the student's score?
    A. 50   B. 41   C. 32   D. 12

11. Suppose you bought 3 birthday cards for $1.50 each and 2 posters for $2.75 each. How much did you spend in all?

12. Use a calculator to find each sum or difference.
    a. $-85 + 54$ b. $-112 - (-792)$
    c. $384 + (-556)$ d. $3,077 - (-1,902)$

13. Identify the quadrant in which each point lies.
    a. $(4, 2)$ b. $(-6, -5)$
    c. $(9, -15)$ d. $(-8, 3)$

14. Below is part of the profit and loss statement for Balloons Galore.

Month	Profit/Loss
January	–$985
February	$10,241
March	–$209
April	$17,239

   a. Find the total balance for the four months ending with April.
   b. *Writing* Did Balloons Galore have a profit or a loss during that time? Explain.

Choose the best answer.

1. Which statement is false?

   A. A square is always a rectangle.
   B. Some rectangles are rhombuses.
   C. All quadrilaterals are parallelograms.
   D. Parallelograms can be divided into two congruent triangles.

2. Which could be a net for a rectangular prism?

   A.   B.

   C.   D.

3. Find the best estimate for 43% of 87.

   A. 50   B. 36
   C. 30   D. 25

4. Suppose you bought 9 apples, 6 oranges, 12 pears, and 8 plums. What was the ratio of the number of plums bought to the number of pears bought?

   A. $\frac{2}{3}$ B. 9 to 12
   C. 12 : 8   D. 4 : 2

5. A hardware store sells window glass in thicknesses of $\frac{3}{16}$ inch, $\frac{5}{16}$ inch, and $\frac{7}{32}$ inch. A homeowner plans to install glass that is at least $\frac{1}{4}$ inch thick. Which thickness should the homeowner use?

   A. $\frac{3}{16}$ inch
   B. $\frac{7}{32}$ inch
   C. $\frac{5}{16}$ inch
   D. either $\frac{7}{32}$ or $\frac{3}{16}$ inch

6. Find the perimeter of a square with sides 5 m.

   A. 10 m   B. 20 m
   C. 25 m   D. 125 m

7. Evaluate the expression $b - a - 8$ when $a = 7$ and $b = 24$.

   A. -25 B. -9
   C. 9   D. 11

8. Write the numerical expression that is represented by the set of tiles. Then find the sum.

   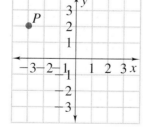

   A. $-5 + 7; 2$
   B. $5 + (-7); -2$
   C. $5 + 7; 12$
   D. $-5 + (-7); -12$

9. On a scale drawing, the scale shown is 1 in. : 10 ft. The length of a room is 2.5 in. on the drawing. How long is the actual room?

   A. 4 in.   B. 25 in.
   C. 4 ft   D. 25 ft

10. What is the correct ordered pair for point P?

    A. $(-3, -2)$
    B. $(-2, -3)$
    C. $(3, -2)$
    D. $(-3, 2)$

11. How many lines of symmetry does a parallelogram have?

    A. 4   B. 2   C. 1   D. 0

Exploring Probability

11

| WHAT YOU WILL LEARN IN THIS CHAPTER | • How to identify fair and unfair games | • How to find experimental and theoretical probabilities | • How to use probability to make predictions |

NOW PLAYING

Suppose you and a friend have to choose among three movies, and you can't make up your mind. Should you flip a coin? You'd probably agree that assigning "heads" to one movie, "tails" to the second, and "lands on edge" to the third would not give the third movie much of a chance. What should you do?

Design a Three-Choice System Your project will be to design a device or system that is equally fair to three different outcomes. You will test your system to make sure each outcome can be expected one third of the time in a large number of trials.

Steps to help you complete the project:

p. 491   Project Link: *Simulating*
p. 496   Project Link: *Designing*
p. 506   Project Link: *Analyzing*
p. 517   *Finishing the Chapter Project*

• How to use simulations to solve problems

PROBLEM SOLVING

What You'll Learn

▼ To find experimental probability

▼ To find possible outcomes

...And Why

You can use experimental probability to determine whether games and contests are fair.

Here's How

Look for questions that

▪ build understanding

✔ check understanding

THINK AND DISCUSS

▼ Experimental Probability

A game is **fair** if each player has the same chance of winning. Players are *equally likely* to win in a fair game.

Play these three games with a partner. For each game, place the given numbers of colored cubes in a bag. Then draw cubes without looking. Answer Question 1 before each game. Answer Questions 2 and 3 after each game.

Game 1	Game 2	Game 3
1 red and 1 blue	2 red and 2 blue	3 red and 1 blue
Draw 1 cube.	Draw 1 cube. Then draw a second cube.	Draw 1 cube. Then draw a second cube.
Red: A wins.	Same color: A wins.	Same color: A wins.
Blue: B wins.	Two colors: B wins.	Two colors: B wins.

1. ▪ *Think About It* Before playing, decide whether the game seems fair or unfair. Which player seems more likely to win?

2. ▪ *Data Collection* Play the game 20 times. Record your results in a table like the one below. For more data, combine your results with the results of two other groups.

	Your Group	3 Groups Combined
Number of times A won	▪	▪
Number of times B won	▪	▪
Number of games played	20	60

3. ▪ *Draw a Conclusion* Does the game seem fair or unfair now? Explain.

You can write a ratio to show the fraction of games that a player wins. This ratio is the **experimental probability** of winning.

EXPERIMENTAL PROBABILITY

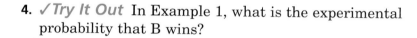

$$\text{Probability(A wins)} = \frac{\text{number of games A won}}{\text{total number of games played}}$$
$$\text{Probability(B wins)} = \frac{\text{number of games B won}}{\text{total number of games played}}$$

■ EXAMPLE 1

In 20 rounds of Game 2, Player A won 8 and Player B won 12. What is the experimental probability that A wins?

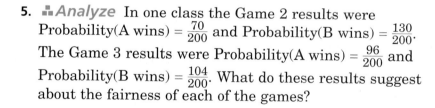

$$\text{Probability(A wins)} = \frac{8}{20} \quad \longleftarrow \text{number of games A won}$$
$$\qquad\qquad\qquad\qquad \longleftarrow \text{total number of games played}$$
$$= \frac{2}{5}$$

The probability that A wins is $\frac{2}{5}$.

4. ✓*Try It Out* In Example 1, what is the experimental probability that B wins?

5. ∴*Analyze* In one class the Game 2 results were Probability(A wins) $= \frac{70}{200}$ and Probability(B wins) $= \frac{130}{200}$. The Game 3 results were Probability(A wins) $= \frac{96}{200}$ and Probability(B wins) $= \frac{104}{200}$. What do these results suggest about the fairness of each of the games?

6. ∴*Reasoning* If you play the games tomorrow, will the experimental probabilities be the same as today? Explain.

▼2 *Possible Outcomes*

You can decide if a game is fair or unfair by finding the *possible outcomes*. Then compare the possible outcomes to the game rules.

7. ∴*Look Back* In Game 1, the 2 possible outcomes are red and blue. Are they equally likely to occur? How do you know?

8. ∴*What If . . .* Imagine a game in which all the cubes in the bag are the same color. How many possible outcomes would there be?

HISTORY
The Mandan people who lived along the Missouri River played a game by tossing decorated bone disks in a basket. The score depended on which sides of the disks landed facing up.

You can make an organized list to find all the possible outcomes. Some outcomes are identical. For Game 2, drawing Red 1, Red 2 is the same as Red 2, Red 1. You can cross out duplicate outcomes.

Red 1, Red 2   ~~Red 2, Red 1~~   ~~Blue 1, Red 1~~   ~~Blue 2, Red 1~~

Red 1, Blue 1   Red 2, Blue 1   ~~Blue 1, Red 2~~   ~~Blue 2, Red 2~~

Red 1, Blue 2   Red 2, Blue 2   Blue 1, Blue 2   ~~Blue 2, Blue 1~~

There are 6 possible outcomes.

Here's another way to find possible outcomes for Game 2. This method eliminates duplicate outcomes.

■ EXAMPLE 2

Draw a diagram of the possible outcomes of Game 2. List the possible outcomes.

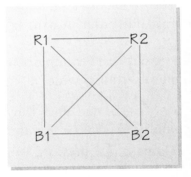

First red cube = **R1**
Second red cube = **R2**
First blue cube = **B1**
Second blue cube = **B2**

Each line represents a possible draw of 2 cubes.

The six possible outcomes are: R1 R2, R1 B1, R1 B2, R2 B1, R2 B2, and B1 B2.

9. Recall that A wins Game 2 if the cubes are the same color, and B wins if they are different. How many outcomes of Game 2 give Player A a win? How many give Player B a win? Are A and B equally likely to win?

10. a. ⬥*Explain* Is Game 2 fair or unfair?
   b. ⬥*Modeling* Find the experimental probabilities of winning Game 2 for Player A and Player B. How are these results related to your answer to Question 10(a)?

11. a. ✔*Try It Out* Draw a diagram for Game 3. List the possible outcomes.
   b. Is Game 3 fair or unfair? Explain.

1. Ki-Jana and Dwayne played Game 1. The first 3 cubes drawn were blue. Is the fourth cube more likely to be red or blue?

2. The table at the right shows the scores of two players. Find Probability(A wins) and Probability(B wins).

3. Suppose Probability(A wins) = Probability(B wins). What can you say about the fairness of the game?

4. Si and Karen played a fair game. Karen won 7 times and Si won 13 times. How can this happen if the game is fair?

Game Results	
A wins	ЖН IIII
B wins	ЖН ЖН I
Times played	ЖН ЖН ЖН ЖН

List all the possible outcomes for each game.

5. Place 1 red, 1 blue, and 1 yellow cube in a bag. Draw 2 cubes.

6. Place 1 green and 3 yellow cubes in a bag. Draw 2 cubes.

7. Spin a spinner with sections labeled 1–4. Then flip a coin.

8. **Choose A, B, or C.** You and your friend want to play a game, but your only number cube is chipped. To try to make a fair game, you toss the cube 100 times and record the results.

Number	1	2	3	4	5	6
Times rolled	4	10	21	7	23	35

Which of the following games seems fair? Explain.
   A. You win if you roll a 6, and your friend wins if she rolls a 4.
   B. If the number is even, you win. If it is odd, your friend wins.
   C. If the number is 1, 2, or 3, you win. If it is 4, 5, or 6, your friend wins.

9. a. *Data Collection* Toss 2 coins at least 25 times. If you toss 2 heads or 2 tails, Player A wins. If you toss 1 head and 1 tail, Player B wins. Record your results in a table.
   b. Does the game seem fair or unfair? Explain.
   c. *Reasoning* Consider all possible outcomes for the game. Is the game fair? Support your answer without using your recorded data.

10. *Open-ended* Design one game that is fair and one that is unfair. Use coins, number cubes, spinners, or colored cubes.

Use the following information for Exercises 11–13.

Leroy rolled 2 number cubes and found the sum. He played the game many times and recorded the sums in the line plot below.

Sum   2   3   4   5   6   7   8   9   10   11   12

11. Find each experimental probability.
   a. Probability(3)   **b.** Probability(8)   **c.** Probability(12)
   d. Probability(5)   **e.** Probability(2)   **f.** Probability(1)

12. Complete a grid like the one at the right to show all possible outcomes. Which sum appears most likely? How does this compare to Leroy's results?

13. Leroy said to Tim, "If the sum of the 2 number cubes is prime, you win. If the sum is not prime, I win." Use your grid from Exercise 12. Is this game fair or unfair? Explain.

14. *Writing* Elan and Litisha played a game 10 times and decided it was unfair. Jaime and Marek played the same game 50 times and decided it was fair. Who do you think is correct? Why?

Mixed Review

Find the area of each parallelogram. *(Lesson 9-1)*

15. $b = 15$ in., $h = 10$ in.   **16.** $b = 28$ cm, $h = 21$ cm   **17.** $b = 16$ mm, $h = 42$ mm

Compare. Write <, >, or =. *(Lesson 10-1)*

18. -7 ▩ -9 **19.** 2 ▩ -2 **20.** 25 ▩ -50 **21.** 0 ▩ -8 **22.** 6 ▩ 0 **23.** -11 ▩ 13

24. Find all the numbers less than 100 that have the prime factors 2, 5, and 7. *(Lesson 5-1)*

11-2 Simulate a Problem

THINK AND DISCUSS

You can solve many probability problems by *simulating* them. Make a model and collect data from the model. Then use the data to solve the problem.

SAMPLE PROBLEM........

Each day, Sam delivers Mr. Hay's newspaper sometime between 6:30 A.M. and 7:30 A.M. Mr. Hay leaves for work between 7:00 A.M. and 8:00 A.M. What is the probability that he gets his paper before he leaves for work?

READ

Read for understanding. Summarize the problem.

1. Will Mr. Hay get the newspaper before he leaves for work if Sam delivers it before 7:00 A.M.? After 7:00 A.M.?

2. Sam is equally likely to deliver Mr. Hay's paper at any time between 6:30 A.M. and 7:30 A.M. How much of the time does he deliver Mr. Hay's paper before 7:00 A.M.? After 7:00 A.M.?

3. Mr. Hay is equally likely to leave for work at any time between 7:00 A.M. and 8:00 A.M. How much of the time does he leave before 7:30 A.M.? After 7:30 A.M.?

4. Two times are important: the time at which Sam delivers the paper and the time at which Mr. Hay leaves for work. Do these times depend on each other, or are they independent?

PLAN

Decide on a strategy.

You can't collect data on Sam and Mr. Hay. Instead, simulate the situation with a model. You can draw colored cubes, toss coins, spin spinners, or roll number cubes.

5. a. The spinner at the right models the times at which Sam delivers the paper. Make your own version of this spinner.

b. Make another spinner that models the times at which Mr. Hay leaves for work.

Sam's Delivery Times

Spinning each spinner once simulates what may happen on any given day. Each time you simulate the problem, you complete one **trial.**

SOLVE

Try the strategy.

6. Simulate the problem. Make a table like the one below. Perform at least 20 trials. Spin both spinners for each trial. Record the time Sam delivers the newspaper and the time Mr. Hay leaves for work.

Trial	Time Sam Delivers	Time Mr. Hay Leaves	Did Mr. Hay Get a Paper?
1	6:45 A.M.	7:15 A.M.	Yes
2	7:21 A.M.	7:00 A.M.	No

7. Use the data in your table to find the experimental probability that Mr. Hay will get his newspaper before he leaves for work. This probability is the *number of times he gets his paper* divided by *the number of delivery days.*

LOOK BACK

Think about how you solved the problem.

8. ⁂*Summarize* Based on your experiment, about how often might Mr. Hay expect to get his paper before leaving for work?

EXERCISES *On Your Own*

Simulate and solve each problem. Show all your work.

1. *Music* Suppose you practice piano for 15 minutes each weekday between 4:00 P.M. and 5:00 P.M. Your father gets home from work between 4:30 P.M. and 5:30 P.M. Find the experimental probability that your father gets home during your practice.

2. *Sports* A professional basketball player makes 75% of his free throws. Find the experimental probability that he will make two free throws in a row.

3. *Collecting* Suppose each box of cereal contains a coupon for one of four collectible figures. Each box of cereal costs $3.50. About how much will it cost for you to get all four coupons?

Use any strategy to solve each problem. Show all your work.

4. *Statistics* How many people do you need to gather to be sure that at least two of them have birthdays in the same month? Explain your reasoning.

5. *Movie Theaters* A survey reports that 73% of moviegoers buy a container of popcorn at the theater. A theater pays 45¢ for a container of popcorn and sells it for $1.50. What profit can the theater expect on a day when it has 1,000 customers?

6. *Restaurants* A restaurant has 25 of each sticker: soup, sandwich, salad, and drink. A sticker is put on each menu. Each time you visit the restaurant, you receive a different menu. The item listed on the sticker is free. How many times will you need to visit the restaurant to get every free item?

7. *Games* An 8-by-8 checkerboard is missing two opposite corners. One domino covers two squares of the board. Can you exactly cover the entire surface with dominoes?

8. *Writing* Suppose you want to order a new bedroom carpet. Write down all the information you would need to find out before you leave for the carpet store.

9. *Biology* Jumping spiders can jump 40 times their body length. About how far in centimeters might a 15-mm spider jump?

Mixed Review

Use tiles to find each sum. *(Lesson 10-3)*

10. $12 + (-3)$ 11. $-8 + (-3)$ 12. $7 + (-7)$ 13. $-4 + 6$ 14. $-2 + (-1)$ 15. $4 + (-7)$

Find the area of each triangle. *(Lesson 9-3)*

16. $b = 16$ m, $h = 11$ m   17. $b = 7.7$ cm, $h = 6.6$ cm   18. $b = 19$ in., $h = 8\frac{1}{2}$ in.

19. *Choose a Strategy* Susan and Deepa made a total of 33 pairs of gloves. Deepa made twice as many pairs as Susan. How many pairs did each girl make?

11-3 Simulations and Random Numbers

What You'll Learn

▼ To use random numbers to simulate probability problems

...And Why

You can use random numbers to find experimental probability quickly.

Here's How

Look for questions that
- ⚓ build understanding
- ✔ check understanding

THINK AND DISCUSS

It can take a lot of time to simulate a problem by spinning a spinner or flipping a coin. A quicker way is to use *random numbers*. This list shows how a computer printed out the digits 1 and 2 at random. Because the list is random, both digits are equally likely to occur.

List of Random 1's and 2's								
2	1	1	2	1	2	1	2	2
2	1	1	2	2	1	2	1	2
1	1	1	1	1	2	1	2	1
2	1	2	1	2	2	2	1	2
2	2	2	1	2	1	1	1	1
2	1	2	1	2	2	2	2	1
1	1	2	1	2	1	1	2	2
1	1	1	1	2	2	2	1	2

1. a. ⚓*Modeling* Suppose the number 1 represents a coin toss landing heads. Use the table above. Out of 72 trials, how many times might a coin land on heads?

   b. Suppose the number 2 represents a coin toss landing tails. How many times might a coin land on tails?

■ EXAMPLE

Modeling Use the random number table above. Find the experimental probability of tossing a coin three times and getting three heads in a row.

2 1 1	2 1 2	1 2 2	Make groups of 3 to
2 1 1	2 2 1	2 1 2	simulate 3 tosses.
1 1 1	1 1 2	1 2 1	
2 1 2	1 2 2	2 1 2	Let 1 represent heads, and
2 2 2	1 2 1	1 1 1	look for groups of 111.
2 1 2	1 2 2	2 2 1	
1 1 2	1 2 1	1 2 2	3 groups out of 24 show
1 1 1	1 2 2	2 1 2	3 heads in a row.

$$\text{Probability(3 heads)} = \frac{\text{number of groups of 3 heads}}{\text{total number of groups}}$$

$$= \frac{3}{24} = \frac{1}{8}$$

The experimental probability of tossing three heads in a row is $\frac{1}{8}$.

2. Copy the random number table on page 488.
   a. ✔ *Try It Out* Find the experimental probability of tossing two tails in a row.
   b. ⋅ *Think About It* Find the experimental probability of tossing heads, then tails, then heads, then tails.

You can use a graphing calculator or a random number generator program on a computer to generate random numbers.

3. ⋅ *Technology* Generate and print at least 500 random 1's and 2's. Model four coin tosses.
   a. Find the number of times 3 heads were tossed, followed by heads again (1111). Write Probability(3 heads, then heads).
   b. Find the number of times 3 heads were tossed, followed by tails (1112). Write Probability(3 heads, then tails).

4. ⋅ *Reasoning* Suppose a 500-digit random number table represents 125 groups of 4 coin tosses. About how many groups out of 125 would you expect to consist of 4 heads? Explain.

Work Together
Using Random Numbers

Technology Work with a partner to find the experimental probability of tossing heads. Use any section of your 500-digit random number table from Question 3.

5. a. Copy and complete the table below. Simulate tossing a coin 10 times. Then simulate 50 tosses, and so on.

Number of Tosses	Number of Heads	Number of Tails	Probability(Heads) = $\frac{\text{Number of Heads}}{\text{Number of Tosses}}$
10	▦	▦	▦
50	▦	▦	▦
100	▦	▦	▦
200	▦	▦	▦
500	▦	▦	▦

   b. Make a line graph to show what happens to Probability(heads) as the number of tosses increases.
   c. ⋅ *Writing* Describe any trends or patterns in the graph.
   d. ⋅ *Reasoning* What do you think will happen to Probability(heads) if you simulate another 1,000 tosses?

Choose **Use technology or the random number table on page 488. Find the experimental probability of each set of coin tosses.**

1. the probability of getting two heads in a row

2. the probability of getting two heads, then tails

3. the probability of getting two tails, then heads

4. the probability of getting three tails in a row

5. *Reasoning* Do you think your answers to Exercises 1–4 will be different if you use a different random number table? Why or why not?

Describe a way to use random numbers to find each probability.

6. You toss four coins and get four heads.

7. On a spinner divided into two equal sections of different colors, you spin the same color five times in a row.

8. You roll a number cube and get a prime number.

9. *Modeling* A theater prints one digit 0–9 on each ticket. If you collect every digit, you get a free ticket. How many movies will you see before you get a free ticket? Use the random digits at the right to simulate this problem.

List of Random Numbers, 0–9							
5	8	2	0	3	2	1	9
8	4	5	6	0	3	2	1
6	6	1	9	8	7	2	3
0	4	7	2	8	2	2	7
0	1	3	6	3	9	3	9
0	2	6	5	8	3	1	0
8	8	6	8	4	2	9	7
5	0	1	8	2	3	9	5

10. **Choose A, B, or C.** The forecast calls for a 50% chance of rain for each of the next three days. Which method will *not* work to find the probability of three days of rain?

   A. Toss a coin. Let heads be "rain" and tails be "no rain."
   B. Use a computer to list random digits 0–9. Let 0–4 be "rain" and let 5–9 be "no rain."
   C. Spin a spinner with three equal sections: one day of rain, two days of rain, and three days of rain.

11. *Writing* A basketball player makes 50% of her free throws. Explain how to use a simulation to find the experimental probability that she makes 7 of 10 free throws.

12. *Modeling* A game involves tossing three coins. If you get exactly two heads or two tails, you win. Otherwise, your opponent wins. Use a simulation to decide whether the game is fair or unfair.

13. a. *Modeling* How likely are "doubles" when you roll two number cubes? Use the list at the right to do a simulation. Use two digits at a time. Complete the table below.

List of Random Numbers, 1–6							
2	3	4	1	6	3	2	4
1	1	2	5	3	4	5	2
4	3	5	1	4	2	6	3
5	2	3	2	4	3	4	6
4	4	2	4	1	2	3	3
6	2	3	1	3	2	6	4
5	5	4	3	6	3	1	1
4	1	3	4	2	4	5	3
1	4	1	5	2	6	2	2

Number of Doubles	▣
Number of Times the Pair of Number Cubes Was Rolled	▣
Probability(Doubles)	▣

b. Now find the probability by listing all possible outcomes. How does your answer compare to the answer you got using a simulation?

Mixed Review

Find the circumference and area of each circle. Round to the nearest unit. *(Lesson 9-5)*

14. $r = 7$ cm   **15.** $d = 19$ m   **16.** $r = 2.6$ m   **17.** $d = 37$ mm   **18.** $d = 11$ cm

Use tiles to find the difference. *(Lesson 10-4)*

19. $-9 - 1$ **20.** $4 - (-5)$ **21.** $-14 - (-3)$ **22.** $-9 - 4$ **23.** $-2 - (-7)$

24. *Choose a Strategy* For the student meeting, 75% came on time. Of the students who came late, 50% were no more than ten minutes late. Four students were more than ten minutes late. How many students came to the meeting?

CHAPTER PROJECT

PROJECT LINK: SIMULATING

Design a method of choosing among three different movies. Use a computer, a list of random digits, a spinner, or number cubes to simulate the situation. Test your method for 100 trials and record your data in a table. Use the data to find the experimental probability of each outcome.

Theoretical Probability

Work Together

Exploring Theoretical Probability

Work with a partner. Look back at Game 3 on page 480. It involves 3 red cubes and 1 blue cube in a bag.

1. ⚬ **Explain** Suppose you draw 1 cube from the bag. Which are you more likely to pick, red or blue? How do you know?

2. ⚬ **What If . . .** Suppose you draw 1 cube from the bag, and then put it back. If you do this many times, what fraction of the outcomes would you expect to be red? What fraction would you expect to be blue?

3. ⚬ **Reasoning** Are all 4 cubes equally likely to be drawn?

THINK AND DISCUSS

1 _Finding Theoretical Probability_

You can find experimental probability by doing simulations. You can find **theoretical probability** without a simulation. When all outcomes are equally likely, the theoretical probability of an event is the ratio below.

$$\text{Probability(event)} = \frac{\text{number of favorable outcomes}}{\text{number of possible outcomes}}$$

You can write this ratio as a fraction, a decimal, or a percent.

■ EXAMPLE

Suppose you draw one marble from the bag at the left. What is the probability that you draw a red marble?

$$\text{Probability(red)} = \frac{\text{number of favorable outcomes}}{\text{number of possible outcomes}}$$

$$= \frac{\text{red marbles}}{\text{all marbles}}$$

$$= \frac{2}{5}$$

$$\text{Probability(red)} = \frac{2}{5} = 0.4 = 40\%$$

4. **Reasoning** Look at the bag of marbles.
   a. How many yellow marbles should you add to the bag to make Probability(yellow) equal Probability(red)?
   b. After you add yellow marbles to the bag, what is the probability of drawing yellow? Drawing red?

5. ✔**Try It Out** A bag contains 3 red cubes and 1 blue cube. Suppose you draw one cube.
   a. Are all cubes equally likely to be drawn?
   b. How many possible outcomes are there? How many outcomes are favorable for red?
   c. Find Probability(red). Write it as a fraction, as a decimal, and as a percent.

6. **Explain** Look at the formula for theoretical probability on page 492. What does the word *favorable* mean?

▼2 *Types of Events*

When the probability of an event is 1, the event is *certain* to happen. When the probability of an event is 0, the event is *impossible*. Events with probabilities between 0 and 1 are *possible*. Possible events can be likely or unlikely.

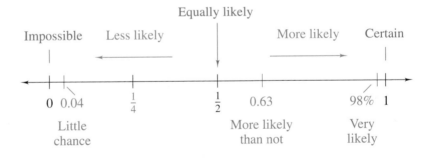

7. **Think About It** Name an example of each type of event.
   a. certain   b. impossible   c. possible

8. ✔**Try It Out** Find the probability of each example you gave. Write each probability as a fraction, a decimal, and a percent.

9. Suppose you roll a number cube once.
   a. List all the possible outcomes.
   b. What is the theoretical probability of rolling an odd number?
   c. **Go a Step Further** Find the sum Probability(odd) + Probability(not odd). What does this sum represent?

Find the theoretical probability for one roll of a number cube. Write each as a fraction, a decimal, and a percent.

1. Probability(4)

2. Probability(9)

3. Probability(not 5)

4. Probability(1 or 3 or 6)

5. Probability(2 or 5)

6. Probability(even or odd)

Find the theoretical probability of each event.

7. A spinner has equal sections of red, blue, pink, green, and yellow. You spin blue or pink.

8. You toss two coins. Both tosses are heads.

9. The sum of the numbers rolled on two number cubes is 7.

10. Find the theoretical probabilities of spinning red and spinning blue for the spinner at the right.

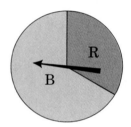

11. *Prize Drawing* Suppose your teacher writes the name of each student in your class on a card. To select a winner, your teacher draws one card from a box. Use your class data to find Probability(you win). Find Probability(you do not win).

12. *Raffles* One thousand raffle tickets are sold. Suppose you buy two of them. One winning ticket is drawn.
a. What is the probability that you will win?
b. What is the probability that you will not win?

Ten cards are numbered 1–10. Find the theoretical probability of each event below. Write each as a fraction, a decimal, and a percent.

13. Probability(6)

14. Probability(even number)

15. Probability(odd number)

16. Probability(not 6)

17. Probability(1 or 2 or 3)

18. Probability(1 through 10)

19. A bag contains only red and green cubes. You select one cube without looking. Probability(red) = $\frac{3}{8}$.
a. Find Probability(green).
b. How many of each color cube might the bag contain?
c. Draw a spinner you could use to simulate this problem.

20. *Reasoning* Suppose you toss an *icosahedron*, a solid with 20 faces. All outcomes are equally likely. Each face is colored red, blue, yellow, or green. You know that Probability(yellow) = Probability(blue) = Probability(green) = Probability(red). How many faces are colored red?

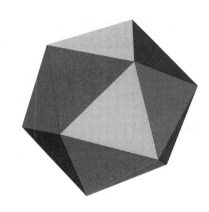

21. *Writing* Does it make more sense to you to think of probability as a fraction, a decimal, or a percent? Explain.

22. a. *Open-ended* Make a spinner with Probability(A) = 50%, Probability(B) = 10%, Probability(C) = 0%, and Probability(D) = 40%.
   b. Use a simulation to find the experimental probabilities of spinning the different letters. Then compare the experimental probabilities to the theoretical probabilities.

Use the letters at the right. Write the theoretical probability of each event as a fraction. Copy the number line and show where each probability lies.

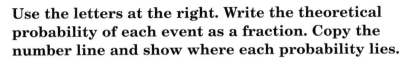
A, B, C, D, E, F, G, H, I, J

23. Probability(H)

24. Probability(A or B)

25. Probability(M)

26. Probability(vowel)

27. Probability(consonant)

28. Probability(A through J)

Classify each event as *certain*, *likely*, *unlikely*, or *impossible*.

29. You spin a wheel numbered 1–30 and land on a multiple of 2, 3, or 5.

30. You roll three number cubes. Their sum is 19.

31. You roll five number cubes. Their sum is at least 5.

32. A meteorite lands in your schoolyard.

33. Order the following events from most likely to least likely.
   A. The sun rises tomorrow.
   B. You have a homework assignment tonight.
   C. The next coin you toss comes up heads.
   D. It snows somewhere in your state this week.
   E. You live to be 195 years old.
   F. You make a basket next time you play basketball.

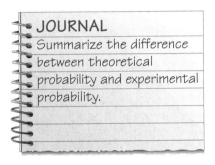
JOURNAL
Summarize the difference between theoretical probability and experimental probability.

Find the perimeter and area of each square or rectangle.
(Lesson 9-2)

34. $s = 54$ mm   **35.** $\ell = 17.5$ m, $w = 8$ **36.** $\ell = 4$ m, $w = 3.2$ m   **37.** $s = 4\frac{1}{2}$ in.

Model each integer in two ways. *(Lesson 10-2)*

38. -7 **39.** 15 **40.** -4 **41.** -9 **42.** 11 **43.** -21

44. *Survey* Jennifer surveyed all 28 members of her home economics class about their favorite food. In the survey, 75% of the students chose pizza. How many students did not choose pizza? *(Lesson 7-9)*

✓ CHECKPOINT 1   Lessons 11-1 through 11-4

1. Five cards are numbered 1–5. Find the theoretical probability of each event. Write as a fraction, a decimal, and a percent.
   a. Probability(3) **b.** Probability(odd number) **c.** Probability(2 or 3)

2. Lei-Li and Earline played a game and completed the table at the right.
   a. Find the experimental probability that Earline wins.
   b. Find the experimental probability that Lei-Li wins.
   c. Is the game fair? Explain.

Game Results	
Earline wins	14
Lei-Li wins	16
Times played	30

3. **Choose A, B, C, or D.** Which event is most likely?

   A. "tails" when you toss a coin
   B. "consonant" when you randomly choose a letter A–Z
   C. "9" in a list with the digits 0–9
   D. "not 3" when you roll a number cube

CHAPTER PROJECT

PROJECT LINK: DESIGNING

Design a three-dimensional shape that would result in three equally likely outcomes. (Look back at Lesson 9-6 if necessary.) How would you use the shape so that a fair situation results? Test this method for 100 trials and record your data. Use the data to find the experimental probability of each outcome.

EXPLORATION

Complement of an Event

After Lesson 11-4

The *complement of an event* includes all ways that the event *cannot* happen. Suppose you draw one of the marbles at the right without looking. The complement of picking a marble that has a star on it is picking a marble that does *not* have a star on it. If the probability of an event is Probability(event), then the complement of the event is Probability(*not* event).

■ EXAMPLE

Find Probability(star). Then find the probability of the complement of that event.

Probability(star) = $\dfrac{3}{5}$ ◀— favorable outcomes (marbles that have a star)

◀— all possible outcomes (total number of marbles)

Probability(not star) = $\dfrac{2}{5}$ ◀— favorable outcomes (marbles that do not have a star)

◀— all possible outcomes (total number of marbles)

Suppose you toss a number cube. Find each probability.

1. Probability(3)
2. Probability(not 3)
3. Probability(3 or 6)

4. Probability(not 3 or 6)
5. Probability(1, 2, 3, or 4)
6. Probability(not 1, 2, 3, or 4)

Suppose you draw one of the marbles shown at the right without looking. Find each probability.

7. Probability(plain white marble)
8. Probability(not plain white marble)

9. Probability(plain black marble)
10. Probability(not plain black marble)

11. Probability(happy face marble)
12. Probability(not happy face marble)

13. Probability(star marble)
14. Probability(not star marble)

15. *Writing* Look at the results of Exercises 7–14.
    a. Find the sum Probability(event) + Probability(not event).
    b. Is this statement true or false?
       Probability(not event) = 1 − Probability(event)
    c. If Probability(event) is $\frac{5}{8}$, what is Probability(not event)?

What You'll Learn

▼1 To use tree diagrams to find possible outcomes and probabilities

▼2 To use the counting principle to find possible outcomes and probabilities

...And Why

Tree diagrams and the counting principle can help you make choices in everyday life.

Here's How

Look for questions that

⚓ build understanding

✔ check understanding

THINK AND DISCUSS

▼1 Using a Tree Diagram

Suppose you want to choose among three after-school activities. You can choose the photography club, the yearbook club, or the computer club for a ten-week period. After ten weeks, you choose again for the next ten weeks. You can choose the same activity.

1. How many choices do you have for the first activity?

A tree diagram displays all possible choices. Each branch shows one choice. Use a tree diagram when all outcomes are equally likely to occur and when an event has two or more stages.

■ **EXAMPLE 1**   *Real-World Problem Solving*

Draw a tree diagram for the after-school activities. How many different ways can you choose?

Use P for the photography club, Y for the yearbook club, and C for the computer club.

First Activity	Second Activity	Possible Choices
P	P	PP
	Y	PY
	C	PC
Y	P	YP
	Y	YY
	C	YC
C	P	CP
	Y	CY
	C	CC

There are 9 different ways to choose activities.

2. ✔*Try It Out* Draw a tree diagram that shows all possible outcomes when you toss 3 coins.

You can use a tree diagram to find the probability of an event.

■ **EXAMPLE 2**

Use the tree diagram in Example 1. Suppose you choose randomly. What is the probability you choose the computer club for the second period?

$$\text{Probability} = \frac{\text{number of favorable outcomes}}{\text{number of possible outcomes}}$$

$$= \frac{3}{9} \qquad \longleftarrow \text{There are 3 favorable outcomes:}$$
$$\qquad\qquad\qquad \text{PC, YC, and CC.}$$

$$= \frac{1}{3}$$

Probability(computer club in second period) $= \frac{1}{3}$

3. ⁂*Reasoning* Is there a relationship between the number of first- and second-period activities and the number of possible choices? If so, what is it?

4. ⁂*Analyze* Do you see a way to count all possible outcomes without using a tree diagram or a grid? Explain.

▼ *Using the Counting Principle*

Another way to find the number of possible outcomes is to use *the counting principle*.

THE COUNTING PRINCIPLE

The number of outcomes for an event with two or more distinct stages is the product of the number of outcomes at each stage.

■ **EXAMPLE 3**   *Real-World Problem Solving*

Food Suppose you want to buy a pizza. The menu is at the left. Thick and thin crusts cost the same. You have enough money for only one topping. How many different types of pizza can you buy?

Use the counting principle.

Topping (6 choices)	Crust (2 choices)	Types of pizza
6	× 2	= 12

You can buy 12 different types of pizza.

Pizza Palace

Toppings	Crusts
mushrooms	thick
onions	thin
pepperoni	
sausage	
peppers	
extra cheese	

5. ✔ *Try It Out* Suppose Pizza Palace decides to offer one more topping. Now how many types of pizza can you buy?

6. ⁂ *Visual Thinking* What information do you get with a tree diagram that you do not get with the counting principle?

You can also use the counting principle to find the probability of an event.

■ **EXAMPLE 4**

Use the menu from Example 3. Suppose you choose a pizza at random. What is the probability that you choose a mushroom pizza with a thin crust?

Number of possible outcomes = $6 \times 2 = 12$ ⟵ Use the counting principle.

Probability = $\frac{\text{number of favorable outcomes}}{\text{number of possible outcomes}}$

$= \frac{1}{12}$

Probability(mushroom, thin crust) = $\frac{1}{12}$

7. ✔ *Try It Out* Find the probability of randomly choosing each type of pizza.
   a. a thick crust
   b. a pepperoni pizza

EXERCISES *On Your Own*

1. **Cars** A white car comes with a gray, blue, or black interior. A silver car also has the option of a red interior. Draw a tree diagram showing all possible color combinations. How many are there?

2. Small and large blocks in a set come in five shapes: cube, pyramid, cone, cylinder, and triangular prism. List all the different types of blocks in the set.

3. A spinner has equal sections of red, blue, and green. Use a tree diagram to find the probability of no more than one result of red in two spins.

4. **Writing** Write a problem that can be solved using the tree diagram at the right. Solve your problem.

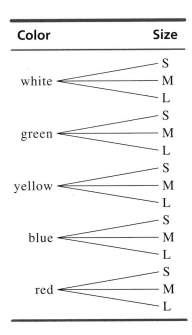

Color	Size
white	S M L
green	S M L
yellow	S M L
blue	S M L
red	S M L

5. *Menu Planning* A cafeteria always serves the same three main courses and three desserts. Each day, you choose a combination of one main course and one dessert. How many meals can you eat before you repeat a combination?

6. *Games* To play a game, you spin a spinner and take a card. The spinner has sections that tell you to move 1, 2, 3, or 4 spaces. The cards read Free Turn, Lose a Turn, or No Change. Find the probability that you move 3 spaces and lose a turn.

7. *Travel* Four airlines fly nonstop from Baltimore to Columbus. Five airlines fly nonstop from Columbus to Seattle. How many different pairs of airlines can you use to fly from Baltimore to Seattle through Columbus?

8. a. Suppose you roll two number cubes. Use the counting principle to find the number of possible outcomes.
   b. Why is using the counting principle easier than drawing a tree diagram?
   c. Find the probability of rolling two 5's.

9. *Consumer Issues* The table below gives some of the choices available when you buy a computer. Suppose you choose one keyboard, one monitor, and one printer.

Keyboards	Monitors	Printers
Standard $50	Color 15-in. $369	Inkjet $149
Extended $90	Color 17-in. $699	Color Inkjet $369
Adjustable $130	Color 19-in. $1,399	Laser $819

a. How many outcomes are possible?
b. You want a monitor larger than 15 in., but you do not want an adjustable keyboard. How many outcomes are left?
c. Which combination costs the least? Which combination costs the most? What is the range of costs?

Mixed Review

Sketch each three-dimensional figure. *(Lesson 9-6)*

10. square prism

11. rectangular pyramid

12. octagonal pyramid

Make a function table for each function. *(Lesson 10-6)*

13. meters as a function of kilometers

14. hours as a function of days

15. *Choose a Strategy* Randy delivers 270 newspapers during a seven-day week. He delivers twice as many on the weekend as on the weekdays. How many newspapers does he deliver on the weekend?

What You'll Learn

▼ To identify independent events

▼ To use multiplication to find probabilities of independent events

...And Why

The probability of independent events is a factor in many games.

Here's How

Look for questions that

🔹 build understanding

✔ check understanding

THINK AND DISCUSS

▼ Exploring Independent Events

Look again at Game 3 on page 480.

1. 🔹**Look Back** Recall your results for Game 3. Is Game 3 fair or unfair? If you need to, play the game again or draw a diagram to consider all possible outcomes.

2. 🔹**Data Analysis** Change Game 3 to Game 3A, described below. Play Game 3A with a partner at least 20 times. To get more data, combine your results with the results of two other groups. Do you think Game 3A is fair or unfair? Explain.

Game 3A

Place 3 red cubes and 1 blue cube in a bag. Draw a cube from the bag without looking. Record the color, put the cube back into the bag, and draw a second cube. If the 2 cubes are the same color, Player A wins. If not, Player B wins.

The tree diagram at the right shows 16 possible outcomes.

3. Is the tree diagram for Game 3, Game 3A, or both games?

4. 🔹**Analyze** Use the tree diagram to decide whether this game is fair or unfair.

5. In Game 3A, are all 4 cubes equally likely to be drawn on the first draw? On the second draw? Does the second cube drawn depend on the first cube drawn?

6. In Game 3, does the second cube drawn depend on the first cube drawn? Why or why not?

Outcomes

```
        ┌ R ──── RR
    R ──┤ R ──── RR
        ├ R ──── RR
        └ B ──── RB
        ┌ R ──── RR
    R ──┤ R ──── RR
        ├ R ──── RR
        └ B ──── RB
        ┌ R ──── RR
    R ──┤ R ──── RR
        ├ R ──── RR
        └ B ──── RB
        ┌ R ──── BR
    B ──┤ R ──── BR
        ├ R ──── BR
        └ B ──── BB
```

When the outcome of one event does not depend on the outcome of another event, the events are **independent.**

7. Which game has independent events, Game 3 or Game 3A?

President John F. Kennedy was inaugurated on January 20, 1961.

8. ✔*Try It Out* Are the two events independent? Why or why not?
   a. It snows in Washington, D.C. A new President of the United States is inaugurated.
   b. A card is drawn from a deck and is not replaced. Another card is drawn from the deck.
   c. Your team scores the most points. Your team wins.
   d. At a soccer game, a coin is tossed and comes up heads. At the next game, the coin comes up tails.
   e. You take a dish from the kitchen cabinet. The dish falls and breaks.

9. ⚏*Think About It* List some events that are independent and some that are not. Think of events that are not already described in this chapter.

▼2 *Multiplying Probabilities*

When events are independent, you can find the probability that both or all of them occur by multiplying the probabilities.

$$\text{Probability(A and B)} = \text{Probability(A)} \times \text{Probability(B)}$$

■ EXAMPLE

For Game 3A, find Probability(both red).

Since the draws are independent, multiply their probabilities.

$$\text{Probability(both red)} = \text{Probability(red)} \times \text{Probability(red)}$$
$$= \frac{3}{4} \times \frac{3}{4}$$
$$= \frac{9}{16}$$

10. ✔*Try It Out* Use multiplication to find Probability(both blue).

11. **⠿ Go a Step Further** Use multiplication to find the probability of tossing 3 tails in a row. Complete: Probability(tails, tails, tails) = Probability(tails) × Probability(tails) × Probability(tails) = ▨ × ▨ × ▨ = ▨.

12. *Clothes* Mei-Ling has 3 sweaters: pink, white, and blue. She has 2 pairs of jeans: white and blue. She has 5 pairs of socks: 3 white, 1 blue, and 1 pink. She randomly selects 1 sweater, 1 pair of jeans, and 1 pair of socks. What is the probability that all are blue?
    a. Use the counting principle to find the number of possible outcomes. Then find the probability.
    b. Use multiplication to find the probability.
    c. Compare your answers for parts (a) and (b). Which method do you prefer for finding the probability? Why?
    d. Explain why you might not want to use a tree diagram to find this probability.

EXERCISES *On Your Own*

Decide whether the events are independent. Explain your answer.

1. You take a coin from your pocket. Then you take another coin from your pocket.

2. It snows one night. The next day you go sledding.

3. A card is drawn from a deck and replaced. Another card is drawn from the deck.

4. You reach into your drawer and take a pencil. At the same time, you take a pen.

5. The local basketball team wins the league championship. That same year, the local baseball team also wins its league championship.

6. **Choose A, B, or C.** Which events are *not* independent?
    A. Your computer randomly lists a 1 and then a 2.
    B. You draw a blue card from a deck of colored cards. Then you draw a red card.
    C. You roll a number cube twice and get 6 both times.

7. *Writing* Use your own words to explain to a friend what independent events are. Give some examples.

8. *Biology* Assume "boy" and "girl" are equally likely outcomes for a baby. Is having two babies of the same sex as likely as having two babies of different sexes? Use a tree diagram to show your solution.

Use the spinner for Exercises 9–11. It is spun twice.

9. Are the two spins independent events? Explain.

10. Draw a tree diagram to show all possible outcomes. Find the probability that the two spins are the same color.

11. Use multiplication to find the probability that the first spin is blue and the second spin is red.

You roll a number cube, and you spin a spinner that is half red and half yellow. Find the probability of each result.

12. any number and red

13. any odd number and red

14. the number 1 and yellow

15. a number less than 3 and either color

16. a number less than 7 and either color

17. a number greater than 6 and either color

Use the two boxes at the right for Exercises 18–20. Box 1 contains 4 cards. Box 2 contains 5 cards.

18. A card is drawn from Box 1. Find Probability(M).

19. A card is drawn from Box 1. Then a card is drawn from Box 2. Find Probability(ME).

20. A card is drawn from Box 1 and put back. Then another card is drawn. Find Probability(HA).

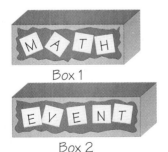

Box 1

Box 2

21. In a game you toss a coin and roll two number cubes. How many possible outcomes are there for each of the following?
    a. one coin
    b. one cube
    c. one coin and one cube
    d. the game

22. *Biology* Assume "boy" and "girl" are equally likely outcomes for a baby. What is the probability of having five girls in a row? Show your solution in at least two different ways.

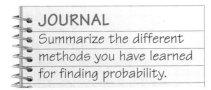

JOURNAL
Summarize the different methods you have learned for finding probability.

Calculator **Find the diameter of a circle with the given circumference. Round to the nearest unit.** *(Lesson 9-4)*

23. 112.3 cm   **24.** 19.5 m   **25.** 265.6 mm   **26.** 131.7 in.   **27.** 160 ft   **28.** 178 km

Give the measures of the complement and the supplement for each angle. *(Lesson 8-3)*

29. 27°   **30.** 58°   **31.** 62°   **32.** 73°   **33.** 87°   **34.** 14°

35. *Choose a Strategy* Mr. Oblas is ordering wrapping paper. He can order ten 12 in.-by-12 in. sheets for $2.95 each or a roll that measures 30 in. by $2\frac{1}{2}$ ft for the same price. Which is the better buy?

CHAPTER PROJECT

PROJECT LINK: ANALYZING

Compare the experimental method you used on page 496 with the one you used on page 491. Which method do you prefer? Using your preferred method, conduct and record 150 more trials. Then compare the experimental probability of each event to its theoretical probability. Do you think you made the right decision? Explain.

Math at Work

BOARD GAME DESIGNER

A career as a board game designer could be just right for you if you love games. Game design requires an eye for color and a creative mind. It also calls for mathematical skills. Many games involve the use of spinners or number cubes. That's where probability comes in. Data analysis is used to evaluate marketing information about a game.

For more information about designing games, visit the Prentice Hall Web site: www.phschool.com

Exploring Arrangements

What You'll Learn

1 To use a tree diagram or a list to find number of arrangements

2 To use the counting principle to find number of arrangements

...And Why

You can use arrangements to solve problems involving hobbies and sports.

Here's How

Look for questions that
- **⁘** build understanding
- ✔ check understanding

Work Together

Exploring Order

Work in groups of four.

1. **⁘ Predict** In how many different ways do you think you can arrange your group members in a line?

2. **⁘ Data Collection** Form a line of your group members. Then form as many different lines as you can. How many could you form?

3. **⁘ Modeling** Simulate the problem. Represent each member with an object, such as a pencil or a book. Arrange the objects in as many different lines as you can. Do you get the same result as in Question 2?

4. **⁘ Modeling** Represent each group member with a letter or number. Make an organized list of all possible arrangements.
   a. How many arrangements are in your list?
   b. Compare this number with your prediction and your answers to Questions 2 and 3.

THINK AND DISCUSS

1 Using a Tree Diagram or List

You can use a tree diagram or an organized list to count possible arrangements. An arrangement in a particular order is called a **permutation.**

5. The tree diagram shows the arrangements of the numbers 1, 2, and 3.
   a. Draw a tree diagram that shows all possible arrangements of the numbers 1, 2, 3, and 4.
   b. How many permutations of 1, 2, 3, and 4 are there?

Outcomes

$1 <$ 2 — 3 — 123
        3 — 2 — 132

$2 <$ 1 — 3 — 213
        3 — 1 — 231

$3 <$ 1 — 2 — 312
        2 — 1 — 321

Use a calculator to find each value.

9. 6!   **10.** 10!   **11.** 8!   **12.** 7!   **13.** 13!   **14.** 4! + 4

15. *Literature* A library receives a new seven-volume set of *The Chronicles of Narnia* by C. S. Lewis.
   a. In how many ways can the books be arranged in a row?
   b. The seven books are placed in a random order on a shelf. What is the probability that the books are in the correct order from left to right?

16. *Reasoning* Lola tells Ana that her phone number includes one of each digit from 3 through 9. Ana decides to try each possible number until she reaches Lola. If Ana is as unlucky as possible, how many tries will it take to reach Lola?

Mixed Review

Find the surface area of each rectangular prism. *(Lesson 9-7)*

17. $\ell = 8$ m, $w = 10$ m, $h = 7$ m   **18.** $\ell = 6.4$ m, $w = 5.2$ m, $h = 2.1$ m

Graph each point on a coordinate plane. Label it with its letter. *(Lesson 10-7)*

19. $A(2, -2)$ **20.** $B(-2, 2)$ **21.** $C(-3, -5)$ **22.** $D(2, 4)$ **23.** $E(-3, 0)$ **24.** $F(0, -5)$

25. *Fitness* Kay exercises $\frac{1}{6}$ h the first day, $\frac{1}{4}$ h the second day, and $\frac{1}{3}$ h the third day. If she continues this pattern, how long will Kay exercise on the fifth day? *(Lesson 2-2)*

✓ CHECKPOINT 2   *Lessons 11-5 through 11-7*

1. A blue, red, or yellow chip is selected, and a coin is tossed.
   a. Draw a tree diagram to show all possible outcomes.
   b. Find Probability(yellow and tails).

2. When ordering the luncheon special, you can choose from 3 entrees, 2 soups, and 2 desserts. Use the counting principle to find the number of possible choices.

3. A bag contains 3 green cubes and 4 red cubes. A cube is drawn and replaced. Another cube is drawn. What is the probability that 2 red cubes are drawn?

4. In how many different ways can 6 students be lined up shoulder-to-shoulder for a photograph?

PROBLEM SOLVING PRACTICE

★★★★★

Choose the best answer.

1. Suppose you pick one letter at random from the word MATHEMATICS. What is the probability that the letter will be a vowel?

   A. $\frac{4}{11}$ **B.** $\frac{1}{2}$ **C.** $\frac{4}{7}$ **D.** $\frac{7}{11}$

2. Suppose you roll a number cube and toss a coin. What is the probability that the number cube will show 6 and the coin will show heads?

   F. $\frac{1}{2}$ **G.** $\frac{1}{6}$ **H.** $\frac{1}{8}$ **J.** $\frac{1}{12}$

3. In playing a game, Tosha won 8 times, Pete won 7 times, and Maurice won 10 times. Based on this information, how many times would you expect Maurice to win if they play the game 100 more times?

   A. 10   **B.** 15   **C.** 25   **D.** 40

4. How many different 4-letter "words" can be formed by using the letters *L, O, V,* and *E* if each letter is used only once and the words do not have to make sense?

   F. 12   **G.** 16   **H.** 24   **J.** 256

5. You want to draw a map of your neighborhood on a piece of paper that is $8\frac{1}{2}$ in. by 11 in. What scale should be used to map an area 1,000 yd by 750 yd?

   A. 1 in. = 75 yd   **B.** 1 in. = 80 yd
   C. 1 in. = 85 yd   **D.** 1 in. = 95 yd

6. What is the volume of a rectangular prism 2 m long, 35 cm wide, and 0.4 m high?

   F. 280 m^3 **G.** 28 m^3
   H. 2.8 m^3 **J.** 0.28 m^3

7. At an ice cream shop you have a choice of 14 flavors of ice cream and 6 choices of topping. Suppose you order a sundae made with 2 scoops of different flavors and 1 topping. How many different sundaes could be ordered?

   A. 33   **B.** 34   **C.** 1,092   **D.** 1,176

8. At a restaurant last night, 8 people ordered steaks, 10 ordered seafood, 18 ordered chicken, and 14 ordered pasta. From this information, how many people out of 100 would you expect to order pasta?

   F. 28   **G.** 50   **H.** 280   **J.** 450

Please note that items 9 and 10 each have *five* answer choices.

9. Use the data below. If one person from the survey is picked at random, what is the probability that the person will prefer news?

Favorite Television Program

Type of Program	Number of People
Situation comedy	13
Sports	16
Drama	11
News	10

   A. $\frac{1}{10}$ **B.** $\frac{1}{5}$ **C.** $\frac{1}{4}$
   D. $\frac{4}{5}$ **E.** Not Here

10. Suppose your pocket contains four coins: a nickel, two dimes, and a quarter. What is the probability you pick a dime?

   F. 0   **G.** $\frac{1}{4}$ **H.** $\frac{1}{2}$
   J. 1   **K.** Not Here

11-8 Making Predictions from Data

What You'll Learn

1 To identify samples from a given population

2 To make predictions about a population based on a sample

...And Why

Sampling methods let you draw conclusions about elections, natural resources, and manufacturing quality control.

Here's How

Look for questions that
- build understanding
- ✔ check understanding

THINK AND DISCUSS

1 Identifying Samples

Tourism A survey was sent to over 8,000 adults in the United States. Only about 2,000 people responded. The survey asked "Have you ever visited the White House?" and "Have you ever visited Disneyland or Disney World?" Here are the results.

Site	Yes	No
White House	60%	40%
Disneyland or Disney World	70%	30%

Source: *The First Really Important Survey of American Habits*

1. **Data Analysis** According to the data, have more adults visited the White House or Disneyland/Disney World?

2. Of 2,000 people who responded, how many have visited the White House?

3. What is the probability that a person who responded to the survey visited the White House? Disneyland or Disney World?

A **population** is a group about which you want information. A **sample** is a part of the population you use to make predictions about the population.

To predict accurately, a sample must be *representative* of the population. In a **random sample,** choosing any population member is equally likely. A random sample is usually representative.

4. **⊡ Look Back** For the survey on page 512, what is the population? What is the sample?

5. a. **✔ Try It Out** Do you think the sample was representative of all people in the United States? Explain.
   b. About one fourth of those questioned returned their surveys. Why is this a problem?

There are several methods of conducting a survey. You could do it at just one location, such as a grocery store. This method is known as *convenience sampling*, because the method is convenient for the one taking the survey. A sample is **biased** if it is not random and may therefore give results that are not representative of the population.

6. **⊡ Think About It** Suppose the city of Orlando, Florida, (home of Disney World), asks people on the street the question "Have you ever visited Disney World?" Do you think the results would be biased? Why or why not?

▼ *Making Predictions*

You can use a random sample to make predictions about a larger population. Write a proportion using the random sample and the population. Then solve for the unknown.

■ **EXAMPLE**   *Real-World Problem Solving*

Quality Control From 15,000 pairs of sports shoes, a manufacturer takes a random sample of 300 pairs. The sample has 4 defective pairs. Predict the total number of defective pairs.

Write a proportion.

$$\text{defective pairs in sample} \rightarrow \frac{4}{300} = \frac{n}{15{,}000} \leftarrow \begin{array}{l}\text{defective pairs in population} \\ \leftarrow \text{pairs in population}\end{array}$$

pairs in sample

$$300n = 4 \times 15{,}000 \quad \leftarrow \text{Solve.}$$
$$n = 200$$

The company can predict that 200 pairs are defective.

7. **What If . . .** Suppose the sample in the Example had contained only 20 pairs of shoes. Would you expect the prediction to be more or less accurate? Explain.

8. **Go a Step Further** Find the probability that a pair of shoes in the Example is defective.

9. ✔**Try It Out** A later sample shows 4 pairs of 500 are defective. Predict how many of 20,000 pairs are defective.

Work Together _____ *Using Random Samples*

Work in teams to experiment with random samples. Take turns being Team 1 and Team 2. Then answer the questions.

Team 1: Create a population of objects (such as marbles, cubes, or beans) that differ only in color. Use 2, 3, or 4 colors. Record the number of objects of each color. Tell Team 2 only the size of your population and the number of colors you used.

Team 2: Take a random sample of the population. From it, predict the distribution of colors in the population. For example, if the population contains 400 white or red cubes, you might predict that there are 100 white cubes and 300 red cubes.

10. **Explain** How did you make sure that the samples were random?

11. **Data Collection** How many objects did you use for a sample? Why?

12. **Data Analysis** How well did your sample represent the population? Explain.

EXERCISES *On Your Own*

In a survey, 1,580 parents were asked which trait they ranked as most desirable in their children. The table shows the results.

1. Which trait was considered most desirable?

2. Of the 1,580 parents surveyed, about how many ranked "good judgment" as the most desirable trait?

Trait	% Ranked as Most Desirable
Honest	36%
Good judgment	18%
Obeys parents	16%

Source: *Statistical Handbook on the American Family*

Is each sample described in Exercises 3–6 random? Is it representative? Explain.

3. A company wants the opinions of sixth graders in a town. They place the name of every sixth grader in town in a revolving bin and draw 30 names.

4. To find the national cost of a two-bedroom apartment, 100 New Yorkers who live in two-bedroom apartments are polled.

5. To determine the most popular car in your city, you survey the cars in the high school parking lot.

6. To taste a bowl of soup, you take a spoonful.

7. *Writing* Why would you take a random sample instead of counting or surveying the whole population?

8. *Reasoning* Can you have a sample that is representative but not random? Can you have a sample that is random but not representative? Explain using examples.

9. *Health* Suppose 6 of the 22 students in your mathematics class are out with the flu. Is this a good sample to use to predict how many of 484 students in the school have the flu? Why or why not?

The survey below appeared in a magazine sold all over the United States. Use it for Exercises 10 and 11.

WHAT DO YOU THINK?

Call the number below to give your opinion. Each call costs 75¢. Use only a touch-tone phone. Press 1 for YES. Press 3 for NO. After you answer the questions, enter your age. This opinion poll lasts only until midnight Eastern Standard Time on Tuesday May 15. This magazine will publish the results in a future issue.

10. Identify the population and sample for this survey.

11. Give at least three reasons why the survey data will not be representative of the population.

Exercises 12–15 describe random samples. Out of a group of 24,000 of each item, predict how many have the given quality or flaw.

12. Of 400 grapefruit, 52 are "premium."

13. Of 250 computer chips, 2 are defective.

14. Of 160 eggs, 96 are Grade AA.

15. Of 75 pairs of jeans, 7 have fabric or stitching flaws.

16. Use the data from Exercise 15.
   a. Find the probability that a pair of jeans randomly chosen has fabric or stitching flaws.
   b. Does it matter whether you use 75 pairs of jeans or 24,000 pairs of jeans to find the probability in 16(a)? Explain.

17. *Natural Resources* Random samples of crushed ore from part of a gold mine show 2 ounces of gold in 17 tons of ore. How much gold would you expect from 120,000 tons of ore?

18. *Research* Find a newspaper or magazine article that includes survey data. Write and send a letter to the editor, asking about the sample, the population, and the survey methods.

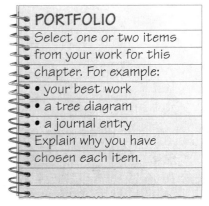

PORTFOLIO
Select one or two items from your work for this chapter. For example:
• your best work
• a tree diagram
• a journal entry
Explain why you have chosen each item.

Mixed Review

Find the volume of a rectangular prism with the given dimensions. *(Lesson 9-8)*

19. $\ell = 15$ cm, $w = 10$ cm, $h = 2$ cm

20. $\ell = 12$ cm, $w = 15$ cm, $h = 8$ cm

21. $\ell = 6.4$ cm, $w = 5$ cm, $h = 5$ cm

22. $\ell = 9.1$ cm, $w = 4.2$ cm, $h = 6.5$ cm

Choose **Use a calculator, mental math, or paper and pencil.** *(Lesson 10-8)*

23. $-52 - 12$

24. $-1{,}423 + 3{,}256$

25. $-320 - (-523)$

26. $85 - 987$

27. *Measurement* Catherine lives $1\frac{1}{4}$ mi from the park. Sharon lives $1\frac{1}{2}$ mi from the park. How much farther is Sharon's trip to and from the park than Catherine's? *(Lesson 6-5)*

CHAPTER PROJECT

NOW PLAYING

Design a Three-Choice System The Project Links on pages 491, 496, and 506 should help you complete your project. This checklist will help you gather together the parts of your project.

✔ your table of data from using a computer, random digits, a spinner, or number cubes

✔ your table of data from using a three-dimensional object

✔ one of the tables above with data from additional trials

Pretend that you want to sell your three-outcome system and that your classmates are your clients. They will base their decision to "buy" or "not buy" your system on the strength of your test procedures, data, and explanations. Prepare a presentation that demonstrates or explains your system. Prove that it works using your test data and calculations.

Reflect and Revise

Give a practice presentation to a friend or family member. Is your data believable and clearly presented? Are your calculations accurate? Is your chosen system the best choice? If necessary, make changes to improve your system and your presentation.

Web Extension

Prentice Hall's Internet site contains information you might find helpful as you complete your project. Visit www.phschool.com/mgm1/ch11 for some links and ideas related to statistics.

A game is **fair** if each player has the same chance of winning. One way to decide if a game is fair or unfair is to consider all the possible outcomes of the game.

You can also play the game many times to determine if it is fair. **Experimental probability** is a ratio that shows the fraction of times that a player wins a game (or that any given event occurs).

1. Players take turns tossing two number cubes. If the sum of the numbers on the two cubes is even, Player A scores a point. If the sum is odd, Player B scores a point.
   a. List all possible outcomes of rolling two cubes.
   b. *Writing* Is the game fair or unfair? Explain.

2. Results of a game are shown below.

A wins				
B wins	Ж		
Times played	Ж Ж

   a. Find Probability(A wins) and Probability(B wins).
   b. Does the game seem fair or unfair? Explain.

You can represent many probability situations with a model. You can **simulate** an experiment with a model or a list of random digits like the one at the right.

List of Random Digits, 1–6
23 41 63 24 11 25 34 52 22
51 42 63 52 32 43 41 11 24
12 33 62 31 32 64 55 43 63
11 41 34 24 51 14 15 26 32

3. How likely are consecutive numbers when you toss two number cubes? Use the list of random digits at the right to simulate this problem.

4. You walk Spot for 20 minutes each weekday any time between 5:00 P.M. and 6:00 P.M. Your mother returns from work any time between 5:30 P.M. and 6:30 P.M. Explain how to use a spinner, number cubes, or random digits to find the experimental probability that your mother will return during your walk.

You can describe the **theoretical probability** of an event as the ratio of the number of favorable outcomes to the number of possible outcomes.

5. A bag contains the letters of the word CIVILIZATION. Find each probability.
   a. selecting the letter I   b. selecting the letter R   c. selecting a vowel

6. Give an example of a certain event and an impossible event. What are their probabilities?

Tree Diagrams, Counting Principle, and Independent Events 11-5, 11-6

You can use a **tree diagram** or the **counting principle** to find the number of possible outcomes. You can find the probability that more than one **independent event** will occur by **multiplying probabilities.**

7. Three on/off switches are set at random. Make a tree diagram and find the probability that at least two are set to "off."

8. A company makes 5 car models. Each comes in 6 colors, 4 interior styles, and with automatic or standard transmission. Harold wants one of each kind of car for his lot. How many cars must he order?

9. Find the theoretical probability that the first spin of the spinner at the right is yellow and the second spin is green.

Arrangements and Making Predictions   11-7, 11-8

You can find the number of arrangements, or **permutations**, of a set of objects by making a list, drawing a tree diagram, using the counting principle, or simulating the problem.

A sample is *random* if each member of a population has an equal chance of being in the sample.

10. Zalika will play 5 songs for her piano recital. In how many ways can Zalika order the songs?

11. To find the favorite sport of boys in your school, you survey all boys on the soccer team. Is the sample random? Explain.

1. Sal and Matt played a game. The results are below.

Game Results	
Sal Wins	7
Matt wins	13
Times Played	20

  a. Find the experimental probability that Sal wins.

  b. Find the experimental probability that Matt wins.

  c. *Writing* Does this game seem fair? Explain.

2. A number cube is rolled twice. What is the theoretical probability of getting a 2 on the first roll and a 5 on the second roll?

3. Use the counting principle to find the number of possible outcomes.

  a. selecting a meal from 5 entrees, 4 soups, and 3 desserts

  b. tossing a coin four times

  c. selecting groups of three letters for a monogram

4. **Choose A, B, C, or D**. The probability of a *certain* event is ▨.

  A. 0   **B.** 1   **C.** $\frac{1}{2}$ **D.** $\frac{1}{4}$

5. Determine if the events are independent.

  a. Two number cubes are thrown. One shows a 3. The other shows a 1.

  b. You choose a red marble from a bag containing red and yellow marbles. You do not put the marble back. You choose again and get another red marble.

6. The spinner below is spun three times.

  a. Make a tree diagram to show all possible outcomes.

  b. Find Probability(green, red, green).

  c. Find Probability(all red).

7. A bag contains blue and green chips. The probability of drawing a blue chip is $\frac{5}{12}$.

  a. Find Probability(green).

  b. Draw a spinner you could use to simulate this problem.

8. Find the theoretical probability that a digit selected at random from the number 216,394 is a multiple of 3.

9. A number cube with 12 faces numbered 1–12 is rolled. All outcomes are equally likely. Find each theoretical probability.

  a. Probability(even number)

  b. Probability(13)

  c. Probability(7 or 8)

  d. Probability(number less than 10)

10. Suppose you tossed a coin 20 times with these results: 12 heads, 8 tails. Use this data to find the experimental probability of getting heads.

11. Suppose you read in the newspaper that the probability of rain is 10%. Write this probability two other ways and describe it using words.

12. What is the theoretical probability of getting two 6's when you roll two number cubes?

Choose the best answer.

1. Find the next two terms in the number pattern 2, 6, 12, 20, . . .

   A. 28, 36   **B.** 30, 42   **C.** 24, 32   **D.** 32, 44

2. You and a friend play the game "Rock, paper, scissors." Each of you puts your hand behind your back and then brings it forward in one of the three shapes. What is the probability that you both show "paper"?

   A. $\frac{1}{2}$ **B.** $\frac{1}{3}$ **C.** $\frac{1}{6}$ **D.** $\frac{1}{9}$

3. What is the value of m if $\frac{2m}{21} = \frac{8}{35}$?

   A. 12   **B.** 7   **C.** $\frac{13}{5}$ **D.** 2.4

4. Which event is least likely to occur?

   A. You roll a number cube once and get a 6.
   B. You toss a coin twice and get two heads.
   C. A single digit produced by a random digit generator is 4.
   D. One of the next 7 days is Saturday.

5. Which value of d will make the sum $\frac{8}{1} + \frac{3}{d}$ greatest?

   A. 4   **B.** 5   **C.** 6   **D.** 7

6. What is the *best* name for the triangle below?

   A. acute   **B.** obtuse
   C. scalene   **D.** right

7. Solve the equation $0.2x = 46$.

   A. 2.3   **B.** 9.2   **C.** 23   **D.** 230

8. Without measuring, choose the best estimate for the perimeter of the triangle shown in Exercise 6.

   A. 7 mm   **B.** 7 cm   **C.** 7 m   **D.** 7 km

9. Find the circumference and area of a circle with a diameter of 4.6 m. Round to the nearest tenth.

   A. $C = 16.6$ m, $A = 124.4$ m^2
   B. $C = 28.9$ m, $A = 66.4$ m^2
   C. $C = 14.4$ m, $A = 16.6$ m^2
   D. $C = 4.6$ m, $A = 5.29$ m^2

10. Look at the button.

    Which drawing shows a rotation of the button?

    A.   **B.**

    C.   **D.**

11. Which of the following is given in increasing order?

    A. $\frac{1}{2}, \frac{3}{4}, \frac{2}{3}, 0.8, \frac{9}{10}$
    B. $0.5, \frac{2}{3}, 0.75, \frac{4}{5}, 0.9$
    C. $\frac{1}{3}, \frac{1}{2}, 0.67, 0.9, \frac{4}{5}$
    D. $\frac{1}{4}, 0.3, \frac{8}{5}, 0.5, \frac{2}{3}$

12. Find the sum of $6\frac{3}{4}$ and $2\frac{4}{5}$.

    A. $8\frac{11}{20}$ **B.** $8\frac{7}{9}$ **C.** $9\frac{1}{20}$ **D.** $9\frac{11}{20}$

Make a frequency table and a line plot for each set of data. ■ LESSON 1-1
Then find the range.

1. books read each month: 3, 1, 4, 2, 4, 1, 3, 2, 4, 4, 2, 1

2. words per minute: 65, 35, 40, 35, 55, 65, 40, 40, 55, 35, 35, 70

Find the mean, median, and mode. ■ LESSON 1-3

3. 23, 26, 22, 25, 22, 28, 22, 10, 11

4. 102, 202, 102, 302, 102, 402, 102, 402, 201

The spreadsheet below shows the number of medals the ■ LESSONS 1-4, 1-6
United States earned during the 1996 Summer Olympics.
Use the data in the spreadsheet for Exercises 5–7.

	A	B	C	D	E
1	Country	Gold	Silver	Bronze	Total
2	United States	44	32	25	

5. What is the value in C2? What does this number mean?

6. Write the formula for cell E2.

7. **a.** Would you use a bar graph or a line graph to display the data in the spreadsheet? Explain your choice.
   b. Graph the data.

Choose the most appropriate type of graph to display ■ LESSON 1-5
each set of data. Explain your reasoning.

8. amount of rainfall in Costa Rica each month for 1 year

9. number of students from each grade who play soccer

10. Use the data in the table at the right to draw two different line graphs.
    a. In the first line graph, mark 0 to 120 in units of 20.
    b. In the second line graph, mark 80 to 110 in units of 5.
    c. How does the change in scale affect each representation?

■ LESSON 1-7

Number of People Watching Television During Prime Time (in millions)

Monday	99.2
Tuesday	97.2
Wednesday	89.7
Thursday	95.9
Friday	86.7
Saturday	87.8
Sunday	107.2

Find the next three terms in each number pattern. Write a rule to describe each number pattern. ■ **LESSON 2-1**

1. 1, 4, 16, 64, . . .

2. 0, 3, 6, 9, . . .

3. 1, 3, 5, 7, . . .

4. 2, 6, 18, 54, . . .

5. 7, 11, 15, 19, . . .

6. 80, 74, 68, 62, . . .

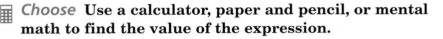 *Choose* **Use a calculator, paper and pencil, or mental math to find the value of the expression.** ■ **LESSON 2-3**

7. $2 + 6 \times 3 + 1$

8. $6(5 + 5)$

9. $(14 + 44) \div 2$

10. $4(1 + 4)$

11. $3 + 64 \div 4 - 10$

12. $7 \times 8 \div 2$

13. $50 \div (25 - 15)$

14. $144 + 56 \div 4$

Mental Math **Evaluate each expression.** ■ **LESSON 2-4**

15. $7x$ for $x = 7$

16. $n - 7$ for $n = 16$

17. $3b - 24$ for $b = 8$

18. $22 - 2n$ for $n = 5$

19. $a + 30$ for $a = 170$

20. $4c + 6$ for $c = 11$

21. $2b + 7$ for $b = 3$

22. $14 - x$ for $x = 5$

23. $10n - 3$ for $n = 7$

Write a variable expression for each word phrase. ■ **LESSON 2-5**

24. one less than b

25. twice as many p

26. four greater than b

27. three more than x

28. three times k

29. half of n

Choose **Use algebra tiles, mental math, or paper and pencil to solve each equation.** ■ **LESSON 2-6**

30. $4 + b = 77$

31. $20 = y + 1$

32. $27 + a = 163$

33. $c - 35 = 75$

34. $b - 11 = 36$

35. $x + 17 = 45$

36. $25 = p - 42$

37. $t - 10 = 24$

38. $302 = h + 5$

Choose **Use algebra tiles, mental math, or a calculator to solve each equation.** ■ **LESSON 2-7**

39. $3n = 21$

40. $62 = 2b$

41. $a \div 3 = 3$

42. $b \div 5 = 25$

43. $178 = 10d$

44. $b \div 7 = 7$

45. $48 = 3c$

46. $15t = 600$

47. $40 = k \div 5$

Write each decimal in words. ■ LESSON 3-1

1. 0.8 **2.** 0.35 **3.** 0.12 **4.** 0.045 **5.** 0.07 **6.** 0.17

Write each number in standard form. ■ LESSON 3-2

7. three thousand forty **8.** fifty-seven hundredths **9.** sixty-six and seven hundredths

10. one hundred forty-two thousandths **11.** two hundred twenty-two thousandths

Find the value of the digit 9 in each number.

12. 0.9 **13.** 1.009 **14.** 52.39 **15.** 0.4829 **16.** 351.09

Use >, =, or < to complete each statement. ■ LESSON 3-3

17. 1.11 ■ 1.09 **18.** 0.2357 ■ 0.23 **19.** 11.521 ■ 11.53 **20.** 13.10 ■ 13.1

Use models to find each sum or difference. ■ LESSON 3-5

21. 0.8 + 1.5 **22.** 1.2 − 0.62 **23.** 2.01 + 0.67 **24.** 1.41 − 0.61

Round each number to the underlined place. ■ LESSON 3-6

25. 0.1̲7 **26.** 4.556̲38 **27.** 3356.7̲76 **28.** 0.0005̲43 **29.** 14.534̲2 **30.** 0.4̲5332

Find each sum or difference. ■ LESSON 3-7

31. 1.14 + 9.3 **32.** 9 − 3.5 **33.** 4.11 − 2.621 **34.** 3.541 + 1.333

35. Measure each side of the triangle in millimeters and centimeters. ■ LESSON 3-8

36. What metric unit would you use to measure each item? ■ LESSON 3-9
a. mass of a book **b.** mass of a pencil **c.** amount of water in a pool

Find the elapsed time between each pair of times. ■ LESSON 3-10

37. 3:45 P.M. and 5:15 P.M. **38.** 8:10 P.M. and 11:55 P.M. **39.** 11:45 A.M. and 6:23 P.M.

40. 4:05 A.M. and 4:10 P.M. **41.** 3:25 P.M. and 5:02 P.M. **42.** 8:10 A.M. and 11:55 A.M.

Extra Practice

Estimation **Round to the nearest whole number to estimate the product or quotient.**

■ LESSON 4-1

1. 3.7×6.8 **2.** 4.8×3.2 **3.** 11.69×4.1 **4.** 5.3×6.9

5. $30.2 \div 4.9$ **6.** $21.49 \div 3.16$ **7.** $12.28 \div 5.59$ **8.** $120.4 \div 2.89$

Simplify each expression.

■ LESSON 4-2

9. $7 + 5^2 \times 6 \div 3$ **10.** $5^4 \times 3 + 5$ **11.** $6^3 \div 2 + 5 \times 3$ **12.** $8 \times 8 \times 8$

13. $(3^2 \times 5) \times (6 \div 2)$ **14.** $3^3 \times (7 + 5)$ **15.** $8^3 \div (1.25 + 0.75)$ **16.** $5 \times 5 \times 5 \times 5$

Use the distributive property to rewrite and simplify each expression.

■ LESSON 4-3

17. 7×78 **18.** $3 \times (10 + 5)$ **19.** 6×66 **20.** $4 \times (50 - 5)$

Modeling **Model each product.**

■ LESSON 4-4

21. 2×0.7 **22.** 1.5×0.2 **23.** 4×0.5 **24.** 1.4×0.6

Find each product.

■ LESSON 4-5

25.	**26.**	**27.**	**28.**	**29.**	**30.**
1.2	0.33	3.5	0.96	0.55	6.15
$\times\ \ 9$	$\times\ 15$	$\times\ 0.4$	$\times\ 0.15$	$\times\ 2.8$	$\times\ 2.4$

Modeling **Model each quotient.**

■ LESSON 4-6

31. $0.6 \div 0.3$ **32.** $1.5 \div 0.3$ **33.** $0.24 \div 0.06$ **34.** $1.8 \div 0.09$

Find each quotient.

■ LESSON 4-7

35. $6.72 \div 4$ **36.** $6\overline{)105}$ **37.** $7\overline{)64.4}$ **38.** $21.12 \div 4$

Find each quotient. Estimate first.

■ LESSON 4-8

39. $28 \div 0.5$ **40.** $12.25 \div 0.25$ **41.** $0.6\overline{)0.306}$ **42.** $0.25\overline{)54.72}$

Mental Math **Complete each statement.**

■ LESSON 4-10

43. $35 \text{ mm} = \blacksquare \text{ cm}$ **44.** $10.8 \text{ km} = \blacksquare \text{ m}$ **45.** $\blacksquare \text{ L} = 2{,}400 \text{ mL}$ **46.** $1{,}008 \text{ g} = \blacksquare \text{ kg}$

Extra Practice

Mental Math **Decide whether each number is divisible by** ■ LESSON 5-1
2, 3, 5, 9, or 10.

1. 324 **2.** 2,685 **3.** 540 **4.** 114 **5.** 31 **6.** 981

Tell whether each number is prime or composite. ■ LESSON 5-2

7. 24 **8.** 49 **9.** 7 **10.** 81 **11.** 37 **12.** 29

Find the GCF for each set of numbers. ■ LESSON 5-3

13. 10, 30 **14.** 15, 18 **15.** 25, 35 **16.** 28, 36 **17.** 45, 72 **18.** 8, 12, 20

Modeling **Model each fraction.** ■ LESSON 5-4

19. $\frac{3}{5}$ **20.** $\frac{1}{10}$ **21.** $\frac{4}{4}$ **22.** $\frac{5}{12}$ **23.** $\frac{4}{6}$ **24.** $\frac{7}{12}$

Simplify each fraction. ■ LESSON 5-5

25. $\frac{6}{60}$ **26.** $\frac{30}{35}$ **27.** $\frac{27}{36}$ **28.** $\frac{40}{50}$ **29.** $\frac{32}{48}$ **30.** $\frac{42}{70}$

Write each improper fraction as a mixed number. ■ LESSON 5-6

31. $\frac{25}{7}$ **32.** $\frac{39}{12}$ **33.** $\frac{12}{5}$ **34.** $\frac{10}{7}$ **35.** $\frac{7}{2}$ **36.** $\frac{100}{16}$

Write each mixed number as an improper fraction.

37. $1\frac{7}{8}$ **38.** $2\frac{3}{5}$ **39.** $11\frac{1}{9}$ **40.** $5\frac{6}{8}$ **41.** $10\frac{1}{8}$ **42.** $3\frac{2}{25}$

Find the LCM for each set of numbers. ■ LESSON 5-7

43. 4, 8 **44.** 6, 14 **45.** 15, 25 **46.** 20, 36 **47.** 3, 4, 12 **48.** 8, 10, 15

Compare using <, >, or =. ■ LESSON 5-8

49. $\frac{1}{2}$ ■ $\frac{2}{3}$ **50.** $\frac{3}{8}$ ■ $\frac{2}{6}$ **51.** $\frac{8}{24}$ ■ $\frac{4}{12}$ **52.** $1\frac{1}{5}$ ■ $1\frac{1}{4}$ **53.** $\frac{3}{10}$ ■ $\frac{1}{3}$ **54.** $\frac{5}{6}$ ■ $\frac{7}{9}$

Order each set of numbers from least to greatest.

55. $\frac{4}{7}, \frac{4}{5}, \frac{4}{9}$ **56.** $\frac{6}{16}, \frac{7}{16}, \frac{5}{16}$ **57.** $\frac{2}{3}, \frac{5}{6}, \frac{7}{12}$ **58.** $\frac{3}{4}, \frac{4}{6}, \frac{7}{9}$ **59.** $2\frac{3}{4}, 2\frac{1}{8}, 2\frac{1}{2}$ **60.** $\frac{3}{8}, \frac{3}{5}, \frac{9}{20}$

Write each fraction as a decimal. ■ LESSON 5-9

61. $\frac{2}{3}$ **62.** $\frac{3}{4}$ **63.** $\frac{2}{5}$ **64.** $\frac{1}{4}$ **65.** $\frac{1}{2}$ **66.** $\frac{3}{5}$

Extra Practice

Estimate each sum or difference.   ■ **LESSON 6-1**

1. $\frac{1}{2} + \frac{1}{8}$ 2. $\frac{5}{6} - \frac{1}{2}$ 3. $12\frac{3}{4} - 7\frac{4}{9}$ 4. $5\frac{7}{9} + 9\frac{3}{5}$

Find each sum or difference.   ■ **LESSON 6-2**

5. $\frac{5}{8} + \frac{1}{8}$ 6. $\frac{4}{5} - \frac{2}{5}$ 7. $\frac{11}{12} + \frac{5}{12}$ 8. $\frac{7}{8} - \frac{3}{8}$

Find each sum or difference.   ■ **LESSON 6-3**

9. $\frac{5}{6} + \frac{2}{3}$ 10. $\frac{7}{8} - \frac{3}{4}$ 11. $\frac{3}{5} + \frac{5}{8}$ 12. $\frac{3}{8} - \frac{1}{12}$

Find each sum.   ■ **LESSON 6-4**

13. $6\frac{2}{3} + 1\frac{1}{2}$ 14. $3\frac{2}{3} + 3\frac{1}{2}$ 15. $7\frac{5}{6} + 9\frac{3}{4}$ 16. $5\frac{7}{8} + 1\frac{3}{4}$

Find each difference.   ■ **LESSON 6-5**

17. $7\frac{3}{8} - 1\frac{2}{3}$ 18. $11\frac{1}{6} - 2\frac{3}{4}$ 19. $7\frac{5}{6} - 2\frac{1}{10}$ 20. $4\frac{2}{3} - 4\frac{1}{8}$

Find each product.   ■ **LESSON 6-7**

21. $\frac{1}{2}$ of $\frac{2}{3}$ 22. $\frac{1}{4} \times \frac{5}{6}$ 23. $\frac{1}{3}$ of $\frac{1}{5}$ 24. $\frac{7}{8} \times \frac{3}{4}$

25. $\frac{1}{2} \times 4\frac{1}{4}$ 26. $\frac{1}{20} \times 100$ 27. $\frac{8}{7} \times 21$ 28. $\frac{7}{6} \times 42$

Find each product.   ■ **LESSON 6-8**

29. $7\frac{1}{2} \times 2\frac{2}{3}$ 30. $4\frac{1}{2} \times 3\frac{5}{6}$ 31. $6\frac{1}{3} \times 7\frac{1}{5}$ 32. $5\frac{7}{8} \times 2\frac{1}{2}$

33. $8\frac{1}{3} \times 6\frac{1}{4}$ 34. $12\frac{1}{4} \times 6\frac{2}{3}$ 35. $10\frac{4}{5} \times 11\frac{1}{3}$ 36. $4\frac{5}{6} \times 2\frac{2}{3}$

Find each quotient.   ■ **LESSON 6-9**

37. $2 \div \frac{4}{5}$ 38. $\frac{2}{3} \div \frac{2}{5}$ 39. $2\frac{1}{4} \div \frac{2}{3}$ 40. $4\frac{1}{2} \div 3\frac{1}{3}$

41. $6\frac{2}{5} \div \frac{2}{25}$ 42. $5\frac{2}{3} \div 1\frac{1}{2}$ 43. $7\frac{1}{3} \div 3\frac{1}{3}$ 44. $12\frac{1}{2} \div 3\frac{3}{4}$

Complete each statement.   ■ **LESSON 6-10**

45. 4 ft = ■ yd   46. 48 oz = ■ lb   47. 32 qt = ■ gal   48. 8,000 lb = ■ T

49. 10 lb = ■ oz   50. ■ ft = 60 in.   51. 64 c = ■ pt   52. 9 mi = ■ ft

53. $5\frac{1}{4}$ ft = ■ yd   54. $6\frac{3}{4}$ mi = ■ yd   55. $6\frac{1}{2}$ qt = ■ pt   56. $4\frac{1}{2}$ gal = ■ qt

Extra Practice

Write a ratio in three ways for each statement. ■ LESSON 7-1

1. Mix 2 parts berries with 3 parts cream. **2.** Combine 1 cup water to 2 cups broth.

Write in simplest form. ■ LESSON 7-2

3. 30 to 60 **4.** 5 : 15 **5.** 13 to 52 **6.** 7 : 77 **7.** 18 : 72

Find the value of n. ■ LESSON 7-3

8. $\frac{n}{30} = \frac{3}{15}$ **9.** $\frac{64}{n} = \frac{5}{10}$ **10.** $\frac{13}{3} = \frac{n}{6}$ **11.** $\frac{5}{225} = \frac{2}{n}$ **12.** $\frac{9}{12} = \frac{12}{n}$

13. $\frac{n}{50} = \frac{3}{75}$ **14.** $\frac{18}{n} = \frac{3}{10}$ **15.** $\frac{51}{17} = \frac{n}{3}$ **16.** $\frac{2}{16} = \frac{n}{24}$ **17.** $\frac{3}{45} = \frac{4}{n}$

A scale model measures 2 cm × 5 cm. Find the dimensions ■ LESSON 7-5
of the actual object with the given scale.

18. 1 cm : 10 km **19.** 1 cm : 3 cm **20.** 1 cm : 4.5 m **21.** 1 mm : 1 km

Modeling **Model each percent using a 10 × 10 square grid.** ■ LESSON 7-6

22. 10% **23.** 30% **24.** 100% **25.** 75% **26.** 13% **27.** 2%

Write each fraction or decimal as a percent. ■ LESSON 7-7

28. 0.77 **29.** $\frac{10}{25}$ **30.** 0.06 **31.** 0.9 **32.** $\frac{13}{50}$ **33.** $\frac{18}{60}$

Write each percent as a decimal and then as a fraction in
simplest form.

34. 42% **35.** 96% **36.** 80% **37.** 1% **38.** 87% **39.** 88%

Estimation **Estimate each amount.** ■ LESSON 7-8

40. 50% of 168 **41.** 60% of 75 **42.** 75% of 34 **43.** 10% of 171 **44.** 15% of 55

Find each percent. ■ LESSON 7-9

45. 20% of 80 **46.** 15% of $17.50 **47.** 50% of 86 **48.** 90% of 100

Sketch a circle graph with the percentages given. ■ LESSON 7-10

49. 30%, 20%, 50% **50.** 29%, 71% **51.** 33%, 41%, 22%, 4% **52.** 15%, 85%

Use the figure at the right for Exercises 1–9.
Name each of the following.

■ **LESSON 8-1**

1. 3 acute angles

2. 4 obtuse angles

3. 3 noncollinear points

4. 6 rays

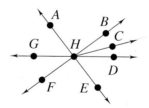

Use a protractor to find the measure of each angle.

■ **LESSONS 8-2, 8-3**

5. $\angle BHF$

6. $\angle FHC$

7. $\angle FHG$

8. $\angle CHD$

9. $\angle AHC$

10. Draw and measure an acute $\angle Z$. Find the measure of the angle
that is complementary to $\angle Z$.

Classify the triangle with the given side lengths as scalene,
isosceles, or equilateral.

■ **LESSON 8-4**

11. 7 cm, 9 cm, 7 cm

12. 3 m, 3 m, 3 m

13. 18 in., 16 in., 5 in.

Classify the triangle with the given angle measures as
acute, obtuse, or *right.*

14. 2°, 176°, 2°

15. 30°, 60°, 90°

16. 45°, 65°, 70°

Complete each statement with *All, Some,* or *No.*

■ **LESSONS 8-5, 8-6**

17. ▨ triangles have three sides.

18. ▨ quadrilaterals have two congruent sides.

19. ▨ circles are polygons.

20. ▨ rectangles are squares.

21. Draw two rectangles that are similar to one with length
8 cm and width 3 cm.

■ **LESSON 8-8**

22. Find the number of lines of symmetry
in the octagon at the right.

■ **LESSON 8-9**

Find the unknown length in each circle.

■ **LESSON 8-10**

23. $r = 24$ in.; $d = $ ▨

24. $d = 70$ ft; $r = $ ▨

25. $d = 3$ m; $r = $ ▨

26. $r = 65$ cm; $d = $ ▨

27. *Writing* Explain what is meant by the terms *translation,*
reflection, and *rotation.*

■ **LESSON 8-11**

Extra Practice

The area of each square is 1 cm². Estimate the area of each figure.

■ LESSON 9-1

1.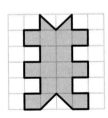

2.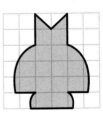

3.

Find the area of each figure.

■ LESSON 9-2, 9-3

4.
9.5 ft

5.5 ft

5.
4 m   5 m

6 m

6.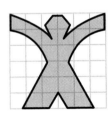
18 cm

10 cm   8 cm

Find the circumference of a circle with the given radius or diameter. Round the answer to the nearest unit.

■ LESSON 9-4

7. $d = 26$ yd   **8.** $d = 10.6$ ft   **9.** $r = 30$ in.   **10.** $r = 11$ cm   **11.** $d = 8.5$ m

12. Find the area for each circle noted in Exercises 7–11. Round each answer to the nearest tenth of a unit.

■ LESSON 9-5

Sketch each three-dimensional figure.

■ LESSON 9-6

13. triangular prism   **14.** hexagonal prism   **15.** cylinder   **16.** cone

Find the surface area of each rectangular prism.

■ LESSON 9-7

17.
8 ft
5 ft
10 ft

18.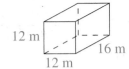
12 m   16 m
12 m

19.
4 m
2 m
4.5 m

Find the volume of the rectangular prism with the given dimensions.

■ LESSON 9-8

20. $\ell = 5$ ft, $w = 3$ ft, $h = 4$ ft

21. $\ell = 2$ in., $w = 6$ in., $h = 2$ in.

22. $\ell = 7$ m, $w = 8$ m, $h = 10$ m

23. $\ell = 22$ cm, $w = 14$ cm, $h = 4$ cm

Extra Practice

Compare using <, >, =. ■ LESSON 10-1

1. $-3 \blacksquare -1$ **2.** $5 \blacksquare 7$ **3.** $-5 \blacksquare -7$ **4.** $-6 \blacksquare 0$

5. $-3 - 1 \blacksquare -3 + (-1)$ **6.** $4 - 8 \blacksquare 8 - 4$ **7.** $-5 - (-2) \blacksquare -5 - 2$

Modeling **Model each integer in two ways.**   ■ LESSON 10-2

8. 3 **9.** -2 **10.** 0 **11.** -4 **12.** 6 **13.** -5

Find each sum or difference.   ■ LESSONS 10-3, 10-4

14. $-14 + 28$ **15.** $31 - (-52)$ **16.** $-72 + (-53)$ **17.** $-83 - (-3)$

18. $19 - (-18)$ **19.** $-101 + 121$ **20.** $65 + (-5)$ **21.** $-217 - (-217)$

Graph each function.   ■ LESSON 10-6

22.

Input	Output
9	4
10	5
11	6
12	7
13	8

23.

Input	Output
0	0
1	8
2	16
3	24
4	32

24.

Input	Output
3	1
6	2
9	3
12	4
15	5

Use the graph at the right for Exercises 25–36. Name the coordinates of each point.   ■ LESSON 10-7

25. A **26.** B **27.** C **28.** D **29.** E

Name the point with the given coordinates.

30. $(4, 2)$ **31.** $(4, 5)$ **32.** $(2, -1)$

33. $(-4, 1)$ **34.** $(-3, 3)$ **35.** $(-2, -4)$

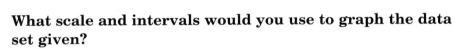

36. In which quadrant are points C, E, and J?

37. On graph paper, graph the points $L(-3, 2)$, $M(5, -4)$, and $N(0, 5)$.

What scale and intervals would you use to graph the data set given?   ■ LESSON 10-8

38. $0, -35, 25, 15, -17, 5, -4.1$ **39.** $-12, 0, 12, -7, -6, 3, -8, 6$

Extra Practice

1. Harvey rolls a number cube. If he rolls an even number, he wins. If he rolls an odd number, his sister wins. Is this a fair game? Explain.

■ **LESSON 11-1**

2. Suppose you take a four-question true–false test. You guess all the answers. What is the probability that you will guess three correct answers? Use a simulation to solve the problem.

■ **LESSON 11-3**

3. Use the number 3,486,335,206 to find each theoretical probability. Write each probability as a percent and a fraction.
   a. probability that a digit selected at random is a 3
   b. probability that a digit selected at random is a 2

■ **LESSON 11-4**

4. Make a tree diagram to show all possible sandwich combinations. Assume you choose one from each category.

■ **LESSON 11-5**

   Sandwiches

Fillings:	Egg Salad, Tuna Salad
Breads:	Bagel, Whole Wheat, White
Toppings:	Lettuce, Tomatoes, Onions

5. Suppose you flip a coin and roll a number cube. Find the theoretical probability of each result.
   a. the number 6 and heads   b. any even numbers and tails

■ **LESSON 11-6**

6. How many possible arrangements are there for the letters in the word TYPE?

■ **LESSON 11-7**

▦ *Calculator* **Use a calculator to find each value.**

| **7.** 5! | **8.** 11! | **9.** 2! | **10.** 9! | **11.** 3! |

| **12.** 4! | **13.** 8! | **14.** 6! | **15.** 7! | **16.** 10! |

Is each sample random? Representative?

■ **LESSON 11-8**

17. A school district wants to find out which fruits to sell in its school cafeterias. They survey all the students in one school.

18. A teacher wants to know the opinions of all her students on the upcoming elections. She places each student's name in a box and draws 15 names.

TABLE 1 *Measures*

Metric

Length

10 millimeters (mm) = 1 centimeter (cm)

100 cm = 1 meter (m)

1,000 m = 1 kilometer (k)

Area

100 square millimeters (mm^2) = 1 square centimeter (cm^2)

10,000 cm^2 = 1 square meter (m^2)

Volume

1,000 cubic millimeters (mm^3) = 1 cubic centimeter (cm^3)

1,000,000 cm^3 = 1 cubic meter (m^3)

Mass

1,000 milligrams (mg) = 1 gram (g)

1,000 g = 1 kilogram (kg)

Capacity

1,000 milliliters (mL) = 1 liter (L)

1,000 L = 1 kiloliter (kL)

United States Customary

Length

12 inches (in.) = 1 foot (ft)

3 feet = 1 yard (yd)

36 in. = 1 yd

5,280 ft = 1 mile (mi)

1,760 yd = 1 mi

Area

144 square inches ($in.^2$) = 1 square foot (ft^2)

9 ft^2 = 1 square yard (yd^2)

4,840 yd^2 = 1 acre

3,077,600 yd^2 = 1 square mile (mi^2)

Volume

1,728 cubic inches ($in.^3$) = 1 cubic foot (ft^3)

27 ft^3 = 1 cubic yard (yd^3)

Weight

16 ounces (oz) = 1 pound (lb)

2,000 lb = 1 ton (T)

Capacity

8 fluid ounces (fl oz) = 1 cup (c)

2 c = 1 pint (pt)

2 pt = 1 quart (qt)

4 qt = 1 gallon (gal)

Time

1 minute (min) = 60 seconds (s)

1 hour (h) = 60 min = 3,600 s

1 day (d) = 24 h = 1,440 min

1 year (yr) ≈ 52 wk ≈ 365 d

TABLE 2 Formulas

Circles

area:	$A = \pi r^2$
circumference:	$C = \pi d$ or $C = 2\pi r$
diameter:	$d = 2r$
radius:	$r = \frac{d}{2}$

Area

parallelogram:	$A = base \times height$
	$A = b \times h$
rectangle:	$A = length \times width$
	$A = l \times w$
square:	$A = side \times side$
	$A = s \times s$
	$A = s^2$
triangle:	$A = \frac{1}{2} base \times height$
	$A = \frac{1}{2} b \times h$

Perimeter

rectangle:	$P = l + w + l + w$
	$P = 2l + 2w$ or
	$P = 2(l + w)$
square:	$P = s + s + s + s$
	$P = 4s$

Volume

rectangular prism:

$V = length \times width \times height$
$V = lwh$

Surface Area

rectangular prism:

$SA = 2(l \times w) + 2(l \times h) + 2(w + h)$

Simple Interest

amount deposited $\times$ interest rate $\times$ number of years = simple interest

Probability

Probability (Event) = $\frac{\text{number of favorable outcomes}}{\text{number of possible outcomes}}$

Probability (A and B) =
            Probability (A) $\times$ Probability (B)

TABLE 3 Symbols

$>$	is greater than	$\overline{AB}$	segment AB	$\lvert 5 \rvert$	absolute value of 5
$<$	is less than	$\overrightarrow{AB}$	ray AB	7^3	seven to the power of three
$=$	is equal to	$\overleftrightarrow{AB}$	line AB		
$\neq$	is not equal to	$\angle ABC$	angle ABC	$30°$	degrees
$\leq$	is less than or equal to	∟	right angle ($90°\angle$)	10%	percent
		mi/h	miles per hour	unit^2	square unit
$\geq$	is greater than or equal to	mi/gal	miles per gallon	π	pi; ≈ 3.14
$\approx$	is approximately equal to	$+8$	positive 8	$a : b$	ratio of a to b
		-8	negative 8		

Place Value of Whole Numbers

The digits in a whole number are grouped into periods. A period has 3 digits, and each period has a name. Each digit in a whole number has both a place and a value.

Billions Period			Millions Period			Thousands Period			Ones Period		
Hundred billions	Ten billions	Billions	Hundred millions	Ten millions	Millions	Hundred thousands	Ten thousands	Thousands	Hundreds	Tens	Ones
9	5	1	6	3	7	0	4	1	1	8	2

The digit 5 is in the ten billions place. So, its value is 5 ten billion, or 50 billion.

■ **EXAMPLE**

a. In what place is the digit 7?
millions

b. What is the value of the digit 7?
7 million

EXERCISES *On Your Own*

Use the chart above. Write the place of each digit.

1. the digit 3　　　　　**2.** the digit 4　　　　　**3.** the digit 6

4. the digit 8　　　　　**5.** the digit 9　　　　　**6.** the digit 0

Use the chart above. Write the value of each digit.

7. the digit 3　　　　　**8.** the digit 4　　　　　**9.** the digit 6

10. the digit 8　　　　　**11.** the digit 9　　　　　**12.** the digit 0

Write the value of the digit 6 in each number.

13. 633　　　　　**14.** 761,523　　　　　**15.** 163,500,000　　　　　**16.** 165,417

17. 265　　　　　**18.** 4,396　　　　　**19.** 618,920　　　　　**20.** 204,602

21. 162,450,000,000　　**22.** 7,682　　　　　**23.** 358,026,113　　　　**24.** 76,030,100

25. 642,379　　　　　**26.** 16,403　　　　　**27.** 45,060　　　　　**28.** 401,601,001

Reading and Writing Whole Numbers

To read a number, you read the number in each period followed
by its period name (except for the ones period).

Billions Period			Millions Period			Thousands Period			Ones Period		
Hundred billions	Ten billions	Billions	Hundred millions	Ten millions	Millions	Hundred thousands	Ten thousands	Thousands	Hundreds	Tens	Ones
6	0	7	3	2	4	0	7	0	2	3	4

607 billion, 324 million, 70 thousand, 234

To write a number in standard form, use commas to show the
periods. Add zeros if you need to so that each period has 3 digits.

607,324,070,234

■ EXAMPLE

Write each number in standard form.

a. 21 million, 4 thousand, 37

21,004,037

b. 125 billion, 2 million

125,002,000,000

EXERCISES *On Your Own*

Complete each statement.

1. 7,360,900 = ▦ million, ▦ thousand, ▦

2. 92,170,000,000 = ▦ billion, ▦ million

3. 67,013,005 = ▦ million, ▦ thousand, ▦

4. 85,000,400 = ▦ million, ▦

Write each number in standard form.

5. 232 billion, 753 thousand

6. 65 million, 2 thousand, 42

7. 321 thousand, 29

8. 38 billion, 37 thousand, 90

9. 322 million, 135

10. 430 million, 15 thousand, 6

11. 5 billion, 4 million, 12 thousand

12. 5 billion, 32 million, 269 thousand

Comparing and Ordering Whole Numbers

The numbers on a number line are in order from least to greatest. So, a number line can be used to compare numbers.

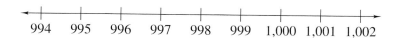

994   995   996   997   998   999   1,000   1,001   1,002

■ EXAMPLE

Use > or < to compare the numbers.

a. 995 ▓ 998

995 is to the left of 998.

995 < 998

b. 1,001 ▓ 999

1,001 is to the right of 999.

1,001 > 999

c. 12,875 ▓ 12,675

Compare the digits starting with the highest place values.

1 = 1, 2 = 2, 8 > 6, so 12,875 > 12,675

d. 84,662 ▓ 840,667

The number on the left has fewer digits, so it is less.

84,662 < 840,667

EXERCISES *On Your Own*

Use > or < to compare the numbers.

1. 366 ▓ 36

2. 54,001 ▓ 54,901

3. 8,801 ▓ 810

4. 84,123 ▓ 9,996

5. 29,286 ▓ 29,826

6. 129,631 ▓ 142,832

7. 31,010 ▓ 30,101

8. 4,328 ▓ 4,238

9. 98,410 ▓ 98,140

10. 40,000 ▓ 300,009

11. 611,401 ▓ 611,701

12. 478,296 ▓ 478,269

13. 1,801,342 ▓ 801,142

14. 27,248,315 ▓ 27,283,718

Write the numbers in order from least to greatest.

15. 1,367; 1,437; 1,747; 1,374

16. 20,403; 20,304; 23,404; 23,040

17. 9,897; 9,987; 9,789

18. 54,172; 51,472; 57,142; 51,572

19. 17,444; 18,242; 17,671; 17,414

20. 7,910; 7,890; 7,901

Use > or < to make each sentence true.

21. 60,789 ▓ 60,798 ▓ 62,532

22. 24,861 ▓ 18,000 ▓ 12,501

23. 42,101 ▓ 42,077 ▓ 41,963

24. 10,455 ▓ 11,400 ▓ 11,483

Adding Whole Numbers

When you add, line up the digits in the correct columns. You may need to regroup from one column to the next.

■ EXAMPLE 1

Add 463 + 58.

Step 1

$$\begin{array}{r} ^{1} \\ 463 \\ +\ 58 \\ \hline 1 \end{array}$$

Step 2

$$\begin{array}{r} ^{11} \\ 463 \\ +\ 58 \\ \hline 21 \end{array}$$

Step 3

$$\begin{array}{r} ^{11} \\ 463 \\ +\ 58 \\ \hline 521 \end{array}$$

■ EXAMPLE 2

Find each sum.

a. 962 + 120

$$\begin{array}{r} 962 \\ +\ 120 \\ \hline 1,082 \end{array}$$

b. 25 + 9 + 143

$$\begin{array}{r} ^{1} \\ 25 \\ 9 \\ +\ 143 \\ \hline 177 \end{array}$$

c. 3,887 + 1,201

$$\begin{array}{r} ^{1} \\ 3,887 \\ +\ 1,201 \\ \hline 5,088 \end{array}$$

EXERCISES *On Your Own*

Add.

1. 45 + 31	**2.** 56 + 80	**3.** 25 + 16	**4.** 43 + 29	**5.** 66 + 78	**6.** 87 + 35
7. 81 + 312	**8.** 406 + 123	**9.** 207 + 72	**10.** 480 + 365	**11.** 217 + 347	**12.** 675 + 329
13. 2,051 + 843	**14.** 786 + 4,109	**15.** 5,227 + 1,527	**16.** 3,104 + 2,698	**17.** 5,337 + 1,812	**18.** 4,282 + 7,518

19. 78 + 56   **20.** 35 + 96   **21.** 105 + 71   **22.** 29 + 342   **23.** 654 + 103

24. 286 + 42   **25.** 55 + 77   **26.** 242 + 83   **27.** 32 + 68   **28.** 108 + 13

29. 589 + 318   **30.** 642 + 975   **31.** 2,308 + 451   **32.** 976 + 4,035

33. 8,228 + 1,024   **34.** 5,417 + 2,391   **35.** 6,470 + 9,828   **36.** 7,121 + 5,359

Subtracting Whole Numbers

When you subtract, line up the digits in the correct columns.
Begin by subtracting the ones. Regroup if the bottom digit is
greater than the top digit.

■ EXAMPLE 1

Subtract 725 − 86.

Step 1

$$\begin{array}{r} {\scriptstyle 115} \\ 72\!\!\!/5 \\ -\ \ 86 \\ \hline 9 \end{array}$$

Step 2

$$\begin{array}{r} {\scriptstyle 11} \\ {\scriptstyle 6\,\cancel{1}\,15} \\ 7\cancel{2}\cancel{5} \\ -\ \ 86 \\ \hline 39 \end{array}$$

Step 3

$$\begin{array}{r} {\scriptstyle 11} \\ {\scriptstyle 6\,\cancel{1}\,15} \\ 7\cancel{2}\cancel{5} \\ -\ \ 86 \\ \hline 639 \end{array}$$

■ EXAMPLE 2

Find each difference.

a. 96 − 27

$$\begin{array}{r} {\scriptstyle 8\ 16} \\ 9\cancel{6} \\ -\ 27 \\ \hline 69 \end{array}$$

b. 625 − 273

$$\begin{array}{r} {\scriptstyle 5\ 12} \\ 6\cancel{2}5 \\ -\ 273 \\ \hline 352 \end{array}$$

c. 3,127 − 1,648

$$\begin{array}{r} {\scriptstyle 10\ 11} \\ {\scriptstyle 2\ \cancel{0}\,\cancel{1}\ 17} \\ 3,12\cancel{7} \\ -\ 1,648 \\ \hline 1,479 \end{array}$$

EXERCISES *On Your Own*

Subtract.

1. 81 − 37	**2.** 59 − 23	**3.** 41 − 19	**4.** 83 − 25	**5.** 99 − 78	**6.** 87 − 31
7. 781 − 312	**8.** 619 − 83	**9.** 247 − 72	**10.** 881 − 391	**11.** 517 − 287	**12.** 973 − 529
13. 7,411 − 583	**14.** 3,789 − 809	**15.** 6,227 − 1,127	**16.** 4,178 − 2,098	**17.** 5,337 − 1,812	**18.** 8,282 − 4,118

19. 78 − 19

20. 231 − 99

21. 534 − 71

22. 629 − 382

23. 918 − 133

24. 827 − 125

25. 517 − 291

26. 973 − 228

27. 721 − 119

28. 522 − 146

29. 642 − 223

30. 427 − 193

31. 444 − 345

32. 988 − 489

33. 601 − 425

Multiplying Whole Numbers by One-Digit Numbers

When you multiply by a one-digit number, multiply the one-digit number by each digit in the other number.

■ EXAMPLE 1

Multiply 294 × 7.

Step 1: Multiply 7 by the ones digit.

$$
\begin{array}{r}
2 \\
294 \\
\times \quad 7 \\
\hline
8
\end{array}
$$

Step 2: Multiply 7 by the tens digit.

$$
\begin{array}{r}
62 \\
294 \\
\times \quad 7 \\
\hline
58
\end{array}
$$

Step 3: Multiply 7 by the hundreds digit.

$$
\begin{array}{r}
62 \\
294 \\
\times \quad 7 \\
\hline
2{,}058
\end{array}
$$

■ EXAMPLE 2

Find each product.

a. 681 × 4

$$
\begin{array}{r}
681 \\
\times \quad 4 \\
\hline
2{,}724
\end{array}
$$

b. 402 × 9

$$
\begin{array}{r}
402 \\
\times \quad 9 \\
\hline
3{,}618
\end{array}
$$

c. 7 × 96

$$
\begin{array}{r}
96 \\
\times \quad 7 \\
\hline
672
\end{array}
$$

EXERCISES *On Your Own*

Multiply.

1. 81 × 3	**2.** 47 × 2	**3.** 58 × 6	**4.** 37 × 5	**5.** 76 × 4	**6.** 39 × 3
7. 678 × 5	**8.** 412 × 7	**9.** 326 × 4	**10.** 228 × 9	**11.** 864 × 5	**12.** 717 × 3
13. 25 × 6	**14.** 87 × 3	**15.** 62 × 8	**16.** 312 × 3	**17.** 456 × 7	**18.** 915 × 2

19. 7 × 45   **20.** 62 × 3   **21.** 213 × 4   **22.** 8 × 177   **23.** 673 × 9

24. 5 × 41   **25.** 3 × 82   **26.** 94 × 6   **27.** 63 × 4   **28.** 58 × 3

29. 4 × 76   **30.** 32 × 3   **31.** 371 × 8   **32.** 562 × 1   **33.** 946 × 7

34. 8 × 111   **35.** 443 × 5   **36.** 199 × 2   **37.** 138 × 3   **38.** 224 × 8

One-Digit Divisors

$6\overline{)466}$ and $466 \div 6$ are two ways of writing the same division problem. In the problem, 466 is the dividend and 6 is the divisor. The answer is a quotient with a remainder.

■ EXAMPLE 1

Find $6\overline{)466}$.

Step 1

$$
\begin{array}{r}
7 \\
6\overline{)466} \\
-42 \\
\hline
4
\end{array}
$$

Step 2

$$
\begin{array}{r}
77 \\
6\overline{)466} \\
-42 \\
\hline
46 \\
-42 \\
\hline
\end{array}
$$

Step 3

$$
\begin{array}{r}
77\,\text{R}4 \\
6\overline{)466} \\
-42 \\
\hline
46 \\
-42 \\
\hline
4
\end{array}
$$

■ EXAMPLE 2

Find each quotient.

a. $568 \div 5$

$$
\begin{array}{r}
113\,\text{R}3 \\
5\overline{)568} \\
-5 \\
\hline
06 \\
-5 \\
\hline
18 \\
-15 \\
\hline
3
\end{array}
$$

b. $232 \div 8$

$$
\begin{array}{r}
29 \\
8\overline{)232} \\
-16 \\
\hline
72 \\
-72 \\
\hline
0
\end{array}
$$

Be careful to place the first digit of the quotient over the correct digit in the dividend.

EXERCISES *On Your Own*

Divide.

1. $7\overline{)29}$
2. $3\overline{)20}$
3. $2\overline{)11}$
4. $8\overline{)70}$
5. $4\overline{)18}$

6. $9\overline{)659}$
7. $7\overline{)96}$
8. $9\overline{)347}$
9. $4\overline{)82}$
10. $8\overline{)232}$

11. $89 \div 7$
12. $90 \div 8$
13. $66 \div 4$
14. $68 \div 6$
15. $95 \div 5$

16. $359 \div 3$
17. $941 \div 9$
18. $148 \div 5$
19. $929 \div 8$
20. $735 \div 6$

21. $965 \div 5$
22. $845 \div 4$
23. $294 \div 7$
24. $487 \div 6$
25. $532 \div 4$

Zeros in Quotients

When you divide, after you bring down a digit you must write a digit in the quotient. In this example, the second digit in the quotient is zero.

■ EXAMPLE 1

Find 8)3,208.

Step 1

$$
\begin{array}{r}
4 \\
8\overline{)3208} \\
-32 \\
\hline
0
\end{array}
$$

Step 2

$$
\begin{array}{r}
40 \\
8\overline{)3208} \\
-32 \\
\hline
00
\end{array}
$$

Step 3

$$
\begin{array}{r}
401 \\
8\overline{)3208} \\
-32 \\
\hline
008 \\
-8 \\
\hline
0
\end{array}
$$

■ EXAMPLE 2

Find each quotient.

a. 423 ÷ 7

$$
\begin{array}{r}
60\,R3 \\
7\overline{)423} \\
-42 \\
\hline
03 \\
-0 \\
\hline
3
\end{array}
$$

b. 1,158 ÷ 23

$$
\begin{array}{r}
50\,R8 \\
23\overline{)1158} \\
-115 \\
\hline
08 \\
-0 \\
\hline
8
\end{array}
$$

c. 7,211 ÷ 9

$$
\begin{array}{r}
801\,R2 \\
9\overline{)7211} \\
-72 \\
\hline
01 \\
-0 \\
\hline
11 \\
-9 \\
\hline
2
\end{array}
$$

EXERCISES *On Your Own*

Divide.

1. 7)212

2. 9)367

3. 3)271

4. 8)485

5. 6)483

6. 34)1,371

7. 19)1,335

8. 62)1,881

9. 54)1,094

10. 41)3,710

11. 282 ÷ 4

12. 143 ÷ 7

13. 181 ÷ 3

14. 400 ÷ 8

15. 365 ÷ 9

16. 1,008 ÷ 5

17. 3,018 ÷ 6

18. 4,939 ÷ 7

19. 1,682 ÷ 4

20. 3,647 ÷ 6

21. 2,488 ÷ 31

22. 3,372 ÷ 67

23. 1,937 ÷ 48

24. 4,165 ÷ 59

25. 1,686 ÷ 82

Dividing by Powers of 10

You can use patterns to divide by powers of ten, such as 10, 100, or 1,000. To find the quotient, move the decimal point of the dividend to the left as many places as the number of zeros in the divisor.

■ EXAMPLE 1

Find each quotient.

Step 1: Count the number of zeros in the divisor.

Step 2: Move the decimal point in the dividend that many places to the left.

a. $46 \div 10$ $= 4.6$ ← 1 place to the left
b. $46 \div 100$ $= 0.46$ ← 2 places to the left
c. $46 \div 1,000$ $= 0.046$ ← 3 places to the left

■ EXAMPLE 2

Find each quotient.

a. $78 \div 100$

$78 \div 100 = 0.78$

b. $29.5 \div 1,000$

$29.5 \div 1,000 = 0.0295$

c. $453 \div 10$

$453 \div 10 = 45.3$

EXERCISES *On Your Own*

Find each quotient.

1. $25 \div 10$
2. $467 \div 1,000$
3. $890 \div 10$
4. $4.3 \div 100$

5. $10.8 \div 100$
6. $70 \div 10$
7. $0.014 \div 100$
8. $12.2 \div 10$

9. $1.4 \div 1,000$
10. $36.1 \div 1,000$
11. $40.5 \div 10$
12. $309 \div 100$

13. $8 \div 10$
14. $455 \div 100$
15. $6,890 \div 100$
16. $90.5 \div 10$

17. $0.09 \div 100$
18. $0.085 \div 10$
19. $66.6 \div 100$
20. $4 \div 1,000$

Use mental math to divide by each multiple of ten.

21. $360 \div 30$
22. $420 \div 20$
23. $1,400 \div 70$
24. $500 \div 50$

25. $8,000 \div 200$
26. $60 \div 30$
27. $2,000 \div 20$
28. $900 \div 300$

Reading Thermometer Scales

The thermometer at the right shows temperature in degrees Celsius (°C) and degrees Fahrenheit (°F).

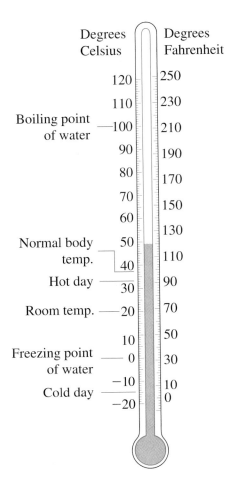

■ EXAMPLE 1

How do you read point *A* on the Celsius thermometer below?

Each 1-degree interval is divided into 10 smaller intervals of 0.1 degree each. The reading at point *A* is 36.2°C.

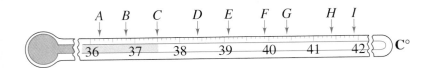

■ EXAMPLE 2

How do you read point *V* on the Fahrenheit thermometer below?

Each 1-degree interval is divided into 5 smaller intervals. Since $10 \div 5 = 2$, each smaller interval represents 0.2 degree. Count by 0.2, beginning with 98.0. The reading at point *V* is 98.6°F.

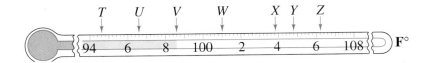

EXERCISES *On Your Own*

Use the thermometers above to write the temperature reading for each point. Tell whether the reading is in degrees Celsius (°C) or degrees Fahrenheit (°F).

1. *B* **2.** *C* **3.** *D* **4.** *T* **5.** *U* **6.** *Z*

Use the thermometers above to name the point that relates to each temperature reading.

7. 40.4°C **8.** 41.9°C **9.** 39.9°C **10.** 104.8°F **11.** 101°F **12.** 103.8°F

Roman Numerals

The ancient Romans used letters to represent numerals. The table below shows the value of each Roman numeral.

I	V	X	L	C	D	M
1	5	10	50	100	500	1,000

Here are the Roman numerals from 1 to 10.

1	2	3	4	5	6	7	8	9	10
I	II	III	IV	V	VI	VII	VIII	IX	X

Roman numerals are read in groups from left to right.

If the value of the second numeral is the same as or less than the first numeral, add the values. The Roman numerals II, III, VI, VII, and VIII are examples in which you use addition.

If the value of the second numeral is greater than the first numeral, subtract the values. The Roman numerals IV and IX are examples in which you use subtraction.

■ EXAMPLE

Find the value of each Roman numeral.

a. CD

$500 - 100$

400

b. MXXVI

$1,000 + 10 + 10 + 5 + 1$

$1,026$

c. XCIV

$(100 - 10) + (5 - 1)$

$90 + 4 = 94$

EXERCISES *On Your Own*

Find the value of each Roman numeral.

1. XI   **2.** DIII   **3.** XCV   **4.** CMX   **5.** XXIX

6. DLIX   **7.** MLVI   **8.** LX   **9.** CDIV   **10.** DCV

Write each number as a Roman numeral.

11. 15   **12.** 45   **13.** 1,632   **14.** 222   **15.** 159

16. 67   **17.** 92   **18.** 403   **19.** 1,990   **20.** 64

Rounding Decimals to Thousandths

After Lesson 3-6

You can use a number line to round decimals.

7.1473

7.147   7.1475   7.148

To round 7.1473 to the nearest thousandth, note that 7.1473 is between 7.147 and 7.148. It is closer to 7.147, so 7.1473 rounds down to 7.147.

You can also use this rule: If the digit to the right of the place to which you are rounding is greater than or equal to 5, round up. If the digit to the right of that place is less than 5, round down.

■ EXAMPLE

a. Round 1.0725 to the nearest thousandth.

1.07**2**5   ⟵ 5 ≥ 5, so round up.

1.0725 ≈ 1.073.

b. Round 0.30614 to the nearest ten-thousandth.

0.306**1**4   ⟵ 4 < 5, so round down.

0.30614 ≈ 0.3061.

EXERCISES *On Your Own*

Round each decimal to the nearest thousandth.

1. 5.2175   **2.** 0.3187   **3.** 2.5091   **4.** 100.0308   **5.** 23.8079

6. 9.0078   **7.** 0.6213   **8.** 0.0897   **9.** 16.5374   **10.** 5.4001

Round each number to the nearest ten-thousandth.

11. 0.04312   **12.** 0.89012   **13.** 0.90099   **14.** 0.10797   **15.** 0.030304

Round each number to the underlined place value.

16. 2<u>9</u>.41   **17.** <u>2</u>,981.3   **18.** 147.1<u>5</u>2   **19.** 10.01<u>4</u>8   **20.** <u>9</u>23.72

21. 0.06<u>9</u>94   **22.** 0.04<u>3</u>8   **23.** <u>1</u>.74   **24.** 3.106<u>0</u>2   **25.** 207.137<u>9</u>

26. 8.<u>7</u>23   **27.** 9.040<u>6</u>7   **28.** 0.40<u>4</u>3   **29.** 2<u>4</u>.18   **30.** 5.<u>2</u>943

31. 0.107<u>3</u>3   **32.** <u>7</u>6.41   **33.** 13.10<u>5</u>5   **34.** 90.4<u>0</u>6   **35.** 41.77<u>2</u>2

Estimating Lengths Using Nonstandard Units

Jan wanted to find a way to estimate lengths when she did not have any measuring tools. She measured her hand in several ways, the length of her foot and the length of her walking stride. Then she used these "natural units" as measuring tools.

After Lesson 3-8

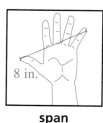

span

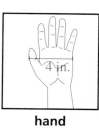

finger width

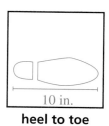

hand

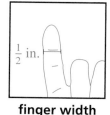

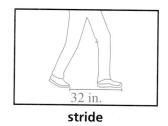

heel to toe

stride

■ EXAMPLE

Jan used strides to measure the length of her room. She counted about 5 strides. What is the approximate length of the room? Give the answer in feet.

$$\underset{\text{strides}}{5} \times \underset{\text{per stride}}{32 \text{ in.}} \approx 160 \text{ in.} \quad \longleftarrow \text{ Change strides to inches.}$$

$$160 \text{ in.} \div \underset{\text{per ft}}{12 \text{ in.}} \approx 13 \text{ ft} \quad \longleftarrow \text{ Change inches to feet.}$$

The approximate length of the room is 13 ft.

EXERCISES *On Your Own*

Measure your "finger width," "hand," "span," and "heel to toe." Use these natural units to find the indicated measure for each object. Then give the approximate measure in inches, feet, or yards.

1. thickness of a math book
2. height of a chair
3. height of a door

4. length of an eraser
5. height of your desk
6. length of a new pencil

7. distance across a room
8. thickness of a door
9. length of a chalkboard

10. *Open-ended* Measure your stride. Then measure something such as a long hallway in strides, and approximate the length in feet and yards. Tell what distance you measured.

Mental Math: Breaking Numbers Apart and Compensation

Mental math strategies can help you quickly compute exact answers without pencil and paper or a calculator. One strategy is to break numbers into parts, then use the distributive property to find the product.

After Lesson 4-3

■ EXAMPLE 1

Mental Math   **Find each product.**

a. 25×14

$$25 \times 14 = 25 \times (10 + 4)$$
$$= (25 \times 10) + (25 \times 4)$$
$$= 250 + 100$$
$$= 350$$

b. 15×18

$$15 \times 18 = 15 \times (20 - 2)$$
$$= (15 \times 20) - (15 \times 2)$$
$$= 300 - 30$$
$$= 270$$

Another strategy is **compensation.** A sum remains the same if you add a number to one addend and subtract it from another addend. A difference remains the same if you add the same number to both numbers, or if you subtract the same number from both numbers. Decide what number to add or subtract in order to make the computation easier.

■ EXAMPLE 2

Mental Math   **Find each sum or difference.**

a. $47 + 29$

$$47 + 29 = (47 - 1) + (29 + 1)$$
$$= 46 + 30$$
$$= 76$$

b. $245 - 98$

$$245 - 98 = (245 + 2) - (98 + 2)$$
$$= 247 - 100$$
$$= 147$$

EXERCISES *On Your Own*

Mental Math   **Find each answer using one of the mental math strategies above.**

1. 7×98

2. $132 - 97$

3. $396 + 87$

4. $88 - 59$

5. $468 + 80$

6. $440 - 102$

7. 250×22

8. $98 + 56$

9. 40×203

10. $89 + 91$

11. $234 - 95$

12. 8×99

13. 20×198

14. 50×28

15. $503 + 78$

16. 6×55

17. $772 - 568$

18. 30×17

19. $804 - 297$

20. $112 + 59$

Rounding Fractions and Mixed Numbers

You can use a number line to round fractions and mixed numbers to the nearest whole number. For mixed numbers, round up if the fraction part is $\frac{1}{2}$ or greater. Otherwise, round down.

After Lesson 5-6

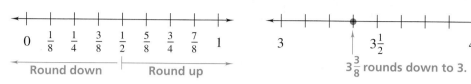

Without using a number line, you can tell if a fraction is more or less than $\frac{1}{2}$ by comparing the numerator and denominator. If twice the numerator is less than the denominator, the fraction is less than $\frac{1}{2}$.

■ EXAMPLE

Round to the nearest whole number.

    a. Round $\frac{11}{16}$ to the nearest whole number.

        $2 \times 11 = 22$ and $22 > 16$, so $\frac{11}{16}$ is greater than $\frac{1}{2}$.
        Round $\frac{11}{16}$ up to 1.

    b. Round $4\frac{4}{15}$ to the nearest whole number.

        $2 \times 4 = 8$ and $8 < 15$, so $\frac{4}{15}$ is less than $\frac{1}{2}$.
        Round $4\frac{4}{15}$ down to 4.

EXERCISES *On Your Own*

Round each fraction or mixed number to the nearest whole number.

1. $2\frac{4}{5}$	**2.** $\frac{1}{2}$	**3.** $\frac{2}{11}$	**4.** $3\frac{1}{9}$	**5.** $5\frac{3}{4}$	**6.** $\frac{5}{12}$
7. $10\frac{8}{9}$	**8.** $4\frac{7}{20}$	**9.** $6\frac{5}{16}$	**10.** $4\frac{13}{32}$	**11.** $\frac{11}{12}$	**12.** $7\frac{4}{9}$
13. $12\frac{9}{13}$	**14.** $8\frac{2}{3}$	**15.** $1\frac{5}{12}$	**16.** $\frac{17}{24}$	**17.** $4\frac{1}{8}$	**18.** $\frac{29}{4}$
19. $\frac{19}{8}$	**20.** $\frac{34}{7}$	**21.** $\frac{49}{12}$	**22.** $\frac{67}{10}$	**23.** $\frac{16}{9}$	**24.** $\frac{15}{2}$

Decimals Written as Products

After Lesson 4-10

You have learned how to multiply and divide numbers by powers of 10 using mental math. Now you will learn to write decimals as products of whole numbers and **powers of 10.** Numbers such as 10, 100, and 1,000, are called powers of 10 because they can be expressed using 10 with an exponent.

$$10^1 = 10 \quad 10^2 = 100 \quad 10^3 = 1,000$$

Other positions on a place-value chart such as 0.1, 0.01, 0.001, and 0.0001 are also powers of 10. Each place is 10 times the value of the place to the left. Study how the numbers in the chart are written as a whole number times a power of 10.

thousands (1,000)	hundreds (100)	tens (10)	ones (1)	tenths $\left(\frac{1}{10}\right)$	hundredths $\left(\frac{1}{100}\right)$	thousandths $\left(\frac{1}{1000}\right)$
			2 .	3		
			0 .	2	3	
			0 .	0	2	3

Whole Number × Power of 10

$= 23 \times 0.1$ ⟵ Multiply by tenths because 3 is in the tenths place.

$= 23 \times 0.01$ ⟵ Multiply by hundredths because 3 is in the hundredths place.

$= 23 \times 0.001$ ⟵ Multiply by thousandths because 3 is in the thousandths place.

You can also count decimal places when deciding which power of 10 to use.

■ EXAMPLE

Use the chart. Write each number as a product of a whole number and a power of 10.

a. 0.007

0.007 ⟵ To write 0.007 as a whole number, move the decimal point 3 places to the right; that is, multiply by 1,000.

$0.007 = 7 \times 0.001$ ⟵ Then, to undo multiplying by 1,000, multiply by $\frac{1}{1,000}$, or 0.001.

b. 402.07

402.07

$402.07 = 40{,}207 \times 0.01$ ← To write 402.07 as a whole number, move the decimal point 2 places to the right; that is, multiply by 100.

← Then, to undo multiplying by 100, multiply by $\frac{1}{100}$, or 0.01.

EXERCISES *On Your Own*

Use the chart. Write each number as the product of a whole number and a power of 10.

1. 35.09

2. 506.2

3. 0.88

4. 0.056

5. 70.99

6. 0.035

7. 200.003

8. 120.09

9. 32.4

10. 21.005

11. 1.55

12. 2.808

13. 0.218

14. 8.0004

15. 0.2

16. 990.4

17. 442.006

18. 0.709

19. 10.605

20. 45.5

21. 2.204

Multiply or divide. Then write each result as the product of a whole number and a power of 10.

22. 0.39×0.1

23. $0.5 \div 100$

24. 0.0694×100

25. $2.404 \div 0.01$

26. 2.73×0.01

27. 70.45×10

28. 1.506×10

29. $3{,}205 \div 1{,}000$

30. $100.43 \div 10$

Choose A, B, C, or D. Which of the four choices is *not* equal to the others?

31. A. $24.3 \div 0.001$ **B.** $2{,}430 \times 10$ **C.** $243 \div 0.01$ **D.** $2.43 \times 1{,}000$

32. A. $5.006 \times 1{,}000$ **B.** 50.06×100 **C.** $5{,}006 \times 10$ **D.** 500.6×10

33. A. 0.14×100 **B.** 1.4×10 **C.** $0.014 \times 1{,}000$ **D.** 14×10

34. A. 30.032×100 **B.** $30.032 \times 1{,}000$ **C.** 300.32×100 **D.** $3.0032 \times 10{,}000$

Review of Properties

After Lesson 10-3

Properties of numbers help you find sums, differences, and products mentally.

Property	Description	Examples
Commutative	Changing the order of the addends or factors does not change the sum or product.	$1 + 7 = 7 + 1$ $8 \times 3 = 3 \times 8$
Associative	Changing the grouping of numbers does not change a sum or product.	$(9 + 3) + 7 = 9 + (3 + 7)$ $(6 \times 2) \times 5 = 6 \times (2 \times 5)$
Identity	The sum of 0 and any number is that number. Zero is called the identity for addition. The product of 1 and any number is that number. One is called the identity for multiplication.	$9 + 0 = 9$ $0 + a = a$ $3 \times 1 = 3$ $1 \times a = a$
Zero property of multiplication	The product of any nonzero number and 0 is 0.	$3 \times 0 = 0$ $0 \times a = 0$
Distributive	Numbers added or subtracted within a set of parentheses can be multiplied by a number outside the parentheses.	$7 \times (3 + 4) = (7 \times 3) + (7 \times 4)$ $5 \times (12 - 1) = (5 \times 12) - (5 \times 1)$
Inverse	The sum of a number and its additive inverse, or opposite, is 0. The product of a nonzero number and its multiplicative inverse, or reciprocal, is 1.	$2 + (-2) = 0$ $4 \times \dfrac{1}{4} = 1$

EXAMPLE 1

Mental Math   **Evaluate (25 + 16) + 75.**

$(25 + 16) + 75 = (16 + 25) + 75$ ← Commutative property of addition
$= 16 + (25 + 75)$ ← Associative property of addition
$= 16 + 100$ ← Add mentally.
$= 116$ ← Add mentally.

EXAMPLE 2

Mental Math   **Evaluate 6 × (20 + 4).**

$6 \times (20 + 4) = (6 \times 20) + (6 \times 4)$ ← Distributive property
$= 120 + 24$ ← Multiply mentally.
$= 144$ ← Add mentally.

EXERCISES *On Your Own*

Identify the properties illustrated in each exercise.

1. $19.75 \times 0 = 0$

2. $25 \times 98 = 25 \times (100 - 2) = (25 \times 100) - (25 \times 2)$

3. $27 + (13 + 48) = (27 + 13) + 48$

4. $\left(4 \times \frac{1}{4}\right) \times 16 = 16$

5. $17.1 + 6.3 + 4.9 = 17.1 + 4.9 + 6.3$

6. $1 \times 343 = 343$

Find the value of each expression. Tell which properties you used.

7. $493 + (7 + 56)$

8. $(7.2 + 0.9) + 13.1$

9. $29.1 + 7.9 + 0$

10. $65 + 156 + 635$

11. $4 \times (25 \times 37)$

12. $73 + (-15 + 15)$

13. $80 \times 36 \times 0$

14. $\left(25 \times \frac{1}{25}\right) \times 357$

15. $4 \times (100 + 6)$

16. $(14 + 75) + 25$

17. $17 \times (-12 + 12)$

18. $(23 \times 4) + (23 \times 6)$

19. $500 \times (2 \times 47)$

20. $10 \times \left(4 + \frac{1}{2}\right)$

21. $(-34 + 34) + 26$

22. $\frac{1}{12} \times 12 + (-17)$

23. $24 \times \left(\frac{1}{6} + \frac{1}{8}\right)$

24. $(5 \times 129) \times 20$

Examples

A

Absolute value (p. 438)   The absolute value of a number is its distance, in either direction, from zero on a number line.

$|-10| = 10$

Acute angle (p. 333)   An acute angle is any angle that measures less than 90°.

Example: The measure of $\angle 1$ is between 0° and 90°.

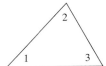

Acute triangle (p. 340)   A triangle that contains all acute angles is an acute triangle.

Example: The measures of $\angle 1$, $\angle 2$, and $\angle 3$ are each less than 90°.

Altitude (p. 392)   See *Triangle*.

Angle (p. 331)   An angle is made up of two rays with a common endpoint.

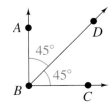

Angle bisector (p. 336)   An angle bisector is a ray that divides an angle into two congruent angles.

Example: $\overrightarrow{BD}$ bisects $\angle ABC$.

Area (p. 143)   The number of square units inside a figure is the area.

Example: $\ell = 6$ ft, and $w = 4$ ft, so the area is 24 ft^2.

Each square equals 1 ft^2.

Associative Property of Addition (p. 74)   Changing the grouping of the addends does not change the sum.

$16 + (4 + 8) = (16 + 4) + 8$

Associative Property of Multiplication (p. 74)   Changing the grouping of the factors does not change the product.

$(7 \times 5) \times 2 = 7 \times (5 \times 2)$

Bar graph (p. 22)   A bar graph compares amounts.

Example: This bar graph represents class sizes for grades 6, 7, and 8.

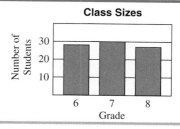

Base (p. 139)   When a number is written in exponential form, the number that is used as a factor is the base.

$$5^4 = 5 \times 5 \times 5 \times 5$$

base

Bases (p. 408)   See *Cone, Cube, Cylinder, Prism, Pyramid, Triangle.*

Box-and-whisker plot (p. 32)   A box-and-whisker plot shows how data are distributed. This type of plot also identifies high, low, and median values.

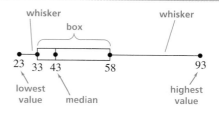

C

Capacity (p. 119)   Capacity is a measure of the amount of space an object or a liquid occupies.

A juice bottle has a capacity of about 1 L.

Central angle (p. 365)   A central angle is an angle with its vertex at the center of the circle.

Example: In circle O, $\angle AOB$ is a central angle.

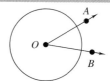

Chord (p. 364)   A chord is a segment with endpoints on a circle.

Example: $\overline{BC}$ is a chord of circle O.

Circle (p. 364)   A circle is the set of points in a plane that are all the same distance from a given point, called the *center*.

Circle graph (pp. 23, 315) A circle graph is a graph of data where the circle represents the whole. Each wedge in the circle graph represents a part of the whole.

Example: The circle graph represents the different types of plays William Shakespeare wrote.

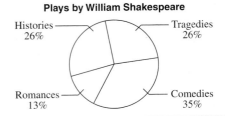

Plays by William Shakespeare

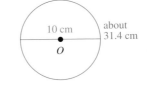

Circumference (p. 398) Circumference is the distance around a circle. You calculate the circumference of a circle by multiplying the diameter by pi, or π, ($C = \pi \times d$). Pi is approximately equal to 3.14.

Example: The circumference of a circle with a diameter of 10 cm is approximately 31.4 cm.

Collinear (p. 327) If a line can be drawn through a set of points, the points are collinear.

Example: Points *B, C, R,* and *S* are collinear.

Common factor (p. 189) Factors that are the same for two or more numbers are common factors.

4 is a common factor of 8 and 20.

Common multiples (p. 206) Multiples that are shared by two or more numbers are common multiples.

12 is a common multiple of 4 and 6.

Commutative Property of Addition (p. 74) Changing the order of the addends does not change the sum.

$7 + 8 = 8 + 7$

Commutative Property of Multiplication (p. 74) Changing the order of the factors does not change the product.

$9 \times 5 = 5 \times 9$

Compass (p. 364) A compass is a tool that is used to draw circles or parts of circles called arcs.

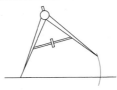

Compatible numbers (p. 134) Compatible numbers are numbers close in value to the numbers you want to multiply or divide. Estimating products or quotients is easier when you use compatible numbers. Compatible numbers are easy to multiply or divide mentally.

Example: To estimate the quotient $151 \div 14.6$, use the compatible numbers 150 and 15.

$151 \approx 150$

$14.6 \approx 15$

$150 \div 15 = 10$, so

$151 \div 14.6 \approx 10$

Compensation (p. 548)   A sum remains the same if you add a number to one addend and subtract it from another addend. A difference remains the same if you add the same number to both numbers, or if you subtract the same number from both numbers.

$$757 + 35 = (757 + 5) + (35 - 5)$$
$$1386 - 998 = (1386 + 2) - (998 + 2)$$

Complement of an event (p. 497)   The complement of an event is all the ways that the event cannot happen.

For a toss of a coin, the complement of tossing heads is tossing tails.

Complementary angles (p. 337)   Two angles are complementary if the sum of their measures is 90°.

Example: $\angle A$ and $\angle B$ are complementary.

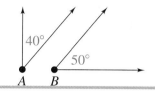

Composite number (p. 185)   A number that has more than two factors is called a composite number.

24 is a composite number that has 1, 2, 3, 4, 6, 8, 12, and 24 as factors.

Cone (p. 409)   A cone is a three-dimensional figure with one circular base and one vertex.

Congruent angles (p. 338)   Congruent angles are angles that have the same measure.

Example: The measures of $\angle C$ and $\angle B$ are each 60°, so $\angle C$ is congruent to $\angle B$.

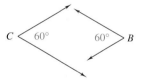

Congruent figures (p. 356)   Figures that have the same size and shape are congruent.

Example: $\overline{AB}$ is congruent to $\overline{QS}$, $\overline{CB}$ is congruent to $\overline{RS}$, and $\overline{AC}$ is congruent to $\overline{QR}$.

$\angle A$ is congruent to $\angle Q$, $\angle C$ is congruent to $\angle R$, and $\angle B$ is congruent to $\angle S$. Triangles ABC and QSR are congruent.

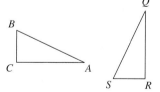

Congruent segments (p. 341)   Congruent segments are segments that have the same length.

Example: $\overline{AB}$ is congruent to $\overline{WX}$.

Coordinate plane (p. 463)   A coordinate plane is formed by the intersection of a horizontal number line, called the x-axis, and a vertical number line, called the y-axis.

Glossary/Study Guide

Coordinates (p. 464)   Each point on the coordinate plane is identified by a unique ordered pair of numbers called its coordinates. The first coordinate tells you how to move from the origin along the *x*-axis. The second coordinate tells you how to move from the origin along the *y*-axis.

Example: The ordered pair (−2, 1) describes the point that is two units to the left of the origin and one unit above the *x*-axis.

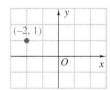

Corresponding parts of polygons (p. 357)   The matching parts of similar figures are called corresponding parts.

Example: $\overline{AB}$ and $\overline{EF}$ are corresponding segments.

$\overline{AC}$ and $\overline{ED}$ are corresponding segments.

$\overline{BC}$ and $\overline{FD}$ are corresponding segments.

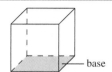

Counting principle (p. 499)   The number of outcomes for an event with two or more distinct stages is the product of the number of outcomes at each stage.

Suppose you flip a coin and roll a number cube. The total number of possible outcomes is $2 \times 6 = 12$.

Cross products (p. 285)   The cross products of the proportion $\frac{a}{b} = \frac{c}{d}$ are $a \times d$ and $b \times c$.

The cross products of the proportion $\frac{2}{15} = \frac{6}{45}$ are 2×45 and 15×6.

Cube (p. 409)   A cube is a rectangular prism with six congruent faces. Each face is a base of the cube.

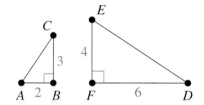

Customary system (p. 266)   The customary system of measurement uses units of inches, feet, yards, cups, pints, quarts, ounces, and pounds.

Cylinder (p. 409)   A cylinder is a three-dimensional figure with two circular, parallel, and congruent bases.

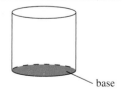

D

Database (p. 138)   A database is an electronic spreadsheet. The information can be organized and reorganized for a variety of purposes.

Decagon (p. 345) A decagon is a polygon with ten sides.

Degree (°) (p. 331) Angles are measured in units called degrees.

Example: The measure of $\angle A$ is 45°.

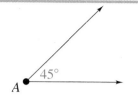

Diagonal (p. 347) A diagonal of a polygon is a segment that connects two vertices that are not next to each other.

Example: $\overline{AC}$ is a diagonal of quadrilateral $ABCD$.

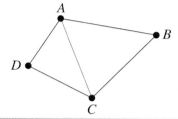

Diameter (p. 364) A diameter is a segment that passes through the center of a circle and has both endpoints on the circle.

Example: $\overline{RS}$ is a diameter of circle O.

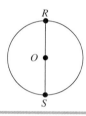

Distributive Property (pp. 144, 552) Numbers added or subtracted within a set of parentheses can be multiplied by a number outside the parentheses.

$$a \times (b + c) = (a \times b) + (a \times c)$$
$$6 \times (4 + 2) = (6 \times 4) + (6 \times 2)$$
$$a \times (b - c) = (a \times b) - (a \times c)$$
$$6 \times (4 - 2) = (6 \times 4) - (6 \times 2)$$

Divisible (p. 182) One number is divisible by another number if the remainder is zero.

15 and 20 are both divisible by 5, because $15 \div 5 = 3$ R0 and $20 \div 5 = 4$ R0.

E

Edge (p. 409) An edge is a segment where two faces of a three-dimensional figure meet.

edges

Elapsed time (p. 124) The time between two events is called elapsed time.

The elapsed time between 8:10 A.M. and 8:45 A.M. is 35 min.

Glossary/Study Guide

Equal ratios (p. 281)   Ratios that make the same comparison or describe the same rate are equal ratios.

$\frac{2}{3}$, $\frac{4}{6}$, and $\frac{24}{36}$ are equal ratios.

Equation (p. 66)   A mathematical sentence that contains an equal sign, =, is an equation.

$6 + 17 = 23$

Equilateral triangle (p. 340)   An equilateral triangle is a triangle with three congruent sides.

Example: $\overline{SL}$ is congruent to $\overline{LW}$ and $\overline{LW}$ is congruent to $\overline{WS}$.

Equivalent (p. 85)   Numbers or values that represent the same amount are equivalent.

$0.7 = 0.70$, $\frac{1}{10} = 0.1$, and 2 pt = 1 qt.

Equivalent fractions (p. 197)   Fractions that have the same simplest form are equivalent fractions.

$\frac{1}{2}$ and $\frac{25}{50}$ are equivalent fractions because they have the same simplest form of $\frac{1}{2}$.

Evaluate an expression (p. 58)   To evaluate an expression, replace each variable with a number. Then follow the order of operations.

To evaluate the expression $3x + 2$ for $x = 4$, substitute 4 for x.

$3x + 2 = 3(4) + 2 = 14$

Even number (p. 182)   An even number is a nonzero whole number that is divisible by 2.

2, 4, 6, 8, . . .

Expanded form (p. 89)   Expanded form shows the place and value of each digit.

0.85 can be written in expanded form as $0.8 + 0.05$.

Experimental probability (p. 481)   Experimental probability is used to describe how likely an event is, based on collected data.

Probability (A wins) =

$$\frac{\text{number of games A won}}{\text{total number of games played}}$$

Exponent (p. 139)   An exponent tells you how many times a number, or base, is used as a factor.

exponent

$3^4 = 3 \times 3 \times 3 \times 3$

Read 3^4 as *three to the fourth power*.

Exterior angle (p. 338)   Angles 1, 2, 7, and 8 are outside the parallel lines. These are exterior angles.

F

Examples

Face (p. 408)   A flat surface on a three-dimensional figure is called a face.

face

Factor (p. 185)   One number is a factor of another if it divides that number with no remainder.

1, 2, 3, 4, 6, 9, 12, 18, and 36 are factors of 36.

Factor tree (p. 186)   A factor tree is used to find a number's prime factors.

Example: The prime factors of 78 are 2, 3, and 13.

Fair game (p. 480)   A game is fair if each player has the same chance of winning.

Predicting whether a coin will land "heads" or "tails" is a game where each player has the same chance of winning, so it is a fair game.

Formula (p. 19)   A formula is a statement of a mathematical relationship.

$A = \ell \times w$
or
=A1+B1+C1 (spreadsheet formula)

Fraction model (p. 193)   A fraction model shows a fraction's numerator and denominator as shaded parts and total parts.

is a fraction model of $\frac{2}{3}$.

Frequency table (p. 4)   A frequency table lists items together with the number of times, or frequency with which, they occur.

Household Telephones

Phones	Tally	Frequency
1	卌 |||	8
2	卌		6
3						4

Front-end estimation (p. 105)   To use front-end estimation to estimate sums, first add the front-end digits. Then adjust by estimating the sum of the remaining digits. Add the two values.

Example: $3.09 + $2.99 ≈ $6

Estimate $3.09 + $2.99.

$3.09	$3.09	$5
+ $2.99	⇒ $2.99	⇒ $1
$5	$1	$6

Function (p. 457)   A function is a relationship in which each member of one set is paired with exactly one member of another set.

Number of Nickels	Value in Cents
0	0
1	5
2	10
3	15

Function table (p. 457)   A function table shows the input and the output values of a function.

The table above is a function table.

Glossary/Study Guide

G

Gram (g) (p. 118)   A gram is the standard unit of mass in the metric system.

A paper clip has a mass of about 1 g.

Greatest common factor (GCF) (p. 189)   The greatest common factor of two or more numbers is the greatest number that is a factor of all the numbers.

12 and 30 have a GCF of 6.

H

Height (p. 392)   The height, or altitude, of a parallelogram or triangle is the length of a perpendicular segment from a vertex to the line containing the base.

Hexagon (p. 345)   A hexagon is a polygon with six sides.

Horizontal (p. 327)   A horizontal line is parallel to the horizon.

$\overleftrightarrow{BC}$ is a horizontal line.

I

Identity Property of Addition (pp. 74, 552)   The sum of 0 and any number is that number. Zero is called the identity for addition.

$7 + 0 = 7 \quad 0 + 7 = 7$
$a + 0 = a \quad 0 + a = a$

Identity Property of Multiplication (pp. 74, 552)   The product of 1 and any number is that number. One is called the identity for multiplication.

$5 \times 1 = 5 \quad 1 \times 7 = 7$
$a \times 1 = a \quad 1 \times a = a$

Image (p. 370)   A point, line, or figure that is moved to a new position is the image of the original point, line, or figure.

Example: Shape B is an image of Shape A.

Shape A

Shape B

Improper fraction (p. 202)   A fraction whose numerator is greater than or equal to its denominator is called an improper fraction.

$\frac{73}{16}$ and $\frac{12}{12}$ are improper fractions.

Independent events (p. 503)   Two events are independent if the outcome of one event has no effect on the outcome of the other.

Rolling a number cube and tossing a coin are independent events.

Examples

Inequality (p. 438)   An inequality is a statement comparing expressions that are not equal.

$2 < d < 3$ means that d is greater than 2 and less than 3.

Integers (p. 434)   Integers are the set of whole numbers and their opposites.

$\ldots -3, -2, -1, 0, 1, 2, 3, \ldots$ are integers.

Interior angles (p. 338)   Angles 3, 4, 5, and 6 are inside the parallel lines. They are interior angles.

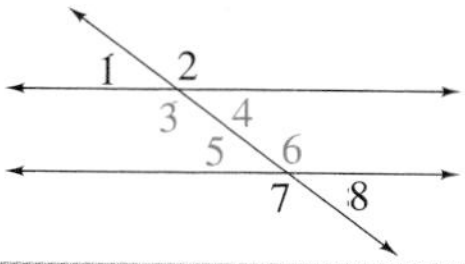

Inverse Property of Addition (p. 552)   The sum of a number and its additive inverse, or opposite, is 0.

$4 + (-4) = 0 \quad (-6) + 6 = 0$
$(-a) + a = 0 \quad a + (-a) = 0$

Inverse Property of Multiplication (p. 552)   The product of a nonzero number and its multiplicative inverse, or reciprocal, is 1.

$2 \times \frac{1}{2} = 1 \quad \frac{1}{4} \times 4 = 1$
$\frac{1}{a} \times a = 1 \quad a \times \frac{1}{a} = 1$

Isosceles triangle (p. 340)   An isosceles triangle is a triangle with at least two congruent sides.
Example: $\overline{LM}$ is congruent to $\overline{LB}$. Triangle LMB is isosceles.

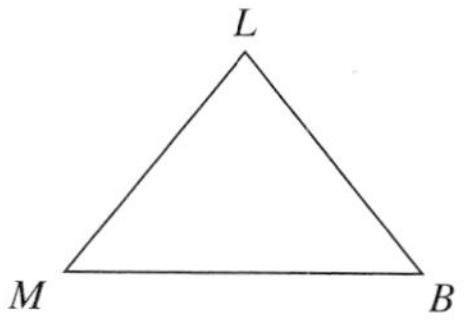

L

Least common denominator (LCD) (p. 209)   The least common denominator of two or more fractions is the least common multiple of their denominators.

The LCD of the fractions $\frac{3}{8}$ and $\frac{7}{10}$ is 40.

Least common multiple (LCM) (p. 206)   The least number that is a common multiple of two or more numbers is the least common multiple.

The LCM of 15 and 6 is 30.

Line (p. 326)   A line continues without end in opposite directions.

Line graph (p. 23)   A line graph shows how an amount changes over time.

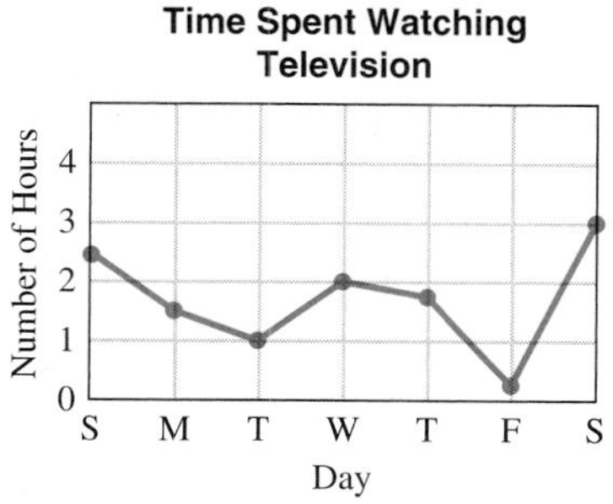

Line of reflection (p. 371)   See *Reflection*.

Line plot (p. 5)   A line plot displays data using a number line.

Example: This line plot shows video game scores during 13 sessions of play.

Video Game Scores

```
                    ×
            ×    ×
        ×   ×    ×    ×
    ×   ×   ×    ×    ×    ×
    ────────────────────────
    45  46  47  48  49  50
```

Line (of) symmetry (p. 360)   A figure has line symmetry if a line can be drawn through the figure so that one side is a mirror image of the other.

Example: The figure shown has one line of symmetry, ℓ.

Liter (L) (p. 119)   A liter is the standard unit of capacity, or liquid volume, in the metric system.

A pitcher holds about 2 L of juice.

M

Magic square (p. 56)   A magic square is a special arrangement of numbers in a square. The sum of the numbers in every row, column, and diagonal is the same.

Magic Square

2	2	5
6	3	0
1	4	4

Mass (p. 118)   Mass is a measure of the amount of matter in an object.

A brick has more mass than a feather.

Mean (p. 12)   The mean of a set of data is the sum of the data divided by the number of pieces of data.

The mean temperature for the set of temperatures 44°F, 52°F, 48°F, 55°F, 60°F, 67°F, and 59°F is 55°F.

Median (p. 13)   The median is the middle number in a set of data when the data are arranged in numerical order.

Temperatures for one week arranged in numerical order are 44°F, 48°F, 52°F, 55°F, 58°F, 60°F, and 67°F. The median temperature is 55°F because it is the middle number in the set of data.

Meter (p. 113)   A meter (m) is the standard unit of length in the metric system.

A doorknob is about 1 m from the floor.

Metric system (p. 113)   The metric system of measurement uses units of millimeters, centimeters, meters, kilometers, grams, kilograms, and liters.

Mixed number (p. 202)   A mixed number shows the sum of a whole number and a fraction.

$3\frac{11}{16}$ is a mixed number: $3\frac{11}{16} = 3 + \frac{11}{16}$.

Mode (p. 14)   The mode is the item that appears most often in a set of data.

The mode of the set of prices $2.50, $3.75, $3.60, $2.75, $2.75, and $3.70 is $2.75.

Multiple (p. 206)   A multiple of a number is the product of that number and any nonzero whole number.

The number 39 is a multiple of 13.

N

Net (p. 410)   The pattern that you cut out and fold to form a three-dimensional figure is called a net.

Noncollinear (p. 327)   If there is no line that can be drawn through all the points in a set, the points are noncollinear.

Example: Points S, Q, R, and T are noncollinear.

Number pattern (p. 44)   A number pattern is a list of numbers that follow a rule. Each number in the pattern is called a term.

65, 60, 55, 50, . . .
The next three numbers in the pattern are 45, 40, 35.

Numerical expression (p. 56)   An expression that contains only numbers and operation symbols is a numerical expression.

$2(5 + 7) - 14$ is a numerical expression.

O

Obtuse angle (p. 333)   An obtuse angle is any angle that measures greater than 90° and less than 180°.

Example: The measure of $\angle K$ is between 90° and 180°. $\angle K$ is an obtuse angle.

Obtuse triangle (p. 340)   An obtuse triangle has one obtuse angle.

Example: The measure of $\angle J$ is greater than 90°. Triangle NJX is an obtuse triangle.

Octagon (p. 345)   An octagon is a polygon with eight sides.

Odd number (p. 182)   An odd number is a nonzero whole number that is not divisible by 2.

1, 3, 5, 7, . . .

Opposite numbers (p. 434)   Two numbers that are the same distance from zero on a number line, but in different directions, are opposites.

3 and -3 are opposites.

Order of operations (pp. 51, 140)
1. Do all operations within parentheses.
2. Do all work with exponents.
3. Multiply and divide in order from left to right.
4. Add and subtract in order from left to right.

$2^3(7 - 4) = 2^3(3) = 8 \cdot 3 = 24$

Ordered pair (p. 464)   An ordered pair is a pair of numbers that describe the location of a point on a coordinate plane. The first value is the *x*-coordinate and the second value is the *y*-coordinate.

Example: The *x*-coordinate of the point $(-2, 1)$ is -2; the *y*-coordinate is 1.

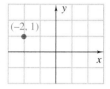

Origin (p. 464)   The origin is the point of intersection of the *x*- and *y*-axes on a coordinate plane.

Example: The ordered pair that describes the origin is $(0, 0)$.

P

Parallel lines (p. 327)   Parallel lines are lines in the same plane that do not intersect.

Example: $\overleftrightarrow{EF}$ is parallel to $\overleftrightarrow{HI}$.

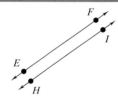

Parallel segments (p. 327)   Parallel segments lie in parallel lines.

Example: $\overline{JK}$ is parallel to $\overline{LM}$.

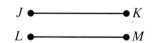

Parallelogram (p. 349)   A parallelogram is a quadrilateral with both pairs of opposite sides parallel.

Example: $\overline{KV}$ is parallel to $\overline{AD}$ and $\overline{AK}$ is parallel to $\overline{DV}$.

Pentagon (p. 345)   A pentagon is a polygon with five sides.

Percent (%) (p. 297)   A percent is a ratio that compares a number to 100.

The ratio 50 to 100 is a percent because 50 is compared to 100. $\frac{50}{100} = 50\%$

Perimeter (p. 387)   The perimeter of a figure is the distance around it.

Example: The perimeter of rectangle $ABCD =$
2 ft + 4 ft + 2 ft + 4 ft = 12 ft.

Permutation (p. 507) A permutation is an arrangement in a particular order.

The permutations of the letters A, B, and C are ABC, ACB, BAC, BCA, CAB, and CBA.

Perpendicular bisector (p. 336) A perpendicular bisector is a line perpendicular to a segment that passes through the midpoint of the segment.

Example: $\overleftrightarrow{AB}$ is the perpendicular bisector of $\overline{CD}$. $\overline{CE}$ has the same length as $\overline{ED}$.

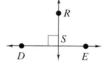

Perpendicular lines (p. 333) Lines that intersect to form right angles are perpendicular.

Example: $\overleftrightarrow{DE}$ is perpendicular to $\overleftrightarrow{RS}$.

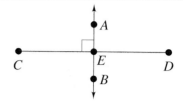

Pi (π) (p. 399) See *Circumference.*

Pictograph (p. 36) A pictograph is a graph that uses picture symbols to represent numerical data.

Example: In this pictograph, 45 girls and 30 boys play soccer.

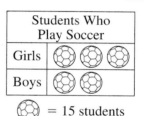

Students Who Play Soccer	
Girls	⚽ ⚽ ⚽
Boys	⚽ ⚽

⚽ = 15 students

Place value (p. 93) The place value system allows us to represent any number using one or more of 10 digits. The value of a digit depends on its place within the number.

26: The 6 represents six ones.
604: The 6 represents six hundreds.

Plane (p. 326) A plane is a flat surface that extends indefinitely in four directions. It has no thickness.

Point (p. 326) A point is a position in space. It has no size, only location.

Point of rotation (p. 372) See *Rotation.*

Polygon (p. 344) A polygon is a closed plane figure formed by three or more line segments that do not cross.

Example: *CDEFG* is a convex polygon. *VWXYZ* is a nonconvex polygon.

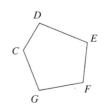
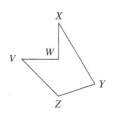

Population (p. 512)   A population is a group about which information is gathered.

In a survey regarding the hobbies of teenagers, the population would be all aged 13 through 19.

Power (p. 139)   A number that is expressed using an exponent is called a power.

2^4 is two to the fourth power.
$2^4 = 2 \times 2 \times 2 \times 2 = 16$
16 is a power of 2.

Power of 10 (p. 550)   A number that can be expressed using an exponent and base of 10 is called a power of 10.

1, 10, 100, 1000, . . .
0.1, 0.01, 0.001, . . .

Precision in measurement (p. 386)   The precision of a number refers to its degree of exactness. A measurement cannot be more precise than the precision of the measuring tool used.

A ruler divided into centimeters cannot be used to measure precisely in millimeters.

Prime factorization (p. 187)   Writing a composite number as the product of its prime factors is called prime factorization.

The prime factorization of 30 is $2 \times 3 \times 5$.

Prime number (p. 185)   A number that has exactly two factors, 1 and the number itself, is a prime number.

13 is a prime number because its only factors are 1 and 13.

Prism (p. 408)   A prism is a three-dimensional figure with two parallel and congruent faces called bases.

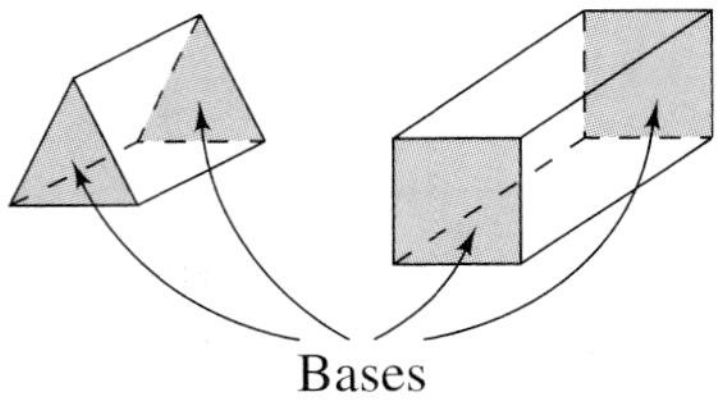

Bases

Probability (p. 481)   Probability is used to describe how likely it is that an event will happen.

See *Experimental probability* and *Theoretical probability*.

Proportion (p. 285)   A proportion is an equation that states two ratios are equal. The cross products of a proportion are always equal.

The equation $\frac{3}{12} = \frac{12}{48}$ is a proportion because $3 \times 48 = 12 \times 12$.

Protractor (p. 332)   A protractor is a tool used to measure and draw angles.

Example: The measure of $\angle A$ is 40°.

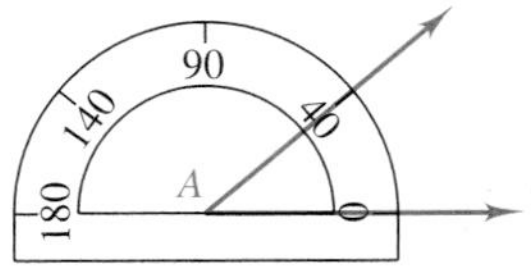

Pyramid (p. 409)   Pyramids are three-dimensional figures with only one base. The base is a polygon and the other faces are triangles. A pyramid is named for the shape of its base.

Example: The figure shown is a rectangular pyramid.

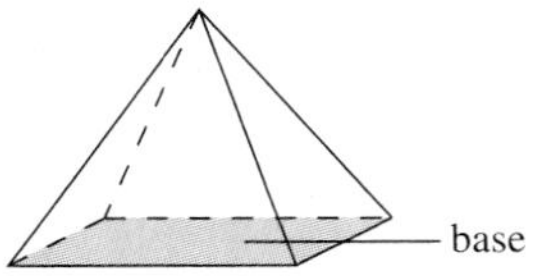

base

Q

Quadrant (p. 465)   The *x*- and *y*-axes divide the coordinate plane into four regions, called quadrants.

Quadrilateral (p. 345)   A quadrilateral is a polygon with four sides.

R

Radius (plural is radii) (p. 364)   A radius is a segment that has one endpoint at the center and the other endpoint on the circle.

Example: $\overline{OA}$ is a radius of circle *O*.

Random sample (p. 513)   A random sample of a group is a subgroup selected at random from the group.

A random sample could be obtained by shuffling all the quizzes from several math classes together and selecting a certain number of them without looking at them.

Range (p. 5)   The range of a set of data is the difference between the greatest and the least values in the set.

Data set: 62, 109, 234, 35, 96, 49, 201
Range: 234 − 35 = 199

Rate (p. 282)   A rate is a ratio that compares two quantities measured in two different units.

A student typed 1,100 words in 50 min, or 22 words/min.

Ratio (p. 278)   A ratio is a comparison of two numbers.

A ratio can be written in three different ways: 72 to 100, 72 : 100, and $\frac{72}{100}$.

Ray (p. 327)   A ray is a part of a line. It consists of one endpoint and all the points of the line on one side of the endpoint.

Example: $\overrightarrow{SW}$ represents a ray.

Reciprocal (p. 263)   Two numbers are reciprocals if their product is 1. Dividing by a number is the same as multiplying by the reciprocal of that number.

The numbers 5 and $\frac{1}{5}$ are reciprocals because $5 \times \frac{1}{5} = 1$.

Rectangle (p. 349)   A rectangle is a parallelogram with four right angles.

Example: The measures of ∠*R*, ∠*S*, ∠*W*, and ∠*H* are each 90°.

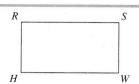

Glossary/Study Guide

Reflection (p. 371)   A reflection flips a figure across a line.

Example: Shape B is a reflection of Shape A.
$\overleftrightarrow{XY}$ is the line of reflection.

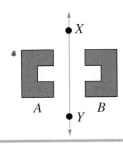

Repeating decimal (p. 215)   A decimal whose digits repeat without end is a repeating decimal. A bar indicates the digits that repeat.

0.6666 . . . or $0.\overline{6}$

Representative sample (p. 513)   A representative sample of a group is a subgroup that has the same characteristics as the larger group.

A representative sample of last week's math quizzes would include quizzes from each of several math classes.

Rhombus (p. 349)   A rhombus is a parallelogram with four congruent sides.

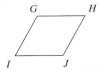

Right angle (p. 333)   A right angle is an angle with a measure of 90°.

Example: The measure of ∠D is 90°.

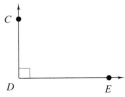

Right triangle (p. 340)   A right triangle is a triangle with a right angle.

Example: The measure of ∠B is 90°. Triangle *ABC* is a right triangle.

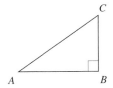

Rotation (p. 372)   A rotation turns, or rotates, a shape.

Example: Shape B is a rotation of Shape A.

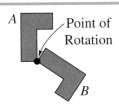

Sample (p. 512)   A sample of a group is a smaller subgroup selected from within the group.

Your English teacher might read one or two poems from the poems written by your class.

Scale (p. 292)   A scale is a ratio that compares a length on a model to the actual length of the real object.

A map may have a scale where 1 in. represents 50 mi.

Scalene triangle (p. 340)   A scalene triangle is a triangle with no congruent sides.

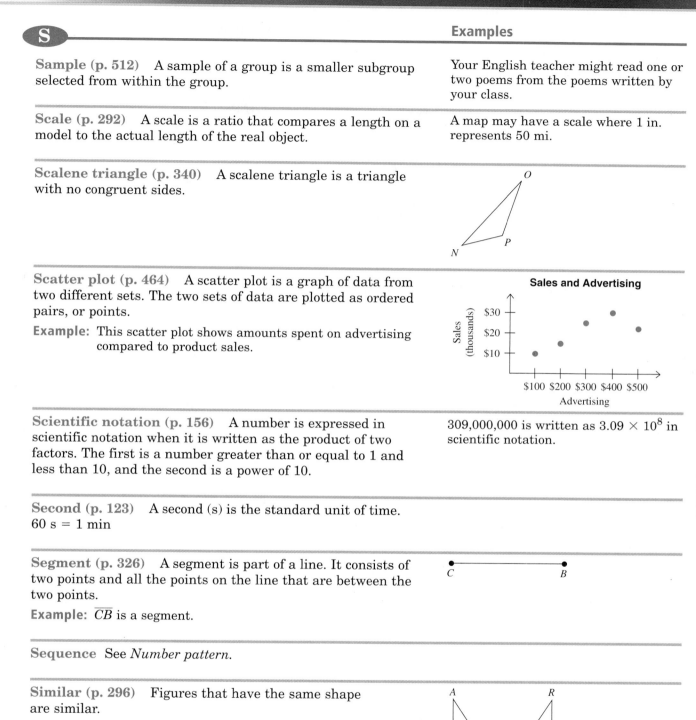

Scatter plot (p. 464)   A scatter plot is a graph of data from two different sets. The two sets of data are plotted as ordered pairs, or points.

Example: This scatter plot shows amounts spent on advertising compared to product sales.

Scientific notation (p. 156)   A number is expressed in scientific notation when it is written as the product of two factors. The first is a number greater than or equal to 1 and less than 10, and the second is a power of 10.

309,000,000 is written as 3.09×10^8 in scientific notation.

Second (p. 123)   A second (s) is the standard unit of time.
60 s = 1 min

Segment (p. 326)   A segment is part of a line. It consists of two points and all the points on the line that are between the two points.

Example: $\overline{CB}$ is a segment.

Sequence See *Number pattern.*

Similar (p. 296)   Figures that have the same shape are similar.

Example: Triangle *ABC* is similar to triangle *RTS*.

Simplest form of a fraction (p. 198)   A fraction is in simplest form when the only common factor of the numerator and denominator is 1.

The fraction $\frac{3}{7}$ is in simplest form because the common factor of 3 and 7 is 1.

Simulation (p. 485)   A simulation is a model of a real-world situation.

A baseball team has equal chances of winning or losing the next game. You can toss a coin to simulate the outcome.

Skew lines (p. 328)   Skew lines are lines that lie in different nonparallel planes. They are neither parallel nor intersecting.
Example: $\overleftrightarrow{AB}$ and $\overleftrightarrow{CD}$ are skew lines.

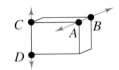

Solution of an equation (p. 66)   The solution of an equation is the value of the variable that makes the equation true.

4 is the solution of $x + 5 = 9$.

Solve (p. 66)   To solve an equation you replace a variable with a number that makes the equation true.

To solve the equation $x + 2 = 5$, subtract 2 from both sides.
$$x = 3$$

Sphere (p. 409)   A sphere is the set of points in space that are the same distance from a given point called the center.

Spreadsheet (p. 18, 138)   A spreadsheet is a tool used for organizing and analyzing data using a computer. Spreadsheets are arranged in rows and columns. A *cell* is the box on a spreadsheet where a row and a column meet. The names of the row and column determine the name of the cell. A cell may contain data values, labels, or formulas.

Example: In the spreadsheet shown, column C and row 2 meet at the shaded box, cell C2. The value in cell C2 is 2.75.

	A	B	C	D
1	0.50	0.70	0.60	0.50
2	1.50	0.50	2.75	2.50

Square (p. 350)   A square is a rectangle with four congruent sides.

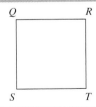

Standard form of a number (p. 88)   To write a number in standard form, use commas to separate periods and add zeros so that each period has 3 digits.

230 thousand, 8 in standard form is 230,008.

Stem-and-leaf plot (p. 32) A stem-and-leaf plot displays a set of data to show the frequencies of values.

Example: This stem-and-leaf plot shows recorded times in a race. The stem represents the number of seconds. The leaves represent tenths of a second.

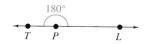

```
stem    leaves
 \       /
27 | 7
28 | 568
29 | 69
30 | 8
```

27 | 7 means 27.7

Straight angle (p. 333) An angle that measures 180° is called a straight angle.

Example: The measure of ∠TPL is 180°.

Straightedge (p. 336) A straightedge is a tool used to draw lines, rays, and segments. It is similar to a ruler, but does not have marks to indicate measure.

A ruler, if you ignore the markings, can be used as a straightedge.

Supplementary angles (p. 337) Two angles are supplementary if the sum of their measures is 180°.

Example: ∠1 and ∠2 are supplementary angles.

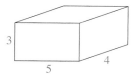

Surface area of a prism (p. 414) The surface area of a prism is the sum of the areas of the faces.

Example: Surface area = $2(3 \times 5) + 2(3 \times 4) + 2(4 \times 5) = 94$

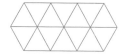

Symmetry (p. 360) A figure has symmetry when one side of the figure is the mirror image of the other side.

See *Line of symmetry.*

 T

Term (p. 44) A term is a part of a variable expression or a number sequence.

The expression $2x + 12$ has two terms, $2x$ and 12. The number sequence 38, 34, 32 has three terms.

Terminating decimal (p. 215) A terminating decimal is a decimal that stops, or terminates.

Both 0.6 and 0.7265 are terminating decimals.

Tessellation (p. 397) A tessellation is a repeated geometric design that covers a plane with no gaps and no overlaps.

Theoretical probability (p. 492) Theoretical probability describes how likely it is that an event will happen based on all the possible outcomes. The ratio for the probability of an event occurring is $P(\text{event})$.

$$P(\text{event}) = \frac{\text{number of favorable outcomes}}{\text{number of possible outcomes}}$$

The probability of spinning the number 4 is $\frac{1}{8}$.

Three-dimensional figure (p. 408)   Figures, such as buildings, that do not lie in a plane are three-dimensional. The dimensions are length, width, and height.

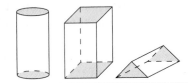

Translation (p. 370)   A translation slides a figure.

Example: Shape B is a translation of Shape A.

Transversal (p. 338)   A transversal is a line that intersects a pair of lines.

Example: Line C is a transversal.

Trapezoid (p. 350)   A trapezoid is a quadrilateral that has exactly one pair of parallel sides.

Example: $\overline{UV}$ is parallel to $\overline{WY}$.

Triangle (p. 340)   A triangle is a polygon with three sides.

Tree diagram (p. 498)   A tree diagram displays all the possible outcomes of an event.

Example: There are 4 possible outcomes for tossing 2 coins: HH, HT, TH, TT.

Trial (p. 486)   A trial is one repetition of a simulation.

One spin of a spinner is one trial.

Two-step equation (p. 453)   A two-step equation is an equation that has two operations.

$2x + 3 = 10$

U

Unit rate (p. 282)   A unit rate compares a quantity to a unit of one.

Miles per hour is a unit rate that compares distance traveled to a unit of time, such as 60 mi/h.

V

Variable (p. 56)   A variable is a symbol, usually a letter, that stands for a number.

x is a variable in the equation $9 - x = 3$.

Variable expression (p. 56)   A variable expression is an expression that contains at least one variable.

$7 + x$

Vertex (p. 331)   A vertex is any point where two rays of an angle or two sides of a polygon meet. See *Angle*.

Example: *C, D, E, F,* and *G* are all vertices of the pentagon shown.

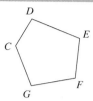

Vertex (p. 409)   In a three-dimensional figure, a vertex is the point where edges meet. See also *Cone*.

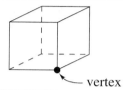

vertex

Vertical (p. 327)   A vertical line is perpendicular to the horizon.

Example: $\overleftrightarrow{AB}$ is a vertical line.

Volume (p. 418)   The volume of a three-dimensional figure is the number of cubic units needed to fill the space inside the figure.

Example: The volume of the rectangular prism is 36 in.^{3}.

each cube = 1 in.^{3}

X

x-axis (p. 463)   The x-axis is the horizontal number line that, together with the y-axis, forms the coordinate plane. See *Coordinate plane*.

Y

y-axis (p. 463)   The y-axis is the vertical number line that, together with the x-axis, forms the coordinate plane.

Z

Zero pairs (p. 439)   Zero pairs are pairs of tiles that represent the number zero.

Zero Property of Multiplication (p. 552)   The product of zero and any number is zero.

$6 \times 0 = 0 \qquad 0 \times 3 = 0$
$a \times 0 = 0 \qquad 0 \times a = 0$

Glossary/Study Guide

TOOLS FOR PROBLEM SOLVING

The Four Step Approach	page xxii

ON YOUR OWN   **1.** 6   **3.** $205

Using Strategies	page xxv

ON YOUR OWN   **1.** 72 in., 80 in.   **3.** 64 calls

Working Together	page xxvii

ON YOUR OWN   **3.** yes; no

Preparing for Standardized Tests	page xxix

ON YOUR OWN   **1.** B   **3.** C

CHAPTER 1

Lesson 1-1	pages 4–7

ON YOUR OWN

1a.

Letter	Tally	Frequency
a	III	3
e	I	1
i	III	3
o	HHI	6
u		0

3.

Cost	Frequency
$122	3
$125	3
$135	1
$138	1

9.   Test Scores
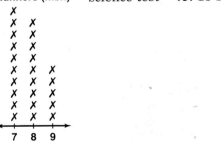

11. Speeds of Runners (mi/h)

13. 5   **15.** 4   **17.** grades on a science test   **19.** 13 students

21a.   Birth States of U.S. Presidents
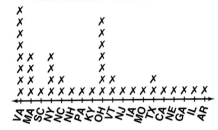

MIXED REVIEW   **25.** 1,139   **27.** 18,629   **29.** 9,818
31. 2 pennies, 1 nickel, 2 dimes, 1 quarter

Lesson 1-2	pages 8–10

ON YOUR OWN   **1.** 13 ways   **3.** 16 race cars and
12 tugboats   **5.** 45, 40, 35, 30, 25, 20, 15   **7.** 1:10 P.M.
9. 2 links   **11.** 6 outfits

MIXED REVIEW

13.   Student Heights (inches)

52 53 54 55 56 57 58 59 60

15. 4,096 members

Toolbox	page 11

1. 30 R2   **3.** 93 R1   **5.** 80 R3   **7.** 503   **9.** 429 R2
11. 50 R22   **13.** 34 R21   **15.** 98 R20   **17.** 47 R11
19. 25   **21.** Round the dividend and the divisor to
two numbers that are easy to divide mentally.

Lesson 1-3	pages 12–16

ON YOUR OWN   **1.** 10   **3.** 2   **5.** 19   **7.** 22   **9.** 40
11. player's scoring in basketball games: 15, 12, 9,
15, 32, 21, 23, 19, 22   **13a.** 12.5; 12   **15.** 19   **17.** 51
19. 810   **21.** 17   **23.** 2   **25.** 0 and 1   **27.** 9 and 12
29. 31   **31.** no mode   **33.** C   **35.** Median; 114
affects the mean too much.   **37.** Mode; the data
are not numeric.

MIXED REVIEW   **39.** 1,488   **41.** 31   **43.** 77

CHECKPOINT   **1.** 20   **2.** 20   **3.** 15
4.

Grams of Fat	Frequency
0	8
1	9
2	5
3	3

1. B   **3.** C   **5.** D   **7.** C   **9.** C

Lesson 1-4   pages 18–21

ON YOUR OWN   **1.** column C   **3.** F2   **5.** E4
7. D6   **9.** = B2 + C2 + D2; = B3 + C3 + D3;
= B4 + C4 + D4; = B5 + C5 + D5; = B6 + C6 +
D6   **11.** Multiply the mean in cell F3 by 3. Then
subtract the values in B3 and C3.   **13.** No; you
could use the formulas for the mean directly in
column F.   **15.** 5   **17.** 3   **19.** 6   **21.** Subtract B2
from C2.   **23.** Multiply the value in D6 by 6, or
add E2, E3, E4, and E5.   **25.** Subtract B5 from
C5.   **27.** = C2 − B2; = C3 − B3; = C4 − B4;
= C5 − B5; = D2 + D3 + D4 + D5; = D6 / 4;
= D2 * 6; = D3 * 6; = D4 * 6; = D5 * 6; = D6 * 6;
= D7 * 6;   **29a.** $72   **b.** E6

MIXED REVIEW   **31.** 17   **33.** 11

Lesson 1-5   pages 22–26

ON YOUR OWN   **1.** ME; RI   **3.** Maine has about
3 times as much land as Vermont.   **7.** 1983–1986
and 1992–1994   **9a.** 650 balloons   **b.** 850 balloons
11. No; the wedge for 4 teachers is much larger
than the wedge for 1 teacher.   **13.** Line graph; the
graph shows change in time.   **15.** Line graph; the
graph shows change in time.   **17.** The longer the
bar, the more money it represents.

MIXED REVIEW   **19.** 155; 155; 155   **21.** 21 and 22

Lesson 1-6   pages 27–31

ON YOUR OWN   **1.** 1,000 or 5,000; a graph with
smaller units would either be too large or too
difficult to read.   **3.** 5,000; a graph with smaller
units would either be too large or too difficult to
read.   **5.** 5; a graph with larger units would not
show enough detail.   **7.** C   **9.** No; the number of
stories and the height use different units.

11.
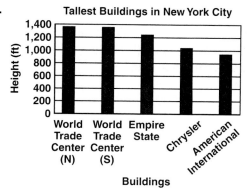
Tallest Buildings in New York City

21. The bars have unequal width.   **23.** The
horizontal gridlines are unevenly spaced.

25a.
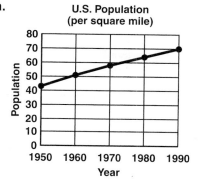
U.S. Population (per square mile)

b.
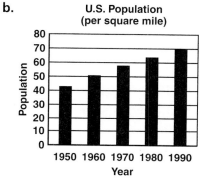
U.S. Population (per square mile)

MIXED REVIEW
27.
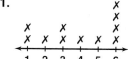

29.
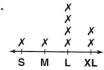

31.
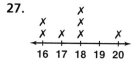

33. bar graph

CHECKPOINT   **1.** C
2.
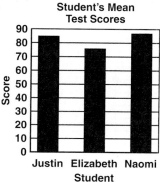
Student's Mean Test Scores

3. Army
4. 239 medals

1. 47 min **3b.** 43 min; 35 min **5.** 49; 27 **7.** The data above the median are spread out more than the data below the median.

Lesson 1-7 pages 33–36

ON YOUR OWN 7. ii; the gap in the scale makes B's margin appear much greater. **9.** i; the wider bar directs attention to candidate A.

11.

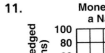

Money Pledged During a National Telethon

13. Use the broken line or zig-zag symbol to represent a gap in the scale.

MIXED REVIEW 17. 120 **19.** 1,211 **21.** 1,000
23. 10 **25.** 1,000,000
27.

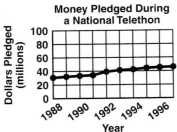

Snowiest Cities

Albany, NY	❄ ❄ ❄ ❄
Boston, MA	❄ ❄
Juneau, AK	❄ ❄ ❄ ❄ ❄
Omaha, NE	❄ ❄

Key: ❄ = 20 in.

Wrap Up pages 38–39

1.

Vowel	Frequency
a	22
e	28
i	10
o	9
u	5

2.

```
X
X        X
X        X
X   X    X
X   X    X
the and a are
```

3. 6 **4.** 18 **5.** 10 **6.** 9 ways **7.** 12 ways
8. 3 quarters **9.** 45; 49 **10.** 6; 7 **11.** 16; 15
12. M **13.** 18 **14.** 8 **15.** B2 and B3 **16.** $65
17. = B2 + C2 + D2 **18.** $940
19.

Ticket Prices

20.

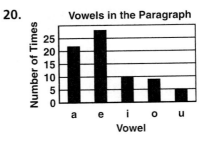

Vowels in the Paragraph

21. Line graph; the graph shows change over time.
22. Circle graph; the data are parts of a whole.
23. The bars have unequal width.
24. The range of the vertical scale is too great. The graph appears flat. **25.** The gap in scale makes it appear that toaster C sold much better.

Cumulative Review page 41

1. A **3.** C **5.** C **7.** C **9.** B

CHAPTER 2

Lesson 2-1 pages 44–47

ON YOUR OWN
1a.  **b.** 1, 2, 4, 8, 16, 32, . . .
3.

5. 12, 14, 16 **7.** 26, 32, 38 **9.** 37, 43, 49 **11.** 4, 2, 1
13. 125, 150, 175 **17.** 486; 1,458; 4,374; start with 6 and multiply by 3 repeatedly. **19.** 42, 52, 62; start with 2 and add 10 repeatedly. **21.** 60, 45, 30; start with 120 and subtract 15 repeatedly.
23. 103, 97, 91; start with 127 and subtract 6 repeatedly. **25.** 18, 6, 2; start with 1,458 and divide by 3 repeatedly.

MIXED REVIEW

27.

Ages	Frequency
8	1
9	3
10	1
11	1
14	2
15	2
18	1

29. 12; 11; 9 and 7; 7; 5 and 8

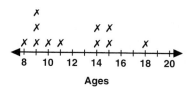

Ages

31.

x	$x + 6$
1	7
4	10
7	13
10	16
14	20

33.

x	$100 - x$
20	80
35	65
50	50
72	28
88	12

35. D

MIXED REVIEW **39.** 256; 1,024; 4,096 **41.** 27, 9, 3 **43.** 95 people

Lesson 2-5 — pages 61–64

ON YOUR OWN **11.** + **13.** + **15.** × **17.** − **19.** ÷ **21.** B **23.** $k - 34$ **25.** $50 + d$ **27.** $7 + b$ **29.** $h \times 150$ or $150h$ **31.** $s - 8$ **33.** $h + 2$ **35.** $r + s$ **37a.** $45t$ **b.** $\frac{3}{4}t$ **41.** $a + 3$ **43.** $p \div 2$

MIXED REVIEW **45.** 1992

Toolbox — page 65

1. 632 **3.** 346 **5.** 4,170 **7.** 335 **9.** 355 **11.** 365 **13.** 71 **15.** 41 **17.** 6,212 **19.** 1,005 **21.** 4,361 **23.** 5,492

Lesson 2-2 — pages 48–50

ON YOUR OWN **1.** 66 handshakes **3.** 5 h **5.** 35 cars **7.** pages 24 and 25

MIXED REVIEW **9.** 15 ways **11.** 20 **13.** 429

Lesson 2-3 — pages 51–54

ON YOUR OWN **1.** × **3.** × **5.** − **7.** 12 **9.** 13 **11.** 60 **13.** 20 **15.** 2 **17.** 210 **21a.** i. 45; ii. 29; iii. 29 **23.** > **25.** = **27.** < **29.** $(12 + 6) \div 2 - 1 = 8$ **31.** $(1 + 2) \times (15 - 4) = 33$ **33.** $14 - (3 - 2) \times 3 = 11$ **35.** 5 **37.** 8 **39.** 26 **41.** 15 **43.** 2 **45.** −; ×; ×

MIXED REVIEW **49.** 176 lockers

CHECKPOINT **1.** 34 **2.** 11 **3.** 2 **4.** 5,625; 28,125; 140,625 **5.** 34, 29, 24 **6.** 28, 35, 42

Problem Solving Practice — page 55

1. C **3.** D **5.** D **7.** C **9.** D

Lesson 2-4 — pages 56–60

ON YOUR OWN

5.  **7.**

11. 20 **13.** 56 **15.** 4 **17.** 8 **19.** 193 **21.** 3 **23.** 18 **25.** 50 **27.** 46 **29.** 2,100

Lesson 2-6 — pages 66–70

ON YOUR OWN **1.** true **3.** true **5.** C **7.** yes **9.** yes **11.** no **13.** no **17.** 3 **19.** 2 **21.** 0 **23.** 5 **25.** 9 **27.** 3 **29.** 8 **31.** 16 **33.** 76 **35.** 21 **37.** 129 **39.** 6 **41.** 9 **43.** 54 days **45.** 2,174 **47.** 46,851 **49.** 17,165

MIXED REVIEW **53.** about 88 million people **55.** 0

CHECKPOINT **1.** 33 **2.** 8 **3.** 6 **4.** 33 **5.** 63 **6.** $12 + y$ **7.** $b + 5$ **8.** $6w$ **9.** $20 - r$ **10.** 50 **11.** 385 **12.** 2 **13.** 9 **14.** D

Toolbox — page 71

1. 16,536 **3.** 18,120 **5.** 48,480 **7.** 1,150 **9.** 5,456 **11.** 2,697 **13.** 1,404 **15.** 67,837 **17.** 3,128 **19.** 31,540 **21.** 15,040 **23.** 35,002 **25.** 17,856 **27.** 20,200 **29.** 30,350 **31.** 10,400 **33.** 20,860 **35.** 18,000 **37.** 7,661 **39a.** i. 15,000; ii. 1,500; iii. 1,500; iv. 1,500; v. 15,000

Lesson 2-7 — pages 72–76

ON YOUR OWN

1.  **3.**

5. no   **7.** yes   **9.** no   **11.** 7   **13.** 8   **15.** 2   **17.** 5
21. 125   **23.** 4   **25.** 200   **27.** 42   **29.** 165   **31.** 15
33. 5   **35.** 108   **37.** 100,000   **39.** B   **41.** 83
43. 18,564,595   **45.** 18,036,201   **47.** C   **49.** 34 ft

MIXED REVIEW
51.

Number of CDs	Cost ($)
1	18.37
2	34.36
3	50.35
4	66.34
5	82.33

53. February and March

1. 162; 486; 1,458   **2.** 55, 67, 79   **3.** 35, 25, 15
4. 112, 224, 448   **5.** 5, 12, 19, 26, 33   **6.** 39 cents
7. 46   **8.** 49   **9.** 37   **10.** 4   **11.** 15   **12.** 240
13. 13   **14.** 2   **15.** <   **16.** >   **17.** 8   **18.** 49   **19.** 42
20. 6   **21.** 27   **22.** 18   **23.** $x - 5$ **24.** $y \div p$
25. $20 + b$ **26.** $h \times 4$ or $4h$ **27.** $2t$ **28.** 5
29. 433   **30.** 5,640   **31.** 128   **32.** 56   **33.** 23
34. 8   **35.** 5   **36.** D

1. D   **3.** D   **5.** C   **7.** B   **9.** A

CHAPTER 3

ON YOUR OWN   **1.** 0.8   **3.** 0.75
5. **7.**

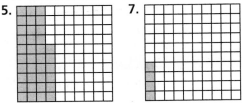

11. two tenths   **13.** forty hundredths   **15.** thirty
hundredths   **17.** 0.40   **19.** 0.5   **21.** 0.31   **23.** 0.12
25. 20   **27.** 80   **29.** 40   **35.** about 0.94

MIXED REVIEW   **37.** 4,250 lb   **39.** 153   **41.** 190
43. <   **45.** =

ON YOUR OWN   **1.** 3; 460; 800   **3.** two hundred
five   **5.** six thousand, seven hundred forty-five
7. forty-five million, six hundred fifty-four

thousand, three hundred thirty-two   **9.** 4,600
11. 478,027   **13.** 213,000,125   **15.** 6,023,158,000
17. 300,020   **19.** four tenths   **21.** four hundred-
thousandths   **23.** four ones   **25.** four ten-
thousandths   **27.** four hundreds   **29.** three
hundred fifty-two and three tenths   **31.** eleven
and two thousand, eight hundred fifty-nine ten-
thousandths   **33.** six hundred fifty-seven hundred-
thousandths   **35.** 2.00004   **37.** 42.3794   **39.** $.8
41. $.49   **43.** As you move left to right, the value
decreases by a factor of 10.   **45a.** i. $.006; ii. $.207;
iii. $.053; iv. $.328   **b.** 1 cent; 21 cents; 5 cents;
33 cents   **47.** 4.7 pt/d   **49.** 0.001 s   **51.** 0.17 mi/h

MIXED REVIEW   **53.** 4,527,982; 3,201,455; 3,097,854;
2,852,238; 2,684,387; 978,897

ON YOUR OWN
1.

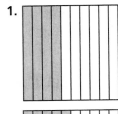

The shaded area for 0.4 is less
than the shaded area for 0.5,
so 0.4 < 0.5.

3.

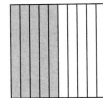

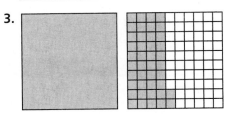

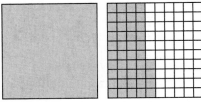

The shaded area for 1.42 is less than the
shaded area for 1.44, so 1.42 < 1.44.
5. The shaded area for 0.2 is greater than the
shaded area for 0.02, so 0.2 > 0.02.   **7.** >   **9.** >
11. <   **13.** >   **15.** <   **17.** =

19.

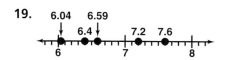

21. C   **23.** 4.28, 4.37, 8.7, 11.09, and 11.4 light-years

25. Check students' work.

MIXED REVIEW   27. 5   **29.** 11   **31.** 7,079   **33.** 65

CHECKPOINT   1. nine tenths   **2.** one hundredth
3. seventy-three hundredths   **4.** sixty hundredths
5. fifty-six hundredths   **6.** ninety-nine hundredths
7. 0.3   **8.** 0.02   **9.** 0.92   **10.** 0.36   **11.** 6 tenths
12. 7 hundredths   **13.** 8 ones   **14.** 3 thousandths
15. 6 tenths   **16.** 1 hundredth   **17.** =   **18.** >
19. >   **20.** <   **21.** <   **22.** =   **23.** >   **24.** <

Lesson 3-4   pages 96–98

ON YOUR OWN   1. 43 tickets   **3.** 80 adult tickets
5. $1,309   **7.** 19 quarters   **9.** 243 passengers

MIXED REVIEW   11. nine hundred seventy-three million, four hundred thirty thousand, six hundred twenty-four   **13.** sixteen billion, seven hundred sixty-five million, eight hundred three thousand, five hundred seventy-eight   **15.** 20   **17.** 22
19. 10,880 ft

Lesson 3-5   pages 99–102

ON YOUR OWN   1. 1.3   **3.** 1   **5.** 0.7   **7.** 0.31
9. six; sixteen   **11.** five; fifteen   **13.** 0.9 + 0.5
15. 0.72 + 0.48   **19.** 4.88   **21.** 11.07   **23.** 0.44
25. 6.51   **27.** 4.24   **29.** 6.27   **31.** 3.55

MIXED REVIEW   35. 5.13   **37.** 0.00006   **39.** 332
41. 600   **43.** 20

Toolbox   page 103

1. 70   **3.** 4,440   **5.** 3,550   **7.** 300   **9.** 1,100
11. 6,400   **13.** 13,700   **15.** 6,100   **17.** 16,000
19. 89,000   **21.** 16,000   **23.** 164,000   **25.** 102,000
27. If the digit to the right of the ten thousands' place is 5 or greater, round up. Otherwise, round down.

Lesson 3-6   pages 104–107

ON YOUR OWN   1. 2.64; 2.6   **3.** 0.74; 0.7
5. 23.45; 23.5   **7.** 0.69; 0.7   **9.** 4.06; 4.1
11. 491.30; 491.3   **15.** 0.402   **17.** 0.01   **19.** 0.6
21. $7   **23.** $15   **25.** $7   **27.** $4   **29.** Higher; each number is rounded up. Yes; the actual answer is 21.112.   **33.** B   **35.** $14   **37.** $58   **39.** $14

MIXED REVIEW   41. 26, 37, 50; start with 2, then add 3, then continue by adding a number 2 greater than the one added before it.   **43.** 625; 3,125; 15,625; start with 1, then multiply by 5 repeatedly.
45. 30   **47.** 18   **49.** 3

Lesson 3-7   pages 108–111

ON YOUR OWN   1. 4; 4   **3.** 9; 8.771   **5.** 13; 13.025
7. 13.5; 13.21   **9.** 5; 5.1   **11.** 9.5; 9.461   **13.** yes
15. C   **17.** 2; 1.7   **19.** 1; 1.16   **21.** 0.7; 0.674   **23.** 5; 5.15   **25.** 8; 7.79   **27a.** 1; the total amount of energy produced   **b.** 0.66; yes; 0.5 is half of 1 and 0.66 > 0.5.   **c.** gas and firewood/charcoal
d.

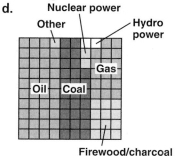

29. 0   **31.** 9.01
33. 5.866   **35.** 22.412
37a. $67.45   **b.** $6.95
c. $80.90

MIXED REVIEW   39. 40   **41.** 25   **43.** 9.004, 9.04, 90.4, 900.4   **45.** $70

Toolbox   page 112

1. The amount in cell F3, $75.47, is the difference between the balance on 11/14, in B3, $173.47, and the withdrawal on 11/14, in C3.   **3.** F2 and B3, F3 and B4; the ending balance after one transaction is the initial balance for the next transaction.

Lesson 3-8   pages 113–117

ON YOUR OWN   1. 28 mm; 2.8 cm   **3.** 92 mm; 9.2 cm   **5c.** 16 cm   **7a.** 136 mm   **b.** 11 cm   **9.** 18 m
11a. 3.3 cm, 4.8 cm, 6.7 cm   **b.** 14.8 cm   **13.** m
15. km   **17.** cm   **19.** cm   **21.** m   **23.** yes   **25.** yes

MIXED REVIEW   29. >   **31.** =   **35.** 12 packages

CHECKPOINT   1. 7; 7.32   **2.** 8; 8.26
3. 18; 18.19   **4.** 29; 29.2   **5.** 1,354; 1,354.356
6. 12.04   **7.** 2   **8.** 9.066   **9.** 53.9   **10.** 0.44   **11.** 23.57   **12.** A   **13.** 105 mm; 10.5 cm

---

Lesson 3-9   pages 118–121

ON YOUR OWN   1. g   **3.** mg   **5.** kg   **7.** g   **9.** g
11. L   **13.** L   **15.** L   **17.** L   **19.** capacity
21. mass   **23.** mass   **25.** mass   **27.** mass

29. capacity   **37.** False; mL is not a unit of mass.
39. true   **41.** true

MIXED REVIEW   **45.** $58   **47.** $6   **49.** six hundred thirty-eight thousand, nine hundred seventy **51.** two and forty-three hundredths   **53.** one thousand three and two hundred eighty-nine thousandths   **55.** $56.25

Problem Solving Practice   page 122

1. C   **3.** C   **5.** D   **7.** F

Lesson 3-10   pages 123–126

ON YOUR OWN   **1.** 90 min   **3.** 179 min   **5.** 615 min   **7.** 372 min   **9.** 2 h 27 min   **11.** 5 h 46 min **13.** 2 h 59 min   **15.** 4 h 5 min   **17.** 12 h 34 min **19.** 13 h 33 min   **21a.** 12:15 P.M.   **c.** yes; 1:15 P.M. **d.** 12:50 P.M.   **23a.** 3 h   **b.** 45 min; 45 min; 1 h

c.
Time	Activity
11:00 A.M.	Friends arrive, play outside
12:00 noon	Clown show
12:45 P.M.	Lunch
1:30 P.M.	Open presents
2:30 P.M.	Friends leave

25. The Beast **27.** 6:00 P.M.

MIXED REVIEW   **29.** 60 times   **31.** 9 thousand **33.** 9 hundred thousand   **35.** 9 thousandths

Wrap Up   pages 128–129

1. 50   **2.** 200   **3.** 310   **4.** 90   **5.** 33   **6.** C   **7.** >
8. >   **9.** >   **10.** >   **11.** 14, 14.02, 14.1, 14.18, 14.2
12. 11 small feeders   **13.** 0.7   **14.** 0.23   **15.** 0.931
16. 53.642   **17.** 357.48   **18.** $14   **19.** 59   **20.** 2
21. 624   **22.** km   **23.** kg   **24.** L   **25.** Each prefix describes how different units are related to each other. The units of length, mass, and capacity measure different kinds of quantities.   **26.** yes; 8:15 P.M.

Cumulative Review   page 131

1. B   **3.** B   **5.** A   **7.** B   **9.** B

CHAPTER 4

Lesson 4-1   pages 134–137

ON YOUR OWN   **1.** 45   **3.** 12   **5.** 36   **7.** 0   **9.** 93

MIXED REVIEW   **51.** 50 mi/h

53.
Q	1 1 1 0 0 0 0 0
D	2 1 0 4 3 2 1 0
N	0 2 4 1 3 5 7 9

Toolbox   page 138

1. 5 records

Lesson 4-2   pages 139–142

ON YOUR OWN   **1.** 4, 5   **3.** 6, 3   **5.** 8, 1   **7.** 6^3; 6, 3   **9.** 8^4; 8, 4   **11.** $1,500^3$; 1,500, 3   **13.** 625 **15.** 343   **17.** 4,096   **19.** 5   **21.** 1   **23.** 2^3 **25a.** 10,000; 10^5, 100,000   **b.** The number of zeros is the same as the exponent.   **c.** 1,000,000; 10,000,000; 100,000,000   **d.** 1, 0.1, 0.01 **27.** When written using exponents, the sequence is $1^3, 2^3, 3^3, 4^3, 5^3, 6^3, \ldots$ **29.** 25   **31.** 2,187 **33.** 10,000,000,000   **35.** 19   **37.** 112   **39.** 147 **41.** 41   **43.** 82

MIXED REVIEW   **45.** 10.725   **47.** 19.61   **49.** 178.17 **51.** 20   **53.** 40   **55.** Yes; the total cost is only $3.87.

Lesson 4-3   pages 143–147

ON YOUR OWN   **1.** 15 in.^{2}, 24 in.^{2}, 40 in.^{2}
5. $(4 \times 5) + (4 \times 5)$; 40 units^2 **9a.** 20 in.^{2}, 864 in.^{2}
b. 52 in.^{2}
11.
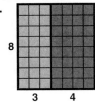
13.

15. 6, 2   **17.** 8, 3   **19.** 13, 8, 7   **23.** $4 \times (6 + 3)$; 36 **25.** $(12 \times 4) + (12 \times 10)$; 168   **27.** $13 \times (6 + 4)$; 130   **29.** $(11 \times 50) - (11 \times 4)$; 506 **31.** $6 \times (22 - 18)$; 24   **33.** 132   **35.** 1,260

MIXED REVIEW   **37.** 405; 1,215; 3,645   **39.** 400; 800; 1,600
41.
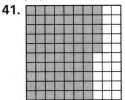
43.
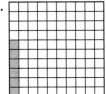

47. 7 h 57 min

CHECKPOINT   **1.** 18   **2.** 52   **3.** 60   **4.** 1,000 **9.** 128   **10.** 468   **11.** 4   **12.** 14   **13.** C

Lesson 4-4 — pages 148–150

ON YOUR OWN **1.** 0.6 **3.** 0.6 **5.** 4.0 **7.** 0.9 **9.** 1.8 **11.** 4.0 **13.** 2.4 **15.** 1.6 **17.** $0.9 \times 0.6 = 0.54$ **19.** $0.5 \times 0.5 = 0.25$ **21.** $1.5 \times 0.3 = 0.45$ **23.** 0.04 **25.** 0.26 **27.** 0.99 **29.** 0.72 **31.** 1.44

MIXED REVIEW **35.** 38 **37.** 2 **39.** 0.38 **41.** 3.95 **43.** 0.18

Lesson 4-5 — pages 151–155

ON YOUR OWN **1.** 2.015 **3.** 261.5 **5.** 405.24 **7.** 31.714 **9.** 18.65 **11.** 149.28 **13.** 14.72 **15.** 17.100 **17.** 5 cm **19.** 17.1 **21.** 878.75 **23.** 213.78 **25.** 2.478 **27.** 0.124 **29.** 0.1152 **31.** 1.05 **33.** 0.616 **35.** 0.1485 **37.** 105 calories **41.** 0.015 **43.** 0.0945 **45.** 0.072 **47.** 0.010075 **49.** 0.708 **51.** 0.26 **53.** 820 **55.** 160 **57.** 0.00482 **59.** 100 **61.** 0.8 **65.** Each product involves multiplying the factors 3 and 4, but for 0.3×0.4, you must place a decimal point in the product. **67.** false; $3.5 \times 4.2 = 14.7 = 4.2 \times 3.5$

MIXED REVIEW **69.** 8 **71.** 15 **73.** 16 **75.** < **77.** >

Toolbox — page 156

1. 3.4×10^4 **3.** 6.54321987×10^8 **5.** 8×10^5 **7.** 9.415027392×10^9 **9.** 164,000 **11.** 823.4

Lesson 4-6 — pages 157–159

ON YOUR OWN **1.** 0.8 **3.** 1.6 **5.** 0.05 **7.** 0.06 **9.** A **11.** 2 **13.** 4 **15.** 3 **17.** 3 **19.** 7 **21.** 3 **23.** 90 **25a.** 3 times greater. **b.** 8 times greater

MIXED REVIEW **27.** 3 **29.** 6 **31.** 32 pieces

Lesson 4-7 — pages 160–162

ON YOUR OWN **1.** 68 **3.** 36.5 **5.** 2.5 **7.** $6.60 **9.** 1.9 **11.** 3.45 **13.** 25.88 **15.** 1.36 **17.** D **19.** Sample: Write a number sentence $15 \times \square \ \cancel{c} = 75\cancel{c}$, then guess numbers that multiply to make 75¢. **21.** $2.07 **23.** 0.015 **25.** $8.03 **27.** 2.44 **29.** 0.817 **31.** 44.3

MIXED REVIEW **37.** = **39.** >

Lesson 4-8 — pages 163–166

ON YOUR OWN **1.** 72.5 **3.** 850 **5.** 132 **7.** 0.05 **9.** 0.73 **11.** 0.211 **13.** 3.31 **15.** 12.5 **17.** 41.5 **19.** 13.9 **21.** 9 **23a.** 5.56 times greater **b.** about 2.69 times greater **25.** 20.30 **27.** 0.21 **29.** 6.6

31. 0.02 **33.** 64 **35.** 99 **37.** 8.25 **39.** 4.40 **41.** 12.4 mi/gal

MIXED REVIEW **43.** $14 + x$ **45.** $\frac{p}{q}$ **47.** forty-five and nine hundred twenty-seven thousandths **49.** four hundred fifty-seven million, two hundred fifty-eight thousand, six hundred fifty-four **51.** fifty-four ten-thousandths

CHECKPOINT **1.** 32.76 **2.** 1.9598 **3.** 16.4 **4.** 5.022 **5.** 24 oz **6.** 13 test tubes **7.** $308.75

Problem Solving Practice — page 167

1. A **3.** A **5.** C **7.** D **9.** C

Lesson 4-9 — pages 168–170

ON YOUR OWN **1a.** $10.95 **b.** cost for two tires **c.** 1.45 lb **d.** weight of two tires **3a.** 0.75 lb **b.** curtain cost and measurements **5.** either 12 blue and 13 red or 12 red and 13 blue **7.** 19.5 hands **9.** You need to know the number of stores. **11.** nine $.79 cards and six $1.19 cards

MIXED REVIEW **13.** 23 **15.** 2,580 **17.** 579,000 **19.** 8.1 **21.** 658.4 **23.** Jerry; $.15 more

Lesson 4-10 — pages 171–174

ON YOUR OWN **1.** 1,300 m **3.** 0.2 m **5.** 3.7 m **7.** 5 L **9.** 3.07 L **11.** 0.503 L **13.** 8,000 g **15.** 240 g **17.** 0.5 g **19.** A **21.** 0.86 **23.** 108 **25.** 2,100 **27.** 4.5 **29.** 1,200,000 **31.** 500,000 **35.** 299,792.458 km/s

MIXED REVIEW **41.** x divided by 5 **43.** 9 times a **45.** 42 more than two times c

Wrap Up — pages 176–177

5. 16,384 **6.** 20 **7.** 28 **8.** 31 **9.** 0.12 **11.** 90 **12.** 30 **13.** 120 **14.** 80 **15.** 96 **16.** 236 **17.** 342 **18.** 29 **19.** $0.1 \times 0.3 = 0.03$ **20.** $0.5 \div 0.1 = 5$ **21.** 0.1286 **22.** 46.08 **23.** 0.75 **24.** 30 **25.** 6.64 **26.** 645 **27.** 0.6 **28.** 0.1125 **29.** Not possible; you need to know the number of students in the class. **30.** 153.5 cm **31.** 2,500 **32.** 57 **33.** 1.257 **34.** 8.09 **35.** 0.3 **36.** 15

Cumulative Review — page 179

1. A **3.** D **5.** D **7.** C **9.** C **11.** D

CHAPTER 5

Lesson 5-1 — pages 182–184

ON YOUR OWN **1.** yes **3.** no **5.** no **7.** yes
9. yes **11.** yes **13.** 1, 3, 5 **15.** 1, 2, 3, 5, 10
17. 1, 2, 3, 9 **19.** 4 **21.** 7 **23.** 4 **27.** B **29a.** yes

MIXED REVIEW **31.** 3.96 **33.** 32,000 **35.** 0.5
37. 4.97 L

Lesson 5-2 — pages 185–188

ON YOUR OWN **1.** 1, 2, 4, 8, 16

3. 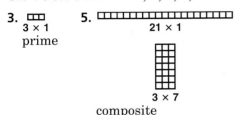 3 × 1 prime **5.** 21 × 1

3 × 7
composite

7. composite **9.** composite **11.** composite
13. prime **15.** prime **17.** composite **19.** prime
21. composite **23.** prime **25.** composite
27. 3; 3; 3 **29.** 10; 3; 5; 2; 5 **31.** $3^2 \times 7$
33. $5^2 \times 11$ **35.** 2^5 **37.** $2 \times 3^2 \times 5$ **39.** $2^5 \times 5$
41. $3^2 \times 59$ **43.** 3, 5; 5, 7; 11, 13; 17, 19; 29, 31;
41, 43; 59, 61; 71, 73 **45.** 440,657

MIXED REVIEW **47.** 0.9 **49.** 6 **51.** 21 **53.** 436

Lesson 5-3 — pages 189–191

ON YOUR OWN **1.** 7 **3.** 2 **5.** 3 **7.** 1 **9.** 5
11. 3 **13.** 2 **15.** 3 **17.** 6 **19.** 4 **21.** 1 **23.** 17
25. 1; each number has only two factors. The
second factor is the number itself. Since the
numbers are different, so are the second factors.

MIXED REVIEW **27.** 7 **29.** 76 **31.** 1.3 **33.** 1.46
35. 1.71 **37.** 2.05 **39.** 0.4518 **41.** 18 numbers

Problem Solving Practice — page 192

1. C **3.** D **5.** C **7.** C

Lesson 5-4 — pages 193–195

ON YOUR OWN **1.** $\frac{3}{4}$ **3.** $\frac{6}{6}$ **5.** $\frac{7}{12}$

7. 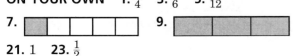 **9.**
21. 1 **23.** $\frac{1}{2}$

MIXED REVIEW **27.** 2.5; 2.6 **29.** 22; 22.35
31. 65; 64.79

Toolbox — page 196

5. $\frac{13}{16}$

Lesson 5-5 — pages 197–200

ON YOUR OWN
1a.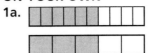

29. The first engineer wrote the time in minutes,
the second wrote it in hours.

31. no; $\frac{2}{3}$ **33.** yes **35.** no; $\frac{3}{11}$ **37.** yes
39. no; $\frac{1}{3}$ **41.** no; $\frac{4}{5}$

MIXED REVIEW **45.** 1 **47.** $\frac{1}{2}$ **49.** $\frac{1}{2}$ **51.** 3.2
53. 5 **55.** flum

CHECKPOINT **1.** 1, 2, 3, 5, 10 **2.** 1, 3, 9
3. 1, 2, 3, 5, 10 **4.** 1, 2, 3, 5, 10 **5.** 1, 3, 5
6. $2^3 \times 5$ **7.** $3^2 \times 11$ **8.** $2^6 \times 3 \times 5$ **9.** 3^5
10. $2 \times 3 \times 5 \times 7 \times 11$ **11.** 8 **12.** 1 **13.** 3
14. 6 **15.** 150 **16.** $\frac{3}{4}$ **17.** $\frac{2}{3}$ **18.** $\frac{7}{9}$ **19.** $\frac{1}{6}$ **20.** $\frac{1}{2}$

Toolbox — page 201

1. $\frac{6}{17}$ **3.** $\frac{6}{11}$ **5.** $\frac{4}{13}$ **7.** $\frac{4}{5}$ **9.** $\frac{2}{5}$ **11.** $\frac{3}{4}$ **13.** $\frac{7}{9}$
15. $\frac{5}{6}$ **17.** $\frac{23}{33}$ **19.** $\frac{7}{18}$

Lesson 5-6 — pages 202–205

ON YOUR OWN **3.** $\frac{7}{5}$ **5.** $\frac{11}{4}$ **7.** $\frac{23}{8}$ **11.** $\frac{67}{10}$ **13.** $\frac{60}{7}$
15. $\frac{11}{4}$ in.; $2\frac{3}{4}$ in. **17.** $9\frac{1}{2}$ in., $5\frac{1}{2}$ in.; $\frac{19}{2}$ in.,
$\frac{11}{2}$ in. **19.** $1\frac{6}{7}$ **21.** $3\frac{1}{12}$ **23.** $3\frac{1}{5}$ **25.** $2\frac{1}{4}$
27. $\frac{11}{9}$ **29.** $2\frac{3}{8}$ **31.** $2\frac{1}{6}$ **33.** $2\frac{7}{23}$ **35.** $4\frac{5}{8}$ **37.** $1\frac{4}{5}$

MIXED REVIEW **39.** 5:50 P.M. **41.** 73 **43.** 7

Lesson 5-7 — pages 206–208

ON YOUR OWN **1.** 12 **3.** 30 **5.** 60 **7.** 60
9. 24 **11.** 24 **13a.** 40 **15.** D **17.** 72 **19.** 60
21. 300 **23.** 260 **25.** 56 **27.** 108 **29a.** i. 6; 36;
216; 216; ii. 5; 100; 500; 500; iii. 4; 168; 672; 672
b. The product of the GCF and the LCM is equal to
the product of the numbers.

MIXED REVIEW **31.** 5.7 **33.** 5.176 **35.** $k - 28$
37. $12 + y$ **39.** 12 people

Lesson 5-8 — pages 209–212

ON YOUR OWN **1.** > **3.** = **5.** < **7.** >
9. Timothy **11.** B **13.** $\frac{2}{7}, \frac{2}{5}, \frac{2}{3}$ **15.** $1\frac{2}{3}, 1\frac{3}{4}, 1\frac{5}{6}$
17. $2\frac{5}{6}, 2\frac{8}{9}, 2\frac{17}{18}$ **19.** $\frac{1}{3}, \frac{7}{15}, \frac{7}{12}$ **21.** $\frac{5}{7}, \frac{3}{4}, \frac{11}{14}$
23. $\frac{8}{15}, \frac{23}{40}, \frac{7}{12}, \frac{19}{30}$

MIXED REVIEW **27.** 253 min **29.** 499 min
31. 156 min **33.** 31.713 **35.** 8.9
37. The collector made $7.

Lesson 5-9 — pages 213–217

ON YOUR OWN **1.** $\frac{3}{10}$ **3.** $2\frac{5}{8}$ **5.** $5\frac{1}{2}$ **7.** $1\frac{31}{50}$
9. $\frac{7}{100}$ **11.** $\frac{8}{125}$ **13.** $\frac{1}{125}$ **15.** $\frac{29}{200}$ **17.** $\frac{113}{200}$
19. $\frac{3}{2,000}$ **21.** $\frac{11}{20}$ **25.** 0.18 **27.** $0.8\overline{3}$ **29.** 0.875
31. 10.75 **33.** 0.35 **35.** $0.5\overline{4}$ **37.** 0.56 **39.** 4.7
41. $0.208\overline{3}$ **43.** $3.\overline{36}$ **45.** $10.625 **47a.** 0.34, $0.\overline{3}$,
0.32, $0.34\overline{6}$ **b.** $\frac{8}{25}, \frac{1}{3}, \frac{17}{50}, \frac{26}{75}$

MIXED REVIEW **49.** 3.5 **51.** 8.2 **53.** 6.3
55. No; the numbers in the last column are
declining, but not at a constant rate.

CHECKPOINT **1.** 96 **2.** 504 **3.** 360 **4.** 140
5. 0.4 **6.** 0.07 **7.** 0.375 **8.** $0.1\overline{6}$ **9.** $5.\overline{5}$ **10.** $\frac{13}{25}$
11. $\frac{1}{25}$ **12.** $\frac{3}{4}$ **13.** $15\frac{1}{40}$ **14.** $1\frac{3}{8}$ **15.** D

Lesson 5-10 — pages 218–220

ON YOUR OWN **1.** 11 **3.** 90 cards **5.** Saturday
7. after 1 h 54 min **9.** 13 people **11.** $8
13. 12 dimes and 3 nickels

MIXED REVIEW **21.** 18,000 **23.** 0.85

Wrap Up — pages 222–223

1. 1, 3 **2.** 1, 2 **3.** 1, 3, 9 **4.** 1, 3, 5, 9 **5.** 1, 2
6. 1, 2, 5, 10 **7.** B **8.** $2^3 \times 3^2$ **9.** $2^3 \times 3 \times 5$
10. 3×11 **11.** $2^4 \times 5$ **12.** $2 \times 3^2 \times 13$
13. $3 \times 5 \times 23$ **14.** 20; 280 **15.** 1; 924 **16.** 3; 72
17. 5; 75 **18.** 6; 1,260 **19.** 2; 240 **20.** $\frac{1}{2}$ **21.** 1
22. 0 **23.** 0 **24.** $\frac{1}{2}$ **25.** $\frac{1}{2}$ **28.** $\frac{1}{2}$ **29.** $\frac{3}{5}$ **30.** $\frac{8}{9}$
31. $\frac{3}{8}$ **32.** $\frac{2}{7}$ **33.** $\frac{19}{4}$ **34.** $4\frac{2}{5}$ **35.** $8\frac{1}{7}$ **36.** $\frac{19}{8}$
37. $2\frac{1}{2}$ **38.** $\frac{57}{11}$ **39.** $\frac{35}{36}, 1\frac{3}{4}, 1\frac{7}{9}, 1\frac{5}{6}$ **40.** $\frac{1}{25}$ **41.** $3\frac{7}{8}$
42. $2\frac{7}{50}$ **43.** 0.425 **44.** $0.\overline{8}$ **45.** $0.5\overline{4}$ **46.** $39

Cumulative Review — page 225

1. A **3.** C **5.** C **7.** C **9.** D

Lesson 6-1 — pages 228–231

ON YOUR OWN **1.** $\frac{1}{2}$ **3.** $1\frac{1}{2}$ **5.** $1\frac{1}{2}$ **7.** $1\frac{1}{2}$ **9.** 1
11. $1\frac{1}{2}$ **13.** $1\frac{1}{2}$ **15.** 2 **17.** $3\frac{1}{2}$ in. **19.** 9 **21.** 12
23. 1 **25.** 4 **27.** 31 **29.** 21 **31.** 2 **33.** $15.00
35. 24 ft

MIXED REVIEW **37.** $\frac{3}{4}$ **39.** $\frac{3}{14}$ **41.** $\frac{24}{25}$

43. Ages of First Cousins

Ages	Frequency
8	1
9	3
10	1
11	1
12	1
13	1
15	2
16	1
20	1

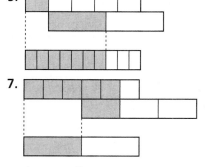

Ages of First Cousins

45. $21

Lesson 6-2 — pages 232–235

ON YOUR OWN **1.** $\frac{2}{6} + \frac{3}{6} = \frac{5}{6}$ **3.** $\frac{3}{12} + \frac{4}{12} = \frac{7}{12}$
5. 1 **7.** $\frac{1}{2}$ **9.** $\frac{5}{6}$ **11.** 1 **13.** $\frac{3}{4}$ **15.** $\frac{71}{100}$ **17.** $\frac{7}{10}$
19. $\frac{9}{10} - \frac{7}{10} = \frac{2}{10}$ or $\frac{1}{5}$ **21.** $\frac{5}{8} - \frac{3}{8} = \frac{2}{8}$ or $\frac{1}{4}$ **23.** no; $\frac{1}{3}$
25. yes **27a.** Subtract. **b.** $\frac{1}{8}$ in. **29.** $\frac{2}{5}$ **31.** $\frac{1}{4}$
33. $\frac{1}{3}$ **35.** $\frac{1}{4}$ **37.** $\frac{1}{5}$ **39.** $\frac{1}{2}$ **41.** $\frac{7}{8}$ **43a.** $\frac{1}{2}$ tbsp **b.** $\frac{1}{4}$ c
MIXED REVIEW **47.** 6^4 **49.** 5.8^5 **51.** 5 **53.** 9
55. Jan: $2.00; Leah: $3.25

Lesson 6-3 — pages 236–240

ON YOUR OWN **1.** $\frac{2}{3} - \frac{5}{12} = \frac{3}{12}$ or $\frac{1}{4}$ **3.** $\frac{2}{5} + \frac{1}{2} = \frac{9}{10}$
5.

7.

9. $\frac{3}{10}$ **11.** $\frac{7}{10}$ **13.** $\frac{1}{2}$ **15.** $\frac{11}{12}$ **17.** $\frac{1}{5}$ **19.** less than
21. less than **23.** $1\frac{5}{12}$ yd **25.** $\frac{11}{15}$ **27.** $\frac{3}{10}$ **29.** $\frac{29}{30}$
31. $1\frac{7}{40}$ **33.** $\frac{1}{3}$ **35.** $1\frac{1}{4}$ **37.** $\frac{1}{4}$ **39.** $1\frac{7}{36}$ **41.** $\frac{9}{20}$

43. $\frac{1}{40}$ **45.** Belize, Panama, Costa Rica, Nicaragua, Honduras, El Salvador, Guatemala

47. El Salvador **49.** $\frac{3}{10}$ **51.** $1\frac{5}{12}$ **53.** $1\frac{1}{4}$ **55.** $1\frac{3}{8}$

57. $\frac{9}{10}$ **59.** no

MIXED REVIEW **61.** line graph **63.** Saturday

CHECKPOINT **1.** 1 **2.** 0 **3.** 10 **4.** 18 **5.** 2

6. $\frac{1}{4} + \frac{1}{4} = \frac{2}{4}$ or $\frac{1}{2}$ **7.** $\frac{7}{10} - \frac{3}{10} = \frac{4}{10}$ or $\frac{2}{5}$

8. $\frac{1}{3} - \frac{1}{6} = \frac{1}{6}$ **9.** $\frac{3}{5}$ **10.** $\frac{1}{3}$ **11.** $\frac{1}{2}$ **12.** $\frac{3}{8}$ **13.** $\frac{1}{2}$

14. $\frac{1}{10}$

Lesson 6-4   pages 241–244

ON YOUR OWN **1.** $1\frac{1}{6}$ **3.** $15\frac{1}{3}$ **5.** 9 **7.** $5\frac{1}{6}$

9. $13\frac{7}{16}$ **11.** $7\frac{3}{4}$ **13.** $13\frac{15}{16}$ **15.** $56\frac{11}{15}$ **17.** $8\frac{17}{20}$

19. $13\frac{7}{12}$ **23.** 5 **25.** 13 **29.** $5\frac{7}{8}$ **31.** $5\frac{1}{2}$ **33.** $3\frac{1}{8}$

35. $9\frac{2}{15}$ **37.** $30\frac{3}{10}$ **39.** $44\frac{13}{20}$ **41.** $12\frac{3}{10}$

43a. $7\frac{5}{8}$ ft **b.** Add **45.** $24\frac{1}{5}$ **47.** $27\frac{2}{3}$ **49.** $4\frac{1}{3}$

51. $31\frac{11}{12}$ **53.** $24\frac{1}{3}$ **55.** $10\frac{1}{4}$ **57.** $171\frac{1}{3}$ **59.** $36\frac{17}{24}$

61. $5\frac{1}{8}$ in. **63.** D **65.** \$77.50

MIXED REVIEW **67.** 2,574 **69.** 380 **71.** 369

73. 972; 2,916; 8,748

Toolbox   page 245

1. $\frac{7}{20}$ **3.** $\frac{7}{10}$ **5.** $\frac{13}{24}$ **7.** $\frac{7}{90}$ **9.** $\frac{7}{45}$ **11.** $13\frac{1}{2}$

13. $4\frac{7}{18}$ **15.** $8\frac{11}{12}$ **17.** $8\frac{1}{12}$ **19.** $10\frac{4}{5}$

Lesson 6-5   pages 246–249

ON YOUR OWN **1.** 4 **3.** $1\frac{1}{3}$ **5.** $2\frac{1}{2}$ **7.** $1\frac{1}{16}$

9. $10\frac{1}{16}$ **11.** $8\frac{1}{8}$ **13.** $4\frac{11}{20}$ **15.** $25\frac{1}{10}$ **17.** $1\frac{5}{8}$

19. $3\frac{8}{15}$ **21.** $16\frac{5}{6}$ **23.** $\frac{9}{16}$ **25.** $7\frac{11}{16}$ **27.** $2\frac{1}{6}$ **29.** $7\frac{5}{6}$

33. $3\frac{1}{2}, 2\frac{1}{3}$

35.

Spruce Tree	Length of Cone (in.)
Black	$\frac{7}{8}$
Red	$1\frac{1}{4}$
White	$1\frac{5}{8}$
Norway	$5\frac{1}{2}$

37. black and red, red and white **39.** 2 ft $5\frac{3}{4}$ in.

41. $9\frac{1}{4}$ **43.** $10\frac{11}{16}$ **45.** $9\frac{3}{10}$ **47.** $4\frac{1}{4}$ **49.** $14\frac{7}{8}$

51. $12\frac{1}{4}$ **53a.** $2\frac{3}{4}$ in. **b.** Subtraction

MIXED REVIEW **55.** $\frac{12}{25}$ **57.** 0.12 **59.** 0.84

61. 9,300,000 **63.** 5.62 **65.** 0.133

Lesson 6-6   pages 250–252

ON YOUR OWN **1.** 1 ft by 11 ft, 2 ft by 10 ft, 3 ft by 9 ft, 4 ft by 8 ft, 5 ft by 7 ft, 6 ft by 6 ft; 6 ft by 6 ft **3.** 39 in. **5.** 19 boxes **7.** 8 different sandwiches **9.** 8:45 A.M.

MIXED REVIEW

11.

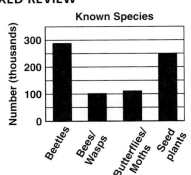

Known Species

13. price for one box of juice

Lesson 6-7   pages 253–256

ON YOUR OWN **1.** $\frac{1}{2} \times \frac{1}{2} = \frac{1}{4}$ **3.** $\frac{2}{3} \times \frac{2}{3} = \frac{4}{9}$

5. 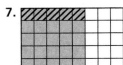 **7.**

9. C **13.** $\frac{2}{5}$ **15.** $\frac{1}{4}$ **17.** $\frac{1}{10}$ **19.** $\frac{1}{20}$ **21.** $\frac{9}{20}$ **23.** $10\frac{5}{6}$

25. $27\frac{9}{10}$ **27.** $10\frac{2}{3}$ **29.** $17\frac{1}{4}$ **31.** $27\frac{1}{2}$ **33.** 33 million people

MIXED REVIEW **35.** prime **37.** composite **39.** prime **41.** 3 tenths **43.** 3 thousandths **45.** 3 ten-thousandths

Problem Solving Practice   page 257

1. B **3.** B **5.** B **7.** B **9.** D

Lesson 6-8   pages 258–261

ON YOUR OWN **1.** 4 **3.** 80 **5.** 18 **7.** 54

9. about 150 in.^{2} **11.** $33\frac{3}{4}$ **13.** $49\frac{5}{6}$ **15.** $13\frac{7}{8}$

17. $2\frac{4}{5}$ **19.** 6 **21.** $9\frac{5}{6}$ **23.** 20 **25.** $17\frac{1}{4}$ **27.** $4\frac{3}{8}$ in.^{2}

29. 3 in. by 3 in. **31.** $13\frac{1}{2}$ in.

MIXED REVIEW **33.** 30 **35.** 360 **37.** 1,260 **39.** 0.191 **41.** 0.0367 **43.** \$3.00

CHECKPOINT **1.** $10\frac{7}{8}$ **2.** $5\frac{3}{16}$ **3.** $28\frac{1}{2}$ **4.** $4\frac{9}{10}$
5. $8\frac{4}{15}$ **6.** $10\frac{1}{4}$ **7.** $23\frac{5}{8}$ **8.** $\frac{9}{16}$ **9.** $13\frac{17}{24}$ **10.** C
11. $\frac{1}{10}$ **12.** 15 **13.** $2\frac{1}{4}$ **14.** $10\frac{1}{8}$ **15.** $11\frac{1}{3}$

Lesson 6-9 page 262–265

ON YOUR OWN
1. **3.**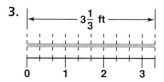

5. $\frac{1}{3}$ **7.** 5 **9.** $\frac{6}{17}$ **11.** 15 **13.** 35 **15.** 36
17. 6 pieces **19.** 20 **21.** 36 **23.** 49 **25.** $\frac{5}{6}$
27. $1\frac{1}{3}$ **29.** $7\frac{3}{4}$ **31.** $3\frac{3}{5}$ **33.** $\frac{22}{25}$ **35.** $\frac{2}{5}$ **37.** $34\frac{1}{2}$
39. 16 servings **41.** 24 pieces **43a.** 10 **b.** divide

MIXED REVIEW **45.** 50 **47.** 3 **49.** 2,400
51. Taro is the pharmacist, Alma is the stock broker, and Wanell is the teacher.

Toolbox page 266

1. pounds **3.** gallons **5.** ounces or cups

Lesson 6-10 pages 267–270

ON YOUR OWN **1.** 3 **3.** 4 **5.** 96 **7.** 16
9. $2\frac{1}{12}$ **11.** 5 **13.** $1\frac{1}{2}$ **15.** 34 **17.** $10\frac{1}{2}$ **19.** 66
21a. division **b.** multiplication **c.** multiplication
23. $6,665\frac{1}{8}$ in. **25.** 4 c **27.** 3 yd 2 ft **29.** 7 lb 15 oz
31. No; if each person eats 3 oz per serving, together they should eat 18 oz, or $1\frac{1}{8}$ lb.
33. No; $3\frac{1}{8}$ ft are needed. **35a.** 45,000,000 gal
b. about 3,000 T **37.** = **39.** < **41.** = **43.** >
45. < **47.** =

MIXED REVIEW **49.** 0.0072 **51.** $9\frac{4}{5}$ **53.** $8\frac{1}{6}$
55. $\frac{53}{6}$ **57.** 2 dimes and 1 nickel

Wrap Up pages 272–273

1. $\frac{1}{2}$ **2.** $1\frac{1}{2}$ **3.** 5 **4.** 6 **5.** $\frac{1}{5} + \frac{1}{2} = \frac{7}{10}$
6. $\frac{5}{6} - \frac{2}{6} = \frac{3}{6}$ or $\frac{1}{2}$ **7.** $\frac{7}{9}$ **8.** $\frac{1}{2}$ **9.** $1\frac{1}{12}$ **10.** $\frac{1}{30}$ **11.** $\frac{13}{40}$
12. 6 **13.** $3\frac{13}{20}$ **14.** $5\frac{1}{24}$ **15.** $4\frac{1}{15}$ **16.** $4\frac{23}{36}$

17a.
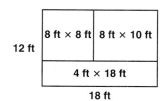

18. $\frac{1}{2}$ **19.** $\frac{1}{12}$ **20.** $8\frac{1}{8}$ **21.** $\frac{19}{20}$ **22.** 11 **23.** $73\frac{1}{3}$
24. 40 **25.** 6 **26.** $20\frac{1}{6}$ yd

Cumulative Review page 275

1. A **3.** C **5.** D **7.** D **9.** C **11.** C

CHAPTER 7

Lesson 7-1 pages 278–280

ON YOUR OWN **1.** $\frac{3}{1}$, 3 to 1, 3 : 1 **3.** $\frac{1}{2}$, 1 to 2, 1 : 2
11. 1 to 2, 1 : 2, $\frac{1}{2}$ **13.** 14 to 12, 14 : 12, $\frac{14}{12}$
15. 35 to 24, 35 : 24, $\frac{35}{24}$ **17.** 24 to 11, 24 : 11, $\frac{24}{11}$
19. 24 to 70, 24 : 70, $\frac{24}{70}$ **29.** 5 : 7

MIXED REVIEW **33.** 106.2 **35.** 17.78 **43.** 12.2 homes; about 146 homes

Lesson 7-2 pages 281–284

ON YOUR OWN **13.** $\frac{2}{5}$ **15.** $\frac{21}{25}$ **17.** $\frac{3}{2}$ **19.** $\frac{6}{1}$
21. $\frac{4}{5}$ **23.** $\frac{9}{5}$ **27.** 2 : 3 **29.** 2 : 5 **31.** 3 : 4 **33.** 3
35. 5 **37.** 33 pages/h **39.** 4 mi/h **41.** \$3 per toy
43. 2.5 mi/practice

MIXED REVIEW **45.** 165 **47.** 48 **49.** 7

Lesson 7-3 pages 285–288

ON YOUR OWN **1.** yes **3.** no **5.** yes **7.** yes
9. no **11.** 36 = 36 **13.** $\frac{2}{5} = \frac{6}{15}$, $\frac{5}{2} = \frac{15}{6}$, $\frac{2}{6} = \frac{5}{15}$,
$\frac{6}{2} = \frac{15}{5}$ **15.** 84 **17.** 27
19. 35 **21.** 63 **23.** 60
25. 1 **27.** 27 **29.** $\frac{3}{8}$ or 0.375 **31.** 108 in. **33.** 5 h

MIXED REVIEW **37.** $\frac{1}{8}$ **39.** $\frac{11}{32}$ **41.** $\frac{3}{20}$
43. 180 **45.** 4 **47.** yes; 7 cm taller

CHECKPOINT **7.** \$.89 per taco **8.** \$.35 per battery
9. 12 **10.** 18 **11.** 8 **12.** 15 **13.** 78 **14.** C

Lesson 7-4   *pages 289–291*

ON YOUR OWN   **1a.** 2 times; 120 times
b. 1,051,200 times; find the number of hours in
1 yr. Then multiply it by 120.   **3.** 63,072,000 times
5. $91.25; $912.50   **7.** no

MIXED REVIEW   **9.** 60   **11.** 20.58   **13.** 34   **15.** 4
17. 0.18   **19.** 0.48   **21.** 1.65   **23.** 2 squirrels

Lesson 7-5   *pages 292–295*

ON YOUR OWN   **1.** 1 in. to 4 ft   **3.** 1 ft to 25 ft
11. 400 km   **13.** 70 km   **15.** 1.25 cm   **17.** 40 cm
19. 10 m × 35 m   **21.** 2 m × 7 m   **23.** 6 m × 21 m
25. 20 km × 70 km   **29.** $\frac{6}{25}$ in. or 0.24 in.
31. $1\frac{31}{50}$ in. or 1.62 in.   **33.** 6 cm   **35.** 36 in.
37a. 4 × 12   **b.** The height remained the same,
but the length doubled.

MIXED REVIEW   **39.** 11.43   **41.** 1.5   **45.** 6:58 A.M.

Toolbox   *page 296*

1. 12 ft   **3.** $7\frac{1}{2}$ ft

Lesson 7-6   *pages 297–299*

ON YOUR OWN
1. 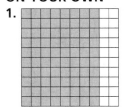   **3.**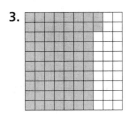

7a. 32%; 46%   **b.** Subtract both results from 100%.
c. 22%   **9.** 97% of the days last summer were
sunny.   **11.** 85% of the answers are correct.
15. 52%; 48%   **17.** 33%   **19.** 25%

MIXED REVIEW   **21.** $1\frac{7}{30}$ **23.** $1\frac{1}{2}$ **25.** $6\frac{11}{20}$ **27.** $5\frac{1}{4}$
29. $28\frac{33}{40}$ **31.** $7\frac{9}{10}$

Lesson 7-7   *pages 300–303*

ON YOUR OWN
1. 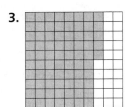   **3.**

7. 0.15; $\frac{3}{20}$ **9.** 0.88; $\frac{22}{25}$ **11.** 0.5; $\frac{1}{2}$ **13.** 0.07; $\frac{7}{100}$

15. 0.625; $\frac{5}{8}$ **17.** 0.274; $\frac{137}{500}$ **19.** 0.42; $\frac{21}{50}$
21. 0.17; $\frac{17}{100}$ **23.** 0.44; $\frac{11}{25}$ **25.** $\frac{4}{5}$, 0.8; $\frac{1}{5}$, 0.2
27. 23%   **31.** 95%   **33.** 14%   **35.** 70%   **37.** 3%
39. 11%   **41.** 100%   **43.** 99%   **45.** 1%   **47.** 40%
49. Move the decimal point two places to the right
and append the % sign.   **51a.** 25%; 34%; 44%;
55%; 69%; 77%

b.

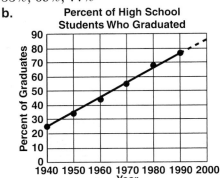

Percent of High School
Students Who Graduated

53. 26.7%
55. 26.7%
57. 14.3%
59. 56.7%
61. 13.3%
63. 85.7%

MIXED REVIEW   **65.** >   **67.** <   **69.** 14   **71.** $105

Problem Solving Practice   *page 304*

1. C   **3.** B   **5.** D   **7.** C   **9.** D

Lesson 7-8   *pages 305–308*

ON YOUR OWN   **1.** $64   **3.** $27   **5.** 36   **7.** 13
9. 12.5   **11.** 3   **13a.** $11.90   **b.** $91   **15.** $20
17a. 80%   **c.** No; $22 < $24 or $25.60.   **19.** 45
21. 10   **23.** 5   **25.** 480   **27.** 87   **29.** 30   **31.** 20
33. 20   **41.** Double the 10% tip to get the 20% tip.
Add half the 10% tip to the 10% tip to get the
15% tip.

MIXED REVIEW   **43.** $2\frac{2}{9}$ **45.** $\frac{230}{261}$ **47.** $1\frac{16}{99}$ **49.** 5
51. 15   **53.** 7   **55.** 64 teams

Lesson 7-9   *pages 309–313*

ON YOUR OWN   **1.** 9.6   **3.** 64.8   **5.** 28   **7.** 4.3
9. 9   **11.** 65.34   **13.** 30.6   **15.** 72.6   **17.** 50.05
19. 8.64   **21.** 190 girls   **23.** 5 girls
25. 647 children and teenagers   **27.** 112 A's
29. 42 I's   **31.** 36   **33.** 48   **35.** 510   **37.** 52
39. 16   **41a.** 39 people   **43.** 21 games   **45.** $200

MIXED REVIEW   **47.** 0.05693   **49.** 3.6   **51.** 5
53. 11   **55.** $10.50

1. 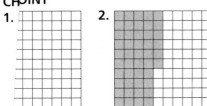 **2.**

7, 8. 45% **9.** 67% **10.** 60% **11.** 95%
1 **13.** 7 **14.** 32 **15.** 24 **16.** 50 **17.** 30
1 .5 km **19.** D

7-10   **page 314–317**

OUR OWN

3. 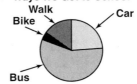 **7.**

23. **Reading for Pleasure**

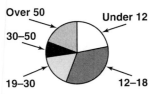

Don't know
Too much
About right
22%
25% 53%
Too little

ED REVIEW **31.** 75 **33.** 228 **35.** 120
136 **39.** 52

lbox   **page 318**

Age of People Eating at Freddy's Fast Food

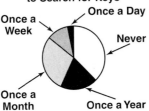

Over 50
Under 12
30–50
19–30
12–18

How Often Adults Need to Search for Keys

Once a Week
Once a Day
Never
Once a Month
Once a Year

1. $\frac{1}{4}$ **2.** $\frac{3}{7}$ **3.** $\frac{3}{7}$ **4.** $\frac{1}{4}$ **5.** $\frac{1}{3}$ **6.** $\frac{45}{100}$, 45 : 100, 45 to 100 **7.** $1.99; $1.88; package of 3 tapes
8. 21 **9.** 27 **10.** 3 **11.** 16 **12.** 3 **13.** 9 **14.** 21
15. 72 **16.** 0 **17.** 6 **18.** 3 m **19.** 1 m **20.** 24 ft
21. 1.5 m **22.** 1,440 times **24.** 24%; $\frac{6}{25}$; 0.24
25. 55%; $\frac{11}{20}$; 0.55 **26.** 12%; $\frac{3}{25}$; 0.12 **27.** 25%; $\frac{1}{4}$; 0.25 **28.** 40%; $\frac{2}{5}$; 0.40 **29.** 20%; $\frac{1}{5}$; 0.20
30. 0.65; $\frac{13}{20}$ **31.** about $72 **32.** C **33.** 30
34. 4.37 **35.** 48 **36.** 23.5 **37.** $.80
38. **Ways We Get to School**

Walk
Car
Bike
Bus

1. B **3.** B **5.** A **7.** C **9.** C **11.** B

CHAPTER 8

ON YOUR OWN **1.** d **3.** c **7.** A, B, C **11.** $\overleftrightarrow{AC}, \overleftrightarrow{DE}$
13. • • • • • **15.** not possible
  A B C D E
17. $\overline{XY}$ and $\overline{WZ}$ **19.** no parallel segments
21. never **23.** always **25.** never **27.** never

MIXED REVIEW **37.** 289 **39.** 192 **41.** 10 **43.** 11 **45.** 1
47. groups of 1, 2, 3, 4, 6, 9, 12, 18 or 36 students

ON YOUR OWN **1.** vertex: R; sides: $\overrightarrow{RQ}$ $\overrightarrow{RS}$
3. vertex: S; sides: $\overrightarrow{SD}, \overrightarrow{SE}$
5. $\angle KLM, \angle KLN, \angle MLN; \angle MLK, \angle NLK, \angle NLM$
7.   **19.** 60°; 58° **21.** 30°; 28°
          23. 30°; 30° **25.** obtuse
          27. straight **29.** acute
31a.   **b.** 4 right angles **35.** A

T
R S
W

MIXED REVIEW **43.** 9 **45.** 28 **47.** 2

Toolbox

page 336

1.

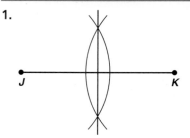

Lesson 8-3

pages 337–339

ON YOUR OWN   1. sometimes   **3.** never   **5.** 64°
7. 90°   **9.** 85°; 95°   **11.** congruent: ∠2 and ∠5, ∠3
and ∠7, ∠4 and ∠6, ∠8 and ∠9, ∠10 and ∠11;
complementary: ∠3 and ∠8, ∠3 and ∠9, ∠7 and
∠8, ∠7 and ∠9; supplementary: ∠4 and ∠10, ∠4
and ∠11, ∠6 and ∠10, ∠6 and ∠11

MIXED REVIEW   19. 30   **21.** 0.4   **23.** $2,440

Lesson 8-4

pages 340–343

ON YOUR OWN   1. isosceles   **3.** scalene
5. isosceles   **7.** scalene   **9.** scalene   **11.** isosceles
13. right   **15.** right   **17.** acute   **19.** obtuse   **21.** e
23. b, f   **25.** a, b, c   **27.** acute, isosceles,
equilateral; equilateral   **29.** Isosceles, isosceles,
isosceles; isosceles triangles have two angles of
equal measure.   **31.** acute, isosceles, equilateral;
equilateral

33.   **35.**

MIXED REVIEW   43. 30.72   **45.** 61.2   **47.** <
49. =   **51.** <

Lesson 8-5

pages 344–348

ON YOUR OWN   1. not convex   **3.** not convex
5. convex   **9.** triangle   **11.** hexagon
13. quadrilateral   **15.** quadrilateral   **17.** Each is
a polygon.   **19a.** 9 diagonals

MIXED REVIEW   21. $\frac{13}{20}$ **23.** $51\frac{21}{25}$ **25.** 18

27. 0.0006   **29.** 0.0044

CHECKPOINT   1. $\overleftrightarrow{KN}$, $\overleftrightarrow{LM}$ **8.** ∠LJN or ∠KJM
9. not possible   **10.** $\overleftrightarrow{LM}$, $\overleftrightarrow{PJ}$ **11.** B   **12.** 10 sides
13. 8 sides   **14.** 4 sides   **15.** 6 sides

Lesson 8-6

pages 349–3

ON YOUR OWN   1a. i, ii, iii, v, vi, vii, viii, ix
b. i, v, vi, vii, viii, ix   **c.** i, vii, viii   **d.** i, v, vii
e. i, vii   **f.** ii

3.   **5.**   **11.** No
13. All

15. No   **17.** All   **19.** Some

21. parallelogram, | rectangle |

23. parallelogram, | rhombus |

25a. They are congruent.   **b.** isosceles
27. rectangle, square

MIXED REVIEW   31. 5   **33.** 27   **35.** $\frac{3}{2}$, or 1.5

Lesson 8-7

pages 353–355

ON YOUR OWN   1. 4 students   **3.** $9\frac{1}{2}$ in.

5a. 17 customers   **b.** 4 customers
7. 6 combinations

MIXED REVIEW   9. 4; 800   **11.** 7; 4   **13.** 19.25
15. 4.65   **17.** 82°F

Lesson 8-8

pages 356–359

ON YOUR OWN   1. A, D   **5.** C   **7.** similar
9. congruent   **11.** 4 congruent triangles;
4 triangles are similar to the large triangle
13. A and E, I and L   **15b.** No; some rhombuses
have four right angles and some do not.   **c.** Yes;
all squares have four right angles and their sides
are always proportional.

MIXED REVIEW   17. $6\frac{1}{3}$ **19.** $15\frac{2}{3}$ **21.** $3\frac{3}{5}$
23. 18%   **25.** 3 wore neither.

Lesson 8-9

pages 360–363

ON YOUR OWN   1. yes   **3.** yes   **5.** yes   **7.** no
9. none   **11.** 16
13.

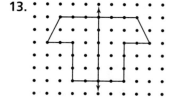

17. A, B, C, D, E, H, I,
M, O, T, U, V, W, X, Y
21. No; if you fold the
figure along the line,
the two sides do not
align.

23. No; if you fold the figure along the line, the two
sides do not align.

MIXED REVIEW   25. 4,959.665   **27.** 462.2499
29. 0.00174   **31.** $\frac{1}{2}$ **33.** $\frac{1}{2}$ **35.** 5 games

O|JR OWN   **1.** $\overline{OR}$, $\overline{OS}$, $\overline{OT}$ **3.** $\overline{ST}$, $\overline{RT}$
5.   **7.** 70 ft   **9.** 92 cm   **11.** 24 m
13. 2 mm   **15.** 0.125 ft
17. 6.2 m   **19.** 10 ft   **21a.** 60°
b. equilateral   **23.** C

N REVIEW   **25.** $2^2 \times 3 \times 5$ **27.** $2^2 \times 5^3$
$2 \times 5 \times 31$ **31.** 13 students

(POINT   **1.** A square is a parallelogram with
|ongruent sides and four right angles.
|ustomers   **b.** 21 customers   **3a.** A, B, E
|3, D, E   **4.** A   **5.** 20 in.   **6.** 90 ft   **7.** 2.5 m
|cm

|e results are the same.   **5.** Their measures
|he same.

3. D   **5.** C   **7.** D   **9.** D

|YOUR OWN

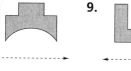

9.

13. translation
15. yes
17. yes   **19.** no
21. A, B, C, D, E
23. You turn a
shape to show
a rotation.

|XED REVIEW   **25.** $7\frac{1}{3}$ **27.** $5\frac{2}{5}$
|. seventy-three hundredths   **31.** three hundred
|ghty-six and nine hundred eight thousandths
|. four hundred seven thousand, six hundred
|ghty-three and seven hundredths
|. 28 handshakes

.   **B**   **2.** J   K   **3.** 3 segments;
A   **C**   M   N   6 rays; 1 line
   4. straight
   5. acute
   6. obtuse   **7.** B

|. 5 students   **9.** similar   **10.** neither
|2. $\overline{OV}$, $\overline{OX}$, $\overline{OY}$ **13.** $\overline{VX}$ **14.** $\overline{VW}$, $\overline{VX}$, $\overline{WY}$

1. C   **3.** B   **5.** D   **7.** B   **9.** C

CHAPTER 9

ON YOUR OWN   **1.** 8 cm^2 **3.** 8 cm^2 **5.** 20 in.^{2}
7. 52 cm^2 **9.** 54 cm^2

MIXED REVIEW   **15.** $\frac{4}{5}$ **17.** $1\frac{1}{8}$ **19.** $1\frac{1}{12}$
21. 1 to 3; 1 : 3; $\frac{1}{3}$ **23.** 1 to 2; 1 : 2; $\frac{1}{2}$ **25.** 5 days

1. $\frac{1}{8}$ in.   **3.** $\frac{1}{16}$ in.   **5.** $1\frac{5}{16}$ in.

ON YOUR OWN   **1.** 26 cm; 30 cm^2 **3.** 26 ft;
36 ft^2 **5a.** 180 ft   **b.** 60 sections   **7.** 50 yd;
150 yd^2 **9.** 38 yd; 84 yd^2 **11.** 21.8 cm; 26.64 cm^2
13. 1.5 cm and 2 cm; 7 cm; 3 cm^2 **15.** 2.5 cm and 1.5
cm; 8 cm; 3.75 cm^2 **17.** 7 ft; 28 ft^2 **19.** 3 ft   **21.** 18
in.; 20.25 in.^{2} **23.** 84 mm; 441 mm^2 **25.** 6 cm; 2.25
cm^2 **27.** 400 ft; 10,000 ft^2 **29.** 1 yd × 24 yd, 2
yd × 12 yd, 3 yd × 8 yd, 4 yd × 6 yd   **33.** 4 cm^2
35. 144 in.^{2} **37a.** 16 in.^{2} **b.** The perimeter would
be 8 in.; the area would be 4 in.^{2}.

MIXED REVIEW   **39.** 4   **41.** 1.3   **43.** 0.23

ON YOUR OWN   **1.** 36 ft^2 **3.** 48 km^2 **5.** 9.6 cm^2
7. 54 in.^{2} **9.** 16 yd^2 **11.** 12.25 m^2 **13.** 8 units^2
15. 6 units^2 **17.** 30 m^2 **21.** 30 units^2
23. 21 units^2 **25.** 12 units^2 **27.** 16 units^2

MIXED REVIEW   **29.** $1\frac{13}{16}$ **31.** $23\frac{1}{3}$ **33.** $31\frac{1}{2}$

CHECKPOINT   **1.** 240 in.   **2.** 80 in.; 175 in.^{2}
3. 84 in.^{2} **4.** 72.25 cm^2 **5.** 78 m^2 **6.** 1,000 ft^2

1. yes   **3.** no

ON YOUR OWN   **1.** about 15 cm   **3.** about 6 in.
5. about 120 mi   **7.** 157 m   **9.** 402 m   **11.** 12 m
13. 55 ft   **15.** 10,000 m   **17.** 20 mm; 10 mm
21. 27.1 cm   **23.** 17.8 m   **25.** 0.6 yd   **27.** 21.9 cm
29. 6.3 m   **31.** about 11 times

Selected Answers

Lesson 9-5   pages 403–407

ON YOUR OWN 1. 1,134.1 cm^2 3. 72.4 m^2
5. about 12 in.^{2} 7. about 300 cm^2
9. about 27 mm^2 11. 314.0 m^2 13. 12.6 yd^2
15. 706.5 in.^{2} 17. 28.3 mm^2 19. 50.2 in.^{2}
21. 95.0 ft^2 23. 60.8 cm^2 25. 452.2 ft^2
27. 19.6 m^2 29. 6,358.5 mi^2 31. 10.2 m^2
33. 360 days 35. 38.5 cm^2 37. 50.3 ft^2
39. 3.1 mm^2 41. 1,017.9 m^2 43. 95.0 in.^{2}
45. 176.7 ft^2 47. 227.0 in.^{2} 49. 1,963.5 in.^{2}
51. 0.8 cm^2 53. 66 m^2 55. 19 m^2
57. 12.6 units^2 59. 14.3 units^2

MIXED REVIEW 61. obtuse 63. acute 65. 20
67. 2.5 69. 80

Lesson 9-6   pages 408–412

ON YOUR OWN 1. triangular prism
3. hexagonal prism 13. 4; C, F, G, H
15. rectangular prism 17. sphere
19. square prism or cube 21. cylinder 25. C

MIXED REVIEW 27. some 29. all 31. $\frac{1}{5}$

Toolbox   page 413

1.

front right top

3.

front right top

5. 11 or 12 cubes

Lesson 9-7   pages 414–417

ON YOUR OWN 1. 14 cm^2 3. 36 cm^2
5. rectangular prism; 80 cm^2 7. rectangular prism;
112 cm^2 9. 600 ft^2 11. 150 cm^2 13. 1,440 cm^2
15. 132 in.^{2} 17. C 19. Find the sum of the
areas. Then double it.

MIXED REVIEW 23. 4.5 m × 7.5 m
25. 30 km × 50 km

Lesson 9-8   pages 418–422

ON YOUR OWN 1. A 3. 96 cm^3 5. 48 cm^3
7. 27 m^3 9. 42 ft^3 11. 320 ft^3 13. $V = s^3$;
the three dimensions of a cube are the same.
15. 245 cm^3 17. 112 mm^3 19. 440 cm^3 21. C
23. 7 yd 25. 9 ft 27. 5 in.

29. 1 cm × 1 cm × 32 cm, 1 cm × 2 cm × 16 c
1 cm × 4 cm × 8 cm, 2 cm × 2 cm × 8 cm, 2 c
4 cm × 4 cm

MIXED REVIEW 35. 71 37. $7\frac{1}{4}$ 39. 28 41.

CHECKPOINT 1. 13 m; 12.6 m^2 2. 82 in.;
530.7 in.^{2} 3. 38 km; 113.0 km^2 4. square pri
5. triangular prism 6. cube 7. square pyram
8. 62 cm^2; 30 cm^3 9. 54 cm^2; 27 cm^3
10. 121 cm^2; 90 cm^3

Problem Solving Practice   page 423

1. A 3. C 5. D 7. D

Lesson 9-9   pages 424–426

ON YOUR OWN 1. right-side-up
3. 204 grapefruit 5. 64 in.; 64 in. 7a. 6 cuts
b. 27 pieces c. 1 piece 9. 1 × 1 × 12
11. 1 m × 17 m, 2 m × 16 m, 3 m × 15 m, 4 m ×
14 m, 5 m × 13 m, 6 m × 12 m, 7 m × 11 m,
8 m × 10 m, 9 m × 9 m

MIXED REVIEW 13. no lines 15. 2 lines
17. $33\frac{1}{3}\%$

Wrap Up   pages 428–429

1. about 19 m^2 2. 13.5 cm^2; 22 cm 3. 34 m
4. 45.6 cm^2 5. 38 in. 6. 24 m 7. 77 cm
8. 118 ft 9. 78.5 in.^{2} 10. 530.9 m^2 11. 69.4 m^2
12a. square pyramid b. 5 faces; 8 edges; 5 vertices
13. A rectangular prism has six rectangular faces,
with two parallel bases. 14. 64 m^2; 28 m^3 15. B
16. 26 people

Cumulative Review   page 431

1. B 3. B 5. C 7. D 9. D

CHAPTER 10

Lesson 10-1   pages 434–437

ON YOUR OWN 1. 1 3. 5
5.

−1 3 6 7
−9

−8 −4 0 4 8

7. −14 9. −1,565
11. −13 13. −150
15. 1 19. −8

21. −6 23. < 25. > 27. > 29. <
31. −2, −1, 3, 4 33. −5, −2, −1, 3, 4

MIXED REVIEW 41. about 452 or 452.16 mm^2
43. about 95 or 94.99 in.^{2} 45. 6:30 A.M.

Toolbox   *page 438*

1.
3.

7. 17   9. 0   11. 180

Lesson 10-2   *pages 439–441*

ON YOUR OWN

1.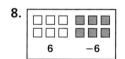
3.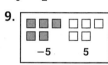

7. 2   9. -2 11. 4
13. -4 23a. 4   b. -4
c. -6

MIXED REVIEW   25. $10\frac{1}{2}$ 27. $19\frac{1}{24}$ 29. $21\frac{8}{9}$
31. 18   33. 0   35. $2\frac{2}{3}$

Lesson 10-3   *pages 442–446*

ON YOUR OWN   1. 6   3. -9 5. -14 7. 0
9. -5 11. $-4 + (-2) = -6$ 13. $-2 + (-8) = -10$
15. $-2 + 6 = 4$ 17. positive   19. positive
21. negative   23. -15 25. 0   27. 5   29. 7   31. 0
35. $<$ 37. $>$ 39. 2 floors down   41. -5 45. 5
47. 0

MIXED REVIEW   49. 6   51. 49   53. 30   55. 33.8
57. 98.7   59. 36 bottles

CHECKPOINT   1. $<$ 2. $>$ 3. $<$ 4. $>$ 5. $<$
6. 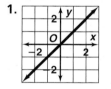   7. 1

8.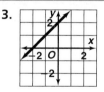
9.

14. -5
15. 2   16. 0
17. -12
18. 3

Problem Solving Practice   *page 447*

1. B   3. A   5. D   7. D

Lesson 10-4   *pages 448–452*

ON YOUR OWN   1. $-1 - 2 = -3$ 3. $-2 - (-6) = $
4   5. -5 7. 4   9. 4   11. -3 13. 6   15. -13
17. 15   19. -8 21. -21 23. -8 25. 4   27. 0
29. -10 31. $=$ 33. $=$ 35. $>$ 37. 9 P.M., New
Year's Eve   39. 10:15 A.M.   41. $-8, -13, -18$
43. 0, 3, 6

MIXED REVIEW   49. 5   51. Valli   53. $1\frac{3}{5}$ 55. $\frac{9}{100}$
57. $2\frac{1}{8}$ 59. 21 students

Toolbox   *page 453*

1. 1   3. 4   5. 2   7. -2 9. -3 11. -1
13. 2   15. 0

Lesson 10-5   *pages 454–456*

ON YOUR OWN   1. September 22   3. 981 mi
5. $-31°F$ 7. 50 miles

MIXED REVIEW   15. 96   17. 36   19. 21 and 13

Lesson 10-6   *pages 457–461*

ON YOUR OWN   1. 16; 20   3. 75; 90

5.

Input (ft)	Output (in.)
1	12
2	24
3	36
4	48
5	60

7.

Input (m)	Output (cm)
1	100
2	200
3	300
4	400
5	500

9.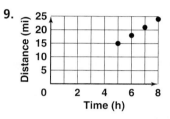

13. A   15a. 11; 14; 17
b. The cost of tees is
three times the
number of tees plus
five.

MIXED REVIEW   17. 225 cm^2 19. 2.89 ft^2 21. $\frac{1}{64} \text{ ft}^2$
23. 27   25. 28.75   27. 4.5

Toolbox   *page 462*

1.   3.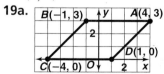

Lesson 10-7   *pages 463–467*

ON YOUR OWN   7. A   9. J   11. L   13. $(-5, 0)$
15. $(0, 3)$ 17. F
19a.

b. quadrilateral or
parallelogram
c. parallelogram   21. I
23. III   25. II   27. B
31. Africa; Europe

MIXED REVIEW   39. equilateral   41. scalene
43. 22   45. 26   47. 1.5   49. $190.35

CHECKPOINT   1. E   2. G   3. N   4. A   5. $(4, 2)$
6. $(4, -1)$ 7. $(-2, 4)$ 8. $(-1, 0)$ 9. $(-4, -4)$
10. $(2, 4)$ 11. $(-3, -1)$ 12. $(2, 0)$ 13. -20
14. 128   15. 585   16. $-1,996$

Lesson 10-8 — pages 468–472

ON YOUR OWN **1.** 193 **3.** −1,110 **5.** 22
7. −1,118 **9.** −7 **11.** 47 **13.** 0 **15.** −200
23a. $9; $18; −$9; $17; −$12; −$1; −$17
b.

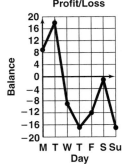

Profit/Loss

25. = B2 + C2;
= B3 + C3; = B4 + C4;
= B5 + C5 **27.** −$2,256;
$984; $194; −$1,196;
$15,931; −$18,205;
−$2,274

MIXED REVIEW **31.** 1 **33.** 3 **35.** 8 m
37a. $1,946.80 **b.** $1,357.46

Wrap Up — pages 474–475

1. −7 **2a.** 7 **b.** −1 **c.** 8 **d.** 14 **e.** −89 **f.** 100
5. > **6.** > **7.** < **8.** < **9.** < **10.** −1 **11.** 3
12. 1 **13.** 2 **14.** 5 **15.** −7 **16.** 8 **17.** −10
18. 0 **19.** 2 **20.** −14 **21.** 12 **22.** −10 **23.** 4

24a.

Input (min)	Output (dollars)
1	$.10
2	$.20
3	$.30

25. C **26.** G **27.** N
28. A **29.** H **30.** K
31. $(-3, -2)$
32. $(1, -3)$
33. $(0, -4)$ **34.** $(-2, 2)$
35. $(4, 0)$ **36.** $(-1, -4)$

b.

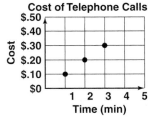

Cost of Telephone Calls

37. $486; $2,000; −$266; $673

Profit and Loss for Royale Bakery

38. 12 NOON

Cumulative Review — page 477

1. C **3.** B **5.** C **7.** C **9.** D **11.** D

CHAPTER 11

Lesson 11-1 — pages 480–484

ON YOUR OWN **1.** equally likely to be red or blue
3. probably fair **5.** RB, RY, BY **7.** 1H, 1T, 2H,
2T, 3H, 3T, 4H, 4T **9c.** Yes; the outcomes are
equally likely. **11a.** $\frac{1}{10}$ **b.** $\frac{7}{30}$ **c.** 0 **d.** $\frac{1}{15}$ **e.** $\frac{1}{30}$
f. 0 **13.** Unfair; only 15 of the 36 outcomes are
prime.

MIXED REVIEW **15.** 150 in.^{2} **17.** 672 in.^{2} **19.** >
21. > **23.** <

Lesson 11-2 — pages 485–487

ON YOUR OWN **5.** $766.50 **7.** no **9.** 60 cm

MIXED REVIEW **11.** −11 **13.** 2 **15.** −3
17. 25.41 cm^2 **19.** Susan: 11 pairs, Deepa: 22 pairs

Lesson 11-3 — pages 488–491

ON YOUR OWN **5.** Yes, the answers are affected
by the order of the numbers.

MIXED REVIEW **15.** 60 m; 283 m^2 **17.** 116 mm;
1,075 mm^2 **19.** −10 **21.** −11 **23.** 5

Lesson 11-4 — pages 492–496

ON YOUR OWN **1.** $\frac{1}{6}$; $0.1\overline{6}$; ≈17% **3.** $\frac{5}{6}$; $0.8\overline{3}$; ≈83%
5. $\frac{1}{3}$; $0.\overline{3}$; 33% **7.** $\frac{2}{5}$ **9.** $\frac{1}{6}$ **13.** $\frac{1}{10}$; 0.1; 10%
15. $\frac{1}{2}$; 0.5; 50% **17.** $\frac{3}{10}$; 0.3; 30% **19a.** $\frac{5}{8}$ **23.** $\frac{1}{10}$
25. 0 **27.** $\frac{7}{10}$ **29.** likely **31.** certain

MIXED REVIEW **35.** 51 m; 140 m^2 **37.** 18 in.;
20.25 in.^{2}

CHECKPOINT **1a.** $\frac{1}{5}$; 0.2; 20% **b.** $\frac{3}{5}$; 0.6; 60%
c. $\frac{2}{5}$; 0.4; 40% **2a.** $\frac{7}{15}$ **b.** $\frac{8}{15}$ **c.** Probably yes; the
experimental probabilities of winning are fairly
close. **3.** D

Toolbox — page 497

1. $\frac{1}{6}$ **3.** $\frac{1}{3}$ **5.** $\frac{2}{3}$ **7.** $\frac{3}{10}$ **9.** $\frac{2}{5}$ **11.** $\frac{1}{5}$ **13.** $\frac{1}{10}$
15a. 1 **b.** true **c.** $\frac{3}{8}$

Lesson 11-5 — pages 498–501

ON YOUR OWN

1.

white car: gray, blue, black — 7 outcomes
silver car: gray, blue, black, red

3. $\frac{8}{9}$ **5.** 9 days **7.** 20 pairs
9a. 27 outcomes **b.** 12 outcomes

MIXED REVIEW

11.

13.

Kilometers	Meters
1	1,000
2	2,000
3	3,000
4	4,000

15. 180 newspapers

Lesson 11-6 — pages 502–506

ON YOUR OWN 1. Dependent; the second outcome depends on the first. **3.** Independent; the second outcome does not depend on the first. **5.** Independent; the second outcome does not depend on the first. **9.** Yes; the outcome of the second spin does not depend on the first.

11. $\frac{4}{25}$ **13.** $\frac{1}{4}$ **15.** $\frac{1}{3}$ **17.** 0 **19.** $\frac{1}{10}$

21a. 2 outcomes **b.** 6 outcomes **c.** 12 outcomes
d. 72 outcomes

MIXED REVIEW 23. 36 cm **25.** 85 mm **27.** 51 ft
29. 63°, 153° **31.** 28°, 118° **33.** 3°, 93°
35. 12-in. × 12-in. sheets

Lesson 11-7 — pages 507–510

ON YOUR OWN 1. yes; AIM
3.

	Outcomes
G → S — I	GSI
G → I — S	GIS
S → G — I	SGI
S → I — G	SIG
I → G — S	IGS
I → S — G	ISG

5. 120 orders
7. 720 ways **9.** 720
11. 40,320
13. 6,227,020,800
15a. 5,040 ways **b.** $\frac{1}{5,040}$

MIXED REVIEW 17. 412 m^2 **25.** $\frac{1}{2}$ h

CHECKPOINT

1a.

	Outcomes
B — H	BH
B — T	BT
R — H	RH
R — T	RT
Y — H	YH
Y — T	YT

b. $\frac{1}{6}$ **2.** 12 meals **3.** $\frac{16}{49}$
4. 720 ways

Problem Solving Practice — page 511

1. A **3.** D **5.** D **7.** C **9.** B

Lesson 11-8 — pages 512–516

ON YOUR OWN 1. Honest **3.** Yes; probably; a random sample is usually representative. **5.** No; no; the sample is biased toward high school students and teachers. **7.** Answers may vary. Sample: The whole population is usually too large. **9.** No; they were all in close contact with each other. **13.** 192 computer chips **15.** 2,240 pairs of jeans **17.** about 14,118 oz

MIXED REVIEW 19. 300 cm^3 **21.** 160 cm^3
23. −64 **25.** 203 **27.** $\frac{1}{2}$ mi

Wrap Up — pages 518–519

1a.

	1	2	3	4	5	6
1	2	3	4	5	6	7
2	3	4	5	6	7	8
3	4	5	6	7	8	9
4	5	6	7	8	9	10
5	6	7	8	9	10	11
6	7	8	9	10	11	12

b. Fair; the number of even sums equals the number of odd sums. **2a.** $\frac{3}{10}, \frac{7}{10}$ **b.** Probably unfair; one player seems more likely to win.

3. $\frac{1}{4}$ **5a.** $\frac{1}{3}$ **b.** 0 **c.** $\frac{1}{2}$

7.

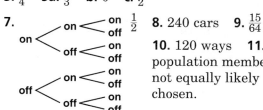

8. 240 cars **9.** $\frac{15}{64}$
10. 120 ways **11.** No; the population members are not equally likely to be chosen.

Cumulative Review — page 521

1. B **3.** D **5.** A **7.** D **9.** C **11.** B

EXTRA PRACTICE

CHAPTER 1

1.

Books Read Each Month	Frequency
4	4
3	2
2	3
1	3

Books Read Each Month

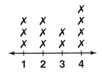

3. 21; 22; 22
5. 32; United States won 32 silver medals.
9. bar graph

CHAPTER 2
1. 256; 1,024; 4,096; multiply by 4
3. 9, 11, 13; add 2   **5.** 23, 27, 31; add 4   **7.** 21
9. 29   **11.** 9   **13.** 5   **15.** 49   **17.** 0   **19.** 200
21. 13   **23.** 67   **25.** $2p$ **27.** $x + 3$ **29.** $\frac{n}{2}$ **31.** 19
33. 110   **35.** 28   **37.** 34   **39.** 7   **41.** 9   **43.** 17.8
45. 16   **47.** 200

CHAPTER 3
1. eight tenths   **3.** twelve hundredths   **5.** seven hundredths   **7.** 3,040
9. 66.07   **11.** 0.222   **13.** thousandths
15. ten-thousandths   **17.** >   **19.** <   **21.** 2.3
23. 2.68   **25.** 0.2   **27.** 3,356.8   **29.** 14.534
31. 10.44   **33.** 1.489   **35.** 10 mm, 15 mm, 23 mm;
1 cm, 1.5 cm, 2.3 cm   **37.** 1 h 30 min
39. 6 h 38 min   **41.** 1 h 37 min

CHAPTER 4
1. 28   **3.** 48   **5.** 6   **7.** 2   **9.** 57   **11.** 123   **13.** 135   **15.** 256   **17.** $(7 \times 70) + (7 \times 8) = 546$ **19.** $(6 \times 60) + (6 \times 6) = 396$ **21.** 1.4   **23.** 2
25. 10.8   **27.** 1.4   **29.** 1.54   **31.** 2   **33.** 4   **35.** 1.68
37. 9.2   **39.** 56   **41.** 0.51   **43.** 3.5   **45.** 2.4

CHAPTER 5
1. 2, 3, 9   **3.** 2, 3, 5, 9, 10   **5.** none
7. composite   **9.** prime   **11.** prime   **13.** 10   **15.** 5
17. 9
19. **21.**
25. $\frac{1}{10}$ **27.** $\frac{3}{4}$ **29.** $\frac{2}{3}$ **31.** $3\frac{4}{7}$ **33.** $2\frac{2}{5}$ **35.** $3\frac{1}{2}$
37. $\frac{15}{8}$ **39.** $\frac{100}{9}$ **41.** $\frac{81}{8}$ **43.** 8   **45.** 75   **47.** 12
49. <   **51.** =   **53.** <   **55.** $\frac{4}{9}, \frac{4}{7}, \frac{4}{5}$ **57.** $\frac{7}{12}, \frac{2}{3}, \frac{5}{6}$
59. $2\frac{1}{8}, 2\frac{1}{2}, 2\frac{3}{4}$ **61.** $0.\overline{6}$ **63.** 0.4   **65.** 0.5

CHAPTER 6
1. $\frac{1}{2}$ **3.** 6   **5.** $\frac{3}{4}$ **7.** $1\frac{1}{3}$ **9.** $1\frac{1}{2}$
11. $1\frac{9}{40}$ **13.** $8\frac{1}{6}$ **15.** $17\frac{7}{12}$ **17.** $5\frac{17}{24}$ **19.** $5\frac{11}{15}$

21. $\frac{1}{3}$ **23.** $\frac{1}{15}$ **25.** $2\frac{1}{8}$ **27.** 24   **29.** 20   **31.** $45\frac{3}{5}$
33. $52\frac{1}{12}$ **35.** $122\frac{2}{5}$ **37.** $2\frac{1}{2}$ **39.** $3\frac{3}{8}$ **41.** 80
43. $2\frac{1}{5}$ **45.** $1\frac{1}{3}$ **47.** 8   **49.** 160   **51.** 32   **53.** $1\frac{3}{4}$
55. 13

CHAPTER 7
1. 2 to 3, 2 : 3, $\frac{2}{3}$ **3.** 1 to 2   **5.** 1 to 4
7. 1 : 4   **9.** 128   **11.** 90   **13.** 2   **15.** 9   **17.** 60
19. 6 cm × 15 cm   **21.** 20 km × 50 km
23. 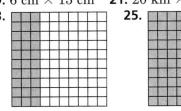   **25.**

29. 40%   **31.** 90%   **33.** 30%   **35.** 0.96, $\frac{24}{25}$
37. 0.01, $\frac{1}{100}$ **39.** 0.88, $\frac{22}{25}$ **41.** 48   **43.** 17
45. 16   **47.** 43

49. 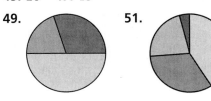   **51.**

CHAPTER 8
5. 180°   **7.** 37°   **9.** 110°   **11.** isosceles
13. scalene   **15.** right   **17.** all   **19.** no
21. 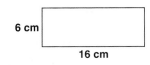   **23.** 48 in.   **25.** 1.5 m

CHAPTER 9
1. 16 cm²   **3.** 15 cm²   **5.** 12 m²
7. 82 yd   **9.** 188 in.   **11.** 27 m
13.   **15.**   **17.** 340 ft²   **19.** 70 m²
21. 24 in.³
23. 1,232 cm³

CHAPTER 10
1. <   **3.** >   **5.** =   **7.** >   **15.** 83
17. −80   **19.** 20   **21.** 0
23.   **25.** (2, 3)   **27.** (−3, −1)
29. (−1, −1)   **31.** F **33.** H
35. J

37.

39. −13 to 13 by 1's

CHAPTER 11 **1.** Fair game; the chances of rolling even (2, 4, 6) or odd (1, 3, 5) are equally likely.

3a. 30%, $\frac{3}{10}$ **b.** 10%, $\frac{1}{10}$ **5a.** $\frac{1}{12}$ **b.** $\frac{1}{4}$ **7.** 120

9. 2 **11.** 6 **13.** 40,320 **15.** 5,040
17. representative

SKILLS HANDBOOK

PAGE 535 **1.** ten millions **3.** hundred millions
5. hundred billions **7.** 3 ten million
9. 6 hundred million **11.** 9 hundred billion
13. 6 hundred **15.** 6 ten million
17. 6 ten **19.** 6 hundred thousand
21. 6 ten billion **23.** 6 thousand
25. 6 hundred thousand **27.** 6 ten

PAGE 536 **1.** 7; 360; 900 **3.** 67; 13; 5
5. 232,000,753,000 **7.** 321,029 **9.** 322,000,135
11. 5,004,012,000

PAGE 537 **1.** > **3.** > **5.** < **7.** > **9.** > **11.** <
13. > **15.** 1,367; 1,374; 1,437; 1,747 **17.** 9,789;
9,897; 9,987 **19.** 17,414; 17,444; 17,671; 18,242
21. < < **23.** > >

PAGE 538 **1.** 76 **3.** 41 **5.** 144 **7.** 393 **9.** 279
11. 564 **13.** 2,894 **15.** 6,754 **17.** 7,149 **19.** 134
21. 176 **23.** 757 **25.** 132 **27.** 100 **29.** 907
31. 2,759 **33.** 9,252 **35.** 16,298

PAGE 539 **1.** 44 **3.** 22 **5.** 21 **7.** 469 **9.** 175
11. 230 **13.** 6,828 **15.** 5,100 **17.** 3,525 **19.** 59
21. 463 **23.** 785 **25.** 226 **27.** 602 **29.** 419
31. 99 **33.** 176

PAGE 540 **1.** 243 **3.** 348 **5.** 304 **7.** 3,390
9. 1,304 **11.** 4,320 **13.** 150 **15.** 496 **17.** 3,192
19. 315 **21.** 852 **23.** 6,057 **25.** 246 **27.** 252
29. 304 **31.** 2,968 **33.** 6,622 **35.** 2,215 **37.** 414

PAGE 541 **1.** 4 R1 **3.** 5 R1 **5.** 4 R2 **7.** 13 R5
9. 20 R2 **11.** 12 R5 **13.** 16 R2 **15.** 19 **17.** 104 R5
19. 116 R1 **21.** 193 **23.** 42 **25.** 133

PAGE 542 **1.** 30 R2 **3.** 90 R1 **5.** 80 R3 **7.** 70 R5
9. 20 R14 **11.** 70 R2 **13.** 60 R1 **15.** 40 R5
17. 503 **19.** 420 R2 **21.** 80 R8 **23.** 40 R17
25. 20 R46

PAGE 543 **1.** 2.5 **3.** 89 **5.** 0.108 **7.** 0.00014
9. 0.0014 **11.** 4.05 **13.** 0.8 **15.** 68.9 **17.** 0.0009
19. 0.666 **21.** 12 **23.** 20 **25.** 40 **27.** 100

PAGE 544 **1.** 36.8° C **3.** 38.4° C **5.** 96.6° F
7. G **9.** F **11.** W

PAGE 545 **1.** 11 **3.** 95 **5.** 29 **7.** 1,056 **9.** 404
11. XV **13.** MDCXXXII **15.** CLIX **17.** XCII
19. MCMXC

ADDITIONAL TOPICS

PAGE 546 **1.** 5.218 **3.** 2.509 **5.** 23.808 **7.** 0.621
9. 16.537 **11.** 0.0431 **13.** 0.9010 **15.** 0.0303
17. 3,000 **19.** 10.015 **21.** 0.0699 **23.** 2 **25.** 207.138
27. 9.0407 **29.** 24 **31.** 0.1073 **33.** 13.106
35. 41.772

PAGE 547 Answers may vary.

PAGE 548 **1.** 686 **3.** 483 **5.** 548 **7.** 5,500 **9.** 8,120
11. 139 **13.** 3,960 **15.** 581 **17.** 204 **19.** 507

PAGE 549 **1.** 3 **3.** 0 **5.** 6 **7.** 11 **9.** 6 **11.** 1 **13.** 13
15. 1 **17.** 4 **19.** 2 **21.** 4 **23.** 2

PAGE 551 **1.** 3,509 × 0.01 **3.** 88 × 0.01 **5.** 7,099
× 0.01 **7.** 200,003 × 0.001 **9.** 324 × 0.1 **11.** 155 ×
0.01 **13.** 218 × 0.001 **15.** 2 × 0.1 **17.** 442,006 ×
0.001 **19.** 10,605 × 0.001 **21.** 2,204 × 0.001 **23.** 5
× 0.001 **25.** 2,404 × 0.1 **27.** 7,045 × 0.1 **29.** 3,205
× 0.001 **31.** D **33.** D

PAGE 553 **1.** zero property for × **3.** assoc., +
5. comm., + **7.** 556, assoc., + **9.** 37.0, identity
property for + **11.** 3,700, assoc., × **13.** 0, zero
property for × **15.** 424, distributive **17.** 0, inverse
property for + and zero property for × **19.** 47,000,
assoc., × **21.** 26, inverse property for + and
identity property for + **23.** 7, distributive

Index

Aztec calendar, 406

Babbage, Charles, 46
Balance (profit and loss), 468
Bank statement, 112
Bar graph, 22, 24–27, 34–35, 39, 302
Base
 of an exponent, 139
 of a parallelogram, 392
 of three-dimensional figures,
  408–409
 of a triangle, 392
Biased sample, 513
Bicycle designer, 60
Bisecting
 angles, 336
 segments, 336
Board game designer, 506
Box-and-whisker plot, 32
Breaking numbers apart, 548

Calculator
 area of a circle, 404–407
 balances, finding, 468
 change-sign key, 435, 468
 circumference, 400–402
 decimals, adding and subtracting,
  109
 decimals, multiplying, 151
 equations, solving, 68, 73, 75, 76
 exercises using, 7, 46, 51–54, 59,
  68–70, 73, 75, 76, 87, 106, 142,
  153, 155, 157, 161, 162, 172, 173,
  184, 188, 201, 216, 242, 245, 287,
  301, 303, 317, 390, 400–402,
  404–407, 416, 428, 435, 437, 462,
  468, 470, 471, 476, 489, 506,
  509–510, 516
 exponents, simplifying, 140, 142
 fraction calculators, 201, 245
 fractions, simplifying, 201
 fractions, writing as decimals,
  213–216
 fractions, writing as percents, 301
 graphing calculators, 462, 489
 hints, 52, 237, 242, 259, 300
 math toolboxes using, 201, 245,
  462
 mean, finding the, 12
 order of operations, 52
 percent key, 300
 percents, 309, 311
 pi (π) key, 400, 402
 random numbers, generating, 489
 simplifying powers, 140–142
 See also Technology

Capacity
 customary units, 266, 533
 metric units, 119–121, 421, 533
Careers. *See* Math at Work
Carpenter, 412
Cartoonist, 348
Cell (spreadsheet), 18–21, 39
Celsius, 205, 544
Centi- prefix, 172
Centimeter cubes, 418–422
Central angles, 365
Central tendency. *See* Mean;
 Median; Mode
Chance. *See* Probability
Chapter Assessment, 40, 80, 130,
 178, 224, 274, 322, 378, 430, 476,
 520
Chapter Projects,
 astronomy: making scale models,
  276–277, 284, 288, 295, 319
 consumer issues: comparing prices,
  82–83, 95, 102, 121, 127
 history: drawing time lines,
  432–433, 441, 452, 461, 473
 patterns: building forts, 42–43, 47,
  64, 76–77
 planning: celebrations, 132–133,
  137, 155, 162, 175
 proofs: designing demonstrations,
  226–227, 231, 256, 261, 271
 puzzles, creating, 324–325, 339,
  343, 352, 359, 375
 sports: comparing basketball
  statistics, 180–181, 195, 212, 217,
  221
 statistics: designing three-choice
  systems, 478–479, 491, 496, 506,
  517
 surveys, conducting, 2–3, 7, 16,
  36–37
 technology: designing Web pages,
  380–381, 391, 402, 407, 412, 427
Chapter Wrap Up, 38–39, 78–79,
 128–129, 176–177, 222–223,
 272–273, 320–321, 376–377,
 428–429, 474–475, 518–519
Checkpoints, 16, 31, 54, 70, 95, 117,
 147, 166, 200, 217, 240, 261, 288,
 313, 348, 367, 396, 422, 446, 467,
 496, 510
Chef, 240
Choose a Strategy exercises, 7, 26,
 36, 50, 54, 70, 91, 95, 126, 137, 150,
 155, 159, 162, 166, 174, 188, 191,
 195, 200, 208, 212, 231, 235, 239,
 244, 249, 256, 261, 265, 270, 280,
 291, 299, 303, 308, 312, 317, 330,
 335, 339, 343, 347, 352, 359, 363,

367, 374, 385, 402, 407, 417, 426,
 437, 452, 456, 461, 472, 487, 491,
 501, 506
Chord, 364–366
Circle, 364–367
 area of, 403–407
 central angle, 365
 chord, 364–366
 circumference, 398–402
 definition, 364
 diameter of, 364, 399–402
 radius, 364–366
Circle graph, 23, 39
 constructing on computer, 318
 reading, 23–25
 sketching, 314–317
Circumference, 398–402
Classifying
 angles, 333–335
 polygons, 344–347
 quadrilaterals, 349–352
 triangles, 340–343
Collinear points, 327, 426
Colored tiles, 439–445, 448–451,
 474
Common denominator, 209
Common factors, 189
Common multiples, 206
Communication
 Cooperative learning, xxvi–xxvii, 4,
  12, 24, 29, 45, 51, 61, 66, 72, 85,
  99, 109, 113, 118, 123, 134, 143,
  148, 151, 158, 161, 182, 185, 189,
  202, 206, 213, 230, 241, 253, 262,
  298, 300, 314, 328, 337, 340, 344,
  349, 356, 361, 370, 383, 389, 392,
  403, 415, 418, 444, 450, 459, 463,
  489, 492, 507, 514
 Journal, 16, 21, 26, 60, 70, 102,
  121, 150, 170, 188, 208, 244, 256,
  284, 312, 343, 363, 396, 417, 441,
  456, 495, 505
 Portfolio, 36, 76, 126, 174, 220, 270,
  316, 374, 426, 471, 516
 Reasoning, 4, 7, 20, 24, 25, 27, 32,
  33, 46, 53, 60, 63, 70, 71, 74, 88,
  96, 101, 106, 109, 113–116, 118,
  125, 134, 141–143, 146, 153, 158,
  164, 165, 172, 183–186, 193, 200,
  202, 203, 208, 213, 228, 262, 263,
  269, 281, 283, 286, 287, 292, 295,
  297, 300, 303, 307, 310, 311,
  329–332, 335, 341, 342, 346, 349,
  350, 352, 357, 359, 361, 364–366,
  372, 374, 385, 387, 401, 415, 417,
  418, 420, 421, 436, 441, 442, 462,
  465, 481, 483, 489, 490, 492, 493,
  495, 499, 510, 515
 Writing, 6, 7, 11, 15, 20, 26, 30, 32,

Index

Communication *(Continued)*
35, 40, 46, 53, 59, 63, 65, 68, 71, 75, 79, 80, 86, 91, 94, 96, 102, 103, 106, 108, 110, 115, 117, 121, 124–126, 129, 130, 137, 138, 142, 145, 150, 154, 155, 158, 161, 166, 170, 174, 176, 178, 182, 184, 188, 191, 195, 200, 201, 205, 208, 211, 216, 220, 222, 224, 231, 235, 239, 243, 245, 248, 256, 260, 265, 266, 269, 273, 274, 280, 284, 287, 295, 296, 298, 303, 308, 312, 317, 322, 330, 335, 336, 339, 342, 344, 346, 351, 358, 362, 366, 367, 372, 373, 377, 378, 384, 386, 390, 395, 398, 405, 411, 417, 420, 429, 430, 437, 440, 445, 451, 453, 460, 461, 466, 471, 475, 476, 484, 487, 490, 495, 497, 500, 505, 509, 515, 520

Commutative property
of addition, 74, 552
of multiplication, 74, 552

Comparing
customary units, 268–270
decimals, 92, 94
fractions, 209–212
integers, 435–437, 474
symbols for, 92, 438, 534
whole numbers, 537

Compass, 364

Compatible numbers, 134–137

Compensation, 548

Complement of an event, 497

Complementary angles, 337

Complex figures, area of, 394–396

Composite numbers, 185–188

Compound event, 494–496

Computer
circle graphs, 318
databases, 138
geometry software, 368
graphing programs, 318
random numbers, 489
spreadsheets, 18–21, 30–31, 112, 138, 368, 470–471
See also Technology

Cone, 409–410

Congruent angles, 336, 338

Congruent figures, 356–359, 377

Connections to careers. *See* Math at Work

Connections, interdisciplinary
art, 4, 56, 238, 333, 339
biology, 45, 91, 156, 219, 246–248, 291, 456, 487, 505
earth science, 93, 151, 283, 301
geography, 5, 24, 171, 270, 294, 383, 451, 466–467

health, 220, 515
history, 40
language, 68, 311, 347, 465
literature, 6, 98, 426, 510
music, 15, 18, 23, 64, 212, 287, 306, 486, 508
physical education, 332
physical science or physics, 174, 205, 302
science, 46, 90, 94, 150, 152, 153, 156, 207, 229, 287, 330, 347
social studies, 6, 7, 35, 92, 136, 239

Connections to math strands. *See* Algebra; Data analysis; Geometry; Measurement; Patterns; Probability; Statistics

Connections to real-world applications
accounting, 468
advertising, 145
airplanes, 12–13
amusement parks, 63, 126, 365
animal studies, 27
archery, 400
architecture, 30, 269, 294, 339
baby-sitting, 391
baking/cooking, 219, 235, 244, 260, 265, 269
bank statements, 112
basketball, 404
bell ringing, 508
bicycles/cycling, 401, 402
bus schedules, 124
business, 260, 469
calendar, 76, 219
camp, 278
car sales, 34, 50
carpentry, 210, 244, 249, 252, 260
cars, 500
chess, 219
clothes, 10, 38, 355, 504
coin collecting/coins, 8–9, 148, 425
collectibles/collecting, 14, 138, 355, 487
communications, 16, 405
community planning, 253
commuting, 252
computers, 21, 150
conservation, 393
construction, 214, 260, 417
consumer issues, 98, 106, 110, 291, 501
cost of living, 165, 170
crafts, 263, 285, 466
customer service, 456
design, 204
dogs, 464
drafting, 342, 402
dressmaking, 170
eclipse, 330

education, 25, 29
energy, 270
entertainment, 5, 13, 97, 142, 178, 220, 268, 298, 312
environment, 315
finance, 216
fitness, 208, 309, 510
food, 24, 63, 252, 281, 287, 355, 419, 499
fund-raising, 62, 97, 317
games, 10, 219, 341, 407, 487, 501, 509
gardening, 251, 383, 390, 422, 425, 455
gas mileage/prices, 89, 282
geology, 238
golf, 435–436
hobbies, 30, 162, 170, 219
hockey, 73
home improvement, 358, 391
in-line skating, 23
interior decorating/design, 169, 373
jewelry, 10
jobs, 21, 50, 137, 170, 283, 308, 425, 458
landscaping, 256, 388, 389
leisure, 366
library science, 137
marine biology, 155, 205
marketing, 252
money, 38, 91, 98, 105, 111, 135, 162, 169, 184, 216, 220, 355, 445
natural resources, 516
navigation, 456
newspapers, 9, 258
nutrition, 16, 104, 107, 136, 173, 174, 269
optics, 343
package design/packaging, 136, 414
pediatrics, 307
pets, 163, 251, 401
photography, 335
pollution, 76
population, 28, 256
quality control, 174, 513
quilting, 169
radio, 509
recreation, 25, 307
recycling, 22
sailing, 342
sales, 305
savings, 49, 137, 169, 220, 291, 311, 425
scheduling, 220, 252
shopping, 178, 211, 216, 219, 307
space, 64
sports, 7, 15, 26, 89, 97, 108, 109, 146, 252, 283, 284, 287, 299, 307, 311, 312, 317, 354, 445, 486, 509

Divisor, 158

Dot paper, 340, 349, 356–359, 362, 397

Draw a diagram, xxiii–xxv, xxviii, 250–252

Drawings, scale, 246, 292–295

Dürer, Albrecht, 56

Earth, 330
coordinate system, 466

Edge of a prism, 409

Eisenhower, Dwight D., 64

Elapsed time, 124–126

Endpoint, 326, 327
See also Points

Equal ratios, 281

Equations, 66, 79
graphing, 462
with decimals, 109, 111, 152, 154, 165
with fractions, 237, 239, 242–244
with integers, 449, 451
with mixed numbers, 247–249
modeling, 67, 69, 72, 74–75, 80, 449, 453
solved by addition/subtraction, 66–70, 79, 109, 111, 235, 237, 239, 241–244, 247–249, 274, 449, 451
solved by multiplication/division, 72–76, 79, 154, 165, 419–421
solving two-step equations, 453
verbal models, 61–63, 73, 241, 246–247, 263, 449

Equator, 466

Equilateral triangle, 340

Equivalent decimals, 85–86

Equivalent fractions, 197–201, 209–212, 223, 237, 238

Estimation
angle measure, 334
area, 382–385
area of a circle, 404–407
breaking apart numbers, 548
circle graphs, 314–317
compatible numbers, 134–137
compensation, 548
decimal products, 134–137
decimal quotients, 135–137
decimal rounding, 134–137
decimal sums and differences, 105–107, 441
decimals, 87, 110, 195
exercises that use, 45, 87, 105–108, 116–117, 121, 130, 228–230, 238, 240, 245, 248, 257–258, 260, 331,

334
fraction sums and differences, 228–231, 238
fractions, 193–195, 224
front-end, 105–107
graphs and, 45
length, 547
mean, 13
metric length, 116
mixed number products, 258
mixed number sums and differences, 229–231
mixed numbers, 248
money, 130
natural units, 547
percent, 298, 305–308
rounding, 103–107, 193–195
whole number products, 134
whole number quotients, 135

Estimation strategies
breaking numbers apart, 548
compatible numbers, 134–137
compensation, 548
rounding, 103–107, 193–195

Euclid, 145

Even numbers, 182

Events
complement of, 497
independent, 502–505, 519
predicting, 513–516
types of, 493, 495, 519

Expanded form/notation, 89–90

Experimental probability, 480–491, 518

Exponent, 139
order of operations and, 140

Exponential notation, 139–142

Exponential patterns, 142

Expressions
evaluating, 51–54, 57–60, 154
modeling, 57–59
numerical, 51, 56, 66, 79
variable, 56–60, 61–64, 79
verbal models, 61–63
writing variable, 61–64, 66

Exterior angles, 338

Extra Practice section, 522–532
See also Mixed Review

Faces, 408

Factor, 185–191
common factor, 189
greatest common factor, 189–191, 222
prime factorization, 186–188, 190–191, 207–208, 222

Factor tree, 186–188, 190

Factorial notation, 509, 510

Factorization, prime, 186–188, 190–191, 207

Fahrenheit, 205, 544

Fair games, 480–484, 502, 518

Field (database), 138

Figures
congruent, 356–359
similar, 296, 357–359
three-dimensional, 408–411

Flip, 370, 373

Folding paper, 361, 370

Foot, 266, 533

Formula, 19, 39, 534
area of a circle, 403
area of a parallelogram, 393
area of a rectangle, 387
area of a square, 388
area of a triangle, 393
circumference, 400
counting principle, 499
creating from data table, 398, 418
creating from a pattern, 398, 403
diameter, 365
experimental probability, 481
perimeter of a rectangle, 60, 387
perimeter of a square, 388
probability of independent events, 503
simple interest, 312, 534
on spreadsheets, 19
surface area, 414
table of, 534
theoretical probability, 492
volume of a rectangular prism, 418

Four-step plan, xx–xxii
See also Problem Solving Strategies

Fractions
adding, 232–234, 236–239, 245
calculator and, 201, 245
comparing, 209–212
decimals and, 214–216
dividing, 262–265
equivalent, 197–201, 209–212, 223, 237, 238
estimating with, 228–231, 238
improper, 202–205, 223
least common denominator (LCD), 209–212, 223
measurements using, 196, 198, 202–205
mixed numbers, 202–205, 223
modeling, 193–195, 197–199, 202–204, 209–212, 224–225, 232–236, 253–256, 262–264
multiplying, 253–256

Index

Inch ruler, 196, 230

Independent events, 502–505, 519

Indirect measurement, 296

Inequalities, 438

Input/output tables, 457–459, 475

Integers, 434–476
    adding, 442–445, 474
    comparing, 435–437, 474
    graphing, 434–438, 468–471,
      474–475
    modeling, 439–445, 448–451, 474
    multiplying and dividing, 452
    negative number, 434, 439, 442,
      443
    and number lines, 434–437, 474
    opposites, 434, 474
    ordering, 435–437, 474
    positive number, 434, 439, 442,
      443
    subtracting, 448–452, 474
    zero pairs, 439–440, 474

Interdisciplinary connections. *See* Connections

Interest, 112, 312

Interior angles, 338, 346

Internet, 156
    accounting careers, 87
    astronomy, 319
    bicycle design, 60
    cartoonist, 348
    chef links, 240
    consumer issues, 127
    game designers guide, 506
    history, 473
    Internet help provider, 313
    meteorologists, 472
    National Air and Space Museum,
      191
    National Park Service, 26
    patterns, 77
    pi, calculating, 400
    planning, 175
    prime numbers search, 186
    projects, 37, 77, 127, 175, 221, 271,
      319, 375, 427, 473, 517
    proofs, 271
    puzzles, 375
    sports, 221
    statistics, 517
    surveys, 37
    technology, 427
    veterinarians, 159
    weather reports, 449
    woodworking, 412

Internet help provider, 313

Intersecting lines, 327

Inverse properties, 552

Isolation of a variable, 67–70

Isosceles triangle, 340

Journal
    16, 21, 26, 60, 70, 102, 121, 150,
    170, 188, 208, 244, 256, 284, 312,
    343, 363, 396, 417, 441, 456, 495,
    505
    See also Portfolio; Writing

Kilo- prefix, 118, 119, 172

Latitude, 466

**Least common denominator
(LCD),** 209–212, 223, 237

Least common multiple (LCM),
    206–208, 222

Length
    customary units, 196, 230, 266,
      293–296, 386
    estimating, 116, 547
    metric units, 113–116, 292–295,
      298, 342, 386, 390, 392–396
    natural units, 547

Less than symbol, 92, 438

Like denominators, 209, 232–235

Likely events, 493, 495

Line, 326
    classifying, 327–328
    graphing, 458–461
    intersecting, 327
    number, 92, 103–104, 434–436, 438,
      474
    parallel, 327
    perpendicular, 333
    of reflection, 371
    skew, 328
    of symmetry, 360–363
    transversals, 338

Line graph, 23–26, 28–30, 33–36,
    303, 458–461, 469–471

Line of symmetry, 360–363

Line plot, 5–7, 14, 15, 38

Line segment. *See* Segment

Linear equation. *See* Equation

Liter, 119

Logical reasoning, 4, 7, 20, 24, 25,
    27, 32, 33, 46, 53, 60, 63, 70, 71,
    74, 75, 88, 96, 101, 106, 109,
    113–116, 118, 125, 134, 141–143,
    146, 153, 158, 164, 165, 172,
    183–186, 193, 200, 202, 203, 208,
    213, 228, 262, 263, 269, 281, 283,
    286, 287, 292, 295, 297, 300, 303,
    307, 310, 311, 329–332, 335, 341,
    342, 346, 349, 350, 352–355, 357,

    359, 361, 364–366, 372, 374, 385,
    387, 401, 415, 417, 418, 420, 421,
    436, 441, 442, 462, 465, 481, 483,
    489, 490, 492, 493, 495, 499, 510,
    515

Longitude, 466

Look Back, 14, 19, 23, 27, 28, 68, 93,
    106, 171, 247, 259, 268, 281, 306,
    331, 394, 481, 502, 513

Look for a Pattern, xxiii–xxv, xxix,
    48–50, 454–455

Lowest terms. *See* Fractions

Magic squares, 56, 59, 446

Make a Model, 424–426

Make a Table, xxiii–xxv, xxix, 8–10

Manipulatives
    algebra tiles, 57–59, 67, 69, 72,
      74–75, 80, 188, 453
    centimeter cubes, 413, 418, 480
    colored tiles, 439–445, 448–451, 474
    compass, 364
    cutouts, 397, 412
    dot paper, 340, 349, 356–359, 362,
      397
    folding paper, 361, 370
    fraction models, 193–195, 197–199,
      202–204, 209–212, 224–225, 228,
      232–236, 238, 253–256, 262–264
    geoboards, 340, 349, 463
    graph paper, 143, 185–188,
      250–252, 292, 302, 392
    inch rulers, 196, 230
    metric rulers, 114–116, 292–294,
      298, 342, 390, 395
    number cubes, 450, 482–485,
      490–491, 494–495, 497, 501,
      505
    protractor, 332–335, 342, 359
    spinner, 486, 490, 494–495, 500,
      505, 519–520
    square tiles, 389
    stencils, 370
    straightedge, 336
    tiles, 397
    tracing paper, 362, 397
    See also Modeling

Mass, 118–121

Math at Work
    accountant, 87
    bicycle designer, 60
    board game designer, 506
    carpenter, 412
    cartoonist, 348
    chef, 240
    Internet help provider, 313
    meteorologist, 472
    park ranger, 26

Index

Quad- prefix, 347

Quadrants, 465–466

Quadrilaterals, 345, 349–352
parallelogram, 349
rectangle, 349
rhombus, 349
square, 350
trapezoid, 350

Quart, 266, 533

Quick Review, 92, 99, 158, 172, 209,
213, 233, 237, 286, 298, 306, 398,
399, 434, 435

Quotient, 158, 541–543
checking, 11, 163
estimating, 135
zeros in, 542
See also Division

Radius, 364, 398–407

Random numbers, 488–491, 518

Random samples, 513–516, 519

Range, 5–7, 38

Rate, 282–284
unit rate, 282–284

Rational numbers. *See* Decimals;
Fractions; Integers; Whole numbers

Ratios
defined, 278
equal, 281–284
and fractions/decimals, 278–279,
281–282, 285, 292–293, 296,
300–301
and predictions, 513–514
and probability, 480–484, 488–489,
492–495, 497, 499–500, 518–519
and proportions, 281–282, 285–287,
357–359
rate, 282–284
scale drawings, 292–295
writing, 278–281, 283–284

Ray, 327

Real-world applications. *See*
Connections

Reasonableness of solutions, 9,
96–97, 103, 106, 108–109, 115, 134,
229, 259, 265, 386, 425

Reasoning
demonstrate understanding, 32, 53,
70, 75, 88, 96, 109, 113, 114, 125,
141, 158, 172, 184, 193, 202, 332,
341, 349, 350, 365, 366, 372, 401,
442, 443
develop a formula or a procedure,
60, 63, 106, 113, 115, 116, 118,
142, 143, 146, 153, 164, 165, 172,

183, 203, 208, 269, 287, 292, 297,
310, 417, 420, 421, 441, 442, 493,
499, 510
justify or rationalize conclusions, 4,
7, 20, 24, 27, 33, 71, 74, 106, 146,
228, 281, 311, 331, 332, 357, 385,
481, 483, 490
make comparisons, 24, 134, 185,
186, 200, 262, 263, 283, 300, 303,
342, 346, 359, 365, 387, 436, 462,
465
make conjectures, 7, 46, 70, 101,
213, 286, 295, 307, 329, 330, 335,
352, 361, 364, 374, 415, 417, 462,
489, 492, 495, 515
See also Logical reasoning; Problem
solving; Proportional reasoning;
Spatial reasoning

Reciprocal, 263

Record (database), 138

Rectangle, 349
area of, 143, 387–391
perimeter of, 387–391

Rectangular prism
surface area of, 414–417
volume of, 418–422

Reflection, 371, 373

Remainder, 11, 182, 541

Renaming, 197–200, 202–205,
237–238, 247–249

Repeating decimals, 215–216

Research exercises, 6, 94, 106, 162,
205, 255, 279, 339, 451, 466, 516

Reviews. *See* Chapter Wrap Up;
Checkpoints; Cumulative Review;
Extra Practice; Math Toolbox;
Mixed Review; Quick Review

Rhombus, 349

Right angle, 333

Right triangle, 340

Roman numerals, 545

Rotation, 372, 374

Rounding
data, 104–107
decimals, 104–107, 134–137, 160
fractions, 193–195
whole numbers, 103

Rulers, 196, 198, 203–204, 386

Sales tax, 306, 308

Sample, random, 513

Samples, 512–516

Scale, 27–30, 292

Scale drawing, 246, 292–295

Scalene triangle, 340

Scatter plot, 464

Schedules, reading and using,
124–126

Scientific calculator.
See Calculator; Technology

Scientific notation, 156

Segment, 326
bisecting, 336
congruent, 340
parallel, 327

Sequence. *See* Number patterns;
Patterns

Sides
of an angle, 331
corresponding, 357
of a polygon, 345

Similar figures, 296, 357–359

Simple interest, 312

Simpler problem, solving, 289–291

Simplest form of fraction, 198–201,
223

Simulate a Problem, 485–487

Simulation
as problem solving strategy,
485–487
of random numbers, 488–491

Skew lines, 328

Skills Handbook, 535–545

Slide, 370–371, 373–374

Software, 368

Solids. *See* Three-dimensional figures

Solution (of an equation), 66

Solve a Simpler Problem, 289–291

Sort (database), 138

Spatial reasoning, 341, 397, 399,
410, 411, 413, 415, 418, 426, 500

Sphere, 409

Spinner, 486, 490, 494–495, 500, 505,
520

Spreadsheet, 18–21, 30–31, 39, 112,
368, 470, 471

Square, 350
area of, 388–391
perimeter of, 388–391

Square centimeter, 382, 403

Square inches, 382

Square number, 140, 388

Square tiles, 389, 391

Squared, 140

Standard form/notation
of decimals, 89–90
of whole numbers, 88–90, 142,
156

Standard units, 113